THE SELF-DETERMINATION OF PEOPLES

*Published in association with
the Liechtenstein Institute on Self-Determination,
Princeton University*

THE SELF-DETERMINATION OF PEOPLES

COMMUNITY, NATION, AND STATE IN AN INTERDEPENDENT WORLD

EDITED BY
Wolfgang Danspeckgruber

LYNNE
RIENNER
PUBLISHERS

BOULDER
LONDON

Published in the United States of America in 2002 by
Lynne Rienner Publishers, Inc.
1800 30th Street, Boulder, Colorado 80301
www.rienner.com

and in the United Kingdom by
Lynne Rienner Publishers, Inc.
3 Henrietta Street, Covent Garden, London WC2E 8LU

Library of Congress Cataloging-in-Publication Data
The self-determination of peoples : community, nation, and state in an interdependent
world / Wolfgang Danspeckgruber, editor ; foreword by Prince Hans Adam II
of Liechtenstein.
    p. cm.
    Includes bibliographical references and index.
    ISBN 1-55587-768-0 (alk. paper)
    ISBN 1-55587-793-1 (pbk. : alk. paper)
    1. Self-determination, National.   2. National state.   3. International relations.
I. Danspeckgruber, Wolfgang F.
KZ1269.S454   2001
320.1'5—dc21
                                        2001019009

British Cataloguing in Publication Data
A Cataloguing in Publication record for this book
is available from the British Library.

Printed and bound in the United States of America

 The paper used in this publication meets the requirements
of the American National Standard for Permanence of
Paper for Printed Library Materials Z39.48-1984.

5   4   3   2   1

Dedicated to Edgar L. Rachlin and his generation,
who laid the foundation for international security,
peace, justice, and prosperity

CONTENTS

FOREWORD

Prince Hans Adam II of Liechtenstein

Coming from a very small state and having grown up at a time when the prevailing wisdom was "the bigger the better," I invested quite some time in exploring what factors influenced the size of states throughout history. The results of this effort are somewhat speculative. Nevertheless, there is good evidence that changes in technology, especially in the military sector, influence the size of states.

When military technology favored the defender, small states or very decentralized large states prevailed. A small number of soldiers behind high walls were able to defend a city or a castle quite effectively against a larger army, especially when transportation was difficult and expensive. When military technology favored the aggressor, larger armies and therefore larger and more centralized states prevailed.

But war is an expensive business, and over a longer period of time economic factors became more important than military technology. In the past, small states could keep their independence only if they were able to pay for their military defense (the Principality of Liechtenstein, having excellent relations over the centuries with its two neighbors, Switzerland and Austria, is the exception rather than the rule). Historically, small states could compete economically with large states only when they were able to rely on international trade. Small states have to import what they cannot produce locally, whereas a large state typically can rely much more on internal resources: a bad harvest in one province can be balanced by a good harvest in another. To pay for all the necessary imports, a small state has to export a much larger portion of its national product.

If we look at the economic and military disadvantages of a small state compared to a large one, it is surprising that any small states have survived. Yet, many reasons for their survival can be found: for example, small states, like small companies, are easier to manage, more flexible, and often more open to innovation. The small city-states in ancient

Greece and in Italy during the Renaissance were extremely productive in most areas of human activity, despite the fact that, with few exceptions, they had fewer than 100,000 inhabitants.

In contrast, in larger states, it seems that sooner or later bureaucracy becomes the major growth industry and centralization the prevailing political trend, until the large centralized state loses its competitive edge compared to the smaller state. For a large state, it is even more difficult to reduce an inefficient bureaucracy and to decentralize than it is for a large company. Political decentralization often means the creation of an additional layer of bureaucracy and a slowdown in the decision-making process. Finally, the large state collapses into smaller units or is taken over by a new, more decentralized large state and the whole cycle starts again.

At the end of the Middle Ages, a new trend toward large centralized states began in Europe and, by the end of the nineteenth century, had spread over the entire world. In the face of the development of artillery, the high walls that had given the city-states at least some protection from aggressors became more or less useless. This dramatic military technological revolution was soon reinforced by the industrial revolution. Large states started to improve their internal transport systems; they also centralized decisionmaking institutions in the capitals. Up to this point, finished goods had been produced in small quantities by artisans. The introduction of large-scale industrial production dramatically reduced the price of those products—but unfortunately for the small city-state, this type of industrial production was only possible in a state with a large population. The small city-state had lost not only its military protection, but also its economic base. Meanwhile, the large European states secured supplies of cheap raw materials through expanding colonial empires.

After World War II, however, as these colonial empires broke up, the large nation-states began to realize that free trade was in their own economic interest and trade barriers had to be removed globally—and the situation began to change dramatically for the surviving small states, like Liechtenstein, that were able to take advantage of the new international environment. Simultaneously, raw materials and traditional industrial goods produced in large factories lost their importance in international trade, relative to the growing demand for innovative specialized products that could be produced best in small factories. The economic balance between small and large states had been restored at least to the level seen before the industrial revolution; one could even argue that it was now more favorable to the small state.

At the same time, I also saw that the reversal of the trend toward the large centralized state would bring further political unrest to Europe and the world: civil wars when the large states collapse, and wars of aggression when small states grow in size. Ironically, the bright economic future of Liechtenstein would be threatened by the general trend toward smaller states. There was little doubt in my mind that the Soviet empire would collapse one day and with it the longest peace in Europe since the end of the Roman Empire.

What can guarantee continued peaceful development? Perhaps if military technology and strategy would again move in a direction that favored the defender and the small states, there would at least be some hope for more stability. But even if a military solution could be found and implemented, I am convinced for at least two reasons that it is critical to search for a political solution in order to manage the changing size of states in a peaceful manner.

First, technology today offers weapons far more destructive and dangerous than in the past. And this progress in military technology is extremely difficult to control, especially because most of our technology is "dual use"—it can be used to accomplish peaceful tasks, as well as for war.

Second, in the past war was a rather local business: it was terrible for those directly affected, but the rest of the world or even the region could go on as usual. Globalization through improved means of communication and transport changed this. Unrest in one part of the world can bring bombs, terror, and refugees to another, where public sentiment may lead to intervention in the conflict one way or the other; thus, local conflicts are globalized.

Again, where do we look for a solution?

Simply freezing the present borders of all states is an unworkable solution; similar proposals have failed in the past, and there is no reason to believe that they will work in the future.

The current policy of the international community is not much better. People everywhere are told that they have the right to self-determination. Nevertheless, if this right is suppressed by a sovereign state, the international community supports territorial integrity until a war of independence is successful. As in the past, the entire problem is settled on the battlefield. As long as civil wars remain local affairs and military technology favors the large states, such a policy—though cynical—does maintain a certain stability in the world. But there are indications that military technology can shift the balance toward the small state, which increases the chances for a breakaway region to be successful in a civil war—and thus encourages violent secession movements. If the international community does not change its present policy, we will probably soon see the collapse of more large states in civil wars.

I believe that the ideal and most democratic solution would be for the people themselves, down to the smallest community, to decide if they want to have more autonomy, belong to another state, or become independent. Is it not true that people created states to serve and protect them, and not the other way around? Does our common humanity not demand that we replace the power of the weapon with the power of the vote, and the battlefield by the ballot box?

Some fifteen years ago I began to work on a convention on self-determination. Though I continue to hope that the vision of complete self-determination will be achieved one day around the world, I knew from the start that a workable approach must be a compromise; otherwise it has no chance of winning international acceptance. But there is room for compromise only if the idea of autonomy is accepted as a solution. In many cases, neither minority rights nor democratic rights are sufficient to solve the problem—even a democracy can become a dictatorship of the majority and lead to civil war. Decentralization of power may often be the only way to bring decisions nearer to the people and to make the state itself more efficient. Graduated levels of autonomy can give the state and the people time to adapt to a new structure. Political leaders who demand more self-determination or even independence for their people must first prove at different levels of autonomy that they can fulfill their promises and the people's expectations. A gradual approach to self-determination avoids situations in which new states are created with leaders who have no experience in self-government.

A major problem thus far has been the creation of new states with new minorities whose right of self-determination was not respected and who would have preferred to remain in the old state or to create their own states. German minorities, whose right to self-determination was ignored after World War I and who were integrated into newly created states, were one reason why Adolph Hitler could lead Germany into World War II. Croatia and Bosnia-Herzegovina are other examples of this critical problem. It is therefore extremely important to bring self-determination to the smallest community. To grant the right of self-determination exclusively to those people who have a distinct ethnic, religious, or cultural background not only creates the danger of ethnic or religious cleansing, but also increases the danger that existing states will be destroyed rather than decentralized.

The wisdom of successful empires in the past, "divide and rule," has been somewhat forgotten by many elites in modern states. Croatia might not have chosen the path of independence if the right of self-determination had been established on the community level rather than in a limited way on a much larger regional level. The Serbian minority inside Croatia would have chosen to remain in Yugoslavia, and Croatia would have lost a large part of its territory through independence. With the exception of Slovenia, all of the states that emerged after the collapse of Yugoslavia have large minorities that probably would have preferred to stay inside a modern decentralized Yugoslavia, rather than experience the present situation. Small communities quickly realize that they cannot solve all their problems alone and instead have to cooperate with other communities and delegate some of their authority to higher levels. It is unfortunately too easy for nationalistic leaders to convince masses of people that independence is the only solution.

There is another reason to offer the right to self-determination to communities. Communities and their inhabitants are much easier to define than the rather theoretical concept of "peoples." Where does a resident of Sarajevo belong if her mother is a Serb, her father a Muslim, and her spouse a Croat? The different ethnic or cultural identities of a city or a village can give its whole population an identity and cultural richness that is destroyed when borders are drawn according to some theoretical definition of what it means to constitute a "people," instead of drawn according to the wishes of the population in each community.

The time has come to address this problem in a systematic way and on different levels. I first raised the matter at the United Nations in 1991, and since then it has been a regular topic of the Liechtenstein delegation to the UN and in other international organizations. Since 1994 we have also dealt with issues relating to self-determination on the academic level. I am grateful to Princeton University for deciding to become involved in this enormous and important research task, and I am confident that we will achieve our ultimate goal. Nevertheless, I have no illusion that it will not take many years and much effort before solutions to the problems I have described are found and implemented.

ACKNOWLEDGMENTS

Self-determination, interdependence, the role of communities and states, and the question of boundaries have always been at the center of international relations—not just since President Woodrow Wilson's Fourteen Points. At the end of the Cold War, Prince Hans Adam II of Liechtenstein's convictions about the importance of the rights of self-determination and democracy to peoples throughout the world led eventually to Liechtenstein's UN Initiative on Self-Determination, as well as to the establishment of the Liechtenstein Research Program on Self-Determination at Princeton University. This book is the result of one of the research program's core projects. Thus, I would like to express my gratitude to Prince Hans Adam for his support and vision.

The interest of colleagues and friends at Princeton and elsewhere made it possible for me to expand research activities and teaching related to self-determination and to organize the project and this volume. I would especially like to mention Michael Doyle, Richard Falk, Claudia Fritsche, James Gow, Jeffrey Herbst, Walter Hinderer, Atul Kohli, Jeremiah Ostriker, the late Edgar L. Rachlin, Albert Rohan, Michael Rothschild, Harold Shapiro, Dusan Sidjanski, James Trussell, Arthur Watts, William Weaver, and Thomas Wright. I also am very grateful for the devoted support and assistance of the staff of the research program: Melissa Magliana, and especially Tyler Felgenhauer, who provided outstanding editorial and research assistance, and Elizabeth Herron, whose efforts have been instrumental in keeping the program running.

Last but certainly not least, I would like to express to my beloved wife, Annegret, my deep gratitude for all her support in the ups and downs of such an undertaking, and to my daughters, Carolina and Mariella, my thanks for their understanding the travails of Daddy's sometimes overbearing work.

May this volume influence and provide knowledge to all who must deal with issues of self-determination, and may it in some small ways help to avoid the bloodshed and destruction that have made so many recent self-determination crises so infamous.

—Wolfgang Danspeckgruber

INTRODUCTION

WOLFGANG DANSPECKGRUBER

The drive for self-determination has been one of the major causes of the world's humanitarian crises in the post–Cold War era. Struggles for autonomy and secession have been the source of tremendous human suffering and destruction in Africa, Europe, and Asia. The dilution of the international system's bipolar rigidity, global interdependence, intensified economic-technological cooperation, and real-time communication have added a crucial challenge to traditionally existing problems between communities and central authorities. Today many communities are torn between their desire to participate in the global marketplace and maximize their international contacts and the wish to obtain maximum freedom for their cultural-religious, linguistic, and other important traditions while asserting themselves vis-à-vis their respective central authority. This conflict offers ample chances for problematic or crises-ridden situations.

The bloody and destructive events accompanying the disintegration of Yugoslavia (that is, the conflicts in Bosnia-Herzegovina and Kosovo) and the upheavals in the Caucasus (for instance, the war in the Russian republic of Chechnya) and in Kashmir in South Asia—to name just a few examples—have proven that separation by force and the intention to redraw external boundaries can lead to large-scale suffering and destruction. Moreover, ruthless leadership and commercial interests, combined with an increasingly global interaction among organized-crime networks and easier access to weapons of mass destruction, have made self-determination crises much more dangerous, costly, and difficult to manage. The process of establishing new international boundaries can create winners and losers and frequently brings about involvement by outside powers.

Background

As the idealistic element of state formation, self-determination has been responsible for the shattering of large empires and smaller states alike. It was a major contributing factor to bloodshed and destruction in the international system of the nineteenth century, at the beginning of the twentieth, during and following World War I, in the immediate post–World War II era, and after the fall of the Berlin Wall in 1989. The notion of self-determination served the assertion of statehood and national identity at the expense of large multiethnic empires (Austro-Hungarian, German, Ottoman, and czarist Russian) and contributed to the dissolution of colonial empires, the sovereignty of the colonies, the unification of Germany, and the disintegration of Yugoslavia, the Soviet Empire, and Czechoslovakia.[1]

At the beginning of the twenty-first century the international system is in a transitional phase. It remains in search of new overarching mechanisms and structures to operate in an ever more interdependent world at the same time that its traditional foundation, national sovereignty, is in decline and mobility and the flow of goods, services, and information increase.[2] Sovereignty has experienced mounting challenges from increased public education about and awareness of basic human rights and global real-time information (from such sources as CNN and the Internet). Particularly the right of a government to exert its power at home in unlimited and *n' aporte quelconque* fashion is coming under serious scrutiny. In fall 1999 UN Secretary-General Kofi Annan questioned the right of any state to hide behind sovereignty while committing flagrant violations of human rights. He invoked "individual sovereignty" (that is, "individual" as enshrined in the UN Charter)—namely the human rights and fundamental freedoms of each and every citizen.[3] Annan also argued that "the state is now widely understood to be the servant of its people—and not vice versa."[4] Interestingly, in 1997 Prince Hans Adam II of Liechtenstein presented a

---

1. For an interesting compilation of studies see Thomas D. Musgrave, *Self-determination and National Minorities* (Oxford: Clarendon Press, 1997); and Metta Spencer, ed., *Separatism: Democracy and Disintegration* (Lanham, Md.: Rowman and Littlefield, 1998).

2. See the important work by Gidon Gottlieb, *Nation Against State* (New York: Council on Foreign Relations, 1993).

3. United Nations Secretary-General Kofi Annan, *Address to the United Nations General Assembly*, New York, September 20, 1999. See also Kofi Annan, "By Invitation: Two Concepts of Sovereignty," *The Economist* (November 1999).

4. Annan, "By Invitation."

similar position in his exposé "Democracy and Self-Determination," where he argued that the state should principally offer services to its citizens; they in turn should have the right to "choose their states and citizenship freely—in self-determination."[5] Arguably, as states and their international organizations interact, change, and develop, sovereignty and autonomy will be "mitigated."[6] But sovereignty will remain to be a critical determinant of the emerging international system.

Since the end of the Cold War, the international system has evolved from a bipolar structure based on hegemony and nuclear deterrence to an at times unipolar one with the United States as the leading superpower. At that juncture when unipolarity reigns, signs of an increasingly multipolar structure are detected: regional major powers emerge as weapons of mass destruction become more available, and population giants such as China, India, Indonesia, and Brazil play an increasingly relevant commercial (as regards producers and markets) and strategic role. Moreover, reemerging nationalism (in part as a reaction against globalization) and (religious) fundamentalism (in part due to the absence of ideology), ruthless leadership interests, powerful global media, and global interdependence in information, trade, and finance and in culture and language have further complicated the issues traditionally related to self-determination, such as sovereignty, communal interests, secession, and borders.

Conceptual Discussion

In a sense, classical self-determination—that is, the search for full independence and sovereignty by a community with the result to redraw international boundaries at the expense of the existing state—represents a dichotomy between the traditional perspective of state formation, the international system as known till the end of the Cold War, and the emergence of a new global structure characterized by interdependence, high levels of real-time information, mobility, and a global marketplace.

Propagated and employed by President Woodrow Wilson—and even earlier by Joseph Stalin—the concept of self-determination in

---

5. Prince Hans Adam II of Liechtenstein, "Democracy and Self-Determination," Schloss Vaduz, Liechtenstein, 1997.

6. Luzius Wildhaber argued that "[self-determination] must be mitigated by the exigence of interdependence," as quoted by Ruth Lapidoth, *Autonomy: Flexible Solutions to Ethnic Conflicts* (Washington, D.C.: U.S. Institute of Peace Press, 1996), p. 47.

reality goes back to the American and French Revolutions. It was finally enshrined in the Charter of the United Nations (UN) more than fifty years ago, at the end of World War II.[7] Following the demise of major colonial powers and the end of the Cold War, the concept's initial impetus (in the context of decolonization) was largely spent. In an increasingly interdependent world, which allows greater specialization and prosperity of even the smallest units, self-determination gained new meaning and relevance. The close link of that principle with human rights was a source of strength initially, when, after World War II, "first generation" human rights were evolving. But with social, industrial, and technological evolution, and heightened interdependence, there was growing pressure to develop human rights so as to encompass rights for groups and communities as well as for individuals within them. Especially puzzling is the definition of the "self" who determines the group's future path of political development. This problem is particularly acute in a world slowly moving away from the relatively tidy system of nation-states toward a more uncertain world in which national sovereignty is being eroded both from above (at the level of regional integration) and below (at the level of smaller-scale political units drawing their cohesion from such factors as religious, ethnic, cultural, and linguistic similarity). We need, therefore, to determine which entity can justifiably argue for self-determination and thus autonomy—a community, a (suppressed) people, a former colony?[8] We must also consider the distinction between the holders of the right to

---

7. Antonio Cassese elaborates that it was really Joseph Stalin who already by 1913 "had written a detailed pamphlet on the matter." He quotes Stalin's pamphlet: "The right of self-determination means that only the nation itself has the right to determine its destiny, . . . no one has the right to forcibly interfere . . . to destroy schools and other institutions, to violate its customs, to repress its language, or curtail its rights. . . . The right to self-determination means that a nation can arrange its life on the basis of autonomy [and] that it has the right to complete secession, [and] that all nations are equal." Quoted from J. Stalin, *Marxism and the National and Colonial Question; A Collection of Articles and Speeches* (London, 1941), pp. 18–19, in Antonio Cassese, *Self-Determination of Peoples: A Legal Reappraisal* (Cambridge: Cambridge University Press, 1995), p. 14, n. 7.

Apparently Lenin developed this idea further in 1915–1916 while he was writing his book *On Imperialism*. See ibid. as well as Lenin's *Thesis on the Socialist Revolution and the Right of Nations to Self-Determination* (New York: International Publishers, 1916); and Arno J. Maier, *Wilson Versus Lenin: Political Origins of the New Diplomacy, 1917–1918* (Cleveland: Alfred A. Knopf, 1964).

8. Wolfgang Danspeckgruber and Arthur Watts, "Introduction" in Wolfgang Danspeckgruber with Arthur Watts, eds., *Self-Determination and Self-Administration: A Sourcebook* (Boulder, Colo.: Lynne Rienner, 1997).

self-determination, which can be a majority or a minority within one state or community, or separated by boundaries.[9]

Nationalism, the search for identity and sociocultural autonomy, and the scrupulous exploitation of nationalist objectives by ruthless leaders have highlighted the destructive dimensions of a concept originally conceived as a basis for state formation, for the liberation of oppressed peoples, and for increasing the democratic power of the individual citizen. Self-determination's two dimensions—the "internal" dimension, that is, the possibility to democratically elect the leadership and to develop the domestic politics and national institutions of a state; and the "external" dimension, referring to the community's or state's right to sovereignty and independent external relations—are increasingly being challenged by the pressure of greater education and contacts abroad, increased mobility, economic and strategic interdependence, and the globalization of the media, but also by an emerging reinsistence upon the traditional national/communal values in decisionmaking, culture, laws, and administration. This tension makes the future development of the concept of self-determination less predictable and questions the general assumption of a reduced role of the state.

History

During the Cold War, the rigidity of the bipolar international system largely suppressed the possibility to strive for greater independence and sovereignty in and around Europe. Self-determination was limited to cases of decolonization and the related geopolitical adjustments (Biafra, Kashmir, Bangladesh, Tibet, East Timor). At the time, this suppression of self-determination contributed to the erroneous image of a stable and calm international community without self-determination and secession movements.[10]

---

9. For an excellent discussion of this issue see Cassese, *Self-Determination of Peoples*, pp. 141–157. See also the classic volumes on this issue by Benedict Anderson, *Imagined Communities: Reflections on the Origin and Spread of Nationalism* (London: Verso, 1983), and by Donald L. Horowitz, *Ethnic Groups in Conflict* (Berkeley: University of California Press, 1985).

The relevant "International Covenant on Civil and Political Rights, 1966, Article 1" and "Excerpts from Judgements and Advisory Opinions of the International Court of Justice Bearing on Self-Determination" can be found in Danspeckgruber with Watts, *Self-Determination and Self-Administration*, p. 468.

10. For an excellent legal discussion of self-determination see Cassese, *Self-Determination of Peoples*.

Once the Berlin Wall fell and the Soviet Union and its empire disintegrated, however, those interested in self-determination, heightened autonomy, or secession began to advance their objectives more aggressively, and leaders tried to exploit the new opportunities. At the beginning of the twenty-first century, struggles over self-determination have emerged in many different places on the globe—from southeastern Europe via the Black Sea region and the Caucasus to central and southern Asia. Since the end of the Cold War, secessionist movements have mobilized in states in Africa and Central America as well as in highly industrialized states such as Canada, Belgium, France, Italy, Russia, and the United Kingdom. But each case harbors its own, very specific background and level of development and differs in intensity and orientation. Causes range from economic and leadership interests and quests for sovereignty by communities to lingering unresolved interethnic problems. Responses vary from suppression and domination to deliberate manipulation and incitement as well as outside power involvement.

However, the international community, still possessing the attitudes and strategies toward self-determination that were developed before and during the Cold War, has responded neither effectively nor consistently. Rarely has it acted in a timely fashion or shown much innovation. For instance, Somaliland (the northwest portion of Somalia previously governed by the British) has claimed independence, but the international community still looks to the government in Mogadishu to grant recognition to the breakaway province before acting (the formal method of dealing with secession movements developed during the Cold War). Yet there is no government in Mogadishu to grant independence to Somaliland.[11] In the case of Bosnia-Herzegovina and Kosovo, the local population had to suffer massive violence and significant destruction before a concerted international reaction could garner momentum; in the case of Kosovo, the reaction led to the North Atlantic Treaty Organization's (NATO) largest air operation in Europe since World War II. In Chechnya, however—within the sovereign territory of the Russian Federation—even rampant human rights violations could not induce any meaningful international reaction.[12]

Contrary to widespread assumption, the intensification of globalization has not diminished the frequency—or violence—of struggles for self-determination and secession. Apparently, even in highly industrial-

---

11. See Jeffrey Herbst, *States and Power in Africa: Comparative Lessons in Authority and Control* (Princeton: Princeton University Press, 2000).

12. See Wolfgang Danspeckgruber, Michael Doyle, Jeffrey Herbst, and Gilbert Grozman, "National and International Responses to Self-Determination Conflicts," Carnegie Corporation of New York, 2000.

ized states, communities and peoples can see a clear distinction between the different worlds they inhabit: although accepting economic and industrial interdependence—or perhaps precisely because of it—they may be eager to maintain communal and sociocultural independence so as to be able to conduct their lives according to communal values and traditions, perhaps even in their specific language (for example, Quebec, Scotland,[13] and Corsica).[14] Many reasons may exist for this insistence: it may be a counterreaction to ever intensifying integration and globalization, may be born of the geographical distance of the scenes of secession-related crisis, or may be born out of a longstanding communal desire for freedom from central authorities.[15]

Thus a thorough analysis of the classical concept of self-determination and the examination of a new role and meaning in the emerging global system has become important. In our time the search for self-determination and autonomy ought not necessarily or automatically cause the breakup of sovereign states or the change of external boundaries. Rather, the introduction of *self-governance*—maximum autonomy in combination with (regional) integration and the acceptance of multiple identities—should satisfy the aspirations of the community looking for greater independence while enabling the state to continue existence within its sovereign (albeit altered) boundaries.[16] Such an adapted concept of traditional self-determination should offer a safety valve for the community seeking autonomy while keeping it from the slippery slope toward independence, help avoid bloodshed and destruction, and save the international community cost and effort.

---

13. Regarding the development of the situation in and around Scotland, see John Lloyd, "Losing Scotland," *Financial Times,* September 16, 1998; and the letter to the editor by David Martin, "Scotland: Autonomy Not Independence in Europe," *Financial Times,* September 22, 1998, p. 16. Martin describes the European Union's "three level development," apparently based on the experience of the Free State of Bavaria, as "the autonomous nations or region, the member state, and the EU."

14. For an interesting debate of issues like ethics, philosophy, and nationalist dimensions of self-determination see Margaret Moore, ed., *National Self-Determination and Secession* (New York: Oxford University Press, 1998).

15. Observe the significant impact of a recent publication on perceived, alas dangerously realistic assumption of the reemergence of a global religious-fundamentalist conflict scenario: Samuel Huntington, "The Clash of Civilizations?" *Foreign Affairs* 72, no. 3 (Summer), pp. 22–50. It remains to be seen, though, how this contributes to the explanation of the tensions between Iran and the Taliban in Afghanistan.

16. Wolfgang Danspeckgruber, "Self-Governance: A Novel Solution for Traditional (European) Problems" (Belgrade, Princeton, 1998).

Objective of the Book

The objective of this book is to examine both empirically and conceptually the causes and impacts of strivings for self-determination and autonomy and the relevant dimensions: legal, political-administrative, ethnic-cultural, economic, and strategic. The empirical analysis attempts to consider examples in all major regions.

The leitmotiv of this study is threefold: the phenomenon of self-determination in theory and practice; the effects of the evolving international system on states, nations, and communities; and the potential of adaptation of the classical notion of self-determination to contemporary challenges. The main concern is the tension between further development, evolution, and adaptation on the one hand and resistance and insistence on the status quo on the other. The current evolution of the international system is caused by technological progress, political goals, generally accessible information, and intensified international trade and mobility.[17] Words such as *interdependence, integration, regionalization, globalization, networks, real-time communication, Internet, mobility,* and *global culture* suggest that the rigidity of borders, the exclusivity of sovereignty, and the omnipotence of state power are challenged. Though it is to be expected that states will fight back and administrations will resist change, change in the international system will occur and will affect the concept of self-determination itself.

The book is divided into three parts. In Part 1, an examination of the conceptual foundations, challenges, and limitations of self-determination, Chapters 1–5 elaborate the various dimensions concerning self-determination in the international system. Two of them are the future of the nation-state in a changing global environment (Chapter 1) and its effect on the classical perspective of self-determination under international law (Chapter 2). Chapters 3–5 are critical evaluations of, respectively, the international responses to self-determination crises and the question of national sovereignty, the limits of self-determination, and the danger of creating a legislated communal identity. Part 2 contains case studies of self-determination struggles in countries and regions around the globe in light of some of the concerns and issues addressed in Part 1. Part 3 consists of a final assessment and an extensive appendix. The final assessment puts the various case studies into the context

---

17. For the classical work on change in the international arena, see Robert Gilpin, *War and Change in World Politics* (New York: Cambridge University Press, 1981).

of the emerging international system and delineates two mechanisms to address and anticipate issues of self-determination in a given state: the introduction of modes and mechanisms in a national constitution, and the elaboration of a new option to satisfy communal aspirations of freedom and equality with the longings and needs of the individual citizen in our interdependent world—commual self-governance plus regional integration.

This discussion is followed by a detailed commentary (see Appendix B) on the so far most sophisticated proposal within the United Nations—the Liechtenstein Draft Convention on Self-Determination Through Self-Administration. Sir Arthur Watts, who with Prince Hans Adam II of Liechtenstein developed this legal document, offers an elaborate commentary that in turn should provide incentives and ideas for the establishment of appropriate communal, national, and regional regulations. The appendixes include a list of crises and conflicts since the Cold War and an overview of major international documents.

Part 1

CONCEPTUAL AND INTERNATIONAL FRAMEWORK

Global Change and the Future of Existing Nation-States

JEFFREY HERBST

The history of the twentieth century is, in good part, the history of the fracturing of large political units. Since 1900, the Austro-Hungarian, Belgian, British, Danish, Dutch, Ethiopian, French, German, Italian, Japanese, Ottoman, Portuguese, Russian, Soviet, and Spanish empires have all collapsed, leaving in their wake a large number of smaller states. The trend toward smaller political units, as well as the recent and dramatic breakups of the Soviet Union and Yugoslavia, demands an examination of whether even smaller states can be viable in the future, especially given the profound global political, economic, and military changes that are becoming apparent at the new millennium. Unfortunately, examinations of recent instances of state-shattering have all but ignored the international context, preferring instead to find domestic explanations as to why the formerly communist countries shattered.[1] Rather, the usual view has been that international forces, notably the stress on sovereignty and international support for the

---

1. For instance, the voluminous literature on the breakup of the Soviet Union does not emphasize the international dimension. See, for instance, Gail W. Lapidus and Victor Zaslavsky, eds., with Philip Goldman, *From Union to Commonwealth: Nationalism and Separatism in the Soviet Republics* (Cambridge: Cambridge University Press, 1992); Alexander J. Motyl, ed., *The Post-Soviet Nations: Perspectives on the Demise of the USSR* (New York: Columbia University Press, 1992); Timothy J. Colton and Robert Legvold, eds., *After the Soviet Union: From Empire to Nations* (New York: W. W. Norton, 1992); and John B. Dunlop, *The Rise of Russia and the Fall of the Soviet Union* (Princeton: Princeton University Press, 1993).

integrity of nations, act as counterbalances to the centrifugal forces that arise from domestic politics and threaten to shatter states.[2]

A focus on the possibilities of smaller states also raises the question of whether forms of political organization other than the nation-state may be viable in the future. Indeed, with the reemergence of self-determination as an important norm for the international community to respect, there has recently been a flurry of debate regarding the future of the nation-state.[3]

An immediate terminological problem relates to what exactly is meant by *small*. Economists define small countries as those that are price takers, that is, those whose domestic policies do not affect the international economy.[4] If we use this definition, almost every country in the world, including Korea, Turkey, Canada, and China, is small. Other definitions use population size but, inevitably, vary on how to demarcate *small*. For instance, Paul Streeten defines *small* as populations under 10 million people, Bimal Jalan identifies *small* as under 5 million, and the David Davies Memorial Institute study of small states focuses on those countries with fewer than 1 million people.[5] Other scholars have used a variety of measures, including gross domestic product (GDP), electrical consumption, and military expenditures, either singly or in some combination, to reach a definition of *small*.[6] The problem with these studies is that the demarcation between small and not small is usually arbitrary. Equally important, the definition of *small* is not related to the analytic question at hand, making the classifications largely an exercise in scholasticism.

This chapter eschews a single definition of *small* because it is large-

---

2. See, for instance, Crawford Young, "The National and Colonial Question and Marxism: A View from the South," in Alexander J. Motyl, ed., *Thinking Theoretically About Soviet Nationalities: History and Comparison in the Study of the USSR* (New York: Columbia University Press, 1992), p. 91.

3. See, for instance, Gidon Gottlieb, *Nation Against State: A New Approach to Ethnic Conflicts and the Decline of Sovereignty* (New York: Council on Foreign Relations, 1993).

4. Vittorio Corba and Fernando Ossa, "Small Open Economies: The Main Issues," in Vittorio Corba, Anne O. Krueger, and Fernando Ossa, eds., *Export-Oriented Development Strategies* (Boulder, Colo.: Westview Press, 1985), p. 5.

5. Paul Streeten, "The Special Problems of Small Countries," *World Development* 21 (February 1992), p. 197; Bimal Jalan, "Introduction," in Bimal Jalan, ed., *Problems and Policies in Small Economies* (London: Croom Helm, 1982), p. 1; and David Davies Memorial Institute of International Studies, *Small Is Dangerous: Micro States in a Macro World* (New York: St. Martin's Press, 1985), pp. 4–6.

6. One example is Harold Codrington, "Country Size and Taxation in Developing Countries," *Journal of Development Studies* 25 (July 1989), p. 509.

ly concerned with the pressures on a country to become smaller, irrespective of the original size. Such an approach allows a focus on the pressures affecting many countries that may cause them to splinter or at least alter the calculations of those who, in the past, may have called for retention of the existing nation-state because smaller units would not have been viable. Focusing on trends rather than absolute size is important, not least because the Soviet Union split into fifteen different countries, two of which—Russia and Ukraine—seem large by most definitions. Similarly, even if Nigeria were to split into three different countries, each of the new countries would probably be among the seven or so largest countries in Africa.

The Nation-State's Rise and the Advantages of Size

In the past fifty years, the nation-state has become the almost universal mode of political organization across the world. Indeed, the nation-state's dominance has become so total that it is often forgotten that its current hegemony is really fairly recent. Even the generally accepted marker for the ascendance of the nation-state—the Treaty of Westphalia in 1648—is really not that auspicious. Westphalia largely initiated a system of interstate relations but did not guarantee the presence of nation-states everywhere, even in Europe, as the subsequent history of both Germany and Italy makes clear. It was not until the nineteenth century that the postfeudal political entities were converted into national states in Europe.[7] In 1900, the organizing principle across much of the world outside of Europe was not the nation-state but empire, as a large fraction of globe was ruled from Lisbon, London, and Paris.

The true triumph of the nation-state occurred between 1948 and 1963, when dozens of countries gained independence and chose as the vehicle to independence the nation-state as defined politically and geographically by their former colonizers. The revolution in international relations was that these new states were accorded the same sovereign rights as any other country irrespective of the strength of their domestic institutions or long-term prospects.[8] Just how profound this change was can be observed in Africa. In precolonial Africa, a wide variety of political organizations—villages, city-states, nation-states, and empires—

7. Anthony D. Smith, *The Ethnic Origins of Nations* (Oxford: Basil Blackwell, 1986), p. 11.
8. Robert H. Jackson, *Quasi States: Sovereignty, International Relations, and the Third World* (Cambridge: Cambridge University Press, 1990), p. 15.

rose and fell. However, that heterogeneous political heritage was brushed aside in the rush by nationalists to seize the reins of power of the nation-state as defined politically and geographically by their European colonizers. Ironically, even as Kwame Nkrumah, Julius Nyerere, and Ahmed Sekou-Toure (as well as Ho Chi Minh, Jawaharlal Nehru, and Kusnasosro Sukarno) were proclaiming a break with Europe and the West, they uniformly seized upon that most Western of political organizations—the nation-state—to rule. As a reward, they were accorded sovereign status equal to that of their former rulers or the superpowers despite the tremendous differences in national capabilities.

At the same time that the nation-state has assumed a virtual monopoly in terms of political organization, individual nation-states have been remarkably stable. Between 1945 and 1989, there was unprecedented boundary stability, perhaps most vividly expressed by a European peace that depended on a bizarrely divided Berlin. One of the implicit rules of the superpower competition was that support of other countries' efforts to change boundaries was not part of the competition. In fact, the great powers usually intervened (as was the case with Zaire, Chad, and Ethiopia) to protect the integrity of existing states. Thus, between the end of World War II and 1989, the only forcible boundary changes that were unrelated to the end of colonialism were the creation of Bangladesh, the annexation of the Golan Heights, and the absorption of South Vietnam.[9] This was a remarkable development in a world where forcible boundary change was once a fairly common event. The most stunning aspect of the Iraqi invasion of Kuwait in 1990 was not that it happened but that this sort of armed effort has not occurred more often in a world made up mainly of weak states that cannot defend their boundaries.

To understand whether in the future even smaller nation-states and other types of political organization could become viable, it is first important to understand the confluence of factors that prompted the unprecedented rise of the nation-state in Europe and then throughout the world.[10] The nation-state rose to dominance largely because its

---

9. Given the strange geography of postindependence Pakistan, even the creation of Bangladesh could arguably be traced to decolonization.

10. This is a huge topic that can be discussed only in a cursory manner here. The major works include Joseph R. Strayer, *On the Medieval Origins of the Modern State* (Princeton: Princeton University Press, 1970); Charles Tilly, "Reflections on the History of European State-Making," in Charles Tilly, ed., *The Formation of Nation States in Western Europe* (Princeton: Princeton University Press, 1975); E. J. Hobsbawm, *Nations and Nationalism Since 1780: Programme, Myth, Reality* (Cambridge: Cambridge University Press, 1991); Michael Mann, *The Sources of Social Power*, vol. 2 (Cambridge: Cambridge University Press, 1993); and Brian M. Downing, *The Military Revolution and Political Change* (Princeton: Princeton University Press, 1992).

unique ability to unite a market and population under sovereign rule provided leaders in successive centuries with important economies of scale in military, economic, and political affairs that could not be achieved any other way. The first prompt for the creation of the nation-state was clearly its unique ability to marshal resources for war beginning in medieval Europe. In past centuries, when warfare was common in Europe, many political entities disappeared after being conquered by their neighbors. Not surprisingly, there was something of a Darwinian evolution that rewarded the design of institutions that might better mobilize resources to defend themselves and defeat others. The comparative advantages of the postfeudal state became progressively more important as warfare became much more expensive and increasingly involved the long-term funding of standing armies conscripted from the national population, funded through domestic taxes, and led by a professional staff that had to be able to adapt to continual changes in military technology. After some failed experiments with mercenary armies, it became clear by 1800 that only the new type of state could support the new type of warfare.[11] Such were the advantages offered by the nation-state that Joseph Strayer was forced to conclude that "the development of the modern state . . . made possible such a concentrated use of human resources that no other type of social organization could avoid being relegated to a subordinate role."[12] Those who had been colonized by the European states understood the modern state's formidable advantages as a means of mobilizing resources and controlling territory, tasks central to the postcolonial project of nationalists across the world.

Second, the relatively large national territories that the nation-state unified to create a single market gave it profound economic advantages over other types of political organization such as the city-state. From Adam Smith to current times, economists have argued, in the words of Charles Kindleberger, that "in economic terms the state should be large to achieve economies of scale."[13] Economists continued to believe that larger internal markets were intrinsically better because the boundaries of the nation-state, in accord with the theory of comparative advantage, were seen as barriers to economic exchange. As Robinson argued, "The boundary of the nation represents a point of discontinuity; it represents a change in the degree of mobility of almost all the factors of production of labor more especially but in hardly less degree also of capital and credit, since currency and banking systems are coterminous with

---

11. Charles Tilly, *European Revolutions, 1492–1992* (Oxford: Blackwell, 1993), p. 32.

12. Strayer, *On the Medieval Origins of the Modern State,* p. 4.

13. Charles P. Kindleberger, *Multinational Excursions* (Cambridge: MIT Press, 1984), p. 28.

nations; it represents above all a discontinuity in the mobility of goods."[14]

In the third world, industrialization through import substitution (ISI), the dominant development ideology from the 1950s until the 1980s, exemplified the fixation with the size of the domestic market. The larger the domestic market, the more viable the strategy became because the approach assumed that growth would be governed by domestic demand. Indeed, ISI institutionalized a bias against those who wanted to export to the international economy.

Finally, in the West, there has been a significant intellectual tradition, exemplified by Herbert Spencer, Emile Durkheim, Karl Marx and Friedrich Engels, and Talcott Parsons, that considered a critical part of modernization to be an evolution from small structures based on familial and ethnic identities to more complex social structures such as the nation.[15] The increasing scale and complexity of political arrangements as societies moved from gemeinschaft to gesellschaft was perceived as perforce good and desirable, whereas smaller political units such as tribe, village, and city-state, which previously were so important to the West, were increasingly seen as anachronistic.[16] The fact that, during the global decolonization process, there was almost no discussion of alternatives to the modern nation-state suggests how dominant its association with modernity had become.

The unique attractiveness of the nation-state as a political organization was furthered by a furious effort on the part of theorists and practitioners to prove that the relative largeness of the nation-state was an unambiguous democratic advantage. Classic political theory stressed the importance of small political units, ideally city-states.[17] Plato calculated the optimal number of citizens at 5,040; Aristotle believed that all the citizens should be able to assemble in one place and hear a speaker. Later, Rousseau and Montesquieu would also stress the importance of the relationship between size and democracy. The framers of the U.S. Constitution were particularly concerned that Montesquieu, who had a profound influence on Thomas Jefferson, seemed to be a size determin-

---

14. E.A.G. Robinson, "Introduction," in E.A.G. Robinson, ed., *Economic Consequences of the Size of Nations* (London: St. Martin's Press, 1960), p. xiv.

15. See, for instance, Karl Marx and Friedrich Engels, *Manifesto of the Communist Party*, p. 477, reprinted in Robert C. Tucker, *The Marx-Engels Reader*, 2nd ed. (New York: W. W. Norton, 1978).

16. Smith, *The Ethnic Origins of Nations*, p. 153.

17. This discussion relies heavily on Robert Dahl and Edward Tuftee, *Size and Democracy* (Stanford: Stanford University Press, 1973), pp. 4–7.

ist, arguing not only that city-states would be democratic but that larger units would inevitably be ruled by despots. Critically, James Madison brilliantly turned the argument on size and democracy on its head by arguing not only that large political units were not inherently undemocratic but that they had substantial advantages over smaller units by being able to limit the damage of factions.

The nation-state triumphed because of a series of complex factors, all of which played to its strength of being able to mobilize resources from a relatively large population and provide economies of scale for military, economic, and political activity. Given these advantages, it is hardly surprising that the nation-state was reproduced throughout the third world, even by those who had little patience for most European political and intellectual traditions. Further, the new leaders of the third world cooperated with the great powers in helping to design an international system, structured around the United Nations, that did not allow for anything other than sovereign states. As a result, decolonization was very much a transfer of power between elites rather than an effort to change existing macropolitical structures or to develop new ones.

The Diminishing Advantage of Size

After several centuries when powerful military, economic, and political considerations favored the establishment and continuation of relatively big nation-states, there is now some reason to believe that the advantages provided by size need to be recalculated. In particular, the utility of a relatively large unified market and polity that is the cornerstone of the nation-state may be less advantageous than before. At the same time, an alternative intellectual tradition has begun to stress the problems associated with political organizations that transfer responsibility away from communities. Some of these trends have been at work since 1900 and have helped to prompt the disintegration of the old colonial empires. Other factors have appeared relatively recently and may further strengthen the need to question whether existing nation-states, already so much smaller than the political organizations at the turn of the century, are really desirable or necessary.

The most important of these trends may be the long-term decline in the value of size, defined as population, land mass, or aggregate economic activity. Countries do not become rich today by mining a vast hinterland or by dint of large labor forces. Rather, they become rich by possessing advanced manufacturing sectors that produce semiconductors and supertankers and service sectors that write software and sell insurance to the world market.[18] The most successful economies since World War II—Japan, Korea, and Taiwan—succeeded despite the fact that they had very little land and the territory they possessed was notably bereft of natural resources. Peculiarly poor resource endowment may actually have propelled these countries to success because their leaders knew (unlike those of Argentina or Australia) that they could not rely on their wealth in the ground but had to develop skilled labor forces and efficient manufacturing sectors.

Indeed, there is no statistical relationship between country size and growth performance.[19] Even economists such as Michael Porter, who continue to believe that the size of the home market is important, note that the influence of other factors, including the composition of domestic demand and the similarities between domestic and international markets, means that even a relatively large internal market does not guarantee economies of scale.[20]

Furthermore, the dominant economic strategy in the 1980s and 1990s centers on export-led growth, implying that the size of the domestic market is not nearly as important as previously thought. An export orientation is particularly attractive because the world economy is growing quickly and developing countries have been successful in capturing an increasing share of manufactured exports.[21] Put simply, if a country is producing for the world market, does the size of its domestic market matter? Given that small countries, almost by definition, devote a larger share of their economy to foreign trade than large countries,[22] it could be that those small countries with proper macroeconomic policies are best positioned to take advantage of expanding interna-

---

18. Commodity producers since 1960 have grown significantly slower than diversified exporters or exporters of manufactured goods or services. World Bank, *Global Economic Prospects and the Developing Countries, 1994* (Washington, D.C.: World Bank, 1994), p. 32.

19. Chris Milner and Tony Westaway, "Country Size and the Medium-Term Growth Process: Some Cross-Country Evidence," *World Development* 21 (February 1993), p. 211.

20. Michael E. Porter, *The Competitive Advantage of Nations* (New York: Free Press, 1990), pp. 92–97.

21. The World Bank projects that international trade will increase at an average rate of 5.9 percent annually through the year 2003. The G-7 countries are expected to grow by only 2.7 percent a year during the same period. Between 1982 and 1988, world trade in manufactures grew by 13 percent a year, and manufactured goods exported by developing countries increased 18 percent annually. See World Bank, *Global Economic Prospects and the Developing Countries*, pp. 2–3; and I.M.D. Little et al., *Boom, Crisis and Adjustment: The Macroeconomic Experience of Developing Countries* (New York: Oxford University Press, 1994), p. 118.

22. Streeten, "The Special Problems of Small Countries," pp. 199–200.

tional trade. Even exceptional vulnerability to external shocks—traditionally believed to be the major drawback to an open economy—may be significantly obviated by good government management of sudden price increases or decreases.[23]

An export orientation combined with a relatively buoyant international economy addresses what has traditionally been seen as another major economic disadvantage of small states—the economies of scale. For instance, in the 1960s, Simon Kuznets could argue that small states (defined by him as under 10 million in population) could often not engage in production of high technology items because their small markets and concomitant small production runs would cause costs to be unacceptably high.[24] He could not have anticipated a world where Singapore can hope to become a leading exporter of such advanced technology products as microelectronics, robotics, or new-materials engineering because of its concentration of skills and its proven ability to export.[25] Although Singapore's performance has in many ways been exceptional, its example could point the way for many other countries.

Another factor reducing the utility of size has been the dramatic changes in international capital markets. Turnover in the global foreign exchange market now amounts to an astounding $2 trillion a day, up approximately fiftyfold from 1980.[26] The revolutions in computers and telecommunications have meant that much of this money can be transferred between currencies and countries almost instantly. Perhaps even more important are the huge increases in international portfolio investment, the ownership of assets by foreigners. The global stock of financial assets (stocks, bonds, bank deposits, and cash) has increased twice as fast as economic growth in rich economies and now totals $80 trillion, up from $12 trillion in 1980. This figure will only increase in the future as stock markets, especially in developing countries, allow foreign participation and institutional investors in the industrialized world seek to further internationalize their portfolios in order to escape low domestic yields.

As a result, national boundaries are no longer barriers to the movements of factors of production, especially capital, because international

---

23. David Bevan et al., *Controlled Open Economies: A Neoclassical Approach to Structuralism* (Oxford: Clarendon Press, 1990), p. 353.

24. Simon Kuznets, "Economic Growth of Small Nations," in Robinson, *Economic Consequences of the Size of Nations*, p. 17.

25. Chan Hwa Loon, "Develop Specialties to Play in the Big League," *Strait Times*, December 13, 1992, p. 6.

26. Statistics in this paragraph are from "Finance: Trick or Treat," *The Economist,* October 23, 1999, p. 91.

capital markets are integrated to allow for the almost instantaneous movement of funds. Thus, the fundamental advantage of a relatively large unified market under sovereign control provided by the nation-state is no longer nearly as important as it once was.

The military advantages associated with size have also changed fundamentally. Although there are today an unparalleled number of weak states that cannot defend their own boundaries, they are not invaded. Part of this change undoubtedly has to do with international norms. But part also is due to the fact that the economic value of land and other resources traditionally taken in wars of conquest is far less than it used to be.[27] The relationship of U.S. to Iraqi power expressed in the ratio of 146 U.S. deaths to approximately 50,000 Iraqi fatalities during the Gulf War is certainly on the order of many of the colonial wars of expansion fought in Africa a century ago.[28] However, no one believes that the economic problems of the United States will change fundamentally if it starts conquering other countries. Correspondingly, the nation-state's advantage in mobilizing resources for warfare has to be reevaluated.

At the same time, the beginnings of a significant change in the perceived political advantages of size are evident. In particular, the international community has in recent years placed much more stress on self-determination. After World War II, the right to self-determination was used by many nationalists to stress their case for independence. However, the global community, usually at the prompting of the same nationalists once they came to power, viewed self-determination as relating solely to freedom from colonial rule. The fate of ethnic groups within the nation was seen as solely a domestic issue even when severe human rights violations, sometimes involving the deaths of tens of thousands of people, occurred.

In the post–Cold War world, self-determination has assumed greater importance, thereby challenging the Madisonian notion that scale was unambiguously an advantage in the design of nations. For instance, in 1992 Hans Brunhart, Liechtenstein's head of government, in putting forward his country's initiative on self-determination at the United Nations, noted that much suffering and violence are caused by the problem of "the frustration of distinctive communities when they

---

27. Richard H. Ullman, *Securing Europe* (Princeton: Princeton University Press, 1991), p. 23.

28. The Iraqi figure can only be an estimate. Data are from Rick Atkinson, "Fratricide Problem Defies Decades of Efforts," *Washington Post,* April 14, 1994, p. A19; and "Staffer Who Released Iraq War Toll to Be Dismissed," *New York Times,* March 8, 1992, p. C4.

are denied the legitimate expression of their communal identities and aspirations."[29] The Liechtenstein initiative's stress on self-determination and the importance of every community having some level of autonomy within the nation-state and of increasing some communities' ability to act vis-à-vis the central state in many ways goes against much of Western intellectual thought over the past 200 years regarding both the optimal design of nations and the nation-state as the ultimate expression of modernity.

The current calls for self-determination are a substantial break from the tradition associated with Woodrow Wilson. Wilson's argument for self-determination was to stop "the aggression of the great powers upon small." He saw the foundations of war as being "the folding together of empires of unwilling subjects by the duress of arms."[30] It was this view of self-determination—protection of the nation from being absorbed by others—that so motivated the nationalists of this century. The view, as expressed by the Liechtenstein initiative, that communities—not necessarily nations—ought to have control over their own affairs, even if they have not been physically conquered by an empire, reflects a new affinity for smaller political units. Wilson was primarily concerned with protecting Poles and Czechs from the Germans, whereas the Liechtenstein initiative is also concerned with protecting groups such as the Welsh from their own central governments, a very different issue.

Implications for the Design of Nation-States

Whereas it seems clear that an array of forces is present in the international political economy that will make smaller states increasingly viable, the implications for the domestic politics of individual countries are less certain. Citizens do not undertake perpetual recontracting of their nation, constantly examining whether their country is the optimal size. Indeed, nearly the opposite is probably true. The inertia of the national experience, the fact that most nations have had stable boundaries for two or more generations, and the lack of any precedent in living memory, until recently, of other nations' changing their boundaries all combine to make the demarcation of the nation-state a nonissue in

---

29. Hans Brunhart, "Statement at the Forty-Seventh Session of the General Assembly," September 23, 1992, p. 3.

30. Woodrow Wilson, "Address to the Representatives of All the Allied and Associated Nations at the Paris Peace Conference, 25 January 1919," reprinted in Hamilton Foley, ed., *Woodrow Wilson's Case for the League of Nations* (Princeton: Princeton University Press, 1923), pp. 217–218.

most countries most of the time, even if there are powerful forces changing the economies of scale. As Boris Yeltsin wrote in his journal after the August 1991 coup, "The economy follows politics, after all."[31]

The New Attractiveness of Smallness

In times of political upheaval, however, the design of the nation-state will often be reexamined. This is especially true in the current era of democratization because the first issue that the new democrats must address is the nature of the polity. Thus Alexander Mokanu, then chairman of the Moldavian Supreme Soviet's presidium, noted during the First Congress of People's Deputies, "Perestroika makes it essential to find optimal forms of national-state organization."[32] Especially given the "demonstration effect" of the former Soviet Union, former Yugoslavia, former Czechoslovakia, and former Ethiopia, those seeking radical reform within their countries no longer have as much reason to believe that boundaries are immutable.

As a result, for countries where fundamental reforms are on the agenda, the powerful forces promoting smallness have, in fact, affected politics in several ways. First, politicians throughout the world no longer see much, if any, relationship between size and success. For instance, in a trip that would, rather oddly, be repeated several times by other world leaders in other places, Mikhail Gorbachev ventured to Lithuania (population 3.8 million) in January 1990 to argue against Baltic independence by stressing the advantages of being part of a large economic union. He prophesied, "Independence means paying the prices of the world market, and you will sink." Hélène Carrère d'Encausse notes that these arguments were met with "frosty silence."[33] Soon after, Estonia (population 1.6 million), Latvia (population 2.6 million), and Lithuania seceded.

In fact, the Baltics did, in a relatively short time, disprove much of Gorbachev's argument. Estonia, the economic leader of the Baltics, managed to dramatically change trade relations quickly. In 1991, Russia

---

31. Boris Yeltsin, *The Struggle for Russia* (New York: Random House, 1994), p. 105.

32. See Oleg Glebov and John Crowfoot, eds., *The Soviet Empire: Its Nations Speak Out* (New York: Harwood Academic, 1989), p. 36.

33. Hélène Carrère d'Encausse, *The End of the Soviet Empire: The Triumph of the Nations* (New York: Basic Books, 1991), p. 155. Of course, Gorbachev's argument that only a vast union could protect the fortunes of individual republics was long a staple of Soviet thought. See, for instance, Joseph Stalin, *Marxism and the National Question* (New York: International, 1942), p. 102.

supplied 85 percent of Estonia imports but only 30 percent in 1993. Similarly, Russia was the destination for 95 percent of Estonia's exports in 1991 but bought only 38 percent of Estonian goods sent overseas in 1993. The country's success moved Anthony Robinson to note that Estonia demonstrated "that a combination of political independence, a strong currency and a rational market-determined price structure can lead to dramatic shifts in both the direction, volume and usefulness of foreign trade."[34]

Gorbachev tried to use a similar argument regarding economies of scale to try to persuade Russia, the great prize, from "seceding" from its own empire. In June 1990, he argued, "Does someone think, maybe, that Russia outside the Union would develop more successfully? This is nothing more than an illusion. How can one make a rapid breakthrough in economic and social spheres without combining the potentials of the republics using the advantages of intra-Union cooperation and division of labor that took shape over decades of joint life and work?"[35] The Russians were unmoved by this appeal. Boris Yeltsin, almost alone among the political actors or academics who have even tried to put the fall of the Soviet Union in comparative perspective, wrote: "A united empire is a powerful and basic force, evoking both awe and respect; but how long could it have remained an empire? By that time all the other empires of the world had collapsed—British, French, and Portuguese."[36]

Yeltsin felt that Russia could develop only if it broke away from the Communist Party, the Council of Ministers, the state supply office, and other institutions of central control. He said that these bodies had only been a hindrance to Russia as a nation. Rather, "Russia had only interested them as a source of raw materials, labor, and cannon fodder."[37]

Other appeals to keep the economies-of-scale argument were equally unsuccessful. For instance, President George Bush visited Kiev in August 1991 to lecture the Ukrainians on the advantages of staying inside the Soviet Union: "The vast majority of trade conducted by Soviet companies, imports and exports, involves . . . trade between republics. The Nine Plus One Agreement holds forth the hope that republics will combine greater autonomy with greater voluntary

---

34. Anthony Robinson, "Survey of Estonia," *Financial Times*, April 19, 1994, pp. 29–31.

35. Mikhail Gorbachev, "Speech to the RSFSR Communist Party Conference, 19 June 1990," in Charles F. Furtado and Andrea Chandler, eds., *Perestroika in the Soviet Republics: Documents on the National Question* (Boulder, Colo.: Westview Press, 1992), p. 330.

36. Yeltsin, *The Struggle for Russia*, p. 113.

37. Ibid., p. 113.

action—political, social, cultural, economic—rather than pursuing the hopeless course of isolation."[38]

This statement was particularly strange because Bush, whose administration constantly prodded other countries to be more export oriented, assumed that the republics could not break from the Soviet Union and integrate with the international economy. However, a few months later, Ukrainians rejected Bush's pleas to avoid "suicidal nationalism" and chose independence.

Similarly, Secretary of State James Baker visited Yugoslavia in June 1991 and demanded that Croatia (population 4.7 million) and Slovenia (population 2 million) not leave Yugoslavia (population 23 million). Baker said that the United States would not recognize either country "under any circumstances" and promised that neither would get aid. In response, Slovenian finance minister Dusan Sesok said that his country was prepared "for financial war," and both countries immediately proclaimed their independence.[39] Slovenia, in particular, had been heavily influenced by the new opportunities provided by the international economy. As Laura Silber noted: "In the past, critics dismissed the prospects for Slovene independence because of its small size and population. But this now appears to be an asset. A diplomat put it simply: 'Slovenia is small enough to be flexible.' Furthermore, the volume of Slovene exports will never be large enough to upset its neighbors, but if it is increased it will guarantee most Slovenes a comfortable standard of living."[40] Ljubljana has been so successful in its new strategy that Slovenia was one of the first former communist states to begin to grow again despite, or perhaps because of, its size.

Remarkably similar warnings were made to Eritrea, Africa's newest nation, whenever independence was considered. For instance, the Fabian Society had written in 1948, "Looking further ahead, Eritrea is almost certainly not a viable unit on its own. If we are to think in terms of eventual independence, its people can stand no chance unless they link themselves to bigger and more viable neighbors."[41] The Eritreans, who number 3.5 million, were unmoved by this or successive arguments that they should stay part of Ethiopia (population 55 million).

---

38. "After the Summit: Excerpts from Bush's Ukraine Speech," *New York Times,* August 2, 1991, p. A8.

39. Marcus Tanner, "Defiant Slovenia Plans Its Rebirth as a Sovereign State," *The Independent,* June 24, 1991.

40. Laura Silber, "Survey of Slovenia," *Financial Times,* August 12, 1994, p. 31.

41. Fabian Society, *The Fate of Italy's Colonies* (London: Fabian Society, 1948), p. 89.

Undoubtedly, their belief in their own viability was strengthened by the success of other small states. For instance, Nerayo Teklemichael, head of the Eritrean Relief and Rehabilitation Agency, envisions that his country will be successful by emulating the "Asian Tigers."[42]

It remains to be seen whether any of these countries, or other smaller political units that may soon appear on the world stage, are actually successful in finding their niche in the extraordinarily competitive international market. However, the perception is that the international economy is accessible and that export-led growth is an option for a country of almost any size. Nowhere can this better be seen than by the international rush to become "the next Hong Kong." Not surprisingly given its success, Tallinn, Estonia, has repeatedly declared itself the "Hong Kong of the Baltics."[43] Similarly, Poland hopes to become the "Hong Kong of Central Europe"; El Salvador's ambition is to be the "Hong Kong of Central America"; Ciudad del Este, Paraguay, is often called the "Hong Kong of South America"; Ghana wants to become the "Hong Kong of Africa"; Jamaica's goal is to be the "Hong Kong of the Caribbean"; Crimea, in the Ukraine, thinks that it will be the next Hong Kong; and Vladivostok aims to be the "Hong Kong of Siberia."[44] Perhaps inevitably, the title "Hong Kong of the Middle East" is contested: Dubai, Gaza, and Tel Aviv all hope to duplicate the performance of Britain's small colony.[45]

The Inability to Prevent State-Shattering

Beyond rejecting sheer size as a basis for viability, the changes in the international economy may force many to reevaluate the specific advan-

---

42. Associated Press, "Nation Busts Africa Stereotype," August 21, 1994.

43. "The Baltics' Would-Be Hong Kong," *The Economist*, November 6, 1993, p. 95.

44. See, respectively, "An Emerging Market," *Warsaw Voice*, March 27, 1994; Daniel Alder, "El Salvador Emerging as Business Center," *UPI Press Report*, August 15, 1992; James Brooke, "Free Trade Fatefully Near for Paraguay's 'Hong Kong,'" *New York Times*, March 25, 1991, p. D1; Moyiga Nduru, "Ghana: Aiming to Become the Hong Kong of Africa," *Inter Press Service*, October 9, 1991; "Jamaica Sells Textile Mill to Hong Kong Interests," *Agence France Presse*, November 8, 1993; Celestine Boholen, "Russia vs. Ukraine," *New York Times*, March 23, 1994, p. A3; and Gerald Nadler, "A Parley to Create the Hong Kong of Siberia?" *United Press International*, September 30, 1988.

45. Marcia Scott Harrison, "Dubai," *Los Angeles Times*, February 13, 1994; Sam Aboudi, "Gaza Sees Construction Boom with Self Rule," *Reuter European Business Report*, May 12, 1994; and Charles W. Holmes, "With Middle East Peace Comes Hope for Profits," *Times-Picayune*, July 31, 1994, p. A24.

tages that their central government can provide. In particular, the benefits of transfers, subsidies, and other special arrangements that previously might have kept a region quiescent may be relatively less attractive if the nascent country believes that it can go it alone in the
international economy. Gorbachev argued that "the development of
cooperative production arrangements, cooperation and mutual assistance among the republics is in the highest interests of our multinational
state and of each republic."[46] However, the republics were again
unmoved. As one Estonian in the Congress of People's Deputies noted,
the experience of other countries shows that "modern civilization is
moving towards international integration, but not by centralizing and
subordinating."[47]

For instance, Slovakia (population 5.3 million), in what may have
been a disastrous decision, left Czechoslovakia (population 15.6 million) at least in part to break ties with Prague and to try its hand with
the international economy despite the fact that it received subsidies
from the Czech lands. Anthony Robinson notes, "Before the 'velvet
divorce,' Slovak nationalists complained that seven decades of cohabitation had left Slovakia as little more than a maker of components and
industrial products, such as steel, which is sold mainly to the Czech
Republic. With independence, they believed, Slovakia would finally
be able to sell more of its produce abroad."[48] A particularly contentious issue before the split was the Havel government's determination to close down the arms industry, which is largely based in
Slovakia. Instead, a central part of Slovakia's economic strategy is to
become a major player in the world's arms market by selling to almost
anyone.[49]

More generally, transfers, subsidies, and other bargaining arrangements will be of limited utility during times of profound change. First,
the region of a country most likely to leave is the richest, after developing a deep resentment against subsidizing others. For instance, there
was nothing that the former Yugoslavia could offer Slovenia to change
its calculus that it was better off as independent and able to export,

---

46. Quoted by Gertrude E. Schroeder, "Nationalities and the Soviet
Economy," in Rachel Denber, ed., *The Soviet Nationality Reader: The
Disintegration in Context* (Boulder, Colo.: Westview Press, 1992), p. 279.
47. Klara Hallik, quoted in Glebov and Crowfoot, *The Soviet Empire: Its
Nations Speak Out*, p. 39.
48. Anthony Robinson, "Breaking Up Was the Easy Part," *Financial Times,*
August 6, 1993, p. 13.
49. Bernd Debusmann, "Slovakia Shoots for a Place in World Arms Market,"
Reuters Business Report, December 31, 1992.

given that it was the richest region of the federation. Since secessionist thoughts will probably be kindled by prolonged economic failure, financial inducements to prevent state-shatt ring are unlikely to be persuasive. Also, once dramatic changes begin, transfer arrangements may be disrupted, further increasing the impetus of regions to leave their former nation-state.[50] Given that, in times of disruption, there can be few guarantees that delicately arranged political and economic power-sharing agreements will be enforced, regions may be more certain of their prospects by facing the international economy alone.

The Weakness of International Sanctions

In the face of incentives for states to become smaller, the international community has been notably unsuccessful in promoting boundary stability. Despite Olympian threats from various world leaders who predicted that separation would be disastrous, many regional leaders do not believe that their fate will be determined by their size. President Bush was seen as doing no more than carrying President Gorbachev's water when he pressed the republics not to leave the USSR. Similarly, Slovenia called Secretary of State Baker's bluff in a particularly brazen manner and was recognized a few months after he guaranteed them international isolation forever. Finally, in May 1991, the rebel advance on Addis Ababa forced Assistant Secretary of State for African Affairs Herman Cohen to switch, almost overnight, his preference for keeping Ethiopia whole to encouraging the occupation of the capital and the inevitable emergence of Eritrea.

The U.S. and European preference for boundary stability sometimes, as in the postcoup Soviet Union, simply becomes irrelevant given the powerful domestic forces in favor of disintegration. In the post–Cold War world, there are few incentives for the great powers to intervene forcibly to keep a country together. If the Europeans can tolerate the instability of the former Yugoslavia, there is no reason to believe that the instability caused by other countries shattering will move the great powers to react decisively. The lack of will on the part of the great powers to keep countries together is in sharp contrast to the Cold War period, when national stability was a high priority. For instance, the United States and France did not rush to aid the Zairian government of Mobutu Sese Seko when it faced (an eventually) suc-

---

50. See, for instance, David D. Laitin, "The National Uprisings in the Soviet Union," *World Politics* 44 (October 1991), p. 176.

cessful rebel movement in 1997, a notable change from the 1970s, when both great powers helped defend Zaire's territorial integrity.

Also, preferences for national stability may conflict with other goals, notably democratization and self-determination. The dilemma for the great powers is likely to be particularly acute because the region breaking away will often have a particularly good case that it has been repressed. For instance, in an age when self-determination is being stressed, it was difficult for anyone to argue that the Eritreans would be better off staying within Ethiopia after their decades-long repression at the hands of successive Amharic rulers. Similarly, sanctions on Slovenia were particularly hard to maintain given that its democratic government and rational economic planning were so at odds with what was happening to the south as Yugoslavia broke up.

Conclusion

Although trying to predict the actual number of countries a generation from now would be foolish, this examination of the international political economy suggests that there are powerful political, economic, and military forces that fully support the geographer's view of a world with an increasing number of small nation-states. The trends supporting smaller states are clear, but there is as yet little reason to believe that the nation-state's monopoly on global political organization will be significantly challenged. The era of the nation-state, incorrectly foretold as ending after centuries, may, in fact, just be beginning as an increasing number of political communities find that the international political and economic systems do not discriminate on the basis of size but do offer profound incentives to organize as nation-states. Thus, future debate on self-determination and other issues will have to take account of the fact that state-shattering, far from being an unusual event, may become routine in the future.

The major uncertainty concerning the trends favoring smallness revolve around security. Clearly, if new security threats emerge, many of the economic and political advantages of smallness will have to be reconsidered. In the former Soviet Union, for instance, there may be real security threats to some of the smaller republics that may make them reconsider their national design and perhaps prompt closer ties with Russia. However, for most countries in the third world, there is no evidence of an increasing security threat. Quite the opposite is true: although there is some suggestion of increasing violence in the third world, almost all of these conflicts are internal. As a result, leaders may increasingly base their decisions on the political and economic trends favoring smaller national units.

2

Self-Determination Under International Law: The Coherence of Doctrine Versus the Incoherence of Experience

RICHARD FALK

What makes the right of self-determination so difficult to clarify is that its exercise involves a clash of fundamental world order principles. On the one side is the basic geopolitical norm that the existing array of states is close to the maximum that can be accommodated within existing diplomatic frameworks. Any significant further fragmentation of existing states is widely seen as producing an unwieldy and inefficient world order compared with present arrangements for global and regional governance. There is also the fear that nurturing the dream of statehood for the several thousand distinct peoples in the world will provide continual fuel for strife.

On the other side of self-determination is the sense that peoples should be treated equally and that since some peoples have the benefit of statehood, others should be entitled as well. Further, involuntary patterns of relations between state and society are seen to be basically inconsistent with the drive, deriving from the American and French Revolutions, to spread human rights and democracy to all persons on the planet. In this regard, the right of self-determination has been a powerful mobilizing instrument by which to resist various patterns of involuntary governance. Also, the claim by one people of a right of self-determination can often be satisfied only by its denial to other peoples, partly because ethnic and other identities are increasingly intermingled in relation to geographical space.

The attempted resolution of these opposed viewpoints reflects a shifting balance among political, legal, cultural, and moral forces. The dynamics of denial and attainment are bound to be arbitrary, reflecting the vagaries of geopolitical priorities and constraints more often than the relative weight of equitable arguments. The Kurdish struggles in the Middle East, including even in Iraq, are illustrative of the geopolitical impulse both to manipulate restive peoples when it suits the purposes of major powers and yet to avoid the breakup of existing states in the region, even though their stability in several instances depends on extreme forms of coercion over long periods of time.

Given such harsh truths, the most challenging question is whether tools can be provided to mitigate strife and provide parties with the means to reach compromises that accommodate the basic goals of both sides. Compromise is not always possible, or even appropriate, and if it is unattainable, the outcome is likely to be shaped by a contest of wills often accompanied by severe violence that can persist for years, even decades or centuries. At the end, either one side prevails and the other retreats or some sort of battle fatigue leads, even after decades of bloody struggle, to the acceptance of compromise. The Liechtenstein proposal represents one effort to enhance the attractiveness of compromise as a feasible alternative to violence against the background of contemporary doctrine and practice relating to the right of self-determination.

The Controversy About the Scope and Application of the Right of Self-Determination

The right of self-determination has at least two mostly separate lives in international law. One is unproblematic, associated with the uncontested status of self-determination as the underpinning for all individual claimants seeking the legal protection of human rights, as expressed in Article 1 of both the Covenant on Civil and Political Rights and the Covenant on Economic, Social, and Cultural Rights.[1] The other role has recently become problematic, involving a wide range of claims by peoples as peoples to establish independent sovereign states, or at least to exert effective control over their collective destiny. It is this second dimension of self-determination that is the focus of inquiry in this chapter, although with some minor consideration of the human rights dimension to the extent it is relevant.

Aside from the end of the Cold War and the related Soviet collapse,

---

1. See Burns H. Weston, Richard A. Falk, and Anthony D'Amato, eds., *Supplement of Basic Documents to International Law and World Order,* 3rd ed. (St. Paul, Minn.: West, 1997), pp. 375–379, 428–445.

the most astonishing feature of the 1990s has been the expanded scope of successful claims of secessionist political movements leading to the emergence of a series of new and additional sovereign states. Attention to issues of self-determination also has been a result of several protracted, violent struggles to establish autonomy or statehood for a people living within an existing state that has so far prevailed, as in Tibet, Chechnya, and Kashmir. That these claims to autonomy and independence have been articulated by reference to the right of self-determination has both strained prior conceptual boundaries and created an increasingly awkward gap between doctrinal and experiential interpretations of the right of self-determination.

Such strains have been particularly associated with the traumatic disintegration of the Soviet and Yugoslav states in the early 1990s, generating several violent ruptures arising from contradictory claims of self-determination put forward by movements of antagonistic and previously suppressed nationalisms. Such experience has been most vividly embodied in the wars fought over the shape of political arrangements in Croatia, Bosnia, and Kosovo as well as in several of the states and substatal administrative units that were formerly republics (or associated with republics) in the Soviet Union. Earlier a consensus had held in international society that the right of self-determination was a matter to be resolved *under all conditions* within existing international boundaries, no matter how ethnically artificial or nationalistically oppressive. This consensus was generally upheld despite several prominent secessionist challenges in sub-Saharan Africa throughout the post-1945 decades of decolonization. International law doctrine, as will be discussed, generally confirmed this political and moral consensus that the "self" in self-determination was meant to signify in *all* circumstances the existing *states* constituting international society. The only acceptable exceptions to this legal norm of limitation were in situations of secession by agreement, that is, a voluntary arrangement agreed upon by the government of the existing state and authenticated representatives of those favoring some type of secession. This exception can be illustrated by the instance of Czechoslovakia voluntarily splitting into the Czech Republic and Slovakia. Canada and Quebec have also proceeded on the basis that a voluntary accommodation of competing claims on the basis of democratic procedures (referenda and negotiation) would eventually resolve the encounter between the federal government of Canada and the potentially secessionist province of Quebec without either side having recourse to violence. A problematic question of a subsidiary character is how to take account of the antisecessionist sentiments of ten "nations" constituted by indigenous peoples living in Quebec.[2]

There have been several forces converging in the past decade to erode and possibly undermine this always fragile, somewhat arbitrary, *doctrinal* clarity about the right of self-determination. There was, first, a broad moral and political sympathy in the West for the Baltic peoples who had been forcibly annexed by the Soviet Union in a way that extinguished their prior international status as sovereign states. As the Gorbachev leadership softened the Soviet approach to impose control over subject peoples, the resurgence of Baltic nationalism succeeded in reestablishing the independent states of Latvia, Estonia, and Lithuania. In one sense, this particular outcome could be perceived and presented in nonthreatening doctrinal terms as merely reestablishing the sovereign rights of existing states that had temporarily been suppressed by illegal Soviet annexation, and thus their reemergence as independent entities would not genuinely represent an expansion of the right of self-determination.

Yet in another sense, the prior unity of the Soviet Union as a single sovereign entity was being successfully challenged on many additional, more ambiguous fronts by the coupling of a range of nationalisms with assertions of the right of self-determination as entailing new and separate states (at least in the place of a former identity as a constituent Soviet republic). What made political independence for the Baltic states relatively unproblematic was far less so with regard to the other constituent republics, which had enjoyed little autonomy and no international status during the Soviet era and had been incorporated into czarist Russia prior to 1918. Not only was their assertion of sovereign rights and political independence of a state-shattering character, but a collision of national and ethnic ambitions produced civil violence of considerable ferocity at the republic level in Georgia, Azerbaijan, Armenia, Tajikistan, and even Russia. In these circumstances of a nationalist claim for self-determination, the threatened minority tends to opt either for the old order with its tendency to suppress all subordinate nationalisms or for an additional cycle of self-determination that shifts adherents to a more congenial and less vulnerable delimitation of boundaries and political authority. Then, ironically, it is the original claimant of self-determination that changes roles and is now protective

---

2. For comprehensive discussion of these issues see "Canada's Fiduciary Obligation to Aboriginal Peoples in the Context of Accession to Sovereignty by Quebec," in vol. 1 of *International Dimensions: Report of Royal Commission on Aboriginal Peoples*, 3 vols. (Ottawa: Canada Communications Group, 1995).

of territorial unity and sovereignty as reconfigured at the level of the former federal units, resisting a further cycle of fragmentation implicit in claims of self-determination based on ethnic or religious identity.

This third-order type of self-determination involves constituent peoples, entrapped within new sovereign boundaries, who seek to avoid what their representatives believe is a subordinate status that may be aggravated under the new political arrangement.[3] In these circumstances, asserting their distinct right as a people entitled to independence can be understood either as a prudent reaction to the dangers posed by the first and second cycles of self-determination or as an opportunistic move to take advantage of a moment of historical fluidity when the restructuring of boundaries is, in any event, taking place. Their claim resembles the other claims to establish independent statehood except that their claim cannot invoke the federal boundaries of the former state. Yet the geographical extent of their claim may be equally clear, and the geographic area in question often has been governed as a subfederal administrative unit in the earlier federal state. The recurrent brutal suppression of such claims posited by Chechnya to break away from Russia is illustrative of this downward disintegrative spiral and the consequent backlash, in this case initiated by Moscow's refusal to countenance any territorial dismemberment of Russia. Why should the former federal boundaries count for so much and the administrative boundaries or endangered circumstances of distinct peoples be treated as irrelevant to the exercise of the right of self-determination? Often a people may be persecuted and in need of separate existence to a far greater extent when entrapped within a unitary state. In each instance, federated units might or might not have a strong human rights justification for asserting a claim of statehood. Chechnya and Kosovo manifest these concerns with particular poignancy. If a crucial part of the rationale for self-determination is in relation to human rights, why should the claims of the Chechens or Kosovars count for so much less than those of the Georgians and Azerbaijanis?

The arbitrariness of the doctrinal approach arises because the basis for claiming the right is similar in each of these settings, but the validation of the claim is doctrinally routine only at the level of the state. Under some circumstances, especially during the past several years, validation of self-determination claims has been extended to the *internal* federal units. This leaves out in the cold those peoples who qualify as nations and yet are trapped within these internal boundaries.

---

3. See the appendix to this chapter for a delineation of the main categories of self-determination claims.

What the Soviet experience suggested, and the Yugoslav sequel confirmed, is that claims of self-determination in situations of ethnic, religious, and national diversity can provide occasions for bitter warfare if the attempted result is the articulation of new states in the full sovereign sense. Slovenia has avoided such a bloody fate largely because its former boundaries encompassed a generally homogeneous population, in contrast to Croatia and Bosnia. Thus the challenge to traditional doctrine is not necessarily attributable to state-shattering alone but to the particular mix of economic, political, cultural, and historical factors weighting the balance between retaining the former degree of unity and insisting on some measure of autonomy, if not outright independence. Both Slovenia and Slovakia emerged as states by relatively peaceful means, if amid controversy. What seems most inflammatory and threatening is state-shattering in circumstances of heterogeneous populations, especially if substantial minorities feel that separation is likely to lead them to be freshly and more menacingly entrapped. Such peoples can be manipulated by their own leaders, who may perceive the breakup of the prior federal state as a rare window of opportunity in relation to their dreams of leadership and separate nationhood and their nightmares associated with certain historically resonant recollections of persecution and defeat. It is difficult to evaluate these concerns, which involve such an explosive mixture of genuine and opportunistic motivations. The tragic fates of Bosnia and Kosovo are illustrative of the sort of ordeal that can be brought about by the assertion and denial of overlapping contradictory claims of self-determination.

Yet the rejection of such claims by forcible means does not provide a solution in most instances. Chechnya, Kashmir, Tibet, and the various Kurdish populations are examples of entrapped peoples for whom the legal and political ideal of territorial unity causes moral havoc and harsh degrees of social, economic, and cultural injustice, producing great suffering and endless strife for these peoples. Such oppression seems legally correct according to the stricter international law accounts of the doctrine of self-determination as limited to repudiation of alien rule only at the level of the state. The obligation to respect human rights, if upheld, would offer a measure of protection to all persons, thereby presumably weakening the impulse to insist on secession. These accounts suppress contrary practices—that is, de facto independence—by treating them as facts rather than law, a jural fiction that formalistically reconciles doctrine with experience, but at the expense of relevance. Worse still, the validation of successful claims due to factual circumstances tends to reward recourse to violence by separatist or anti-separatist movements and provides no procedure by which to assess separatist controversies on a case-by-case basis from the standpoint of nonviolence or the justice of the cause. That is, those who seek independence yet wait for justice to be done seem doomed to perpetual frustration and disappointment.

Not all claims possess the same moral and political weight. For instance, a separatist claim in a deeply divided societal unit is far more likely to produce disaster than if the claiming unit is homogeneous.[4]

There are other problems as well with the standard legal solution of limiting the right of self-determination to the level of the state unless the fission of an existing state is amicably arranged. One problem is that other types of political evolution are not treated as proper instances of self-determination but must somehow be handled extralegally as political facts. The right of self-determination of indigenous peoples is in deep jeopardy despite being acknowledged in international law and enshrined in Articles 3 and 31 of the 1994 Draft Declaration on the Rights of Indigenous Peoples.[5] This right is in jeopardy partly because it is not formally reconcilable with the UN-era conceptualization of self-determination—despite the colonialist character of suppression of indigenous peoples in many instances, which is quite unreasonably ignored—and partly because the geographic scope of the claimed right did not correspond to the colonial units. Resistance to this new set of self-determination claims is reinforced by political worries that endowing indigenous peoples with such a right of self-determination could be used to validate extreme scenarios of statist fragmentation, there being several thousand potential claimants on a global scale if all "peoples," numbering in all about 250 million, are included. Such an extreme scenario is put forward to justify resisting the acknowledgment of a right of self-determination for indigenous peoples, even though it is widely appreciated that the existential goal of such claimants in almost every instance is autonomy in an economically, politically, and culturally

---

4. But even here there are no clear categories. If the former federal unit is itself divided between two ethnic, religious identities, then the pursuit of self-determination by the dominant group can encourage a process of ethnic cleansing on both sides: first, to ensure a clear identity for the new polity and second, to pave the way for a separatist, reactive claim on behalf of the weaker group. Kosovo before and after the NATO air campaign of 1999 illustrates both phases of ethnic cleansing.

5. The status of this document is uncertain. It has not yet been approved by the UN General Assembly and may never be in its 1994 form precisely because of the unconditional endorsement of a right of self-determination for all indigenous peoples. For a comprehensive study of this controversy, and a proposed path of resolution, see Maivân Clech Lâm, *At the Edge of the State: Indigenous Peoples and Self-Determination* (Ardsley, N.Y.: Transnational, 2000).

viable form within existing boundaries rather than an effort to create formally separate international states.

The impasse persists, however, because representatives of indigenous peoples insist on the full dignity of their status as a people, and this dignity has become irreversibly fused with the possession of an unconditional, first-class right of self-determination even if there is rarely an intention to exercise such a right in a secessionist manner. This right, in turn, implies the theoretical option of a people, however small in number, to claim sovereignty and political independence for a given geographical unit. Such a posture is then interpreted by those in power as a threat, if not a plan, to break up existing states into fragments and is stubbornly resisted, keeping relations between states and indigenous peoples at a low boil.

At several recent international meetings I have heard influential diplomats argue that it is now time to eliminate self-determination as a *collective* legal, political, and moral right and limit its relevance in the postcolonial setting to its human rights role of empowering individuals and minorities to equitable treatment within existing state structures of authority. Such an approach urges claimants to abandon the discourse of self-determination in favor of seeking specific constituent rights concerning resources, self-government, and territorial delimitation.

Such advocacy generally falls on deaf ears or, worse, engenders a hostile response that aggravates discord. It reminds me of the early North-South environmental dialogues in which the newly independent countries felt they were being told to forgo affluence to avoid causing further pollution of the planet. At this stage, it is too late to put the genie of self-determination back in its colonialist bottle. Too many additional claims have now been validated; too large a meaning has been invested in the language of self-determination. It is too late for a rhetorical, or even a doctrinal, retreat. The symbolic battle lines have been indissolubly drawn, even though their substantive implications are uncertain.

For these reasons the Liechtenstein Convention proposals are especially apropos. The framework validates an extension of rights of self-determination but associates its normal application with self-administration. As such, the framework allows *symbolic* flexibility while avoiding state-shattering *substance*. Of course, there are some possible traps: the convention can be seen as an empty symbolic gesture that effectively deprives self-determination of its content or, contrariwise, keeps open the floodgates of expanded self-determination without providing any reliable assurance that modesty at the level of application will really occur.

Against such a background of controversy, this chapter traces the evolution of the right of self-determination within the domain of international law, including responses to the two sets of recent challenges mounted by noncolonial separatist claims in Europe and Asia and by the international movement on behalf of indigenous peoples. On this basis it briefly examines the problematic challenges posed by the Kurdish circumstance in the Middle East and by the interplay in Canada arising from conflicting enactments of self-determination by indigenous peoples and by Quebecois separatists.

The Right of Self-Determination in History and International Law

The right of self-determination emerged as a serious element in international life during the latter stages of World War I. It was then expressed in two forms that prefigured, in their essence, the ideological rivalry between East and West that decades later ripened into the Cold War. The more radical, but less overtly influential, proposal was articulated prior to the Bolshevik revolution by Lenin, who in his writings as a revolutionary proclaimed self-determination as an indispensable condition for peace in the world and intended it to apply unconditionally to the non-European peoples being held in thrall by the colonial order. In Lenin's words, "the liberation of all colonies, the liberation of all dependent, oppressed, and non-sovereign peoples" is necessary for the maintenance of international peace.[6]

A far more constricted version of the right of self-determination, the one more prominently associated with the international development of the right since World War I, is of course associated mainly with Woodrow Wilson. In his Fourteen Points, Wilson put forward an authoritative and influential statement of the U.S. approach to the peace process in 1918. Wilson intended the principle of self-determination to apply immediately and unconditionally to the peoples of Europe and made particular reference to those peoples who had been ruled by the Ottoman Empire and to a lesser extent by the Austro-Hungarian Empire. Wilson also intended, but stated this intention in an ambiguous and halfhearted manner, that self-determination would have an uncertain and eventual application in non-European settings. Wilson's fifth point embodies this aspect of his approach: "A free, open-minded, and

---

6. See Vladimir Lenin's "Fourth Letter from Afar," March 25, 1917, quoted in Antonio Cassese, *International Law in a Divided World* (New York: Oxford University Press, 1986), p. 131.

absolutely impartial adjustment of all colonial claims, based upon a strict observance of the principle that in determining all such questions of sovereignty the interests of the populations concerned must have equal weight with the equitable claims of the government whose title is to be determined." The U.S. secretary of state at the time, Robert Lansing, was disturbed by the wider implications of such a formulation of self-determination and made an effort to distinguish Wilson's views from those of Lenin. Lansing insisted that Wilson's advocacy be understood as intending only the promotion of self-government *within* the colonial order, not the dissolution of the order itself, a prospect that Lansing (and Wilson) believed would be dangerous for "the stability of the future world."[7] This restrictive view was also expressed in Wilson's steadfast refusal at Versailles to meet with representatives, including a youthful Ho Chi Minh, of anticolonial movements for national independence.

The Wilsonian restrictive version of self-determination prevailed at first. The legitimacy of colonial rule was not challenged after World War I, and the victorious colonial powers acquired considerable control over additional peoples by way of the mandates system established in connection with the creation of the League of Nations. This system was a means of lawfully incorporating the former colonial peoples of the losing side in World War I into the colonial empires of the victorious side without explicitly extending colonialism as such. The mandates system rested on a variable fiction, depending on practice and the classification given to a particular mandate. The administering states were accountable to the League for the well-being of the peoples involved as a "sacred trust of civilization," as this latter idea was expressed in Article 22 of the League's covenant. The operational authority rested with the colonial power, and the paternalistic language stressing the duty to promote well-being often meant little in practice. True, there was a commitment to work toward independence for mandated peoples, and there was a sharp set of differences in the legal conception between the three classes of mandates. Class A mandates, for example, were viewed as temporary, to be eventually replaced by political independence for the mandated peoples. Operationally, it seems evident that the mandates system was a holding operation that delayed decolonization to varying degrees; the attainment of independence supposedly reflected the relative capacity of a given society for self-rule. But the mandates

---

7. Helpful discussion is in Cassese, *International Law in a Divided World*, pp. 132–134.

system also set in motion a process of self-assertion that eventually led in every instance to political independence and full statehood.

In retrospect, the Wilsonian top-down approach to self-determination was of limited application. The Leninist approach, although never designated as such, gradually caught on as a rationale for the extension of the ethos of anticolonial nationalism that was to sweep across the planet in the aftermath of World War II. In its essence, despite efforts to craft a conception of self-determination that does not disturb the established order, the idea is subversive to the legitimacy of all political arrangements between distinct peoples that do not flow from genuine and continuing consent. It is this subversive feature that worked its way through the history of international relations during the latter part of the twentieth century, giving a variable and expanding content to the right of self-determination, whether the right was considered in relation to the identity of its claimants or to the substantive claims being advanced.

As World War II came to an end there was a repetition of the split between Leninist and Wilsonian views, but it was not so labeled. The Soviet Union supported those elements in international society that were challenging the colonial order. The European powers, although weakened by war, remained committed to retaining their colonies by force if necessary. The United States positioned itself in the middle, allied with the colonial powers in strategic and ideological respects yet normatively sympathetic, in part due to its own historical legacy, to the claims of peoples seeking independence. The UN Charter embodied this compromise in its specification of guiding principles, especially in the language of Article 1(2): "To develop friendly relations among nations based on respect for the principle of equal rights and self-determination of peoples."[8] The Charter deliberately refers to self-determination as a "principle" rather than a "right." It is only later on in both human rights and decolonization settings that official UN terminology confirms that peoples enjoy a *right* of self-determination. Arguably, this distinction is inconsequential as a substantive aspect of international law. To the extent that such a principle exists and is actualized, it implies the existence of rights and duties to ensure its application, or at least encompasses the prospect that such rights will, as appropriate, be specified and realized.

The limits envisioned for the application of the principle of self-determination by the UN are also illuminated by reference to Chapter XI of the Charter dealing with non-self-governing territories. In Article

---

8. This language is repeated in Article 55 in the setting of human rights.

73 the well-being of the inhabitants is affirmed as "paramount," but implementation is essentially left in the hands of the administering state. In all instances this vested legal authority is in a European or North American state (except for the geographic, yet not political or ethnic, exception of South Africa). The central commitment is expressed in Article 73(b) as one of working "to develop self-government," but not necessarily national independence. Article 76(b) does anticipate "advancement of the inhabitants of the trust territories, and their progressive development towards self-government or independence as may be appropriate to the particular circumstance of each territory and its peoples and the freely expressed wishes of the peoples concerned."

Again, the normative content is ambiguous, due partly to the vague textual language. The tone is paternalistic with respect to administration yet subversive if considered in relation to historical trends and the expected aspirations of subordinated peoples. This trust concept introduced into UN operations is relevant to the rights and circumstances of dependent peoples, but it was not meant to have any relevance to the legal circumstances of indigenous peoples. Such peoples have never been offered, nor have their representatives claimed, a trust status as understood in the UN Charter.

The right of self-determination has matured along three distinct, often overlapping, and sometimes uneven and confusing paths: those of morality, politics, and law. Indeed, the incorporation of self-determination into international law has consistently lagged behind advocacy based on aspirations and considerations of justice (the moral debate) and political movements and their results (the political experience). The developments of the twentieth century in their several stages ebbed and flowed with respect to the multiple reality of self-determination but cumulatively moved toward a legal acknowledgment and application of self-determination across an expanded spectrum of circumstances.

This expansion can be understood by reference to four sets of factors: (1) the weakening of the capacity of the European colonial powers as a result of the two world wars; (2) the rise of an ideology of nationalism, reinforced by the basic democratic perspective that governing arrangements, to be legitimate, should be genuinely consensual and participatory in relation to their citizenry; (3) the unconditional ideological, diplomatic support extended to anticolonial struggles by the Soviet Union and its bloc after 1945, and the concern by the United States that the West would lose out geopolitically in the third world if it tied its destiny indefinitely to the defense of the colonial order; and (4) the increasing importance accorded to the international implementation of basic human rights.

Against this background, the evolving dynamics of decolonization gradually deepened the acknowledgment of a right of self-determination by stages. The great moment of acceptance within the United Nations came with the adoption of the famous Declaration on the Granting of Independence to Colonial Peoples in the form of a General Assembly resolution (GA Res.) in 1960.[9] The thinking expressed in Resolution 1514 remains important in understanding the most recent postcolonial phases of struggle with respect to the application of the right of self-determination. The resolution does not attempt to clarify the specific legal content of the right; nor does it identify the circumstances of its application and their outer limits.[10] Indeed, one source of difficulty is that the language is so general that the resolution can be read to support a wide range of aspirants seeking political independence even if leading governments understood the language more narrowly as referring primarily, or even exclusively, to claims posited in relation to colonial rule.

The preamble of the declaration sets forth a litany of considerations that, by 1960, came to express the content of the anticolonial movement. The preamble recognizes "that the peoples of the world ardently desire the end of colonialism in all its manifestations" and that "the process of liberation is irresistible and irreversible and that . . . an end must be put to colonialism." Of particular relevance to current concerns about the scope of the right of self-determination is the incorporation into this declaration on anticolonialism of a potentially far broader ethos encompassing "all dependent peoples" and extending to vesting permanent sovereignty over "natural wealth and resources" in such peoples.[11]

---

9. GA Res. 1514 (XV), Declaration on the Granting of Independence to Colonial Countries and Peoples, December 14, 1960. The vote was 89–0 with nine significant abstentions including Portugal, Spain, South Africa, the United Kingdom, the United States, Australia, Belgium, the Dominican Republic, and France. Note that Canada voted with the majority. For text see Weston, Falk, and D'Amato, *Supplement of Basic Documents to International Law and World Order*, pp. 404–405.

10. See also GA Res. 1541 (XX), December 15, 1960, for amplification.

11. This thinking is made manifest and is expressed more fully and authoritatively two years later in the General Assembly Resolution on Permanent Sovereignty over Natural Resources, GA Res. 1803 (XVII), December 14, 1962; and GA Res. 3171 (XXVIII), December 17, 1973. Text in Weston, Falk, and D'Amato, *Supplement of Basic Documents to International Law and World Order*, pp. 695–696, 703–704.

The approach taken by the 1960 declaration to the right of self-determination is instructive, both in terms of its attempt to confirm the right in relation to colonialism and to deny some forms of wider application. It is important to keep in mind the inevitable tension between the exercise of this right and the parallel set of rights associated with the territorial integrity of existing and emerging sovereign states. Operative provision 2 reads: "All peoples have the right of self-determination; by virtue of that right they freely determine their political status and freely pursue their economic, social and cultural development." Provision 3 adds that "inadequacy of political, economic, social or educational preparedness should never serve as a pretext for delaying independence." These affirmations are then qualified by the now familiar deference to the territorial integrity of existing states contained in provision 6: "Any attempt at the partial or total disruption of the national unity and the territorial integrity of a country is incompatible with the purposes and principles of the Charter of the United Nations." This approach culminated in the adoption of the influential Declaration of Principles Concerning Friendly Relations Among States, adopted as General Assembly Resolution 2625 in 1970.[12] This authoritative formulation significantly accepted the principle of self-determination (linked to the notion of "equal rights of peoples") as one of only seven constitutive norms of international order in the Cold War era and conferred moral, political, and legal stature all at once.

Africa endorsed this approach during the peak decade of decolonization, the 1960s, via the Organization of African Unity (OAU). The OAU, by resolution in 1964 and frequently in various formats thereafter, agreed that colonial frontiers, even if arbitrary and unjust, were to provide the only acceptable basis for delimiting sovereign states in Africa as colonial entities achieved independence. In effect, the African consensus on self-determination was intended to deny ethnic and tribal claimants any right of secession or independence in the midst of decolonization, thereby validating an approach that could be given a more legalistic explanation by reference to the Roman principle of *uti possidetis*. Rosalyn Higgins, commenting on this development, argues that the OAU approach does not provide direct legal authority for *uti possidetis* but reflects the African acceptance of "an underlying norm—that

---

12. GA Res. 2625 (XXV), October, 24, 1970. Text in Weston, Falk, and D'Amato, *Supplement of Basic Documents to International Law and World Order*, pp. 92–96.

of commitment to territorial integrity and international stability."[13] The African fear was that the moment of independence, if coupled with the invalidation of colonial boundaries, would open up the continent to devastating civil strife, possibly producing a pattern of ethnically oriented and nonviable states that had little chance of coping with the challenges of modernity.

But as former professor and now World Court judge Rosalyn Higgins recognizes, matters are not so simple. Self-determination as a right came also to be accepted as an anchoring norm for human rights in settings unrelated to decolonization. She attempts to resolve the tension by reference to the World Court treatment of the relationship in *Mali v. Burkina Faso*, relying on an assertion by Professor Georges Abi-Saab, the distinguished judge ad hoc of Mali, that "without stability of frontiers, the exercise of self-determination is in reality a mirage. Turmoil is not conducive to human rights."[14] But such an assertion, without further elaboration, doesn't resolve the question of the stability of *which* frontiers.

Unfortunately, Abi-Saab's observation is not generalizable; its degree of persuasiveness depends completely on the context. In some settings, it seems evident that only by perpetuating colonial boundaries can turmoil be overcome and stability restored. The effort to maintain an abusive structure of dominance with respect to independence will often depend on a systematic and severe denial of human rights, as was the experience of Tibet and East Timor. East Timor has recently moved toward independence, benefiting from a series of developments within Indonesia and globally but also enduring a final effort by Indonesia to thwart the East Timorese move, which enjoyed UN validation, toward independence. What changed East Timor's prospects were, in main, the fall of Suharto in the wake of the 1997 Asian financial crisis, the increased leverage of the international community with respect to Jakarta, and, above all, the end of the Cold War and its consequent weakening of Indonesia's geopolitical position as a crucial ally of the West. In contrast, none of these developments affected China, and its hold over Tibet has not diminished despite the changed regional and global conditions.

What may have seemed convincing in Africa in the 1960s as decol-

---

13. Rosalyn Higgins, *Problems and Progress: International Law and How We Use It* (New York: Oxford University Press, 1994), pp. 122–123; see also Professor Higgins's discussion relating to the determination of the boundaries of Guinea-Bissau (pp. 123–126).

14. Ibid., p. 123.

onization was taking place seems selectively problematic in light of the current climate of severe ethnic tensions producing violent suppression and even genocidal onslaughts. Closely related to this political observation is the argument being made here that the contours of the right of self-determination have never been and are not now fixed in the concrete of rigid legal doctrine. The right is intrinsically unstable and has been continuously evolving conceptually and experientially in response to the pressure of events, reflecting changing geopolitical priorities, according varying degrees of respect to the prevailing moral and political climate, and taking account of the specifics of a given context. This combination of factors tends to produce a confusing pattern of precedents, leaving considerable room for widely disparate interpretations bearing on the legal doctrine governing the right of self-determination, and its application to a particular claim.

Expressing the potency of the anti-apartheid movement and the general revulsion against racism, the 1970 Declaration on Friendly Relations goes further than Res. 1514 by expanding the scope of self-determination in a manner not earlier anticipated. The language used in the declaration is again instructive with respect to understanding the expansionist evolution of the right of self-determination and the impossibility of pinning down the acceptable limits of a plausible legal claim. The principle of territorial integrity is reasserted but, significantly, in a more conditional form. The declaration insists that nothing about the right of self-determination

> shall be construed as authorizing or encouraging any action which would dismember or impair, totally or in part, the territorial integrity or political unity of sovereign and independent States conducting themselves in compliance with the principle of equal rights and self-determination of peoples . . . and thus possessed of a government representing the whole people belonging to the territory without distinction as to race, creed or color.

The language of this passage is notable in its generality, as it ensures a potential receptivity to and loopholes for self-determination claims that are not strictly reconcilable with the unconditional primacy previously accorded to territorial integrity and political unity. The assurance of territorial unity is now made conditional on the government being representative of the whole people and nondiscriminatory in relation to "race, creed, or color."

There had always been a second, rather bewildering, dimension to the struggle for self-determination—individual and group quests for human rights rather than a collective struggle for national independence. In that setting the exercise of the right of self-determination did not normally imply, as it did in the anticolonial context, an insistence on the potential exercise of sovereign rights associated with statehood. Such a distinction led to discussions of "internal" self-determination as appropriate for the protection of minority rights, which amounted to the avoidance of discriminatory and exclusionary policies arising in relation to race and religion. In group settings, internal self-determination involved the linking of movements for cultural and political autonomy for distinct peoples with the right of self-determination.[15] But again, even this foreshortened view of self-determination cannot be derived from the plain meaning of the textual language as it appears in the common Article 1 of the two covenants on human rights, which affirms the right without placing any limitations on its exercise. Nor can the scope of the right be convincingly restricted to Article 27 of the Covenant on Civil and Political Rights, which declares that individuals belonging to "ethnic, religious or linguistic minorities" shall "not be denied the right, in community with the other members of the group, to enjoy their own culture, to profess and practice their own religion, or to use their own language."

Suppose after decades of repression and suffering a people demands secession as a foundation for exercising its right of self-determination. Can we say conclusively, on the basis of international law doctrine and practice, that such a demand is inherently unacceptable? The position of this chapter is that we cannot reach such an invariable conclusion but must assess the merits and overall reasonableness of such a claim in its particular context. The outcome of such an assessment will almost always be controversial. An international mechanism for assessment is more likely to embody a compromise between the capacity to assert the claim effectively and its seeming legal and moral merit. There is a specious legal clarity insisted upon by those who continue to rely on a cautious reading of the Friendly Relations Declaration and some of the rather tangential findings and assertions of the International Court of Justice (ICJ), especially in the *Western Sahara Case*.[16]

This chapter adopts a view close to the position of Judge Hardy Dillard, especially as expressed in the oft-quoted phrase appearing in his separate opinion on *Western Sahara:* "It is for the people to determine the destiny of the territory and not the territory the destiny of the people."[17] Judge Higgins criticizes Dillard's orientation by showing

---

15. Cassese, *International Law in a Divided World*, p. 134.
16. *ICJ Reports*, 1975.
17. Ibid., p. 122.

clearly that the court only confirmed the relevance of the right of self-determination once it concluded that Western Sahara should be regarded as a Spanish colonial possession of separate identity and not as belonging within the sovereign domain of either Morocco or Mauritania. Such an assessment is persuasive within the four corners of the dispute about the delimitation of Western Sahara, but Judge Dillard is both accurate and prophetic with respect to the most appropriate legal comprehension of the variable content of the right of self-determination.

In the international law literature on self-determination, two main tendencies are pulling in opposite directions. The first is to hold the line against expanding the right of self-determination by insisting on a restrictive view of rights that must defer to the persisting relevance of the territorial unity of existing states, thereby still providing an unconditional limitation on its exercise. The second tendency acknowledges and, to varying degrees, validates recent state-shattering practice in a reformulated legal approach that admits that the character and scope of the right are more unsettled than ever but are nevertheless expansionary. This latter view takes due note of the degree to which diplomatic recognition and admission to the UN has been granted to federal units formerly encompassed as nonsovereign components of the Soviet Union and Yugoslavia.[18]

Judge Higgins, in supporting her continuing adherence to the more restrictive view of self-determination, wrote that the long struggle to establish the right as legal "now faces a new danger: that of being all things to all men."[19] Yet the whole history of the right of self-determination is, for better and worse, the story of adaptation to the evolving struggles of peoples variously situated to achieve effective control over their own destinies, especially in reaction to circumstances that are discriminatory and oppressive. For a period, states successfully held the line, agreeing that self-determination would not have secessionist implications except in colonial settings. Even here, it was more a matter of changed status and only secessionist in relation to the colonial empire. This attitude was acceptable to the Soviet Union, which appreciated the explosive danger to itself of encouraging either captive nationalities within its sovereign boundaries or the various captive peoples restive within its East European sphere of influence to assert independence

---

18. Some of these issues will be discussed in later sections on the breakup of Yugoslavia and the Soviet Union.

19. Higgins, *Problems and Progress*, p. 128. There is a subtle irony here: A noted female jurist persists in the use of a colloquially correct yet paternalistic trope—"men" as encompassing "all persons," that is, both men and women.

claims as a matter of right. At the same time, as already suggested, the former colonial peoples were in general agreement that opening up the colonial boundaries to revision could contribute to political disarray and widespread warfare, especially in Africa and parts of Asia.

The large-scale bloodshed accompanying the 1948 breakaway of Pakistan from India, and then Bangladesh from Pakistan in 1972, gave credence to the view that altering colonial borders would be extremely destabilizing. Furthermore, the United States and other countries in the Western Hemisphere were aware that indigenous peoples within their boundaries continued to insist on their status as sovereign nations and were fearful of the implications of an acceptance of such longings. There was thus a political and moral consensus among governments that shaped the legal conception of the right of self-determination during the Cold War, but it was a historically conditioned and pragmatic conception that has not held since 1989. Although NATO formally supports claims of the Kosovar Albanians only to the extent of autonomy and human rights, it presides over a transition on the ground that seems, as of 2000, to be leading to de facto independence, or to de facto partition; most of Kosovo is moving toward independence, and the Serbian remnant in the North is being absorbed into the Federal Republic of Yugoslavia.

Since 1995, the practice of states, the transnational assertiveness of indigenous peoples, and the moral force of groups rights in various situations have expanded the scope of the legal right of self-determination. The right is now closer to that associated with Judge Dillard's dictum than to various positivist attempts to deny recent practice relating to self-determination any legal status, or only a very restrictive one. The more flexible international law approach that is sensitive to context and trends in official practice gives a more realistic picture of the relevance of law to current discussions of self-determination than does its restrictive counterpart, which purports a clarity and definiteness that seem increasingly out of touch with the ways in which self-determination claims have been validated by diplomatic recognition, UN admissions procedures, and geopolitical priorities. Arguably, criticisms can be made of this variable legal content recently accorded self-determination claims, but to deny such a content is to pretend by legalistic sleight-of-hand that the self-determination genie remains in the doctrinal box of a statist world. Yet such a world has eroded before our eyes, and to contend otherwise is to place an unacceptable strain on the descriptive and prescriptive character of international law, as well as to finesse the need for a morally and politically persuasive way to recapture the genie of self-determination, or, more realistically, to admit that recapture is only partially possible at this stage. The various political prospects of resolving such high-profile situations as East Timor, Kosovo, Chechnya, and Kashmir are constantly reshaping the general understanding of the scope of the right of self-determination and creating ever new settings for controversy about the benefits, burdens, and even the character of the right.

Practice Versus Doctrine Since 1989

The striking feature of recent practice is both the extension of the right of self-determination beyond earlier conceptions and the variability of arrangements that satisfy particular claims of self-determination. Earlier doctrinal conceptions are no longer descriptive of practice; nor is it accurate to equate every movement for self-determination with secessionist ambitions. In this section, this recent pattern of state-shattering practice is depicted in relation to doctrinal efforts to avoid the legal implications of such practice. The intent is to deny expansionist practices as possessing authority to operate as precedents for the future and thereby limit the availability of self-determination as a collective right of people.

International practice until 1989 embodied the UN consensus of an emergent right of self-determination for peoples held under colonial, alien, or racist rule to be exercised in a manner that did not challenge prior *external* boundaries. Even in this pre-1989 period, the secession of East Pakistan from Pakistan to form Bangladesh, in the wake of atrocities perpetrated by the armies of the central government, was generally accepted by international society; Bangladesh was quickly accorded diplomatic recognition by other states. Not long afterward Bangladesh became a UN member even though its emergence altered the external boundaries of the former Pakistan as well as generated a new sovereign state. Such an outcome was substantively an exercise of the right of self-determination by the peoples involved, even if it was not so described at the time. The quest for a national homeland by the Palestinians, the various Kurdish national movements, and the struggles for independence by a series of ethnic groups in the former Soviet Union should all be regarded as efforts to assert rights of self-determination. Self-determination claims can be satisfied either internally through a variety of autonomy arrangements or externally by the establishment of a new state. Such movements may "succeed" in achieving self-determination even if political independence is not claimed and no attempt is made to join international institutions or establish distinct diplomatic relations. There is no assured or necessary link between exercising the right of self-determination and a particular outcome. As the political debate on the future of Puerto Rico over the years has illustrated, the majority of a particular people may under certain conditions reject the option of independence and favor remaining in a subordinated status within a larger political entity even if that status evolved out of a colonialist background and involves a certain sacrifice from the perspective of identity. In the case of Puerto Rico, the economic subsidies associated with remaining within the United States are a factor, as is the prospect of massive poverty if political independence is granted.

The disintegration of the Soviet Union and Yugoslavia in 1991 involved establishing a series of new, sovereign states that sought diplomatic recognition and full membership in international institutions. In effect, these emergent states shattered the territorial unity of the former federated entities and departed from the apparent UN guidelines premised on the exercise of the right of self-determination *within* existing states, seemingly making the right unavailable at the level of the federal units that together constitute a state. This recent practice is a significant confirmation of the extent to which the effective political outcomes that are consistent with geopolitical preferences and are welcomed by important countries produce *legal* results incompatible with earlier conceptions of legal doctrine. Community responses to such state-shattering practice are registered by way of diplomatic recognition and admission to international institutions. Such actions amount to international rituals of a legitimizing effect that is quite inconsistent with earlier efforts to reject self-determination claims of a state-shattering variety, even if the claim seemed morally justified. Despite these recent developments, most state-shattering self-determination political movements continue to be viewed unsympathetically by representative leadership of states at regional and global levels. These attitudes are hardly surprising. Such movements pose a challenge to the unity and integrity of existing states by drawing into question the inviolability of territorial boundaries. This combination of factors generates strong pragmatic pressure to avoid treating recent secessionist results as precedent setting in situations that have yielded new states by diminishing or fracturing the territorial domain of a former state.

This tension between practice and doctrinal preference has been clearly evident in the opinions of the Badinter Commission, composed of leading European judges and established by the European Community (EC) to evaluate the legal consequences of the disintegration of Yugoslavia, as well as in a quite separate report prepared by a distinguished international law specialist and submitted to the Quebec Assembly; this report assessed the effects of Quebec's possible accession to sovereignty should its separatist movement succeed in gaining a majority in a subsequent referendum. Both of these efforts to formulate doctrinal contours of the right of self-determination in the face of actual and potential expansionist practice have produced confusing and unconvincing legal analyses that are exceedingly vulnerable to technical and policy lines of criticism. Such efforts at reconciliation have not put the issues to rest but rather have called further attention to the challenge.

The Badinter Commission and the Former Yugoslavia

A prime example of this confusion is the work of the Arbitration Commission, established by the European Community in 1991 as part of the EC's effort to minimize and contain the violent conflict attending the breakup of Yugoslavia. The commission was composed of five presidents of constitutional tribunals in European countries and headed by Robert Badinter, president of the French Constitutional Council. This Arbitration Commission, or Badinter Commission, as it came to be known, lacked legal authority to make decisions and possessed only an advisory role in relation to then ongoing Balkan diplomacy. Despite its name, the commission had no arbitration functions. Lord Carrington, president at the time of the International Conference on Yugoslavia, put several questions to the commission, as did the government of Serbia.[20]

In Opinion 2 the commission addressed self-determination in the context of Serbian claims on behalf of ethnic minorities in relation to Croatia and Bosnia, concluding that although the right of self-determination is not spelled out, "it is well established that, whatever the circumstances, the right to self-determination must not involve changes to existing frontiers at the time of independence (*uti possidetis juris*) except where the States concerned agree otherwise." In its tersely worded opinion the commission said that Serbians are entitled to full protection as "minorities" and that the right of self-determination is a matter of human rights, allowing Serbs acting as individuals, if they so wish, to insist that their distinct national identity be respected by Bosnia and Croatia.

The Badinter Commission never discussed the crucial issue relating to when a minority becomes or chooses to become a people, and thus it seems to have missed the main point. The right of self-determination is a collective right of a people, the scope of which is fixed by a mixture of context (suppose, as in Bangladesh, the claimant people were being victimized by systematic atrocities or, as was closer to the reality, feared such atrocities and, at the very least, discrimination on the basis

---

20. For more details on the Badinter Commission see the note by Marizio Ragazzi introducing the texts of the opinions thus far rendered. *International Legal Materials*, vol. 31 (Washington, D.C.: American Society of International Law, 1992), pp. 1488–1519.

of earlier experiences), geopolitical climate, and effective outcomes (the facts created).[21] As Hurst Hannum aptly points out, the commission members "appear to have based their judgments on geopolitical concerns and imaginary principles of international law, rather than on the unique situation in Yugoslavia."[22] He contends, "The principle that borders should not be altered except by mutual agreement has been elevated to a hypocritical immutability that is contradicted by the very act of recognizing the secessionist states."[23]

Furthermore, the extension of the *uti possidetis* approach by the Arbitration Commission in Opinion 3 to *internal* administrative boundaries of a fragmented or federalist state rests on extremely shaky grounds of policy and legal authority. The emergent legal authority in the decolonization setting was directed at the maintenance of *external* boundaries. The opinion of the Badinter Commission invokes some language of the International Court of Justice in the dispute between Burkina Faso and Mali to the effect that *uti possidetis* "is a general principle, which is logically connected with the phenomenon of the obtaining of independence, wherever it occurs. Its obvious purpose is to prevent the independence and stability of new States being endangered by fratricidal struggles."[24]

As Hannum notes, the commission left out the end of the sentence in the ICJ decision, which reads "provoked by the challenging of frontiers following the withdrawal of the administering power."[25] Further, the court's dictum concerning *uti possidetis* is explicitly limited to situations arising out of decolonization. None of these considerations seem to apply, even indirectly, to the breakup of federated states in which federal boundaries do not correspond with the ethnic or religious affiliations of the peoples living in the overall, wider territory and may collide badly with their own loyalties or anxieties. The fundamental question posed is not one of frontiers, in the first instance, but of the rearrangement of power and authority in a manner that poses severe threats to the security of newly entrapped minorities. Validating such patterns of fragmentation is neither a matter of mechanically upholding or rejecting claims of self-determination nor properly a matter of acknowledging a

---

21. See the devastating critique of the work of the Badinter Commission by Hurst Hannum, "Self-Determination, Yugoslavia, and Europe: Old Wine in New Bottles?" *Transnational Law and Contemporary Problems* 3, pp. 59–69.

22. Ibid., p. 69.

23. Ibid., p. 68.

24. Frontier Dispute (*Burkina Faso v. Mali*), 1986 ICJ 554 (December 22), at p. 565.

25. See Hannum, "Self-Determination, Yugoslavia, and Europe," pp. 66–67 for criticism; also Benedict Kingsbury, "Claims by Non-State Groups in International Law," *Cornell International Law Journal* 25 (1992), p. 481.

de facto set of realities. It is, above all, a question of democratic procedures and the secure protection of minority and group rights while recognizing certain realities of power. Some beleaguered peoples are able
to succeed in their efforts, whereas others are doomed to failure.

A crucial point here is that the unconditionality of respect for territorial unity has been decisively breached in relation to the former
Yugoslavia, and the separatist movements launched by these developments were operationally invoking their right of self-determination
even if this specific language was not emphasized. This entire process
of constituting new states without protecting the constituent peoples or
respecting their wishes was indirectly validated by according widespread diplomatic recognition to these new states, as well as by their
rapid admission to the United Nations, which thereby legitimized these
particular challenges to prior conditions of territorial unity under the
auspices of the Federal Republic of Yugoslavia. In effect, what is
accepted as valid by organized international society cannot be adequately understood by consulting abstract legal guidelines. The fact that the
claims of independent statehood have generally corresponded with prior
internal boundaries does not alter the breach of the fundamental effort
of international law during the Cold War era to reconcile the territorial
unity of existing states with the exercise of the right of self-determination. During that period, colonies were uniformly considered as unified
entities even if composed of antagonistic peoples with subfederal and
transnational ethnic and religious identities more binding than their
overall shared identity. In effect, the *juridical* criterion of statehood was
accorded absolute priority over psychosocial criteria of *identity*.

The Pellet Report and Quebec

A confusion similar to that arising from the opinions rendered by the
EC's Arbitration Commission is expounded in a far more extended
legal analysis in the form of a report prepared by five international
lawyers in response to a series of questions set by the Committee of the
Quebec National Assembly on May 8, 1992, to clarify the legal consequence of a possible accession of Quebec to sovereignty. The report is
generally referred to as the Pellet Report, arising from the formative
role of Alain Pellet, a distinguished French jurist who apparently draft-
ed the initial set of responses.[26] It is, first of all, important to appreciate

---

26. "The Territorial Integrity of Québec in the Event of Its Accession to
Sovereignty," a study commissioned by the Committee of the Quebec National
Assembly, but not officially presented to it, May 8, 1992. Hereafter cited as the
Pellet Report.

the limited scope of the Pellet Report. The authors are careful to restrict their responses to the questions put to them, which in my judgment do not properly cover the topic, especially in relation to the extent and meaning of participatory rights that belong to aboriginal peoples during any negotiation of separation for Quebec as a whole. Also, the report makes a point of suggesting that the questions "were asked exclusively from a legal perspective, and this study intends to situate itself solely within the field of law."[27] If such language means only that "in no way does it reflect any political preferences" of the authors, then it is quite unexceptional. But if the authors purport, as does seem to be the case throughout their analysis of the issues, that the law is autonomous and clear, then the language is quite misleading; alternative lines of interpretation are posited by diverse, often contradictory, political and moral perspectives. The issues posed are so challenging in part because their disposition cannot be resolved solely by law; they therefore inevitably confer on the government of Canada an opportunity and responsibility to address these claims in a manner that best contributes to the clarification of respective rights and duties of the various peoples affected.

Insofar as the rights of indigenous peoples are concerned, the Pellet Report concentrates on whether a right of self-determination inheres in their claims. The assumption is that if it does, the crucial question is whether a claim of territorial independence is thereby included and validated. True, such a claim is one outer limit of an unconditional right of self-determination. But within the setting of the issues posed by possible accessions to sovereignty there are many additional intermediate questions posed, including the bearing of any self-determination claim on behalf of one people on the rights of other peoples and minorities encompassed by the territory. There are several specific implications of potential Quebec separatism for the eleven distinct resident indigenous peoples. The reported preference of these peoples, with one possible exception, is to remain part of Canada. The question raised, then, is whether such peoples can block separatist claims by insisting on their right to remain part of Canada, in which case Quebec cannot become a separate entity whatever the majority sentiments of its nonindigenous population. If accession to sovereignty by Quebec could be taken as already established, as is sometimes argued, the assertion by aboriginal peoples of a right to remain part of Canada would seem to have the odd legal appearance of challenging the territorial unity of the hypothesized

---

27. Pellet Report, p. 2.

new state of Quebec.[28] Such a mode of analysis seems highly artificial given the unresolved character of the underlying separatist claims and the claim of the right to participate, posited by indigenous peoples in whatever process is established to resolve the future status of Quebec and its relationship to Canada.

On the nature of self-determination, which the Pellet Report correctly notes to be "the heart of the controversy," the basic view of the right is delimited as one "of variable geometry" to be applied in each instance in accordance with the wishes of the people involved. This, too, is accurate. What is more dubious, however, is the false clarity of asserting that the right of self-determination "is sufficient *only in colonial situations* to found the right of a people to acquire independence to the detriment of the State to which it is attached" (emphasis added).[29] On the basis of both the more open-ended textual authorities, including the Declaration on Friendly Relations and diplomatic practice since 1989 (starting with the Baltic republics), the possibility of such claims of independence in noncolonial situations is certainly not legally or politically precluded; nor are the parameters of such a right yet, if they ever will be, firmly fixed. The law on self-determination (especially pertaining to indigenous peoples) is in flux and is likely to remain so for the indefinite future. This fluidity reflects the inconsistencies of practice on the ground and doctrine as interpreted by various concerned actors, and it expresses above all the realities of power and the vagaries of geopolitics that produce uneven and arbitrary results with respect to self-determination claims.

The Pellet Report also conveys a false impression of definiteness in law with respect to the treatment of the breakup of the former Yugoslavia. Unlike the Arbitration Commission, the Pellet Report, when discussing the "Case Concerning the Frontier Dispute" (*Burkina Faso v. Mali*), manages to acknowledge that the circumstances of Quebec are different from those arising in the setting of decolonization. It contends, nevertheless, the applicability of this Yugoslav experience on the basis of its "logic" pertaining to all situations "of accession to independence."[30] Such a generalization is unfortunate and precedes a misleading inference:

---

28. The Pellet Report itself confirms such an interpretation when it says that the questions it responds to "are situated 'downstream' from accession to independence. That event is postulated, and it is a matter of determining the effect of international law after it has occurred" (p. 7).

29. Ibid., p. 5.

30. Ibid., p. 24.

All new States issuing from secession from a pre-existing State have retained their pre-existing administrative boundaries, be they Singapore, Yugoslav republics, or States produced by the [collapse] of the Soviet Union; and in the latter two cases, the international community has very firmly manifested its conviction that there is a rule in such situations that needed to be respected.[31]

In fact, the international community has exhibited considerable ambivalence with regard to the preexisting boundaries internal to Yugoslavia, especially with regard to its efforts to resolve the war in Bosnia. The Vance-Owen and Owen-Stoltenberg diplomatic initiatives, as well as those developed with broad UN backing by the Contact Group, centered on various plans for a radical redrawing of boundaries within Bosnia and indicated great flexibility as to the practical implementation of self-determination in circumstances of ethnic conflict. The war in Bosnia came to an end in late 1995, being resolved by the Dayton Accords, which formally treated Bosnia as a unitary state yet accepted autonomous ethnic zones that reflected battlefield outcomes. These negotiations and diplomacy refute the firmness of internal boundaries as the territorial basis for the division of a given state into two or more sovereign states. Acceptable international boundaries depend on an assessment of the context, including the battlefield results of struggles among the various "selves" that had been conflated to produce a "self."

Perhaps the most confusing dimension of the Pellet Report is its insistence that the emergence of a new state "is not a problem of law, but of fact."[32] Of course, if the existence of a new state is postulated, the assertion is true; it is also trivial. Such a formulation deflects attention from the most crucial question of the situation: Given diverse and inconsistent claims based on a diversity of exclusive appeals to the right of self-determination, under what conditions can a new state come into existence validly, assuming validity to be primarily assessed by the extent and character of diplomatic recognition in the international community and by the ease of admission to international institutions? Providing guidance on this question was outside the scope of inquiry of the Pellet Commission, but such a limitation greatly restricts the relevance of its findings and recommendations. Such a limitation of scope also renders dubious the central conclusion of the Pellet Report as applied to Quebec, namely that under no circumstances can there be

31. Ibid.
32. Ibid., p. 28.

acceptable grounds to alter its territorial domain, although it was not previously an international entity, in the course of accession to sovereignty.[33] This impression of limits is very misleading here because a process of accession is often a matter of negotiations where competing and even antagonistic claims need to be reconciled to the extent possible on the basis of legal guidelines and their enlightened application. In other words, even a negotiated secession may not be acceptable if constituent peoples resist or effectively mount their opposition to a change in status that is perceived to diminish their well-being and purports to shift their formal allegiance without their consent.

A similar line of objection applies to the Pellet Report's treatment of the emergent right of self-determination enjoyed by indigenous peoples. It argues unpersuasively that the full right of self-determination (that is, including secession) pertains only in colonial situations. For one thing, the report assumes without argument that aboriginal peoples are not appropriately entitled to claim such rights on the basis of their experience of subordination despite its resemblance in many regards to "colonial" subordination—indeed, to an extreme form of it. The literature on the subject suggests a growing disposition to view indigenous and aboriginal peoples as victimized by particularly harsh variants of colonization that often resulted in virtual extinction.[34] If the treatment of indigenous people is denominated as colonial, such designation would entitle such peoples, even at this late stage, to act upon such an identity and exercise whatever legal rights this status confers. For another, the crucial immediate issue here for the people in question is one of participatory rather than secessionist rights, which is acknowledged by the Pellet Report to pertain to all peoples (including those not entitled to claim independence because of their noncolonial status).[35] Yet because the report takes accession to be consummated, it does not explore the ramifications of such participatory rights except in the most general terms, formulated as follows: "For colonial peoples, this choice includes the possibility of independence; for others, it excludes independence, but signifies at once the right to one's own identity, the right to choose, and the right to participate."[36] It seems evident from context and reference to Thomas Franck's article on the emergent entitlement to democracy that participation in the Pellet Report means democratic

33. Ibid., p. 35.
34. See Lâm, *At the Edge of the State,* for a comprehensive analysis along these lines.
35. Ibid., pp. 40–42.
36. Ibid., p. 41.

inclusion in the relevant political community on a nondiscriminatory basis, and nothing else.[37]

As argued here, it is the interpretation of the significance of this right of participation by objecting peoples that needs to be clarified with respect to any attempted accession to sovereignty. It is only by artificially postulating an already independent Quebec as an established fact that the Pellet Report can make the question of secession so central and base any rights of the aboriginal peoples in relation to a consummated process.

The Pellet Report helpfully confirms that the rights of aboriginal peoples are emergent, gaining steadily in recognition under contemporary international law. The report also notes that the positing of a right of self-determination in the Draft Declaration on the Rights of Indigenous Peoples, which has yet to be presented to the UN General Assembly for formal adoption, is likely to exert a significant influence despite the appreciation that its degree of authoritativeness and impact will remain uncertain and controversial for a considerable period of time. But the whole matter of the existence of such a right is determined to be "of little consequence" by the Pellet line of argument because even in "the broadest conception of rights contemplated for aboriginal peoples, nowhere [is it] provide[d] that they should have a right of secession."[38] This argument puts the whole matter of self-determination for indigenous peoples as it relates to Quebec in a quite misleading posture. There is no claim being currently made or contemplated on the issue of secession by aboriginal nations. This issue is, at most, a matter of deciding whether there exists an outer limit restricting the right of self-determination should secession be claimed. The central claims of the aboriginal peoples in present Quebec, however, do not pertain directly to secession but to their rights to avoid any change of circumstances that is perceived to be harmful to their existing arrangements and future prospects, as well as to a prior right of consultation and participation equivalent to that enjoyed by representatives of Quebec as a whole. Quebec's aboriginal peoples do not want to be merely an afterthought or be placed in a reactive posture of responding due to Quebec's separation being accepted as a fait accompli.

---

37. Thomas Franck, "The Emerging Right of Democratic Governance," *American Journal of International Law* 86, no. 1 (1992). It is not evident that rights of democratic inclusion mean more than participation in periodic, free elections, which may be quite irrelevant to the sort of situation presented by the controversy over Quebec secession.

38. Ibid., p. 55.

These issues of participation are important whenever existing states break into two or more parts. If objecting groups claim to be a people, themselves entitled to exercise the right of self-determination, then it is important to have a mechanism to evaluate such a claim and draw appropriate legal conclusions. If the objecting groups are content with the status of being a minority, then it seems most helpful to view complaints as a series of human rights challenges, possibly requiring special regimes of guaranty and protection in the course of rearranging sovereign boundaries. The failure to take such steps for the benefit of Serbian minorities in Croatia and Bosnia undoubtedly contributed to the downward spiral in the 1990s that erupted into vicious warfare. Though we cannot excuse in any way the atrocities committed by the Bosnian Serbs, their sense of abuse and neglect in 1990–1991 was understandable and reasonable, especially given their recall of historical persecution and Germany's encouragement of the Yugoslav breakup by way of extending diplomatic recognition to Slovenia and Croatia prior to any reasonable effort to reassure Serb minorities. There were also serious irregularities associated with the initial Bosnian claim of independence, which violated the constitutional requirement of legislative approval by a plurality—a requirement that deliberately gave the Serb minority an effective veto on any move by Bosnia to withdraw from the Yugoslav Federation.

These events, which generated the Bosnian war, reinforce the need for peacekeeping approaches that rely on preventive diplomacy, acting before social, political, economic, and political tensions generate violence and thereby offering parties an alternative to war. The right of self-determination in circumstances of multiple claims should be subject to a process of participation, negotiation, and assessment under respected neutral auspices. This kind of approach will fail on some occasions, but it seems evident that if the global community is to learn from Bosnia and elsewhere, the postcolonial extensions of the right of self-determination cannot be allowed to unfold on their own as if no framework of principles and procedures exists. It is instructive to note that where the breakup is mainly voluntary and the new entity does not contain significant objecting or threatened minorities, as was the case in Slovenia, such a cautious, preventive orientation is neither needed nor appropriate. The presence of indigenous peoples within the seceding entity presents a special problem if their representatives object to the contemplated change of status, as has been the case in relation to the separatist option for Quebec.

Three sorts of questions are raised. Do such peoples enjoy their own right of self-determination? Is the territorial government obligated to represent the fiduciary interests of such peoples in the course of any negotiations relating to secession? Are indigenous peoples entitled to exercise a full or partial right to take part in any negotiations that might produce an accession to sovereignty? This matter of an emergent right of self-determination for indigenous peoples is explored in the next section. It introduces a special dimension into the conceptual discussion: the peoples involved do not normally aspire to constitute themselves as a modern sovereign state.

The Claims of Indigenous Peoples
to Possess a Distinct Right of Self-Determination

Another recent development of some consequence is the insistence by indigenous peoples and their representatives on their core right of self-determination, which befits their generally shared avowal of sovereignty and nationhood. The degree to which such a right of self-determination is currently part of international law remains uncertain and controversial.[39] There is, to be sure, no binding formal instrument that establishes such a right, or clarifies its scope, particularly in relation to international sovereign states within whose territory or territories such indigenous peoples and nations are situated.

At the same time, there has been a notable evolution of political consciousness with respect to such a claim, as well as a process of acknowledgment to a degree within the UN and on the part of many existing states. It can be argued that the right of self-determination inheres in a people and need not be established on its own or that the path of customary international law has been cleared to a sufficient degree to admit of the legal existence of a right of self-determination. Such matters are embedded in a gray sector of legal controversy and indefiniteness and are likely to remain so for the next decade or so at the very least.

What seems evident is that the presence of an array of potential claims by indigenous peoples around the world relating to the right of self-determination adds to the current confusion as to the status of the right and contributes to nervousness on the part of many diplomats about the persistence and character of a right of self-determination in this postcolonial era. Of course, it is not strictly a postcolonial era, as certain colonies in a traditional sense continue to exist. France retains colonial possessions in the Pacific and Caribbean and gives no sign of a

---

39. For an overview on these matters, see Lâm, *At the Edge of the State*. See also S. James Anaya, *Indigenous Peoples in International Law* (New York: Oxford University Press, 1996).

willingness to give them up. It seeks, rather, to avoid the colonial opprobrium by characterizing its colonies as integral parts of France that are affirmed as such by the inhabitants, making them voluntary political communities.

Also relevant here is the contention by supporters of the claims of indigenous peoples that their exercise of the right of self-determination occurs within a colonial context, that such peoples have been severely colonized and are as entitled, if not more so, to self-determination as are those peoples who were formally categorized and denominated as colonial. There is historical and ethical merit in such a perspective. However, it seems that anything like its full acceptance might be very destabilizing, making even its serious consideration politically unacceptable to the entrenched interests of the established order. Any validation of such rights could conceivably confront many states with gigantic territorial claims whose satisfaction would lead to devastating economic, political, and social effects for the vast majority of their population, which would presumably resist implementation by violence if necessary.

What adds to the confusion in this setting is the intermixing of symbolic and substantive goals and the deliberate blurring of the distinction by both sides. If the claims to the right of self-determination were clearly symbolic as to full international statehood, it would seem less threatening for existing states to acknowledge the right. Unfortunately, an integral part of the symbolic value of the right of self-determination is its affirmation of the unencumbered right of a people to choose its destiny, including, *in theory*, territorial sovereignty. The fact that such a claim cannot be successfully exercised and practically implemented within the setting of present world conditions does not altogether provide states with sufficient reassurance that they will not be faced with challenges to their unity and present character. If a right of self-determination is confirmed in a noncircumscribed form, its full exercise can be threatened in order to achieve benefits in bargaining or negotiating circumstances, and there is no assurance that larger demands will not actually be made even if it would be irresponsible for an indigenous people under most circumstances to attempt to become a fully independent state. The impracticality of exercising a right of self-determination is no assurance that it will not be exercised.

No end of this problematic challenge is currently in sight. As with other aspects of controversy about the proper scope of the right of self-determination, it is too late to deny altogether its applicability to the situation of indigenous peoples. To attempt to do so would intensify conflict and would not be accepted by those who support the general improvement in the protection of indigenous peoples and regard such peoples as victims of acute injustice.

It is also worth noting the legal progress that indigenous peoples have made in recent decades, moving from the category of unprotected victims of the modernizing process to individuals entitled to protection by way of assimilationist norms of nondiscrimination and then to groups whose autonomous way of life deserves protection. The question posed is whether this latter goal, which is now widely enough endorsed by states to qualify as a norm of customary international law, also implies a full right of self-determination or whether the safeguarding of indigenous autonomy is necessarily a matter for negotiation, compromise, and conflict resolution and should be treated as a category of its own. The unresolved issue is how to confer on indigenous peoples an appropriate entitlement that belatedly rectifies, to some extent, past injustices without in the process creating an explosive situation with respect to contemporary realities.

In this regard, the assertion by indigenous peoples of their claims to the right of self-determination based on historical and sacred attachments to specific land now collides with parallel rights of self-determination by the people of the modern territorial state that is the encompassing reality. These latter rights are themselves legally protected and entrenched, and present beneficiaries feel little or no responsibility for the injustices allegedly committed by their ancestors. In other words, the *full* exercise of the right of self-determination claimed by either people would infringe on the perceived rights of the other. Some process of mutual adjustment is called for that somehow accommodates the essential claims of both sides to the extent that is feasible. With goodwill and sensitivity such an outcome seems attainable in most situations, perhaps invoking the mediating good offices of the UN, if the indigenous substantive claim relates to ensuring a capability to retain at least what such indigenous people currently possess.[40] Such a claim also needs to include symbolic acknowledgment of the injustices of the past and some credible gesture of rectification.[41] There may be virtually insoluble problems in the event that valuable mineral or energy resources are found on land previously

---

40. Lâm concludes her excellent book *At the Edge of the State* with a series of proposals along these lines.

41. The government of Canada, for example, has moved toward reconciliation by issuing a formal apology for 150 years of mistreatment of aboriginal peoples under its authority and by establishing a trust fund that would be available to such peoples in their efforts to sustain their way of life.

possessed by indigenous people but developed by those who long ago displaced them.

Finally, this aspect of the self-determination debate raises issues similar to the challenge posed by secessionist claims made in the face of opposition by the prior unified political structure and by minorities that will find themselves unhappily subject to a new sovereign authority. There are two clusters of problems: The first involves whether the right of self-determination applies and, if so, whether it allows for secession; the second involves the process—whether those affected by a proposed breakup of a state are entitled to participate and whether their consent is needed to validate a change in political arrangements. In these respects, the situation of the Serbian minorities in Croatia and Bosnia structurally resembles that of indigenous nations in Quebec (ten of eleven object to the secessionist movement there) that are insisting that there can be no valid change in constitutional structure without their participation and consent. Since the movement for secession in Quebec has engendered strong support but has not up to this point succeeded at the referendum stage, the issues raised are unlikely to be tested fully and will remain unresolved. There are also comparable questions pertaining to the rights of the objecting, largely English-speaking minority of modern Quebec.

Conclusion

The evolution of the right of self-determination is one of the most dramatic normative developments in this century. The range of claims to exercise this right are schematically classified in the appendix to this chapter. During the height of the decolonization process, affirming the rights of self-determination seemed fully in step with the march of history—such affirmation had an overall positive effect on the human condition and freed hundreds of millions from colonial bondage. Decolonization extended sovereignty and statehood to all corners of the planet for the first time and built the UN into a genuinely universal body representing virtually the whole of humanity.

The identification of the right with people in a world in which many peoples lack a state of their own or are victimized by an oppressive state is bound to produce problems if a contrary objective is to keep the existing territorial arrangement of states reasonably stable. The breakup of the Soviet Union and Yugoslavia have dramatized these concerns, generating intense civil strife due to an array of efforts to reconstitute states in a manner that newly entraps resisting peoples and hence creating a collision of political wills and passions. Whereas the larger political entity may have tried to contain and accommodate several overlapping expressions of nationalist identity, the smaller fragment may be a vehicle for a particular nationalism and, as such, hostile to alternative nationalisms. Such a dynamic tends to provoke defensive reactions by those who fear the repressive consequences of the new arrangement even more than they may have resented the older, more generalized pattern of oppression.

Yet to dismiss self-determination as an option is impossible at this stage. Its reality has sunk too deeply into political and legal consciousness, and there remain in the world too many distinct peoples enduring alien and oppressive rule. The idea of self-determination recognizes that the legitimacy of *any* political arrangement depends on the will of the people subject to its authority and is closely associated with ideas of democracy and fundamental human rights.

There are no fully satisfactory solutions. In some settings, self-determination struggles can be avoided by the timely establishment of a regime for the protection of group rights. In others, struggle is avoided with a phased process that moves from human rights to autonomy and then, possibly, on to independence. In still others, self-determination claims can be satisfied by moderate solutions that ensure self-rule and self-administration in the spirit of the Liechtenstein proposal. The Liechtenstein proposal has the great merit of preserving the symbolic aura of self-determination while restricting its most threatening substantive implications. The limited situation arises where substance, as well as symbol, is of essence and takes the form of a state-shattering movement in a setting where there is opposition from the old unified state and from ethnic minorities in the new proposed state. In such circumstances, patient dialogue and diplomacy, the avoidance of violence on both sides, neutral good offices, and the effective protection of human rights seem the most constructive approach.

In the background remains the core issue of seeking an overall stability at the level of the state, which includes limiting the total number of states to around 200 with an upper limit of 250. To do this, outer limits on state-shattering exercises of the right of self-determination must be kept at a minimum. And yet the promise of self-determination to all peoples, of which at least 5,000 exist, makes it very difficult to find a principled basis in law for denying claimants who seem to be a people and have the will and capability to be a sovereign state. Possibly, the evolution of regional community frameworks will allow peoples to achieve meaningful forms of autonomy without feeling the need to break out of an existing state. If states deepen democracy to ensure the equitable participation and protection of all peoples subject to their authority, secessionist motivations are reduced, if not eliminated. In the event of such favorable developments, self-determination in its various contemporary dimensions may be eventually reconcilable with the maintenance of political stability. At present, patterns of governmental abuse and exploitation, dreams of freedom, and the mystique of statehood are so prevalent as to make state-shattering claims based on self-determination likely to persist for years to come.

Appendix: Classifying Self-Determination Claims

There are several different types of self-determination claims based on the historical context and the character of the entity asserting the claim. One set of claims derives from collective processes demanding secession, autonomy, self-rule, self-administration, and the like. There is a second set of claims deriving from demands for human rights, grounded in the conferral of a right of self-determination in Article 1 of both the Covenant on Civil and Political Rights and the Covenant on Economic, Social, and Cultural Rights.

Table 2.1   Types of Self-Determination Claims

Type A Claims of Secession and Autonomy
First order	decolonization; foreign rule (Indonesia, India, Tunisia)
Second order	secession by federal units in relation to a central government (Slovenia, Croatia, Kashmir, Aceh, Bosnia and Herzegovina, Quebec, and Slovakia)
Third order	administrative subunits (Chechnya, Kosovo, Dagestan)
Fourth order	indigenous communities or nations (Cree, Navajo, Zapatistas)

Type B Claims of Human Rights and Democracy
First order	the option of colonial status (Falkland Islands)
Second order	the option of federalism
Third order	the option of legal regimes of guaranty and protection that confer rights of access, participation, and equality
Fourth order	the option of fiduciary arrangements administered by traditional territorial sovereign with an undertaking to preserve traditional rights to sacred land (including hunting and fishing rights) and the ways of life of minorities and indigenous peoples

3

UN Intervention and National Sovereignty

Michael W. Doyle

Since the end of the Cold War, the community of nations has experienced a near revolution in the relation between what is in the legitimate realm of state sovereignty and what is subject to legitimate international intervention. Employing a strikingly intrusive interpretation of United Nations Charter provisions concerning international peace and security, the UN's member states have endorsed a radical expansion in the scope of collective intervention. In the 1990s the new interventionism has both vastly widened legitimate collective interventions and considerably narrowed the scope of legitimate unilateral intervention by individual states. Both serve to reduce the scope of state sovereignty. This widening of the domain of global authority and the shrinking of state sovereignty have had two effects on national self-determination: the traditional rights of states have been fettered, and the rights of some oppressed nations have been (partly) recognized. Yet unfulfilled commitments and escalating use of force have provoked a severe crisis in UN peace enforcement, driving the new interventionism to a political dead-end in Bosnia and Somalia. At the same time, the basic human rights of all people and peoples found a new protector as the UN

This chapter was written with the generous support of the Liechtensten Research Program on Self-Determination. It also draws on research supported by the Ford Foundation, which I conducted while serving as vice president of the International Peace Academy, and on "Forcing Peace," Dissent (Spring 1994), pp. 167–171, and The UN in Cambodia: UNTAC's Civil Mandate (Boulder, Colo.: Lynne Rienner, 1995). I would like to thank the Liechtenstein Research Program on Self-Determination, the International Peace Academy, the Ford Foundation, and, in particular, Emilio Cárdenas, Jean Cot, Ibrahim Gambari, Jeffrey Herbst, Ian Johnstone, Hurst Hannum, F. T. Liu, Hisashi Owada, Laurence Pearl, Danilo Turk, and John Waterbury for their valuable advice. None of the above bear responsibility for the views advocated in this chapter.

opened new opportunities for individual and communal self-expression in countries ranging from Cambodia to El Salvador to Croatia.

Beginning with a description of the revolution in state sovereignty, I show how the rights of collective intervention have increased and the rights of once legitimate sovereignty, including unilateral intervention, have narrowed. Here I draw some comparisons both to Cold War UN doctrine and to the traditional legal and moral standards of international ethics and law. I then offer a brief account of the political origins of global sovereignty, discussing how and why this occurred. For the UN, this ideological revolution produced a crisis of overcommitment and a failure of (UN Charter) Chapter VII enforcement by the UN. In the third section I illustrate how this crisis of credibility created havoc in the UN Protection Force for the Former Yugoslavia (UNPROFOR) and in the UN Operation in Somalia (UNOSOM). Both failures contributed to the retrenchment that UN Secretary-General Boutros Boutros-Ghali acknowledged in 1995 and that Secretary-General Kofi Annan now challenges. Annan, in his speech to the 1999 UN General Assembly, identified "a new international norm in favor of intervention to protect civilians from wholesale slaughter."[1] Acknowledging all the difficulties, he particularly challenged nation-states to find a path to intervention that avoids Security Council inaction in the face of genocide (the Rwanda precedent) and regional action without Security Council authorization (the Kosovo precedent).

I conclude with a suggestion for how to respond to both the limitations Secretary-General Boutros-Ghali identified and the challenges Secretary-General Annan has noted, thus taking into account both the overburden on limited UN resources and the need to protect global human rights and enhance both national and communal self-determination. Drawing on the examples of the UN operations in Cambodia and El Salvador, I argue that the UN needs to foster a political engagement with national sovereignty, an internationalist alternative based on an enhancement of Chapter VI–based consent. Successfully carried out, such engagements can promote the development of law and order while supporting communal autonomy. The recent operation in Eastern Slavonia (UNTAES) illustrates some steps in that direction.

The UN Challenges State Sovereignty

Recent years have witnessed a massive expansion of UN action in international peace and security. In 1999 there were seventeen peacekeeping

---

1. Kofi Annan, "Two Concepts of Sovereignty," *The Economist,* September, 18, 1999.

and peace enforcement operations, whereas the UN previously had two or three truce supervision or observation operations at any one time. The annual cost of these operations is about half the total cost of all UN operations since 1947, but measures of the number and cost of the operations do not reveal the change in their nature. The UN has been, is, and is likely to long remain an organization of states. Yet at the end of the Cold War there was a willingness on the part of the international community to challenge state sovereignty and to restrict states in defining the essential nature of domestic sovereignty; these challenges were made in the name of an emerging global view of human rights and national self-determination, both external and internal.[2] International law, as embodied in the UN Charter (1945), Article 2(4), precludes states from the "threat or use of force" against the "territorial integrity or political independence" of any other state. Article 2(7) further provides that the UN itself is not authorized to intervene in matters "essentially" within the domestic jurisdiction of states except when the Security Council acts under Chapter VII concerning matters that are "threats to the peace, breaches of the peace, or acts of aggression." Yet 1990s practice was strikingly different:

• Security Council Resolution 687 (the Gulf War Resolution) envisaged a comprehensive, intrusive interference in Iraqi sovereignty. Resolution 687 was not an agreed-upon peace treaty with a defeated nation or a preemptive measure against a current threat to the peace but a set of sanctions imposed for the sake of global order with the goal of reforming a proven international outlaw. It set extraordinary precedents: it regulates permissible weapons, creates an observation force, demarcates the country's borders with Kuwait, enforces reparations, and mandates the practices of the Iraqi government vis-à-vis the exercise of human rights and the protection of internal dissidents, the Kurds and Shiites.[3]

• Security Council Resolution 688 offered specific protection to an Iraqi minority—the Kurds. It did so by declaring the possible flow of refugees to be a threat to international peace.

• Acting presumably in the name of national self-determination and overriding the opposition of Yugoslavia, the UN admitted four of its

---

2. For a legal analysis of changing norms of state sovereignty and national self-determination, see Chapter 2 by Richard Falk in this volume.

3. See Ian Johnstone, *Aftermath of the Gulf War: An Assessment of UN Action,* IPA Occasional Paper (Boulder, Colo.: Lynne Rienner, 1994); and Stephen Stedman, "The New Interventionism," *Foreign Affairs* 72, no. 1 (1993), pp 1–16, for a valuable discussion of interventionist trends in post–Cold War international politics.

former territorial units—Macedonia, Slovenia, Croatia, and Bosnia—as sovereign member states.

• Security Council Resolution 648, the Libya-Lockerbie case, declared a failure to extradite alleged terrorists to be a threat to the peace and invoked Chapter VII mandatory economic sanctions.

• In Security Council Resolution 794, the UN judged the starvation of thousands of human beings in Somalia to be a threat to the peace and so authorized the Unified Task Force, led by the United States. It then reiterated the same view in Resolution 814 and created a mandate for a comprehensive regime of law, order, and national self-determination.[4] The UNOSOM regime in 1993 began to resemble colonial rule, albeit for a benign purpose.

• Security Council Resolution 841, concerning Haiti, enforced an embargo and blockade to restore former President Jean-Bertrand Aristide, legitimately elected by 70 percent of the vote and ousted in a coup in September 1991. Here we see an act of war (the blockade) imposed for the sake of restoring democratic rule.

• Later Security Council sanctions continued the border-leaping pattern.[5] The UN imposed sanctions against an internal guerrilla movement—UNITA (National Union for the Total Liberation of Angola) in Angola—for its failure to abide by the results of the election won by its opponents. The UN had monitored the election and certified that it had been conducted in a free and fair manner.

• Concerning Kosovo in 1999, the Security Council sent mixed signals. On the one hand, the Council refused to give NATO authorization to protect the Kosovar Albanian population (Russia and China especially resisted such an authorization). On the other hand, the Council overwhelmingly voted in March 1999 (the vote was 12–3) against condemning the NATO bombing when NATO went ahead without Council

---

4. UNOSOM deliberately postponed the issue of whether northern Somalia would be included in Somalia, but its mandate presupposed a unified Somalia. For the operations of UNOSOM, see Samuel Makinda, *Seeking Peace from Chaos: Humanitarian Intervention in Somalia,* IPA Occasional Paper (Boulder, Colo.: Lynne Rienner, 1993). Somalia soon became the classic "failed state," subject to what amounted to a UN trusteeship. The term *failed state* was introduced by Gerald Helman and Steven Ratner, "Saving Failed States," *Foreign Policy* (Winter 1992–1993), pp. 3–21.

5. The UN's actions have significant precedent: the UN sanctions against South African apartheid, which significantly were affirmed by the International Court of Justice. The Security Council in Res. 253 (1969) also imposed sanctions under Chapter VII against the racist, undemocratic regime of Southern Rhodesia for its "inhuman executions" despite the fact that Southern Rhodesia posed no direct threat to the territorial integrity or political independence of any other state; nor was it a weak or "failed state."

authorization. Equally startling was the trusteeship-like role that the UN assumed under Resolution 1244 (1999) in cooperation with NATO.

• East Timor in some respects is classic peacekeeping: Indonesia formally consented to all the peace operations. But the issue of internationally managed national self-determination within the territory of a recognized UN member state was a departure, as was (on the Kosovo model) the trusteeship-like role that the UN has assumed in East Timor.

Pre-Charter international law lent little support to post–Cold War globalism. Traditional law was a set of "club rules" for sovereigns, back-scratching principles designed to protect their sovereignties while permitting extensive interference and colonial activity in the nonrecognized parts of the world remote from "civilized" Europe and North America. Traditional law allowed any state to assist any recognized government at, but only at, its request. Such interventions by invitation were often designed to help suppress a popular rising by a state's own people. Conversely, traditional law permitted intervention against the government in aid of rebels only when the rebels had established a control of territory sufficient to be recognized as a belligerency (for example, the Confederacy in the U.S. Civil War) and then only if other states were first aiding the government side. These standards were reaffirmed by the disposition of the Nicaragua case before the International Court of Justice, in which a variety of U.S. justifications for its intervention against Nicaragua were rejected.

These traditional prohibitions against intervention were made even stronger by UN majorities in the General Assembly. Though not recognized as binding international law, these jurisprudential declarations and resolutions strictly condemned "interference" in any form—political, economic and cultural—"in the domestic affairs of sovereign states."[6]

Human rights–oriented (liberal) moral argument was more permissive of intervention, but it allowed intervention only when the basic purposes by which national sovereignty is justified—national self-determination and individual autonomy—were so egregiously violated that state sovereignty lost its meaning. It thus allowed intervention in support of: (1) national secessions when there are two nations, one

---

6. General Assembly Resolution 2625, "Declaration on the Principles of Friendly Relations and Cooperation Among States, 1970." The only major formal erosion of state sovereignty in the Cold War system was directed against South Africa and colonial regimes, whose African, Asian, and Caribbean colonies were declared to have a right to national independence.

struggling to free itself from the control of another; (2) counterintervention in a civil war when a foreign force seeks to tilt a domestic struggle for sovereignty; (3) an effort to halt genocide when the survival of the people is made an object of direct and dire threat.[7]

Let us note the difference between tradition and the 1990s: The UN intervened to reshape Iraq's borders and determine its treatment of minorities and to decide on its permissible military capacity. It determined to restore democracy in Haiti; extradite terrorists from Libya; force UNITA to abide by an election; establish law and order and a democratic regime—by March 1995, no less—in Somalia; and, recently, to permit the self-determination of the East Timorese and preserve the basic human rights and self-government of the Kosovar Albanians.

The new interventionism did not appear to reflect a complete global consensus on global responsibility. A number of states formerly part of the second and third worlds saw a danger of tyranny in the process of Security Council decisionmaking. They asserted that too much was done in secret and the process was too dominated by the P-5 (the five permanent members of the Security Council: the United States, Russia, France, China, and Britain). The P-5, moreover, were in fact led by the Western P-3, who, in their turn, are really led by the United States—P-1.[8]

Despite, however, the dissent on process, there was less dissent in substance. It was African states who condemned the UN in 1991–1992 for failing to intervene in Somalia, a poor, black people's, African disaster, contrasting its neglect there to its heavy commitment in the former Yugoslavia, a rich, white people's, European disaster. In Bosnia, moreover, the effort in the Security Council to enforce human rights was led not by the five permanent members but by the then Non-Aligned Movement members of the Security Council—Cape Verde, Djibouti, Morocco, Pakistan, and Venezuela—and by Muslim states outside the Council.[9]

---

7. An illuminating discussion of these considerations can be found in Michael Walzer, *Just and Unjust Wars* (New York: Basic Books, 1978).

8. These issues are thoroughly explored in Olara Otunnu, "Maintaining Broad Legitimacy for United Nations Action," in John Roper et al., *Keeping the Peace in the Post–Cold War Era: Strengthening Multilateral Peacekeeping, A Report to the Trilateral Commission* (New York: Trilateral Commission, 1993); and David Caron, "The Legitimacy of the Collective Authority of the Security Council," *American Journal of International Law* 87, no. 4 (October 1993), pp. 552–590.

9. In particular, see the Security Council debate on June 29, 1993, on whether to raise the arms embargo on Bosnia. Venezuelan ambassador Diego Arria made an eloquent speech in defense of the right of self-defense and the duties of collective self-defense. He drew specific analogies between the plight of small states and their leaders—Bosnia in 1993 and Czechoslovakia in 1938, Izetbegović and Beneš—and the duty to avoid appeasing aggressors.

In addition to UN interventions to support global human rights, other UN interventions diminished national sovereignty in yet another way, one that was equally revolutionary. Recent UN practice contracted the traditional sovereign rights to engage in and support counterintervention in civil wars as well as national secession. Under traditional law and ethics, states challenged by an armed group could request assistance. Complementarily, a recognized, "legitimate" belligerent could request assistance against foreign intervention supporting the government side. Yet Bosnia, a recognized member state of the UN, was prevented by the UN arms embargo from acquiring such assistance. It could neither request aid against Serb and Croat rebels, as a sovereign state could, nor request counterinterventionary assistance, as a legitimate belligerent in the midst of a civil war, against the massive support the former Yugoslav National Army (JNA) gave the Bosnian Serbs. Instead, the UN arms embargo applied against all, making Bosnia very much less than the sovereign state and member of the UN it had been formally recognized as being. In another instance, the Kurdish nation inside Iraq is protected by the UN from Iraqi oppression, but at the same time, it is prevented from requesting assistance as a recognizable belligerent and a national liberation movement. Once the Security Council decides on a matter of peace and security, all member states are required to support that decision (Articles 41 and 43).

The Political Origins
of the UN Claim to Global Sovereignty

In recent years, two interpretive axioms have slipped into the practice of the world community, shrinking domestic sovereignty from two directions and together paving the way for the new interventionism. First, UN member states have subtly altered the definition of what is "essentially" sovereign in Article 2(7). Now global standards of human rights, as expressed in the First (civil and political) and perhaps even the Second (economic and social) Covenants, have become definitive of, universal to, and constraining on what constitutes domestic sovereignty and what is a legitimate matter of international attention. Human rights, then, are claimed to be inherently global, and domestic sovereignty cannot override them.[10] In this view, the Vienna Conference on

---

10. Thomas M. Franck, "The Emerging Right of Democratic Governance," *American Journal of International Law* 86, no. 1 (1992); and Tom Farer, "Collectively Defending Democracy in a World of Sovereign States," *Human Rights Quarterly* 15 (1993).

Human Rights (June 1993) was but the formal endorsement of the claim to a universal jurisdiction over human rights. The earlier relativistic objections of the Bangkok Group, composed of third world states, were overcome. In return for a vague promise to pay more attention to assisting international development, the conference's dissenting members signed an agreement that explicitly linked democracy to human rights and held that levels of economic development would be taken into account in assessing how to judge the implementation of human rights, not in assessing whether human standards applied.[11]

Second, the Security Council has also expanded the meaning of the Article 2(7), Chapter VII–based conditions regarding when sovereignty may be overridden: "threats to peace, breaches of the peace, acts of aggression."Article 2(7) now appears to include all the infringements of traditional sovereignty formally endorsed by the Security Council in the resolutions previously noted. Indeed, "threat to the peace" and so forth has come to mean severe domestic violations of human rights, civil wars, and humanitarian emergencies—almost whatever a Security Council majority (without a P-5 veto) says it is.[12]

These two developments, in turn, have roots in striking changes in the international system since the end of the Cold War. First, the new spirit of cooperation manifested by the USSR, beginning with President Gorbachev's reforms, met a new spirit of tolerance from the United States now that the USSR appeared to be verging on democracy and had decided to end its "empire" over Eastern Europe and the Baltic states. Together they broke the forty-year gridlock in the Security Council. Post–Cold War cooperation meant the Security Council became functional, operating as the global guardian of peace and security, a continuation of the World War II Grand Alliance, and thus very much in the spirit anticipated by Franklin D. Roosevelt and Winston Churchill and manifested in its Charter design.

Second, we now see an emerging community of democratic values that gives specific content to the cooperative initiatives of recent years. Initiatives coming out of the Vienna Conference on Human Rights and Gorbachev's plea before the General Assembly for "global human values" signify that human rights are no longer merely a Western but a global principle of good governance.

Third, the U.S. "unipolar moment" and temporary commitment to

---

11. Vienna Declaration and Programme of Action (draft reference number: A/CONF 157/23).

12. For a discussion of the traditional Cold War interpretations of "threat to the peace" and so forth, see Leland M. Goodrich, E. Hambro, and Anne Simons, *Charter of the United Nations* (New York: Columbia University Press, 1969), pp. 293–300.

assertive multilateralism, which was evident between the Gulf War and the October 3, 1993, disaster in Mogadishu, provided a degree of commitment and resourceful leadership in the Security Council that the UN had rarely seen before. Eschewing the national role of "globocop" in order to address a pressing domestic agenda, the United States encouraged Secretary-General Boutros-Ghali to take an ever more assertive role in international crises. The dissenting minority in the Security Council (China, on some occasions) was not prepared to resist the United States other than on issues that were of paramount national interest. Kosovo proved to be just such an issue for Russia, and NATO chose to bypass the Security Council until, having persuaded Russia to take a role in the negotiations, NATO and Russia came back to the UN for implementing the agreed peace.

For many in the United States, multilateral action seemed to be the ready solution to a difficult dilemma. It reconciled an advocacy of collective security, universal human rights, and humanitarian solidarity overseas with the need to refocus Cold War spending on domestic reform at home. Multilateral action under the UN Charter was not only the prescribed legal route to world order, it appeared to be a practical solution to human solidarity when each nation caring a little seemed sufficient to ensure that all together cared enough. The successful reversal of Saddam Hussein's aggression in the Gulf and the December 1992 U.S.-led rescue of the Somali population from starvation heralded what appeared to be a remarkable partnership. The Security Council decreed; the United States delivered. For a while, conveniently, many other states paid and supported.

Together these developments made the new globalism feasible and legitimate. Collective intervention, intervention by the UN, was acceptable where unilateral intervention was not. Because it appeared more impartial, not self-serving, the UN community was perceived to be acting as the whole, speaking for the whole community of nations. Traditional suspicion of intervention was thus allayed. The traditional restraints, moral and political, were lifted—in retrospect, perhaps too readily.

Globalism in Crisis

Fears that Russia might decide to abandon its multilateralism in the former Yugoslavia and instead act in support of the special interests of its fellow Slav brethren, the Serbs, proved exaggerated until the clash over Kosovo illuminated deep Russian (and Chinese) concerns over growing NATO and U.S.hegemony. But earlier, the twin crises in Somalia and Bosnia produced a crisis in UN "assertively multilateral" peace enforcement that recent experience in Kosovo and East Timor have not yet put to rest.[13]

Somalia

The UN effort in the large part of Somalia outside of General Aidid's southern Mogadishu proceeded according to plan. By early 1993, starvation was not an issue in the areas within the reach of UN protection. By contrast, 300,000 Somalis died in 1991–1992 in a famine induced by the murderous competition of the Somali warlords. In 1993, with UNOSOM II's protection, the UN Children's Fund (UNICEF) was assisting 40,000 pupils. Thirty-two hospitals and 103 mobile vaccination teams were active (75 percent of the children under five had received the measles vaccine), and 70,000 Somali refugees returned from Kenya. Thirty-nine district councils and six regional councils were formed; UNOSOM began to recruit 5,000 former Somali policemen to perform basic police functions. Tens, perhaps hundreds, of thousands of lives were saved by the UNITAF (Unified Task Force) and UNOSOM II peace operations.

Nonetheless, the October 3, 1993, disaster and the killing of eighteen U.S. soldiers (about 500 Somalis also were killed and a thousand or more were wounded),[14] the earlier crisis on June 5 in which twenty-four Pakistani peacekeepers were killed, and the fruitless effort to capture General Aidid over the summer together exposed what had become a politically bankrupt attempt to enforce law and order on an increasingly resistant population. With the advantage of hindsight, we can identify policy mistakes, without which Somalia might look very different today.[15] A more thorough partnership with Somalia's regional neighbors in a mediation effort in 1991;[16] a more extensive mandate for the U.S.-led UNITAF in December 1992, when controlling the heavy and light weapons of the clans would have been easier; and, above all, a smoother political transition from UNITAF's partial successes in nego-

---

13. The following paragraphs draw on my "Forcing Peace," *Dissent* (March 1994).

14. Mark Bowden, *Black Hawk Down* (New York: Atlantic Monthly Press, 1999), p. 310.

15. See Jonathan Stevenson, "Hope Restored in Somalia," *Foreign Policy* 91 (Summer 1993), pp. 138–154; Jeffrey Clark, "Debacle in Somalia: The Failure of Collective Response," in Lori Damrosch, ed., *Enforcing Restraint* (New York: Council on Foreign Relations, 1993); and Jane Perlez, "Somalia Self-Destructs and the World Looks On," *New York Times,* December 29, 1991, p. A1.

16. For this argument, see Mohammed Sahnoun, *Somalia: The Missed Opportunities* (Washington, D.C.: U.S. Institute of Peace, 1994).

tiating with the warlords to UNOSOM's more ambitious state-building agenda might have made a difference.

The fundamental problem was a famine induced by drought, by the ravages of the civil war that followed on the collapse of Siad Barre's dictatorship, and by the rapacious extortion of the Somali warlords who taxed relief convoys in order to fund their competition for power. Only a Somali leviathan with a monopoly of violence or a superwarlord capable of playing warlord against warlord could restore order and end the famine. UNOSOM I (with 500 Pakistani troops holed up in the port of Mogadishu) could do very little, not even prevent grain ships from being shelled from shore. UN Special Representative Mohammed Sahnoun valiantly tried to negotiate a peace, appealing to the humanity of the very warlords who ran the famine. In December 1992 the U.S.-led UNITAF became the Somali leviathan, and the roads were opened and the famine broken.[17] UNITAF met almost no opposition because the mass of the people welcomed the relief, and the warlords knew it was temporary and no threat to their power.

In May 1993, UNOSOM II came face-to-face with the fundamental problems. Its mandate included the necessary authority to disarm the factions—a disarmament to which, we should note, the faction leaders had agreed to at the Addis Ababa conference in March 1993.[18] This mandate, however, unlike UNITAF's, threatened the political existence of the warlords. It proposed the establishment of a Somali national authority elected by the people and sustained by a police force trained by the UN. UNOSOM, however, was a paper tiger, lacking the capacity to enforce (or even bargain for compliance with) the agreement. The bulk of its troops were lightly armed and vulnerable to the weapons the warlords withdrew from the temporary UNITAF cantonment. UNOSOM's forces were immobile and dependent on Mogadishu's port facilities, which made the UN too dependent on Aidid to threaten a credible withdrawal from his zone. The entire force relied too much on the military and logistic backbone of the U.S. contingent, and this contingent was poorly coordinated with the overall UNOSOM force. UNOSOM survived casualties inflicted on the Pakistanis in June, but when Aidid attacked the U.S. troops in October he struck UNOSOM's Achilles' heel.

---

17. For President Bush's rationale, see Michael Wines, "Bush Outlines Somalia Mission to Save Thousands," *New York Times,* December 5, 1992, p. A1.

18. *Further Report of the Secretary-General Submitted in Pursuance of Para. 19, Res. 814 (1993) and Para. 5, Res. 865 (1993), S/26738* (November 12, 1993).

Bosnia

The opposite problem to UNOSOM's aggressiveness emerged in the UN Protection Force (UNPROFOR) operation in the former Yugoslavia. There, the UN was not doing what it has been criticized for doing in Somalia, although there, too, its presence has in all likelihood saved tens of thousands of lives. In the former Yugoslavia, the UN was committed to protecting the humanitarian convoys and the safe areas as well as maintaining an arms embargo over the entire area and an economic embargo against Serbia. Yet the failure to provide protection to the Bosnian Muslims (but also Croats and Serbs), to the relief convoys, and even to the peacekeepers themselves left the UN force in a most equivocal position. In Bosnia alone, after the establishment of UNPROFOR, over 140,000 Muslims and 90,000 Serbs and 20,000 Croats died; more than 1 million Muslims and 250,000 Serbs had to flee their homes, according to the estimates of Thorvald Stoltenberg, the former UN mediator.

The protection dilemma was real, however, with more than half the population in the UN-designated safe areas directly dependent on UN convoys for food and medicine. Military action against the predominantly Serb aggressors would be met by a complete cutoff of humanitarian assistance by those same Serbian forces, which then controlled the access routes.[19]

Prior to 1995, none of UNPROFOR's military forces were prepared to undertake a massive military campaign designed to defeat the Bosnian Serb forces. The United States limited its contribution to air forces. Its once preferred strategy—"lift [the 1991 UN arms embargo] and strike [against Serb gunners]"—was designed to level the playing field between Serb forces and the poorly equipped Muslim forces. The United States, however, was never prepared to invest its own soldiers on the ground in a peace enforcement operation or even to ship heavy weapons to Bosnia (presumably by airlift over the Croat and Serb lines) and train the Muslims in their use.[20] Radical Muslim forces from Iran and the Palestine Liberation Organization (PLO) were ready to come to

---

19. Rosalyn Higgins, "The New United Nations and the Former Yugoslavia," *International Affairs* 69, no. 3 (1993), pp. 468–470; James B. Steinberg, "International Involvement in the Yugoslav Conflict," in Lori Fisler Damrosch, ed., *Enforcing Restraint* (New York: Council on Foreign Relations Press, 1993); and Sabrina Ramet, "War in the Balkans," *Foreign Affairs* 71, no. 4 (Fall 1992), pp. 79–98.

20. Michael Gordon, "Pentagon Is Wary of Role in Bosnia, " *New York Times,* March 13, 1994, p. A6.

Bosnia's aid, but they were rejected by Russia and would, it seemed to many observers, merely widen the fighting to Kosovo, Macedonia, and even beyond. The resulting strategy—"constrict [the level of violence] and contain"—was not without costs to its European proponents. By 1995, UNPROFOR, with large contingents of British, French, and Canadian troops, had sustained seventy fatalities. Still, the strategy had two great advantages: it was tolerated by the Russians, and the killing had been contained within Croatia and Bosnia.

Again, with the advantage of hindsight, we can see what appear to be mistakes, most of them occasioned by the Security Council's foisting mandates on the UN forces in the field without giving them the means to implement them. Resolutions were issued that bore upon the Bosnian Serbs; yet the international community had no direct way to exert pressure on them. What pressure there was came from the indirect effects of the misery that the international economic embargo inflicted on the Serbian public. In retrospect, we can see that the UN-protected areas in Croatia lacked adequate buffer zones and sufficient peacekeepers, providing the Serbs with excuses not to disarm and the Croats with the opportunity to engage in incursions. In Bosnia, the declared safe havens were never adequately provided with UN forces. They were too small, militarily vulnerable, and economically nonviable, and they lacked wide enough connecting corridors.[21]

The taproot of error was identified in Cyrus Vance's warnings in December 1991 not to recognize the independence of Croatia and Bosnia outside of the framework of an overall settlement of Yugoslavia. The only separable parts of Yugoslavia immediately recognizable as independent, sovereign nation-states were Slovenia and (arguably) Macedonia. For Serbs, the federal unity of Yugoslavia was what made "small" Serbia tolerable and the non-Serb governments of Croatia and Bosnia safe for their Serbs. For Croats, the inclusion of Bosnia in Yugoslavia was what made Bosnia safe for its Croats. For Bosnian Muslims, the inclusion of Croatia in Yugoslavia was what made the Bosnian republic safe in Yugoslavia; otherwise it would have been dominated by the Serbs. Croatia, some suggest, might have been partitioned between Croats and Serbs, but the ethnic mix was too intimate in Bosnia to allow a peaceable partition.

The failures in Somalia and Bosnia soon claimed victims elsewhere. Following the October 3 crisis in Somalia, U.S. senators clam-

---

21. The UN's candid report on the massacre at Srebrenica documents these and other assessments in considerable detail; see *Report of the Secretary-General Pursuant to GA Resolution 53/35* (1998).

ored for immediate withdrawal of all U.S. forces from UNOSOM. The Clinton administration barely succeeded in holding out for March 31, 1994. Emboldened by the prospective U.S. withdrawal from Somalia, associates of the police force terrorizing Haiti chased UN advisers from the harbor of Port-au-Prince, wrecking the Governor's Island peace plan and eventually forcing the administration to pursue the very risky decision (from the standpoint of U.S. domestic politics) to invade Haiti. Learning to say "no," the United States led the Security Council's rejection of the request to protect thousands of displaced persons in Burundi who were fleeing the coup that slaughtered the elected government and undercut the feeble efforts of some member states to engage the UN in halting the genocide in Rwanda (May 1994).

Generations of UN Peace Operations

Old precepts, painfully learned, from the early days of UN peacekeeping seemed newly relevant. The emergence of a working consensus in the Security Council in favor of a more interventionist international order, however impartial those actions may now be, did not remove the other reasons to be wary of intervention.

In order to explore those reasons in a UN context, it is helpful to think in terms of three categories of peace support operations. In traditional peacekeeping, sometimes called first-generation peacekeeping, unarmed or lightly armed UN forces were stationed between hostile parties to monitor a truce, troop withdrawal, or buffer zone while political negotiations went forward.[22] They provided transparency (an impartial assurance that the other party was not violating the truce). They also raised the costs of defecting from, and the benefits of abiding by, the agreement because of the threat of exposure, the potential resistance of the peacekeeping force, and the legitimacy of UN mandates.[23]

---

22. Traditional peacekeeping is a shorthand term that describes many, but by no means all, Cold War peacekeeping missions—the most notable exception being the Congo operation of 1960–1964. For cogent analysis of different types of peacekeeping, see Marrack Goulding, "The Evolution of United Nations Peacekeeping," *International Affairs* 69, no. 3 (July 1993); and John Mackinlay and Jarat Chopra, *A Draft Concept of Second Generation Multinational Operations* (Providence, R.I.: Watson Institute, 1993).

23. In game-theoretic terms, they solved variable sum "coordination" problems, where both parties have the same best outcome and will reach it if they can trust each other, and prisoner's dilemma problems, where the parties have an incentive to cheat. The peacekeepers provide the missing transparency in the first and alter the payoffs in the second, making the prisoner's dilemma into a coordination game. First-generation operations include both sorts of games.

The second category, called second-generation operations by Secretary-General Boutros-Ghali, involves the implementation of complex, multidimensional peace agreements. In addition to the traditional military functions, the peacekeepers are often engaged in various police and civilian tasks, the goal of which is a long-term settlement of the underlying conflict. I will return to this category later.

Peace-enforcing missions are the third category. They extend from low-level military operations to protect the delivery of humanitarian assistance to the enforcement of cease-fires and, when necessary, assistance in the rebuilding of so-called failed states. Like Chapter VII UN enforcement action to roll back aggression, as in Korea in 1950 and against Iraq in the Gulf War, the defining characteristic of third-generation operations is the lack of consent to some or all of the UN mandate.[24]

With all of Minerva's usual sense of timing, insightful doctrine for these peace-enforcing operations appeared just as Somalia and Bosnia exposed their limitations. Recent studies have thoughtfully mapped out the logic of the strategic terrain between traditional UN peacekeeping and traditional UN enforcement action.[25] Militarily, these operations seek to *deter, dissuade, and deny*.[26] By precluding an outcome based on the use of force by the parties, the UN instead uses collective force (if necessary) to persuade the parties to settle the conflict by negotiation.

---

24. Other recent categories include "preventive deployments" with the intention of deterring a possible attack, as in Macedonia today. There, the credibility of the deterring force must ensure that the potential aggressor knows that there will be no easy victory. In the event of an armed challenge, the result will be an international war that involves costs so grave as to outweigh the temptations of conquest. Enforcement action against aggression (Korea or the Gulf), conversely, is a matter of achieving victory—"the decisive, comprehensive and synchronized application of preponderant military force to shock, disrupt, demoralize and defeat opponents"—the traditional zero-sum terrain of military strategy. See John Ruggie, "The United Nations: Stuck in a Fog Between Peacekeeping and Enforcement," in *Peacekeeping: The Way Ahead?* McNair Paper 25, Institute for National Strategic Studies (Washington, D.C.: National Defense University, 1993). Ruggie draws on "A Doctrinal Statement of Selected Joint Operational Concepts," Office of the JCS, DOD, Washington, D.C. (November 23, 1992).

25. Categories of action are insightfully described in Mackinlay and Chopra, *A Draft Concept of Second Generation Multinational Operations.* Also see John Mackinlay's update, "Problems for U.S. Forces in Operations Beyond Peacekeeping," in *Peacekeeping: The Way Ahead?* McNair Paper 25, Institute for National Strategic Studies (Washington, D.C.: National Defense University, 1993), pp. 29–50.

26. See Ruggie, "The United Nations: Stuck in a Fog Between Peacekeeping and Enforcement."

In the former Yugoslavia, for example, the UN, following this strategy, could have established strong points to deter attacks on key humanitarian corridors. (It did, but the Serbs bypassed them.) Or it could threaten air strikes, as was done successfully around Sarajevo in February 1994, to dissuade a continuation of the Serb shelling of the city. Or it could have denied (but did not) the Serb forces their attack on Dubrovnik in 1992 by countershelling from the sea or air on the batteries in the hills above the city.

This terrain is murky. Forcing a peace depends on achieving a complicated preponderance in which the forces (UN and local) supporting a settlement acceptable to the international community hold both a military predominance and a predominance of popular support, which together permit them to impose a peace on the recalcitrant local military forces and their popular supporters. This strategy, however, was likely to and did encounter many of the problems interventionist and imperial strategies have faced in the past and also revealed fresh problems peculiar to the UN's global character.

First, although the UN seems to have the advantage of global impartiality, which should and often does win it more local acceptance when it intervenes, this is not universally the case. Israel maintains a suspicion of UN involvement dating back to the UN General Assembly's notorious anti-Zionism resolutions of the 1970s. In Somalia, Egypt's support for Siad Barre seems to have tainted the role Boutros-Ghali, former Egyptian foreign minister, sought to play as impartial Secretary-General. And there is lingering distrust of the UN in other parts of Africa due to its role in the Congo.[27]

Second, the very act of intervention, even by the UN, can mobilize nationalist opposition against the foreign forces. In Somalia, it contributed to a significant growth of support for Aidid's Somali National Alliance. Aidid's supporters now roundly condemn UN colonialism.[28] The strategic balance is not static: military intervention tilts both local balances, improving the military correlation of forces but often at the cost of undermining the more important political balance.

Third, the UN is particularly poorly suited to interventionist strate-

27. Recently, this distrust has given way to a sense of urgency about Africa's conflicts, in which UN involvement is seen to be necessary. See *The OAU and Conflict Management in Africa*, report of a joint Organization of African Unity–International Peace Academy consultation, Addis Ababa, May 1993 (New York: International Peace Academy, n.d.).

28. Abdi Hassan Awale, an Aidid adviser in Mogadishu, complained, "The UN wants to rule this country. They do not want a Somali government to be established. The UN wants to stay and colonize us." *New York Times,* March 2, 1994.

gies. Its traditional ideology (despite recent practice) is highly protective of national sovereignty, and (to its credit) it lacks the callousness or psychological distance required to inflict coercive punishment on political movements having even the least degree of popular support.[29] The UN Security Council, moreover, tends to solve international crises rhetorically, by issuing a resounding resolution without providing the means to implement the announced policy. In Bosnia, for example, General François Briquemont, the former Belgian commander of UNPROFOR, denounced "the fantastic gap between the resolutions of the Security Council, the will to execute those resolutions, and the means available to commanders in the field."[30]

Fourth, "peace-enforcing fatigue" is afflicting the UN's contributing countries, whether new or old. States are rarely willing to invest their resources or the lives of their soldiers in war other than for a vital interest (such as oil in the Gulf). In 1999 alone, three UN operations—those in Macedonia, Iraq, and Angola—were closed far from having completed their missions. Yet if states have a vital national interest in a dispute, they are not likely to exercise the impartiality a UN peace operation requires. Nor are they likely to cede decisionmaking control over, or command of, their forces to the UN.

Fifth, coercive intervention for eventual self-determination, as J. S. Mill noted over a century ago, is very often a self-contradictory enterprise.[31] If the local forces of freedom, self-determination, and human rights cannot achieve sovereignty without a foreign military intervention, they are very unlikely to be able to hold on to power after the interventionary force leaves. Either the installed forces of freedom will collapse, or they themselves will employ those very coercive methods that provoked and justified the initial intervention. The Kurds, for example, won widespread sympathy for their resistance to Saddam Hussein and benefited from a UN-endorsed U.S.-French-British intervention in the aftermath of the war against Iraq. But the Kurdish factions soon became so divided that they appeared incapable of establishing law and order in their territory. Instead, three factions divided the region. None yet appears capable of sustaining itself against whatever

---

29. An added problem is that the use of force in civil wars frequently causes casualties among civilians, opening the UN and its members to accusations of neo-colonialism and brutality. Adam Roberts, "The United Nations and International Security," *Survival* 35, no. 2 (Summer 1993).

30. "26 Are Killed in Sarajevo in First 4 Days of Year," *Baltimore Sun*, January 5, 1994, p. 4A (from Reuters, AP).

31. J. S. Mill, "A Few Words on Nonintervention." (1859), in Gertrude Himmelfarb, ed., *Essays on Politics and Culture* (Gloucester: P. Smith, 1973).

attempts Saddam Hussein may make to reincorporate Kurdistan. The international community has thus placed itself in the awkward position of either adopting Kurdistan as a long-term ward or returning it to Saddam Hussein.[32]

Sixth, despite all these limiting constraints, "the need for timely intervention," according to Secretary-General Kofi Annan, has grown, not disappeared. Discovering forms of intervention that avoid the enforcement crises in Somalia and Bosnia, the neglect that met Rwanda's genocide, or the contention that characterized the Kosovo intervention remains a key challenge for the UN community.

An Internationalist Alternative

The existing problems of "enforcement minus," manifested so signally by the UN in Bosnia and Somalia, suggest a search for alternatives that reduce the impact of the constraints previously noted. One alternative is simply fortitude. Both UNPROFOR and UNOSOM, as noted, saved tens of thousands of lives. Carrying such operations forward may be all that can be done, if the UN can find the nations willing to stick it out. Another alternative, centered about the new attention to the possibilities of regional peacekeeping, a strategy recommended in Secretary-General Boutros-Ghali's *Agenda for Peace*, appears designed to elicit a more locally sensitive approach to political disputes. Yet the lack of institutional, military, and financial capacity of the regional organizations (with the exception, perhaps, of NATO) remains a considerable hurdle. For another alternative, Sir Brian Urquhart has issued an eloquent manifesto in favor of a UN army. Small and centrally controlled, it would be suited for the rapid interventions that can sometimes preempt an escalating crisis, such as occurred in Somalia in early 1992 or Rwanda in spring 1994.[33] Delegation to national action, a fourth remedy, is becoming so increasingly prevalent that it is being designated fourth-generation peacekeeping. Stimulated by the temporary success of UNITAF and by the delegations to Russia in Georgia, to France in Rwanda, to the United States in Haiti, and to the Australian intervention force in East Timor, the UN is surmounting contributor fatigue by assigning mandates to the national states willing to accept and perhaps

32. Chris Hedges, "Quarrels of Kurdish Leaders Sour Dreams of a Homeland," *New York Times,* June 18, 1994, p. A1.

33. Sir Brian Urquhart, "For a UN Volunteer Military Force," *New York Review of Books,* June 10, 1993; see also "Four Views," *New York Review of Books,* June 24, 1993.

enforce them. This may indeed be the best compromise available in difficult circumstances, but in itself, it does little to address the longer-run problems of leaving behind a stable form of locally legitimate government; and it may raise difficult issues of control. Can the Security Council be confident that the mandate it assigns will be implemented in ways that fulfill UN principles and serve the interests of the UN as a whole?

The residual problems raised by each of these alternatives suggest the value of innovating within UN traditions, the development of a superior form of "consent plus" that recognizes the continuing political significance of national sovereignty. The UN should seek out a consensual basis for a restoration of law and order in domestic crises and try to implement its global human rights and self-determination agenda in a way that produces less friction and more support.

Taking a substantial step beyond first-generation operations, in which the UN monitors a truce, and keeping a significant step short of the third-generation peace-enforcing operations, in which the UN uses force to impose a peace, second-generation operations are based on consent of the parties. Yet the nature of that consent and the purposes for which it is granted are qualitatively different from traditional peacekeeping. In these operations, the UN is typically involved in implementing peace agreements that go to the roots of the conflict, helping to build a long-term foundation for stable, legitimate government. As former Secretary-General Boutros-Ghali observed in *An Agenda for Peace*,

> Peace-making and peace-keeping operations, to be truly successful, must come to include comprehensive efforts to identify and support structures which will tend to consolidate peace. . . . These may include disarming the previously warring parties and the restoration of order, the custody and possible destruction of weapons, repatriating refugees, advisory and training support for security personnel, monitoring elections, advancing efforts to protect human rights, reforming or strengthening governmental institutions and promoting formal and informal processes of political participation.[34]

The UN Transitional Authority in Cambodia (UNTAC), for example, was based on the consent of the parties, as expressed in the Paris Agreements, but it moved beyond monitoring the actions of the parties to the establishment of a transitional authority that actually implemented directly crucial components of the mandate. Moreover, its scale was

---

34. Boutros Boutros-Ghali, *Agenda for Peace* (New York: UN, 1992), pp. 32–33.

vastly larger than all but the enforcement mandates, and for a variety of reasons it found itself operating without the continuous (in the case of the Khmer Rouge) or complete (in the case of the other factions) cooperation of the factions.

The UN has a commendable record of success in second-generation, multidimensional peacekeeping operations as diverse as those in Namibia (UN Transition Assistance Group, or UNTAG), El Salvador (UN Observer Mission in El Salvador, or ONUSAL), and Cambodia (UNTAC).[35] The UN's role in helping settle those conflicts has been threefold. It served as a *peacemaker*, facilitating a peace treaty among the parties; as a *peacekeeper*, monitoring the cantonment and demobilization of military forces, resettling refugees, and supervising transitional civilian authorities; and as a *peacebuilder*, monitoring and in some cases organizing the implementation of human rights, national democratic elections, and economic rehabilitation.

Though nonenforcing and consent-based, these operations are far from harmonious. Consent is not a simple bright line demarcating the safe and acceptable from the dangerous and illegitimate. Each function will require an enhanced form of consent if the UN is to help make a peace in the contentious environment of civil strife. We need, therefore, to focus on new ways to design peace operations if the UN, in the face of likely resistance, is to avoid having to choose between either force or withdrawal.

Strategies of Enhanced Consent

Peacemaking

Achieving a peace treaty itself often requires heavy persuasion by outside actors. In Cambodia, the USSR and China are said to have informed their respective clients in Phnom Penh and the Khmer Rouge that ongoing levels of financial and military support would not be forthcoming if they resisted the terms of a peace treaty that their patrons found accept-

---

35. Before the UN became involved, during the Cold War when action by the Security Council was stymied by the lack of consensus among the P-5, the international community allowed Cambodia to suffer an autogenocide and El Salvador a brutal civil war without concerted multilateral assistance. Indeed, the great powers were involved in supporting factions that inflicted some of the worst aspects of the violence the two countries suffered. We should keep this in mind when we consider the UN's difficulties in Somalia, Bosnia, and Kosovo.

able. Peace treaties may themselves depend on prior sanctions, threats of sanctions, or loss of aid imposed by the international community.[36]

The construction of a comprehensive agreed-upon peace, however, is more than worth the effort. Going beyond the negotiation of a simple cease-fire, the very process of negotiation among the contending factions can discover the acceptable parameters of an implementable and stable peace that are particular to the conflict. An agreed-upon peace treaty, moreover, can mobilize the support of the factions and of the international community in favor of implementing the peace, as it can establish new institutions designed to further peacekeeping and peace-building.

The UN has developed a set of crucially important innovations that help manage the building of peace on a consensual basis. First among them is the diplomatic device that has come to be called the Friends of the Secretary-General. This group brings together multinational leverage for UN diplomacy to help make and manage peace. Composed of ad hoc, informal, multilateral diplomatic mechanisms that unify states in support of initiatives of the Secretary-General, it legitimates, with the stamp of UN approval and supervision, the pressures interested states can bring to bear to further the purposes of peace and the UN.

The Core Group in New York and the Extended P-5 in Phnom Penh together played a "friends" role in the negotiation and the management of the peace process. Composed of the Security Council P-5 and extended to include Australia, Indonesia, Japan, and other concerned states, the two groups took the lead in the construction of the Paris Agreements. They provided key support to UNTAC, both political and financial, and helped organize ICORC (International Committee on the Reconstruction of Cambodia) aid (almost $1 billion) while providing special funds for various projects. Yet the Extended P-5 lacked a fixed composition. It, of course, included the P-5 but then included or excluded others on an ad hoc basis depending on the issue and topic covered and the message the group wished to send. For example, Thailand was excluded from certain meetings in order to send a signal of concern

---

36. The Governor's Island Accord, which produced the first (ineffective) settlement of the Haitian conflict, resulted from economic sanctions on arms and oil imposed by the UN and the Organization of American States on Haiti as a whole. Sanctions targeted on the perpetrators (the military elite and their supporters) might have been much more effective had they been imposed before summer 1994. Restrictions on the overseas private bank accounts and air travel of the ruling elite would have been both more just and perhaps more effective than general economic sanctions, whose impact was most severe on the most vulnerable and from which the elite may actually have benefited.

about its lack of support for the restrictions imposed on the Khmer Rouge. In Cambodia, moreover, there was not a sovereign government to monitor or support. Much of the Extended P-5's diplomacy was therefore directed at UNTAC itself, protecting, for example, the interests of national battalions. It also served as a back channel for Special Representative Akashi to communicate directly to the Security Council.[37]

In El Salvador, the four friends of the Secretary-General were Venezuela, Mexico, Spain, and Colombia. Frequently joined by a "fifth friend"—the United States—they together played a crucial role in negotiating and implementing the peace accords.[38] So, too, did the Core Group in Mozambique. Hopes also centered on the Contact Group, including Russia, the United States, France, Germany, Italy, and the United Kingdom for the former Yugoslavia and another group of friends for Haiti, consisting of Canada, France, the United States, and Venezuela. Informal diplomatic support groups have also been active in Namibia, Nicaragua, Georgia, Afghanistan, and Guatemala.

In Croatia, the Z-4 (four Zagreb-based mediators—Russia, the United States, the EU, and the UN) began a similar role in crafting an acceptable peace. Following the Croatian offensives of 1995, two mediators, U.S. ambassador Peter Galbraith and UN mediator Thorvald Stoltenberg, took over to shape the final terms presented to both Croatia and the Serb leadership of Eastern Slavonia. The result was the Erdut Agreement, which established the principles underlying the mandate to reintegrate peacefully the former Sector East with its then overwhelmingly Serb population into Croatia.

Playing a crucial role in the Secretary-General's peacemaking and preventive diplomacy functions, these groupings serve four key functions. First, the limited influence of the Secretary-General can be leveraged, multiplied, and complemented by the "friends." The UN's scarce attention, and even scarcer resources, can be supplemented by the diplomacy and the clout of powerful, interested actors. The second value is legitimization. The very act of interested states constituting themselves as a group, with the formal support of the Secretary-General, lends legitimacy to their diplomatic activities that they might not otherwise have. The strategy also allows for constructive diplomacy

---

37. Yasushi Akashi, "UNTAC in Cambodia: Lessons for UN Peace-keeping," the Charles Rostow Annual Lecture (Washington, D.C.: SAIS, October 1993), and Doyle interviews in Phnom Penh, March 1993, and New York, November 1993.

38. Ian Johnstone and Mark LeVine, "Lessons from El Salvador," *Christian Science Monitor,* August 10, 1993; and for UNTAES see Peter Galbraith, "Washington, Erdut and Dayton," *Cornell International Law Journal* 30 (1997), pp. 643–649.

when accusations of special and particular national interest could taint bilateral efforts. In order to address this concern, it is crucial that the UN itself, through the constant participation of a special representative of the Secretary-General, be part of the peacemaking process. Otherwise, the "friends" may exploit the UN label for partisan (even if multinational) purposes. The third value is coordination. The friends mechanism provides transparency among the interested external parties, assuring them that they are all working for the same purposes and, when they are doing so, allowing them to pursue a division of labor that enhances their joint effort. It ensures that diplomats are not working at cross-purposes because they regularly meet and inform each other of their activities and encourage each other to undertake special tasks. And fourth, the friends mechanism provides a politically balanced approach to the resolution through negotiation of civil wars. It often turns out that one particular friend can associate with one faction, just as another associates with a second. In the Cambodian peace process, China back-stopped the Khmer Rouge, just as France did Prince Sihanouk and Vietnam together with Russia did the State of Cambodia. The friends open more flexible channels of communication than a single UN media-tor can provide. They also advise and guide the UN intermediaries, although the process tends to work best when they support, rather than move out in front of, the UN.

Multidimensional Peacekeeping

Even consent-based peace agreements fall apart. In the circumstances faced by failed states or in cases of partisan violence, agreements tend to be fluid. In the new civil conflicts, parties cannot force policy on their followers and often lack the capacity or will to maintain a difficult process of reconciliation leading to a reestablishment of national sover-eignty.[39]

Peace treaties and their peacekeeping mandates thus tend to be affected by two sets of contradictory tensions. First, in order to get an agreement, diplomats assume all parties are in good faith; they cannot question the intentions of their diplomatic partners. Yet to implement a peacekeeping and peacebuilding operation, planners must assume the

---

39. These issues are effectively explored in Mackinlay and Chopra, "Second Generation Multinational Operations"; Adam Roberts, "The United Nations and International Security," *Survival* 35, no. 2 (Summer 1993); William Durch, ed., *The Evolution of UN Peacekeeping* (New York: St. Martin's Press, 1993); Mats Berdal, *Whither UN Peacekeeping?* Adelphi Paper 281 (London: International Institute for Strategic Studies [IISS], 1993); and Thomas Weiss, "New Challenges for UN Military Operations," *Washington Quarterly* 16, no. 1 (Winter 1993).

opposite—that the parties will not or cannot fulfill the agreement made. Moreover, diplomats who design the peace treaty tend to think in legal (authority, precedent) rather than strategic (power, incentives) terms. Treaties thus describe obligations; they tend to be unclear about incentives and capacities.

All these factors militate against clear and implementable mandates. Diplomats seek to incorporate into the treaty the most complete peace to which the parties will agree. UN officials seek to clarify the UN's obligations. Knowing that much of what was agreed to in the peace treaty will not be implementable in the field, the officials who write the Secretary-General's report (which outlines the implementation of the agreement) contract or expand the mandate of the peace operation.[40] Confused mandates are an inevitable result of this tension.

A second tension also shapes the peacekeeping mandate. The mandate, like a natural resource contract, is an obsolescing bargain. When a country begins a negotiation with an oil company for the exploration of its territory, the company holds all the advantages. The costs of exploration are large, whereas the possibility of oil is uncertain. The country must therefore cede generous terms. As soon as oil is discovered, the bargain shifts, as discovered oil is easy to pump and any oil company can do it. The old bargain has suddenly obsolesced.[41] So, too, with a UN peacekeeping operation. The spirit of agreement is never more exalted than at the moment of the signing of the peace treaty; the authority of the UN is never again greater. Then the parties assume that the agreement will be achieved and that all are cooperating in good faith. They depend on the UN to achieve their various hopes. The UN as yet has no investment in resources or political prestige—it holds all the cards. Yet as soon as the UN begins its investment of money, personnel, and prestige, the bargaining relationship alters its balance. The larger the UN investment—these multidimensional operations represent multi-billion-dollar expenditures—the greater the independent UN interest in success and the greater the influence of the parties becomes. Since the parties control an essential element in the success of the mandate, their bargaining power rapidly rises. So, in late spring 1993 as the crucial Cambodian elections approached, UNTAC chief Akashi acknowledged, "I cannot afford not to succeed."[42]

---

40. I first heard a variation on this point from Edward Luck.
41. See Raymond Vernon, "Long-Run Trends in Concession Contracts," in *Proceedings of the Sixty-first Annual Meeting of the American Society of International Law* (Washington, D.C.: ASIL, 1967).
42. Yasushi Akashi, interview in "Peace in the Killing Fields," part 3 of *The Thin Blue Line*, BBC Radio 4, released May 9, 1993.

This dual tension in designing peacekeeping operations emphasizes that time is critical. The UN should be ready to implement the mandate as soon after the peace treaty is signed as is practical. UNTAC suffered a large decrease in authority in early 1992 as time passed and expectations of the factions and the Cambodian people were disappointed.

These tensions also explain how the ideal framework (both legal and political) of a treaty can dissolve in days or months, as the Cambodian peace agreements did, and how the provisions of peace accords become so general, ambiguous, or unworkable that many of the details have to be worked out in the implementation process. To be minimally effective under those circumstances, the UN must innovate. One clear implication is the importance of risk-spreading multidimensionality. The UN should design in as many routes to peace—institutional reform, elections, international monitoring, economic rehabilitation—as the parties will tolerate.

The UN also needs a flexible political strategy to win and keep popular support and create (not just enjoy) the support of local forces of order. In a failed state, as is the case in former colonial societies, what is most often missing is modern organization. This the colonial metropoles supplied, in their own self-interest, as they mobilized local resources to combat local opposition. Over the longer run, "native" forces (the Zamindars, the King's Own African Rifles, and other local battalions), not metropolitan troops, were the forces that made imperial rule effective, preserved a balance of local power in favor of metropolitan influence, and kept it cheap. Learning from the history of imperial institution building (while avoiding imperial exploitation and coercion) can contribute to an effective and affordable strategy for UN peace operations, but the UN faces a greater challenge. It needs to discover ways to generate *voluntary* cooperation from divided local political actors and mobilize existing local resources for *locally legitimate*, collective purposes.[43] And it must do so *rapidly*.

---

43. It is interesting, in this light, that some key, early UN experts in peacekeeping were eminent decolonization experts deeply familiar with the politics of colonial rule, as was Ralph Bunche from the UN Trusteeship Division. See Brian Urquhart, *Ralph Bunche: An American Life* (New York: W. W. Norton, 1993), chap. 5. For a discussion of imperial strategy, see Michael Doyle, *Empires* (Ithaca, N.Y.: Cornell University Press, 1986), chap. 12. Yet there are key differences between the objectives of colonial rule and those of UN operations. Empires were governed primarily in the interests of the metropole; UN peace operations explicitly promote the interests of the host country. And what made imperial strategy work was the possibility of coercive violence, the over-the-horizon gunboats that could be, and often were, offshore. That, for good and bad, is what the UN usually lacks unless it calls in the enforcement capacity of the major powers. Rehabilitation assistance is sometimes an effective carrot but not the equivalent of the Royal Navy.

Recent peacekeeping experience has suggested a second peace-keeping innovation: an ad hoc, semisovereign mechanism designed to manage the peace process and mobilize local cooperation. It has often been remarked that Chapter VI presents the UN with too little authority and Chapter VII offers too much and that Chapter VI is associated with too little use of force and Chapter VII with too much.

The value of these ad hoc, semisovereign artificial bodies is that they provide a potentially powerful, political means of encouraging and influencing the shape of consent. Indeed, these semisovereign artificial bodies can help contain the erosion of consent and even manufacture it where it is missing. Created by a peace treaty, they permit the temporary consensus of the parties to be formally incorporated in an institution with regular consultation and even, as in the Cambodian Supreme National Council, a semiautonomous sovereign will. These mechanisms have proved crucial in a number of recent UN missions. They can represent the once-warring parties and act in the name of a preponderance of the "nation" without the continuous or complete consent of all the factions. They can both build political support and adjust the mandate in a legitimate way, with the consent of the parties, in order to respond to unanticipated changes in local circumstances.

In Cambodia, the Supreme National Council (SNC), constructed by the Paris Peace Agreements, enshrined Cambodian sovereignty. The council, composed of the four factions and chaired by Prince Sihanouk, offered a chance for these parties to consult on a regular basis and endorse the peace process. It also lent special authority to Prince Sihanouk, who was authorized to act if the SNC failed to achieve consensus. Beyond that, it empowered the UN, represented by Special Representative Yasushi Akashi, to act in the interests of the peace process if Sihanouk failed to do so. The artificially created SNC thus established a semisovereign legal personality designed to be responsive to the general interests of Cambodia (even when a complete consensus was lacking among all the factions) and to the authority of the UN Special Representative. Acting in the name of Cambodia—as a step in the implementation of the Paris Agreements—the SNC adopted all the major human rights conventions (including the First and Second Covenants on Human Rights) and authorized the trade embargo against illegal exports of logs and gems. It was the forum that endorsed the protracted and sensitive negotiations over the franchise. It legitimated the enforcement of certain elements of the peace, absent the unanimous consent of the parties and without the necessity of a contentious debate at the Security Council. It could have exercised greater authority, perhaps even designing an acceptable scheme for rehabilitation, if Prince Sihanouk or Akashi had been both willing and able to lead it in that direction.

The Commission on the Peace (COPAZ) in El Salvador played a

related, although much less authoritative, role in the Salvadoran peace process, serving as a forum for consultation among the Frente Farabundo Martí para la Liberacion Nacional (FMLN), the government, and the other political parties. Designed to monitor and establish a forum for the participation of civilian society in the peace process, it was the only political institution that embodied the full scope of Salvadoran politics, the only institution that could legitimately speak for El Salvador. Its minimal role in the peace process was unfortunate. And in Somalia, the Transitional National Council was designed to perform a similar function, but its failure to get off the ground was perhaps the single most disturbing problem in the peacemaking process, one that seriously eroded the attempt to create a peace.

In Eastern Slavonia, UNTAES held an extraordinary mandate to exercise interim "executive authority" independent of the sovereignty of Croatia. With the dynamic leadership of Jacques Klein and the substantial backing of the United States (as well as the support of both Presidents Franjo Tudjman of Croatia and Slobodan Milosevic of Yugoslavia behind the scenes), UNTAES was able to establish control of the region. The mandate was to reintegrate the region peacefully into Croatia by securing a return of refugees and displaced persons, establishing a transitional police force, restoring the normal functioning of public services, monitoring the border, monitoring human rights, and supervising an election.

The UN did what the peace agreement authorized it to do: it governed, practically becoming the colonial administrator or benevolent dictator. The UN oversaw the demilitarization of the region, chased the Serb paramilitaries out of the Djeletovici oil fields, persuaded Croatia to pay the salaries of the local civil administration and public enterprises (from the oil field revenues), and established the multiethnic Transitional Police Force with at first a Serb and then a Croatian commander. UNTAES had to use its executive authority when local Serb or Croatian consent was slow or absent. The result was that by the middle of 1997, the Serbs were registering as Croatian citizens and beginning to acquire a feeling that they had a stake in the Croatian political system. All this was achieved through a combination of means: the backstage support of both Yugoslav president Milosevic and Croatian president Tudjman; the leadership of the forceful U.S. general Jacques Klein; and a substantial presence of armed force including 5,000 soldiers, a tank unit, attack helicopters, and NATO airpower on call.

One key lesson to be learned in the design of these semisovereign, artificial bodies is that one should try (to the extent that one's freedom of negotiation allows) to preview the peace that the parties and the international community seek. For the Paris Peace Agreements for Cambodia, seeking a pluralist democracy should have meant expanding the Supreme National Council to also include other bodies, such as one for civil society. It might have included, for example, Buddhist monks, nongovernmental organizations, and other representatives of society outside the state. These supplementary bodies, it should be noted, need not perform executive or legislative functions. The important point is that civil society participate in the decisionmaking process, at a minimum through formally recognized consultative channels.

The UN must avoid the trade-offs between too much force and too little. The dangers of Chapter VII enforcement operations, whether in Somalia or Bosnia, leave many observers to think that it is extremely unlikely that troop-contributing countries will actually show up for such operations. The risks are much more costly than the member states are willing to bear for humanitarian purposes. Yet when we look at Chapter VI operations, we see that consent by parties easily dissolves under difficult processes of peace. UN operations in the midst of civil strife have often been rescued by the timely use of force, as were the operations in the Congo, when Katanga's secession was forcibly halted, and in Namibia, when SWAPO's (South West African People's Organization) violation of the peace agreement was countered with the aid of South African forces; but both resulted in grave political costs. The UNTAES seizure of oil fields was essential to the successes achieved by the mission. Given those options, the semisovereign artificial bodies offer the possibility of midcourse adjustments and legitimated enforcement. They artificially but usefully enhance the process of consent in the direction of the promotion of peace while avoiding the dangers associated with attempts to implement a forced peace.

Peacebuilding

Multidimensional, second-generation peacekeeping pierces the shell of national autonomy by bringing international involvement to areas long thought to be the exclusive domain of domestic jurisdiction. If a peacekeeping operation is to leave behind a legitimate and independently viable political sovereign, it must help transform the political landscape by building a new basis for domestic peace.

Traditional strategies of conflict resolution, when successful, were designed to resolve a dispute between conflicting parties. Successful resolution could be measured by (1) the stated reconciliation of the parties, (2) the duration of the reconciliation, and (3) changes in the way parties behaved toward each other.[44] Successful contemporary peace-

___

44. For a good account of traditional views of reconciliation, see A. B. Fetherston, "Putting the Peace Back into Peacekeeping," *International Peacekeeping* 1, no. 2 (Spring 1994), p. 11, which discusses a paper by Marc Ross.

building, however, does not merely change behavior but, more important, transforms identities and institutional context.

This is the grand strategy General John Sanderson invoked when he
spoke of forging an alliance with the Cambodian people, bypassing the
factions. Reginald Austin, Electoral Chief of UNTAC, probed the same
issue when he asked about the "true objectives" of UNTAC: "Is it a
political operation seeking a solution to the immediate problem of an
armed conflict by all means possible? Or does it have a wider objective:
to implant democracy, change values and establish a new pattern of
governance based on multi-partisan and free and fair elections?"[45]

UNTAC helped create new actors on the Cambodian political
scene: the electors, a fledgling civil society, a free press, and a continuing international and transnational presence. The Cambodian voters
gave Prince Norodom Ranariddh institutional power, and the Khmer
Rouge was transformed from an internationally recognized claimant on
Cambodian sovereignty to a domestic guerrilla insurgency. The peacebuilding process, particularly the election, became the politically tolerable substitute for the inability of the factions to reconcile their conflicts.

The UN's role in these cases, mandated by these complex agreements rather than by Chapter VII, includes monitoring, substituting for,
renovating, and in some cases helping to build the basic structures of
the state. The UN is called in to demobilize and sometimes to restructure and reform once-warring armies; to monitor or to organize national
elections; to promote human rights; to supervise public security and
help create a new civilian police force; to control civil administration in
order to establish a transitional, politically neutral environment; to
begin the economic rehabilitation of devastated countries; and, as in the
case of Cambodia, to address directly the values of the citizens with a
view to promoting democratic education.

The parties to these agreements, in effect, consent to a limitation of
their sovereignty for the life of the UN-sponsored peace process. They
do so because they need the help of the international community to
achieve peace. But acceptance of UN involvement in implementing
these agreements is less straightforward than, for example, consenting
to observance of a cease-fire. Even when genuine consent is achieved, it
is impossible to provide for every contingency in complex peace
accords. Problems of interpretation arise, unforeseen gaps in the
accords materialize, and circumstances change. The original consent, as
the Salvadoran peace process suggests, can become open-ended and, in
part, a gesture of faith that later problems can be worked out on a consensual basis. In the process, the international community, represented

---

45. Reginald Austin, UNTAC, 1993.

by the UN, exercised a monitoring pressure to encourage progress on the reform of the judiciary, the expansion of the electoral rolls, and the operation of a free press.

Yet authentic and firm consent, in the aftermath of severe civil strife such as that Cambodia endured, is rare. The international negotiators of a peace treaty and the UN designers of a mandate should therefore attempt to design in as many bargaining advantages for the UN authority as the parties will tolerate. Even seemingly extraneous bargaining chips will become useful as the spirit of cooperation erodes under the pressure of misunderstandings and separating interests.[46]

The architects of the UN operation should therefore also design into the mandate as much independent implementation as the parties will agree to in the peace treaty. In Cambodia, the electoral component and refugee repatriation seem to have succeeded simply because they did not depend on the steady and continuous positive support of the four factions. Each had an independent sphere of authority and organizational capacity that allowed it to proceed against everything short of the active military opposition of the factions. Civil administrative control and the cantonment of the factions failed because they relied on the continuous direct and positive cooperation of each of the factions. Each of the factions, at one time or another, had reason to expect that the balance of advantages was tilting against itself and thus refused to cooperate. A significant source of the success of the election was Radio UNTAC's ability to speak directly to the potential Cambodian voters, bypassing the propaganda of the four factions and invoking a new Cambodian actor, the voting citizen. Yet voters are powerful only for the five minutes it takes them to vote if there is not an institutional mechanism to transfer their democratic authority into bureaucratic practice.

In these circumstances, the UN should try to create new institutions in order to make sure votes in UN-sponsored elections count more. The UN needs to leave behind a larger institutional legacy, drawing, for

---

46. For example, the UN counted on the financial needs of the Cambodian factions to ensure their cooperation and designed an extensive rehabilitation component to guarantee steady rewards for cooperative behavior; however, the Khmer Rouge's access to illicit trade (with the apparent connivance of elements of the Thai military along the western border) eliminated this bargaining chip. This link was drawn explicitly by Deputy Secretary Lawrence Eagleburger at the Conference on the Reconstruction of Cambodia, June 22, 1992, Tokyo, where he proposed that assistance to Cambodia be "through the SNC—to areas controlled by those Cambodian parties cooperating with UNTAC in implementing the peace accords— and only to those parties which are so cooperating" (Press Release USUN-44-92, June 23, 1992). Disbursing the aid through the SNC, however, gave the Khmer Rouge a voice, as a member of the SNC, in the potential disbursement of the aid.

example, upon the existing personnel of domestic factions, adding to them a portion of authentic independents, and training a new army, a new civil service, a new police force, and a new judiciary. These are the institutions that can be decisive in ensuring that the voice of the people, as represented by their elected representatives, shapes the future.

Effective postconflict peacebuilding attempts to settle social conflicts by transformation, but peacebuilding should also be seen as the first step in preconflict preventive action. Conflicts in dynamic societies are natural. The key question is whether they are managed peacefully (as through electoral campaigns) or violently (as through civil wars). Ensuring that basic human rights and democratic or internal self-determination are achieved settles some of the causes of past conflict. It also establishes a powerful conflict-resolution mechanism—electoral politics. It was for just these reasons that the peace treaties for Cambodia and El Salvador incorporated commitments to the human rights covenants,[47] democratic elections, and judicial reform.

In Eastern Slavonia, with the very substantial authority UNTAES possessed, considerable progress was made in ensuring the rights of the Serb inhabitants. Numerous employment-guarantee contracts were signed, and agreements were negotiated sector by sector in an effort to ensure that the basic rights of the Serb inhabitants would be protected. But reconstruction and true reintegration were blocked. UNTAES lacked a substantial capacity to launch the economic reconstruction of the region (in part blocked by Croatia), and the return of displaced persons to their homes was stymied by a multilateral stalemate in both Bosnia and Croatia. Refugees were squatting in each other's homes, making the solution for one refugee contingent on accomplishing the return of all. At the end of the UNTAES mandate in January 1998, the longer-term viability of the Slavonian peace was left uncertain, dependent on Croatia and whatever indirect influence the international community could exert through OSCE (Organization for Security and Cooperation in Europe) monitors and the carrots and sticks of foreign aid.[48]

Individual rights and majority rule clearly do not, however, resolve all conflicts. Some involve issues, as in eastern Croatia, of communal

---

47. Both human rights covenants, civil-political and economic-social, were adhered to by the SNC during the Cambodian peace process, before the national election.

48. Information on UNTAES can be found in the Secretary-General's regular reports on UNTAES and in *The United Nations Transitional Administration in Eastern Slavonia and Western Sirmium (UNTAES), January 1996–January 1998: Lessons Learned, Report* (New York: UN, July 1998). I also benefited from extensive interviews in July 1997 and 1998 in the region and in Zagreb.

identity for which the very question in dispute is, Who is the legitimate majority? In this case of communal differences, it would be well advised to incorporate in the peace mandate a specific provision along the lines of the Liechtenstein Draft Convention, allowing for communal rights in education and perhaps even self-administration, including guaranteed places for minorities in local and national administration.[49] If separate communities have no recourse but secession to protect their basic rights, economic welfare, and communal identity, civil war will become the strategy of choice. If these goals can be achieved through communal self-administration (and, in many cases, it appears they can be), then incorporating commitments along the lines of the Draft Convention in the negotiated peace mandate and eventual constitution can preclude the emergence of civil violence.

Conclusion

The lessons of international engagement designed to promote law, order, and (in our time) human rights and democracy in the face of domestic civil disorder have recently become more clear. First, establishing peace in the aftermath of ethnic or civil war requires a considerable transformation—called peacebuilding in UN jargon. Warring parties rarely reconcile; at best, they are transformed or fade away and are replaced by new parties prepared to work together for some common purposes.

Second, that degree of transformation can be achieved by massive long-term force, for example, during colonial occupations such as by Britain of India and by the United States of Germany and Japan following World War II. The UN, however, is incapable of making that kind of long-term "war," if only because the member states are unwilling for it to have that kind of capacity. This is the kind of transformation that only national or, in some cases, multinational forces can achieve. When no one can negotiate a peace and the international community will not tolerate acts of overt aggression such as Iraq's invasion of Kuwait or a looming humanitarian disaster, delegation to national action has become the UN's answer to extreme emergencies.[50] The UN can then

---

49. Arthur Watts, *The Leichtenstein Draft Convention on Self-Determination Through Self-Administration: A Commentary* (Permanent Mission of the Principality of Liechtenstein to the UN, April 1994)—see Appendix B to this volume.

50. For a case for an option similar to this, called "benign spheres of influence," see Charles William Maynes, "A Workable Clinton Doctrine," *Foreign Policy* 93 (Winter 1993–1994), pp. 3–20.

play a key role in the follow-on peacebuilding role (as in Haiti and since June 1999, in Kosovo). But the transition needs to be well planned and reflect a commitment to long-run development. In Somalia, the UNITAF to UNOSOM II handoff failed because peacemaking stopped short of negotiating a comprehensive, implementable agreement that included both the warlords and civil society and because the international community was unwilling to make a multiyear commitment to help foster a Somali coalition prepared to build peace from the ground up, province by province.[51] Instead, the UN attempted to impose law and order from New York and Washington, with all the consequences, and then abandoned the enterprise as soon as it encountered resistance.

A similar problem confronted the peacebuilders in Kosovo in 1999–2000. Because the long-term future of Kosovo was unclear (a province of Serbia? an independent country?), there were regular challenges to the UN's authority from Belgrade and from the local Serb and Kosovar Albanian factions, and efforts to implement law and order appeared temporary and uncertain, having inadequate effect.[52]

Third, the UN should continue to develop a set of "strategies of enhanced consent" that permit societal transformation but that are much less costly because they build upon the engineered consent of once-warring factions. New strategies of peacemaking, peacekeeping, and peacebuilding open up these possibilities. All three were exploited efficiently in Cambodia, El Salvador, and Croatia and help account for the partial successes of the UNTAC, ONUSAL, and UNTAES operations.

These strategies are designed to build the social and institutional capital that such societies lack. One part of that process can be self-administration, acknowledging that something more than equal (but culturally subordinate) citizenship and something less than independence may preclude the ethnic civil wars and national secessions that have wracked the international system since the end of the Cold War.

Employing strategies of enhanced consent, the UN can play a constructive role in the forging of peace and reconstruction in those areas of the world in need of assistance in the establishment of human rights.

---

51. A good discussion of these issues can be found in Ken Menkaus, "International Peacebuilding," in Walter Clarke and Jeffrey Herbst, eds., *Learning from Somalia* (Boulder, Colo.: Westview Press, 1997), pp. 42–63.

52. R. Jeffrey Smith, "Kosovo's Youth Blamed for Brutal Ethnic Crimes," *Washington Post,* December 6, 1999, p. A1; George Robertson, "What's Going Right in Kosovo," *Washington Post,* December 7, 1999, p. A31; and Lucian Perkins, "Building Trust in a Kosovo Village," *International Herald Tribune,* December 28, 1999.

Avoiding the counterproductive effects of armed intervention, whether unilateral or multilateral, the UN can be the legitimating broker in the making, keeping, and building of peace that takes the first steps toward the opening of political space for human rights and participatory communal self-expression, as the UN did in Cambodia, El Salvador, and Eastern Slavonia.

4

The Limits of Self-Determination

EMILIO J. CÁRDENAS AND MARÍA FERNANDA CAÑÁS

> The guarantee of minorities' participation in political life is the sign of a morally adult society and an honor for countries in which all citizens are free to participate in the national life in a climate of justice and peace.
>
> —John-Paul II,
> "Ten Thoughts for the Year 2000," 1994, p. 183

The principle of self-determination originated in the ideal of the corporal integrity of individuals, which was espoused in the English, French, and U.S. bills of rights. Since 1945, probably no other issue has been more divisive among legal scholars than the question whether there is —or is not—a legal right to self-determination.[1] The idea was not articulated in a comprehensive fashion until World War I, when it was elevated to the status of a norm to which the international community rapidly subscribed. Some years later (although it had already been foreseen in the Atlantic Charter of August 14, 1941) self-determination found its way into international law through the UN Charter and became a formal right at the disposal of all "peoples."

Yet as soon as one tries to be specific, narrowing down the meaning of self-determination and examining its concrete application to these peoples, a wide variety of questions surfaces and clear answers are sim-

---

1. B. G. Ramcharang, "Individual, Collective and Group Rights: History, Theory, Practice and Contemporary Evolution," in *International Journal on Group Rights* 1 (1993), pp. 27–43. Also see Aurelia Critescu, *El Derecho a la libre determinación: Desarrollo histórico y actual sobre la base de los instrumentos de las Naciones Unidas* (E/CN.4/SUB 2/404/Rev.1 (1981), as cited in Ian Brownlie, *Principles of Public International Law*, 4th ed. (Oxford: Clarendon Press, 1990), p. 595; and James Crawford, *The Creation of States in International Law* (New York: Oxford University Press, 1979), pp. 85ff.

ply not available. The notion of self-determination is imprecise and ill defined. Its scope is unclear, as are the concepts of self and people, and periodic agonizing about their definition has not produced consensus or concrete results.

According to the UN Charter, all "peoples" have the right to "self-determination" (Article 1, paras. 2, 55). This notion has been reiterated over and over: in the UN General Assembly Resolution 1514 (XV), "Granting of Independence to Colonial Countries and Peoples" (December 14, 1960); in the International Covenant on Human Rights (1966); and in the Declaration on Principles of International Law Concerning Friendly Relations and Cooperation Among States, in Accordance with the Charter of the United Nations (October 24, 1970). Notwithstanding such declarations, the notion has been the object of continued doctrinal disputes with attempts to ascertain both who enjoys its protection and what exactly it entails.

Meanwhile, step by step, the academic community has defined various conceptual categories of self-determination. Some maintain that there is a right to "external" self-determination, which basically translates into the right to political independence and seems to include the right to secession. Furthermore, they also believe that there is a narrower right, the right to "internal" self-determination, which, being of a somehow defensive nature, relates to the basic political right to choose one's government, that is, the right of people to assert their will, while somehow downplaying the notion of sovereignty.

Very few in the international community are eager to accept the divisive forces that encourage state disintegration or the formation of myriad new political units. Any call for such an outcome could make it impossible to preserve a semblance of international consensus or order. Instead, it may lead to either utter chaos or the increase of factionalism. At the same time, however, the international community is undoubtedly concerned by all instances of blatant subjugation of groups or communities regardless of which regime, political front, or umbrella organization is responsible for such conduct.

This concern has motivated actions addressed toward protecting the status of minorities and communal groups. The general acceptance of a common obligation to protect other peoples' rights to individual and collective existence and self-expression is growing beyond the scope of traditional self-determination.

Extending external self-determination beyond the ideal of decolonization has frequently proven overambitious. In practice, the right of self-determination has not at all meant that minorities are granted the right to secede. Attempts aimed at disrupting a state's national unity and territorial integrity are, in fact, met unfavorably by the international community. However, when secession is accomplished peacefully, that is, through negotiations, the international community seems inclined to validate it, accepting reality once it takes effect. Secession, therefore, has rapidly become both the attraction and the tragedy of self-determination.

The contemporary tendency is to grant preference to the principle of territorial integrity. In other words, sovereignty is granted priority when it conflicts with self-determination. This is sensible, since in order to preserve a minority's right to its identity, it is neither necessary nor prudent to revise history or to injure the notion of territorial integrity. However, as there is no place in the world where territorial integrity precisely coincides with ethnic identity, real problems do multiply.

This is not a new occurrence; the outcome of the Åland Islands dispute is one example. At the Paris Peace Conference in 1920, the Swedish inhabitants of these Finnish islands requested annexation to Sweden. They were told that they had no right to secede. Autonomy under an international guarantee was recommended instead, together with the demilitarization and neutralization of the archipelago. In order to preserve the identity of the islands' population, only those Finnish residents already residing in the islands were authorized to purchase real estate therein. This would prevent the well-known practice of transferring population into the area, thus diluting a majority and turning it into a minority by simply flooding it with new residents, as has occurred in Tibet and elsewhere.

Other European islands—Faroe, Greenland, Madeira, and the Azores—have followed the example of Åland, viewing autonomy in a cultural rather than in a political way. Clearly, all of these autonomy-related objectives can be achieved by obtaining or granting greater political autonomy within an existing state. Thus minorities gain better internal political representation without being granted political independence.

We reiterate that although subnational groups or minorities do not, in principle, have a legal entitlement to external self-determination, they do have a right to autonomy as an expression of the right of internal self-determination. Through such autonomy they may govern and influence their own political order, controlling all issues that matter most in their daily life, thus preserving their cultural, ethnic, and historical identity.

The built-in contradictions and possible excesses of self-determination have, for quite some time, not only created unrest and turmoil globally but also generated significant academic debate.[2] The solution to managing both self-determination (which defies tidy definition) and the various claims derived from it has not yet been found. It remains a true gray area in public policy.

President Wilson's own secretary of state, Robert Lansing, was highly critical of his own president's enthusiasm—and even fervor—over the notion of self-determination (Wilson thought of self-determination as a right of colonial peoples). Lansing stated: "The more I think about 'self-determination' the more convinced I am of the danger of putting such an idea into the minds of certain races. It is bound to be the basis of impossible demands. The phrase is loaded with dynamite. What a calamity that the phrase was ever uttered!"[3]

In the early days following the end of World War II, self-determination was understood to mean "achieving independence from colonial domination." It proved to be an important tool through which colonization almost vanished from our world. Thus, self-determination—with its many caveats—provided the legal foundation for decolonization.

By the twenty-first century, the Cold War has ended and the decolonization of the third world is, for all practical purposes, nearly complete. However, self-determination seems to have somehow outlived its usefulness and is instead undermining the potential for peace in many regions around the globe. As L. Buchheit accurately warned us, what "seemed at first heaven-sent to supply a minimally explosive content for the doctrine of self-determination, eventually worked to evolve an

---

2. Lee C. Buchheit, *Secession: The Legitimacy of Self-Determination* (New Haven: Yale University Press, 1978), pp.1–42. This is a remarkable early study of the problems that the interpretation of the notion of self-determination was able to create. See also "Report of the Commission of Jurists (Larnaude, Huber, and Struycken)," *League of Nations Official Journal*, Special Supplement, no 3. (October 1920); J. Barros, *The Aaland Islands Question* (Princeton: Princeton University Press, 1968); Gunnar Jansson, "Self-Determination and Self-Governance," paper presented at the seminar Self-determination, Autonomy and Independence in the Twenty-first Century, held under UN auspices in Vienna, January 16–17, 1995; Christian Tomuschat, ed., *Modern Law of Self-Determination* (Dordrecht, The Netherlands: Martinus Nijhoff, 1993); Thomas D. Musgrave, *Self-Determination and National Minorities* (Oxford: Clarendon Press, 1997); and Antonio Cassese, *Self-Determination of Peoples: A Legal Reappraisal* (Cambridge: Cambridge University Press, 1995).

3. See the citation of Robert Lansing, *The Peace Negotiations: A Personal Narrative* (Boston, 1921), pp. 97–98, by Morton H. Halperin and David J. Scheffer with Patricia L. Small, in *Self-Determination in the New World Order* (Washington, D.C.: Carnegie Endowment for International Peace, 1992), p. 17. See also Clyde Eagleton, "Excesses of Self-Determination," *Foreign Affairs* 31, no. 4 (July 1953), pp. 592–604.

even more vague but certainly more incendiary terminology—that of the right of 'peoples' to self-determination."[4]

Because of the excesses, commentators now speak about "the evils of self-determination."[5] Their concern is, in our view, correct. We probably did spawn—as we were warned—a real Frankenstein's monster.[6]

Having realized this the hard way, we are now told that we must withdraw all moral support and approval from the various movements that attempt to resort to self-determination in order to try to obtain independence. But there are too many of them. They have become a destructive force and, in some cases, a concrete threat to international peace and security. It now appears that the intellectual inheritance on self-determination, as traditionally interpreted, may well prove ill suited to address the cascade of present-day problems.

An overwhelmingly negative consensus has surfaced, for justifiable reasons. We know what self-determination should not and cannot mean: fragmentation or balkanization. We also know that it can rapidly progress toward the dangerous resurrection of the concept of "inner isolationism," which was responsible for the madness that led the people of Germany to genocide.[7] Once again the international community must be reminded and alerted to history's lesson that liberty is impossible without true pluralism.[8]

A Different and Rapidly Evolving World

Today's world is a contradictory one. On the one hand, various conflicts seem to be tearing the globe apart. On the other hand, most states are, at least economically, moving unmistakably toward integration and association. The influence of economics, communications, and technology is becoming more intertwined each day, challenging the traditional definition of borders. Capital, ideas, information, cultures, and even people (we do face a new phenomenon, unknown for centuries, which is the migration of large numbers of people across frontiers) circulate globally and at unprecedented speeds.

Several well-established global issues affect us all: respect for

---

4. Buchheit, *Secession: The Legitimacy of Self-Determination*, p. 7.

5. Amitai Etzioni, "The Evils of Self-Determination," *Foreign Policy* 89 (Winter 1992–1993), pp. 21ff.

6. Buchheit, *Secession: The Legitimacy of Self-Determination*, p. 6.

7. Adolf Hitler, *Mein Kampf* (The Easton Press, 1994), p. 200, particularly Chapter 1, "Race and People."

8. Ernest Gellner, *Conditions of Liberty: Civil Society and Its Rivals* (New York: Penguin Press, 1994), p. 88.

human rights, the environment, corruption, terrorism, and drug trafficking. All will undoubtedly remain for a long while on the global agenda. The logic of this global marketplace of money and ideas is quietly changing our habits and lifestyles while simultaneously eroding the traditional notion of the nation-state. Those who do not realize, for instance, how much the international financial revolution is challenging the assumed sovereign powers of the nation-state are simply not looking at the proper scenario. In this connection, Paul Kennedy reminded us:

> The borderless world implies a certain surrender of a nation's control over both its own currency and its fiscal policies. That surrender might bring prosperity, but if the international financial system is unstable—as it too often happens—there is little or no authority to control potential massive currency flows. With the volume of daily currency exchanges well in excess of the GNP's of many countries, individual governments and finance ministries have much less command over the system than they had just a quarter of a century ago. Simply the awareness of the market's disapproval of certain measures (like raising taxes) can deter the so-called sovereign governments from implementing them.[9]

Today's world is rather different than yesterday's. As a former UN Secretary-General has stated: "The time of absolute and exclusive sovereignty . . . has passed."[10] In all likelihood, tomorrow's world will be even more different.

Yet today's move toward worldwide economic integration seems at odds with the virulent outbreak of tribalism and nationalism precipitated by the end of the Cold War that pushed the world toward political fragmentation. Whereas internationalization has taken over in the private sector and is universally promoted by the business community,

---

9. Paul Kennedy, *Preparing for the Twenty-first Century* (New York: Random House, 1993), pp. 128–129. Also see John Lukacs, *The End of the Twentieth Century and the End of the Modern Age* (New York: Ticknor & Fields, 1993), p. 264; Terry L. Deibel, "Internal Affairs and International Relations in the Post–Cold War World," *Washington Quarterly* 16, no. 3 (Summer 1993), pp. 13–33; and Marvin S. Soroos, *Beyond Sovereignty: The Challenge of Global Policy* (Columbia: University of South Carolina Press, 1986), p. 65. There are problems that transcend national boundaries and can spill over the boundaries of the state in which they originate: John Naisbitt, *Global Paradox: The Bigger the World Economy, the More Powerful Its Smallest Players* (New York: W. Morrow, 1994); Evan Luard, *The Globalization of Politics* (New York: New York University Press, 1990); and Joseph Camilleri and Jim Falk, *The End of Sovereignty? The Politics of a Shrinking and Framenting World* (Brookfield, Vt.: Edward Elgar, 1992).

10. Boutros Boutros-Ghali, *An Agenda for Peace*, UN Doc. A/47/277-S/2411 (New York: UN, June 17, 1992), para. 17.

national chauvinists (espousing ethnic, extremist, demagogic, or xeno-phobic ideas) are pounding the world's table.[11] Claims and demands invoking alleged rights of external self-determination are being made on an unprecedented scale. Well over 900 million people, belonging to 233 increasingly assertive groups or communities, are—one way or another—resorting to such claims, thus massively abusing the tradition-al concept of self-determination. Today's world hosts nearly 200 states—but also 3,000 linguistic groups and 5,000 national minorities.[12] UN Secretary-General Boutros Boutros-Ghali alerted us, back in August 1992, to the dangers of misused self-determination: "If every ethnic, religious or linguistic group claimed statehood, there would be no limit to fragmentation, and peace, security and economic well-being for all, would become even more difficult to achieve."[13]

As Patrick E. Kennon points out, in today's scenario the world where there was one "Big Enemy" (the now defunct Soviet Union) has been suddenly replaced by one with many intrastate conflicts and, therefore, a thousand little enemies. All of a sudden an unexpected form of totalitarianism is surfacing in many corners of the world like a new religion. Unfortunately, it has no use for pragmatism and no room for tolerance. It operates under a rigid code of right and wrong that allows no compromise. This is its deep tragedy.[14]

During the first half of 1999, no fewer than twenty-five armed con-flicts of an *intra*state nature were raging around the world. Many are giving the rest of us a rather primitive message, that "it is safer to flee, fight or even exterminate, than to coexist."[15] The world's arena is unex-pectedly filled with a variety of all-or-nothing patriots unwilling to tol-erate or even compromise. Their minds are entrenched in the past, and they are capable of only further divisiveness. They do not understand that to be united, one must take the past into account but be also willing to accept that there is a future. They lean toward isolationism, reject universal values, systematically refuse to find common ground, and dis-regard the liberties and dignity of others. Although impossible to justify, these views are understandable. As in times of war, one does not have to

---

11. Patrick E. Kennon, *The Twilight of Democracy* (New York: Doubleday, 1995), p. 270. Jason W. Clay, "States, Nations and Resources, an Interdependent Relationship?" in *Fletcher Forum of World Affairs* 19, no. 1 (1995), p. 11, defines the present changes in the world's environment in a hilarious nutshell: "Goodbye Berlin Wall, Hello Berlin Mall!"

12. John Stremlan, "Antidote to Anarchy," *Washington Quarterly* 18, no. 1 (Winter 1995), p. 33.

13. Boutros-Ghali, *An Agenda for Peace*, para. 17.

14. Kennon, *The Twilight of Democracy*, p. 270.

15. Ibid., p. 271.

voluntarily succumb to a sick nationalist ideology, but one can well be sucked into it.[16] Thus there is an urgent need for new approaches that, without ignoring the human dimension of the problems, could help in framing a useful multilateral response.

Self-determination was never intended to be and cannot be turned into an instrument of intolerance. As Jean Bethka Elshtain writes: "The long history of the human race suggests that resentment fuels hate; isolation feeds paranoia; cynicism stokes mistrust; and fear generates flight from neighborliness, large heartedness and the patience necessary to perdure."[17]

The Moral Dimension of the Problem

When confronted with intolerance and militant efforts to destroy the mosaic of a particular society, we must remember that the fostering of human dignity requires respect for other cultures, races, and religions, all of which have their own individual characteristics and heritage. Such respect is paramount even if it is true that all cultures contain their share of prejudices that sometimes become sacralized.

Those who preach the dangerous gospel of religious, cultural, or demographic homogeneity must be told that it goes against the very grain of coexistence. Those who listen must be aware that the so-called ancient ethnic tensions frequently explode in response to provocations by elites who are trying to create a domestic political setting to dominate. The greatest absurdity is that many adherents of such gospel profess to be believers, that is, loyal members of a religion. Thus they murder and massacre in the name of God. As long as this behavior continues, there will be no lasting peace.

The world is, and will always be, made out of the many. Community nevertheless is different from unity. It is a social contract and not an imposition. Society can and must contain a wide degree of cultural or ethnic diversity. It comes out of diversity significantly enriched, since ignorance frequently is replaced by understanding, thus making peace possible. Nothing less may succeed.

The positive-sum game of political pluralism must prevail over the irrational zero-sum politics of ethnic nationalism or fundamentalism. For this purpose, majority governments must be held accountable inside

---

16. Slavenka Drakulic, *The Balkan Express: Fragments from the Other Side of a War* (London: Hutchinson, 1994), p. 52.

17. Jean Bethke Elshtain, *Democracy on Trial* (New York: Basic Books, 1995), p. xii.

their respective territories for creating and granting political guarantees not only for the rights of individuals but for the preservation of their identities as well. The problem is one of properly reconciling minority demands with the exercise of democracy. This reconciliation is a delicate balancing act.

We should consider dialogue as the only way to avoid the two dangerous extremes: monologue and war.[18] There is an urgent need to systematically eliminate corrosive resentment and educate the public on the benefits of national integration and mutual understanding. This dialogue is a process. It goes beyond the discourse of seduction and suggestion and appeals to common sense rather than to the imagination only.[19] Its importance is that it has to do with reality and possibilities.

Modernity should be personified by cooperation and solidarity, not nationalism. It is faith in diversity, built on respect for all individual cultures and personalities. In today's world no one can live in complete isolation; we are all interdependent.[20] Nationalism looks inward, whereas modernism looks, instead, around and forward. Modernism means believing that pluralism can flourish within a unified multicultural state and that ethnic groups need not be suppressed to build community.[21]

The experience of several American and European countries evidences that it is possible to sustain government responsiveness and unity even when having to integrate separate identities and cultures. This approach is what Arend Lijphart calls "consociationalism," where a winner-takes-all attitude is systematically avoided. Consequentially, community-building efforts, and not fragmentation claims, should be accorded the highest priority.[22] This is only possible if and when it is

----

18. Tzverkan Todorov, *On Human Diversity* (Cambridge: Harvard University Press, 1994), pp. xi, xv. See also V. P. Gagnun Jr., "Ethnic-Nationalism and International Conflict," *International Security* 19, no. 3 (Winter 1994–1995), pp. 130ff.

19. Ibid., p. xi.

20. See John Breuilly, *Nationalism and the State*, 2nd ed. (Chicago: University of Chicago Press, 1994), p. ix; and Elie Kedourie, *Nationalism*, 4th ed. (Cambridge, Mass.: Blackwell, 1993), p. 44. Also see Anthony Giddens, *Modernity and Self-Identity: Self and Society in the Late Modern Age* (Stanford: Stanford University Press, 1991), pp. 4ff.; and Jan Rensmelnik, "General Report," *Conscience and Liberty: International Journal of Religious Freedom*, nos. 1–2 (10) (1994), p. 61.

21. Etzioni, "The Evils of Self-Determination," p. 34; and Nicholas Rescher, *Pluralism: Against the Demand for Consensus* (Oxford: Clarendon Press, 1993), pp. 3–4.

22. Anne Phillips, *Democracy and Difference* (University Park: Pennsylvania State University Press, 1953), pp. 150ff.; and Daniel Thürer, "National Minorities: A Global, European, and Swiss Perspective," *Fletcher Forum of World Affairs* 19, no. 1 (Winter/Spring 1995), pp. 53–69.

understood that sovereignty is power over both people and territory and that sharing and even delegating sovereign authority is perfectly possible, as many experiences around the world demonstrate.

A Modern Notion of Self-Determination

The principle of self-determination is probably "best viewed as entitling a people to choose its political allegiance to influence the political order under which it lives" and to preserve its identity.[23] Usually, but for exceptional cases, these objectives can be achieved with less-than-full independence. Self-determination must not be used as an instrument of secession.

Autonomy is the best means of upholding the necessary balance among different communities or minorities in a pluralistic society. International borders correspond to states and not to nations, minorities, or communities. These entities can claim a right to internal self-determination, that is, an autonomy to protect their cultural identity. However, their autonomy must not be abused in order to destroy the bases of the political community in which they live.[24]

The exercise of internal self-determination should not result in having to recognize independent statehood for each and every individual group or unit. There are many other known options: empowering previously marginalized voices by stressing minority rights protection and guarantees, cultural and political autonomy, and so forth. Because there are these other paths to self-determination, the international community has systematically begun to sidestep external self-determination. Instead, it has rapidly moved toward providing greater protection for

---

23. Halperin and Scheffer with Small, *Self-Determination in the New World Order*, p. 47. See also Robert McCorquodale, "Human Rights and Self-Determination," in Mortimer Sellers, ed., *The New World Order: Sovereignty, Human Rights, and the Self-Determination of Peoples* (Washington, D.C.: Berg, 1996), p. 12; and Hurst Hannum, *Autonomy, Sovereignty and Self-Determination: The Accommodation of Conflicting Rights* (Philadelphia: University of Pennsylvania Press, 1990).

24. Thomas Fleiver, "State–Nation–Nationalities–Autonomy, The Nation-State Reconsidered: Basic Concepts for Autonomy, Decentralization, and Minority-Protection in a Post-Modern World," paper presented at the seminar Self-determination, Autonomy and Independence in the Twenty-first Century, held under UN auspices in Vienna, January 16–17, 1995. See also Jerry J. Simpson, "The Diffusion of Sovereignty: Self-Determination in the Post-Colonial Age" in Sellers, *The New World Order.* Simpson states, "Devolutionary self-determination is the name given to official arrangements that distribute power to local groups, regions or centers" (p. 51). Devolution is both decentralization and noncentralization.

the freedom, dignity, and rights of minorities through autonomy, that is, through internal self-determination.

This narrow (internal) interpretation of the concept of self-determination—which must be understood not as an injunction to unanimity but, much to the contrary, as a firm invitation to community—has the potential to prevent the dismemberment of multicultural states and avoid turbulent invitations to chaos that are hidden behind a pseudoright to a limitless (external) version of self-determination.

Through the internal variety of self-determination, minorities should be able to avoid discrimination while conducting their own administration with reasonable autonomy. Internal self-determination includes policies for organizing consultative, legislative, and executive bodies, among other institutions, structured through periodic and free elections. These decentralized democratic governments should deal with matters directly related to the protection of minority identities.

Members of minority communities should be protected so that they may enjoy the same individual rights as other citizens of the state. In such an environment, a minority's language, education, and culture are preserved. Very often this protection will coincide with a high degree of territorial autonomy for the affected group.

Furthermore, it may mean that minorities are entitled to their own democratic government, but only within a scheme whereby a plurality of relatively autonomous subsystems reside within the domain of a single state.[25] This plurality cannot, however, be understood as a conglomeration of diverse but disparate groups or communities that lack an underlying and somehow cohesive society. Pluralism should not evolve into ethnocentrism with the resulting cacophony of competing and disruptive voices. Likewise, a cohesive society must be permanently aware of and actively concerned with avoiding the disfranchisement of its minorities.[26]

A world of segments should not be allowed to replace a world of tolerance. As Amitai Etzioni has recently reminded us, "In a truly democratic state, there is no reason for one culture to try to suppress others, as long as the others seek self-expression rather than cultural domi-

---

25. This is the well-known position of Thomas M. Franck. See "Postmodern Tribalism and the Right to Secession," in Catherine Brölmann et al., *Peoples and Minorities in International Law* (Boston: Martinus Nijhoff, 1993). See also Robert A. Dahl, *Dilemmas of Pluralist Democracy: Autonomy Is Control* (New Haven: Yale University Press, 1982), p. 5.

26. Ted Robert Gurr, *Minorities at Risk: A Global View of Ethnopolitical Conflicts* (Washington, D.C.: United States Institute of Peace, 1993); and Patrick Thornberry, *International Law and the Rights of Minorities* (Oxford: Clarendon Press, 1991).

nance or territorial separatism. Otherwise, the process of ethnic separation will never be exhausted."[27] Democracy provides the sociopsychological framework for social compromise, but it requires tolerance in order to function properly, as tolerance is crucial in negotiations between peoples of divergent identities.

Internal self-determination, therefore, is not an absolute but a relative right, one with clear limits. The mistaken tendency to believe that it is unconditionally available to any group and that it includes the right to secede is rapidly fading away. Such a perspective is simply not tenable.[28] As a relative right, self-determination therefore does not include the right to secession except under very specific circumstances,[29] and this narrow interpretation of the notion prevails in the modern doctrine.

In addition to the general guideline of excluding from the right of self-determination the right to independence, there are three specific situations where the right should be further curtailed. Large groups of immigrants, the ethnic diasporas, are the first case. People who possess a common national identity but reside outside a claimed or an independent home territory cannot resort to invoking the protection of self-determination because they are excluded from its scope. This category of people functions very frequently in the industrialized world as a substitute for the notion of race.[30]

Second, the extent of self-determination is also limited in the case of population transfers, entailing the displacement of people en masse to territories acquired or annexed by the illegal use of force. Claiming a separate territorial status for the purposes of self-determination would, if anything, only reinforce the illegality. This practice is simply another form of colonialism and has occurred in a wide variety of fashions in

---

27. Etzioni, "The Evils of Self-Determination," p. 28.

28. Van Dycke V., "Human Rights of Groups," *American Journal of Political Science* 18 (1974), p. 13. See also McCorquodale, "Human Rights and Self-Determination," p. 14.

29. Max M. Kampelman, "Secession and the Right of Self-Determination: An Urgent Need to Harmonize Principle with Pragmatism," *Washington Quarterly* 16, no. 3 (Summer 1993), pp. 5–12; Lea Brilmayer, "Secession and Self-Determination: A Territorial Interpretation," *Yale Journal of International Law* 16 (1991), pp. 177–201; and Alexis Heraclides, "Secession, Self-Determination and Non-Intervention: In Quest of a Normative Symbiosis," *Journal of International Affairs* 45, no. 2 (1992), pp. 399–420.

30. José A. de Obieta Chalband, "El derecho humano de la autodeterminación de los pueblos," *Tecnos,* 1985, p. 60; and Yossi Shain, "Ethnic Diasporas and U.S. Foreign Policy," *Political Science Quarterly* 109, no. 5 (Winter 1994–1995), pp. 811ff.

many corners of the world.[31] Various techniques have been used: the removal of the population (as was the case with both Diego Garcia and the Falkland/Malvinas Islands);[32] discriminatory immigration policies (for many years in the Falkland/Malvinas Islands); massive settlements of individuals with a different identity in an effort to "dilute" the preexisting population (Tibet); or a combination of these practices. Communities that may have grown through the use of these techniques, that lack the required historical continuity, and that do not reside in ancestral lands cannot benefit from the umbrella of self-determination. This is so despite any disguises they may have resorted to in demanding their "special status." These communities are certainly not excluded, however, from the protection that may apply to them as minorities.

Third, individual minorities who may have settled within a state's boundaries are certainly entitled to legal protection as minorities. This protection can be achieved through a rainbow of possible autonomy schemes—but they are not entitled to a right of external self-determination.[33]

The case of indigenous population is a particular one. An estimated 300 million people distributed over more than seventy countries fall into this category.[34] The vast majority of them do not claim identity

---

31. Christopher M. Goebel, "A Unified Concept of Population Transfer," *Denver Journal of International Law and Policy* 21, no. 1 (Fall 1992), pp. 29ff. Crawford, in *The Creation of States in International Law,* p. 86, even doubts that modern international law could accept the application of self-determination to a situation such as the Åland Islands.

32. On the displacement of the Argentine population from the Falkland/Malvinas Islands, see the excellent book by Julius Goebel Jr., *The Struggle for the Falkland Islands: A Study in Legal and Diplomatic History* (New Haven: Yale University Press, 1927), pp. 434ff.; and V. F. Boyson, *The Falkland Islands* (Oxford: Clarendon Press, 1924), pp. 187ff. When force has been used to seize territory, it must be recalled that title could only accrue should the dispossessed sovereign express its acquiescence. See also Sonia A.M. Viejobueno, "Self-Determination v. Territorial Integrity: The Falkland/Malvinas Dispute with Reference to Recent Cases in the United Nations," *South African Yearbook of International Law* 16 (1990–1991), pp. 1ff.

33. Deborah C. Cass, "Re-thinking Self-Determination: A Critical Analysis of Current International Law Theories," *Syracuse Journal of International Law and Commerce* 18 (Spring 1992), p. 29.

34. On this topic see Douglas Sanders, "Self-Determination and Indigenous People," and Gudmundur Alfresson, "The Right of Self-Determination and Indigenous Peoples," both in Tomuschat, *Modern Law of Self-Determination,* pp. 55 and 41, respectively. Also see C. M. Bralmann and M.Y.A. Zieck, "Indigenous Peoples," in the same volume, p. 191. Brazil may itself have lost one indigenous nation per year for the past 100 years. See J. W. Clay, "The Ethnic Future of Nations," *Third World Quarterly* (October 1989), pp. 223ff.; Mary Ellen Turpel, "Indigenous People's Rights of Political Participation and Self-Determination," *Cornell International Law Journal* 25 (1992); and Harris O. Schoenberg, "Limits of Self-Determination," in *Israel Yearbook on Human Rights* (Tel Aviv: Faculty of Law, Tel Aviv University, 1976).

absolutism but instead believe in unity through diversity, a concept that defines the only enduring and lasting unity. Self-determination from the perspective of indigenous peoples is usually of the internal variety, as they normally claim to be interested in building partnerships with the states in which they reside and emphasize efforts toward the recognition of their cultural, civil, political, economic, and social rights. Self-determination is here limited in that their emerging strategy is thus focused predominately on self-development.

In the past three decades a series of UN conventions have focused on discrimination, proscribing its practice against members of minority as well as majority groups.[35] In December 1992, the UN General Assembly adopted the Declaration on the Rights of Persons Belonging to National, or Ethnic, Religious and Linguistic Minorities. It obligates states to protect the existence and identity of minorities within their respective territories and details the specific rights of minorities that must be the object of such protection. These include the rights to enjoy their own culture; profess and practice their own religions; use their own language; participate effectively in public life, as well as in all decisions having to do with the minority to which they belong; establish and monitor their own associations; and establish and maintain, without discrimination, free and peaceful contacts with other members of their group or other citizens of other states to whom they are related by special ties. The declaration is certainly not a binding legal instrument, but as a standard-setting guideline, it will no doubt be very influential. The international community has not been and does not presently seem to be ready to enact specific rules in a treaty regarding minorities.

In conclusion, the clear legal priority of respecting a state's territorial integrity and political unity over and above self-determination may be conditioned on that state's observance of, and respect for, the human rights of individuals and minorities within its own territory.[36] It is unac-

---

35. See Frank C. Newman, "A 'Nutshell' Approach to the U.N. Human Rights Law Protecting Minorities," *Fletcher Forum of World Affairs* 19, no. 1 (Winter/Spring 1995), pp. 6–7.

36. Kampelman, "Secession and the Right of Self-Determination," p. 8. Christian Tomuschat (in "Self-Determination in a Post Colonial World," in his *Modern Law of Self-Determination*, p. 9) states, "If the state machinery turns itself into an apparatus of terror, which persecutes specific groups of the population, those groups cannot be obligated to remain legally under the jurisdiction of that state." According to Robert McCorquodale, "Only a government of a state that allows all its peoples to decide freely their political status and economic, social, and cultural development can assert an interest in protecting its territorial integrity to limit the exercise of a right of self-determination." McCorquodale, "Human Rights and Self-Determination," p. 20.

ceptable for minorities to be victimized by a majority group. In addition, self-determination redefined does not include the right to secede but, instead, the right to autonomy and democracy—the right to determine one's own identity and destiny instead of having them imposed from above.[37]

The Liechtenstein Draft Convention on
Self-Determination Through Self-Administration

On September 26, 1991, Prince Hans-Adam II of Liechtenstein introduced an initiative on self-determination in the UN General Assembly, anticipating that his delegation would prepare a Draft Convention on the subject. After a series of general debates at a variety of levels on this particularly sensitive issue, a Draft Convention began to circulate.

Our preliminary reaction and comments on it are based on its text as distributed in April 1994. A preamble sets the Draft Convention's general context and motivations. It does not, however, erase our concerns about the convenience of proposing or debating a Draft Convention to implement the principle of self-determination through self-administration unless an unequivocal decision to downgrade unjustified expectations is made and distinctly reflected in the text. This is not yet the case.

The notion of self-determination remains imprecise, its beneficiaries, ill defined. Its own nature (whether a principle or a right) is undefined, and the text on implementation—except for decolonization—is rather incoherent. Moreover, due to its direct relationship with the process of decolonization, it cannot be easily disassociated from independence.

Whereas we certainly must keep trying to discourage the current abusive reliance on self-determination, the road toward a Draft Convention—particularly when an ambitious institutional structure is proposed—must necessarily be a very slow and careful one. We share the general concern behind the drafters' efforts, but some of the proposals deserve further discussion.

For instance, we would suggest that the preamble recognize that the biggest achievement of self-determination in recent history was the world's decolonization after World War II. It is true that the misemploy-

---

37. See T. M. Franck, "Postmodern Tribalism and the Right to Secession," in Catherine Brölmann, Renè Leféber, and Marjoleine Zieck, *Peoples and Minorities in International Law* (Boston: Martinus Nijhoff, 1993), p. 20.

ment of self-determination and the absence of an adequate measure of self-administration, as an option, have led to countless wars and conflicts (as noted by the preamble). At the same time, it is obvious that the permanent search for roads toward independence through the window of self-determination has already been the source of too much bloodshed.

As the Draft Convention convincingly argues, self-determination is definitely not coterminous with and should not always lead to independence. There must be nontraumatic alternatives short of independence at the disposal of conflicting parties. Independence is an exceptional measure, and it should be reserved only for those cases where a state—beyond a doubt—does not respect the identity of a minority.

The text reassurances that self-determination does not constitute a threat to territorial integrity are important and welcome. In this connection Article 1, paragraph (b), is nevertheless not sufficiently clear. Furthermore, Article 3 should specifically refer to the territorial integrity and political unity of States, as being of paramount importance. When a community is presented with the possibility of achieving different and alternative levels of self-administration, it will probably aim high, that is, it will seek to achieve full independence rather than some intermediate level of autonomy. Recent experience seems to suggest this path, particularly in those cases when communities are coming out of authoritarian regimes where unity was maintained by force. Thus the document should specifically state that full independence is a solution only of last resort.

Certain terms in the text need more precise definition. The ambiguity of concepts such as "distinct group" and "sufficient degree of organization" will serve to encourage those (whether state or minority actors) looking for loopholes in the document. Although the International Court of Justice theoretically could decide in the case of dispute over definitions, this solution may not be realistic.

The new concept of community introduced by the Draft Convention, although innovative, does not seem to solve the problem of uncertainty with the classic concept of a people. Geography is the essence of "community" and differentiates it from "minority." Nevertheless, determining the borders of communities will surely be problematic, particularly where members of the same group are spread throughout the world or across the border into neighboring states. This situation could enhance the already strong temptation for states to interfere in the internal affairs of their neighbors and disrupt the communities living across the border. One cannot avoid recalling the recent situations in Burundi, Rwanda, and Uganda, where Tutsis and Hutus moved across the borders depending on the prevailing political situation.

Article 2.2 of the Draft Convention carries an unsettling and almost activist tone when it talks about the aspirations of all communities instead of what is commonly referred to as the wishes or interests of the persons falling under the protection of self-determination. Even more debatable is the idea of the appropriate degree of self-determination, which could well have as many possible interpretations as cases, transforming the Draft Convention into a useless instrument. Something very similar occurs, later in the text, with the concepts of "reasonable period" and "satisfactory experience," which, again, can have as many meanings as parties to the cases.

The main objective of the Draft Convention is to avoid conflicts by making the peaceful use of the principle of self-determination through self-administration easier to invoke and more effective. But in not declaring illegal the use of armed force to achieve self-determination, the document's call for its peaceful implementation is rather weak. The text of the Draft Convention should state explicitly that its implementation is to be achieved only peacefully.

Finally, allowing private capital to fund the establishment of the foundation as provided for by the Draft Convention is risky, as private interests could contradict those of the state parties or even the foundation itself. It seems that for now, while the Draft Convention remains in the development stage, the best way to deal with claims of self-determination is still on a case-by-case basis.

Conclusion

The road to a lasting world peace and the well-being of all peoples is through interconnected communities, not through fragmentation. For the community to prosper, the open moral support historically granted to external self-determination must be clearly qualified.

Minorities must be protected by granting different degrees of autonomy rather than by continually allowing them to demand independence. This aim requires simultaneous efforts to promote democracy and eliminate human rights abuses.[38]

A state, when confronted with a crisis involving one minority living within its territory, should realize that it must not only tolerate but fully respect the identity of such a minority. Otherwise, the support of the international community for the sanctity of the state may rapidly fade away.

38. See Thomas Carothers, "Democracy and Human Rights: Policy Allies or Rivals?" *Washington Quarterly* 17, no. 3 (Summer 1994), pp. 109–120.

The broad interpretation of external self-determination has proven to be a blind alley that destabilizes the international community and is counterproductive for those who demand it. Autonomy, or internal self-determination, fine-tuned to each individual case, is the moderate and modern answer. A fundamental reexamination of all majority-minority relations within states seems unavoidable.[39]

The goal is as urgent as it is ambitious: we should all try to find a creative way to channel conflicts through political structures rather than through war and violence. Such structures, with federalism as a possible central component, must embrace and reflect diversity. As Harland Cleveland writes, "A practical pluralism, not a unitary universalism, is the likely destiny of the human race."[40] A more peaceful world should follow, one in which differences are not only recognized but respected and in which an underlying solidarity is forged across such differences, as none of them should be set in stone.

Nevertheless, "if one sees in democratic principles, including the insistence that we are obliged to reach out to one another rather than to entrench in our violated groups, only a cover for hidden privileges, one stalls as a citizen."[41] In fact, we would do worse than stalling: we would fail to build the bridges that are necessary to preserve and respect diversity in order to live together in a civilized fashion.

Promoting democracy is not an easy task. It requires both (1) "democratic dispositions," which in essence means readiness "to work with others different from oneself towards shared ends";[42] and (2) a common sense of responsibility.

In addition, democracy requires that tolerance and sincere willingness to compromise—the very pillars of democratic politics—are part of the foundation of the society. Without this base, experience shows that there is no lasting dialogue and society rapidly tends to disintegrate. Pragmatism and the ability to compromise—not unbending theology—should prevail in the design of each specific solution or ad hoc institutional arrangement. At least for the time being, we should address these issues on a case-by-case basis.

---

39. Hurst Hannum, "Minority Rights. Introduction," *Fletcher Forum of World Affairs* 19, no. 1 (Winter/Spring 1995), p. 1.

40. Harland Cleveland, *Birth of a New World* (San Francisco: Jossey-Bass, 1993), p. 76.

41. Jean Bethke Elshtain, *Democracy on Trial* (New York: Basic Books, 1995), p. 75.

42. Ibid., p. 2.

5

Avoiding the Iron Cage of Legislated Communal Identity

JOHN WATERBURY

> How many people have ever heard of the Szekels of Transylvania? Yet there are over 800,000 of them, all entitled to a place in the sun and all capable of making trouble if it is denied to them.
> —Walter Lippmann, *The Stakes of Diplomacy,* 1915[1]

> But of all the individuals living in Peyrane during the thirteen-year period from 1946 to 1959, how many lived there for thirteen years? Only 275! And of these, 137 were not born in Peyrane! At this point I begin to wonder what I mean when I refer to "the people of Peyrane."
> —Lawrence Wylie, *A Village in the Vaucluse*[2]

We would not talk of self-determination, as opposed to democratization or the protection of human rights, if there was not a presumption that certain groups should or could legitimately seek some degree of self-rule. Although accepting that broad premise, I argue in this chapter that we have very weak guides as to what constitutes such groups and that in trying to protect them we may endow certain of them with a factitious reality that is neither historically nor dynamically grounded. Indeed, there are no natural, legal units in the international or in most national

I would like to thank the anonymous outside reviewers for their valuable comments.

1. Quoted in Arend Lijphart, "The Power-Sharing Approach," in Joseph Montville, ed., *Conflict and Peacemaking in Multiethnic Societies* (Lexington, Mass.: Lexington Books, 1987), pp. 491–509; and Daniel P. Moynihan, *Pandaemonium: Ethnicity in International Politics* (New York: Oxford University Press, 1993), p. 100.

2. Quoted in Lawrence Wylie, *Village in the Vaucluse* (New York: Harper and Row, 1961), p. 352.

systems. The majority of the population of the famous *hexagon étoilé* did not speak French as its first language until the mid-1800s. Even islands do not make natural units, as Ireland and Britain vividly demonstrate. When one thinks of the contemporary cases of self-definition and self-determination embodied in, say, Georgia, Quebec, Lithuania, or Kurdistan, gratifying the urge for the self-rule of one group complicates, if not denies, similar gratification for groups living in their midst.

The issue is, above all, one of consent. Political systems must allow groups, if they choose to act as groups, to seek representation and to consent to participate in a larger unit. Rather than stimulating the formation and legal participation of groups qua groups, legislation should be neutral and permissive, but not encouraging. It may be advisable in certain circumstances to institutionalize what Arend Lijphart has called a "minority veto," that is, a negative or blocking right, but legislation should not enshrine the rights and entitlements of any particular minority or group.[3] It is equally important that political systems allow individuals to assert their identities as they see fit and to place no legal impediments or disincentives on the individual's ability to redefine herself or himself constantly.

Whatever its contours, the nation-state is no better and no worse than any other context for playing out the process by which individuals come together, cooperate, move apart, and conflict. Self-determination implies some set of protean group interests, historically disembodied and immutable, whereas reality, like Lawrence Wylie's village (in the quote at the beginning of this chapter), is far more malleable and inconstant. To take an example that will be developed further on, Turkey is today a flawed democracy. Its constitution denies participation to groups that espouse ethnic or sectarian causes. Turkey's Kurdish (and, to a lesser extent, Islamic) problem is not one of self-determination but rather one of improving the country's democratic system. Gidon Gottlieb has posited that "autonomy in a state without democracy has scant practical meaning."[4] I would go a step further and argue that in a state in which the mechanisms of representation and the instruments of

---

3. Lijphart, "The Power-Sharing Approach."
4. Gidon Gottlieb, *Nation Against State: A New Approach to Ethnic Conflicts and the Decline of Sovereignty* (New York: Council on Foreign Relations, 1993), p. 79. See also *CSCE Geneva Report of the Meeting of Experts on National Minorities*, as cited in Morton Halperin and David Scheffer with Patricia Small, *Self-Determination in the New World Order* (Washington, D.C.: Carnegie Endowment for International Peace, 1992), p. 58.

accountability work well, the issue of autonomy may lose its relevance (see Kohli's Chapter 11 on India in this volume).

Identity

There may be instances in which the objective characteristics of a group are so salient that if they are in a minority or in some other way vulnerable as a group, it is reasonable and imperative to treat them as a group and to provide them with explicit legal safeguards. Groups defined by race and skin color best fit these criteria, for the option of dissimulating or assimilating to some other racial group is most often denied their members. Perhaps ironically, given the terrible history and legacy of apartheid, whites and "coloureds" are in that position in South Africa today. Neither can hide from or assimilate the other.

Yet such objective situations are relatively rare. More common are situations in which it is at least possible for individuals to move from group to group. Movement from one religion or sect to another is possible, as is the abandonment of faith altogether. Ethnic identity may be so ambiguous and blurred around the edges that no one can be sure who is who. The Rwandan Tutsi adopted the Hutu language, and although they imposed a caste system that subordinated the Hutu, there was movement among castes in all directions; many Rwandans could not be distinguished physically one from another. Tribal scarring and religious tattooing are symbolic of efforts to lock people into identities that they are perfectly capable of abandoning. The quest for self-determination should not lead to the legal equivalent of scarring and tattooing.

It is, of course, true that one cannot change one's origins, and few people want to do so. But one can deemphasize origins as a component of one's identity, and certain political and institutional settings may be more conducive to such deemphasis than others.

There is a fundamental divide in the academics' and politicians' understanding of the dynamics of identity and how best to cope with those dynamics politically. There are those, including myself, who stress the plasticity of identity and who therefore advocate political rules that encourage identity change.[5] For example, Tawfic Farah analyzed surveys showing that between the late 1970s and the late 1980s

---

5. See, inter alia, Nelson Kasfir, "Explaining Ethnic Political Participation," *World Politics* 31, no. 3 (1979), pp. 365–388.

the number of "Arab" respondents identifying themselves as Arabs declined sharply in favor of those identifying themselves as Muslims.[6]

Of a differing view are those such as Walker Connor[7] and Arend Lijphart, who take an essentialist view of identity, one that stresses its protean and prior qualities. For them, the best way to cope with the dynamics of identity is to recognize and, to some extent, legally bless what is and what cannot be changed. I will explore this question further with respect to Lebanon, which constitutionally recognized the fundamental confessional nature of Lebanese society. Yet there are many other examples—successful ones such as India (despite the conflicts in Kashmir and the Punjab) and less successful ones such as Nigeria—where this principle has been applied. The constitution for Ethiopia establishes nine regions, in eight of which a single ethnic group predominates. Each region is granted the right to secede. An Ethiopian minister remarked, "Our ethnic experiment has never been tried before in Africa. . . . We have grabbed the bull by the horns. Instead of pretending that ethnicity doesn't exist, we are prepared to face it."[8]

The Ethiopian constitution offers positive incentives to politicians and voters to act and think ethnically. Once patronage and budget outlays begin to reinforce the ethnic territorial divisions, the system will probably "lock in"; as the Belgians oblige Hutu and Tutsi to be so named on their ID cards, so the Ethiopian solution may create legal straitjackets that ignore shifting, situational identities. If the recognition of minority claims is founded on numerical concentrations in specific territories, as is the case in Ethiopia, then the free movement of citizens, as well as of labor and capital, may be impeded, thereby adding economic suboptimality to political expediency.

I do not in the least belittle the enormous challenges multiethnic, multisectarian states such as Ethiopia face in trying to avoid civil war and political collapse, but there is a difference between legal encouragement and legal permission of the assertion of ethnic or sectarian identity. Legal encouragement, by naming ethnic or sectarian names, runs the risk that such arrangements may transform what can be a personal or group resource into an immutable fact and even a stigma. A Sikh may

---

6. Tawfic Farah, ed., *Pan-Arabism and Arab Nationalism: The Continuing Debate* (Boulder, Colo.: Westview Press, 1987), pp. 1–18.

7. Walker Conner, "Ethnocentrism," in Myron Weiner and Samuel Huntington, eds., *Understanding Political Development* (Boston: Little, Brown, 1987), pp. 103–159.

8. "No Easy Answers; Tribalism Is the Bone of Independent Africa," *The Economist*, September 10, 1994, p. 48.

take pride in his topknot and turban, but a Polish or German Jew surely did not in his yellow badge with the Star of David.

Community

Like individual and group identity, communities are in a constant process of dissolution and redefinition. The range of legal remedies open to them are laws protecting minority rights, rights to lingual and cultural expression, autonomy and self-rule, and, ultimately, statehood. Morton Halperin and his coauthors argue that a people or community is determined by the degree to which its members share ethnic, linguistic, religious, and cultural bonds *and* a perception on the part of its members of "groupness."[9] The danger here is that even if one can satisfy these criteria *at a moment in time*, one may proceed to lock them in. It seems to me that the Bosnian Muslims tried to avoid just such a locking-in—not that, at this point in time, they are not Muslim and Bosnian but that to remain so juridically would deny them the chance to be something else, something less easily targeted by their adversaries.

Communities hold the seeds of both considerable good and considerable evil. Nations, which are the communities that have dominated international politics for the past century or so, contain these same seeds. The analysis of communities and nations produces images of benevolent and malevolent natures. The dividing line seems to be the degree of voluntarism and consent involved in membership.[10] Communitarians such as Amitai Etzioni see as the enemy a dehumanizing individualism that leads to the abnegation of individual and group responsibility to one's immediate fellows, and the abdication of duties and rights to an invasive government. The image one takes away from Etzioni and others is that of porous groups, constantly emptying and

9. Halperin and Scheffer with Small, *Self-Determination in the New World Order*, p. 47.

10. Nadia Urbinati, "Two Ideas of Nation," unpublished paper, European Research Seminar, Princeton University, November 16, 1992. Urbinati contrasts nations joined and held together by political consent with those with the following four characteristics: (1) the individual cannot be understood except in terms of the group to which he or she belongs; (2) the community is an organic whole; (3) traditions and beliefs are good because they are "ours"; and (4) the nation, like an organism, has needs that must be satisfied. This latter understanding, Jonathan Eyal argues, is still dominant in Europe (see his "Liberating Europe from Nationalism Will Not Be Easy," *International Herald Tribune,* May 24, 1994). Guhenno regards as "trompeuses" all those putative nations that have not traversed the hundreds of years of bloodshed and savagery that yielded the real McCoy in Europe. See Jean-Marie Guhenno, *La fin de la democratie* (Paris: Flammarion, 1993), p. 21.

filling without precise criteria for membership, rules of exclusion, mechanisms to sanction and monitor, and a clear resource base.

The good community does, however, have goals such as the protection of the family, dispute resolution, self-help, and the inculcation of benign values, but it is resolutely voluntarist. It is governed by "the gentle prodding of kin, friends, neighbors, and community members," and the government should have a role only if there is a kind of market failure in the community provision of mutual support.[11] Michael Taylor echoes this view and goes further to suggest (based both on iterative game theory and empirical observation) that the altruism fostered in community interaction engenders yet more altruism, as it becomes a norm defining legitimacy within the group.[12]

Etzioni himself recognizes the two faces of community (as does Daniel Moynihan) but implicitly sees two distinct genera rather than an evolutionary process by which the good can become the bad and vice versa.[13] In his *Foreign Policy* article against the evils of self-determination, he worries about the inherent intolerance that characterizes most of those communities seeking to rule themselves. Intolerance, he rightly argues, cannot be accommodated with voluntarism and consent. However, it seems to me unlikely that the "nested" communities of family, neighborhood, towns, and nation that Etzioni espouses would not, over time, risk falling into the same trap of perceiving hostile or inferior "outgroups" and attributing to them characteristics worthy of condemnation, if not open enmity.[14] Altruism and other voluntarily held norms may not be effective substitutes for self-righteousness, contempt, and conflict in maintaining group cohesion. Etzioni's nesting image implies territoriality and contiguity, factors that often militate for intolerance of "outsiders."[15]

---

11. Amitai Etzioni, *The Spirit of Community* (New York: Crown, 1993), p. 15.

12. Michael Taylor, *The Possibility of Cooperation* (Cambridge: Cambridge University Press, 1987), pp. 166–179.

13. Guilain Denoeux demonstrates the "two-edged" nature of political and social networks in major urban centers of the Middle East (Beirut, Cairo, and Teheran). Guilain Denoeux, *Urban Unrest in the Middle East: A Comparative Study of Informal Networks in Egypt, Iran, and Lebanon* (Albany: State University of New York Press, 1993).

14. Amitai Etzioni, "The Evils of Self-Determination," *Foreign Policy* 89 (Winter 1992–1993), pp. 21–35.

15. For a similar argument, see Iris Marion Young, *Justice and the Politics of Difference* (Princeton: Princeton University Press, 1990); and Gellner as cited in Hurst Hannum, *Autonomy, Sovereignty, and Self-Determination: The Accommodation of Conflicting Rights* (Philadelphia: University of Pennsylvania Press, 1990), p. 455.

It is possible to conceive of communities held together by shared (benign) norms, social causes,[16] policy issues, or shared knowledge. Yet such communities, to the extent they exist, appear inherently episodic and ephemeral. Communities that endure typically manage resources and territory. Whether a tribe, a professional association, or an agricultural cooperative, there are rules of membership and of exclusion, and they are perceived by their members to be enduring. If this latter perception is not widespread, members will lack the incentives to honor group norms.[17] Rather than the voluntarism and consent evoked by Etzioni, we have in this perspective the implicit coercion of ostracism and loss of status coupled with access to, or exclusion from, valued resources. This kind of community ever teeters on the brink of xenophobia and contempt for any other group that might encroach on its territory.

Minorities Within Minorities

Solving one minority problem may exacerbate two others. Halperin et al. argue that the post–World War I territorial settlements were doomed because, in the effort to create strategic national buffers against Germany, the new entities contained large, unhappy minorities that often spilled across borders.[18] Careful territorial design, it is implied, could obviate such problems, but such design may lead to the reductio ad absurdum of the Vance-Owen plan for the division of Bosnia. Who could make political or territorial sense of Abkhazia, of whose population the Abkhaz constitute only 17 percent, whereas Georgians account for 46 percent, the Armenians 14.6 percent, and various Slavic peoples 17 percent? Even the Abkhaz themselves are divided among Muslims and Orthodox Christians.[19]

In the Sudan, Iraq, and in colonial Lebanon, as we shall see further on, one minority's oppressor becomes another minority's protector or liberator. Turcoman and Arab Christians living among the majority Kurds of northern Iraq look to Ankara or Baghdad for protection. The equatorial tribes of southern Sudan have looked to Khartoum for protection against the region's dominant Dinka tribe. For this very reason,

---

16. See Iris Marion Young, *Justice and the Politics of Difference.*
17. Elinor Ostrom, *Governing the Commons: The Evolution of Institutions for Collective Action* (New York: Cambridge University Press, 1990).
18. Halperin and Scheffer with Small, *Self-Determination in the New World Order,* p. 19.
19. Paul Henze, "Caucasian Madness," *Turkish Times,* November 15, 1992.

clearly recognized by the players on the ground, the temptation of ethnic cleansing becomes strong. The way to deal with minorities within minorities is to expel or regroup them rather than accommodate them. The sorry history of the nation-state is liable to be replayed in the microentities now seeking self-rule.

Thus the issue today within existing nation-states and in international politics is to avoid offering material and other incentives to would-be mininations. Politicians are all too ready to take advantage of any outside support that will allow them to maintain and consolidate their power. This is not to deny the legitimacy of some such movements, but acknowledging legitimacy is a far cry from Conor Cruise O'Brien's assertion that most self-determination movements have been driven to that position out of desperation.[20] The Quebecois, the Bosnian Serbs, the Kurds of eastern Anatolia, the Punjabi Sikhs, the Kashmiris, the Catalonians, the Scots, the Biafrans, and so on have been politically disadvantaged and culturally confined—but until or unless they resorted to violence, they were not threatened with physical harm as a community.

What should be put in place are legal instruments that are neutral in the face of such demands. National law should allow for the near total freedom to organize nonviolently along whatever lines any subset of its citizens sees fit, but without granting specific groups specific rights. So too should the international community and international organizations urge the same norms upon their constituent parts, supplemented with monitoring and disclosure.

This recommendation is premised on the existence of states that can draft and implement laws, that is, states that, more or less, effectively govern. If violence is so widespread and deep-seated that central authority has collapsed, and if the units in contention are defined by ethnicity or sect, explicit guarantees of group rights and the naming of group names may be the unavoidable price of establishing some semblance of order. That would appear to be the case in Rwanda and Bosnia, but not in Tajikistan, Somalia, or Liberia, where warlords and clans are the contending units.

Case Studies

The cases I examine in order to illustrate the points argued earlier are drawn from the Middle East. There has been an important opening up of

---

20. Conor Cruise O'Brien, as cited in Hannum, *Autonomy, Sovereignty, and Self-Determination.*

the debate in the region over minority rights, including self-determination, in recent years. This is a hopeful sign. But even though the heretofore unchallenged orthodoxy of the unitary, Jacobin state, founded on one supreme national identity rather than political consent, has been subjected to criticism, the old guard is still in power in most places.[21]

The populist, unitary states that have dominated the region since the 1960s are under assault with Islamist movements wielding the greatest numbers and mass appeal. However, if such movements come to power, it seems reasonable to expect that they may do little to undermine the juridical and political character of the states and bounded territories they inherit. Almost certainly, they will make no concessions to minority rights, as the examples of Iran since 1979 and the Sudan since 1989 amply demonstrate.

The other source of assault comes from small, liberalist, generally secular movements that, through human rights organizations, think tanks, and occasionally political parties, promote democratization and the recognition of minority problems and denied rights. In Turkey, it should be noted, a substantial part of the large, secularist intelligentsia

---

21. See Burhan Ghaliyun, *The Sectarian Order: From the State to the Tribe* (Beirut: Arab Cultural Center, 1990) (in Arabic); and Sa'ad Elddin Ibrahim, *Considerations on the Question of Minorities* (Kuwait, Cairo: Dar Su'ad al-Sabah, 1992) (in Arabic).

When Sa'ad Elddin Ibrahim's Ibn Khaldoun Center in Cairo tried to organize a conference on the UN Declaration on the Rights of Minorities and Peoples of the Arab World and Middle East, the criticism was so vociferous that the venue had to be shifted to Cyprus. In particular, chauvinist Islamists such as 'Adil Hussein and old Nasserists such as Mohammed Hassanein Heikal trotted out the threadbare accusations that Ibrahim and his colleagues were playing directly into the hands of those forces bent on subverting the unity and security of the Arab world. Even some of Egypt's most prominent Coptic (Christian) leaders denounced the reference to Egypt's Christians as a minority as opposed to Egyptian citizens who happen to be of Christian faith. See Sa'ad Elddin Ibrahim, "The Wrong Side of History," *Civil Society* (May 14, 1994).

In Turkey over the past decade it has become possible to read the writings and speeches of prominent Kurdish leaders and intellectuals, including those of the now incarcerated Abdullah Ocalan, leader of the Marxist-Leninist PKK (Kurdish Workers Party). The Turkish government maintains emergency law in the southeast of the country and savagely deals with what is justifiably called PKK terrorism. There may be little sympathy for the Kurdish cause among the bulk of the Turkish population, but the cause itself, in all of its expressions from cultural assertion to separatism, is well known and well publicized. See, for example, Metin Sever, *The Kurdish Question: What Our Intellectuals Think* (Istanbul: Cem Yayinevi, 1992) (in Turkish). For a perspective on changes in Kurdish politics both in Iraq and Turkey after the Gulf War and a heightened interest and sympathy for Kurdish claims, see Denise Natali, "International Aid, Regional Politics, and the Kurdish Issue in Iraq After the Gulf War," Occasional Paper, no. 31 (Abu Dhabi: Emirates Center for Strategic Studies and Research, Spring 1999), pp. 27–28.

is as "religiously" committed to the unity of a Turkish nation as it is opposed to the Islamic trend in Turkey. The Turkish and other secular intelligentsia (with the exception of a handful of socialists) are not liberal, and they are for the most part unsympathetic to the Kurdish or other sectarian and ethnic causes.

Southern Sudan

In 1972 Sudan launched an experiment in regional self-rule that was unprecedented for Africa and the Middle East. A radical, populist state devoted to the cause of Arab nationalism and Arab unity, led by the military authoritarian Gaafar Mohammed Nimeiri, negotiated an agreement on regional autonomy with the commanders of the guerrilla fighters of southern Sudan. The three southernmost provinces of Sudan, containing about a third of the country's population, had always been racially (black African Nilotic), linguistically, and religiously distinct from the northern, Arabized, Muslim populations. There is no need to go into the details of this case, which are reasonably well known (see Deng, Chapter 10 in this volume). Rather, I want to highlight certain aspects that speak to points raised earlier.

Since the outbreak of civil war in the South in 1955, on the eve of Sudan's independence, southern grievances have been driven by two interrelated factors. The first is the fear that a numerically superior North, in control of the country's infrastructure, military, and best-trained human resources, would totally subordinate the South in its project for national construction. Second, the South feared that the Arab Muslim North would seek union with Arab Muslim neighbors, thereby diminishing still further the weight and leverage of the South in the new state. Prospects of union with Nasserist Egypt following independence in 1956 triggered the mutinies of southern garrisons in 1955. Again in 1969, Nimeiri led Sudan into the Federation of Arab Republics with Egypt and Libya.[22] In the late 1970s Egypt and Sudan once again pursued integration, and since the late 1980s, with a militantly Islamic military dictatorship in place, the fear has been that the South will be lost in an Islamic sea.

The extraordinary aspect of what transpired in 1972 is that Nimeiri stepped out of character—out of his own as well as out of the general character of Arab populist military leaders. Already in 1971 he had suspended Sudan's membership in the Federation of Arab Republics, and

---

22. Peter Bechtold, "New Attempts at Arab Cooperation: The Federation of Arab Republics," *Middle East Journal* 27, no. 2 (1973), pp. 152–172.

then in Addis Ababa, he signed the act granting the southern provinces regional self-government. The act recognized the three southern provinces as constituting a single region with English as its principal language. The federal government retained control over defense, external affairs, currency and coinage, interregional transport, communications, customs, and foreign trade. The High Executive Council (HEC) was ambiguously responsible to both the president of the republic and to the elected Peoples Regional Assembly. The latter would propose to the president of the republic the name or names of candidates for the presidency of the High Executive Council.

The southern negotiators succeeded in entrenching the entire agreement in the new national constitution, adopted the following year and stipulating that any amendments to the act must accord with its basic provisions. That understanding was to be violated a decade later. Finally, Articles 9 and 16 of the new constitution restricted the extent to which Islamic law could shape regional legislation.

Perhaps all these efforts were doomed to failure: the South was too poor to rely on its own resources to promote development and had constantly to turn to the North for support; the president of the republic's powers to appoint and dismiss were so broad that no local leader could have a secure power base. Probably more important, however, was that when the locus of some decisionmaking and allocation of scarce public goods shifted from Khartoum to Juba, the nature of political rivalries and alliances shifted with them. It became clear that the Dinka tribe, the single largest in the South, would dominate the regional government. In that *rapport de forces* smaller tribes, such as the Nuer and Shilluk, but especially the equatorial tribes in the southern highlands, could now look to their erstwhile enemies in Khartoum as potential protectors.

When the cabinet was headed by the Dinka Abel Alier, it was nonetheless the case that this body and other top positions were filled with careful attention to a myriad of tribal groups. Abel Alier, at least, was fully conscious of the perceived threat of the Dinka and sought to allay the fears of other tribes by distributing political rewards on a tribal basis. Ultimately, this strategy did not save him, the Dinka, or southern autonomy, but it did reinforce a system of incentives that rendered tribes the meaningful units in political competition.

Nimeiri was not long in seizing the opportunities offered him after 1972 to begin to broker the internal politics of the new region. He may have suspected, even in signing the regional autonomy act, that such opportunities would present themselves. One of those who began to cooperate with him in an implicit anti-Dinka alliance was the former guerrilla commander and equatorian, Joseph Lagu. When he was president of the HEC (1978–1980) he made common cause with Khartoum in an effort to set up six provinces in the South, deeply eroding thereby the authority of the HEC in Juba and simultaneously opening up many new patronage opportunities in the provincial governments.[23] An indirect ally in these efforts was Hassan al-Turabi, at the time attorney general and the leader of the Muslim Brethren and someone who wanted ultimately to see the Addis Ababa Agreement scuttled altogether.

Southern Sudan, like many areas in which ethnic or sectarian resistance is met fiercely by central authorities, has strategic value. The sources of the White Nile flow through it so that both northern Sudan and Egypt look to the South as a potential source of disruption, as well as a source of augmented flow, of the White Nile. In the middle 1970s Egypt and Sudan agreed to excavate a jointly funded canal to drain a portion of the Sudd swamps of the South in order to reduce surface evaporation and deliver more water downstream. Southerners saw the canal scheme as part of a strategy to open the South to northern commercial and military penetration and eventually to Egyptian peasants who would be brought in to farm new irrigated areas adjacent to the canal and to dilute the local Nilotic populations with Arab Muslim stock.

To compound matters, in 1979 significant amounts of petroleum were discovered in a zone straddling the line demarcating the southern provinces from the northern, and Khartoum immediately asserted its right to develop the field and to refine the oil outside the southern region.

In October 1981, Nimeiri dissolved the National Regional Assembly and appointed an interim regional government. The culmination of this process came in summer 1983 when Nimeiri officially divided the South into three separate provinces. A year later Sudan signed an integration charter with Egypt, and southern fears that Egyptian peasants would flood into the region were rekindled. For the southerners, the *coup de grâce ou de trop* came in the form of Nimeiri's decree making the Islamic *shari'a* the law of the land. The civil war that had ended in 1972 started once again.[24]

Although Nimeiri himself was deposed in 1985, his military successor, General Siwar al-Dhahab, although rescinding the redivision of the South, did not rescind the application of *shari'a*.[25] For his part,

---

23. Andrew Deng, "Political Power and Decentralization in the Sudan," *Decentralization & Development Review*, no. 1 (Spring 1981), pp. 6–7.

24. See Francis Deng's Chapter 10 in this volume.

25. Hannum, *Autonomy, Sovereignty, and Self-Determination*, p. 315; and Special Correspondent, "Khartoum's Greatest Challenge," *Merip Reports* (September 1985), pp. 11–18.

General John Garang, who formed the Sudan People's Liberation Army (SPLA) in 1983, demanded that the *shari'a* be the law nowhere in Sudan and proclaimed his movement's goal to be the liberation of the entire Sudan from reactionary Islamism and dictatorship. He did not then espouse, and until recently has not espoused, secession.

In 1991 the SPLA split apart, nominally over the issue of whether to fight for secession. Two Nuer military leaders in the SPLA, Riak Machar and Lam Akol, broke from the SPLA and remained passive in the face of a subsequent offensive of northern troops against Garang's forces. It is reasonably clear that what is at play here is the resentment of the Nuer and other tribes of the domination of the SPLA by the Dinka. After repeated and failed rounds of negotiations with the government in Khartoum, Garang himself has moved toward endorsement of a self-determination referendum with the possibility of a confederative solution between two independent states.[26]

In this situation, there is no solution—other than continued slaughter—but one anchored in tribalism, language, and race. The killing has gone on between northerners and southerners since 1955 with an eleven-year hiatus. There is not the remotest chance that the benign, voluntarist communitarianism espoused by Etzioni and others can take root here. These communities, although nested, have been made compulsory through killing. The killing, of course, has been carried out by brother against brother in order to hold the community together, and it has taken place among groups sharing the same nest—Dinka against Nuer against Equatorians—as much as against the Arab Muslim North. If the South asserts its autonomy, it may come internally to resemble Lebanon with tribal cantons, elite deals across tribes, periodic slaughter, and ethnic cleansing. If it remains within Sudan, the price of its remaining will surely be to institutionalize ethnic, religious, and racial proportional representation. An end to the killing may be worth this iron cage, but it will be an inheritance with a high price tag.

Lebanon

For a couple of decades following World War II, Lebanon became one of the darlings of modernization studies—a pluralist, free-market polity and economy led by civilians and openly embracing its sectarianism. In place of the stultifying corporatist and nationalist populism of its Arab neighbors, it maintained a freewheeling cosmopolitanism

---

26. 'Abd al-Malek 'Awda, "Self-Determination in the Sudan," *al-Ahram al-Iqtisadi,* January 24, 1994, p. 90 (in Arabic).

often secretly admired and experienced by its most severe Arab critics. In the boom years of the 1960s, the brief civil war of 1958 was
looked back upon more as a growing pain than a signal of things to
come.

As early as 1926, under French colonial auspices, Lebanon had
begun to devise a system of legalized confessional representation and
government. A census in 1934, the last to be officially taken, showed
the Christians of Lebanon outnumbering the Muslims at a ratio of 6:5.
That ratio, until 1989, was constitutionally graven in stone.[27] Through
the National Pact, negotiated on the eve of independence after World
War II—by which the Christians of Lebanon forswore any attempts to
seek succor from their traditional Western (Christian) supporters and
the Muslims forswore any attempt to bring Lebanon into a larger Arab
(Muslim) entity—the ratio became the guiding principle for allocating
seats in the parliament and in the distribution of all significant posts in
the government and civil service. Article 95 of the constitution states:
"Provisionally . . . and in order to promote harmony and justice, the
communities will be equitably represented in government employment
and in the composition of the ministry without jeopardizing the good of
the State." "Equitably," Pierre Rondot observes, in fact means proportionally to the numerical size of each community.[28]

The foundation of the system was confessional equilibrium, but
subsidiary rules of representation tried to promote cross-confessional
alliances. Electoral districts were multiconfessional, and powerful political chieftains (the famous or notorious *zu'ama*), always prominent
leaders of a particular sect, constructed multiconfessional lists of candidates in order to win a majority in their districts. Note, however, that
even as such alliances were forged, and although they may for a time
have promoted moderation among sects, the only meaningful political
payoffs were to sectarian representation as opposed to parties, ideologies, programs, or economic interests, per se.[29] Michael Suleiman
posits: "Since tradition, fortified by the 1943 national pact, allocates the
high state offices each to one of the major sects, the prominent members in each sect engage in fights to determine which 'clan' is to capture

---

27. Michael Suleiman, *Political Parties in Lebanon* (Ithaca, N.Y.: Cornell
University Press, 1967), p. 50.
28. Pierre Rondot, "The Political Institutions of Lebanese Democracy," in
Leonard Binder, ed., *Politics in Lebanon* (New York: John Wiley, 1966), p. 129.
29. Michael Hudson, *The Precarious Republic: Political Modernization in
Lebanon* (New York: Random House, 1968), p. 217.

the prize: the presidency for the Maronites, the premiership for the Sunnis, the speakership for the Shi'a."[30]

Competition and conflict were thus as much intrasectarian over quotas, so to speak, as they were intersectarian, or more so. Even in the run-up to the 1958 civil war, Maronites were divided over the legitimacy and legality of President Camille Chamoun's effort to change the constitution so that he could succeed himself. As Donald Horowitz observed in his comment on Arend Lijphart's notion of the "grand coalition" in consociational democracy, it "depended upon and exacerbated preexisting subethnic (sic) cleavages, based on family, clan and region. . . . Lebanese subgroups were tailor-made for this system, and they rose to its opportunities."[31]

Lijphart lays out a set of principles for power sharing that may be summarized in five points: (1) there must be participation of "all significant groups"; (2) there must be a high degree of autonomy among all significant groups; (3) there must be proportionality in representation among the groups; (4) minorities must retain a right of veto over vital affairs affecting their fate; and (5) it is best that the majority be underrepresented.[32]

These principles are fine insofar as they suggest solutions within a democratic framework and within existing units. The major concession made to self-determination lies in the autonomy of groups and the minority veto. Lijphart is at pains to allow for groups to change, for some to redefine themselves or disappear altogether. Yet could this possibly happen in political practice? First, who defines or decides what are the "significant groups," and, once having been so defined, will they not be named and given legal blessing? Specific groups are granted autonomy because at a moment in time, they are judged to be significant and able to perpetuate that moment for as long as possible. Lijphart's invocation of flexible identity is analytically comforting but in practice unrealistic unless no "significant groups" are legally identified as such in the first place.

The curious, if not poignant, aspect of Lebanon's confessional system is that it was always underlain by a note of guilt or at least sheepishness. Article 95 of the constitution saw confessional representation as temporary and expedient. So, too, when thirteen years of civil war

---

30. Suleiman, *Political Parties in Lebanon*, p. 51.

31. Donald Horowitz, *Ethnic Groups in Conflict* (Berkeley: University of California Press, 1985), p. 654. See also Arend Lijphart, "Consociational Democracy," *World Politics* 21, no. 2 (1969), pp. 207–225.

32. Lijphart, "Consociational Democracy," p. 503.

came to an end in 1989, confessionalism was once again instituted "temporarily." The 1989 Taif Accords, negotiated in Taif, Saudi Arabia, by the warring sects and including the Palestinians, set forth the principle of abolishing sectarianism in representation, in the civil service, and on identity cards. The accords state: "Until the parliament has laid down an electoral bill which is free from sectarian restraints, the parliamentary seats will be distributed along the following lines: (a) equal numbers for Christians and Muslims; (b) proportionally among the sects of the two groups; and (c) proportionally among the regions."[33]

Sectarianism is thus provisionally alive and well except that the 6:5 ratio has been abandoned for 5:5.[34] The old political incentive system has been reinvented. In summer 1993, seventy high-level civil servants were appointed, and it was obvious that new sectarian *zu'ama*— President Elias Hrawi (Maronite), Prime Minister Rafik Hariri (Sunni), and Speaker Nabih Berri (Shi'a)—had divvied up the posts on a strictly sectarian basis.[35] Further, the Taif Accords greatly diminish the powers of the president and create a balanced confessional troika combined with a decisionmaking process based on majority votes in the Council of Ministers. Ghassan Salam summed up the changes thus: "The institutional diffusion of the former [Maronite] hegemon's power is such that the concept of representation will henceforth prevail, in a most debilitating manner, over the necessity for government. The logic of acceptable representation of the confessional groups, not to mention the different tendencies within each of these groups, brings with it almost complete paralysis of the state apparatus."[36] With protestations to the contrary, the Lebanese, abetted by the Syrians and Saudis, have reinvented a confessional cage.

The Kurds

The Kurdish case is strewn with more complex issues than are manifest in either Sudan or Lebanon. The starting point seems clear and compelling. The Kurds are a people who, measured by precedence of residency, have been throughout recorded history in the mountainous area that today joins Turkey, Syria, Iraq, Iran, and parts of Armenia. They

---

33. FBIS-NES-89-204 (October 24, 1989).
34. Richard A. Norton, "Lebanon After Ta'if: Is the Civil War Over?" *Middle East Journal* 45, no. 3 (1991), pp. 457–473.
35. *Saudi Gazette,* May 1, 1994.
36. Ghassan Salamé, "Small Is Pluralistic: Democracy as an Instrument of Civil Peace," in Ghassan Salamé, ed., *Democracy Without Democrats? The Renewal of Politics in the Muslim World* (London: I. B. Tauris, 1994), p. 104.

predate Arabs, Mongols, and Turks. They have a powerful historical claim to peoplehood. Moreover, that claim was recognized in Wilson's Fourteen Points and in the 1920 Treaty of Sèvres. Southern Sudan was never accorded such international recognition until 1972, and Lebanon was Kurdistan's inverse, a nation created or cobbled together by imperial fiat.[37] Kurdistan was eventually broken asunder by imperial fiat.

The Kurds today may number upward of 23 million (with another 1 million in the diaspora), surely well beyond whatever implicit measure of nationhood the international community retains. In Turkey and Iraq they compose between 20 and 30 percent of the total population,[38] and in Iran the Kurds are about 10 percent of the population. Finally, albeit ineffectively, they have periodically fought for their autonomy and independence. Such violent struggles, however, have never been waged as a people but rather as clans, ideological currents, and even religious brotherhoods. The story of the Kurds today is one of a large single ethnic community fractured along political, economic, geographical, and sociological lines. Whereas nearly all Kurds make claims to common ethnic and cultural origins, they have, since the division of Kurdistan into four main states, developed their sense of national identity alongside the culture and politics in the states in which they reside.

The Kurds are ethnically distinct from the populations among which they live, except for the Iranians. They speak their own language(s), and all are Muslims, predominantly Sunni with some Shi'a in Iran. They are thus "objectively" more cohesive than the southern Sudanese but not more so than the Lebanese (except in the historical sense). Yet that cohesiveness is more apparent than real.

The three major Kurdish dialects, Zaza, Kurmanji, and Sorani, are as much alike as English and German.[39] Conflicts among Kurdish clans—highlanders versus lowlanders, valley versus valley—have been as deep seated as those between Kurds and non-Kurds. In the contemporary era, Kurdish factions in one country have been routinely used by another country to contain its own Kurds. Mulla Mustafa Barzani lent himself to these ends in alliances with the Iranians, and more recently,

---

37. I am not of the school that argues that all colonial creations are artificial. As a North American, I do not believe it takes centuries, much less millennia, for a national or other identity to form. It may be a matter of only a generation or two, and the identity is nonetheless real despite its adolescence (Guhenno notwithstanding). Lebanon was France's brainchild; it is today very much its own.

38. Mohammed M.A. Ahmed, "Demographic Changes in Kurdistan-Iraq, 1957–1988," *Namah* 2, no. 1 (1994), p. 7.

39. Philip G. Kreyenbroek, "On the Kurdish Language," in Philip G. Kreyenbroek and Stefan Sperl, eds., *The Kurds: A Contemporary Overview* (London: Routledge, 1992), p. 71.

both Jalal Talabani and Mas'ud Barzani have cooperated with the Turkish military in suppressing the PKK (the Kurdish Workers Party).[40]

Kurds, like Lebanon's Maronites, have been too ready to seek the backing of regional or great-power neighbors: in the early 1970s Mulla Mustafa Barzani cast in his lot with the United States and Israel, and in 1975, when the Nixon administration, and especially Secretary of State Henry Kissinger, no longer had any strategic use for the Kurds, they were thrown to their fate and crushed by Saddam Hussein. This type of instrumental behavior of seeking outside support to advance their political and economic interests continued as the political context brought new opportunities during the late 1990s. While Barzani strengthened his alliances with Turkey and Baghdad, Talabani turned to Iran, Syria, and cross-border Kurdish parties to balance political power. Although Barzani has no real loyalty to Saddam Hussein, he turned to Baghdad and formed a temporary alliance with Hussein's military forces in September 1996 as a way of controlling his rival Talabani and his Patriotic Union of Kurdistan (PUK).

The Kurdish region, straddling at least three international borders, is interlaced with substantial non-Kurdish minorities. Except for a few families, most Jews of Kurdistan have departed, but there is still a substantial Christian Arab population, especially in Erbil, Mosul, and Kirkuk. In 1932, the British moved Assyrian Christians from Turkey into northern Iraq, especially into the territory inhabited by the Barzani clans. They were, to say the least, not welcome. The Turcoman population, numbering perhaps 200,000, once dominated Kirkuk until the Arab head of state, Abd al-Karim Qassim, began to move the Turcomans out in favor of the Kurds. The Ba'ath regime in the 1970s began to deport Arabs to the Kurdish areas and Sunni Kurds to the Shi'a areas of the south. The fact that many of these movements were forced does not diminish the dilemma the Kurdish region faces today. Autonomy or independence would inevitably raise the level of risk to the minorities remaining in the region. The temptation on the part of these non-Kurdish minorities to reach out to Baghdad, whether to Saddam or to his successor(s), would be natural and irresistible.

The region in which Kurds predominate is of great strategic importance. The discovery of oil at Kirkuk, in present-day Iraq, probably determined that the former Ottoman province of Mosul was, in 1926, formally awarded to the British-mandated Kingdom of Iraq and not to

---

40. Among others, see Hanna Yusif Farij, "The Kurdish National Question in Iraq and Foreign Intervention in the Region," *Political Readings* 2 (Tampa, Fla., 1993), pp. 9–42 (in Arabic).

Turkey. Today the Kirkuk region holds about one-third of Iraq's proven oil reserves. Were Kurdish Iraq to form its own state, as Graham Fuller sees as a distinct possibility, the issue for the rest of Iraq would not be one primarily of the loss of oil revenues, for two-thirds of the reserves would remain in the south of the country, but rather one of the economic viability that an independent Iraqi Kurdistan, containing Kirkuk, would derive from the remaining third.[41] In addition, Kurdistan, writ large, encompasses the headwaters of both the Tigris and Euphrates Rivers, the lifeblood of agriculture in northeast Syria and lower Iraq and Turkey. Self-determination, in this context, faces formidable odds, and no appeals to justice or equity can alter that fact.

In Turkey, more than in Iraq and perhaps more than in Iran, Kurds have become mestizo Turks. Former Turkish president Turgut Özal stated publicly that his mother was Kurdish. One of his foreign ministers, Hikmet Çetin, is fully Kurdish. Over the centuries intermarriage between Kurds and Turks must have been very common, to the extent that many Turks have Kurdish blood. A survey of Turkish businessmen revealed 100 of the most prominent to be of Kurdish origin. For some, their only link to their Kurdish roots was through music and food.[42] It is said that even the notorious leader of the PKK, Abdullah "Apo" Öcalan, has a very poor command of Kurdish and is much more comfortable in Turkish. This observation is not to extol the virtues of perhaps forced assimilation but rather to note that it is a fact that cannot today be ignored.

Thus there is not much straightforward about the Kurdish cause, but there is enough that we must note the historical markers of the denial of nationhood. On the strength of the 1923 Lausanne Treaty, the promises of the Treaty of Sèvres were first overturned and then reversed in the Turkish-Iraqi accord of 1926. Successive Kurdish uprisings in Turkey, in 1925 and 1932, culminated in that of Dersim in 1938. After its brutal suppression, the word *Kurd* and the public speaking of Kurdish were for all practical purposes forbidden. Dersim itself was razed and rebuilt under the name Tunceli.[43] Only toward the end of the 1980s, prodded by President Özal in his last days, was there a begrudging recognition of the Kurdish situation in southeast Anatolia.

That fact had been implicitly recognized years earlier as Turkey

----

41. Graham Fuller, *Iraq in the Next Decade: Will Iraq Survive Until 2002?* Rand Note N-3591-DAG (Santa Monica: Rand, 1993), p. vi.
42. Lamia Torunlu, "100 Rich Kurds," *Nokta* (June 6–12, 1993), pp. 12–18 (in Turkish).
43. Nader Entessar, *Kurdish Ethnonationalism* (Boulder, Colo.: Lynne Rienner, 1992).

marshaled staggering national resources to undertake the Southeast Anatolian Project (or GAP, by its Turkish acronym) that would, when completed in the early twenty-first century, use the headwaters of the Euphrates and the Tigris Rivers to generate hydroelectric power and irrigate some 1.6 million hectares of land in areas partially inhabited by Kurds.[44]

Along with the carrot has come the stick, applied more judiciously by President Özal than by his successor, Süleyman Demirel. Öcalan's PKK stepped up guerrilla activities in southeast Anatolia (with Syrian backing) with the restoration of civilian government and law in 1983. Since 1991 the fighting, the terrorist activities of Kurds against Kurds and the repression of the Turkish government against the Kurds, has become vicious. Emergency law has prevailed in the southeast for over a decade, and Turkish military and police have free rein to pursue whomever they suspect of complicity with the PKK.

Finally, by late 1998 the Turkish military gained the upper hand in the region and forced the remaining PKK forces to retreat. Turkish diplomatic and military pressure compelled the Syrian government to ask Öcalan to leave the country. Subsequently, Öcalan was arrested in Kenya in 1999 and brought back to Turkey. Although he was sentenced to death by a court, the hard-pressed Turkish government decided not to implement the verdict in order to appease the international community, particulary by the EU. This decision played a very significant role in diminishing the PKK's activities.[45]

Thus, while Turkey has in general successfully restored democracy since 1983, and even allowed the election of Kurdish deputies in coalition with a recognized political party, there is virtually no democracy or protection of human rights in southeast Anatolia. The solution to Turkey's Kurdish problem, it seems to me, is neither continued military repression nor regional autonomy, let alone independence, but rather the lifting of emergency law and the extension of real democratic freedoms to the regions in which Kurds predominate. Öcalan, for his part, has at least rhetorically abandoned the quest for independence and accepted that for "at least forty years" the Kurds would need to be part of

---

44. It is moot how many Kurds will ever benefit from this project, as the prime areas for irrigation fall outside of regions in which the Kurds predominate. Yet the combination of industry utilizing hydropower and farms demanding labor are likely to generate employment for Kurdish populations. They may, however, come more to resemble the Palestinians working in Israel than direct citizen beneficiaries of a state-financed regional boom.

45. This paragraph was contributed by an outside reviewer.

Turkey.[46] At his trial Öcalan defended the same thesis and proposed a better understanding between Turkey and Kurds.[47]

In Iraq there has always been an implicit, and sometimes explicit, recognition of the Kurdish situation. The Iraqi state has never put the word *Arab* into its official title, either under the monarchy or since the establishment of the republic in 1958. After 1958, and above all in 1963, Kurdish factions united in opposition to Iraq's inclusion in the United Arab Republic, first formed by Syria and Egypt. A certain number of Kurds were generally co-opted into the Iraqi ministerial cabinet, so that there was power sharing of a sort. The Ba'ath regime in 1970 went so far as to declare Iraq a binational state, and in 1974 President Ahmad Hassan al-Bakr announced a regional autonomy plan for the Kurdish region of Iraq (not including Kirkuk). By this time, the Barzani clans had been recruited by Israeli and U.S. intelligence to try to destabilize the pro-Soviet Ba'ath regime and did not seek to take advantage of the autonomy plan. In March 1975, the Shah of Iran and Saddam Hussein agreed in Algiers to cosovereignty of the waters of the Shatt al-'Arab in exchange for which the Shah stopped all support to the Barzani faction. Iraqi government forces then crushed the Kurdish *peshmerga* (guerrilla fighters).

In the aftermath of Desert Storm, portions of Iraqi Kurdistan, those lying north of the thirty-second parallel, are under U.S.-UN protection. That region now lives in de facto independence, albeit in horrendous economic circumstances. Its three immediate neighbors—

---

46. Remarks to *Hüriyet* in April 1990, cited by 'Ali 'Uthman, "The Kurdish Workers Party and the Future of the Kurdish Question in Turkey," *Political Readings* 2 (Tampa, Fla., 1993), p. 56 (in Arabic).

47. Since Öcalan's arrest he has taken on a new strategy of emphasizing political negotiation and the termination of armed struggle. In the attempt to push a real dialogue with the Turkish elite and encourage democratization, the PKK has altered its political program, surrendered some of its leaders, and appealed to the European Parliament, European governments, and human rights organizations. Given the large and influential diaspora Kurdish community in European capitals, the Kurdish issue has also become integrally tied to Turkey's relationship with Europe and, in particular, its candidature for the European Union. Although Ecevit and his military cliques emphasize the independence of Turkey's internal policy and although the government has upheld Öcalan's death sentence, Western governments, including the EU and the United States, are encouraging Turkey to alter this decision. The European Parliament has also urged Turkey to suspend this decision in the likelihood of being denied its much-wanted EU membership. These issues, as well as the downward spiraling Turkish economy linked to the unresolved Kurdish issue, has created heated debates in Turkish ruling circles over Öcalan and a Kurdish policy. (This comment was contributed by an outside reviewer).

Syria, Iran, and Turkey—whatever else may divide them, have repeatedly gone on record to warn against any effort to make that autonomy de jure.[48]

In most respects, Iraq's Kurds can generate the most bargaining leverage by remaining within Iraq, although they must utilize the threat to leave. Were they to break away, they would leave a Sunni Arab minority to face a Shi'a Arab majority in what remains of Iraq. Because the bulk of Iraqi Kurds are Sunni, they represent an element of security for the Sunni Arabs.

Conclusion

I have argued that no matter how compelling on historical and human rights grounds a case for self-determination may be, caution is the better part of wisdom in honoring such claims. In some cases, ethnic or racial identity is not sufficiently plastic to avoid erecting legal safeguards based on the designation of specific groups. Southern Sudan, were it to remain within the Republic of Sudan, would require such safeguards, but then, if it were to leave, such safeguards would have to be extended to minority populations living within the South.

However, in most instances the legal naming of names should be avoided. The law should allow groups to organize along ethnic or sectarian lines if they see fit, and if they obey the laws of the land, but it should also allow them to disappear if their political raison d'être disappears. For example, it may become politically irrelevant for mestizo populations to sort out their origins. At times sectarian identities may take on greater importance than ethnic, and vice versa. The law should be neutral and permissive but should not provide incentives to organize political participation along ethnic or sectarian lines. Lebanon provided and still provides such incentives, all the while bemoaning that fact.

One cannot fly in the face of ethnic and sectarian realities. No one was more cognizant of that fact than Jawarharlal Nehru of India, who is alleged to have remarked that one can throw money at class differences but not at religious and lingual ones. India's federal constitution has given official recognition to the country's ethnic and lingual differences (but not, for the most part, to its religious differences). West Bengal, Punjab, Tamil Nadu, Gujarat, and other states are testimony to this. Yet

---

48. In 1937, Syria, Turkey, and Iran signed a joint defense agreement known as the Saadabad Pact. Its real motive was to contain any concerted Kurdish movement for autonomy. That pact has been revived informally since 1991.

at the same time, to win power nationally parties must construct broad cross-ethnic and cross-lingual coalitions. The Congress Party, even before independence, learned how to do this. Such coalitions will, as in Lebanon, take on the character of a piebald assemblage of ascriptive units; successful coalitions have had to find programmatic messages that go beyond crude appeals to blood, language, and religion. The same logic of forming broad-based coalitions has not worked well in Nigeria, and in Lebanon it gave way to civil war; but it is one, I argue, that must be followed with all the ingenuity that its authors and practitioners can muster. Why play this game within the confines of India, or Lebanon, or Iraq? Because none of these entities is any more artificial than its constituent parts. It seems more important to introduce sound democratic practice than to focus on autonomy or independence, for such practice is a better guarantee of renewable consent than are units erected on claims of historical injustice and group righteousness.

Part 2

CASE STUDIES

6

Language and the Politics of Self-Expression: Mayan Revitalization in Guatemala

KAY B. WARREN

This chapter focuses on the Pan-Mayan culturalist movement in Guatemala, which is promoting the revitalization of Mayan culture for the 60 percent of the national population that is indigenous. The movement is working to establish common interests across the twenty language groups in the country given their similar cultural, historical, and community backgrounds. Although many of these language communities are relatively small, the largest four number between 350,000 and 1 million speakers each. The Mayan culturalists, as they are called, have proposed a pluricultural model for participatory democracy. This model would define the collective cultural, linguistic, and political rights for Mayan citizens and legitimize their claims to having a cultural and political space in national educational, judicial, and administrative systems.[1] Culturalists hope that these changes will bring Mayans into the mainstream to attack Guatemala's rural poverty and serious development dilemmas.

This analysis focuses on Mayan critiques of bilingual education as failing to meet children's needs and subverting the authority of indige-

I want to thank the Mayan scholars I cite in this chapter for sharing their written work with me and reading the initial draft of this chapter. For additional feedback, my thanks go to John Waterbury, Wolfgang Danspeckgruber, and other participants in the Liechtenstein Research Program on Self-Determination (LRPSD) seminars. A short version of this analysis, which benefited from feedback from David Maybury-Lewis, appeared in Kay B. Warren, "Language and the Politics of Self-Expression: Mayan Revitalization in Guatemala," *Cultural Survival Quarterly* (Summer/Fall 1994), pp. 81–86.

   1. See COMG (Consejo de Organizaciones Mayas de Guatemala), "Derechos específicos del Pueblo Maya/Rujunamil ri Mayab' amaq'" (Guatemala: Mayab' Nimajay Cholsamaj, 1991).

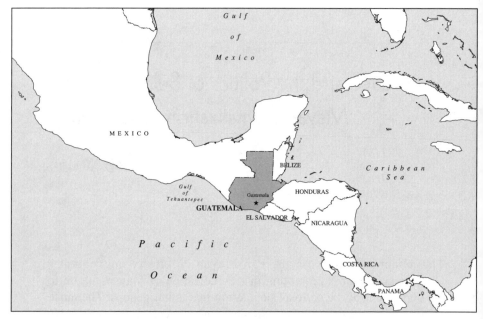

Central America, highlighting Guatemala

nous parents and communities. Dropout and illiteracy rates are extremely high for indigenous communities. In the past, teachers were Spanish
speakers with very limited knowledge of Mayan culture, meaning that
they were unable to communicate directly with incoming students.
Bilingual education demoralized the children, who were pressured to
assimilate Hispanic culture and taught that the Spanish language and
national culture are superior to their own. Since the 1980s, Mayan intellectuals have critiqued this national school policy and formulated alternative models that would reduce alienation, attrition, and illiteracy.

The chapter explores Mayan alternatives for language policy and
elementary education, the rocky experiences of PRONEBI (Programa
Nacional de Educación Bilingüe, the nationally funded organization in
charge of fostering more effective bilingual education), which was
renamed DIGEBI, and Mayan images of federalism that would promote
indigenous culture and self-determination within the structure of the
Guatemalan state.

Mayan Indians in Guatemala are currently promoting a cultural
resurgence and moving toward national unification through an innovative network of research centers and grassroots education programs.
They are working to foster a distinctive sense of *pueblo*, that is, a community of interest for all Mayab' as a people or a nation. In their pluri-

cultural model for participatory democracy, multiple national cultures would be recognized. This project would end the monopoly of the Hispanic standard, historically established by the Spanish colonizers and later transformed and modernized by their cultural descendants, the Ladinos, who authored "national" culture after independence from Spain in the nineteenth century.

To achieve this revitalization, Mayan professionals, teachers, and community activists are utilizing their own substantial resources and backgrounds in law, linguistics, education, agriculture, and religion. Virtually all of these culturalists come from rural backgrounds. Some have stayed in their home communities, working as agriculturalists or teachers or becoming regional and local leaders in the cooperative movement, religious groups, or local development initiatives. Others have relocated to urban centers to pursue professional training and higher education, working as academics, bookstore owners, publishers, social workers, administrators, teachers, and experts for nongovernmental organizations (NGOs) such as the UN Children's Fund (UNICEF). At the end of the workweek, during vacations, and for major events, it is not unusual for professionals to return to their home communities, where close relatives live and where some have families.

This chapter is part of a much larger project to trace the ways in which Mayans as cultural nationalists and agents of globalization are developing projects for self-determination in a climate of continuing political uncertainty.[2] A set of interrelated theses guides my analysis. First, the movement's emphasis on self-determination is part of a historically constituted language for agency that needs to be studied in the context of transnational institutions and Mayan histories of social criticism, community formation, and international involvement. The language itself and the Mayans' emphasis on constituting themselves as a people are the products of an elaboration of rights discourse through organizations such as the UN, which finds itself caught in a field of competing interests given its role as the international custodian of state sovereignty. Second, this analysis argues that the particular cultural forms and social relationships through which Mayans assert their cultural claims are integral aspects of self-determination. Third, Mayan struggles for self-determination are often muted when they are viewed solely in terms of universalizing schemes, whether they be the liberal language of individual rights or the historical materialist language of oppression and class conflict.

---

2. Kay B. Warren, *Indigenous Movements and Their Critics: Pan-Maya Activism in Guatemala* (Princeton: Princeton University Press, 1998).

Mayan studies *(Estudios Mayas)* is an interdisciplinary field of research and social commentary designed by Mayan culturalists to promote resurgence and unification. Reborn in the early 1980s, it has produced alternative histories that denounce the racism of state histories, searing critiques of foreign research practices and scholarship, linguistic scholarship to promote the retention of the Mayan language, critiques of Western models of development, and political psychology concerned with counteracting internalized racism. Through this applied research, Mayan intellectuals have condemned colonialism as an ongoing issue rather than a moment of ethnogenesis five centuries ago at the Spanish conquest.

It would be inaccurate to dismiss this cultural revival as parochial, primordial, or detrimental to modern politics. Mayans are highly aware of global identity politics, even more so since Rigoberta Menchú won the 1992 Nobel Peace Prize. Culturalists bring their own experiences, ideologies, and evolving politics to the international process of ethnic intensification. Culture, history, and politics make Mayan studies and the culturalist movement a related yet different process from both ethnic nationalism and multiculturalism elsewhere in the world.

This chapter deals with the special relevance of language for Mayan cultural revitalization and for images of relations between the state and the nations of which it is composed. Language is self-consciously emphasized as a key aspect of indigenous identity by Mayan activists because it antedates European colonialism and because it is a nonracial mode of identity construction. It also illustrates Mayan constructions of linguistics and comparative politics as aspects of the interdisciplinary field of Mayan studies.

Reading Language as a Political Code

Culturalists such as Luis Enrique Sam Colop and Demetrio Cojtí Cuxil argue that in Guatemala language must be read as a "double-voiced" political code, "as indicators of the existence and the political position of Mayan communities."[3] Culturalist studies of language, with their context-sensitive notion of language-as-practice, examine the regional

---

3. Demetrio Cojtí Cuxil, *Configuración del pensamiento político del Pueblo Maya* (Quetzaltenango, Guatemala: Asociación de Escritores Mayances de Guatemala, 1991a), pp. 65–66.

distribution of language groups in Guatemala; patterns of monolingualism and bilingualism in community and national affairs; the stakes in producing standardized written versions of Mayan languages; state policy with regard to the official language of administration, the courts, and educational systems; and the power structures and ideologies inherent in existing arrangements. This discussion draws on the work of Mayan educators along with other Mayan linguists and anthropologists. My goal is to present a synthesis of the issues they define as central to an "activist linguistics" and the critiques of education and nation that flow from their analysis.

The first reading of language-as-practice reveals patterns of internal colonialism central to Guatemala today. Culturalists observe that language represents key dimensions of the surrounding political and economic worlds; it is an indicator of the relative position of Mayans and Ladinos. Demetrio Cojtí Cuxil notes the powerful mandate and ramifications of designating Spanish as the official language:

> The wide scope of the [constitutional] articles that institute Spanish as the language reserved for education, high culture, official communication, general public administration . . . implies that Mayan languages should carry out secondary functions, that are domestic and informal (in local culture and family life). We can say that the constitution generates linguistic inequality by giving higher rank and formal responsibility to Spanish.[4]

At Guatemala's independence, an 1824 legislative decree not only affirmed a single national language but also encouraged municipal governments and priests to extinguish indigenous languages.[5] The constitutions of 1945, 1956, and 1965 renewed Spanish as the official language while addressing the importance of improving the economic, social, and cultural situation of the indigenous population. Apparently, lawmakers saw little contradiction between improving people's standard of living and working to displace their household and community languages. From 1956 on, constitutions have included formulaic commitments to nondiscrimination on the basis of ethnicity, religion, sex, and so on. This nondiscriminatory language was no doubt influenced by the UN Universal Declaration of Human Rights promulgated in 1948, which in

---

4. Ibid., p. 72.
5. Luis Enrique Sam Colop, "Hacia una propuesta de ley de educación bilingüe," unpublished thesis for the Licenciatura en Ciencas Jurídicas y Sociales, University Rafael Landívar, Guatemala, 1983, p. 49.

the eyes of the culturalists has only continued the odd but revealing contradiction in state policy.

A 1978 Guatemalan law established literacy as a universal right and obligation. Literacy, however, was constructed as synonymous with *castellanización,* that is, teaching Spanish as the path to Hispanic culture, a policy that started in 1935.[6] Culturalists argue that the oral status of Mayan languages results from colonial barriers to their written representation and the "subaltern" status of their communities.[7] Indigenous language literacy became a priority in 1981 when the Protestant Summer Institute of Languages (SIL) suggested this approach might ease the transition to Spanish for monolingual children.[8]

Today, Mayan children from dispersed hamlets in the western highlands, where indigenous people form the majority, often arrive at school with little background in Spanish because their families speak an indigenous language at home. Yet Guatemalan education is conducted overwhelmingly in Spanish, and Ladino teachers routinely use Spanish as the only language of communication inside and outside the classroom. In other schools, Mayan languages are used as a *puente de incorporación,* a bridging transition during the initial years of schooling to foster subsequent incorporation into the "real" Spanish curriculum later in school.

This philosophy governs an educational system in which 70 percent of the schools offered classes only through the fourth year of primary school in 1987, a number that improved to 84 percent by 1998. Yet many students still do not finish elementary school. In 1995, the national illiteracy rate stood at 37 percent for males over the age of fifteen and 51 percent for females over the age of fifteen. These averages mask other disparities, according to 1997 statistics. In the urbanized department of Guatemala, where nonindigenous Ladinos predominate and schools have a history of receiving the lion's share of educational funding, the illiteracy rate for Mayans is only 9.03 percent for males and 11.45 for females. For departments where Mayans are the numerical majority, indigenous illiteracy rates range from 26 to 58 percent of the population; the poorest and largely rural depart-

---

6. Guillermina Herrera, *Estado del arte sobre educación en Guatemala,* (Guatemala: Centro de Información y Documentació Educative de Guatemala and Universidad Rafael Landívar, 1987), p. 16.

7. Cojtí Cuxil, *Configuración del pensamiento político del Pueblo Maya,* p. 67.

8. Sam Colop, "Hacia una propuesta de ley de educación bilingüe," p. 54.

ment of Quiché has an illiteracy rate of 45.64 for males and 67.99 for females.[9]

The effort to make Spanish the universal national language has never succeeded. A substantial percentage of the population still retains Mayan languages as its dominant mode of communication, speaks limited utilitarian Spanish, and is illiterate in all languages. Those with more education are often bilingual in Mayan languages and Spanish. Estimates of the percentage of Mayan speakers are variable, ranging from 36 to 70 percent of the national population;[10] estimates of ethnic Mayans are considerably higher, ranging from 42 to 87 percent of the national population.[11]

The second reading of language-as-practice traces history through Mayan language development beginning thousands of years ago and emphasizes the modern persistence of Mayan languages as a form of grassroots resistance to internal colonialism. The reconstruction of proto-Mayan by linguists stands as a symbol of the unity of Mayan origins and a rationale for current cultural unification. The branching and dispersion of Mayan languages represents the pre-Hispanic history of political and economic development that sustained large language communities. Subsequently, these communities developed into separate nations with the distinctive Mayan languages spoken today (see Table 6.1).

Despite the pressures to Hispanicize or Ladinoize, Mayans have continued to speak their own languages. Dialects of the major languages are now often seen as community-specific identity markers for Guatemala's 326 *municipios* (counties, which function as the units of community). Culturalists hold several explanations for dialect diversifi-

---

9. For these statistics, see Herrera, "Estado del arte sobre educación en Guatemala"; Gabriela Núñez, Beatrice Bezmalinovic, Susan Clay, et al., *Primer encuentro nacional: Educando a la niña: Lograremos el desarrollo de Guatemala* (Guatemala: U.S. Agency for International Development [AID], 1991); CONALFA, *Resultados finales de las coberturas de atención etapa inicial (alfabetización): Estimaciones y projecciones de población* (Guatemala: Departmento de Estadística de CONALFA, 1997); UNICEF, *Estado mundial de la infancia 1999* (New York: UNICEF, 1999); and Ruth Moya and Otilia Lux de Cotí, "La mujer maya en Guatemala: El futuro de la memoria," paper presented at Conferencia Internacional Sobre Género, Etnicidad y Educación, Cochabamba, Bolivia, August 1999.

10. Guillermina Herrera, "Las lenguas indígenas de Guatemala: Situación actual y futuro," in Nora England and Stephen Elliot, eds., *Lecturas sobre la lingüística maya* (La Antigua Guatemala, Guatemala: Centro de Investigaciones Regonales de Mesoamérica, 1990), p. 30; and Sam Colop, "Hacia una propuesta de ley de educación bilingüe," pp. 10, 12.

11. Cojtí Cuxil, *Configuración del pensamiento político del Pueblo Maya,* p. 56.

Table 6.1   Number of Speakers of Mayan Languages in Guatemala

Language	Number of Speakers	Departments	Number of Municipalities
K'iche'	1,000,000	Sololá, Totonicapan, Quetzaltenango, El Quiché, Baja Verapaz, Alta Verapaz, Suchitepéquez, Retalhuleu	73
Mam	687,000	Quetaltenango, Huehuetenango, San Marcos	56
Kaqchikel	405,000	Guatemala, Sacatepéquez, Chimaltenango, Sololá, Suchitepéquez, Escuintla, Baja Verapaz	47
Q'eqchii'	361,000	Alta Verapaz, El Petén, Izabal, El Quiché	14
Q'anjob'al	112,000	Huehuetenango	4
Tz'utujiil	85,000	Sololá, Suchitepéquez	7
Ixil	71,000	El Quiché	3
Ch'orti'	52,000	Chiquimula, Zacapa	5
Poqomchi'	50,000	Alta Verapaz, Baja Verapaz, El Quiché	7
Popti'	32,000	Huehuetenango	6
Poqomam	32,000	Guatemala, Jalapa, Escuintla	6
Chuj	29,000	Huehuetenango	3
Sakapulteko	21,000	El Quiché	1
Akateko	20,000	Huehuetenango	2
Awakateko	16,000	Huehuetenango	1
Mopan	5,000	El Petén	4
Sipakapense	3,000	San Marcos	1
Itzaj	3,000	El Petén	6
Teko	2,500	Huehuetenango	2 (plus 2 in Mexico)
Uspanteko	2,000	El Quiché	1

Source: Oxlajuuj Keej Maya' Ajtz'iib', Maya' Chii' (1993), pp. 10–19; England, 1996.
Note: Approximately twenty Maya languages are spoken in the country depending upon how the difference between dialects and languages is negotiated by speech communities and by linguists. Language communities vary from over a million to a few thousand. The leadership of the Maya movement has been drawn primarily from Kaqchikel and K'iche' speakers who come from communities closer to urban centers and continuing educational opportunities than do other goups. However, many national Mayanist organizations—from the Academy for Maya Languages of Guatemala (ALMG) to Oxlajuuj Keej Maya' Ajtz'iib' (OKMA)—self-consciously seek representation of as many language communities as possible in their organizations.

cation, which they derisively term *babelización*, referring to the sixteenth-century Spanish invasion that decapitated indigenous states, leaving local communities to resist cultural and political domination;[12] the lack of written forms of the languages;[13] and the continuing importance to community members of localized identities.[14]

---

12. Ibid.
13. Sam Colop, "Hacia una propuesta de ley de educación bilingüe."
14. Herrera, "Las lenguas indígenas de Guatemala."

At present, twenty Mayan languages are spoken in Guatemala (see Table 6.1).[15] In the past, linguistic research tended to focus on describing the differences among languages and the proliferation of dialects within each of them. Missionary linguists who worked with SIL and the academic linguist Terrance Kaufman separately developed a variety of alphabets to represent Mayan languages. When the resulting twenty official alphabets—in some cases more than one alphabet for a single language—were recognized by the government's Instituto Indigenista Nacional (IIN), the sense of language divergence was only heightened. Kaufman and the culturalists criticized the IIN alphabets for using Spanish-derived orthography to represent unrelated Mayan sound systems. The IIN promoted this connection between the unrelated languages because it would "facilitate [indigenous] adaptation to Spanish."[16] This philosophy flowed from the 1940s indigenist ideology in Latin America, which called for "incorporating indigenous people into national culture, freeing them from the situation of inferiority in which they maintain themselves."[17]

For the culturalists, these and other analyses have demonstrated that *castellanización, indigenismo, ladinización, mestizaje,* incorporation, and assimilation are variations on a single theme, the attempt to undermine indigenous culture and merge Mayans into a system not of their making. The problem with these frameworks—whether they are used to guide national policy or academic research—is that they lend positive value to images of modernization as a linear process through which indigenous populations will be merged into the Ladino mainstream. They also reinforce the sense that national (Ladino) society can speak for the whole population.[18]

Demetrio Cojtí Cuxil argues that the assimilationist mission confuses objective and subjective criteria when observing change and thus fails to consider the significance of indigenous actions for the people themselves. "The adoption of characteristics from another culture can be undertaken in order to strengthen one's own national identity, not to deny or weaken it. For characteristics can be adopted and made one's own, and upon doing this, they are different from their origin by the dif-

---

15. Readers will see a variety of totals depending on the source. Twenty-nine Mayan languages are spoken throughout southern Mexico and Guatemala. In Guatemala the number currently stands at twenty with an addition of two non-Mayan indigenous languages.

16. Cited in Sam Colop, "Hacia una propuesta de ley de educación bilingüe," p. 28.

17. Ibid., p. 32.

18. Cojtí Cuxil, *Configuración del pensamiento político del Pueblo Maya,* pp. 31–38, 57.

ference in their meanings."[19] By not considering the issue of cultural meaning, analysts of modernization as assimilation have misunderstood the strategic appropriation of colonial culture that Mayans used in oppressive circumstances to rescue and reaffirm their identity. Today, assimilationists fail to make note of coercive situations that pressure Mayans to abandon their distinctive dress or even pass as Ladinos for scholarships or factory work. Cultural resurgence and the struggle for rights will allow these individuals to make other choices as they identify as Mayans outwardly and inwardly.[20] The culturalist counterargument distinguishes objective and subjective (that is, outsider and insider) views of identity to make space for alternatives to the conventional choice of reproducing traditionalist culture or passing into another identity. These analytic moves illustrate the discourse culturalists have elaborated in developing their own brand of constructionism.[21]

Culturalists argue that there is a hidden history of resistance to the impositions of *castellanización* and *indigenismo*. As early as 1945, Adrián Inés Chávez proposed a unified alphabet for indigenous languages at the Primer Convención de Maestros Indígenas in Cobán, and members of the Academia de la Lengua Maya-Quiché discussed another alphabet in 1959 and proposed it to the government three years later. The suggestion was rejected in favor of the alphabets produced by the SIL and the IIN.[22] Nevertheless, culturalists worked through the 1970s and 1980s to produce dialect surveys, dictionaries of major languages, and a unified alphabet. These were important steps in the longer process of language unification. As the projects advanced, linguists such as Sam Colop began to find "a great deal of similarity among the following language families: Chuj, Konjobal, Acatec and Jacaltec; among Quiché, Sipacapec, Sacapultec, Tzutujil, and Cakchikel. This means there are not so many social and regional variants within each language; there is, by contrast, a great deal of similarity."[23]

A wider goal for linguistic research coalesced: "It is not important to see how [languages and dialects] are different from each other, but rather to analyze their reunification in order to strengthen them and achieve greater social cohesion."[24]

Standardizing the written forms of Mayan languages is the ambi-

---

19. Ibid., pp. 36, 38.
20. Ibid., pp. 36–39.
21. Kay B. Warren, "Transforming Memories and Histories: The Meanings of Ethnic Resurgence for Mayan Indians," in Alfred Stepan, ed., *Americas: New Interpretive Essays* (New York: Oxford University Press, 1992), pp. 189–219.
22. Sam Colop, "Hacia una propuesta de ley de educación bilingüe," p. 29.
23. Ibid., p. 8.
24. Ibid., p. 19.

tious next step. The choice of a standard dialect is obvious in only one case: for Q'eqchii' speakers, for example, the Copán dialect is widely accepted as having special prestige. In other cases, standardization will be based on common denominators across dialects.[25] Standardization of written language will allow for mass dissemination of cultural materials, news, creative writings, and texts for formal and nonformal education. Spoken dialects will remain as they are. The role Mayan linguists see for themselves involves carrying out dialect surveys they can use as the basis for standardization, promoting Mayan alternatives for words that have been borrowed from Spanish, and modernizing Mayan languages so that they maintain their vibrancy and capacity to talk about contemporary issues and technologies.

Modernization *(modernización)* would ideally eliminate the present need to switch between Mayan languages for domestic issues and Spanish for technical matters and thus undercut one element of the internal colonialism promoted by *castellanización.* The concern with rooting out borrowed words may seem extreme given that Mayans recognize their active involvement in appropriating and subverting elements from other cultural systems. But for Mayans, the asymmetry of borrowed words reflects the domination of Spanish speakers over Mayan speakers; Mayan lexical emphasis on agriculture and artisan production; the loss of Mayan vocabulary in areas where their culture has been displaced; and their dependency on Spanish-derived vocabulary in the courts, administration, religion, and the arts. These patterns mirror colonial divisions of labor—Mayans specializing in agriculture and crafts and Ladinos in administration and white-collar work—that culturalists have actively challenged in their careers. Culturalists are seeking to displace common images of the limits and inadequacy of indigenous tongues *(lenguas),* and thus their built-in obsolescence, by providing explanations of existing patterns and their underlying power structures and imagining alternative models for the future.[26]

Alternative Educational Models

The culturalist vision claims equal rights and opportunities for all languages in the country. To respond to criticisms they are being utopian or unrealistic, culturalists refer to other countries—Belgium, Switzerland,

---

25. Ibid., p. 24.

26. Cojtí Cuxil, *Configuración del pensamiento político del Pueblo Maya,* pp. 68–69, 96–97; and Oxlajuuj Keej Mayab' Ajtz'iib' Ajpub', Ixkem, Lolmay, Nik'te', Pakal, Saqijix, and Waykan, *Mayab' Chii': Idiomas mayas de Guatemala* (Guatemala: Cholsamaj, 1993).

Spain, Canada, Peru, and Ecuador, among others—where cultural and linguistic diversity has been taken seriously in domestic policy and administration. Other political systems, both Western and Latin American, have forged alternatives to the melting pot. In their view, solutions to the "Indian problem" need to widen the scope of "the problem" and recognize that Guatemala falls within the broader category of multinational societies, many of which already allow different types and grades of autonomy: from federal and semifederal structures to autonomous regions to policies guaranteeing children education in their maternal language and litigants the right to represent themselves in the language they speak. Culturalists take special note of the way other states recognize more than one official language; support regional variations in language use; and allow for some measure of cultural autonomy or federal decentralization of authority over courts, economic policy, and schools.[27]

Culturalists propose the development of alternative educational systems and constructions of state bilingualism. One option is the current official system—bilingualism as fluency in Spanish—which has driven the national school system since 1964. Culturalists see it as a form of institutionalized colonialism in which children are taught that their maternal tongue is inferior to Spanish and individual education and mobility inevitably involves assimilation and Ladinoization: "*Castellanización* is an educative process which tries to give the indigenous population necessary knowledge for understanding and using Spanish with the goal of facilitating communication and living together in the country."[28] It is the asymmetry of obligations and goals for Mayans and Ladinos, that is, the fundamental lack of reciprocity in this formulation, that strikes Mayan culturalists as unjust.

PRONEBI,[29] which focuses on education from kindergarten through the third year of elementary school in 400 schools, became a source of new jobs for young Mayans and the impetus for studies to standardize and modernize Mayan languages. The program, however, has phrased its mission as one of national integration rather than linguistic autonomy. Culturalists have criticized this institution for what

---

27. Sam Colop, "Hacia una propuesta de ley de educación bilingüe," p. 74; and Cojtí Cuxil, *Configuración del pensamiento político del Puebo Maya*, p. 24.

28. Sam Colop, "Hacia una propuesta de ley de educación bilingüe," p. 54.

29. PRONEBI has since been renamed DIGEBI. See Julia Becker Richards and Michael Richards, "Mayan Education: An Historical and Contemporary Analysis of Mayan Language Educational Policy," in Edward Fischer and McKenna Brown, eds., *Mayan Cultural Activism in Guatemala* (Austin: University of Texas Press, 1966) for more details on the history of indigenous education and language policy.

they believe is a hidden agenda antithetical to its avowed goal of bilingualism. By dovetailing its efforts with the national policy of *castellanización*, PRONEBI is seen as hypocritically working to transform
monolingual Mayan speakers into monolingual Spanish speakers.[30]

An alternative plan, this one proposed by the culturalists, calls for a
strategic equilibrium in language use between maternal and second languages. This proposal envisions universal bilingualism in the schools as
the institutionally favored goal, with monolingualism (in either Spanish
or one of the Mayan languages) as an option for specific cases. Because
each language brings its own cultural horizon, this form of bilingualism
is seen as enriching people's lives. By this model, the first two grades of
elementary school would be taught in the language of the region. Third
and fourth grade would involve a transitional period during which the
ratios of maternal to second language would be 75:25 with the goal of a
50:50 split in the fifth year of primary school through the university.
The plan would reinforce rather than undermine the basis of community
authority.[31] Culturalists acknowledge that not all Ladinos would be
interested, so some monolingual schools would operate in the departmental and national capitals. The development of regional Mayan universities is another future possibility.[32]

In the strategic equilibrium model, Mayan linguists would play an
important role in the educational process, as materials in all indigenous
languages would have to be generated for a full primary and secondary
curriculum. The issue, as the culturalists see it, is much more than one
of Mayan linguists' producing translations of the old monolingual curriculum into the new multilingual one:

> Through sociolinguistic investigations [Mayan linguists] will come to
> know factors of great importance such as the prestige of each lan-
> guage spoken in an area; feelings of language loyalty; relations con-
> cerning power, solidarity, ethnic sentiment; [and relations concerning]
> responsibility, maturity, and leadership relative to the cultures and lan-
> guages. They will get to know the stereotypes and attitudes that users
> of a given language have of other languages. All linguistic planning

---

30. Cojtí Cuxil, *Configuración del pensamiento político del Pueblo Maya*, p.
67.

31. Sam Colop, "Hacia una propuesta de ley de educación bilingüe," p. 48.

32. Irma Otzoy and Demetrio Cojtí Cuxil have written important works on
Mayans in higher education. Both make it clear that reforms are needed so that
Mayans do not feel they are foreigners on their own campuses. See Irma Otzoy,
"Identity and Higher Education Among Mayan Women," unpublished M.A. thesis,
Department of Anthropology, University of Iowa, 1988; and Demetrio Cojtí Cuxil,
"Universidades guatemaltecas, universidades colonialistas," paper presented at
Latin American Studies Association (LASA), 1991b.

should have as a fundamental base sociolinguistic study that will provide fundamental data with which to operate adequately.[33]

To accomplish this project, new university degrees would have to be
developed in sociolinguistics, ethnolinguistics, and anthropological linguistics.

In regional affairs, this model of bilingualism would be accompanied by the incorporation of indigenous languages into the official
usage of the courts and administration. In national and international
affairs, however, Spanish would still be the official language. The
model is designed to prepare indigenous students to deal linguistically
with transregional worlds.[34]

In another culturalist view, however, bilingualism is ethnocide, particularly when introduced through primary education in a situation of
political and economic inequality. Instead of being enriching or addi-
tive, second-language acquisition is seen by these culturalists as sub-
tractive, creating a zero-sum game that, when institutionally mandated,
would threaten children's linguistic development and in the long run the
integrity and existence of the maternal language:

> It is clear that schools, proceeding in this way, comply with the coun-
> try's laws. They aid Mayan speakers so that they do not remain lin-
> guistically isolated and equip them with a code that can help them
> defend their rights in the language of the legal system and meet the
> prerequisites so they can progress professionally and academically.
> But [these schools] also contribute to the extermination of Mayan lan-
> guages. The issue is to determine a kind of bilingual teaching that is
> less isolating and also less assimilating.[35]

The problem is that Mayan languages are currently taught as a means.
The inevitable result, according to Demetrio Cojtí Cuxil, is ethnocide
no matter how one defines bilingualism.[36]

Decentralizing school systems so that most education is carried out
in the appropriate regional language is the culturalist solution to this
dilemma. The goal is to foster monolingualism in Mayan languages
accompanied by instrumental Spanish, given its role in state administration. Spanish as a second language could be offered early in school but
would never be given more than 5 percent of classroom time. Or, alter-
natively, the introduction of Spanish could be held off until secondary

---

33. Sam Colop, "Hacia una propuesta de ley de educación bilingüe," p. 94.
34. Ibid., pp. 98–112.
35. Cojtí Cuxil, *Configuración del pensamiento político del Pueblo Maya*, p.
114.
36. Ibid., pp. 107–119, 139.

school. Because all subjects would be taught in Mayan languages, there would be no built-in linguistic division of labor and knowledge.[37]

Clearly Mayan languages will have to be standardized and modernized to take on this role, particularly in scientific and technical fields, and school materials will have to be developed to reflect Mayan culture.[38] Schools themselves would be contributors to standardization. As Cojtí Cuxil asserts, this type of education cannot be enacted without prior commitments to regionalization, the decentralization of development projects, Mayan cultural autonomy, and the recognition of Mayan languages as official languages for their regions. In departmental capitals where Ladinos and Mayans from a variety of language groups reside, the desired formula could be achieved by having specialized schools, separate classrooms in the same school, or bilingual instructors depending on the numbers of students for each language in question. Until Mayan universities are available, advanced education will be in Spanish, but when this system is changed, students might be given the choice of a variety of second languages, including English. The ultimate goal of this model is the dominance of Mayan languages in regional affairs.[39]

Although culturalist models are divergent in their judgment of bilingualism in the schools—one finding enrichment and the other seeing a threat—they share an overarching philosophy. First, they agree that Mayan languages should become the language of instruction for most, if not all, primary education. Second, indigenous languages should be recognized on par with Spanish for the courts and government administration. Third, schools need to evaluate their curricula so that they reflect Mayan culture and so that Mayan parents can be seen as knowledgeable resources rather than as ignorant and marginal to the flow of change. Fourth, both models see a necessity for Mayan linguists to standardize and modernize written forms of indigenous languages in a universal alphabet so that wider written literatures can flourish and be disseminated through schools, development groups, and publishers. Both models make their claims in the spatial language of regionality. Let us now turn to culturalist constructions of nation and state, which culturalists judge integral to any attempt at reform.

---

37. Ibid.

38. Cojtí Cuxil does not develop the issue of the curriculum content. But his essay on differences between Mayan and non-Mayan constructions of authority is suggestive (see "Universidades Guatemaltecas, universidades colonialistas," pp. 153–181). More recently, Mayan-Ladino collaborations have produced texts through the Instituto de Lingüística at the Universidad de Rafael Landívar.

39. Ibid., pp. 128–140.

National Culture or National Cultures

At the heart of culturalist concerns is the state of national culture. National legal and educational systems have not shared this concern; for them, national culture is synonymous with contemporary Ladino culture. By contrast, culturalists argue that this self-satisfaction only masks a submerged identity crisis:

> "National culture" is the set of habits that Ladinos practice, a sum of North American-Hispanic elements that do not diminish [national culture] yet render it dependent. Jean Loup Herbert says of this culture: "They look endlessly for a definition of national culture: *mestizo*, Hispanic-American, Iberian-American, Latin American, or modern— empty terms that reflect the alienated search of a minority." Paradoxically they hope for and predict the disappearance of indigenous culture into this historic nothingness: "Integration does not require that all indigenous people are transformed into Ladinos, but this will probably be their destiny" (Joaquín Noval).[40]

This skepticism deconstructs the rightful authority and authoritativeness of existing constructions of national culture to represent the country.[41] It is clear to culturalists how Ladinos have been able to reproduce the illusion of a hegemonic national culture through their monopoly of the schools, church, and mass media. Yet despite the image of hegemony, alternative realities erupt from time to time to defy its terms even on the highest level. For instance, while addressing the National Congress in 1975 about Ladino land seizures that had victimized Mayan peasants, Representative Fernando Tezahuic Tohon suddenly lapsed into Kaqchikel. He was summarily called to order for not speaking in the official language. The incident was reported in the national press and is still referred to years later. Sam Colop sees this incident not as a tactical move but as a moment when the representative, speaking about an issue that affected him deeply, unconsciously switched to his maternal language in order to express himself more freely. This failure to observe order and the anger it evoked in Congress revealed the arbitrary and imposed nature of the official system.[42] But once one unmasks the instability and arbitrariness of existing arrangements, culturalists argue, it is imperative that Guatemala move on to recognize the national stature of both rather than only one of its cultures. As Cojtí Cuxil

---

40. Sam Colop, "Hacia una propuesta de ley de educación bilingüe," p. 61.

41. Cojtí Cuxil (*Configuración del pensamiento político del Pueblo Maya*, pp. 4–10) takes this a step further by personalizing the identity crisis as one characteristic of Ladinos.

42. Sam Colop, "Hacia una propuesta de ley de educación bilingüe," p. 66.

announces: "Guatemala is a multinational society. . . . That is to say 'Guatemalan culture' cannot be other than a confederation of cultures and languages in which each preserves its originality."[43]

Mayan analysis of language and politics has important implications for models of national political organization. Culturalists and others are proposing new models for democratic organization that range from territorial autonomy to administrative regionalization to class-based and transethnic political blocs acting within existing forms of participatory democracy. For culturalists, the emerging metaphor is "nation" as contrasted with "state." Sam Colop defines nation in the following terms:

> Nation is a state of social consciousness, a psychological phenomenon. It is collective loyalty that unites a society with its collective past and involves it in common aspirations. It is cultural identification, sentiment, and a common means of communication: language. We do not include the term race[44] because this biological terminology has been surpassed. This means that a legislated or objective standard does not make a nation. Rather, we insist that it is the psychological or intellectual self-conception of the human group to which we are referring.[45]

On the one hand, culturalists differentiate between a state as a sovereign instrument of administration and control over a territory and a nation, which does not always have juridic or political power or even territorial expression.[46] Elements of nation emerge from the *hilo invisible de la etnia* (the invisible thread of ethnicity), which involves identification with a group having a common history, its own culture, a collective memory, religion, ways of dress, and future aspirations—in short, a deeply felt essence that no one else shares. One can change in innumerable ways without losing this essence, the thread of common consciousness. Constitutions and statutes do not really have the capacity to argue against this essence, for theirs is another nature: as texts they are vulnerable and ephemeral, as Guatemalan political history certainly shows. A common judicial system does not unify distinct nations into a

---

43. Cojtí Cuxil, *Configuración del pensamiento político del Pueblo Maya*, pp. 6, 84.

44. On race, see also ibid., pp. 6, 17–21, 26–27.

45. Actually, some existing departmental divisions conform roughly to cultural and linguistic regionality. This is even more the case with municipal and hamlet divisions. Yet there has been substantial migration for Mayan businesspeople and the dislocation of hundreds of thousands of Mayans during the civil war of 1978–1985. See Sam Colop, "Hacia una propuesta de ley de educación bilingüe," p. 35.

46. Cojtí Cuxil, *Configuración del pensamiento político del Pueblo Maya*, p. 4; and Sam Colop, "Hacia una propuesta de ley de educación bilingüe," p. 36.

singularity because this imposed abstract uniformity fails to relate to the cultural reality of the indigenous majority.[47]

In imagining a multinational state, Cojtí Cuxil suggests a new role for Mayan languages as indicators of regionalized cultural identities or nationalities, indicators that would serve as the basis for territorial subdivisions and self-government. As such they would become the basis of political mobilization to break with existing models of internal colonialism that subdivide the country into departments without attention to the ways local culture and history shape the landscape.[48]

This is where culturalists differ from the popular movement.[49] The popular movement, headed by Rigoberta Menchú in Guatemala but much more global in its organization and financing, has sought to bring together Guatemalans on the basis of class and work affiliations. In Guatemala, this is a transethnic movement of Ladinos and Mayans that stresses a language of cultural respect and autonomy for indigenous peoples of the Americas. Yet the idea that autonomy might be expressed in administrative regionalization in Guatemala was troubling to the movement's leadership. On the whole, culturalists judge the popular model as calling for indigenous people's assimilation into national society, much as the Guatemalan state has acted in educational policy. Popular organizers are seen as externalizing injustice by focusing their critiques on U.S. imperialism and colonialism—and more recently on global neoliberalism—rather than giving first priority to patterns of Guatemalan racism, internal colonialism, and cultural distinctiveness. Despite these differences, culturalist and popular organizations see important overlaps in their concerns over rights and poverty.

Cojtí Cuxil sees the future of Guatemala as a federation of nations, each with its own government, territory, laws, and means for cultural development. Public administration would speak the language of those governed, not the other way around (as is presently the case); state government would routinely translate documents into regional languages;

---

47. Sam Colop, "Hacia una propuesta de ley de educación bilingüe," pp. 37–39; and Cojtí Cuxil, *Configuración del pensamiento político del Pueblo Maya*, pp. 11, 20, 33–39.

48. Cojtí Cuxil, *Configuración del pensamiento político del Pueblo Maya*, pp. 68–71.

49. Popular movements are work- and class-based organizations: widows' groups (Coordinadora Nacional de Viudas de Guatemala, or CONAVIGUA), peasant groups (Comité de Unidad Campesina, or CUC), student groups, and unions. They often have political roots in working-class movements inspired by historical materialist critiques of capitalism and imperialism. I have resisted the common translation of *popular* as "grassroots," since many other cultural and educational movements in Guatemala are community based as well.

and representatives from national subunits (Mayan and Ladino) would make up the overarching government of the state. Through the late 1990s, these issues fell outside the scope of Guatemalan political parties, which have traditionally shown little interest in indigenous issues outside the electoral courting process. The government repression of indigenous organizations during the counterinsurgency war further inhibited Mayans from creating their own political party. In response, politicized Mayans have turned to local civic communities through which they can run their own mayoral candidates.[50]

The problem is more than one of recognizing different nationalities or assuming that an abstract language of rights will easily transcend diversity. Rather it involves conceiving a formula "to federate diverse nationalities [and] articulate diverse national identities democratically."[51] Without legitimacy, the risk is violence, as those who govern seek to impose their system and those who want to evade domination push for radical decentralization. Without a concern for the multinational character of the country, regional development plans that seek decentralization are bound to be insufficient.[52]

Culturalists use comparative examples to make their case for the viability and necessity of national reform. First, they show that a range of democratic European societies have already achieved what some would dismiss as an apocalyptic goal for Guatemala. Latin American examples are included to establish that reforms have been attempted in New World countries with substantial indigenous populations. Second, they illustrate that peoples caught in much more dramatic diasporas have reunified through the thread of a common consciousness to create viable nation-states. Finally, they show that suppressed ethnicities do not disappear when the larger system mutes them. The failure to negotiate pluricultural alternatives has torn other states apart; the threat is as real as it is oblique.

In their publications and public forums, the Pan-Mayan culturalists have historically concentrated their efforts on cultural revitalization and education rather than on confrontational political activism or party politics. Now they are putting their ideas and cultural politics to the test: Language committees have been set up in communities throughout the highlands; Mayan schools are being created, as reform efforts in public education are too slow or underfunded; and university centers are producing school texts and teacher-training materials. Pan-Mayanists will

---

50. Cojtí Cuxil, *Configuración del pensamiento político del Pueblo Maya*, pp. 12–13, 70–76.
51. Ibid., p. 13.
52. Ibid., pp. 13, 15.

continue to work toward inclusive definitions of *nation* to counteract what they see as continual transformations of a singular national ideology of coercive assimilation practiced by a range of political groups on the right as well as on the left.

The issues of education, cultural rights, and federalism gained political priority and international funding through the recent deliberations to implement the 1996 peace accords, which brought the country's eighteen-year civil war to a formal close. Pan-Mayanist participation in this process through the Assembly of Civil Society and the Truth Commission has given Mayans extensive training in national politics and brought Mayan leaders to national prominence. That some Mayans now successfully run for congressional seats reflects a new stage in the movement's development and increased pressures on political parties to include Mayan representatives and issues, as was clear from the 1999 elections. Certainly the implications of these political developments for the movement's internal debates and activist agendas will be important to monitor in the coming years.

7

Self-Determination and Regionalization in Contemporary Europe

WOLFGANG DANSPECKGRUBER

The quest for self-determination and independence has yielded both creative and destructive forces on the European continent. Since the collapse of the Berlin Wall in 1989, the unification of Germany, and the disintegration of Czechoslovakia, but especially since the violent disintegration of Yugoslavia and the breakup of the Soviet empire, self-determination has obtained unexpected relevance in intra-European relations.

With the fall of the iron curtain and the end of the Cold War, a new wave of disintegration and state formation—not seen since the end of World War I—set in, signaling a renaissance of the classical form of self-determination that implies state formation (for example, sovereignty, independence, and new international boundaries). Yet the search for greater autonomy—and possibly independence—has not been limited to communities in Europe's Central, Eastern, or southeastern parts. It exists also in Western European states such as Belgium, Italy, Spain, the United Kingdom, and even Switzerland.

Self-determination in its classic nineteenth-century interpretation focused on nation and state formation, that is, the establishment of traditional sovereignty and independence. Arguably, the drive of the European Community's (and since 1991 the European Union's) member states toward deeper economic-industrial, fiscal, political, and even strategic integration, along with a wider readiness to cooperate with one another in general, has not eliminated the appeal of self-determination and self-realization *(Selbstverwirklichung)* on the communal level. However, as will be discussed, such integration and cooperation may have changed the approach and objectives of those seeking self-determination: although still aiming for maximum autonomy and self-governance, communities may no longer be looking for sovereignty,

Europe

independence, and new boundaries. Hence, on the European continent at the beginning of the twenty-first century, classical self-determination is evolving to meet changing outlooks and expectations.

This chapter consists of three parts: (1) a discussion of self-determination and self-governance as it developed in Europe, (2) an inquiry into the role and impact of subsidiarity, and (3) an examination of regionalization, particularly its respective impacts on demands for communal autonomy in EU states and in those bordering the EU.

Self-Determination in Europe:
Past, Present, and Perspectives

Past

The unification of small principalities in the seventeenth century, the *levée en masse* in the French Revolution in the eighteenth, and the nationalistic unification of states in the nineteenth were all inspired by social problems, technological progress, and the search for power and economic advantage. Critical in the period of state formation in the nineteenth century (especially after the U.S. victory in the War of 1812), self-determination in its classical form, that is, the search for independence, new boundaries, and statehood (and hence traditional nationalism), played a powerful role in the destruction of Europe's empires in the twentieth century.[1]

The orientations of the romantic period and during the Enlightenment and the Industrial Revolution all favored the notion of state building (see, for instance, Germany in 1866 and Italy in 1864). From the end of the nineteenth century to the years following World War II, the notion of autonomy and independence (as equated with self-determination) offered communities and colonies an ideal objective.[2] This notion eventually split European "mother states" or metropolitan centers such as England and France, the Netherlands, Portugal, and Spain.[3] Continental empires such as Germany and Austria-Hungary (post-1866) experienced equally both the destructive and the state-formative power of the classical concept of self-determination.

---

1. Alfred Cobban, *The Nation State and National Self-Determination* (New York: Thomas Y. Crowell, 1970), pp. 39–55.
   2. See Hendrik Spruyt, *The Sovereign State and Its Competitor: An Analysis of Systems Change* (Princeton: Princeton University Press, 1994), especially chap. 8, "The Victory of the Sovereign State."
   3. See Michael Doyle, *Empires* (Ithaca, N.Y.: Cornell University Press, 1986).

During the Versailles peace conferences (1919), the victorious France and England accepted self-determination for Germans, Austrians, Hungarians, and Turks only to the extent that the concept suited the victors' strategic design and their relationship with the vanquished.[4] Except in certain cases (such as with the Czechs, Slovaks, Serbs, Italians, and Romanians), it was considered inappropriate to offer independence to communities or nations that chose to break away from empires. The redrawing of borders and the shapes of the new states certainly had to be in line with the strategic interests of the great powers rather than with the actual needs of the communities. World leaders realized that the state-shattering effects of self-determination, that is, the emergence of independent nations, might precipitate reactionary insurgencies in their own empires.[5] In the 1920s several self-administrative solutions were installed under supervision of the newly founded League of Nations (for example, the Åland Islands, the Free City of Gdansk).[6]

Following World War II and during the Cold War, self-determination was an important issue for former colonies and elsewhere in the third world. In a rigid bipolar system characterized by a nuclear stalemate between Washington and Moscow, classical self-determination with the possible result of state formation was suppressed, nationalism was squared with ideology, and international borders were rigid.[7] Independence movements and a wave of state building in Africa and parts of Asia became linked to ideology. Even before these developments, however, ideology had been introduced into both the internal and external dimension of self-determination: prior to and during World War I, Joseph Stalin and Valdimir Lenin linked the revolutionary call for bread, land, and peace to self-determination; Woodrow Wilson embraced both self-determination and democracy in his Fourteen Points; and revolutionary leaders in Czechoslovakia, Hungary, and Italy proclaimed self-determination as a tool to search

---

4. Felix Gilbert with David Clay Large, *The End of the European Era: 1890 to the Present*, 4th ed. (New York: W. W. Norton, 1991); John Morton Blum, *Woodrow Wilson and the Politics of Morality* (Boston: Little, Brown, 1956); and Derek Heater, *National Self-Determination: Woodrow Wilson and His Legacy* (New York: St. Martin's Press, 1994).

5. Cobban, *The Nation State and National Self-Determination*, pp. 57–97.

6. For an excellent overview of international mandates by a younger scholar, see Amy Lehr, "Trusteeship for the Twenty First Century," senior thesis, Princeton University, 2000.

7. See the introduction to this volume.

for independence and break away from empire. The ideological component increased during the Cold War, when especially the Soviet Union and the newly independent India supported self-determination in the colonial territories of European powers. The formation of the Non-Aligned Movement in 1955 to offer a "third way" to newly created states added yet another ideological and strategic dimension to the external dimension of self-determination.

During this period, independence and changes of international borders were not an option in either Western or Eastern Europe, where many states remained under U.S. and/or Soviet military occupation. But decentralization and federalism—more autonomy for the provinces, *Länder,* and cantons—was implemented in some European countries such as Germany, Austria, Spain, Switzerland, and Yugoslavia. With the exception of multiethnic Yugoslavia, such ideas were suppressed by the governments in Eastern Europe and the Soviet Union. Many of them, however, granted—though not necessarily implemented—formal constitutional rights for regional administrations to defuse interethnic tensions. For example, the central authorities did offer greater autonomy to select ethnic groups such as the Balts and Tartars in the USSR and the Hungarians and Kosovo Albanians in Yugoslavia. In Central Europe, subregional cooperation, that is, a certain devolution and decentralization, was encouraged in the 1980s by transnational cooperative projects such as the Hexagonale and Alpen-Adria projects (see further on).

Two developments within the international system induced change in the second part of the Cold War subsequent to the Helsinki Accords of 1975: increasing economic discrepancies between the Soviet empire and the West, that is, the United States, Japan, and the EC countries; and rapid technological progress in the West, fostering globalization and integration. Both factors undermined the cohesion of the world's last multiethnic empire, controlled by Moscow. Furthermore, two countervailing developments precipitated a sudden increase in both the number and the types of self-determination movements. Following the fall of the Berlin Wall in 1989 and German unification in 1990, latent centrifugal forces in Eastern Europe and the Soviet Union intensified. Forty-five years after the end of World War II, Germany was united; indeed, this unification represented the first major change of international boundaries since 1945 and the most significant implementation of self-determination. It also proved to be a deadly blow to the political life of an important contributor to the process, Mikhail Gorbachev.

The European integrative dynamic was heavily encouraged by Germany's chancellor, Helmut Kohl, and by various French governments under President François Mitterand. It was Helmut Kohl's desire to alleviate French apprehensions by binding Germany ever more closely to Europe following the success of East Germany's strive for self-determination, that is, German unification. With the ratification of the Treaty of Maastricht on the European Union in 1991, the deepening of European integration and the Single European Market (SEM) made a major step further, to be followed by European monetary integration and European Monetary Union (EMU) and eventually by the agreement on the euro. On the conceptual and strategic plane, de facto German self-determination brought about European integration on a more rapid and perhaps intensified path and was strongly encouraged and supported by the Bonn-Paris axis of Kohl and Mitterand as a trade-off for other concerned Europeans. German unification also implied, however, that "the center of political gravity [moved] steadily eastward" from London, Brussels, and Paris to Bonn and increasingly to Berlin.[8] In addition, the accumulation of wealth and technological progress in the EU spurred interest in the regions north, east, and south of Central Europe to join this truly supranational organization and thus intensified separatist tendencies among the members of the Soviet bloc. Therefore, by the beginning of the 1990s centripetal forces in the West converged with centrifugal ones in the East as many members of the Council for Mutual Economic Assistance (CMEA) began to aspire to EU membership. Following the successful unification of Germany, the Balts, the Czechs, and the Slovaks, as well as the Slovenes, Croats, and Bosnians and the Macedonians and Serbs, found encouragement in the new possibilities of classical self-determination. By 1990–1991, the possible unification and dissolution of states and the formation of new states (with changes in existing boundaries) had become an eminent issue affecting the European geopolitical landscape. And all these prospects existed in an era when the development of a benign global village seemed imminent. In that situation, following the negotiations on the Treaty of Maastricht and some forty-six years after the hostilities of World War II, it seemed inconceivable to Europeans that armed conflict

---

8. John Newhouse, *Europe Adrift* (New York: Council on Foreign Relations, 1997), p. 11. I usually suggest examining the "B words": Baltics, Balkan, Berlin, Belgium, Belgrade, Britain, Brussels, Bosnia-Herzegovina, Bratislava, Byelorussia, Bulgaria, Bosporus, Black Sea, and so on. What an interesting coincidence that many of these words represent critical geopolitical dimensions in European politics and history.

caused by drives for self-determination and ruthless leadership and resulting in millions of refugees could break out on the Continent. In addition to having their own incentives to break up unloved relations and bonds, many Eastern Europeans felt that they were encouraged by the rest of EU Europe to take the path of self-determination and democracy toward freedom from Soviet influence. There were implied promises of EU membership in the very near future (though the East Europeans were soon to be disappointed). This tacit encouragement, along with the enormous economic and social problems caused by the dissolution of the Soviet trading bloc and disruptions in energy supplies, offered additional incentives to political radicalization and the ruthless pursuit of personal power. Separatist tendencies, the settling of old accounts among ethnic groups from the Baltics to the Bosporus, and the removal of the Soviet threat emboldened many a leader in the region. Arguments based on historical suffering, economic injustice, ethnic superiority, and dreams of enhanced international status (Greater Serbia, Greater Croatia, Greater Albania) were employed to foster militant nationalism. After the first rejoicing at the end of the Cold War, the search for (personal) power and self-determination resulted in aggrandizement at its worst when in Eastern and southeastern Europe, ruthless and opportunistic leaders seized power on the basis of cheap nationalism—thus contributing to tensions, civil strife, and bloodshed, many times even involving criminal organizations.[9] Between 1990 and 1993, a series of international crises broke out encompassing the Iraqi aggression against Kuwait, the disintegration of Yugoslavia and the Soviet Union, and the unification of Germany. They were all based on the notion of self-determination, sovereignty, or statehood as a critical juncture.[10]

---

9. In many instances, especially in the former Yugoslavia, self-determination has been employed as a cover and excuse for accumulating personal power and for obtaining geopolitical objectives not always in tune with the real interests of the majority of the populations. See relevant debates in James Gow, *Triumph of the Lack of Will: International Diplomacy and the Yugoslav War* (London: Hurst, 1997); Misha Glenny, *The Fall of Yugoslavia: The Third Balkan War*, 3rd rev. ed. New York: Penguin Books, 1996), esp. chaps. 1, 3; Laura Silber and Allan Little, *Yugoslavia: Death of a Nation* (New York: Penguin Books, 1996), esp. part 1; and Susan Woodward, *Balkan Tragedy: Chaos and Dissolution After the Cold War* (Washington, D.C.: Brookings Institution, 1995).

10. Wolfgang F. Danspeckgruber, "Epilogue," in Wolfgang F. Danspeckgruber with Charles R. Tripp, eds., *The Iraqi Aggression Against Kuwait* (Boulder, Colo.: Westview Press, 1996), pp. 271–312.

Present

At the end of the twentieth century, there was an intriguing paradox on the European continent: whereas regional integration and globalization in its Western part reduced the traditional role of the state and in turn diminished the relative importance of external boundaries, sovereignty, and the power of national government, southeastern Europe presented the international community with some of the bloodiest and most destructive conflicts since World War II in struggles over the traditional notions of sovereignty, state symbols, and territory.[11] New contradictions have arisen: symbolism versus substance, sovereignty versus supranationality, sovereign territory versus subregionalization, secession versus integration, national boundaries versus globalization, and power and industriousness versus poverty and the search for prosperity. As the interpretation and effects of sovereignty change, so do the meaning of self-determination—with self-governance asserting itself.

At the same time, interest in independence from hitherto national and central governments within the EU has been expressed, as seen in the current developments in Scotland and Corsica. But even for a hypothetically sovereign Scotland, England remains the primary neighbor, whereas for Corsica it would still be France, and all would presumably remain members of a supranational EU. That solution certainly would be the most cost effective for the emerging members. All of them will most likely have the same currency, and, increasingly, their domestic and foreign policy will be guided by similar (EU) rules and objectives. In addition, they will have a major say, together with other small states, against the larger EU members. Thus it is rather unlikely that a smaller, emerging state in Europe will opt to remain outside the EU. The key to a successful and peaceful cooperation rests in the acceptance of multiple identities, flexibility, and mutual respect.

Just as states without EU membership were attracted to the Union, certain member states (France, Denmark) began to resist the further transfer of sovereign powers to Brussels once the Cold War security threat subsided. The struggle for self-governance in Europe contributes to a potential polarization between the European Parliament and the

---

11. For literature supporting the argument of a global village and the challenge of sovereignty through interdependence, see Raymond Vernon, *Sovereignty at Bay: The Multinational Spread of U.S. Enterprises* (New York: Basic Books, 1971); and Robert O. Keohane and Joseph S. Nye, *Power and Interdependence,* 2nd ed. (Boston: Scott, Foresman, 1989).

Committee of the Regions on the one hand and the Council of Ministers and the governments of member states on the other. The latter are opposed to granting too independent a voice to their regions in the EU process.[12] In the regions, however, a more independent role in the EU decisionmaking process is seen as the way to reduce the power of the national administrations, introduce a *supra*national dimension, and provide maximum financial, scientific, and technical assistance for the regions' cultural, social, and economic development. For the EU regions, integration brings enhanced autonomy, decentralization, and devolution of power.

Perspectives

According to Konrad Ginther, self-determination in Europe has two principal objectives: the demand of communities to determine their own political and legal fate and the reaction to this demand by a highly organized European state community via the appropriate use and adap-

---

12. Diana Chigas with Elizabeth McClintock and Christophe Kamp, "Preventive Diplomacy and the Organization for Security and Cooperation in Europe: Creating Incentives for Dialogue and Cooperation," in Abraham Chayes and Antonia Handler Chayes, eds., *Preventing Conflict in the Post-Communist World,* Brookings Occasional Papers (Washington, D.C.: Brookings Institution, 1996), pp. 25–98; and Jean E. Manas, "The Council of Europe's Democracy Ideal and the Challenge of Ethno-National Strife," in the same volume, pp. 99–145.

"The participating states will respect the equality and right of self-determination of the peoples, by acting any time in accordance with the objectives and principles of the Charter of the United Nations and the appropriate laws and regulations of the international law, including those which refer to the integrity of states. According to the principle of equality and self-determination of the peoples, all peoples have [at] any time the right to determine freely, and without outside infringement, their internal and external status as well as their political, economic, and cultural development according to their own desires." Article VIII, Conference on Security and Cooperation in Europe (CSCE), Helsinki Final Act (1975) (translation by Wolfgang Danspeckgruber).

For a detailed analysis of the role of the OSCE in dealing with questions of minority protection and self-determination see Rob Zaagman, "Commentary," in Wolfgang Danspeckgruber with Arthur Watts, eds., *Self-Determination and Self-Administration: A Sourcebook* (Boulder, Colo.: Lynne Rienner, 1997), pp. 248–254; and Prince Alois of Liechtenstein, "Der Liechtensteinische Entwurf für eine Konvention über das Selbstbestimmungsrecht im Vergleich zum Heutigen Völkerrecht," master's thesis in science of laws, University of Salzburg, 1993, p. 12.

See also Ruth Lapidoth, "Sovereignty in Transition," *Journal of International Affairs* (Winter 1992), pp. 337–338; and Ruppert Emerson, "Self Determination," *American Journal of International Law* 65 (1971), pp. 459–475.

tation of its laws, regulations, and institutions.[13] The two objectives encompass the principal orientations of self-determination—either internally or externally. The internal dimension relates to the traditional three freedoms, *liberté*, *égalité*, and *fraternité*; the external orientation points to the freedom to form alliances and draft foreign policy.[14]

Disillusionment and dissatisfaction among electorates, caused by the general economic and sociopolitical situation and the concomitant credibility gap and "democracy gap," have spoiled the relationship between elites and voters in Western Europe. This disaffection applies both within EU member states and in the relationship between national (EU) citizens and Brussels EU officialdom (the "European bureaucrats" or Eurocrats).[15] The EU's simultaneous demand for ever-greater integration, standardization, sharing of common values, consideration for the weakest members, and transfer of powers from member governments to EU institutions creates tensions as communities strive to retain their identity. Voters in traditionally independent, Euro-critical states such as Denmark, France, and even (non-EU member) Switzerland remain skeptical about participating in intensified integration out of concern that the disadvantages would outweigh the gains. They feel that

---

13. Konrad Ginther, "Selbstbestimmung in Europa," Herbert-Miehsler Memorial Lecture at the University of Salzburg, June 1992; *Oesterreichisches Handbuch des Völkerrechts*, vol. 1, 2nd ed. (Vienna: Braunmüller Universitäts-Verlagsbuchhandlung, 1991), pp. 323ff; and Konrad Ginther and Herbert Isak, eds., *Self Determination in Europe*, proceedings of an international workshop, Academy of Graz (Vienna, 1991).

14. Historically, with increasing popular sovereignty, the power of the monarch was transferred to the people, and the nation became the operative unit. It was the nation in which the people were to consent to be governed. If people were sovereign as a nation, they had to be free to form their own state, and the state had to be free to establish its own government. Each people had an inherent right not only to choose its own form of government but to determine its own status as a state. These choices mark the difference between internal and external self-determination. The first concerns the right of a people to form a national unit. The second concerns the right of the national unit to determine its own destiny, primarily in the form of a state. The concept of nationalism has come to be associated with the latter; democracy provides the justification and means for the former. Harold S. Johnson, "Self Determination: Western European Perspective," in Yonah Alexander and Robert A. Friedländer, *Self-Determination: National, Regional, and Global Dimensions,* Special Studies in National and International Terrorism (Boulder, Colo.: Westview Press, 1980), pp. 81–85.

15. The EU policy of furthering integration—deepening—as expressed by the Treaty of Amsterdam, has contributed to additional limitations of the sovereign powers and rights of the EU's member states. It has also led to further expansion and centralization of EU authority over technical, socioeconomic, and even financial (euro), political (CFSP, or Common Foreign and Security Policy), and environmental matters.

their domestic social, educational, and environmental standards, as well as foreign policy goals, exceed the requirements of the EU, which frequently represents the lowest common denominator among its members. Furthermore, a generational change in leadership swept to power younger members of Europe's postwar *Wirtschaftswunder* (economic miracle) generation, leaders who are in search of new values and orientations such as prioritizing environmental protection over increased economic wealth.[16] As an ever more mobile and internationally oriented Internet generation—born in affluent and peaceful conditions of the 1950s, 1960s, or later—takes over, heightened mobility and a feeling of belonging to "one Europe" surface. Europe's historic continent-wide wars appear to be events of a distant past, though new tensions become visible, including radical political and religious dimensions, anti-immigrant sentiments, and even certain anti-American feelings.[17] Franz Borkenhagen writes that in Western Europe, a "new nationalism has emerged . . . which superficially flaunts the popular notion that the supranational uniformity of the EU was preventing a national identity and ignoring local needs."[18] Radical ideas can find their way into party programs even now, and certain radical and populist leaders may feel tempted to exploit this yearning for new values by encouraging nationalist feelings. This nationalism in turn could intensify popular resilience against deepened integration, especially during economic downturns or when perceptions of insecurity increase. It would also stiffen the insistence of regions and communities on retaining sufficient control over their communal affairs, values, and cultural heritage and on keeping enough power to independently direct their destiny according to their own traditions. New forms of split or divided sovereignty; partial integration, or integration à la carte; and apportioned self-governance among communities, regions, states, and EU institutions offer a solution.

---

16. William Wallace notes that the "leaders of post–Cold War Europe are only one or two generations removed from the order which collapsed in 1914." Many of them lived the traumas of World War II and the fears and complications of a stringent Cold War with forceful presence by superpowers. William Wallace, "Regionalism in Europe: Model or Exception," in Louise Fawcett and Andrew Hurrell, eds., *Regionalism in World Politics* (New York: Oxford University Press, 1995), p. 207.

17. Sophie Meunier, "The French Exception," *Foreign Affairs* 79, no. 4 (July/August 2000), pp. 104–107.

18. Franz H.U. Borkenhagen, "Regions in Europe," *Aussenpolitik* (November 1994), pp. 182–188; and Ole Waever, "Nordic Nostalgia: Northern Europe After the Cold War," *International Affairs* 68, no. 1 (1992), pp. 77–102.

Marion Levy Jr. argues that integration automatically introduces stronger centralization irrespective of communal and national interests.[19] By definition, the power of national governments will be challenged in all areas that succumb to integration (economics, finance, technology, social standards, and so on). This loss of power may be avoided in areas where integration is limited by, for example, cultural and education policies, or where it is deliberately excluded.

This observation has shed light on a new *quadrangular relationship* involving the community or communities and their respective central authorities as well as communities interacting with communities in other states (and the respective central governments) on the one hand and the communities and the central powers of the EU on the other. In such a central authority, relationship communities may try to negotiate advantageous deals with either of the two authorities, play one community against the other, or try to obtain more aid (financial, legal, and so on) from the supranational unit, the EU, at the expense of the relationship with the central government. This last option represents the intention to exchange one authority for another (see also Figure 13.1). As long as these options of flexible self-governance are available, communities may not endeavor to achieve classical sovereignty or independence. Thus regional integration and maximum autonomy may offer an interesting alternative to the traditional objective of classical self-determination.

These options also reduce the attraction of redrawing sovereign boundaries. In "Euro-space"—under the Schengen Accords—hard external borders between member states have been transformed into softer, more administrative boundaries.[20] A supranational entity automatically downgrades the importance of the borders between its member states. Communities in search of greater self-determination and autonomy will not necessarily be interested in new international borders if they can obtain the benefits of unlimited membership in the supranational entity by other means. Maximum devolution and decentralization of the central government can offer sufficient self-government to the community, enabling it to participate more directly in EU integration and thus in the global marketplace while not necessarily altering the territory of its state or its international boundaries.

Unfortunately, in economically depressed parts of Eastern and

---

19. I am grateful to Professor Marion Levy Jr. for extensive conversations on this subject, Woodrow Wilson School, 1998.

20. Wolfgang Danspeckgruber, "Review Article: Borders, Self-Determination, and the Emerging Concept of 'Self-Governance,'" *Contemporary Austrian Studies* 7 (2000).

southeastern Europe and the former Soviet Union, notions of sovereignty, statehood, and independence are still capable of mobilizing the masses toward nationalism and eventually bloodshed and destruction. There, the doubtful promises of economic growth and prosperity do not necessarily overcome political cleavages, personal and leadership ambitions, or the influence of the old *nomenklatura* and security services. In many instances (such as in Belarus, Romania) there has been little or no generational or leadership change; instead, leaders have merely morphed from communists to "democrats." Deep-seated antagonisms and socioeconomic problems have become aggravated by foreign involvement via diasporas, governments in exile, or international organized crime.[21] Arguably, if the international community had succeeded in enforcing greater autonomy within a stable environment, a higher level of self-governance concomitant with maximum economic freedom in Eastern Europe and the former Soviet Union, the disastrous conflicts in the former Yugoslavia and Chechnya may have been avoided (see also Prince Hans Adam's comments in the foreword).[22]

Many communities and states still outside the EU experience difficulties in reasserting their independence, finding a new (European) identity, and—for those of former CMEA membership—finding assurance that their future will be free of Russian interference. The problem is especially trying for minorities and others who do not belong to the states' predominant ethnic groups. It seems that minorities are treated according to the past experiences of the dominant community. In spite of the fact that every European government has signed the Charter of Paris of 1990, which guarantees the inviolability of today's boundaries except for alterations through peaceful means, some leaders—in the name of self-determination—still toy with the existing boundaries,

---

21. Wolfgang Danspeckgruber, "EU and US Have an Important Role to Play in Beating Organised Crime in the Balkans," *Financial Times,* January, 6, 1999, p. 12; see <http://www.wws.princeton.edu:80/~lisd/ft99.html>.

22. Regarding Yugoslavia, see footnote 9. On Chechnya, see Anatol Lieven, *Chechnya: Tombstone of Russian Power*, new ed. (New Haven: Yale University Press, 1998); Carlotta Gall and Thomas de Waal, *Chechnya: Calamity in the Caucasus* (New York: New York University Press, 1998); Henry S. Bienen, "Self-Determination and Self-Administration in the former Soviet Union," in Danspeckgruber with Watts, *Self-Determination and Self-Administration: A Sourcebook*, pp. 255–266; Marie Beningsen-Broxup, ed., *The North Caucasus Barrier: The Russian Advance Towards the Muslim World* (New York: St. Martin's Press, 1992), esp. the introduction; and Marie Bennigsen, "Chechnia: Political Developments and Strategic Implications for the North Caucasus," *Central Asian Survey* 18, no. 4 (1999). The LRPSD (Liechtenstein Research Program on Self-Determination) report on the colloquium on Chechnya can be reached at <http://www.princeton.edu:80/~lisd/chechnya.html>.

especially where large ethnic communities are separated from the rest of a nation.[23]

However, what can be seen on the EU level—communal pushes for integration replacing the search for traditional independence—may perhaps develop on the global level as well. Large-scale regional integration (for example, the EU and the North American Free Trade Agreement [NAFTA]) and intensifying globalization reduce the value of hard external boundaries. These integration projects reaffirm the emerging, more general integrative, village character of major regions—a "Schengen-like" phenomenon comparable to the EU Europe of the early twenty-first century, where external boundaries are no longer of the same critical importance as they were from the Peace of Westphalia until Versailles and Yalta and the fall of the Berlin Wall. Under certain conditions, communities elsewhere may be able to see the same cost-benefit calculation as in Europe: Obtain maximum autonomy in order to participate in both regional integration and the global marketplace; leave hard external boundaries untouched but soften them over time.

Subsidiarity

Subsidiarity describes "the relationship between different levels of government."[24] It means decentralization, devolution, and the distribution of power, that is, the devolution of power from central authorities to local and communal ones.[25] In the EU context, subsidiarity addresses the extent to which a community, rather than the EU or a member government, has decisionmaking power.[26] In a sense it addresses "govern-

---

23. Hurst Hannum, "Rethinking Self-Determination," *Virginia Journal of International Law* 34, no. 1 (Fall 1993).

24. See Peter McKinlay, "Globalization, Subsidiarity, and Enabling the Governance of Communities," <http://www.mdl.co.nz/readingroom/governance/globalsub.html>, p. 4.

25. The original Article 1(A) in the 1993 Treaty on European Union states that the EU is a "new stage in the process of creating an ever closer union among the peoples of Europe." The Treaty of Amsterdam Amending the Treaty on European Union, The Treaties Establishing the European Communities and Certain Related Acts (1997) expands on this: "The Treaty marks a new stage in the process of creating an ever closer union among the peoples of Europe, in which decisions are taken as openly as possible and *as closely as possible to the citizen*" (emphasis added).

26. For further treatment of subsidiarity in the EC/EU, see Dusan Sidjanski, *The Federal Future of Europe* (Ann Arbor: University of Michigan Press, 2000), pp. 222–225.

ment by the lowest level possible," though it does not by itself force decentralization.[27] It means that the executive and legislative bodies are expected to adopt a decisionmaking process that involves the people they affect—and hence reduce the distance between the Brussels bureaucracy and the people it governs.[28] The Treaty of Amsterdam's Protocol on the Application of the Principles of Subsidiarity and Proportionality explains that "the principle of subsidiarity provides a guide" to indicate how those powers are to be exercised at the community level and that the EU does not have exclusive competence to make those decisions.[29] Subsidiarity, according to Article 3(A) of the Treaties of Maastricht on the EU, reflects "a commitment to create an ever closer union among the peoples of Europe in which decisions are taken as closely as possible to the citizens."[30] The idea was thus to "reassure member state populations . . . that the Community's seemingly inexorable march towards greater legal and political integration would not needlessly trample their legitimate claims to *democratic self-governance* and cultural diversity" (emphasis added).[31]

Subsidiarity allows for the maximum amount of self-governance and autonomy in a centrally governed and expanding EU. The concept has been applauded as a principle for determining how powers should be divided or shared among different levels of government. Subsidiarity draws criticism from those who argue for centralized leadership and who oppose the devolution of power to the periphery or the provinces. But it does offer a sophisticated legal mechanism that can be used to help avoid nationalistic tensions by permitting devolution in areas rele-

---

27. Thomas Christiansen, "Regionalization in Western Europe," in Kirchner, *Decentralization and Transition in Visegrad*, p. 29.

28. Andreas Follesdal, "Subsidiarity and Democratic Deliberation," ARENA working paper 99/21, also at <http://www.sv.uio.no/arena/publications/wp99_21.html>.

29. The Treaty of Amsterdam, 1997; and Protocol on the Application of the Principles of Subsidiarity and Proportionality Amsterdam, 1997.

30. Alain Delcamp, *Definition and Limits of the Principle of Subsidiarity*, Report prepared for the Steering Committee on Local and Regional Authorities (Strasbourg: Council of Europe Press, 1994); Pat Devine, Yannis Katsoulacos, and Roger Sugden, eds., *Competitiveness, Subsidiarity, and Industrial Policy* (New York: Routledge, 1996); and Chantal Millon-Delson, *L'état subsidiaire: Ingerence et non-ingerence de l'état: Le principe de subsidiarite aux fondements de l'histoire europeenne* (Paris: Presses Universitaires de France, 1992).

31. George A. Berman, "Taking Subsidiarity Seriously: Federalism in the European Community and the United States," *Columbia Law Review* 94, no. 2 (March 1994), p. 334.

vant to cultural identity while continuing central governance in other political and economic matters.[32] It may therefore be an efficient way to reconcile nationalistic tendencies. Indeed it may serve as a valve to release such tensions and permit aspirations for self-governance and cultural identity. In a future EU of twenty states or more, extensive devolution of power and self-governance of communities and regions will become a *conditio* sine qua non for a functioning EU. These circumstances should help not only to satisfy communal and regional ambitions for greater autonomy in cultural and other important aspects but also to render the administration and implementation of the EU more effective.[33]

Subsidiarity and Contemporary Europe: Three Versions

In modern European politics, subsidiarity as a concept has remained oriented toward devolution and the circumstances under which public authorities should intervene in social and economic affairs. The Christian Democrats, in power in many European governments during the 1970s, were major supporters of this idea. The German Bundestag especially has been a strong supporter of subsidiarity.[34] Since the Single European Act and the Giscard d'Estaing Report on the application of the principle of subsidiarity, administrative decentralization has proceeded in the EC with the objective of granting *Länder* and regions the power to make and enforce administrative laws and regulations. More

---

32. Commission of the European Communities (CEC) Office in the United Kingdom, "The Subsidiarity Principle," background report no. 34 to the European Council and the European Parliament, London, November 1992; CEC, "Report to the European Council on the Adaptation of Community Legislation to the Subsidiarity Principle," November 1993; Karl-Heinz Neureither, "Subsidiarity as a Guiding Principle for European Community Activities," *Government and Opposition* 28, no. 2 (London, 1993), pp. 206–220; Scott A. Peterson and D. Millar, "Subsidiarity: A Europe of the Regions Versus the British Constitution?" *Journal of Common Market Studies* 32, no. 1 (March 1994), pp. 46–47; and Anthony L. Taesdale, "Subsidiarity in Post-Maastricht Europe," *Political Quarterly* 64, no. 2 (April/June 1993), pp. 187–197.

33. Historically, the concept of subsidiarity derived from Aristotle and Thomas de Aquinas. Pope Pius XI employed subsidiarity in the *Encyclica Quadragesimo Anno* (1931). See Wolfgang Danspeckgruber, "Self-Determination, Subsidiarity, and Regionalization" in Danspeckgruber with Watts, *Self-Determination and Self-Administration: A Sourcebook*, p. 229; and Sidjanski, *The Federal Future of Europe*, pp. 199, 223–225.

34. Andrew Moravcsik, *The Choice for Europe: Social Purpose and State Power from Messina to Maastricht* (Ithaca, N.Y.: Cornell University Press, 1998).

autonomous regions were allowed to participate in meetings of the EC's Council of Ministers.[35]

According to John Peterson, however, there was a problem: the argument for autonomy could be opposed by reasoning that the need to transfer sovereignty to the European Community was in fact justified by the subsidiarity concept, as only common policies in the entire EC territory could match the scale of the problems and create an effective common approach.[36] In the 1980s, subsidiarity gained relevance through the development of the European Economic Area (EEA) and the EC's environmental standards and regulations. In this case, subsidiarity served as a guarantor against the weakening of strong national environmental standards through the imposition of less stringent EC norms.[37] Several schools of thought on the issue of subsidiarity emerged, and Peterson enumerates the following three competing views.[38]

In the Christian Democratic view, small social groups should be autonomous and sovereign in pluralist societies yet united in a common morality that stresses duty and harmony. The state should assist these communities, but it has no right to substitute its administrative capacity for that of the social groups; nor should the state be shackled by their demands. The state should serve the public good and provide the legal framework. Christian Democrats take a dynamic view of politics and envision state intervention only for limited periods to address specific social needs.

The second, alternative ideology is based on the principles of German federalism and specifically defines the duties and powers of different levels of government in Europe. The German *Länder* want to see their substantial powers protected and—if anything—enlarged, as they are guaranteed by the *Grundgesetz* (Federal Constitution) against trespass by EU institutions and deepening European integration.

---

35. Carles Alfred Gasòliba i Böhm, "The Application of Subsidiarity," in Andrew Duff, ed., *Subsidiarity Within the European Community* (London: Federal Trust for Education and Research, 1993), p. 71.

36. John Peterson, "Subsidiarity: A Definition to Suit Any Vision," *Parliamentary Affairs* 47 (January 1994), pp. 116–132.

37. Deborah C. Cass, "The Word That Saves Maastricht? The Principle of Subsidiarity and the Division of Powers Within the European Community," *Common Market Law Review* 29 (Dordrecht, December 1992), pp. 1107–1136; Neunreither, "Subsidiarity as a Guiding Principle for European Community Activities," pp. 206–220; and Peterson, "Subsidiarity: A Definition to Suit Any Vision," p. 118.

38. Peterson, "Subsidiarity: A Definition to Suit Any Vision," p. 118.

Finally, the conservative British interpretation of subsidiarity emerged in the aftermath of the 1991 Inter-Governmental Conference of Maastricht. British conservatives see subsidiarity simply as a principle for limiting the EU's powers. They assume a narrow definition that sanctions EU action only when it is necessary to ensure the "four freedoms" of the Single European Market. British conservatives refuse to accept the Continental version of subsidiarity, which can be used to justify decentralizing powers to subnational units of government. The British conservatives have insisted on a version of "territorial government" that resists any constraints, internal or external, on the autonomy of central government.

Ideological interpretations of subsidiarity, which indeed address self-governance, can be found in the schools of the German *Länder*. The German position is the most favorable toward self-governance, allowing communities to retain maximum power; hence, the *Länder* also fought against transferring too much power to "remote Brussels." Following the Christian Democratic position, maximum social and moral power would be given to "small social groups" within a state. The federal government, in contrast, would be vested with only limited power.

The British version operates according to a restrictive interpretation of EU powers, as it employs subsidiarity to neutralize the EU's restrictive influence in areas that are important for sovereign national interest. However, certain EU members, such as France, have expressed concern about distributing too much autonomy to the provinces. The Maastricht agreements were rejected in the first referendum in Denmark, and France had difficulties with achieving a consensus on ratification. Meanwhile, the governments of the major federal states of Austria, Belgium, Germany, and Spain favored the concept. The regulations in the Treaty of the EU express this ambiguity.[39]

------

39. Articles 1 and 3(A) argue that decisions should be made with the participation of the citizens, ideally at the level of local government whenever possible. Article 3(B) expects that subsidiarity is employed to divide power between the EU and member states, and the appropriate institutions, in order to maximize efficiency. Article 3(A) seems to reflect Germany's and Belgium's interests; Article 3(B) reflects those of the United Kingdom and Denmark, ensuring the primacy of the nation-state in EU decisionmaking as well as in checking the process of integration. Obviously, Article 3(A) has genuine appeal for all peoples interested in decentralization and regionalization, especially the German *Länder,* the Spanish autonomous regions, the Belgian regions, and the Austrian *Bundesländer.* Furthermore, Article 3(A) offers the basis for extensive regional cooperation.

Subsidiarity and EU Deepening

The idea of subsidiarity has encouraged discussions on the role of local government in EU policymaking, especially as it applies to regional development. The regions' political interest in Europe has grown after a period during which most EU states decentralized their powers at home and transferred powers to the EU. In 1996, the Inter-Governmental Committee discussed the possibility of giving local authorities legislative powers at the EU level. One method of implementing the policy would be to empower the Committee of the Regions.[40] Sending representatives of subnational governments to participate in EU decision-making would provide the desired "nearness" of the government to average citizens. However, as Andreas Follesdal argues, "Subsidiarity [also] serves to constrain European integration as . . . member states . . . disagree about common ends, shared standards, and the likely result of . . . common action."[41]

The Amendments of the Treaty of Amsterdam (1997) establish more precisely the conditions for the principles of subsidiarity and "ensure their strict observance and consistent implementation by all institutions."[42] However, the Protocol on the Application of the Principles of Subsidiarity and Proportionality, attached to that treaty, states that "each institution shall ensure [compliance]" (para. 1) and states (in para. 3) that Article 3b relates "to the areas of which the Community does not have exclusive competence." In the words of the protocol, "the principle of subsidiarity provides a guide as to how those powers are to be exercised at the Community level."[43] There is still

40. Marc Wilke and Helen Wallace, "Subsidiarity: Approaches to Power-Sharing in the European Community," RIIA Discussion Papers, no. 27, 1990; "Overall Approach to the Application by the Council of the Subsidiarity Principle and Article 3b of the Treaty of the European Union," EU Conclusion of the Presidency (Edinburgh: December 12, 1992), SN 456/92, Annex 1 to Part A; and "Subsidiarity," EU Conclusion of the Presidency (Edinburgh: December 12, 1992), SN 456/92, Annex 2 to Part A.
41. Andreas Follesdal, "Subsidiarity and Democratic Deliberation," p. 3.
42. The Treaty of Amsterdam Amending the Treaty on European Union, The Treaties Establishing the European Communities and Certain Related Acts, 1997.
43. The Protocol on the Application of the Principles of Subsidiarity and Proportionality of the Treaty of Amsterdam Amending the Treaty on European Union, the Treaties Establishing the European Communities, and Certain Related Acts (1997), which states:

[E]ach institution shall ensure that the principle of subsidiarity is complied with.

room for interpretation, but clearly the Treaty of Amsterdam and this protocol demonstrate the will of the EU to bring policy- and decision-making closer to the peoples and *not* necessarily to the governments of the member states. Subsidiarity thus presents the intellectual underpinning for a viable "Europe of the Regions."

Regionalization

Regionalization reflects the intention of preserving some degree of self-governance on the communal level that is independent of external national boundaries. If subsidiarity means government by the lowest possible level, regionalization means the closest possible interaction among communities and peoples whose intercommunal relations are favored by geography, culture, ethnicity, and tradition. There were several "regionalist waves" in the 1930s, 1950s, and 1960s. Joseph Nye distinguished two categories of regionalization: "microeconomic organizations, involving formal economic integration, and macroregional political organizations concerned with controlling conflict."[44]

At the beginning of the twenty-first century, in a post–Cold War Europe characterized by the disintegration of the CMEA and the Warsaw Pact, the enlargement of the EU and NATO, and a general international trend toward global interdependence, regionalization is of particular relevance. Specifically, communities are torn between partici-

---

The application of the principle of subsidiarity . . . shall respect the general provisions and objectives of the Treaty, particularly as regards the maintaining in full of the *acquis communautaire* and the institutional balance; it shall not affect the principles developed by the Court of Justice. . . .

The principle of subsidiarity does not call into question the powers conferred on the European Community by the Treaty . . . The criteria referred to in the second paragraph of Article 3b of the Treaty shall relate to areas of which the Community does not have exclusive competence. The principle of subsidiarity provides a guide as to how those powers are to be exercised at the Community level. Subsidiarity is a dynamic concept and should be applied in the light of the objectives set out in the Treaty. . . .

For Community action to be justified, both aspects of the subsidiarity principle shall be met: the objectives of the proposed action cannot be sufficiently achieved by Member States' action in the framework of their national constitutional system and therefore can be better achieved by action on the part of the Community. ["Community" in the above refers to the EU]

44. Louise Fawcett and Andrew Hurrell, "Introduction," in Fawcett and Hurrell, *Regionalism in World Politics*, p. 4.

pating in integration, economic advance, technological progress, and the global marketplace on the one hand and, on the other, preserving some of their traditional ethnic-cultural values and structures.[45]

Regionalization may be based on geographical proximity or commonalities, social and cultural affinities, traditional ethnic relations, trade and infrastructure, and even internal and external security.[46] Regionalization furthers decentralization and democratization by encouraging responsibility and autonomy from below, which ought to inspire the regions to develop their own appropriate capabilities to compete with other regions. Since regionalization seems to be able to compensate for missing structural support from central authorities, regions might find the prospect of interregional (fiscal) operations especially appealing. The essence of regionalization is both the intention to overcome boundaries and separation and a defensive reaction against increasing demands for integration and deepening of the EU. Regionalization also expresses the will to participate in integration and the global marketplace directly and not necessarily via the applicable central authority. In the EU, regionalization and greater regional cooperation cannot be realized without subsidiarity. Regionalization also transcends boundaries, hence also the limits of Schengenland, that is, the outer borders of the EU.

Regionalization introduces an administrative layer at the community level (see Figure 13.1). Administration at the regional level is more efficient and democratic than at the state and supranational levels. This administrative layer is closer to the people and communities that the authorities purport to serve.

Regional cooperation can take place between substates (regions, *Länder*, cantons, provinces), between states and substates, and between states and states. Cooperation can thus take place on the highest-developed, state level (the Central European Initiative [CEI], the Black Sea Economic Cooperation Pact [BSEC]) as well as on the subregional level (Arbeitsgemeinschaft Alpenländer [ARGE], or Alpine States Working Group) (see the appendix to this chapter). All three versions can also exist between EU and non-EU members. Regional projects may range from purely economic to cultural and educational; they may concern infrastructural development, environmental protection, or scientific cooperation, even certain foreign policy matters and operations

---

45. Emil J. Kirchner and Thomas Christiansen, "The Importance of Local and Regional Reform," in Kirchner, *Decentralization and Transition in Visegrad*, p. 4.

46. Regionalization understood as the emergence of subregions, of several smaller states or parts of states according to infrastructural needs, is based on similarities in ethnicity, history, geography, and even climate.

such as against organized crime. These projects can involve local authorities and organizations, groups and citizens. Successful regionalization also supports (EU) stability, development and revitalization projects in poorer areas, which in turn soften discrepancies of wealth and even diminish socioeconomic problems and extensive (socioeconomic) migration. Regional cooperation on a bilateral level between states and states or between states and substates also stimulates trade and industrial development without requiring vast financial or other program assistance from Brussels or the national governments; regionalization may thus be cost effective.[47] In addition, regional cooperation among different ethnic groups and nationalities helps overcome possible tensions and furthers understanding and peace.

Problems and Conditions for Regional Cooperation

The renaissance of regionalization and regionalism in Europe means little less than the successful introduction of democratic values and self-governance on the local level, namely, decentralization and federalization. This renaissance has been aided by increased transparency and a greater readiness to exchange information. (In the early days of the CEI, for example, members' lack of accurate information about other member communities was a problem.) Furthermore, regional cooperation also permits the weak to join forces and act with one, powerful voice or to join the strong to launch mutually beneficial projects.

The introduction of a federal system increases the rights and obligations of subregions both within a certain sovereign system and across borders. Regional cooperation between two communities separated by external boundaries could be termed bilateral; in the case of more, it would be multilateral. Frequently, multilateral regional projects, even if they do not result in an organization, tend to have common headquarters and (small) administrations.

There are four general problems that can often be dealt with effectively through regional and subregional cooperation:[48]

1. Economic problems: Regionalization can be a reaction to profound regional differences in income, wealth, employment, or the per

---

47. Emil J. Kirchner, "The Role of the EU in Local and Regional Government," in Kirchner, *Decentralization and Transition in Visegrad,* pp. 209–215; and Paul Krugman, *Geography and Trade* (Cambridge: MIT Press, 1991).

48. For extensive analysis, see Wolfgang Danspeckgruber, "Regionalization, Sub-Regionalization, and Security in Central Eastern Europe," Princeton Pew Papers, Center of International Studies, Princeton University, 1996, pp. 28–34.

capita contribution to GDP. Regionalization may be an expression of the search for more prosperity. The post–Cold War phenomenon of regionalization as part of an intra-EU reaction to enlargement and deepening offers participating communities, states, and regions a strategy to attract special attention and funding by the European Commission and EU institutions. Furthermore, EU administrators may suggest such cooperation as another means to spur industrialization, trade, and economic development not only in a given region but within EU-wide projects.

2. Psychosociological problems: Regionalization offers new ways, above and beyond the use or manipulation of boundaries, to help realize the ethnic and national interests of the group or community involved. Local exploration and support of regional religious and cultural values and identities is perhaps more effective than petitioning a central national authority or a powerful and distant supranational administration for recognition and support. Communities exhausted by trying to achieve support through these traditional channels may be revitalized by the possibility of new avenues for achieving change. Regionalization may result from common concerns such as a perception of threat or disadvantaged situation in an existing international order (as experienced by the Hungarians, South Tyrolians, Slovaks, Slovenes). It may also be encouraged as a result of personal relationships—for instance, CEE (Central and Eastern Europe) intellectuals and artists during the 1970s and 1980s and contacts between opposition leaders and certain West European politicians.

3. Displaced relationships: After several decades, regionalization within Central and Eastern Europe has allowed the establishment or reestablishment of relationships among those who were separated. In many cases, peoples forcibly separated following World War I and the post–World War II Yalta order saw regional projects as a means to link up with those with whom they found more affinities. Obviously, the political strategic conditions had to be conducive to such projects. Thus regionalization can also be a reaction to the imposition of a political order and boundaries and permits communities to interrelate irrespective of outside power interests. Cooperation between cities, as in a European city network, has again intensified. For instance, Vienna, Bratislava, and Budapest; Lyon and Geneva; and Hamburg, Berlin, and Stettin have reactivated their historical cooperation in many areas such as high-speed transmission of data and rail infrastructure. Such triangular or quadrangular networks are prone to intensify.

4. Geographical, topographical, and climatic parameters: Regionalization clearly follows routes of trade, communication, and

interaction, for example, sea lanes, valleys, rivers, mountain passes, plains, and so on. Geography and climate also influence communal character and preferences. However, regional stability and peace are a precondition for cooperation based on these parameters.

Europe of the Regions

A "Europe of the Regions" was an idea that rose and fell in accordance with the progress and limitations of European integration. In a sense it suggests a possible European superstate with a degree of decentralization. A number of institutions oversee various partnerships between subregional entities and the EU and the Council of Europe (COE).

The Committee of the Regions (COR) and the Conference of the Europe of the Regions are umbrella organizations. The Maastricht Treaty, which established the COR, contains amendments relating to the rights of regions and subunits and their enhanced powers within the institutional process of the EU.[49] The COR provides for representation of regional and local bodies and must be consulted by the European Commission and the European Parliament.[50] It undertakes to empower the regions to contribute in lawmaking, may submit legal opinions, and perceives "the principle of subsidiarity its *leitmotif.*"[51] The COR may also directly participate in EU Council of Minister meetings.[52]

The Assembly of the European Regions (AER) is the regions' most powerful voice. It has a direct role in EU decisionmaking, a voice in the European Commission and an extensive lobbying mechanism in Brussels and Strasbourg. Founded in 1995, the AER aims to foster intraregional cooperation and strengthen the political representation of the regions in the EU, the Council of Europe, and the Organization for Security and Cooperation in Europe (OSCE). Today AER is composed of more than 290 regions from Western, Central, and Eastern Europe.[53]

In the Council of Europe, the Steering Committee of Local and

---

49. In the 1960s and 1970s, but especially since the Single European Act (SEA) and the Giscard d'Estaing Report on the application of the principle of subsidiarity (1991), administrative decentralization has persisted in favor of *Länder,* nations, and autonomous communities.

50. See Article 198a of the Maastricht Treaty.

51. Kirchner, "The Role of the EU in Local and Regional Government," p. 217.

52. Gasòliba i Böhm, "The Application of Subsidiarity," p. 71.

53. *Jahrbuch der Oesterreichischen Aussenpolitik* (Vienna: Ministry for Foreign Affairs, 1995), pp. 95, 96.

Regional Authorities (CDLR) "provides a forum to exchange information and promote cooperation in the area of local democracy."[54]
The Congress of Local and Regional Authorities of Europe
(CLRAE), established in 1994, is a consultative body for establishing
effective local and regional self-government.[55] It seems important to
recognize that local self-government has a long tradition within the
COE. This is expressed in the 1985 European Charter of Local Self-
Government, which should help define "the principles of local autonomy."[56]

European City Network

The ECOS Program (European Cities Cooperation System) represents a
specific program on cooperation among cities in Europe, particularly
members of CEE. It arose from an initiative of the EU Commission to
emphasize cooperation among counties, towns, and cities in the EU and
Central and Eastern Europe.[57] The emphasis is on local democracy,
urban policy and planning, and environmental protection.[58] The first
projects have focused on cooperation between Berlin, Brussels, Lisbon,
and Budapest on traffic and migration and have been extended to
include Bratislava, Prague, and Warsaw.[59]

---

54. CDLR covers legal and administrative dimensions and is assisted by committees of experts and groups of specialists, particularly the Select Committee of
Experts on Transfrontier Cooperation (IRRCT). See Kirchner, "The Role of the EU
in Local and Regional Government," p. 213.

55. The CLRAE replaces the former Standing Conference of Local and
Regional Authorities of Europe. It has two chambers, the Chamber of Local
Authorities and the Chamber of Regions. They comprise 291 titular members and
291 substitute members representing over 200,000 regional and local authorities in
the COE's forty-one member states. See <http://www.coe.fr/cplre/eng.html>; also
Territorial Authorities, Transfrontier Co-operation and Regional Planning Division,
Council of Europe.

56. Council of Europe, *European Charter of Local Self-Government and
Explanatory Report* (1996).

57. Renate Kicker, Joseph Marko, and Martin Steiner, eds., *Changing Borders,
Legal and Economic Aspects of European Enlargement* (New York: Peter Lang
Verlag, 2000); Beth E. Strutzenberg, "Urban Reawakening: International City
Networks Within the European Union," senior thesis, Princeton University, 1995;
and Stephan Tempel, "Staedtepartnerschaften in der deutsch-polnischen
Zusammenarbeit," *Osteuropa* 47 (1997), pp. 630–665.

58. On the initiative of Berlin, Vienna has been a "voluntary member" of
ECOS since 1993 (as at that time Austria was not yet an EU member).

59. *Wien: StadtAussenpolitische Jahresbilanz 1995* (Vienna: Magistrat der
Stadt, 1995), p. 47.

The EU does not have a specific city policy, but many of its initiatives are run through ERDF (European Regional Development Fund), which addresses socioeconomic, economic, and environmental problems and the revitalization of historic and city centers. Eventually it provided for further programs such as RECITE (Regions and Cities for Europe).[60]

On the one hand, EU Europe knows the greater search for a special status and relative independence by major cities in Europe such as Hamburg, Berlin, Vienna, Frankfurt, and Milan—based in many cases on historical experience. On the other hand, the emerging trend of cooperation among cities across Europe via the Trans-European Network (TEN), in the form of high-speed rail and fiber-optic/satellite communication networks,[61] will permit cities to offer unique advantages to business, industry, and households and may further contribute to an increased rift and uneven development with rural areas. The Rhine-Rhone cities and the so-called Euro cities are further examples of such beneficial cooperation.[62]

Geography

It is significant that today's united Germany shares borders with so many of the major regions of Europe: three of the four members of ARGE (ARGE Alps, ARGE Alpen-Adria, and ARGE Danube Regions) as well as the members of CEFTA (Central European Free Trade Agreement) and CEI (Central European Initiative) border on Germany. Germany's influence extends as well to other areas via these bordering regions: to the Baltic area, the Danubian region, the Mediterranean region via Austria and Switzerland, and the Visegrad Group via the Czech Republic and Poland. The CEE countries are aware of

---

60. Strutzenberg, "Urban Reawakening: International City Networks Within the European Union," pp. 6–7, quotes "Millan Speech at Eurocities Conference," Reuter European Community Report (3/11/93).

61. Panayotis Getimis and Grigoris Kafkalas, eds., *Urban and Regional Development in the New Europe: Policies and Institutions for the Development of Cities and Regions in the Single European Market* (Athens: Urban and Regional Development Policy: TOPOS, 1993); and Mick Dunford and Grigoris Kafkalas, eds., *Cities and Regions in the New Europe: The Global-Local Interplay and Spatial Development Strategies* (London: Belhaven Press; New York: Halsted Press, 1992).

62. Péter Hardi, "Hungarian Foreign Policy: Integration into Europe," in Hans-Peter Neuhold, ed., *New Forms of Cooperation in a Changing Europe: The Pentagonal/Hexagonal Experiment* (Vienna: Braumüller, 1991), p. 17.

Germany's influence, and many an initiative serves to provide a counterbalance. (Nevertheless, Germany is welcomed regarding financial and industrial support; the country is also a reliable *pour-parleur* in the EU and the international community.) Other strategies for counterbalancing that fall just beneath the optimum solution of full EU or NATO membership include the formation of extensive trade ties; the search for direct investment from other major powers, particularly the EU, France, Britain, and the United States; and the enhancement of regional cooperation.

The formation of regional, especially subregional, cooperative ventures is a variation of interstate regional integration with the emphasis on building from below. This strategy may offer increased networking, strengthening, and integration at the local level and hence enhanced democratization at the base. It also builds human ties, enhances stability, and has the ultimate effect of diminishing the relevance of borders.[63]

For the regions of Central Europe, around the territory of the former Austro-Hungarian monarchy, regionalization represents a continuation of a natural sociopolitical interaction that existed before 1914. During the Cold War, regional cooperation initiatives (above and beyond political cooperation) began to demonstrate successful examples of cooperation between democratic states. The governments in both Eastern and West Central Europe also favored certain schemes of cooperation (such as cultural exchange and scientific cooperation) that eventually expanded into more costly projects, for example, transportation technology exchanges, environmental and energy cooperation, and industrial training.[64] These endeavors had considerable momentum by

---

63. Martin Eichtinger, "Oesterreichs Aussenpolitik in Zentral- und Osteuropa nach dem Annus mirabilis 1989," in Ilona Slawinski and Joseph P. Strelka, eds., *Viribus Unitis Oesterreichs Wissenschaft und Kultur im Ausland: Impulse und Wechselwirkungen* (Vienna: Peter Lang, 1996), p. 118; Wolfgang Danspeckgruber, "The European Economic Area, the Neutrals, and an Emerging Architecture," in Gregory Treverton, ed., *The Shape of the New Europe* (New York: Council on Foreign Relations, 1992), pp. 92–130; and Emil Staffelmayr, "Die Dynamik der Entwicklung in Europa," Oesterreichisches Jahrbuch für Politik 1990 (Vienna, 1991), pp. 711–720.

64. For an interesting article on the Pentagonale, see Hans-Peter Neuhold, "Renaissance of Regionalism," *Der Standard* (January 4, 1991), p. 4 (transcribed in FBIS-WEU-91-038, p. 2). Also see Klaus-Peter Weiner, "Between Political Regionalization and Economic Globalization: Problems and Prospects of European Integration," *International Journal of Political Economy* (Spring 1992), pp. 41–61.

the time the Berlin Wall fell in 1989; they have since been overtaken by regionwide efforts to join the EU and NATO.[65] Regionalization can encompass smaller states (for example the CEI states, the Baltics, and the Benelux countries) as well as regions. A really successful example of self-governance in Europe—achieved through patience, negotiations, and goodwill demonstrated by all sides involved and without negative outside interference—is represented by the region of South Tyrol/Alto Adige.[66] Following the successful completion of the

---

65. Barry Jones and Michael Keating, eds., *The European Union and the Regions* (Oxford: Clarendon Press, 1995); Joachim Jens Hesse, ed., *Regionen in Europa = Regions in Europe = Régions en Europe* (Baden-Baden: Nomos, 1995); Claude Du Granrut, *Europe: Le temps des Régions*, preface by Jean-Francois Deniau (Paris: Librarie Générale du Droit et de la Jurisprudence, 1994); Leo van den Berg, *Governing Metropolitan Regions* (Aldershot: Avebury, 1993); Wolfgang Haubrichts and Reinhard Schneider, eds., *Grenzen und Grenzregionen* (Saarbrücken: Saarbrückner Druckerei und Verlag, 1993); Robert Lafont, *La nation, l'état, les regions: Reflexions pour une fin de siécle et un commencement d'Europe* (Paris: Berg International, 1993); R. Cappellin and P.W.J. Batey, eds., *Regional Networks, Border Regions, and European Integration* (London: Pion, 1993); John Bachtler, ed., *Socio-Economic Situation and Development of the Regions in the Neighbouring Countries of the Community in Central and Eastern Europe: Final Report to the European Commission* (Brussels: Commission of the European Communities, Directorate-General for Regional Policies; Lanham, Md.: Unipub distributor, 1992); Robert Leonardi and Raffaella Y. Nanetti, eds., *The Regions and European Integration: The Case of Emilia-Romagna* (London: Pinter, 1990); *Regional Research in an International Perspective* (Munich: V. Florentz, 1984); and Dudley Seers and Kjell Ostrom, eds., *The Crises of the European Regions* (New York: St. Martin's Press, 1983).

66. For an excellent work see Melissa Magliana, *The Autonomous Province of Bolzano-Südtirol: A Model of Self-Governance?* Arbeitshefte, no. 20, Europäische Akademie Bozen, 2000. Also see Duncan Morrow, "Regional Policy as Foreign Policy: The Austrian Experience," *Regional Politics and Policy: An International Journal* 2, no. 3 (1992), p. 39.

For Austrian perspectives, see various issues of the *Aussenpolitische Bericht*, Federal Ministry of Foreign Affairs (Vienna, 1970s to 1990s); Felix Ermacora, *Südtirol: die verhinderte Selbstbestimmung* (Vienna: Amalthea, 1991); Josef Fontana, ed., and Walter Freiberg, *Südtirol und der italienische Nationalismus: Entstehung und Entwicklung einer europäischen Minderheitenfrage, quellenmässig dargestellt* (Innsbruck: Wagner, 1989); Klaus Weiss, *Das Südtirol-Problem in der Ersten Republik: dargestellt an Österreichs Innen und Aussenpolitik in Jahre 1928* (Vienna: Verlag für Geschichte und Politik; München: R. Oldenbourg, 1989); Theodor Veiter, *Bibliographie zur Südtirolfrage* (1945–1983) (Vienna: Braumüller, 1984); and Peter Bettelheim and Rudi Benedikter, eds., *Apartheid in Mitteleuropa? Sprache und Sprachenpolitik in Südtirol: La lingua e la politica delle lingue nel Sudtirolo* (Vienna: J & V, 1982).

For other positions, see Louis Freschi, *Le Haut Adige-Tyrol du Sud: autonomie et developpement* (Grenoble: Editions des Cahiers de l'Alpe, de la Societe Desecrivains Dauphinois, 1988); Klaus Eisterer and Rolf Steininger, *Die Option: Südtirol zwischen Faschismus und Nationalsozialismus* (Innsbrucker Forschung zur Zeitgeschichte, Band 5, Innsbruck: Haymon, 1989); and Felix Ermacora, ed., *Geheimbericht der Südtiroler Delegation zur Pariser Konferenz 1946: mit einer historischen und aktuellen Standortbestimmung* (Vienna: Amalthea, 1987).

Südtirol Packet, modern South Tyrol has benefited dramatically by exploiting the EU's regionalization arrangements in the form of cross-border cooperation initiatives.[67] Factors contributing to South Tyrolean prosperity and self-governance include extensive transfrontier North-South interaction through the Inn Valley, local industry, tourism, and financially rewarding relationships among Bozen, Rome, and Vienna as well as South Tyrol's interactions with Austrian North and East Tyrol, the City of Innsbruck, and the federal state of Vorarlberg.[68] Furthermore, South Tyrol has been active with the Swiss canton of Grisons, (West) German Bavaria, and Italian Lombardy since the first meeting of the ARGE Alpine in 1972.[69]

The ARGE Alpine has provided South Tyroleans with even broader self-determination by bringing South Tyrol into direct relationships with similar regions in other countries.[70] The interest of creating the ARGE lay in the economic opportunities provided by the dynamic growth in northern Italy and southern Germany.[71] Joint efforts by local inhabitants have unified the region further in demanding financial support from the EU, Austria, and Italy to minimize highway congestion

---

67. The package consisted of 137 detailed measures to be taken in favor of the people of South Tyrol. They were intended to guarantee the ethnic, cultural, and economic survival of the German-speaking and Ladin groups. Some favored the minorities (that is, use of languages and access to civil service jobs); others were designed to strengthen the region economically. Alois Mock, "South Tyrol Conflict Resolved: A Contribution to European Stability," *Austrian Information* 45, no. 7–8 (1992), p. 6.

68. South Tyroleans have used their good relationship with Austria to strengthen their voice within their own state of Italy. For instance, Austria encourages young South Tyroleans through financial incentives to come to study and take apprenticeships.

69. North and South Tyrol have exploited all possible opportunities to maximize contacts with each other since the 1970s and have formed the Interregional Parliamentary Commission to work out problems in the provinces. Joint meetings occur regularly between the two provincial assemblies. Annual South Tyrol consultations have brought leading Tyrolean politicians together to participate with Austria's foreign policy elite and form the basis of federal contacts between the Austrian and Italian governments.

70. ARGE Alpine is widely considered to be the brainchild of former Tyrolean *Landeshauptmann* Eduard Wallnöfer, the late chairman of the Tyrolian Peoples Party (ÖVP). See Morrow, "Regional Policy as Foreign Policy: The Austrian Experience," p. 30.

71. The 1972 completion of the Brenner Autobahn, under the auspices of the Alpine Europa Bridge project, provided one of these needed internal links—a transport corridor between Milan and Munich that runs directly through Tyrol. This strategic north-south artery in fact has become too much of a success, as the many thousands of cars and trucks that travel it each day have created local environmental problems.

with a new rail-tunnel system—the new Brenner-Base Tunnel—as part of the TEN. The proposed new tunnel would help further secure North-South Tyrolean relations.

The Euro-Region of Tyrol project, involving Tyrol in Austria and South Tyrol and Trentino in Italy, has been approved as a form of institutionalized transborder cooperation. A related Austro-Italian framework agreement on transborder cooperation by regional authorities permits the conclusion of agreements between authorities of the respective provinces in both states within their respective administrative and legal powers. The working group's success has led to numerous imitations throughout Europe.[72]

Conclusion

Self-determination has played as much a role in shaping the political landscape of the Continent as it has been exposed to and influenced by its dramatic changes over time—from the development of the nation-state and the Peace of Westphalia to our times. In the emerging Europe, leaving aside those areas where nationalism and old-style leadership and even armed clashes still exist, subsidiarity, regionalization, and local self-government are its best expression. Granting decisionmaking powers to regional and local governments facilitates the process of problem solving at the local level, which directly benefits the people concerned. Smaller areas linked by ethnic, religious, cultural, or historic ties certainly benefit from intensified cross-border trade, cooperation, and regionalization.

Arguably, the goal of European unification, stability, peace, and prosperity can be attained only through regional cooperation and extensive adherence to subsidiarity. Via the Treaty of Amsterdam, subsidiari-

---

72. Eastern Alpine regions established the ARGE Alpen-Adria in Venice in 1978. French, Italian, German, and Swiss Alpine regions, provinces, cantons, and departments created COTRAO (Communauté de Travail des Alpes Occidentales, or Working Community of the Western Alps) in 1982. By 1990, ARGE Alp membership grew to eleven, with the addition of Austrian Salzburg, Swiss St. Gallen and Ticino, and West German Baden-Württemberg. In its first twenty years of existence, "the loose collection of neighboring provinces and regions developed an informal infrastructure of intergovernmental consultation and information exchange, administrative cooperation and a series of conferences on important themes for Alpine and transalpine development" (Morrow, "Regional Policy as Foreign Policy: The Austrian Experience," p. 31). ARGE Alpen-Adria was the first to cross truly untouched boundaries. Under the aegis of that ARGE, in 1986 regions from member states of NATO, the Warsaw Pact, nonaligned countries, and neutral states were in one grouping for the first time.

ty has become ingrained in the framework of European integration with the intention to offer the peoples of Europe as much say as possible. This devolution from the center of Brussels, indeed, down to the regions and communes of the EU, is very much in the spirit of self-government. Subsidiarity is hence also a precondition for regionalization, which can happen between substate actors as well as between states. Regionalization introduces another administrative layer and can overcome rivalries, help alleviate ethnic antagonisms (through human contact, trade, and distribution of wealth), and lessen disparities in economic and industrial development. It can also further cooperative efforts in the areas of education, science, technology, and the environment—particularly where regions of the EU cooperate with nonmember states. Arguably regionalization would not be feasible without subsidiarity; nor could it be understood without the objective of greater regional cooperation. Consequently, the Committee on the Regions sees subsidiarity as an essential precondition.[73] Moreover, new international entities within the EU would automatically belong to that supranational unit. This development has the potential to alter the role, position, and meaning of sovereign entities in Europe and beyond and to possibly change the very meaning of international borders. Such entities will presumably keep their exclusionary power for years to come regarding the sovereign powers, defense, and the transit of humans and (certain) goods but open up more regarding the exchange and movement of information, money, and services.

Infringements on regionalization may derive from adverse leadership choices or outside-power resistance, minority issues, and other

---

73. In explaining this drive toward regionalism in Europe, Ginther refers to "internal colonialism," a term used by the Western European regionalization movement that addresses issues of dominance and dependence in the relationship between the metropolitan center and the provinces. He asserts that there are two major defining dimensions to self-determination: the theory of persistency, which relates to regionalization movements of minority and ethnic groups; and the motivation thesis, which concerns why self-determination has (once again) obtained relevance. Indeed, both are attempts to examine the objective and subjective aspects of self-determination.

Regionalization has become an appealing option because change has occurred in the national and continental system. This fluidity invites alteration and demands adaptation, including reform of structures. In such times, greater awareness of the "self" and national virtues can be observed, which motivates citizens to demand greater self-governance. Regionalization concerns all the economic, political, and strategic underpinnings capable of causing change. Thus regionalization occurs once the overall patterns of trade, industrialization, and power structure on a national, regional, and continental scale change, and it will continue until a new equilibrium is found.

polemic issues such as environmental concerns. For instance, migration and cheap imported labor may influence national labor markets and educational structures, hence causing tensions and aversion to regionalization. Incompetence or unwillingness to change plans regarding major construction projects with environmental repercussions, such as hydropower plants or nuclear power plants, can add to interregional political frictions. In sum, it can be argued:

1. In Western Europe, interest in traditional self-determination (autonomy) is not necessarily focused on the modification of borders or the establishment of new sovereign units. Rather, the parties involved typically address questions of language, culture, education, and religion as well as related administrative and economic dimensions. In matters such as industrial policy, economic coordination, or scientific cooperation, the need for central EU guidance is more readily acknowledged. Incidentally, it still is the dream of most European states—including Russia—to get as close as possible to the EU. Such is the case with the new unified currency, the euro. Greater autonomy for any region or province within an EU member state will, at any rate, mean that *all* resulting new entities will still remain members of the supranational entity, the EU. Hence, self-determination and secession have acquired a new meaning in Europe: the focus has shifted from unlimited traditional sovereignty to limited sovereignty within a larger, supranational entity as hard external borders are transformed into soft, internal ones. Seemingly contradictory moves toward both autonomy and integration coexist, hence underlining a readiness to recognize the rights of minorities while accepting multiple identities and a flexible political culture.

2. Striving for secession and autonomy in Eastern and southeastern Europe in the post–Cold War period still indicates a search for classical sovereignty, but combined with immediate membership in the EU. The new states are willing to curtail their sovereign political and economic powers in exchange for the benefits of EU membership, integrated economies, higher standards of living, and even enhanced security.

3. The process of obtaining greater self-determination has to be understood in four dimensions: vertical, horizontal, bilateral, and internal (see Figure 13.1). Each case is unique because each community has its own history, traditions, location, and aspirations, making it difficult to draw general conclusions.

4. There is a new attempt to institutionalize self-determination, that is, to build it into constitutions.

The Principality of Liechtenstein is testing the institutionalization of self-determination by proposing that the right to self-determination be included in the new constitution. The Princely House suggests including a paragraph on self-determination in order to offer communities the possibility of searching for new legal arrangements (see Chapter 13). Obviously, this is a novel proposition.

The successful case of South Tyrol for self-governance and regional integration demonstrates that continuous negotiation, patience, and a readiness to compromise between communities searching for greater autonomy and their respective governments; a malleable political culture; and the absence of negative outside influence can lead to favorable results and contribute to both economic and social success and a fruitful relationship with EU institutions.

*   *   *

Appendix 7.1   Regionalization and Subregionalization in Central and Eastern Europe

Regional and local cross-border cooperation aims to overcome existing borders that prevent the establishment of networks among authorities, enterprises, and peoples. The cooperation provides for transborder economic and infrastructural development, trade, and environmental protection. Other benefits include the protection of the cultural heritages of the cooperating parties, examination of the effects of EU enlargement at its outer boundaries, and an increasing number and effectiveness of people-to-people contact.

Regional Cooperative Endeavors and Interstate Cooperation

Central European Initiative (CEI, formerly Pentagonale)
http://www.digit.it/ceinet
Members: Albania, Austria, Belarus, Bosnia and Herzegovina, Bulgaria, Croatia, the Czech Republic, Hungary, Italy, Macedonia, Moldova, Poland, Romania, Slovakia, Slovenia, Ukraine, and the Executive Secretariat in Trieste (Italy).
    The CEI has the stated goal of bringing states together for enhanced regional cooperation and mutual understanding. The initiative has sixteen working groups—including agriculture, culture, environment, against organized crime, media, migration, minorities, science and technology, tourism, and transport—and more than 130 projects financed by member countries, the EBRD, the EIB, or PHARE.

Visegrád Group (V4)
http://www.visegrad.org/
Members: the Czech Republic, Hungary, Poland, and Slovakia.
    In 1991, as a result of the Bratislava process, Hungary, Poland, and Czechoslovakia formed the Visegrád Group. The group uses its historic, religious, and cultural links to deal with political, economic, and security issues, as well as education and science. Specifically, the group works for trade promotion, EU and NATO integration, and the building of a European security architecture that reinforces cooperation and coordination within existing European and transatlantic institutions.

Central European Free Trade Agreement (CEFTA)
http://stars.coe.fr/doc/doc98
Members: the Czech Republic, Hungary, Poland, Romania, Slovakia, and Slovenia.
    Established in 1993, the CEFTA signifies an important step for countries in the region to cooperate closely in the field of economics. The group also supports its members in their efforts to attain EU membership. A complete lifting of nonagricultural tariffs among members was introduced in 1998.

Council of Baltic Sea States (CBSS)
http://www.baltinfo.org/CBSS.htm
Members: Denmark, Estonia, Finland, Germany, Iceland, Latvia, Lithuania, Norway, Poland, Russia, Sweden, and the European Commission.
    The council was formed to encourage intensified cooperation and coordination among the Baltic Sea states with the aim of achieving democratic development, greater unity among the member countries, and favorable economic development in the Baltic Sea region. The CBSS has working groups on democratic institutions, economic cooperation, and nuclear safety and radiation protection.

Black Sea Economic Cooperation Pact (BSEC)
http://www.bsec.gov.tr
Members: Albania, Armenia, Azerbaijan, Bulgaria, Georgia, Greece, Moldova, Romania, Russia, Turkey, and Ukraine.
    The Bosporus Declaration, signed July 27, 1992, brought together countries in the region with the goal of enhancing cooperation in trade, finance, infrastructure, and cultural and religious contacts.

continues

Appendix 7.1   Continued

Subregional Cooperative Endeavors

Working Community of Western Alps (COTRAO)
http://www.unil.ch/cotrao
Members: Rhone-Alps and Prevence-Alpes-Côte d'Azur (France); Piemont, Liguria, and the
Aosta Valley (Italy); Geneva, Valais, and Vaud (Switzerland).
   COTRAO was created in 1982 to cooperate and exchange information in areas such as
transit needs and policies, mountain agriculture and economy, energy, tourism, environmental
protection and land preservation, urban and rural planning, and culture.

Working Community of Alps (ARGE-Alp)
http://www.argealp.at
Members: Baden-Württemberg and Bayern (Germany); St. Gallen, Graubünden, and Tessin
(Switzerland); Vorarlberg, Tirol, and Salzburg (Austria); Lombardia and Trentino-Südtirol
(Italy).
   Founded in 1972, ARGE-Alp facilitates cooperation between Länder and regions of the
western Alps. The group deals with both local challenges and international and EU issues
related to tourism, transit, and environmental protection. It collaborates closely with Alp-
Adria and COTRAO.

ARGE Alp–Adria
http://www.alpeadria.org
Members: Bavaria (Germany); Oberösterreich, Kärnten, Steiermark, and Burgenland
(Austria); Trentino-Südtirol, Lombardia, Veneto, Emilia Romagna, and Friuli (Italy); Gyoer-
Moson-Sopron, Somogy, Vas, Zala, and Baranja (Hungary); Ticino (Switzerland); Slovenia;
Croatia.
   Founded in 1978 as a forum for cooperation similar to ARGE-Alp, ARGE Alp–Adria
also includes provinces from Hungary and Yugoslavia. It focusses on traffic issues, the envi-
ronment, agriculture, energy, youth and sports, science, and disaster protection and relief.

ARGE Danube Regions
http://www.argedonau.at
Members: Bavaria (Germany); Oberösterreich, Niederösterreich, Wien, and Burgenland
(Austria); Gyoer-Moson-Sopron, Komarom-Esztergom, Pest, Fejer, Bacs-Kiskun, Tolna, and
Baranja (Hungary); Serbia; Moldova.
   ARGE Danube Regions was founded in 1989 at the initiative of Niederösterreich to cre-
ate an effective mechanism for the area to deal with issues on the Danube river such as ship-
ping, the environment, the economy, tourism, and culture.

Selected Euroregions in the CEI countries
Euroregion Baltic: Sweden, Poland, Kaliningrad, Lithuania, Latvia (along the Baltic Sea
   coast)
Euroregion Pomerania: Sweden, Germany, Poland (along Baltic Sea coast)
Euroregion Niemen: Lithuania, Poland, Belarus
Euroregion Bug: Poland, Ukraine, Belarus
Carpathian Euroregion (Polish-Hungarian initiative related to ARGE Alps–Adria): Poland,
   Slovakia,
Hungary, Romania, Ukraine
Euroregion Sumava: the Czech Republic, Germany, Austria
Euroregion Southern Moravia: the Czech Republic, Austria, Slovakia
Danube-Kris-Mures-Tisza Euroregion: Hungary, Yugoslavia-Serbia, Romania
Euroregion Danube-Drava-Sava: Hungary, Croatia, Bosnia and Herzegovina
Lower Danube Euroregion: Ukraine, Moldova, Trans-Dniestr, Romania

8

Self-Determination and State Contraction: Britain and Ireland, France and Algeria, Israel and the West Bank/Gaza

IAN S. LUSTICK

Edward Gibbon summarized his explanation for the decline and fall of the Roman Empire as "the natural and inevitable effect of immoderate greatness." "The causes of destruction," he observed, "multiplied with the extent of conquest; and, as soon as time or accident had removed the artificial supports, the stupendous fabric yielded to the pressure of its own weight." Though Gibbon has passed out of fashion, most explanations for the failure, collapse, decline, or disappearance of the (western) Roman Empire share a notion of a state that had overreached its capacities in the face of increasingly difficult challenges. But these explanations beg the question of why those governing the sprawling empire did not seek to preserve their state by reducing its burdens, that is, by contracting it.[1] Few scholars have addressed the question of why Rome did

---

1. The same can be said of the literature on the Ottoman Empire. Great attention has been paid to the fate of alternative projects for redefining the nature of the empire as strategies to save it during the eighteenth, nineteenth, and twentieth centuries, but virtually none to the question of whether or why before World War I no efforts were made to adapt by strategic contraction. Although I am not equally familiar with the relevant literatures, I would hypothesize that similar patterns of research characterize scholarly traditions pertaining to other empires, such as the Austro-Hungarian and the tsarist empires. It is also relevant that in the sophisticated treatments of organizational evolution, growth, and development, the overwhelming tendency has been to study expansion of organizations and the reasons for their failure or collapse rather than to study patterns of strategic contraction. See, for example, the seminal book by J. D. Thompson, *Organizations in Action* (New York: McGraw-Hill, 1967), which systematically considers the reasons for organizational growth as a strategic response to environmental circumstances and survival requirements but not once entertains the possibility of strategic contraction as an adaptive response to a threatening task environment.

not prudentially shrink its domain to conform to available resources. So too with European imperialism: few scholars have asked why the greatly enlarged states did not contract themselves effectively at a pace that could have secured their continued rule of still large but more realistically designed domains.[2]

One reason for the greater prominence of expansion as opposed to contraction is that instances of strategic expansion far outnumber those of strategic contraction. I here define strategic expansion as the enlargement of a polity's territorial domain as an intended result of policies implemented for military, political, cultural, social, psychological, ideological, or economic reasons; strategic contraction is defined here as the purposeful reduction in a polity's territorial domain *excluding* the collapse, destruction, or dismemberment of polities and effected despite or without reference to the strategic calculus of the ruling elite. But why should expansion occur so much more frequently than contraction? A deceptively simple answer to this question is that it is easier to expand than to contract. This answer, however, conceals within itself a theory of states as institutions and of processes of institutionalization and deinstitutionalization; it is theory that imagines state contraction as a process that is not simply the converse of state expansion.

After outlining a framework for the study of territorial boundaries as institutional norms, I suggest how its application to the British-Irish, French-Algerian, and Israeli-Palestinian cases helps clarify the asymmetries that characterize processes of state expansion versus contraction.[3] I argue that holding state contraction in mind as an option can help solve a number of existing theoretical problems in the literature on state building and imperialism. Since virtually all habitable land on earth is presently ruled by existing states, transferring authority over or in any particular territory for the purpose of enhancing self-determination for its inhabitants will automatically require the territorial or functional

---

2. Although we have studies that compare the dynamics of European imperial expansion to those of Roman expansion or that compare the Roman collapse with the decline of European empires, there is no literature that seeks to learn about the rigidities of European imperial rule from the Roman Empire's failure to contract with the same opportunism with which it expanded. See, for example, P. A. Brunt, "Reflections on British and Roman Imperialism," *Comparative Studies in Society and History* 7, no. 3 (1965), pp. 267–288; Michael W. Doyle, *Empires* (Ithaca, N.Y.: Cornell University Press, 1986); and Gary B. Miles, "Roman and Modern Imperialism: A Reassessment," *Comparative Studies in Society and History* (1990), pp. 629–659.

3. This treatment is summarized from the detailed study of these three cases offered in Ian S. Lustick, *Unsettled States, Disputed Lands: Britain and Ireland, France and Algeria, Israel and the West Bank/Gaza* (Ithaca, N.Y.: Cornell University Press, 1993).

contraction of an existing state. A powerful theory of state contraction will thus be necessary for the design and implementation of any policy that expands opportunities for self-determination. Indeed, implicit within the Liechtenstein Draft Convention on Self-Determination Through Self-Administration is the assumption that such a theory exists.

The Shape of States: Institutionalizing and Deinstitutionalizing Territorial Boundaries

A state is a special kind of institution. An institution is a framework for social action that elicits from those who act within it expectations of regularity, continuity, and propriety. Such a framework is institutionalized to the extent that those expectations are reliably reproduced. Institutionalization is a process by which changing the rules of political competition becomes increasingly disruptive and decreasingly likely to be part of the strategic calculus of competitors within the institutional arena. States are the institutions that enforce property rights and provide order sufficiently to permit people within their purview to design and build other institutions. The boundaries of states, both internal (between national, regional, and local authorities) and external, are crucial components of the set of stable expectations that, ultimately, constitute the state as an institution.

The evolution of Wessex and then England into Great Britain, then into the United Kingdom of Great Britain and Ireland, and most recently into the United Kingdom of Great Britain and Northern Ireland illustrates the fundamental fluidity of states regarding their territorial and cultural composition.[4] But if the morphological variability exhibited by Britain and the United Kingdom indicates the need for a dynamic conception of the state, the long periods through which such discontinuous shifts in size and shape manifest themselves suggest the need to temper awareness of fluidity with expectations that change in the contours of states will not respond smoothly to marginal changes in patterns of popular loyalty, economic interest, elite ideology, or even military strength.

What then endows the nominal border of a state with long-term political significance? To answer this question requires an understanding of the combination of the ultimate fluidity yet sluggishness and discontinuity in patterns of state border change.

---

4. Concerning long-term fluctuations in the shape of the British and French states, see Ian Lustick, *State-Building Failure in British Ireland and French Algeria* (Berkeley: Institute of International Studies, University of California, 1985), pp. 1–16.

Considering a state as an institution, that is, as an established set of expectations, suggests that state borders describe boundaries between political arenas within which it is believed that available power resources will be mobilized according to different sets of norms and legal arrangements. State borders are politically important because they serve as institutionalized constraints that give advantage to certain groups and rival elites within the state at the expense of others. Substantial changes in the territorial shape of a state represent institution-transforming episodes. Struggles over the size and shape of the state must accordingly be understood as struggles over the rules of the game. Boundaries specify who and what are potential participants or objects of the political game and who and what are not. The territorial shape of a state thus helps determine what interests are legitimate, what resources are mobilizable, what questions are open for debate, what ideological formulas will be relevant, what cleavages could become significant, and what political allies might be available.

Territorial expansion or contraction can be expected to trigger shifts in the distribution of power within a state by changing resource allocations among different groups and, ultimately, by changing prevailing norms and legal arrangements to correspond with the interests of newly dominant groups. Accordingly, unless the border of the state is accepted as an immutable given, different groups within the state will, under some circumstances, adjust their perceptions of what the proper border of the state should be based on their chances of achieving and/or maintaining political power.

The usefulness of this formulation is that it suggests both the long-term variability of state borders—flowing from the essentially subjective nature of popular beliefs and linked ultimately to constellations of economic benefit, social status, and political interest—and the potential for stability in the size and shape of states that can attend deeply embedded, widely shared, and uncontested beliefs.

As recent events in Europe, Asia, Africa, and the Middle East conclusively demonstrate, territorial boundaries are far from being a given of a state's existence. Indeed the territorial shape of a state, qua institution, is one of its most salient *contingent* dimensions. Patterns of change and stability in state borders are processes of institutionalization and deinstitutionalization. To be sure, change in the size and shape of states is commonly attributable to success or failure in armed conflicts—a sudden loss or acquisition of territory that in itself does not reflect the institutionalizable character of borders. But the loss of a territory in war does not necessarily mean its permanent separation from the defeated state. Nor does conquest of a territory necessarily lead to its political integration. With respect to territorial expansion and contraction as a *political* problem, a problem of the shaping of an institution, it is precisely those cases where force majeure was not decisive in the determination of outcomes, or where it is not expected to be decisive, that are of the greatest interest.

A well-developed concept of strategic state contraction could have helped the former Soviet Union preserve itself within smaller boundaries or transform itself in an orderly manner. Such a theory could also help assess the feasibility of consolidating existing or enlarged boundaries, as opposed to contracting the state as part of a process leading to less violence and fewer threats to international security. Such a theory is, in fact, necessary for assessing prospects for the successful implementation of the terms of the Liechtenstein Draft Convention. The regime it envisions presumes that states can and will contract, that is, accede to demands that the scope of their authority be territorially (or functionally) reduced.

A Two-Threshold Image of
Territorial State Building and State Contraction

Recognizing states and state boundaries as institutions does not itself suggest a solution to the problem of why there should be such a huge discrepancy in the occurrence of state expansion versus state contraction. To explain why states get smaller with so much more difficulty than they get larger requires a theory of institutions that appreciates this asymmetry. This kind of theory needs to focus on the continuous, gradual, linear processes that affect change in state size and shape. But it also must pay attention to discontinuities in these processes and the thresholds associated with the sudden and drastic changes that can occur in the mix of costs and benefits facing state leaders.

Indeed, it is obvious that the territorial shape of states can change in sudden and drastic ways. Ireland was annexed as an integral part of the United Kingdom on January 1, 1801. The twenty-six counties of the Irish Free State left the authority of the British state on December 5, 1922. France made Algeria three departments of France in 1848. France officially recognized Algerian independence on July 3, 1962. However, the political pressures and psychological processes leading up to these transformations and consequent upon them were cumulative and gradual.

These sharp breaks in the official, legal size of states and in the status of disputed lands are associated with thresholds in the process of institutionalization. A theory of this process can be built around an image of two kinds of discontinuities marked by two different kinds of thresholds. These thresholds can then be understood to divide the state institutionalization process into three parts, or stages. Movement from one stage to another entails a shift in the order of magnitude in the scale of political conflict that would surround efforts to change a particular institution along a salient dimension. The metaphor of threshold is key. It is a kind of gear, and a ratcheting effect. Adding territory to the institutionalized sphere of the state's authority means moving in the direction of the teeth of the gear. Some effort is required to expand, but that effort is rewarded more or less smoothly with increments of territory more deeply and reliably attached to the core of the state, the stability of whose political life is unlikely to be jeopardized. State contraction, in contrast, means moving backward against the teeth of the gear. The idea is that reversing an expansionary or institutionalization process is possible, but if that process has crossed either or both thresholds, that is, if the gears have ratcheted into place, then moving backward can be expected to entail considerable and even violent disruptions in the political life of the core state.

Drawing on this asymmetric model of expansion and contraction, we can portray the process of territorial state building as a process of change in the character of political conflict within the core state that would attend efforts to *disengage* from the new territory. More precisely, the scale of the internal political dislocation expected by the political class within the core state to be associated with efforts to disengage from an outlying territory measures the extent to which that territory has been built, or integrated, into the central state. The regime and ideological hegemony thresholds divide political conflicts pertaining to the territorial shape of the state into three types or institutional stages. These stages correspond to struggles over incumbency; incumbency and regime integrity; and incumbency, regime integrity, and ideological hegemony (see Figure 8.1).

Conflict at the incumbency stage, over a government policy designed to achieve disengagement from a closely held territory, might be intense. Indeed, the political future of incumbents and their rivals may be at stake in any effort to move toward disengagement. But if competition is limited to political bargaining, threats to bolt from the ruling coalition, and so on, it is easily contained within the political institutions of a developed polity. The rules of the allocative game are not the issue. Neither the integrity of the regime nor the underlying balance of power enshrined by state institutions is threatened. It is precisely for this reason that such conflict can be interpreted to mean that integration of the peripheral territory into the state-building core is in its early stage.

The territory can be considered much more closely integrated into

Figure 8.1   Model of Territorial State Building and State Contraction

Incumbency Stage	Regime Stage	Ideological Hegmony Stage
Disengagement means struggles over incumbency	Disengagement means struggles over regime integrity	Disengagement means struggles over ideological hegemony
(Decolonization)		(Secession)
Regime Threshold		Ideological Hegemony Threshold

State contraction ◄

State expansion ►

the core state if proposals for disengagement from the territory raise in the minds of competitors for political power not only the danger of losing coalition partners, partisan advantages, or career opportunities but also the real possibility of violent opposition and the mounting of extralegal challenges to the authority of state institutions. Clearly, state building has proceeded much further if conflict over disengagement is conducted about the rules of the game, that is, about state institutions and not within them. At this regime stage of political struggle over the inclusion or exclusion of the territory, the question is not only Should the state, for its own interests or the interests of those it is deemed to represent, disengage from the territory? but also Should the future of the territory as a part of the state be legitimately entertained as a question of interests, costs, and benefits, by government officials or by participants in the wider struggle for power in and over the state?

The fundamental characteristic of institutions is that they establish certain parameters of political competition not only as difficult to change but as operational givens that permit decisionmaking, bargaining, and other forms of political activity to proceed normally. By effectively ruling out many of the most basic questions that could otherwise be raised in any political context, well-developed institutions permit political actors to focus on particular issues, calculate the consequences of different outcomes, and make appropriate trade-offs. The establishment of a belief as a part of common sense has the effect of privileging it—of protecting it from reevaluation in the face of events or pressures that might otherwise affect it, and of diverting political responses to strains associated with the state of affairs it describes. This agenda-shaping aspect of deep-seated, unquestioned beliefs represents a qualitatively different kind of protection against deinstitutionalization than the incumbency- or regime-level concerns of political actors.

We may think of two different thresholds that must be crossed by a state if some outlying territory is to be incorporated on as permanent a basis as possible. The first threshold is the regime threshold (see Figure 8.1), the point at which a government interested in relinquishing the areas finds itself more worried about civic upheavals, violent disorders, and challenges to the legitimate authority of governmental institutions than about possible defections from the governing coalition or party. The second, ideological hegemony threshold is crossed when the absorption of the territory ceases to be problematic for the overwhelming majority of citizens of the central state, that is, when hegemonic beliefs prevent the territorial question from occupying a place on the national political agenda. The presence of such beliefs is revealed when, in public, ambitious politicians systematically avoid questioning, even by implication, the permanence of the integration of the territory. The absence of struggle about the shape of the state indicates its successful institutionalization.

In the case of state expansion, a hegemonic level of institutionalization is attained as politicians who might otherwise have reason to oppose permanent incorporation of the target territory adopt vocabularies and rhetorical strategies that imply presumptions of its inclusion within the state. State contraction, accordingly, is conceived as a process of moving backward through these thresholds, first by legitimizing public discussion of disengagement as a credible or sensible option and then by eliminating from public debate and private calculation the threat of challenges to the legal order should a coalition favoring disengagement be in a position legally to implement its preferences.

Plotting Patterns of State Expansion and Contraction: Three Cases

I have sought to test and elaborate this framework for the study of state expansion and contraction by systematically comparing the Algerian, Irish, and Palestinian–West Bank–Gaza Strip problems in French and British political history and Israeli politics, respectively. Each case presents several examples of more or less successful attempts to institutionalize (and deinstitutionalize) state boundaries. In the summary of my analysis of these cases I illustrate how it is possible to use the two-threshold model I have sketched to plot shifts in the character of the relationship between core states and outlying territories and then explain those changes in terms of the extent to which putative borders of the state have been institutionalized. Each case features an episode of state contraction accomplished (or, in the Israeli case, being accomplished) after decades of hesitation. In each case the contraction was intended to enhance the interests of the central state.

Britain and Ireland: 1801–1922

In the British-Irish relationship, state contraction occurred in its most concrete form in 1922, when British rule was withdrawn from three-quarters of Ireland. The United Kingdom of Great Britain and Ireland, inaugurated in 1801, was transformed into the United Kingdom of Great Britain and Northern Ireland and the Irish Free State. Within ten years the Irish Free State transformed itself into Eire, or the Republic of Ireland. The disposition of Northern Ireland is still in dispute, but it remains under British sovereignty.

From a political and institutional perspective, however, the contraction of the British state from most of Ireland did not occur in, or only in, 1922. Instead the partition of Ireland marked the culmination of a long process of deinstitutionalization of the territorial shape of the British state as it was established, on a hegemonic basis within Britain itself, early in the nineteenth century.

After centuries of conquest, land expropriation, and settlement by English and Scottish Protestants, Catholic Ireland was formally and legally incorporated into the United Kingdom by the Act of Union of 1801. After nearly thirty years of struggle, Catholics secured limited political rights. In the 1830s and 1840s Irish bids for autonomy (a repeal of the union) were rejected within the British political arena as insane, ridiculous, and impossible. The debate was not over the pros and cons of Irish autonomy but whether the issues should even be placed on the agenda. The defeat, in Britain, of Irish efforts to raise the issue of repeal signaled the successful defense of the ideologically hegemonic status of the conception of Ireland as an integral part of the United Kingdom.[5] We can therefore locate the Irish issue in British politics between 1834 and 1843, as labeled A in Figure 8.2.

---

5. See Ian S. Lustick, "Becoming Problematic: Breakdown of Hegemonic Conception of Ireland in Nineteenth Century Britain," *Politics and Society* 18, no. 1 (1990), pp. 39–73.

Figure 8.2   Model of Territorial State Building and State Contraction:
Great Britian and Ireland

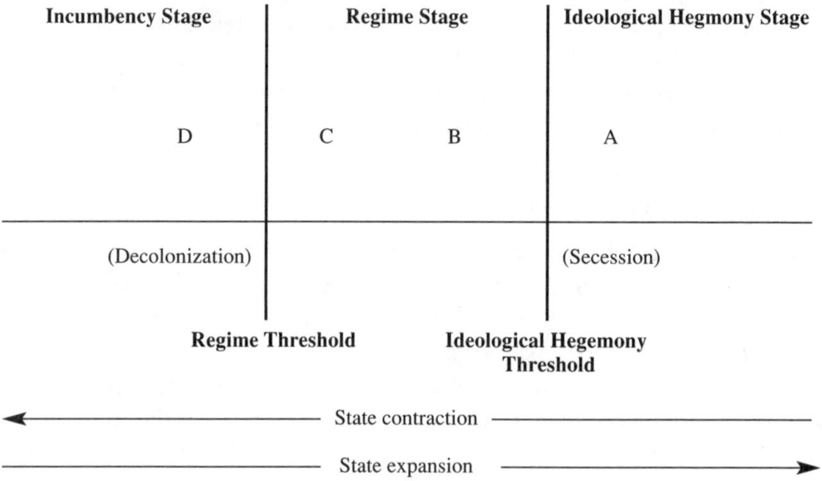

Incumbency Stage	Regime Stage		Ideological Hegmony Stage
D	C	B	A
(Decolonization)			(Secession)
Regime Threshold		Ideological Hegemony Threshold	

◄─────────────────── State contraction ─────────────────

─────────────────── State expansion ──────────────────►

The boundary of the British state, including Ireland as an integral part of its territorial shape, was institutionalized in the early nineteenth century beyond both the regime and ideological hegemony thresholds. For state contraction to occur, for Britain to withdraw from Ireland, therefore required both the overthrow of a hegemonic belief within the British ruling class (that Ireland was a natural, commonsensical part of the British state) and, subsequently, the running of risks of regime destabilization in order to produce conditions for a straightforward policy decision to withdraw British authority over Ireland.

Such political debate was, in fact, the political trajectory followed by the Irish Question in British politics from the 1830s to the 1920s. The end of the repeal movement gave rise to long, indeed ghastly struggles for economic and social reforms within the framework of the Union of Britain and Ireland. Between 1845 and 1851 at least 1.5 million Irish men, women, and children died of starvation and disease as a result of the great potato famine and British economic and social policies. One million more emigrated. Reforms that were implemented in the late nineteenth century were both too little and too late. They served only to intensify demands by Irish Catholics for self-government, spurring an attempted armed revolt in 1867, scattered terrorism, rent-refusal campaigns, Gaelic revivalism, and political movements (first for "home government" and then "home rule"), all dedicated toward loosening or severing the links that bound Ireland to England.

In 1886 the British parliament again defeated, and by a decisive margin, William Gladstone's proposal of home rule for Ireland. His proposal was not very different at all from the earlier proposal to repeal the union. But the arguments used by those who defeated this bid for Irish autonomy were dramatically different from those used in the 1830s and 1840s. The issue was first of all on the agenda. Not only were opponents of Irish autonomy battling a specific proposal formally laid before the parliament for its consideration but they were doing so by mobilizing instrumentalist arguments that appealed to the larger interests of their audiences. The fact that these arguments prevailed is less significant than that by engaging in cost-benefit analysis instead of outraged appeals to common sense and sanity, opponents of Irish autonomy provided evidence that between the early 1840s and the mid-1880s the ideologically hegemonic status of the conception of Ireland as an integral part of the United Kingdom had broken down.[6] The location of the Irish problem in 1886 is designated in Figure 8.2 by B.

That a discontinuous change had occurred in the meaning of the Irish Question in British politics was well understood by both Gladstone, whose legislative efforts and party went down in crushing defeat, and Lord Salisbury, whose Unionist Party enjoyed political ascendancy in Britain for most of the next twenty years. Salisbury bemoaned the fact that the fate of Ireland had become "a momentous issue before the country" and called for renewed efforts to re-create beliefs in the inevitable and permanent rule of Britain over Ireland. In rather specific terms he called upon Unionists to reconstruct the ideologically hegemonic status of the idea of British Ireland that had been lost. This would require, he emphasized, an act of will on the part of Englishmen and their adherence to beliefs that would drive debate over future proposals for home rule from the realm of legitimate political discourse. He urged his followers to abandon lines of argumentation that even implied home rule as a conceivable option to be compared against others. Gladstone saw, in the 1886 defeat of his first home rule bill, an even more fundamental victory. It signaled, he argued, a new stage in the evolution of the Irish question. Accordingly, he predicted that precisely because the issue had been addressed as an instrumentalist problem, Ireland would, eventually, be granted a measure of self-government.[7]

From 1885 to 1914 the Irish Question divided the British polity more profoundly than any other. The Liberals and the Irish Home Rule Party, on one side, argued for a devolution of British authority over

---

6. Ibid., pp. 55–62.
7. *Times,* December 20, 1887, p. 7.

Ireland that would allow, implicitly if not explicitly, mechanisms for the expression of national self-determination by Irish Catholics. On the other side of the great debate were the Conservatives (also known as the Tories, or Unionists) and the Liberal Unionists (who had split from the Liberal Party on the Irish issue). They fought vigorously against any substantive political or constitutional change in Ireland's status that would imply acceptance of the idea of an Irish nation whose political rights contradicted the permanent integration of both "British" Isles into one sovereign state.

In early 1914 the British parliament finally passed the Home Rule for Ireland Bill, which would have granted political autonomy to the entire island. The Asquith government's commitment to the project was grounded not only in the long-standing policy of the Liberal Party (since Gladstone's day) of supporting Irish home rule as a means of removing the burden of Ireland from British affairs, but also in Asquith's need for the votes of the Irish Nationalists in parliament. The measure was vehemently opposed by the Unionist Party and the Protestant (Loyalist) population of Ireland, concentrated in Ulster. Nearly half a million of these "settlers" signed a covenant swearing their readiness to defy any government that would abandon them to Irish Catholics. The British officer corps was sympathetic to calls for defiance of the government and to Unionist condemnation of any "trai-torous" bargain with the Irish Catholics. High-ranking officers and the most prestigious retired commanders in Britain even helped to train and arm a 100,000-man Protestant militia that gave disciplined expression to Unionist and Loyalist warnings of civil war over Ireland.

This struggle over the character of the link between Britain and Ireland came to a climax in March 1914. Emboldened by Unionist Party declarations that civil war would be preferable to acceptance of home rule and unwilling to confront the large, highly disciplined paramilitary force organized by Ulster Protestants, commanders of the British army stationed in Ireland announced their refusal to implement home rule in Ulster. With war clouds gathering in Europe the government backed down before these threats, deciding to forgo a final decision on the implementation of home rule until after the war.[8]

By the end of World War I, home rule, though finally supported by majorities in both houses of parliament, could no longer satisfy the

---

8. Indeed, among British historians it is commonly argued that only the out-break of World War I saved Great Britain from clashes that could have led to civil war.

demands for independence from Britain advanced by Sinn Fein (the Irish nationalist forerunner of the Irish Republican Army). The vast majority of Englishmen were still staunchly opposed to the final separation of what had, for so long, been thought of as an integral part of their country. But World War I had left Britain emotionally exhausted. Indeed, from 1916 on, none of the many schemes for devolution, home rule, or autonomy for southern Ireland ever sparked regime-level threats by opponents or fears of regime destabilization by government advocates of these schemes. The problem, redefined and stripped of Northern Ireland, had been relocated to the incumbent stage. The process of state contraction had moved another political notch toward actual separation.

In 1916 a violent rebellion in Dublin was crushed swiftly by the British army. The Easter Rising nevertheless effectively cast Irish demands for independence as a national struggle for self-determination. On the basis of Wilson's Fourteen Points it became easier after the war than before it to present convincingly the case for British "decolonization" of Ireland. In 1919 a wave of guerrilla raids, terrorism, and violent disturbances broke out in southern Ireland. Weary of bloodshed and strife, public opinion turned strongly against the brutal measures adopted by government forces for Ireland's pacification. By this time it also became clear that against the backdrop of enormous war losses and the staggering problems of postwar reconstruction, many leading Conservatives had lost their former enthusiasm for the demands of the Unionist diehards and the Orangemen of Ulster. Though Irish nationalists were at the brink of military defeat by the time negotiations between the Sinn Fein "terrorists" and the British government began in July 1921, the coalition that had blocked Irish autonomy for 120 years had finally collapsed. The politically crucial fact is that the Irish problem had been recategorized from a problem whose resolution appeared to put the regime at risk to a more or less typical colonial problem with consequences for incumbent competition but not for regime stability. As a result, the physical capacity of the British army to hold Ireland ceased to be significant. Instead the exorbitantly high price that Britain paid for ruling Ireland and the few benefits enjoyed thereby could be and were decisive in gaining practical and, soon, formal independence for most of Ireland.

It is appropriate, then, to understand a regime crisis to have occurred in spring 1914 over the Irish Question as it was defined at that time and to note that this crisis was resolved by decomposing the Irish Question into the fate of the Catholic majority South, a question that did not arouse regime-threatening mobilization within Britain, and the

Protestant majority North, which did. In other words, the location of the Irish Question, now defined as the disposition of the twenty-six southern counties, moved from B in Figure 8.2 in the mid-1880s to D in 1914, but at the cost of leaving a chunk of Ireland institutionalized within the British state at the regime level, labeled C.

France and Algeria: 1871–1962

In the French-Algerian case, advocates of *Algérie française* did not succeed in establishing a hegemonic belief in France that Algeria was an integral, natural, and immutable part of the French state. However, in contrast to France's failure to institutionalize its rule of Indochina, French West Africa, Madagascar, Tunisia, and Morocco within France itself, French efforts to institutionalize Algeria's incorporation into the French state did succeed in pushing the status of Algeria as part of France beyond the regime threshold. The degree of dislocation associated with French separation from Algeria was, accordingly, of an order of magnitude greater than that associated with the decolonization of France's other overseas possessions.

European settlers flocked to Algeria following the French conquest in 1830 and Algeria's gradual pacification. Encouraged and protected by the French government and military administration, these settlers prospered, benefiting especially from the systematic transfer of indigenous lands to their proprietorship. More intensively colonized than any other French dominion, Algeria was annexed as an integral part of France in 1871. In principle, French citizenship was open to native Algerians. In actuality, the requirement that Muslims renounce Islam in order to become eligible for French citizenship made it impossible for all but a negligible minority to enjoy the rights of French citizens, including the right to vote.

In this context the European settlers emerged as the real rulers of Algeria and its 7 million (1954) Muslim inhabitants. In Paris, coalitions of European settlers, French businessmen with interests in North Africa, and right-wing parties doomed successive efforts to introduce comprehensive reforms of France's Algerian policies. Nonetheless, in World War I hundreds of thousands of Algerian Muslims fought in the trenches to defend France. In the 1920s the Muslim intellectual elite, reformist leaders, and even modernist clerics accepted the prevailing view of Algeria as a French domain and organized civil rights associations and political parties to further their demands as French citizens or subjects. Despite the brutality associated with the French conquest and rule over Algeria, the fact that even in the 1920s Algerian Muslim elites were demanding French citizenship suggests that the effective incorporation of the Algerian territory into the French state could have occurred.[9] But repeated attempts by reform-minded Frenchmen to satisfy these Muslim demands were subverted by the French settler lobby, which was anxious to preserve the privileges of its constituents.[10] As a consequence every substantial reform effort went down in defeat. The revolt in 1954 erupted against a background of the final failure, in 1947, to implement legislation providing genuine opportunities for the assimilation of Algerian Muslims into the French political system.[11]

In debates over French policy in Algeria before World War II, speakers seldom, if ever, implied that they considered separation of that territory from France to be a possibility. In terms of the model discussed here, this suggests that the inclusion of Algeria within the territorial ambit of the French state may have achieved ideologically hegemonic status. However, because there was no serious attempt to bring about Algerian autonomy during this period, a dominant discourse whose implicit assumptions rejected the idea as insane and impossible cannot be found. There is, accordingly, no way to be sure on which side of the ideological hegemony threshold the problem was located in the 1920s and 1930s.

However, subsequent treatment of the problem during the 1940s suggests that the ideological hegemony of Algeria as France, if it had existed prior to the war, did not survive it. In the tumultuous aftermath of World War II, Frenchmen recalled the occupation of half of their country and the humiliation of the Vichy regime. They also discovered how intense international opposition was to the continuation of their African and Indochinese empires. In this context, as the very nature of France came before the body politic for discussion, the perceived permanence of Algeria's connection to France came into question.

Meanwhile, native political elites in Algeria had during the war formed a small but important nationalist movement. Their demands

---

9. See Charles-Robert Ageron, "Les Algériens musulmans et la France, 1871–1919," *Revue Historique*, no. 494 (April/June 1970), pp. 355–366; Vincent Confer, *France and Algeria: The Problem of Civil and Political Reform, 1870–1920* (Syracuse, N.Y.: Syracuse University Press, 1966), pp. 115–121; and Malcolm Lynn Richardson, "French Algeria Between the Wars: Nationalism and Colonial Reform, 1919–1939," Ph.D. dissertation, Duke University, 1975, pp. 87–88, 110–113, 195–198, 233–239, and 246–248.
10. The Europeans of Algeria numbered 150,000 in the 1850s and over 1 million by the 1950s.
11. For a discussion of colonial subversion of metropolitan French efforts to grant Algerian Muslims political rights within French institutions, see Lustick, *State-Building Failure in British Ireland and French Algeria*, pp. 47–76.

ranged from full-fledged autonomy for Algeria within a French-led federal system that emphasized cultural ties and economic cooperation to an independent Algerian republic operating entirely outside the orbit of French influence. Nationalist agitation, combined with the terror inspired in the European community in Algeria whenever the native population showed signs of resistance, accounts for the massacre of tens of thousands of Algerian Muslims in May 1945, following demonstrations and riots in the towns of Setif and Guelma. During subsequent debates the French political class was forced to confront the question of Algeria's status.

Analysis of these debates shows that no ideologically hegemonic conception of Algeria's relationship to France was present in the postwar years. In the 1947 parliamentary debate over the Organic Statute for Algeria, representatives from all parties leveled substantive and explicit arguments against one another over whether Algeria should properly be considered a part of metropolitan France, a nonmetropolitan department of France, an overseas department of France, a collection of overseas departments with a special personality and singular status, a pillar of the French union but not part of France itself, or an exploited colony in need of opportunities to exercise a sovereign choice to associate or not with France. Thus although Algeria was firmly institutionalized as an integral part of France under the regime of the Fourth Republic, the terms of discourse about the territory showed that no successful candidate for an ideologically hegemonic conception of its status had been found; the problem's location in French politics was at E in Figure 8.3.

As late as 1957 and despite French disengagement from Indochina, Tunisia, Morocco, and other colonies, French public opinion polls showed that Algeria was still not perceived as belonging to the decolonization category, and fewer than 20 percent of all French were willing to accept the permanent separation of Algeria from France. Yet *Algérie française* had failed as a hegemonic project. If French Algeria was not institutionalized at the hegemonic level, it was, however, embedded within France at the regime level. France's contraction from Algeria involved not only risks of regime collapse but, in the event, both the collapse of one regime, the Fourth Republic, and severe threats to the existence of its successor, the Fifth Republic.

The Fourth Republic lurched through six governments from 1954 to 1958. Horrified by revelations of brutal methods used by French officers and men to combat the FLN (National Liberation Front, the organizers of the Algerian revolution against French rule), many intellectuals, clerics, and professionals declared their support for Algerian self-

Figure 8.3   Model of Territorial State Building and State Contraction: France and Algeria

Incumbency Stage	Regime Stage	Ideological Hegmony Stage
H	G E F	

(Decolonization)		(Secession)

Regime Threshold   Ideological Hegemony
                        Threshold

◄─────────────────── State contraction ───────────────────

─────────────────── State expansion ───────────────────►

determination. When social and economic reforms were threatened by the taxes and inflation associated with the war, both businesspeople and trade unionists began to question the importance of *Algérie française.* When governments turned tentatively toward options for negotiating an end to the war in Algeria, the Fourth Republic found itself unable to cope with the deep divisions within France over the prospect of state contraction from Algeria. In 1958 the regime succumbed, overthrown by an alliance of Gaullists, army officers, and Algerian settlers.

But almost as soon as he took power de Gaulle began turning on his erstwhile allies. Instead of affirming his commitment to *Algérie française,* he used the extraordinary political opportunities associated with establishment of the Fifth Republic to move decisively toward complete disengagement from Algeria. By declaring himself in favor of Algerian self-determination and then humiliating and removing General Jacques Massu from his Algerian command in 1959, de Gaulle provoked the *pieds noirs* into the Barricades Rebellion of January 1960 and an attack that cost the lives of fourteen gendarmes and wounded more than 100. Declaring the attack as a "stab in the back for France" and exploiting widespread fears in the metropole of civil war, de Gaulle isolated active supporters of *Algérie française* from a wider strata of sympathizers. In a referendum on the question of self-determination for Algeria held in January 1961, a majority of 75 percent voted yes. After purging the army he declared, in April 1961, that "Algeria costs us, to say the least, more than she is worth to us. . . . And that is why, today,

France considers with the greatest composure a solution such that Algeria would cease to be a part of her domain."[12]

After diehards within the military led a putsch attempt in April 1961, de Gaulle again relied on metropolitan fears of a Spanish civil war scenario if he was not given support in his stand against the *Algérie française* extremists. He declared a state of emergency and shifted the terms of the crisis from whether France would abandon its departments in Algeria to whether parliamentary democracy would remain intact and whether the lives and property of ordinary Frenchmen would be secure. When the French masses responded to his call for loyalty to the French Republic and conscripts refused to follow the orders of their rebellious commanders, the revolt collapsed. The regime threshold was crossed in the state-contracting direction.

De Gaulle's avoidance of partition in Algeria (referred to as the Palestinian option) as a means of mollifying his opponents paid off. Once the problem had been relocated to the incumbency stage, de Gaulle's government abandoned French claims to the Sahara and to the protection of the *harkis* (Algerians who had fought with the French army) and moved swiftly and decisively toward implementing its agreement with the FLN. In April 1962, 90 percent of the French electorate, in another referendum, approved the Evian agreements ending the Algerian war. These agreements provided for the separation of Algeria from France, setting the stage for the FLN to declare the country's immediate independence.

The drastic change in the character of the Algerian problem for France, from one that threatened regimes to one that threatened no more than governing coalitions and careers, reflects France's passage back through the regime threshold, or a deinstitutionalization of the status of Algeria as a part of France, which is the meaning of state contraction. Thus the location of the problem can be seen to have shifted from E in Figure 8.3 in the late 1940s and early and mid-1950s to F by late 1957 (at the high-water mark of the hegemonic project of *Algérie française*), to G in 1960 and early 1961 to H following the failure of the generals' revolt in April 1961.

The Israeli-Palestinian Case: 1967–1988

During the 1948 war the new state of Israel managed to expand the borders allotted to it by the UN to include large areas of the Galilee, the Negev, and a significant strip of land along what is now known as the

---

12. Charles de Gaulle, speech reprinted in *L'Année Politique* (1961), p. 645.

West Bank. The majority of Arab inhabitants of these territories were evicted or kept out after fleeing the fighting. Their lands and almost half the lands of those Arabs remaining in the state were expropriated for exclusively Jewish use. Despite Arab majorities in western and central Galilee and in the strip adjoining the West Bank, which is known as the Little Triangle, these areas have been incorporated into Israel as integral parts of the state, hegemonically established as commonsensical parts of Israel whose ultimate disposition is not an important focus of public debate by Jews or Arabs.

The negotiations between Israel and the Palestinian Authority pertain to other predominantly Arab territories occupied and settled by Israel—the West Bank and Gaza Strip, acquired by Israel as a result of the 1967 war. These territories, despite the best efforts of powerful groups in Israeli society who have sought to erase the Green Line between Israel proper and the territories conquered in 1967, have not been institutionalized hegemonically as part of the Jewish state—neither in the minds nor in the discourse of Jews or Arabs.

However, the annexationist campaign conducted halfheartedly by the elements within the Labor Party governments from 1967 to 1977, and enthusiastically and systematically by the Likud governments in place from 1977 until 1992, did have the effect of institutionalizing Israeli rule of the West Bank (including expanded East Jerusalem) past the regime threshold. Elsewhere I have demonstrated that this institutionalization occurred between 1982 and 1984.[13] Here I only wish to note that because of this successful but incomplete institutionalization of an expanded Israel to include the West Bank, efforts by some Israeli governments to contract the shape of the state, as a strategic response to the necessity for peace with the Palestinians and the Arab world as a whole, have confronted and will confront Israeli leaders with the necessity to weather, overcome, or adapt to regime-threatening opposition.

Passage of the regime threshold in the state-building direction was spurred by the 1977 parliamentary elections, in which the right-wing Likud Party defeated Labor. The result was an ultranationalist government supported enthusiastically by a powerful Jewish fundamentalist movement (Gush Emunim) and the National Religious Party. From 1977 to 1984 this coalition ruled Israel, using all the assets of the government to pursue its single most valued objective: to expand the Jewish state by creating such a thick network of linkages between Israel and the occupied territories, as well as such a widespread pattern of Jewish settlement there, that no options for peace negotiations based on

---

13. Lustick, *Unsettled States, Disputed Lands,* pp. 366–373.

the idea of territorial compromise could be pursued by future Israeli governments. The success of this effort, involving billions of dollars, tens of thousands of new settlers, and, indirectly, a war in Lebanon, transformed debate in Israel over the issue of the occupied territories. By 1983 arguments in Israel no longer concerned simply what *should* be done with the territories. Increasingly the debate became focused on what the Israeli political system *could* do with them.[14] The radical shift in the scale of anticipated internal disruption associated with efforts to disengage from the West Bank and Gaza Strip indicates that between 1977 and 1984 the location of the relationship between Israel and these areas shifted from point K in Figure 8.4 to point L, thereby crossing the regime threshold.

The effects of having passed this regime threshold were evident in the political crisis of 1989–1990, which ensued when the Likud-Labor "unity government" broke up, and for several months, neither Shimon Peres's Labor Party nor Yitzhak Shamir's Likud Party was able to form a government. After months of uncertainty and political strife, Yitzhak Shamir managed to exploit fears by Rabbi Eliezer Shach, spiritual leader of two small ultraorthodox parties, that the peace policies of a Labor government would lead to civil war. Shach's decision to oppose Labor Party efforts to form a government led directly to Shamir's formation of a narrow, far-right government—the government that ruled Israel until the June 1992 elections brought Yitzhak Rabin to power. Rabin's assassination by a right-wing Jewish fundamentalist was shocking proof of the regime-level status of the West Bank's institutionalization as part of the Israeli state, and a costly lesson for antiannexationists.

In terms of the model, the location of the relationship between the State of Israel and the Galilee, Negev, and Little Triangle territories acquired in 1948 quickly passed through both thresholds to I in Figure 8.4. From 1967 to 1977 the Israeli West Bank–Gaza relationship can be understood as moving gradually from J to K in Figure 8.4. Both points are located within the incumbency stage of state expansion, which is to say that during this time the most serious concern deterring governing elites from withdrawal was threats to coalition integrity, party prospects, or their own personal careers. Movement toward the regime threshold, represented by the distance from J to K, reflects the steady increase in the political weight of the interests (economic, ideological, settlement related, military, and infrastructural) that came to surround demands to maintain Israeli rule of the areas.

By 1986 and 1987 many activists within the Gush Emunim and the

---

14. Ibid., pp. 1–20.

Figure 8.4   Model of Territorial State Building and State Contraction: Israel and the West Bank/Gaza

Incumbency Stage	Regime Stage	Ideological Hegmony Stage
J	K N L M	I

(Decolonization)		(Secession)

Regime Threshold   Ideological Hegemony Threshold

◄─────────────── State contraction ───────────────

─────────────── State expansion ───────────────►

Likud began to argue that for all intents and purposes what they call "Judea, Samaria, and the Gaza District" had been irreversibly absorbed into Israel. The Green Line (the armistice line of 1948 between Israel and the occupied territories), they argued, had been erased. Indeed, those Israelis arguing for territorial compromise increasingly found themselves forced to assume three burdens of proof: first, that Israelis could any longer distinguish between "Israel proper" and the "occupied territories";[15] second, that Israeli rule over the territories entailed substantial risk or cost; and third, that political decisions to disengage from the substantial portions of the territories in return for peace could ever be implemented. This shift in the character of the dominant discourse reflects gradual but definite movement in the period between 1983 and 1987 from L toward M in Figure 8.4. While the annexationist right was seeking to push the relationship past the ideological hegemony threshold, the dovish left was reduced to preventing that—fighting to keep the issue defined as an issue, and on the Israeli political agenda.

Israel permitted virtually no organized political activity by West Bank and Gaza Palestinians under the occupation. But in December 1987, a major Palestinian uprising, the intifada, broke out. The ultimate

---

15. Faced with a generation of Israelis who had come to maturity without ever knowing an Israel without the occupied territories, peace activists resorted to literally painting the Green Line on the ground in order to remind Israelis of its existence.

effect of this semiviolent rebellion was vividly to remind Israelis that there was a difference between Israel and the territories.

Accompanied by a more assertive U.S. policy toward the issue under the Bush administration (1988–1992), the intifada shifted the debate in Israel over what to do with the West Bank and Gaza Strip. With the election of a narrow but extremely dovish (in Israeli terms) government in 1992, the Labor Party and its allies began a serious effort to contract the state from the occupied territories. Taking advantage of the public's widespread fear of and distaste for the teeming and impoverished Arab towns and refugee camps of the Gaza Strip, the Rabin government began its state contraction program there with a token grant of autonomy to a tiny area around the isolated West Bank town of Jericho.

In terms of the comparative framework for understanding state expansion and contraction presented here, the location of the West Bank problem in Israeli politics can thus be seen to have shifted to the left, in the state contraction direction, from M to N in Figure 8.4. Following the Israel-PLO accord in September 1993, the Labor Party government in Israel, allied tacitly but effectively with parliamentarians from predominantly Arab parties, faced the kind of opposition to its policies toward withdrawal from the West Bank and Gaza Strip that reflects the prior regime-level institutionalization of those areas as part of the State of Israel. As part of the "Oslo peace process" the government contemplated further moves toward Palestinian empowerment and an eventual Palestinian state in the West Bank and Gaza. However, Rabin was forced to confront trade-offs between the short-term risks of regime-threatening and even violent Jewish opposition to government policies and the possibilities for arriving, in the long term, at a political arrangement with the Palestinians that could be the basis for a lasting peace. The cautious delays he implemented afforded many opportunities for disruption to both Israeli and Arab "rejectionists." In November 1995 Prime Minister Rabin was assassinated by a Jewish fundamentalist convinced of Rabin's "traitorous" commitment to surrender portions of the land of Israel to non-Jewish rule. The killing dealt a severe blow to the peace process—to Israel's contraction from Palestinian territories. It provided tragic but dramatic corroboration of predictions of the state contraction theory presented here.[16]

At the incumbent level, Rabin's assassination cleared the way for

---

16. See Lustick, *Unsettled States, Disputed Lands*, pp. 426–427, for predictions of this kind of disruption, including assassination attempts on Israeli leaders moving toward state contraction.

the Likud Party's Benjamin Netanyahu, who exploited violence by Palestinian extremists to unseat the Labor Party coalition. From 1996 to 1999 Netanyahu implemented a policy of entrenchment in the territories combined with deceptive and legalistic negotiating tactics designed to delegitimize the Oslo process without formally rejecting it.[17] Although the Labor Party's Ehud Barak defeated Netanyahu in the 1999 elections, Barak did little to change Israeli policies on the ground. Fearing the kind of regime-threatening opposition that had led to Rabin's murder, Barak waited until 2000 before signaling a readiness to take the risks necessary to achieve state contraction (withdrawal from almost all the territories, dividing "Yerushalayim" from "al-Quds" as a solution for Jerusalem and finding a mutually acceptable formula vis-à-vis the refugee problem). By this time, however, the Palestinian Authority, unable to prevent waves of new settlers or to enhance Palestinian living conditions, had lost much of its support. Margins for error on both sides had become impossibly narrow, making it likely that the accidents of history and the usual array of tactical blunders would lead to a break-down of the entire process. Last-ditch efforts to get the Oslo process back on track were overwhelmed by the bloody events associated with the "Al-Aqsa Intifada" (fall and winter 2000) and what, at this writing, appears to be the political demise of Ehud Barak.[18]

With Ariel Sharon now in power, it is unlikely that Israel will contract from the territories until another cycle of violence and deep political dissatisfaction is endured. We can say, in other words, that the location of the territories problem in Israeli politics remains where it has been since the early 1980s—oscillating between a regime threshold that prevents the question from being decided without threats to the stability and legitimacy of the regime and an ideological hegemony threshold that prevents Israelis from experiencing the status of the West bank and Gaza as natural and permanent portions of the State of Israel.

Conclusion

The "other" side of self-determination is contraction in the scope and range of authority exercised by existing states and those they represent. This is an obvious point, but it is virtually ignored by existing theory

---

17. Ian S. Lustick, "Ending Protracted Conflicts: The Oslo Peace Process Between Political Partnership and Legality," *Cornell International Law Journal* 30, no. 3 (1997), pp. 741–757.

18. Ian S. Lustick, "Yerushalayim and al-Quds: Political Catechism and Political Realities," *Journal of Palestine Studies* 30, no. 1 (2000), pp. 5–21.

and by most policymakers. State contraction, whether defined in territorial or functional terms, is a severely undertheorized notion even though it is a logical requirement of enhanced self-determination for groups ruled by existing states. Not all problems of self-determination and state contraction are likely to be as difficult as have been in the case of the Irish, Algerian, and Palestinian problems for Britain, France, and Israel. But if the framework and attendant theory I have developed can illuminate these protracted and exceedingly difficult problems, it will certainly help establish reasonable expectations about the kind of obstacles that will attend enhancement of self-determination and self-administration opportunities in other cases. Yet the conclusions that can be drawn from the data and theoretical material presented here are limited. Precisely speaking, the framework presented here for studying patterns of state expansion and contraction is not itself a theory of how the transformations from one state of institutionalization to another are accomplished or a theory of what different consequences are associated with different mechanisms used to move across these thresholds in the state-expanding or state-contracting direction.[19]

Instead, the framework here presented helps address a wide range of important policy problems resulting from previous failures to recognize state contraction as a distinctive political phenomenon. It does this by conceiving of boundaries as institutional features of states and by imagining two thresholds within a process of institutionalization that produce asymmetric processes of expansion and contraction. For example, the notion of asymmetric thresholds is helpful in the Israeli case. The categories and expectations associated with the double-threshold theory encourage the identification and correction of errors made by many analysts either that Israel's absorption of Palestinian territories was irreversible or that ending the occupation would be a simple matter

---

19. In my larger work I do present such a theory. I analyze political struggles around the regime threshold as wars of maneuver and struggles around the ideological hegemony threshold as wars of position. Theoretical propositions about how the thresholds are crossed in each direction spring from considering the logic of different strategies available for winning, or surviving, these different struggles. With respect to the regime threshold, for example, that theory suggests that the choices Israeli leaders now make in deciding how they will contend with regime-threatening opposition to the peace process will partially determine whether Israel will suffer from a Northern Ireland type of problem for decades to come or whether, as in France, a sharper test of strength will result in a more radical but more complete and stable set of political arrangements in both Israel and the West Bank. For my analysis of Rabin's rescaling strategy and my predictions for the Israeli-Palestinian case using the theories tested in the British and French cases, see my *Unsettled States, Disputed Lands,* pp. 385–438.

of calculating that the benefits of continuing it were no longer worth the costs.[20]

Another contribution of this framework is in the study of that particular kind of state contraction known as decolonization. By posing decolonization as a subspecies of state contraction, analysts can adopt a nonlegalist, nonteleological means of distinguishing between decolonization and secession. The framework also permits students of decolonization to go beyond the modal conclusion of their studies, namely that metropolitan states relinquish control once the costs of that control outweigh the benefits. As the Irish, Algerian, and Palestinian cases have shown, the crucial consideration for metropolitan states whose coercive capacity to hold on to the territories is not in question when costs outweigh benefits but (1) whether cost-benefit calculations are allowed to be placed on the political agenda and (2) whether larger fears about the stability of the regime inhibit elites from acting on those calculations.

By integrating decolonization, secession, state building, and imperialism within one state expansion versus contraction framework, this approach also addresses the issue of internal colonialism. It does so by eliminating teleological distinctions between internal colonialism, within states whose institutional consolidation is deemed a fact of life, and imperialism, conducted within empires deemed incapable of institutional consolidation. Without a concept of the shape of the state as an institutionalized dimension of its existence, and without qualitative measures of institutionalization, analysts must rely on a priori or legalist demarcations of state boundaries. Even among the most careful practitioners, this reliance leads to serious taxonomic problems. Michael Hechter, for example, classified Ireland as an internal colony while treating Irish independence as the result of secession rather than decolonization.[21]

The theory also addresses the issues as seen from separatist movements within well-institutionalized states (such as the Bretons in France or the Basques in Spain). The first challenge for separatist movements is to break apart hegemonic conceptions within the political class of the central state. Victory in this "war of position" will be signified not by movement toward satisfaction of demands for autonomy or a greater

---

20. For a detailed analysis using the notion of state contraction to unravel the debate in Israel over the supposed irreversibility of the occupation, see ibid., pp. 11–37.

21. Michael Hechter, *Internal Colonialism: The Celtic Fringe in British National Development*, 1536–1966 (Berkeley: University of California Press, 1975), pp. 60–64 and 348–351.

share of resources but by a shift in the ground of rejection of the separatist program. Once separatist demands are discussable among politically ambitious elites, alliances can be formed with metropolitan sympathizers or at least with those able to profit from a struggle to reduce the size of the state—a struggle that could lead eventually to a war of maneuver. A successful outcome at this stage would transform the question of state contraction into a policy question for successive governments rather than a problem portending a regime crisis for any government wishing to solve it by satisfying separatist demands.

There are also substantial public policy benefits to asking explicit questions about state contraction. By making the category analytically salient and by offering explicit theories for how it is accomplished, analysts can identify available options for reducing the size and scope of the state, however risky or unattractive those options might usually appear to be, while avoiding false impressions of irreversibility or political impossibility. A theory integrating state contraction and expansion can also provide a basis for judging how strategies for state contraction can best be devised and implemented.

Finally, regarding territorial issues, the kind of theoretical framework offered here should afford more flexibility to states as they seek to respond to the competing and changing demands of the communities and peoples they are putatively designed to serve. Such an orientation, for example, would help move us beyond the no longer hegemonic idea that borders are immutable and encourage appreciation of the circumstances in which redrawing of territorial boundaries can be considered a viable policy instrument. Contemporary self-determination conflicts could all be addressed productively by loosening expectations that existing states cannot profit from territorial contraction. It may well be argued, for example, that it has been Canada's willingness to tolerate state contraction from Quebec that accounts for the generally peaceable nature of the dispute over that province's future.

If one great cause of misery and bloodshed in our world is the mismatch between the domains of existing states and the distribution of peoples capable of identifying with those states, then adding state contraction as an alternative to expansion, assimilation, annihilation, expulsion, collapse, or forcible dismemberment would seem not only intellectually necessary but downright useful.

9

Self-Determination and the Stability of the Russian Federation

WILLIAM WOHLFORTH AND TYLER FELGENHAUER

> I want you to know that the country really needs what you have been doing here. I do not merely mean protection of the honor and dignity of the country. I mean more serious things. We are talking about putting an end to the disintegration of Russia. This is our task here.
> —Acting Russian President Vladimir Putin to Russian soldiers in Chechnya (*Trud,* January 6, 2000, p. 7,)[1]

If the Russian Federation collapses in 2010, observers then will see the collapse as the inevitable consequence of developments now. Twice in the 1990s, Moscow sent troops into Chechnya, in part to forestall the further disintegration of the federation. As the century came to a close, no stable resolution of the Chechen question was visible on the horizon, and the underlying reasons for Russians to question the stability of their state seemed as salient as ever: deep economic, political, social, and moral crises afflicting a formerly socialist state with a large number of ethnically defined federal units. Add to that volatile mix a weak central leadership in dubious control of poorly trained but heavily armed soldiers, but still bent on preserving the integrity of the state and fearful of the domino effect that concessions on local sovereignty might bring. In these circumstances, it is little wonder that scholars have begun to ponder the disintegration of the Russian Federation as a realistic prospect.

Now is thus the time to address the new intellectual and political challenges today's Russia presents to the old contradiction between state sovereignty and self-determination. It is time, in particular, to

---

1. As cited in Henry E. Hale, ed., *Russian Election Watch*, no. 7 (February 4, 2000), Strengthening Democratic Institutions Project, Harvard University, p. 4.

The Russian Federation

bring together scholars working on the problem of Russian regionalism with those who study the international politics and law of self-determination. Our purpose in this chapter is to begin such a synthesis. We start by outlining the critical background necessary for any analysis of Russian federalism today. The colonial map that Eurasia inherited from the USSR is as ramshackle a construction as any analogous imperial legacy in Africa and Asia. But the specific mix of vulnerabilities presented by the Soviet Union's socialist ethnofederalism needs to be considered carefully before comparisons to other regions can be made usefully.

Second, we survey the rich literature on Russian regionalism that has emerged since the dissolution of the Soviet Union. Notwithstanding alarm bells ringing in some scholarly quarters, the overwhelming preponderance of expert analysis suggests that Chechnya is the exception. National or ethnic separatism, the consensus holds, is not the main issue. Rather, the rhetoric of self-determination is part of a complex set of bargaining games over the evolution of Russia's federal system, the distribution of economic surplus and political benefits, and the basic problem of providing effective governance in the context of crisis-ridden economic transition and political development. The stakes in this struggle are immense—no less than the future of Russian statehood. Yet the ability of the outside world to affect its outcome is marginal.

The consensus we outline reflects rigorous research by scores of local, Russian, European, and U.S. scholars. Nevertheless, like any such expert consensus, it reflects the assumption that key underlying trends that characterized Russian politics in the 1990s will continue. Although the Chechen case is exceptional on most grounds, it does show what can happen when poor leadership choices and dangerous elite dynamics contradict these underlying trends. And some of the most in-depth local research by regional experts reveals developments that in other cases have engendered state-shattering forms of self-determination. In the third section, we provide a checklist of such developments. Major change in any of these basic trends could undermine the current equilibrium that undergirds the stability of the Russian Federation and bring forth the challenge of ethnic or national self-determination with a vengeance.

We conclude by exploring the relevance to the Russian Federation of the Liechtenstein Initiative on Self-Determination at the United Nations. Russia's regions are at the very least a laboratory for exploring the many different ways local groups come to terms with central authorities on economic, political, and cultural issues. In addition, there may be instances in which local leaders and activists as well as central authorities are searching for new ways to settle their differences without altering hard external borders. The scholarly and policy communities need to be ready in such cases with ideas that help actors resolve practical problems of governance and cultural well-being without violence or threats to the territorial integrity of states.

Why Group Identity, Politics, and Economics Fuse

The key feature of Russian regional politics is the frequent fusion of political, economic, and national or ethnic claims such that the relative importance of each motivation is hard to disentangle. This fusion is the consequence of two critical historical developments: Soviet ethnofederalism and the specific events that precipitated post-Soviet Russia's de facto decentralization.

Soviet Ethnofederalism and the Russian Federation

The borders of most sovereign states today were once administrative boundaries within long-gone empires. Despite their arbitrary nature, the colonial maps of Africa and North and South America have been remarkably stable.[2] The map of today's Eurasia is largely the product of

---

2. Robert Jackson, *Quasi-States: Sovereignty, International Relations and the Third World* (Cambridge: Cambridge University Press, 1990); and Jeffrey Herbst, "War and the State in Africa," *International Security* 14, no. 4 (Spring 1990), pp. 117–139.

Bolshevik nationality policy. The Soviet Union was formally a federation of sovereign, ethnically designated republics that was in reality a centralized dictatorship. The combination proved fatal—to both the USSR and its sister socialist federations in Czechoslovakia and Yugoslavia. The policy of restructuring the administration of ethnic groups into ancestral homelands played a critical role in the formation of nations and in the development of national territoriality.[3] From the 1920s until the mid-1930s, the Bolsheviks redrew and renamed the old provincial *(guberniya)* borders of the Russian empire and formed the majority of the boundaries that exist today in the post-Soviet era. By drawing this often arbitrary "complicated patchwork of constituent units," they effectively created non-Russian ethnic homelands. Ironically, however, these areas often contained a majority ethnic Russian population rather than a majority of the titular nationality.[4] Centralized power and periodic repression fostered grievances, whereas naming territories after national groups and conferring specific political rights and privileges on these territories created incentives for the development of national identities.[5]

The legacy of Soviet-drawn administrative boundaries powerfully determines the extent and nature of self-determination claims in the former Soviet Union. The USSR was dissolved by agreement among leaders of the Soviet Union republics. The legitimacy of that settlement hinges on maintaining a distinction between the boundaries of former Soviet Union republics and all other Soviet federal units. For this reason, most Soviet successor states face strong incentives to support this distinction—as does the rest of the international community. The logic is identical to the African case, in which the arbitrary borders drawn in Berlin in 1885 are widely seen as better than any feasible alternative.

Arbitrary borders are common, and often stable. Unlike European colonialists, the Bolsheviks paid formal obeisance to the principle of

---

3. The Soviet case is thus a strong one for advocates of a constructivist as opposed to primordial view of national identity. However, regardless of one's position in this debate, Soviet nationalities policies had the effects we describe. See Robert John Kaiser, *The Geography of Nationalism in Russia and the USSR* (Princeton: Princeton University Press, 1994); and Ronald Grigor Suny, *Revenge of the Past* (Stanford: Stanford University Press, 1992).

4. Kathryn Stoner-Weiss, "Federalism and Regionalism," in Stephen White, Alex Pravda, and Zvi Gitelman, eds., *Developments in Russian Politics 4* (London: Macmillan, 1997), p. 230.

5. See Denis J.B. Shaw, *Russia in the Modern World: A New Geography* (Oxford: Blackwell, 1999), p. 184; and Margorie Mandelstam Balzer, "Dilemmas of Federalism in Siberia," in Mikhail A. Alexseev, ed., *Center-Periphery Conflict in Post-Soviet Russia: A Federation Imperiled* (New York: St. Martin's Press, 1999), p. 153.

national self-determination. Hence, despite its hypocrisy, Soviet nation-alities policy did not result in unusually bad borders from the standpoint of stability. Although they did occasionally play divide-and-rule by drawing borders designed to foster conflict, the Soviets just as often tried to make administrative boundaries correspond to their best esti-mate of demographic and economic realities.[6]

Nevertheless, the Soviet colonial map *is* arbitrary. Many of the for-mer Soviet Union republics are themselves little empires. And like the Soviet Union itself, many are also organized on the ethnofederal princi-ple. Chief among these is the Russian Federation. At the end of the Soviet period there were a total of eighty-eight administrative units in the Russian Socialist Federated Soviet Republic (RSFSR) higher than the city and district *(rayon)* level. The most common units were the forty-nine oblasts, populated primarily by ethnic Russians and lacking any special ethnic status. The oblasts and six *krais*, mainly large, sparsely populated territories, were essentially administrative units, although the *krais* did have some ethnic character. The cities of Moscow and St. Petersburg had a special status relatively equal in the hierarchy to that of oblasts. Today around 80 percent of the country's population lives in either an oblast or a *krai*.

The sixteen Autonomous Soviet Socialist Republics, or ASSRs, within Soviet Russia were established according to the location of the traditional homelands of the hundred or so non-Russian ethnic groups. The national-territorial principle was also applied to the five smaller autonomous oblasts (ethnic units within *krais*) and ten autonomous *okrugs* (lower-level ethnic units within oblasts and *krais*). The autonomous oblasts and *okrugs*, which were directly subordinate to the territories in which they were located, had substantially fewer rights and representation at the center than the autonomous republics, which were subordinate to the RSFSR. The autonomous republics also suppos-edly had slightly more independence from Moscow than the regular oblasts.

After years of Soviet development and in-migration the population mixes of these ethnic homelands were often changed substantially. As of the last Soviet census (1989), in only seven of the sixteen autonomous republics in the RSFSR was the titular nationality the largest ethnic group in the republic.[7]

---

6. See Kaiser, *The Geography of Nationalism in Russia and the USSR,* for this argument.

7. The North Caucasus Republic of Dagestan, which has the lowest percent-age of Russians, is the only one of the autonomous republics that was not designat-ed for a specific ethnic group or groups. See Kathryn Stoner-Weiss, *Local Heroes:*

Several changes have occurred in Russia's administrative boundaries since the fall of the Soviet Union. All sixteen of the autonomous republics in the RSFSR now have the status of "republic of the Russian Federation" with more autonomy than they had in Soviet times. Four of the five autonomous oblasts have now also acquired this new republic status: Adigai, Borno-Altai, Karachi, and Khakassia, with the Jewish autonomous oblast remaining. Finally, the former Checheno-Ingush ASSR split into two republics, the Chechen Republic and the Ingush Republic.[8] Today, thirty-four non-Russian and ethnically based political entities (including Chechnya) coexist in the Russian Federation.[9] (See Tables 9.1 and 9.2.)

De Facto Decentralization

Thus Soviet Russia was a structural replica of the USSR itself. And like the Soviet Union, the RSFSR was a federation in name only.[10] In reality it was a centrally controlled party dictatorship, where the center's control had been in a state of decay since at least the 1970s. The contradic-

Table 9.1   Russian Federation Demography (from the 1989 census)

	Population	Percent of Total
Total Population of Russia	147,021,869	—
Russians	119,865,946	81.5
Non-Russians	27,155,923	19.5
Tatar	5,522,096	3.8
Ukrainians	4,362,872	3.0
Chuvash	1,773,645	1.2
Bashkir	1,345,273	0.9
Belorussian	1,206,222	0.9
Mordva	1,072,939	0.8
Chechen	989,999	0.7

Source: Margorie Mandelstam Balzer, "Dilemmas of Federalism in Siberia," in Mikhail A. Alexseev, *Center-Periphery Conflict in Post-Soviet Russia: A Federation Imperiled* (New York: St. Martin's Press, 1999), p. 138.

The Political Economy of Russian Regional Governance (Princeton: Princeton University Press, 1997), pp. 62–63; Darrell Slider, "Federalism, Discord, and Accommodation: Intergovernmental Relations in Post-Soviet Russia," in Theodore H. Friedgut and Jeffrey W. Hahn, *Local Power and Post-Soviet Politics* (Armonk, N.Y.: M. E. Sharpe, 1994), pp. 239, 241; and Daniel S. Treisman, "Russia's 'Ethnic Revival': The Separatist Activism of Regional Leaders in a Post Communist Order," *World Politics* 49 (January 1997), pp. 212–249.

    8. See Stoner-Weiss, *Local Heroes,* p. 81; and Shaw, *Russia in the Modern World,* p. 62.

    9. Balzer, "Dilemmas of Federalism in Siberia," p. 134.

    10. Stoner-Weiss, *Local Heroes,* p. 62.

Table 9.2   Ethnic Components of the Russian Federation

Republics	Ethnic-Based Autonomous *Okrugs*
Republic of Adygeya	Aga Buryat
Altai Republic	Chukchi (Chukotsk)
Republic of Bashkortostan	Evenki
Republic of Buryatia	Khanty-Mansy
Carachai-Cherkess Republic	
Chechen Republic	Komi-Permyak
Chuvash Republic	Koryak
Republic of Dagestan	Nenets
Ingush Republic	Yamalo-Nenets
Kabardino-Balkar Republic	Taymyr (Dolgano-Nenets)
Republic of Kalmykia-Khalmg-Tangch	Ust'-Orda Buryat
Republic of Karelia	
Khakass Republic	Autonomous Oblasts
Republic of Komi	Yevreyskiy (Jewish) Autonomous Oblast
Republic of Marii El	
Republic of Mordovia	
Republic of North Ossetia	Districts
Republic of Sakha (Yakutia)	Buryat
Republic of Tatarstan	Eveno-Bytantaysk
Republic of Tuva	Taimyr (Nganasan)
Udmurt Republic	

Source: Marjorie Mandelstam Balzer, "Dilemmas of Federalism in Siberia," in Mikhail A. Alexseev, *Center-Periphery Conflict in Post-Soviet Russia: A Federation Imperiled* (New York: St. Martin's Press, 1999), p. 134; Constitution of the Russian Federation, 1993, as cited by Kathryn Stoner-Weiss, "Federalism and Regionalism," in Stephen White, Alex Pravda, and Zvi Gitelman, eds., *Developments in Russian Politics 4* (London: Macmillan, 1997), p. 232; and Denis J.B. Shaw, *Russia in the Modern World: A New Geography* (Oxford: Blackwell, 1999).

tion between the actual centralism and the formal federalism of Soviet times was finally reversed in the chaotic politics of 1991–1995; during this period, there was a dramatic devolution of power from the center to the regions *as well as* the creation of a formal constitutional structure that accorded immense power to the presidency. As a result, the country is formally centralized but de facto decentralized.

In March 1992, President Boris Yeltsin induced eighteen of the then twenty republics to sign the Russian Federation Treaty, which gave republics the right of "independent participation" in foreign relations and economic affairs; Moscow would continue to handle issues relating to national defense, the budget, and the money supply. The agreement in effect established an unequal system where republics were placed at the top of a three-tier federal structure.[11] Tatarstan and Checheno-Ingushetia were the only two republics that refused to sign the

---

11. Stoner-Weiss, "Federalism and Regionalism," p. 249.

Federation treaty; Tatarstan later, in February 1994, concluded a separate bilateral treaty with Moscow. Next came Bashkortostan in August 1994, followed by dozens of others over the succeeding years. These agreements negotiated between the center and the regions allowed the Russian Federation to be reconstructed on a treaty basis. The 1993 Russian constitution views all eighty-nine administrative units as subjects of the Russian Federation, although the federation treaty has yet to be adopted as an annex to the constitution, as promised by Moscow.[12]

As the century ended, the Russian Federation remained a stated goal and not a reality. It was still, in effect, a transitional arrangement. Even on paper it was not a federation in the Western sense. One scholar noted that the Russian constitution speaks of exclusive federal rights (Article 71) and shared rights (Article 72), but nowhere are the exclusive rights of subnational units enumerated.[13] Furthermore, the bilateral treaties that Moscow signed with the regions differ considerably, sometimes directly contradict the federal constitution, and are often unobserved.[14] Finally, much of the provincial law on the books contradicts federal law, with figures ranging from 30 percent to as high as 60 percent. And according to the Russian minister of justice, nineteen of the twenty-one republics have adopted constitutions that contain provisions incompatible with the Russian constitution.[15] At the heart of the Russian Federation, therefore, is a set of informal and often downright illegal norms and arrangements.

This present state of de facto decentralization of the Russian state has nothing to do with Kremlin presidential politics or who happens to be governor in a particular region but instead relates to the deep structural issues of a state unable to govern itself effectively.[16] Over the past decade, regional executives have garnered the power to determine important policies in their regions, having gained control over locally elected bodies, local government, the press, and the local economy.[17] Until the Russian state is able to implement an efficient tax-collection

---

12. See Shaw, *Russia in the Modern World,* pp. 66–67; and Morton H. Halperin and David J. Scheffer with Patricia L. Small, *Self-Determination in the New World Order* (Washington, D.C.: Carnegie Endowment for International Peace, 1992), p. 153.

13. *The Crisis in Chechnya: Causes, Prospects, Solutions.* Conference Proceedings, Liechtenstein Research Program on Self-Determination, Princeton University, March 3–4, 2000.

14. Forty-one regions have special bilateral accords with Moscow. See Clifford Kupchan, "Devolution Drives Russian Reform," *Washington Quarterly* 23, no. 2 (Spring 2000), pp. 67–77 at 69.

15. Darrell Slider, "Regional and Local Politics," in White, Pravda, and Gitelman, *Developments in Russian Politics 4*, p. 254.

16. Ibid.

17. Ibid., p. 258.

system and enforce the rule of law on a national level by building effective institutions at the local level, the Russian state will continue to weaken and decentralize.

The Limits of Separatist Self-Determination in Russia

We thus have the chaotic politics of decentralization in a poor, disorganized state that contains many ethnically defined territorial units. On the surface, the Russian Federation appears a likely candidate to suffer the Soviet Union's fate. In this section, we show that this is not the case. We then examine the main argument against this view—namely, Chechnya. On close examination, the Chechen case is the exception that proves the rule. It follows that classical self-determination—the right of a people to its own state—is not the issue in Russia. At issue, therefore, are much more subtle solutions to the problem of group claims. We examine some of these cases in the final subsection.

Why Did the Soviet Union Break Up and Russia Did Not?

Explanations for the territorial stability of the Russian Federation despite the dramatic rise of regional power fall into four categories. The first and by far the most popular explanation concerns demography. By the late 1980s Russians just barely made up a majority of the Soviet Union's population; today they represent over 80 percent of the population of the Russian Federation. Moreover, the titular nationality represents an absolute majority of the population in only five of twenty-one of the federation's ethnic republics; Russians make up a majority in nine. And many of Russia's minorities are in territories surrounded by Russia (for example, Tatarstan), making them poor cases for statehood.

Though important, the numerical preponderance of Russians is insufficient to explain stability. First, we might expect ethnic minorities who are outnumbered even in their own regions to be more interested in secession rather than less. Second, during the perestroika period there were a remarkably high number of Russians in the non-Russian union republics who opted to support the local independence movement.[18] The same is true in Tatarstan, where a high number of Russians support the sovereignty referendum.

18. Stephen E. Hanson, "Ideology, Interests, and Identity: Comparing the Soviet and Russian Secession Crises," in Alexseev, *Center-Periphery Conflict in Post-Soviet Russia*, p. 20.

The second explanation highlights the influence of institutions and economics. Russia's federal structure ensures that elites in Russia's autonomous republics enjoy far less power than did those in the former Soviet republics. At the same time, the central government is too weak to threaten local elites enough to cause them to consider radical separatism. The result is an institutional balance of power. Though imperfect and corrupt, the Russian Federation is at least a protodemocracy. Both local governors and the central executive and legislature are elected; the ballot box can deflect many grievances. With their important role in the federal legislature (both as members of the Federation Council and as powerful players in elections for the State Duma) and in presidential politics, elected regional governors can provide a real constraint on central authority.[19]

Although the central government is weak, 3 or 4 percent of Russia's GDP is still recycled through Moscow—and the regions clamor for their share. In addition, powerful natural monopolies create incentives for regions not to stray too far. Local financial-industrial groups—frequently in crude corporatist cahoots with the local regional governor—are dependent on links to the center. Also critical is institutional stratification: most separatist activism occurs in the non-Russian ethnic republics, whereas the Russian oblasts are strongly integrationist and balance out the few separatists.[20] The Soviet Union lacked this group of integrationist balancers. Local-level institutional factors also act to inhibit separatism. Social and political institutions in many ethnic republics foster interethnic consensus and mediation, create incentives to limit the political power of ethnic radicals, and facilitate integration into Russia's federal structure.[21]

Thus both primordial factors such as demography and geography and institutional factors conspire against separatist variants of self-determination. However, empirical research—in both deep case studies and wide comparative analyses—tends to confirm the greater importance of institutional effects. For example, Daniel Treisman's comprehensive study of separatist tendencies of Russia's ethnic regions over

---

19. See Daniel S. Triesman, "After Yeltsin Comes . . . Yeltsin," *Foreign Policy* (Spring 2000).

20. Hanson, "Ideology, Interests, and Identity," p. 20.

21. Mikhail A. Alexseev, "Asymmetric Russia: Promises and Dangers," in Alexseev, *Center-Periphery Conflict in Post-Soviet Russia,* pp. 258–259. For a case study of such institutions, see Leokadiya Drobizheva, "Comparison of Élite Groups in Tatarstan, Sakha, Magadan, and Orenburg," *Post-Soviet Affairs* 15, no. 4 (October-December 1999), pp. 387–406; and Robert Bruce Ware and Envery Kisriev, "Political Stability in Dagestan: Ethnic Parity and Religious Polarization," *Problems of Post-Communism* 47, no. 2 (March/April 2000), pp. 23–33.

1990–1994 strongly supported the institutional explanation. He found that the higher in administrative rank a region's administrative status, the higher its level of separatist activism. In other words, the best explanation for the level of separatism was simply whether a given territory was an oblast, *okrug*, or republic. Yet although Soviet-era ethnic administrative designations may have played a role in nurturing ethnic identification, such identification did not mean that any of these non-Russian ethnicities were predestined to pursue separatist policies. According to Treisman, preexisting ethnic self-identification, or "primordial ethnicity," with one exception was not decisive in determining which of Russia's ethnic regions staged active separatist campaigns. Finally, regional leaders who were of the titular nationality were not more likely to press separatist demands than those who were Russian. Instead of being the representatives of "nonrational primordial impulses," these leaders are brokers between their region and the center and make their decisions on the basis of a cost-benefit analysis.[22]

The third explanation centers on ideas. To its last days, the Soviet Union was associated with a discredited Marxist-Leninist ideology against which it was easy to mobilize. Thus far, the Russian Federation has not replaced Marxism-Leninism with a similarly powerful or divisive official ideology—such as Russian nationalism. When even a team of Russia's 100 most prominent scholars selected by the Kremlin failed to define the meaning of Russian statehood, it is little wonder that separatists find Russia to be an elusive target.[23] To the extent that it has a coherent ideology, the Moscow government is committed to a market economy and a strong-state version of democracy—ideas that are popular worldwide. Its main problem is a failure to realize those pragmatic aims. The best issue for local mobilization is not the threat from Moscow's strong hand imposing a new order but rather the threat created by Moscow's incompetence, corruption, and venality. Hence, the current ideological climate limits the political import of absolutist national claims as against more pragmatic bargaining issues concerning management and governance.

Finally, scholars point to specific policies and strategies to explain Russia's continued essential stability in the face of massive challenges. Russian presidents Boris Yeltsin and Vladimir Putin have been more willing to use force than Soviet president Gorbachev. At the same time, Yeltsin, at least, proved more adept at using pragmatic accommodative strategies to hold the federation together. Moscow has used its limited

---

22. Treisman, "Russia's 'Ethnic Revival,'" pp. 212–249.
23. Alexseev, "Asymmetric Russia," p. 272.

means to provide selective incentives to obtain cooperation from regional elites. Meanwhile, regional leaders and elites have also chosen their strategies carefully. The same goes for the international community, whose overwhelming majority has expressed official support for Russian statehood and played the regional card with great circumspection.[24]

The Exception: Chechnya

Were it not for the case of Chechnya, the rise of Russia's regions would be seen today as simply one more example of the worldwide trend toward the devolution of state authority.[25] Chechnya naturally draws attention, not least because Russian leaders constantly invoke its implications for the integrity of the Russian state as a justification for brutal use of force against the republic.[26] However, the Chechen case is an outlier on all four of the critical dimensions that explain Russian stability.

First, consider the "primordial" factors. Unlike in the rest of Russia, there is a large preponderance of the titular nationality in the specific territory of Chechnya.[27] Unlike most of Russia's regions, Chechnya has an external border that makes independence at least possible. The Chechen national identity runs strong, in part because Chechens were deported en masse to Kazakhstan in 1944. Moreover, the Chechens are one of the very few Russian subject groups that maintained a steady two-century history of resistance fighting against the Russians. Over the same period the Russians established a reputation for unusual brutality in suppressing the Chechens. Some other republics score highly on one

---

24. For a description of U.S. policy toward the regions, see Kupchan, "Devolution Drives Russian Reform," pp. 67–77.

25. See James Manor, *The Political Economy of Democratic Decentralization* (Washington, D.C.: World Bank, 1999).

26. Putin, in his campaign biography, on the repercussions of the summer 1999 Chechen incursion into Dagestan: "I was struck dumb [by the consequences]. It would have spread to Dagestan, the whole Caucasus would have been taken away, it's clear. . . . Russia as a state [would] cease to exist." David Hoffman, "Miscalculation Paved Path to Chechen War; Conflict Hastened by Russians' Neglect," *Washington Post,* March 20, 2000, p. A1.

27. The latest population statistics are for the Checheno-Ingush Republic, from the 1989 Soviet census: 55 percent Chechens, 22 percent Russians, 12 percent Ingush, and 11 percent other ethnicities. With the split into two separate Chechen and Ingush republics, the proportion of Chechens in their territory has undoubtably grown. See Ian Bremmer and Ray Taras, eds., *New States, New Politics: Building the Post-Soviet Nations* (Cambridge: Cambridge University Press, 1997), Appendix A, p. 712.

or two of these primordial criteria. None, however, combine them all in such extreme degree.

On the institutional criterion, too, Chechnya stands out. Chechnya was the only republic in the post-Soviet transition that emerged from a disintegration of a constituent unit of the Russian Federation (the former Checheno-Ingush Republic). The split was unique to Chechnya and Ingushetia and created an unusual power vacuum in these two units. Elsewhere in the Russian Federation, institutional continuity allowed the essential institutional incentives that foster integration to work. In the former Checheno-Ingush Republic, however, institutional change broke down the old structures and led to a situation in which political entrepreneurs could profit by exploiting separatist ideology. As the Ingush case shows, this situation by no means made separatism inevitable. It simply made other elements critical in determining outcomes.

Chechnya is also an outlier in the third dimension: ideas. Triesman found that the presence of an Islamic religious tradition tended to predispose regions toward greater separatism (as opposed to those regions that were traditionally Christian, Buddhist, or shamanistic), and all three of the most assertively separatist regions were Muslim: Tatarstan, Chechnya, and Bashkortostan.[28] But as has been found, Chechens have the highest level of religious belief and practice among Islamic ethnic groups in Russia.[29] In addition, cultural anthropologists, ethnologists, historians, and other experts on the North Caucasus stress the uniqueness of the Chechens' warrior culture, built on ideas of honor and martial heroism.[30] Finally, as noted, Chechens suffer from more Russian bigotry than almost any other group. As a result, the clash of ideas in the Chechen case was far more dangerous than elsewhere.

Given this volatile mix of primordial, institutional, and ideological factors, the Chechen case put a premium on politics and strategic

---

28. Daniel Treisman, "Russia's 'Ethnic Revival': The Separatist Activism of Regional Leaders in a Post Communist Order," *World Politics* 49 (January 1997): pp. 212–249.

29. Susan G. Lehmann, "Islam and Ethnicity in the Republics of Russia," *Post-Soviet Affairs* 13 (January/March 1997), pp. 78–103, as cited by Gail W. Lapidus, "The Dynamics of Secession in the Russian Federation: Why Chechnya?" in Mikhail A. Alekseev, *Center-Periphery Conflict in Post-Soviet Russia: A Federation Imperiled* (New York: St. Martin's Press, 1999), p. 51.

30. See Yo'av Karny, *Highlanders: A Journey to the Caucasus in Quest of Memory* (New York: Farrar, Straus, and Giroux, 2000); Carlotta Gall and Thomas de Waal, *Chechnya: Calamity in the Caucasus* (New York: New York University Press, 1998); and Anatol Lieven, *Chechnya: Tombstone of Russian Power*, new ed. (New Haven: Yale University Press, 1998).

choice. Yet here again, Moscow and Grozny made a series of spectacular strategic blunders on the path to war. Indeed, so incompetent, erratic, feckless, and irresponsible was the political leadership on both sides that many analysts view strategic choice as the most important cause of the conflict. In other words, the extraordinarily combustible mix of primordial, institutional, and ideological factors was by itself insufficient to cause military conflict in the absence of an incredible series of strategic missteps on both sides.[31] The regime of Dzokar Dudayev set its new republic on course for independence in 1991. As Mikhail Alekseev notes, it was the only regional leadership that refused to participate in the sessions of the Federation Council, Russia's upper house of parliament; it alone among all the regions refused to hold elections to the Russian State Duma and to vote on the referendum on the Russian constitution in 1993; it alone rejected the introduction of the post-Soviet ruble for fear of Russian financial domination[32]

For its part, Moscow showed unusual levels of incompetence in dealing with Chechnya, both prior to and during the first and second Chechen wars of the 1990s (unlike how it dealt with Tatarstan). Moscow's Chechen policy was outstanding in its lack of imagination and flexibility even against Russia's dismal record as imperial steward. This interelite struggle was personified in the individual struggle between Russian president Yeltsin and Chechen president Dudayev. As a consequence of their bitter feud, the two could not even agree on terms for a meeting that could have forestalled the deterioration in relations. But even with this undistinguished policy, the status quo was hardly unsustainable as of 1994, when Yeltsin and his team—against the strong counsel of regional experts—undertook the series of violent actions that culminated in the disastrous invasion of December.

For a great many experts on the North Caucasus, much of the current Chechen problem—especially the radicalization of Chechen Islam and society and the involvement of outside powers—is a direct consequence of the invasion and subsequent war rather than preexisting conditions. To be sure, there would inevitably have been *a* Chechen problem; but *this* Chechen problem in all its intractability is a consequence of more conjunctural factors that are unlikely to recur in other cases.

Thus there is no evidence that Chechnya is a harbinger of things to

---

31. See, for example, Lieven, *Chechnya: Tombstone of Russian Power*; Alexseev, "Asymmetric Russia"; and Gail W. Lapidus, "The Dynamics of Secession in the Russian Federation: Why Chechnya?," in Alexseev, *Center-Periphery Conflict in Post-Soviet Russia*, p. 70. Also see Gall and de Waal, *Chechnya: Calamity in the Caucasus*.

32. Alexseev, "Asymmetric Russia," p. 257.

come. On the contrary, there has been a strong backlash even in the North Caucasus against the Chechens, and especially against their leaders for embarking on such a reckless course.[33] As Yo'av Karny notes, "There is a distinct disinterest on the part of virtually all other ethnic groups in the Caucasus—even those related ethnically to the Chechens—either in seceding from Russia or joining an insurrection against Russia. That applies even to Dagestan, where the Russians are only about five percent of the population, and there is a clear historical Muslim identity."[34]

Chechnya does present a tough problem in self-determination policy for Russia and the outside world. On traditional grounds, the Chechen case for independence is among the strongest in Russia. Given current Russian preferences, however, independence is not an option. In addition, most states—and certainly the most powerful states—in the international system will not support Chechen independence in defiance of Moscow. The implications of our analysis are three. First, because Chechnya is the exception, Russia could let it go without jeopardizing its integrity. Second, given Russia's preference for holding the republic, the use of force and the festering conflict will not spill over to other republics and regions.[35] Third, and most important, Chechnya should not be at center stage in discussions of self-determination in the Russian Federation, since all evidence suggests it is anomalous.

The Rule: Opportunistic Adaptation

Events on the ground across the Russian Federation show a pattern of pragmatic adaptation to the new informally decentralized system. Although these arrangements are hardly models of democratic governance, they do appear to have forestalled more destabilizing pressures. Future drives for further autonomy are likely to reflect a more economic, rather than ethnic, character. The following case of Tatarstan illustrates the pattern.

---

33. See official testimony of Dr. Fiona Hill, director of Strategic Planning, Eurasia Foundation, *The Chechen Crisis and Its Implications for Russian Democracy*, hearing before the Commission on Security and Cooperation in Europe, 106th Congress, 1st session, November 3, 1999 (Washington, D.C.: GPO, 2000), p. 27.

34. Official testimony of independent journalist Yo'av Karny, *The Chechen Crisis and Its Implications for Russian Democracy*, hearing before the Commission on Security and Cooperation in Europe, 106th Congress, 1st session, November 3, 1999 (Washington, D.C.: GPO, 2000), p. 22.

35. Marie Bennigsen, "Chechnia: Political Developments and Strategic Implications for the North Caucasus," *Central Asian Survey* 18, no. 4 (December 1999), pp. 535–574.

At their core, Tatarstan's future efforts to secure and protect its autonomy will be fundamentally of the economic and not ethnic form of self-determination. Having secured with the Russia-Tatarstan Power Sharing Treaty (February 1994) a broad range of rights over republican taxation, budgeting, and local administration, along with several symbolic privileges of republican sovereignty,[36] the republic's elite seem to be concerned with maintaining this semi-independent status.

Tatarstan, which at 3.7 million people is Russia's seventh largest republic, lies completely within Russian borders and straddles Russia's main artery, the river Volga. According to the 1989 Soviet census, Tatarstan is 48.3 percent Tatar, 43.5 percent Russian, and 8.2 percent other ethnic groups. The 1.8 million Tatars in Tatarstan represent only about one-third of the 5.5 million Tatars residing in the Russian Federation. As Alexei Zverev notes, Tatarstan's geographical position and ethnic composition would make successful secession extremely difficult to achieve.[37]

The story of Tatar ethnic mobilization is one of a rise and fall of the Tatar nationalist movement that coincided with falling and then rising economic fortunes of ethnic Tatars within the republic. According to Elise Giuliano, "Nationalists constructed a political program in part around the issue of Tatar under-representation vis-à-vis Russians in Tatarstan's economy." As the Soviet economy tightened in the late 1980s and Russian-Tatar job competition rose, the nationalists' program gained salience. The Soviet system had trained people to equate their professional success with their ethnicity, and ethnic job competition arose as the Soviet economy collapsed. The decline in Tatar nationalism began as the Soviet state ended the use of ethnic quotas to allocate jobs and promotions, and as a private sector emerged in the republic that did not reward or penalize workers because of their ethnicity.[38] Giuliano writes, "In sum, two variables—a structural change in the economy toward decreased inter-ethnic labor competition, and the absence of a connection between ethnicity and people's professional lives—caused

---

36. Regarding the sovereignty issue, see Alexei Zverev, "Qualified Sovereignty: The Tatarstan Model for Resolving Conflicting Loyalties," in Michael Waller, Bruno Coppieters, and Alexei Malashenko, eds., *Conflicting Loyalties and the State in Post-Soviet Russia and Eurasia* (London and Portland, Oreg: Frank Cass, 1998), pp. 118–144. Regarding Tatarstan's autonomous status, see various issues of the EastWest Institute's *EWI Russian Regional Report*, <http://www.iews.org>.

37. Zverev, "Qualified Sovereignty," pp. 118–144.

38. Elise Giuliano, "The Politics of Economic Possibility and Nationalist Decline in Tatarstan," paper presented at the Association for the Study of Nationalities, Fifth Annual World Convention, Columbia University, New York, April 13–15, 2000.

individuals to move their support from the nationalists' program of radical change and republican secession."[39]

Tatarstan declared itself a full-fledged republic on August 30, 1991, and despite condemnation by President Yeltsin it held a referendum on independence on March 21, 1992, with 61 percent of the republic's population voting in favor.[40] But as Kathryn Stoner-Weiss points out, "Even ostensibly ethnic claims to independence made, for example, by the Tatar republic contained a 'Russians against Russia' element," because with 61% voting for independence, "a good proportion of the ethnic Russian population backed independence."[41] And in surveys conducted in 1994 by Leokadiya Drobizheva of a representative sample of Tatars and Russians, 60 percent of Tatars and more than 40 percent of Russians declared themselves in favor of economic sovereignty, while more than half of Tatars and more than one-third of Russians were for political sovereignty as a part of the Russian Federation.[42]

As stated previously, although the negotiations over a power-sharing agreement between Kazan and Moscow were difficult and protracted—and even provoked the threat of Russian military intervention in March 1992—the fact that the Tatar and Russian leaderships were able to discuss their problems, unlike in the case of Chechnya, helped to forestall any preemptive moves to violence by either side.[43]

Today, reports from the republic reveal that most ordinary Tatars now place personal economic gain above sovereignty concerns, and recent nationalist protest demonstrations in Kazan and Naberezhnye Chelny, where the nationalist movement is the strongest, have been weak.[44] Damir Iskhakov, a historian and founding member of the Tatarstan Social Center, which played a key role in the Tatar nationalist movement of the early 1990s, said that paradoxically, some Tatar nationalists "support a greater role for the federal government on the

---

39. Ibid.
40. Halperin and Scheffer with Small, *Self-Determination in the New World Order*, p. 154.
41. Stoner-Weiss, *Local Heroes*, pp. 85–86.
42. Leokadiya Drobizheva, "Comparison of Élite Groups in Tatarstan, Sakha, Magadan, and Orenburg," *Post-Soviet Affairs* 15, no. 4 (October/December, 1999), pp. 387–406.
43. Lapidus, "The Dynamics of Secession in the Russian Federation," p. 70. For more on the comparison between Chechnya and Tatarstan, and on how Tatarstan Republic president Mintimer Shamiev pursued a strategy of inclusive local politics, see Gulnaz Sharafutdinova, "Chechnya Versus Tatarstan: Understanding Ethnopolitics in Post-Communist Russia," *Problems of Post-Communism* 47, no. 2 (March/April 2000), pp. 13–22.
44. The EastWest Institute, *EWI Russian Regional Report* 5, no. 25 (June 28, 2000), <http://www.iews.org>.

theory that it will be less selfish, and less narrow in its distribution of power and resources than the current local elite."[45] According to the same report, many local Tatar and Russian entrepreneurs are looking to the Russian federal government to loosen the stranglehold on private business that is now held by the republic's leaders.[46]

What Might Upset the Equilibrium? A Checklist

The Russian Federation is a work in progress. It has resolved the challenge of self-determination in part by tolerating the large set of extralegal practices that govern center-periphery relations. These practices thrive in an atmosphere of ambiguity and obscure deep and unresolved contradictions between formal centralism and informal devolution. At the same time, ambiguity surrounds the most fundamental questions of national identity. If elites seek clarity concerning either the institutional structure of the state or the real meaning of ethnic and national identity, underlying vulnerabilities in the current arrangement might be exposed. The current provisional stability might evolve into an institutionalized equilibrium, or it might become unhinged, depending on how developments play out in the following areas.

Ideas: The Question of Identity

Russia so far has failed to construct a new identity.[47] It is a country that still cannot agree to the words of its national anthem, and a special presidential commission appointed by Yeltsin to develop the idea of Russian national identity failed to reach a consensus. It is a country in which the questions of the national anthem and the state seals remain controversial, notwithstanding the efforts of President Putin to resolve them.[48] It

---

45. Celestine Bohlen, "Russian Regions Wary as Putin Tightens Control," *New York Times,* March 9, 2000, p. A3.

46. Ibid.

47. Ronald Grigor Suny, "Provisional Stabilities: The Politics of Identities in Post-Soviet Eurasia," *International Security* 24, no. 3 (Winter 1999–2000), pp. 139–178.

48. Regarding the national anthem and state seals, see Michael R. Gordon, "Post-Communist Russia Plumbs Its Soul, in Vain, for New Vision," *New York Times,* March 31, 1998, pp. A1, A6, cited in Suny, "Provisional Stabilities," p. 140, and David Hoffman, "Russia Restores Soviet National Anthem," *Washington Post,* December 9, 2000, p. A30. Regarding the presidential commission, see Mikhail A. Alexseev and Vladimir Vagin, "Fortress Russia or Gateway to Europe? The Pskov Connection," in Alexseev, *Center-Periphery Conflict in Post-Soviet Russia,* p. 194.

is not just among the elites where the definitions are wanting; as Ronald Grigor Suny notes, public opinion is also deeply divided over the question of what constitutes the Russian nation and state.[49]

The roots of the dilemma run deep, as the Russian national identity was suffused first within the multinational tsarist empire and then within the multinational Soviet empire. In both manifestations, the imperial idea contradicted a purely national concept of Russian identity. Over the seventy-year period of communist rule, most Russians had come to accept the regime's attempt to equate their interests as a separate people with those of the entire USSR. As a consequence, the majority of ethnic Russians find themselves living in a state that had little or no meaning for most of them prior to 1991.[50]

During the perestroika period of the late 1980s and very early 1990s, many Russians began the slow process of changing their personal identifications from Soviet to Russian. The transformation was catalyzed in late 1990 when, three months after Russia had declared its sovereignty, the Nobel Prize–winning author Aleksandr Solzhenitsyn published the programmatic brochure *Rebuilding Russia* in a print run of over 25 million. In it he called for the peaceful dismemberment of most of the Soviet Union to preserve its Slavic core of Russia, Ukraine, and Belarus in the form of a "Pan-Russian Union *(Rossiiskii soyuz)."* Because the Russian people simply didn't have the energy left to maintain an empire, Russia had to concentrate on "nation building" on this freely chosen foundation.[51] As for minority peoples within the RSFSR, he had two prescriptions. Those with ethnic homelands such as Tatarstan, whose borders were fully enveloped by Russia, would have to share the same fate as Russia while receiving maximum attention to their special needs. Non-Russian areas that enjoyed external borders would have the choice of seceding if that was decided by local referendum.[52]

Solzhenitsyn's vision of a Russia of freely associated Slavs never came to fruition. A more malignant view of "non-Russians" became prevalent, however, with the growth of anti-Southern (especially anti-Caucasus) and anti-Muslim sentiments. Russian perceptions of south-

49. Suny, "Provisional Stabilities," p. 148.

50. John B. Dunlop, "Russia: In Search of an Identity?" in Ian Bremmer and Ray Taras, eds., *New States, New Politics: Building the Post-Soviet Nations* (Cambridge: Cambridge University Press, 1997), pp. 29, 35; and Shaw, *Russia in the Modern World,* p. 69.

51. Solzhenitsyn assumed that Belarus would choose to stay with Russia, as would the western half of Ukraine, and that the northern tier of Kazakhstan should be ceded to Russia because of the over 19 million Russians living in these areas.

52. Dunlop, "Russia: In Search of an Identity?" pp. 40–41, 60.

erners (especially Chechens and Azeris) as being corrupt and criminal, combined with an outbreak of ethnic clashes in the Caucasus in the early 1990s, led many to demand that the non-Russian parts of the Soviet Union be cast off and left to fend for themselves.[53] Russians remained divided on the status and rights of non-Russians living in autonomous regions within Russia.[54]

Is Russia a multinational state meant to represent all of the peoples now residing within its borders, or is Russia primarily a nation-state of the ethnic Russian majority? The fact that it is a federation, alone among the post-Soviet states, would seem to support the multinational view.[55] This is the liberal notion that Russia is a republic of Russian speakers that perhaps would allow some non-Russian autonomies to separate from the Russian state while integrating the Russian-speaking diaspora.[56] The extreme, and what could be termed antinational, approach to this view is represented by those who question the way the Russian Federation originally came into being. Dennis Shaw writes, "Some anti-Communists . . . have argued that the RSFSR was created in an arbitrary and purely opportunistic way by the Bolsheviks back in the early Soviet period, and that such decisions need not be taken as binding today."[57] A more executable version of this view is that Russia is a multinational state in which the term *Russian* is understood to refer to both Russian ethnicity *(russkii)* and Russian citizenship *(rossiiski)*.[58] The term *rossiyanin* is also used here as an alternative to describe a citizen of the Russian Federation without ethnic connotations.[59]

Yet the 1993 Russian constitution generates some doubt as to the general inclusiveness of the Russian nation, as it names the state both "Russia" and the "Russian Federation."[60] This ambiguity is promoted

---

53. This account follows that of Victor Zaslavsky, "The Evolution of Separatism in Soviet Society Under Gorbachev," in Gail W. Lapidus and Victor Zaslavsky, eds., with Philip Goldman, *From Union to Commonwealth: Nationalism and Separatism in the Soviet Republics,* Strengthening Democratic Institutions Project (Cambridge: Cambridge University Press, September 1992), quoted in Donald L. Horowitz, "Self-Determination: Politics, Philosophy, and Law," in Margaret Moore, ed., *National Self-Determination and Secession* (New York: Oxford University Press, 1998), pp.181–214 at 188.
54. Dunlop, "Russia: In Search of an Identity?" p. 62.
55. Shaw, *Russia in the Modern World,* pp. 69–70.
56. Vera Tolz, "Conflicting 'Homeland Myths' and Nation-State Building in Postcommunist Russia," *Slavic Review* 57, no. 2 (Summer 1998), p. 168, as summarized by Suny, "Provisional Stabilities," pp. 148–149.
57. Shaw, *Russia in the Modern World,* pp. 69–70.
58. Suny, "Provisional Stabilities," p. 149.
59. Dunlop, "Russia: In Search of an Identity?" p. 68.
60. Shaw, *Russia in the Modern World,* pp. 69–70.

by those who adopt a second conception of the Russian national idea, the Solzhenitsyn view of Russia as a Slavic union of Great Russians (Russians), White Russians (Belarussians), and Little Russians (Ukrainians).[61] A third conception of Russia is forwarded by conservative nationalists, the most militant communists, and the so-called Eurasianists, who believe that Russia should take steps to restore the Soviet Union under a different name with as many of the former Soviet republics joining as possible.[62] The communists in particular have argued that the 1991 dissolution of the USSR was illegal and therefore should be reversed, a view that was endorsed by the communist- and nationalist-dominated Duma in March 1996.[63]

The key is that these three visions of Russian identity are fundamentally incompatible.[64] Yet the outcome of the debate will determine how Russia responds to the concerns of minorities within its borders and in other smaller nations outside of its borders. As Ronald Grigor Suny writes, "Whether the nation is conceived as ethnically exclusive or civically inclusive has political consequences of great force."[65] The still unresolved issue of Russian national identity is critical to understanding the future course of Russian development as well as the status of ethnically based administrative units within Russia. At what point does the attempted secession of a part of the Russian Federation mean a loss to the heart of Russia? Does it matter if the part wishing to secede is Slavic or non-Slavic? Russia faces a contradiction: it needs a national idea to get collective action in pursuit of development, but the national idea is potentially destabilizing for both the Russian Federation and the Commonwealth of Independent States (CIS). Until Russia embraces an identity based on civic principles rather than on ethnic guidelines of who and who isn't a legitimate member of Russian society, the self-determination issue will continue to fester.

However, the ambiguity concerning Russian identity dampens incentives for separatism by removing a potential threat to local identities. At the same time, below the surface, regions are building local cultural capital through language and history education.[66] Local elites are

---

61. Tolz, "Conflicting 'Homeland Myths,'" p. 168.
62. Ibid.
63. Shaw, *Russia in the Modern World,* pp. 69–70.
64. Tolz, "Conflicting 'Homeland Myths,'" p. 168.
65. Suny, "Provisional Stabilities," p. 140.
66. See Dmitry Gorenburg, "Regional Separatism in Russia: Ethnic Mobilisation or Power Grab?" *Europe-Asia Studies* 51, no. 2 (March 1999), pp. 245–274; and Drobizheva, "Comparison of Élite Groups in Tatarstan, Sakha, Magadan, and Orenburg."

careful to cooperate with Moscow and do not escalate ethnic rhetoric. At the same time, they exploit their freedom to foster local identity— including the use of affirmative action for educational and governmental posts. On the one hand this is a good sign, as it means the freedom to develop. As long as cultural flowering can continue within the confines of the Russian Federation, destabilization is not inevitable. On the other hand, as this cultural revival continues, the raw material for the separatist version of self-determination can accumulate. Should developments in the Kremlin or in national or ethnic Russian politics cause a shift toward more opposition to the ethnic republics, the republics will be primed to fight back.

Institutions and Politics: A New Recentralization?

A key problem with the post-1995 equilibrium is that one powerful actor—the Russian state—has never been satisfied with it. This dissatisfaction came to the fore first with the rise of Prime Minister Yevgeny Primakov and then more consequentially with the advent of Vladimir Putin. Upon his election as Russia's second president, Putin placed the reassertion of central authority at the center of his agenda. He sought a revitalized Russia that is able to collect its taxes and where the rule of national, and not regional, law prevails.[67] He began with a comparatively strong hand—both national popularity and a relatively strong economy, which combined to give him a temporary mandate to restructure the Russian state.

To this end, Putin quickly proposed three daring changes that amounted to an effort to shift the balance of power from the regions back to the center: (1) permanently oust all eighty-nine governors and the leaders of the regional legislatures from their guaranteed seats on the Federation Council; (2) grant the president legal authority to personally suspend or fire any governor who flouts federal law or defies the Russian constitution, and (3) place the eighty-nine regions under the administrative oversight of seven new *guberniya,* each headed by an official appointed by and responsible to Putin alone.[68] The initiative, Putin surely hoped, would put an end to the decade of negotiated bilateral deals where the center gave in to regions under the implicit threat of secession.

---

67. See Vladimir Vladimirovich Putin with Natalya Timakova Gevorkyan and Andrei Kolesnikov, *First Person: An Astonishingly Frank Self-Portrait by Russia's President,* trans. Catherine A. Fitzpatrick (New York: Public Affairs, 2000).

68. Michael Wines, "Putin's Move on Governors Would Bolster His Role," *New York Times,* May 22, 2000, p. A3.

In response to these announced policies, the mood in Moscow immediately shifted to the expectation that the center would soon reassert itself.[69] In reality, the center-periphery contest will be a battle of many years' duration against deep-laid institutional and economic realities. Any Russian head of state will need to have Bismarck-like qualities to stealthily change the institutional landscape. He must gather forces carefully, divide opponents, and reduce regional rivals in piecemeal fashion. The drama will bear watching. If initial attempts at recentralization fail and Putin decides to use more repressive methods against the regions, the costs and benefits of appeals to ethnic separatism will shift.

The critical place to watch will be the regions themselves. The response of the regions to Putin's initiatives depends largely on how much they fear the power of the Putin presidency. A few regional leaders quickly shifted their strategy in 2000 and embraced the reforms in an attempt to ingratiate themselves with the presidential administration. It remains to be seen, however, whether the Kremlin will be able to scare the regional governors into, in effect, handing the keys over to their personal fiefdoms.[70]

A decade of taking all the sovereignty they can swallow (to use Yeltsin's appeal) gave the regions time to build significant power relative to the Kremlin.[71] After the August 1998 financial crisis, the regions became more self-sufficient and less used to thinking that the federal government would bail them out; most governors have wide influence over political processes in their regions. Local institutions under their control, in particular the local media, can be used to shape the outcome of federal, regional, and local elections conducted in their region. Governors often are able to capture or circumvent federal agencies working in their districts because federal agencies are often dependent on the governors for their office space and other resources. A lack of fiscal transparency and the prevalence of barter, tax write-offs, and other forms of soft budget constraints allow the governors to hide how they are actually spending their money and other resources while evading oversight from the federal government and the public. Regional bosses can block the implementation of federal policies in their regions, as was the case when Moscow mayor Yury Luzhkov successfully campaigned to prevent Anatoli Chubais's federal privatization policy from being implemented in the capital and instead imposed his own program.

---

69. Bohlen, "Russian Regions Wary as Putin Tightens Control," p. A3.

70. Indeed, in the weeks following the announcement the Kremlin and the regions jockeyed for positions in the struggle over recentralization.

71. The EastWest Institute, *EWI Russian Regional Report* 5, no. 10 (March 15, 2000), <http://www.iews.org>.

Given all of these advantages, regional elites will have considerable room to maneuver in the years to come.

As for its effect on the non-Russian ethnic republics, Putin's present attempt at restructuring the Russian Federation does not seem so drastic as to drive non-Russian moderates into the arms of radical nationalists[72] and thus increase the likelihood of secessionist movements. Such a development is plausible, however, if the ethnically Russian oblast leaders are successful in convincing the Kremlin to take away what they see as unfair privileges held by the ethnic republics. Mikhail Alexseev believes that in order for ethnic republics to seriously seek secession and state disintegration, Moscow would have to engage in "significant unilateral, non-consensual moves . . . to consolidate its political and economic control in the regions with reliance on coercive power."[73]

As the drama unfolds, three critical processes in the regions bear watching:

1. The emergence of parties or movements in the regions with ethnopolitical or regionalist agendas and their rise to commanding positions within existing political institutions or within new institutions of their own making that displace the existing ones. Such parties could arise in response to a preceding rise in Russian nationalist parties, giving them a distinctly anti-Russian agenda for political mobilization.
2. Increasing political interactions and ideological consolidation among the Russian ethnic regions, especially in Russia's European core, creating a currently nonexistent political and ideological center from which the non-Russian regions could separate themselves.
3. The emergence of authoritarian political designs among these regional movements, along with an increasing refusal of regional political leaders to participate in the federal political institutions, pay their taxes, and so on.[74]

The preponderance of research findings suggests that each of these developments remains unlikely. At most, Putin will succeed in corralling the regions and forcing them to cough up more taxes; his chances of failing to restructure and recentralize the state are probably higher. The ethnic republics will likely maintain their relatively autonomous status.

---

72. Balzer, "Dilemmas of Federalism in Siberia," p. 154.
73. Alexseev, "Asymmetric Russia," pp. 273–274.
74. Ibid.

Conclusion

It would be easy to dismiss the relevance to Russia of the Liechtenstein Draft Convention on Self-Determination Through Self-Administration. The current draft contains language implying an evolutionary path to self-determination that would raise the hackles of traditionally minded Russian officials.[75] Still, it is important to bear in mind that the draft remains a draft—part of a larger initiative that is endeavoring to update outmoded and contradictory international norms.

The upshot of our analysis is that the initiative is directly relevant to the Russian Federation. It would therefore be in the best self-interest of Russian officials to engage in the ongoing dialogue surrounding the initiative in the UN and other international forums, including conferences held under the auspices of the Liechtenstein Institute on Self-Determination. Three specific conclusions support this argument.

First, state-shattering forms of self-determination are unlikely to be at the forefront of the agenda in Russia. The best scholarly estimate is that this will be the case for many years—unless leaders in Moscow and certain regions conspire to blunder into conflict as they did in Chechnya in 1994. The real issues are governance, economic development, democratization, and, in several crucial cases, self-determination through self-administration—precisely the issues at the heart of the Liechtenstein initiative. Across the Russian Federation, the center and local elites have reached a bewildering array of provisionally stable arrangements that do allow for a great degree of practical self-determination. The main problem that citizens in these regions face is that neither Moscow nor local authorities are capable of effective democratic governance. Citizens' preferences for the relative balance between central and local authorities are in most cases determined by specific and pragmatic considerations of development and administration rather than general ethnic or national principles. Though important and tragic, Chechnya is on most dimensions a special case. The outside world's stance on that question will be determined in the main by geopolitical considerations, though the Liechtenstein initiative may provide a basis for discussions between state and nonstate actors and the parties to the dispute.

Second, Russian federalism is a work in progress. Devolution, regionalization, and local self-determination have become central issues in Russia's search for a new national identity. In this context, new thinking on the international scene about nationality, national sovereignty, and territoriality is critical. Fundamentally, the Liechtenstein ini-

---

75. See Appendix B by Sir Arthur Watts in this volume.

tiative seeks to square the circle of the old sovereignty verus self-determination problem in the context of a globalized world where devolution within states is widespread. The development of new international norms on self-determination that accord with new global political and economic realities is especially important for a state like Russia, which is still struggling to find its place in the world. It is vital that international norms remain unthreatening to the core security of Russia so that Russians can aspire to live up to those norms. Otherwise, traditional thinking about self-determination and sovereignty, which is quite strong in both the structures of the federal government and among some local elites, may come to the fore and help generate more serious clashes between local and central aspirations. At the same time, it is critical for Russians to be part of the discussions concerning new norms so that they can ensure that the problems specific to their region and history are on the table.

Third, although the outsider world's role in the unfolding drama of Russia's federal evolution is marginal, it is still important. International factors played only a small role in Russia's chaotic devolution of power to the regions in the mid-1990s. Domestic determinants prevailed. Still, critical links between international and domestic factors will help shape Russia's federal structure in the years to come. Once again, the Chechen tragedy has distracted attention from other regional issues where outsiders play important roles: Kaliningrad, Karelia, and the Far East, for example. Subjects of the Russian Federation have signed hundreds of agreements on trade, economic, and humanitarian cooperation with foreign countries.[76] Officials on all sides are aware of the absence of a coherent set of rules and norms for governing such interactions. The Liechtenstein initiative represents an important effort to address the problem.

Although some Russian officials might be put off by certain clauses in the Draft Convention, its central thrust—emphasized elsewhere in this book—comports with Russian realities: self-determination should not automatically be equated with independence. A multitude of arrangements that fall short of changing hard, international sovereign boundaries can and do apply.

---

76. Alexander A. Sergounin, "Russia's Regionalization: The International Dimension," Copenhagen Peace Research Institute.

10

Self-Determination and National Identity Crisis: The Case of Sudan

FRANCIS M. DENG

With an estimated combined death toll from war and war-related humanitarian crises at 2 million, Sudan's civil war is one of the worst, longest lasting disasters in the world. Raging intermittently for over four decades, the war has clearly cost more in economic terms than the country can afford. Indeed, Sudan, although rich in natural resources, including vast oil reserves, is now unquestionably one of the poorest countries in the world. Much of this poverty is directly attributable to the war.

It is ironic that the civil war in Sudan should be the result of the country's greatest promise as a microcosm of Africa and a bridge between the continent and the Middle East. The racial, ethnic, cultural, and religious diversities in Sudan's composition are most often described as falling into North and South. The North, two-thirds of the country in land and population, is inhabited by indigenous tribal groups, the dominant among whom intermarried with incoming Arab traders and, over a period preceding Islam but heightened by the advent of Islam in the seventh century, produced a genetically mixed African-Arab racial and cultural identity. In the North, Islam, the Arabic language, and Arabism as a combined ethnic, cultural, and nationalist concept are closely intertwined. Northern Sudanese Muslims therefore see themselves simply as Arabs despite the visible African element in their skin color and physical features. There are, however, non-Arab communities in the North. Though large in numbers proportional to the Arabized tribes, they have been partially assimilated by their conver-

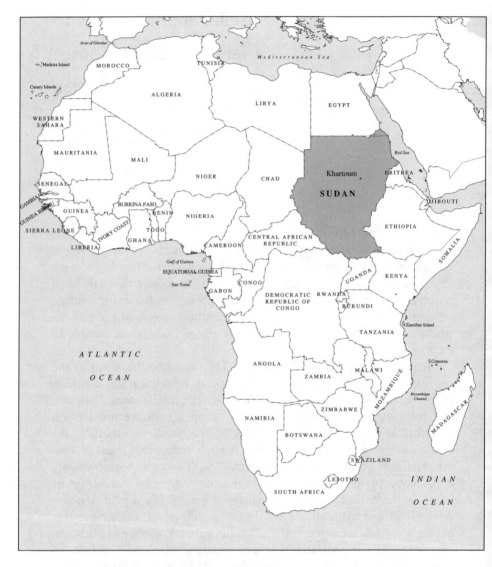

Africa, highlighting Sudan

sion to Islam and adoption of Arabic as the language of communication with the other tribes.[1]

It is in the South, the remaining third of the country in land and population, that the African identity in its racial and cultural composition has withstood assimilation into Arabism and Islam. And it is for the South that a consensus has emerged around the principle of self-determination. Although arrived at with considerable difficulty and still subject to various interpretations, the view is that only through fostering a genuine commitment to the right of self-determination for the people of the South can the war truly end. The Southern Sudan People's Liberation Movement and the Sudan People's Liberation Army (SPLM/SPLA) must choose between the southern people's preferred choice of secession and the movement's own tactical commitment to national unity.

The British colonial policy of administering the North and the South separately reinforced Arabism and Islam in the North, encouraged southern development along indigenous African lines, and introduced Christian missionary education and rudiments of Western culture as elements of modernization in the South. Interaction between the two sets of people was strongly discouraged. While the British administration invested considerably in the political, economic, social, and cultural development of the North, the South remained isolated and undeveloped. The principal objective of colonial rule was the establishment and maintenance of law and order. The separate administration of the two regions left open the option that the South might eventually be annexed to one of the East African colonies or become an independent state. In deference to Egypt, where its paramount interests lay, Britain in 1947 reversed the policy of separate development for the South. However, in the nine years leading up to Sudanese independence in January 1956, the British had neither the time nor the political will to put in place constitutional arrangements that would ensure protection for the South in a united Sudan.

The preoccupying concern among the northerners since independence has been to correct the divisive effect of the separatist policies of

---

1. In Sudan, unlike other African countries with a Muslim population, Islam is closely associated with the Arabic language, culture, and race, perhaps because of the historical association with the Arab world and in particular with Egypt. For the contrasting models of Islam in sub-Saharan and northern Africa, see Omar H. Kokole, "The Islamic Factor in African-Arab Relations," *Third World Quarterly* 6 (July 1984), pp. 687–701. According to the author, while African countries south of the Sahara underwent Islamization, North Africa experienced two processes: Islamization and Arabization. "With time the North Africans came to see themselves as 'Arabs,'" p. 688.

the colonial administration by pursuing the assimilation of the South through Arabization and Islamization. For the South, northern domination has been tantamount to replacing British colonialism with internal Arab "colonialism." Southern resistance first took the form of a mutiny in 1955 by a battalion, then of a political call for a federal arrangement and of an armed struggle for secession or at least the right of self-determination.[2]

The political impasse created by the situation in the South prompted the Sudanese military to seize power in 1958, only two years after independence, with the aim of pursuing the strategies of Arabization and Islamization more vigorously and unhampered by parliamentary democracy. The ruthlessness with which these assimilation policies were pursued in the South aggravated the conflict, which became a full-fledged civil war in the 1960s. The effect of that war on the political situation led to the popular uprising that overthrew the military regime in 1964, after which oppressive policies toward the South were temporarily relaxed. The government organized a conference on the problem of the South. The conference rejected separation or self-determination but mandated the Twelve Men Committee to formulate an appropriate constitutional arrangement that would reconcile southern demands with the preservation of national unity. The committee recommended regional autonomy for the South. However, parliamentary democracy was restored before the committee's recommendation could be implemented by the interim government, and with the return of democracy the traditional political parties assumed control and resumed the assimilation policies with a vengeance. As the violence escalated, the differences between the North and the South became sharper, and the level of political instability rose.

This vicious cycle was broken in 1969, when another military junta, this time under the leadership of Gaafar Mohammed Nimeiri, seized power in alliance with the Communist Party, which believed in autonomy for a socialist South. Following the abortive coup of 1971, when the leftist elements in the government tried to take over power from within,

---

2. For a background on the conflict and a history of the first phase of the war, see Mohamed Omer Beshir, *The Southern Sudan: Background to Conflict* (London: C. Hurst, 1968; republished by Khartoum University Press, 1979). See also Dunstan M. Wai, *The Southern Sudan: A Problem of National Integration* (London: Frank Cass, 1973); and *The African-Arab Conflict in the Sudan* (New York: Africana, 1981). For a southern point of view, see William Deng and Joseph Oduho, *The Problem of the Southern Sudan* (Oxford: Institute of Race Relations, 1963); and Oliver Albino, *The Sudan: A Southern Viewpoint* (London: Oxford University Press, 1970).

Nimeiri's regime eventually negotiated with the Southern Sudan Liberation Movement (SSLM) and in 1972 concluded the Addis Ababa Agreement, which, based on the recommendations of the Twelve Men Committee, granted the South regional autonomy with a democratic parliamentary system.[3]

The regime, however, remained under pressure from Islamic elements, in particular the traditional sectarian parties and the Muslim Brothers (Ikhwan El Muslimeen), a radical rightist religious group with whom Nimeiri eventually entered into an uneasy alliance. Nimeiri also underwent a personal conversion and became a born-again Muslim even though he still hoped that through religious reforms he could pull the rug from under the feet of the sectarian opposition leaders. He also hoped to remove the anomaly of liberal democracy in the South, which was incongruous with the national system of an authoritarian presidency. Nimeiri gradually eroded the South's autonomy, moving relentlessly toward imposing Islamic law, or *shari'a,* and establishing an Islamic state. Eventually he unilaterally abrogated the Addis Ababa Agreement in 1983 by dividing the South into three regions and ordering the transfer of southern troops to the North. This triggered the formation of the SPLM and its military wing, the SPLA, under the leadership of John Garang de Mabior. To the surprise of most people, the declared objective of the movement was not secession but the creation of a new, secular, democratic, and pluralistic Sudan. Within only two years of the resumption of hostilities, a popular uprising, largely fueled by the military situation in the South, led to Nimeiri's own overthrow in April 1985.

After Nimeiri's fall and exile, the Muslim Brothers reorganized themselves into a broader-based political party, the National Islamic Front (NIF), which won the third largest number of seats in the parliamentary elections of 1986. The NIF's Islamic national agenda was endorsed and significantly reinforced when General Omar Hassan al-Bashir, in alliance with the NIF, seized power on June 30, 1989, in the name of the Revolution for National Salvation. The SPLM/SPLA condemned the coup as an Islamist move engineered by the NIF and secret-

---

3. For a detailed account of the Addis Ababa Agreement, see Ministry of Foreign Affairs, *Peace and Unity in the Sudan: An African Achievement* (Khartoum: Khartoum University Press, 1973); and Mohamed Omer Beshir, *Southern Sudan: From Conflict to Peace* (London: Hurst, 1975). For the negotiations that led to the agreement, see Wai, *African-Arab Conflict in the Sudan*; Hizkias Assefa, *Mediation of Civil Wars: Approaches and Strategies—The Sudan Conflict* (Boulder, Colo.: Westview Press, 1987); and Abel Alier, *The Southern Sudan: Too Many Agreements Dishonoured* (Exeter, N.Y.: Ithaca Press, 1990).

ly committed to the division of the country along religious lines.[4] The movement agreed, however, to participate with the government in peace talks. Although the meetings raised no controversies on such generalities as preserving the country's unity, adopting a federal system of government, and correcting the disparities in economic and social development among the regions, the talks broke down for another reason: on the characterization of the problem as southern rather than national, the implication being a fundamental disagreement on the objective of restructuring the system toward creating a new Sudan.[5] Further talks sponsored by various mediators over the years raised issues of detail such as pluralistic democracy, the separation of religion and state, and the right of self-determination, all of which have been severely contentious. The conflict has escalated into a crisis of national identity with far-reaching implications for the future of the country.

The current struggle over national identity is reflected at two principal levels. One has to do with the configuration of Sudanese identity in the light of historical processes that have left the peoples with different layers of civilizations, racial characteristics, and cultural traditions. The other concerns the repercussions for unity in a pluralistic modern nation-state in which the conflict between the identities that give the country its geopolitical significance now threatens the nation with disintegration.

The crisis of national identity manifests itself in discrepancies among self-perceptions of identity, realities of identity, and how the national framework is defined. These discrepancies result in contrasting policy implications. One set of implications argues that the gap between self-perceptions and realities of identity is fictitious: if the divisive, subjective myths of identity are discredited, the common elements can be brought to the fore. Adjusting self-perceptions to harmonize with

---

4. For the reaction of the SPLM/SPLA, see John Garang de Mabior, "Statement to the Sudanese People on the Current Situation in the Sudan," General Headquarters, SPLM/SPLA, August 10, 1989.

5. Between September 9 and October 21, 1989, the government convened the National Dialogue Conference on Peace Issues, whose principal recommendation for solving the country's problems of regional, ethnic, cultural, and religious diversity was a federal constitution. The government endorsed the recommendations of the conference and the SPLM/SPLA acknowledged them, along with recommendations from other sources, as useful bases for constitutional talks. For the official report on the conference, see Steering Committee for National Dialogue on Peace Issues, *Final Report and Recommendations* (Khartoum, 1989), the so-called Red Book. The report was officially endorsed and reissued as "The Government's Peace Programme for Negotiations with the SPLM-SPLA" in November 1989 with an introduction by Colonel Mohamed al Amin Khalifa, a member of the Revolutionary Command Council for National Salvation and chairman of the National Dialogue.

realities helps to bridge the gap between group identities and the national identity. The other set of implications argues that self-perceptions must be accepted as they are and not scrutinized in the interest of a postulated framework of unity that does not exist. Instead, the gap between identities and the national framework should be managed through various forms of diversified unity and equity. This approach may succeed in preserving some form of national unity, although disparities that nurture divisiveness and intensify the call for self-determination (and even secession) are likely to persist.

In this chapter I probe these issues from the perspective of identity politics, perceptions, and the tension between national unity and self-determination. I consider the history in which conflicting identities of the North and the South were shaped and discuss the generic concept of identity as a factor in the Sudanese conflict. I end with a critical analysis of the options confronting the Sudanese in light of the contested issues and the positions of the parties on them.

History of Conflicting Identities

Whether or not a people is entitled to exercise the right of self-determination to the point of secession, how justified are the notions of identity that dichotomize peoples and threaten to tear nations apart on the basis of their inherent racial, ethnic, cultural, or religious differences? Do assumptions of identity match the realities of a country's identity map? These questions are particularly pertinent to the case of Sudan. A close look at the historical evolution of the distinctive identities of the North and the South might provide useful insights and a fuller appreciation of the value of self-determination as a political and human rights principle, as well as the people entitled to enjoy it and the scope of its application within or beyond national unity.

Northern Sudan

The historical process that separated the Arab Muslim North and the African South has its roots in the Arabization and Islamization of the North and in the resistance to those forces in the South. Sudanese contact and interaction with the Middle East via Egypt date back thousands of years before Christ and contributed to the eventual Sudanese identification with the Arabs. The process was continued with the advent of Islam in the seventh century and the Arab Muslim invasion of Sudan in later centuries. Although the Arab settlers were traders and not rulers, their privileged position, more cosmopolitan and universalizing religious culture, and superior material wealth combined with the liberal assimilationist Arab Islamic tradition to open the gates to universal brotherhood and made them an appealing class for intermarriage with the leading Sudanese families.

It was the grassroots power of sectarian Islam that the British rulers eventually recognized and used toward their political ends. When the British saw the rising tide of secular nationalism among the educated youth, they decided to turn to the sectarian leaders as political allies. The colonial exploitation of these traditional leaders in turn provoked an ambivalent reaction toward them from the educated class with the rise of the nationalist independence movement.

The reaction to the conservative sectarian mold of political-religious leadership gave rise to radical movements representing both secularism and Islam; though the movements were antagonistic, they had antisectarianism as a common objective.[6] These were the Communist Party and the two brotherhoods, the Muslim Brothers and the Republican Brothers, the last two differing in their interpretation of Islamic doctrine—one was Orthodox and the other liberal.

Three interrelated and interdependent factors figured in the strategy of the Muslim Brothers: (1) the pursuit of power; (2) the reform of society in the political, economic, social, and cultural fields; and (3) the use of religion as a tool for the mobilization of the community. The difference between the Republican Brothers and the Muslim Brothers may well be in the degree to which Islamic ideals are an end (the Republican Brothers) or a means to other objectives (the dominant faction of the Muslim Brothers). The differences, indeed the conflicts, between the two wings of the Islamic path increased with time. The rift was exacerbated by the September Laws of the military ruler Gaafar Nimeiri (enacted in alliance with the Muslim Brothers), which eventually resulted on January 18, 1985, in the public hanging of Mahmoud Mohamed Taha, who was condemned for apostasy.[7]

From this summary, it is obvious that the Islamic platform of the Muslim Brothers—now the National Islamic Front—has been shared by

---

6. For studies of these two movements, see Mohamed Nuri El-Amin, *The Emergence and Development of the Leftist Movement in the Sudan During the 1930s and 1940s* (Khartoum: Institute of African and Asian Studies, Khartoum University Press, 1984); and Hassan Mekki Mohamed Ahmed, *Harakat El Ikhwan El Muslimeen Fil-Sudan* 1944–1969 (Khartoum: Khartoum University Press, 1987).

7. On Mahmoud Mohamed Taha's trial and execution, see Abdullahi Ahmed An-Na'im, "The Islamic Law of Apostasy and Its Modern Application: A Case from the Sudan," *Religion* 16 (1986), p. 197. Sadiq al-Mahdi also opposed the September Laws. See his views in his *Islam and the Problem of the South*, published by the author (Khartoum, 1984).

virtually all political forces in the North to varying degrees of commitment. The NIF's rise to power has sharpened the differences between the North and the South and placed the national question on the front lines of the conflict of identities.

Southern Sudan

What is particularly significant about the South's confrontation with the North, whether prior or subsequent to the advent of Islam, is that whereas the Arabs persistently invaded the South for slaves, they never penetrated sufficiently, far less attempted to settle. Swamps, insects, tropical humidity, and the fierce resistance of the local tribes kept the contact marginal even as it was devastatingly violent. Furthermore, since the Arab Muslim was interested in the actual or potential value of the Negro as a slave, he did not desire to interact and integrate with him in the manner experienced in the North. To convert the Negroes of the South to Islam would have meant that they could not be justifiably kidnapped for slaves.

The Anglo-Egyptian condominium rule, although objectionable in principle, gave the South the only period of peace, tranquility, and relative independence in the form of "tribal" autonomy that it had experienced for centuries. However, the British did not develop the South but kept it isolated from the North under a system of "closed districts" that would evolve along indigenous lines with the Christian missionaries playing a modest "civilizing" role. The separation of the administration and educational systems meant that graduates from the southern intermediate schools went to Makerere College in Uganda for higher education, and the future of the South was contemplated more in the context of East Africa than in the national framework of Sudan.

There were a few among the British, however, who conceived of the future of the South differently, arguing that it would not be easy to redefine the boundary satisfactorily; that left alone, the North would almost certainly be absorbed by the Arab Middle East, especially by Egypt; that racially, the African blood from the South had been mingled with that of every northern tribe; and that the South possessed the economic potential that also existed in Uganda. They reckoned that "if the South, remaining essentially Southern, could yet become an integral part of an independent Sudan it could help to bridge the inevitable gulf between Muslim and non-Muslim, Asian and African, white or brown and black, in the Africa of the future."[8]

---

8. Kenneth David Druit Henderson, *The Sudan Republic* (London: Ernest Benn, 1965), p. 164.

With the rise of political consciousness in the North, the independence movement, spearheaded by northern elites collaborating with Egypt, began to manifest aspirations for the integration of the South into the national political process. The first step was taken by the Graduates Congress in 1942 when it demanded from the government, among other things, the abolition of restrictions placed on trade and intra-Sudanese travel and the unification of the country's educational system. By 1944, an advisory council was formed in the North, which, though it did not legislate, wielded much influence. The South did not participate in the council. Indeed, the possibility of its either being separated from Sudan and annexed to one of its neighbors in the south or being left completely independent was still in mind. The issue of whether the South should be united with the North or separated remained an open question for the British administration.

Negotiations between Britain and Egypt on the future of Sudan, beginning in December 1945, resulted in the 1946 draft treaty that included a protocol providing for a framework of unity between Egypt and Sudan under the common crown of Egypt. The outraged reaction of the Sudanese and the British political elite led to the immediate abandonment of the plan and a statement by the British foreign secretary to the House of Commons on March 26, 1946, to the effect that the government considered the sole aim of its administration in Sudan to be the welfare of the Sudanese people and that no change in the status of Sudan should be made until the Sudanese had been consulted through constitutional channels. That year, the government convened the Sudan Administrative Conference to plan constitutional changes. It was at that conference that the idea of the unity of the country, North and South, was formally presented and confronted for the first time.[9] In 1946, the governor-general set up an administration conference to help determine steps to be taken toward the devolution of power to the Sudanese. Again, the South did not participate in the consultations. Even after Sir James Robertson (under pressure from Egypt and northern Sudan) decided to reverse the separatist southern policy in favor of ultimate unity of Sudan, the unity of the country was not completely a foregone conclusion.[10]

---

9. Mohamed Ahmed Mahjoub, *Democracy on Trial* (London: Andre Deutsch, 1974), p. 208.

10. The British still seemed to hope that the North might change its mind and reject the South as a financial burden, and in any case, it was still envisaged that certain parts might be severed from Sudan and annexed to East African territories. See "Memorandum on Revision of Southern Policy," CS/SCR/1.C.1, December 16, 1946; Appendix 8 of Muddathir 'Abd al-Rahim, *Imperialism and Nationalism in the Sudan: A Study in Constitutional and Political Development, 1899–1956* (Oxford: Clarendon Press, 1969).

The Juba conference was held on June 12, 1947, to seek southern views on the issue of whether and how the South should be represented in the proposed assembly. At the conference the southerners, although willing to accept Sudan as one country, demanded a separate advisory council until such time as they could have a legislative body on equal footing with the northerners. Meanwhile, they wanted to learn from the forthcoming Legislative Assembly in the North as observers.[11] Mutual suspicion continued, however, with the northerners suspecting the southerners of desiring separation and the southerners suspecting the northerners of wishing to dominate the South. The conference concluded with a halfhearted and vague understanding "to agree," although to what exactly the parties had agreed was unclear.

Only two years after the Legislative Assembly opened in December 1948, a constitutional amendment commission was set up to examine the situation and recommend steps to be taken in the advance to self-government. Northern parties negotiated and agreed with Egypt in January 1953 on a strategy whereby self-determination could be exercised by a parliamentary declaration of independence without the need for the stipulated nationwide plebiscite. Meanwhile, the northern parties had agreed with Egypt and Britain on a process that would begin with a transitional period of self-government and lead to self-determination in three years. Again, the South was not represented in those negotiations.

With the signing of the Anglo-Egyptian Agreement in 1953, southern political consciousness was aroused and the nationalist movement for recognition began to take organized form in the region. The movement arose with the view that the South had not been accorded its due share in the decision processes leading to self-determination; that the constitutional setup envisaged for the independent Sudan did not give due recognition to the southern identity; that under the unitary system, the South would be politically subordinated to, and dominated by, the North; and that unity with the North was possible only under a diversified system of government.

---

11. This conference is often cited by northerners as the occasion when the southerners decided for a fully united Sudan, but this is a disputed view. See Central Office of Information of Sudan, *Basic Facts About the Southern Provinces of the Sudan* (Khartoum: Central Office of Information, 1964), p. 18. The speech of the representative of the Southern Front at the Round Table Conference on the Southern Problem; Deng and Oduho, *The Problem of the Southern Sudan*; and Albino, *The Sudan: A Southern Viewpoint*, pp. 25–28. See also Bona Malwal, *People and Power in the Sudan* (London: Ithaca Press, 1981), pp. 24–30; Wai, *The African Arab Conflict in the Sudan*, pp. 42–44; and Alier, *The Southern Sudan: Too Many Agreements Dishonoured*, pp. 20–21.

After promising to fulfill the demands of southern Sudanese members of parliament for a federal government for the three southern provinces,[12] the Sudanese parliament adopted a unanimous resolution in favor of a declaration of independence on December 19, 1955. Whether northern parliamentarians intended to take this pledge seriously can be judged only from the cursory reference to it and the subsequent dismissal of the southern claim without anything near a "full consideration."[13]

North-South Dichotomy

This historical account of the constitutional developments leading to the independence of Sudan as a unitary state is given in some detail not to provide constitutional justification for the southern call for self-determination but rather to substantiate the politicization and consolidation of the North-South dichotomy and the marginalization of the South from the mainstream nationalism of the country, which continues to be the core of southern grievances and the reason for separatist tendencies among southerners. Rather than endeavor to win the South, the North has since independence perceived it in terms of the separatist policies of the British and especially the encouragement of a Southern identity based on traditional tribal systems combined with the modern influence of Christianity and Western culture. Consequently, the remedy of the North has persistently been aimed at undoing this history through Arabization and Islamization, to remove the Christian Western influence, and to integrate the country along the lines of the Northern model.[14] What northerners do not realize is that a traditional identity and the Christian Western influence have combined to consolidate and

---

12. Mahjoub, *Democracy on Trial*, p. 57.

13. Mansur Khalid, *The Government They Deserve* (London: Kegan Paul International, 1990), p. 231. As Tim Niblock noted, "Southerners remained peripheral to the debate over independence arrangements during 1955, except when their votes were needed in Parliament. Such attention as Northern political parties did give to Southern Sudan, moreover, was motivated by short-term political interest and often had destructive consequences. Promises were made by Northern politicians in the course of the 1953 elections which bore little relation to what these politicians intended, or were able, to do." *Class and Power in Sudan: The Dynamics of Sudanese Politics, 1989–1985* (London: Macmillan, 1987), p. 215.

14. As an Islamist scholar has observed, "For *Ikhwan* [Muslim Brotherhood], the South was perceived as a distant, vaguely symbolic place. Like the rest of the educated [northerners], *Ikhwan* only saw in the South the alienated, lost brother, who had to be retrieved through the spread of Islam, the Arabic language and better communications." Abdel Wahab El-Affendi, *Turabi's Revolution: Islam and Power in Sudan* (London: Grey Seal, 1991), p. 148.

strengthen a modern Southern identity of violent resistance to Islamization and Arabization.

Since the South is deemed by the North to be a spiritual vacuum to be filled by "the universal religion," only the competition of the Christian West could obstruct the progress of Islam in that region. The major political forces in the North are basically agreed on the Arab-Islamic identity of Sudan and the need to spread their mission into black Africa, starting first with the South. They disagree concerning which of them should occupy the chair of power and the degree to which Islam should accommodate the non-Muslims in a pluralistic system.

It is often argued, especially by the opposition groups from both the South and the North, that the ruling Islamists are a small, narrowly based elite that is kept in power only by military dictatorship. Although the military aspect of their rule lends credence to this view, it can also be argued that the regime represents an extreme version of the Islamic agenda that all political parties have pursued in varying degrees. It is also a fact that the political parties that have wielded grassroots majority support have depended on their religious leadership and the loyalty owed them on that basis. It is widely recognized that the overwhelming majority of the Sudanese, even the so-called animists, are devotedly religious. This religious devotion is capable of being manipulated and mobilized by political elites toward conservatism and intolerance. The fact that the Islamists want to build a modern state based on the values and institutions of Islam—to offer an alternative to the failed model from the West—gives their message a sense of optimism that contrasts sharply with the pessimism bred by the continuing crises and disintegration that have characterized developments since independence. Furthermore, the fact that the resistance in the South is misconstrued as a creation of the Christian West, which threatens both Islam and Arabism, intensifies the perception of jihad as a war of survival not only for the Islamic majority but, even more pertinently, for the Arab minority, which sees itself as threatened by the non-Arab majority in the country.

The Addis Ababa Agreement of 1972, although seemingly uniting the country, appears to have had the effect of arousing the fears of the extremists on both sides. It was particularly perceived by the right-wing factions of Arabism and Islam as a victory for their adversaries—southern Christians and secularists—not to mention military dictatorship. And of course, there were southerners who saw the agreement as a virtual surrender and chose to remain outside the settlement. Mohamed Beshir Hamid wrote on the agreements, "The Northerners, while offering some regional devolution of power, stopped short of federation; the southerners, while accepting a unified Sudan, wanted the loosest of confederations."[15]

A serious debate ensued among the Islamists about allowing the South to secede if that was necessary for the setting up of an Islamic state in Sudan. Nimeiri was faced with a dilemma. On the one hand, he needed the South, as it was proving to be his main source of security. On the other hand, he continued to be threatened by the rightist, mostly Islamic opposition groups. He chose the latter and embraced the Islamic agenda, which eventually led to the rise of the Islamists to the summit of power. It is now widely accepted that their seizure of power on June 30, 1989, was prompted by the prospects of an imminent agreement between the government and the SPLM/SPLA that would have compromised the Islamic agenda.

Since then, the various movements that have come and gone in the South have consistently called for secession from the North, and it is widely recognized that the overwhelming majority of the southerners would opt for separation. The stated goal of the SPLM/SPLA, which aims at preserving the unity of the country by creating a "new Sudan" liberated from any discrimination based on race, ethnicity, religion, culture, or gender, has been perceived as incongruous. However, it is not entirely inconceivable that liberal political forces in the North, especially the non-Arab elements, could in the long run ally themselves with the South to bring about such a change. Even though the SPLM/SPLA might indeed have come to believe that such an alliance might be imminent when it was militarily strong in the field, it is now widely recognized that the objective of the movement is unattainable in the short run. The tendency, therefore, is either to see the leaders of the movement as callous warlords who simply want to prosecute an endless war or to suspect that they must have a hidden separatist agenda.

The truth probably lies somewhere in between. Although separation would be the first choice of most southerners, it is obvious that separatism does not resonate well worldwide, especially in Africa. The SPLM/SPLA leaders obviously realized that fighting for justice or equal-

---

15. Mohamed Beshir Hamid, "Confrontation and Reconciliation Within an African Context: The Case of Sudan," *Third World Quarterly* 5, no. 2 (April 1983), pp. 320–329. Peter Woodward viewed the Addis Ababa Agreement as "dependent regionalism" that was "designed to give sufficient regional powers to appease the South, while creating enough ties to band the region into the Sudan as a whole." Under the system the North provided patronage to the South to support national unity. The South was thus attached to rather than incorporated into the national political system. *Sudan: The Unstable State*, pp. 142–146.

ity is more likely to win sympathy and support than calling for seces-sion. In their calculation, even the separatists stand a better chance of achieving their objectives within the framework of equitable unity, coop-erating with those motivated by the prospects of a national alliance behind the goal of a new democratic, secular, and pluralistic Sudan. It would therefore seem that the SPLM/SPLA, or at least its leadership, is following, within the unitary framework, a multifaceted policy that does not exclude and probably even prefers separation as the ultimate goal.

The stated ideal of a new, united democratic Sudan was challenged by factions that broke away from the mainstream movement in August 1991. These internal rebels, though motivated by personal rivalries and ambitions, call for self-determination and separation. The SPLM main-stream, however, still holds to the delicate balance between the higher challenge of unity and the more popular aspiration for self-determina-tion. A southern intellectual-politician articulated what is a widely shared point of view among southerners when he wrote, "It is . . . not impossible to move beyond a traumatic past and look forward to a more just future, if the causes of the evil acts which have been done are explainable, . . . defensible [and corrected]."[16] Describing the war in the South as "a war of genocide, where one race or ethnic group, in total control of power, [has] gone out of [its] way systematically and inten-tionally to destroy another ethnic group," he concludes that the cost of the war in terms of innocent lives lost "without taking into account any of the political issues, would alone justify the current call by the South for self-determination."[17] With this seemingly unbridgeable polarization of the nation, the conflict has decisively shifted from one of negotiable distributional demands to a nonnegotiable contest for the identity of the nation.

Identity as a Factor in the Conflict

Identity involves how people define themselves and are defined by oth-ers on the bases of race, ethnicity, culture, language, and religion. In sit-

---

16. Bona Malwal, "Address to the Sudan Studies Association," November 1994, p. 1.

17. Ibid. It is worth noting that the Nilotics of southern Sudan are among the minorities at risk of victimization according to the global survey conducted by Ted Robert Gurr and James R. Scaritti, "Minorities Rights at Risk: A Global Survey," *Human Rights Quarterly* 11 (August 1989), pp. 375–405. See also Gurr's "Theories of Political Violence and Revolution in the Third World," in Francis Deng and William Zartman, eds., *Conflict Resolution in Africa* (Washington, D.C.: Brookings Institution, 1991), p. 154.

uations where the nation or the country is defined with reference to the identity of a dominant group, whether a majority or a ruling minority, these factors become bases for discrimination. Although constitutional provisions and other legal instruments might prohibit discrimination, so long as the framework is defined in terms that exclude, subordinate, or marginalize those who do not fit the definition of the nation, discrimination becomes inherent.

As Sudan is currently defined in terms that connote race, ethnicity, culture, or religion, there is no way discrimination can be avoided. Arabism, defined in racial and cultural terms, and Islam, crystallized in *shari'a*—which in Islamic doctrine is a comprehensive way of life embracing public and private domains—are clearly the dominant elements. Whereas a person can be converted to Islam and assimilated into Arabism by speaking the Arabic language and adopting Arab culture, one cannot be fully equal as an Arab without genetic or genealogical claims that are visibly authentic.

It is important to recognize, first, that identity is basically a subjective concept; what people perceive themselves to be establishes who or what they are. Second, an important element of such subjective identification, insofar as ethnic identity is concerned, is blood ties; in Sudan, the concept of Arabism is associated with race. Third, recognizing identity (including its blood or racial component) as subjective does not mean that it cannot be challenged by objective facts or criteria. Fourth, if an exclusive identity conflicts with the requirements of national unity in a framework of diverse identities, then a need arises either to remove the divisive elements and redefine national identity to be all inclusive or to allow the diverse parts to go their separate ways. The conflict in Sudan is essentially the manifestation of an acute crisis of national identity based on ethnicity and religion.

Ethnicity usually implies that the ethnic group is in large part biologically self-perpetuating, shares fundamental values realized in overt unity in cultural forms, composes a field of communication and interaction, and has a membership that identifies itself and is identified by others as constituting a category distinguishable from other categories of the same order. These elements of the definition support "the traditional proposition that a race = a culture = a language, and that a society = a unit which rejects or discriminates against others."[18]

Although these criteria are accepted as objective indicators, the general tendency among scholars is to recognize self-identification with

---

18. Frederick Barth, ed., *Ethnic Groups and Boundaries: The Social Organization of Culture Differences* (Boston: Little, Brown, 1969), pp. 10–11.

a particular group as the crucial determinant of identity. As Crawford Young put it, "In the final analysis, identity is a subjective, individual phenomenon; it is shaped through a constantly recurrent question to ego, 'Who am I?' with its corollary, 'Who is he?' Generalized to the collectivity, these become 'Who are we?' and 'Who are they?'"[19]

Young qualifies that "subjective identity itself is affected by the labels applied by others."[20] These labels may become internalized and accepted as part of the subjective sense of self. The main point is that "although identity is subjective, multiple, and situationally fluid, it is not infinitely elastic. Cultural properties of the individual do constrain the possible range of choice of social identities. Physical appearance is the most indelible attribute; where skin pigmentation serves to segment communities, only a handful of persons at the color margins may be permitted any choice of identity on racial lines."[21]

In the African context, the politics of identity often clash with the demands of statecraft and nation building. On the one hand, individual and group identities pervasively rotate around such descent-oriented institutions as the family, the clan (Somalia), the tribe or ethnicity (most African countries), language, and their regional affiliations (Ethiopia, Nigeria, and Sudan). On the other hand, forging national unity requires transcending these concepts and developing an overarching framework. The crisis of national identity may emanate from the conflict between the subjective and the objective elements of identity or from the tendency of dominant, hegemonic groups to impose their identity as the framework for the nation, thereby providing a basis for discrimination.

The myths of superiority associated with the dominance of hegemonic groups nearly always run against the subjective self-esteem and defensive self-assertiveness of disadvantaged minorities or politically weaker groups, which, as the examples of South Africa, Burundi-Rwanda, and Sudan show, could be the majority. Studies of relatively isolated societies indicate that virtually all groups and individuals in their own specific cultural contexts not only demand respect as human beings but ethnocentrically assume that they represent the ideal model.[22]

In Sudan, any claim by northern Sudanese to Arab origins can only

---

19. Crawford Young, *The Politics of Cultural Pluralism* (Madison: University of Wisconsin Press, 1976), p. 20.

20. Ibid.

21. Ibid.

22. This is particularly illustrated by the Nilotics of Sudan, the Dinka and Nuer, who are among the least touched by modernization and yet remain among the most ethnocentric peoples in the world.

be valid for a negligible few. And yet, blood traced through putative Arab genealogies is one of the factors for the overwhelming identification of the North with Arabism and, it must be added, one of the major reasons for the conflict with the South and between the government and the non-Arab elements in the North. In most African countries, identities are based on distinctions within a broadly encompassing racial or ethnic categorization as Africans. Such distinctions are nonetheless grounds for tension and conflict, as Burundi, Rwanda, Somalia, and a host of other countries testify, yet they do not pose the same issues of race and ethnicity as the system of apartheid in South Africa or the situation in Sudan.[23]

According to Nelsen Kasfir, ethnicity in Sudan "encompasses all forms of identity that have at their root the notion of a common ancestor-race as well as tribe."[24] Kasfir goes even further in stretching the concept of ethnicity by linking religion and region with ancestor race and ethnicity.[25] Although he concedes that the choice "depends on the particular situation, not merely on the individual's preference," Kasfir concludes with an emphasis on personal choice: "Though objective ethnic characteristics (race, language, culture, place of birth) usually provide the possible limits, subjective perception of either the identities or the identified—whether objectively accurate or not—may turn out to be decisive for the social situation."[26]

Since the subjective factor implies assumptions of accuracy about objective indicators, Kasfir's analysis leaves one wondering where he places the northern Sudanese claim to be Arab, balancing the assertion that personal choice is the crucial criterion with the recognition that there are limits. In a purely isolated subjective world, this criterion may not matter much; but in the context of a quest for national unity, subjective idiosyncrasies about identity that do not match the facts but also divide the nation without objective justification become legitimate targets for scrutiny.

Thus, northern Sudanese who claim to be Arabs are presented as

---

23. Northern Sudanese intellectuals generally argue that whereas Arabism is a nationalist concept in the sense that there is indeed a notion of an Arab nation, Africanism is merely a geographical concept without a nationalist fervor.

24. Nelsen Kasfir, "Peacemaking and Social Cleavages in Sudan," in Joseph V. Montville, *Conflict and Peacemaking in Multiethnic Societies* (Lexington, Mass., and Toronto: Lexington Books with D.C. Heath, 1990), pp. 365–366.

25. Ibid.

26. Ibid., pp. 340, 366. As Peter Woodward has argued, "Although there may be considerable plasticity in identity, it is not something that is entirely malleable." *Sudan: The Unstable State*, p. 7.

doing so not on the basis of the obvious grounds of race, blood, or color, which (though invoked in support of Arabism) are untenable, but rather on the more plausible grounds of culture, language, and Islam, which, in Sudan, are associated with Arabism as both a racial and a cultural concept.[27] The underlying differentiating sentiments of race, which breed contemptuous pride, prejudice, and discrimination, are thereby covered up, evaded, and exonerated by benign dismissal or neglect.

If the focus is on the concept of a collective national identity, and if a sense of common identity is only possible if the rulers and the people feel that they are bound together in association, the next question is what the common association is or can be.[28] Abstractions like the nation are unlikely to do the trick, as they are not supported by the concrete factors that consolidate the sense of identity. One must therefore search for a basis of identity that can effectively bridge the gap between the mutually hostile ethnic or subnational sentiments and the postulated more conciliatory loyalty to the nation. Clearly Arabism and Islam cannot be acceptable to the South and significant parts of the North as bases for the national identity. Yet both are central to the northern elite's self-perception. Attempts at resolving this dilemma have centered on a flexible and potentially accommodating interpretation of Arabism as a cultural and not a racial phenomenon. The northern predisposition is to see the concept of Arabism as primarily cultural and nonracial, a classic though controversial interpretation that in essence attempts to reconcile the contradictions in the historical experience of the Arab world as reflected in contemporary conditions and especially in its interaction with the non-Arab world.

Lloyd Binagi attributes the Arabs' view of their identity to the success of their policy of assimilation through conquest, conversion to Islam, the spread of the Arabic language, and intermarriage.[29] According to Raphael Patai, the term *Arab* in the post-Islamic period "came to denote all the peoples who, after having been converted to

---

27. For a comparison between black African countries, where Islam is divorced from Arabism as an ethnic and cultural concept, and North African Muslim countries, where Islam is tied to Arabism, see Omari H. Kokole, "The Islamic Factor in African-Arab Relations," *Third World Quarterly* 6, no. 3 (July 1984), pp. 687–702.

28. Lucian W. Pye, "Identity and the Political Culture," in Leonard Binder, et al., *Crisis and Sequences in Political Development* (Princeton: Princeton University Press, 1971), p. 110.

29. Lloyd Binagi, "The Genesis of the Modern Sudan: An Interpretative Study of the Rise of Afro-Arab Hegemony in the Nile Valley A.D. 1260–1826," Ph.D. dissertation, Temple University, 1981.

Islam, gave up their ancestral languages and adopted Arabic instead."[30] The evidence of this historical assimilation provides the basis for an argument that anyone can become an Arab simply by adopting Arab culture, speaking Arabic, and, preferably, converting to Islam. A widely accepted definition in the Arab world is that "Arabs are those who speak Arabic, are brought up in Arab culture, live in an Arab country, believe in Mohammed's teachings, cherish the memory of the Arab empire."[31] As Binagi says in "The Genesis of the Modern Suden," this definition, "like that of the Arab League, which defined an Arab as 'He who lives in our country, speaks our language, is brought up in our culture, and takes pride in our glory' . . . is problematic and obviously questionable." This problematic definition is often applied with little sensitivity to what it means for the fellow Sudanese who are not Arab and for whom the identity of the nation is clearly affected by the Arabism of the North. As John and Sarah Voll have observed, the two critical factors that Arab intellectuals and scholars highlight are language and history perceived in genealogical terms:

A . . . person must be identified in both of these dimensions to be considered an Arab. The person must speak Arabic and consider it to be his or her home language. In addition, however, because many non-Arab Sudanese are native speakers of Arabic, the person must also be identified with a tribe that is believed to have come originally from the Arabian Peninsula or with a group that has been so Arabized in culture and custom that it has no other visible or publicly known identity.[32]

Generally, the racial anomalies of northern identity, the identity crisis implicit in the pluralism of the nation-state, and the racial overtones of the Arab attitude toward the more Negroid Africans, particularly in the South, all combine to make the cultural concept of Arabism particularly appealing to northern Sudanese politicians, intellectuals, and even scholars.[33]

---

30. Raphael Patai, *The Arab Mind* (New York: Charles Scribner's Sons, 1973), pp. 12–15.

31. Husayn Mohammed Tawfig and Nabih Amin Faris, *The Crescent in Crisis: An Interpretative History of the Modern Arab World* (Lawrence: University of Kansas Press, 1955), pp. 177–178.

32. John Obert Voll and Sarah Potts Voll, *The Sudan: Unity and Diversity in a Multicultural State* (London: Croon Helm; Boulder, Colo.: Westview Press, 1985), pp. 7–8.

33. In his statement to the 1965 Round Table Conference on the problem of the South, Prime Minister Sirr El Khatim El Khalifa observed: "Gentlemen, Arabism, which is a basic attribute of the majority of the population of this country and of many African countries besides, is not a racial concept which unites the members of a certain racial group. It is a linguistic, cultural, and non-racial link that binds together

Muddathir Abd Al-Rahim, a scholar-diplomat-politician, argues that northern Sudan is more representative of Africa because it combines elements of Arabism and Africanism that are characteristic of the continent.

> The fact that they are predominantly Muslim and Arab does indeed distinguish the Northern Sudanese from their Southern compatriots but does not mean that they are non-African. As the only region in the continent, and indeed the world, in which the physical, racial and cultural diversities of Africa as a whole are not merely represented but have been synthesized into a unique and unparalleled entity, Northern Sudan may in fact be described as more representative of Africa as a whole than any other country or region, including Southern Sudan.[34]

In noting that "the great majority of [the northern] population rightly feel that they are Arab and African at the same time, to an equal degree, and without any sense of tension or contradiction,"[35] Muddathir Abd Al-Rahim is overgeneralizing from the perspective of an elite, and even then he clearly overstates the case. Certainly, the Arab tribes are proud to be Arab without being aware of the notion of Africanism; they are far less aware of the fact that the two identities, African and Arab, have become fused. Ordinary Sudanese Arabs are at ease with the reality of the African-Arab mold, which they perceive as monolithically Arab.[36] Just as the sophisticated southerner is conscious of his tribal identity or, in the case of the educated elite, his Africanness, the sophisticated northerner is conscious of the Arab-African dualism of northern identity. Indeed, the more aware of the dualism a northern Sudanese is, the more he realizes the inequities involved and the more he feels the tensions and the contradictions of this duality.

As long as Arabism and Africanism are envisaged as dominant in defining the national framework, they will continue to evoke sentiments of descent, ethnicity, and race and therefore remain divisive. To this conflict has now been added the religious dimension in the form of

---

numerous races, black, white, and brown. Had Arabism been anything else but this, most modern Arabs, whether African or Asian, including the entire population of the Northern Sudan, would cease to be 'Arab' at all." See text in Appendix 15 in Muhammad Omer Beshir, *Southern Sudan: From Conflict to Peace*, p. 168.

34. Ibid.

35. Ibid.

36. As Yusuf Fadl Hasan explained in a conversation with the author, it does not occur to the ordinary Arab in the tribes that he can be anything but Arab. He is not even aware that Arabs are supposed to be lighter in skin than he is. Nor is he aware of the dark skin being a characteristic of Negro Africanness.

Islamic revivalism, which in Sudan remains closely associated with the racial and cultural notions of Arabism and which has so far proved even more divisive.

The reaction of southern Sudanese generally is to accept northern racial and cultural self-perception and to deal with northerners as the Arabs they claim to be, which supposedly distinguishes them from the South. Dunstan Wai's view is representative of the South: "Whether the North is both Arab and African or exclusively one or the other, is not crucial. The significant point is that those who wield political power, generally the educated elites, think the North is Arab. Thus, even if biologically they are both Arab and Africans, they have opted in their choice of self-identification for Arabism."[37] Wai's argument is that whether justified or not, northern identification with Arabism should be recognized and Sudan should be fashioned accordingly to give the North its separate nationhood as Arab and the South its nationhood as an African country.

The alternative approach is to question the validity of these exclusive identities and refashion the country's identity to reflect a more uniting concept of national identity. Despite the racial overtones in the North-South dichotomy, northern and southern Sudanese perspectives on close examination reveal that the divisive identity factors in Sudan are both racial and cultural with culture as the determining factor. The explanation rests in a broad, inclusive understanding of culture. Indeed, the tenuousness of northern claims to Arabism in itself underscores the role of culture in cultivating self-perceptions, so that even biological or racial claims are ultimately culture-bound. Culture becomes an overarching social engineer that molds perspectives on identity, even on racial bases. It becomes both a means and an end.

Given this broad perspective on culture, it is obvious that it links perceptions of the various components of identity, which make the dividing line between racial and cultural sentiments too thin to be differentiated in popular consciousness. The result of these ambiguities is that misconstrued and unacknowledged racial cleavage remains unbridged and is indeed deepened by the elites on both sides. One group builds on a fictional notion of Arabism while the other responds with an equally fictional notion of Africanism, both overlooking the realities of the country. As Ali Mazrui put it, "Distinguished Arabic-speakers of the North, and distinguished southerners, have all been

---

37. Dunstan M. Wai, "Revolution, Rhetoric, and Reality in the Sudan," *Journal of Modern African Studies* 17 (March 1979), pp. 71–93.

known to exaggerate the ethnic chasm which separates northerners from the peoples of the South."[38]

The policy orientation of those who emphasize cultural and other objective factors may well be to implicitly undermine these subjective factors on which prejudice, discrimination, and hatred breed. But negative racial sentiments cannot be eliminated by asserting that they do not exist. Exposing the subjective sentiments of identity as half-truths at best or myths at worst should contribute to removing the foundation of the negative or discriminatory sentiments involved and reveal alternative bases for redefining and restructuring a more mutually accommodating concept of national identity. If people are divided by the objective facts of culture, language, or religion, the approach becomes more one of regulating and reconciling the differences rather than arguing that those differences have no bases. Refuting fictitious claims to ethnic or racial differences is to remove the psychological barriers instead of validating them and then attempting to reconcile conflicting interests.

Even if Arabism and Africanism were defined in terms of such objective indicators as culture, language, and religion, there would still be a strong case against giving these labels more than their due because of the amount of intermingling and fusion that has taken place between the respective peoples and their cultures.[39] To subject this hybrid to a monolithic and universalistic notion is not only to distort reality but to endanger the harmony and stability of mutual accommodation, tolerance, and cross-fertilization.

Southern Sudanese identification is predominately in tribal terms now extended to concepts of nationhood that are founded on African, non-Arab identity. Tribal culture in the South, perhaps even more than that of the North, both assimilates and discriminates in the sense that outsiders who join the tribe either as captives or clients become adopted as members of the group and with cultural adaptation are fully integrated in due course, whereas outsiders who retain the symbols of their identity are considered alien and inferior and are judged by the tribal standards of physical, cultural, and moral integrity.

---

38. Ali A. Mazrui, "The Multiple Marginality of the Sudan," in Yusuf Fadl Hasan, ed., *Sudan in Africa* (Khartoum: Khartoum University Press, 1971), p. 243.

39. This mixture pertains even to the field of religion, which, though clear-cut, has been the scene of much eclectic mutual influence. The Islam of Sudan is a peculiar mold that has incorporated indigenous African elements. See, for example, Mohamed Ibrahim El Shoush, "Some Background Notes on Modern Sudanese Policy," *Suden Notes & Records* (Khartoum) 14 (1963), pp. 21–42.

The positive element in the subjective factor is that its dynamic flexibility permits the possibility of reshaping self-identification as a means of resolving or ameliorating conflict between identity groups. All people, it is widely recognized, have multiple identities, and the one that is most salient at any moment is "viewed situationally—in terms of the social, economic, and political contexts in which the various groups interact and attempt to achieve their collective purposes."[40] An individual's identity, therefore, will change to reflect his or her political context and calculations of interest. This is particularly the case in pluralistic societies where identities are more likely to be stratified and opportunities exist for self-enhancement by changing one's own identity or that of one's group to an identity that is inherent in the pluralism. Although such a change might reinforce the status quo by changing national priorities and incentives, it is possible to reshape identities as a matter of public policy.

Self-perceptions may at times come into conflict with the way one is perceived by others, prompting a crisis that requires both subjective and objective resolution. Northern Sudanese who view themselves primarily as Arab, not only culturally but also racially, have been disappointed, even shocked, to find themselves identified differently by the outside world, including other Arabs. In the Western world, northern Sudanese are classified as Africans, blacks, or Negroes and rarely, if ever, as the Arabs they perceive themselves to be. Even when Sudanese speak Arabic abroad, unless it is known that the person speaking is a Sudanese, in which case most informed Arabs would recognize the anomaly, a casual Arab would be surprised to hear that this "black African" claims to be Arab.[41] Whatever their subjective view of themselves, such experiences cannot leave them totally unaffected even though they may nevertheless retain their original belief and rationalize the discrepancy as merely a matter of ignorance on the part of the outside world. This discrepancy in perceptions illustrates what Ali Mazrui called the multiple marginality of Sudan, ambiguously poised between

---

40. Ibid., pp. 119–120.

41. In a case witnessed by the author in 1961, a group of Sudanese students from Khartoum University, almost all of whom were northerners, were strolling in a Cairo park when a group of Egyptian high school students followed them chanting, "Lumumba, Lumumba," obviously thinking they were from a black African country. One of the Sudanese students turned to them and said in Arabic, "Brothers, we are Arabs like you." On hearing the Arabic, the Egyptian students opened their hands wide, chanting, "Welcome, brothers from the Sudan!" In another episode in London, a group of Sudanese students were standing talking in the London underground train when a man who looked European turned to his colleague and said in Arabic, "They speak Arabic."

Arab and African, Muslim and Christian worlds, perceiving its Arab identity as preeminent over its Africanism yet looking more African than Arab, rejected by most Arabs, and viewed by many Africans as betraying the cause by "passing" as Arab.[42] But above all, it poses a challenge of nationhood that the Sudanese must now address if the country is to stop bleeding and avoid collapse as a nation.

The Challenge of Self-Determination

Self-determination raises some serious questions, both internally and regionally. Internally, it is feared that it could result in the fragmentation and disintegration of Sudan. This danger is compounded by the diversities and divisions that characterize both the North and the South. Despite the clear preference of many southerners for separation, a significant number of southerners genuinely believe that Sudan is African, that there is a sizable population of assimilated southerners among the so-called Arabs of the North whom the South should not abandon, and that in the long run there is more to be gained from unity than from secession.

This unionist sentiment from the South threatens the Arab-Islamic establishment in the North and further radicalizes the Islamic fundamentalists who are set on creating an Arab-Islamic state in Sudan. This radicalization among the Muslims has divided the North as well. Northern opposition parties working against the NIF regime have formed ties with the SPLM/SPLA through the National Democratic Alliance (NDA). As partners with southerners in the opposition, and out of the conviction that the southern cause is legitimate, they have come to accept the right of the South to self-determination as a matter of principle. But they remain committed to the unity of the country, not only as a goal but also as the probable outcome of the exercise of self-determination.

Therefore, even if the South were to exercise the right of self-determination to its fullest extent and secede, the liberation struggle of the non-Arabs and secularists in the North would continue. The ominous implication is that a peace settlement between the government and the South will not necessarily bring peace to the country: not only will the northern opposition parties continue their struggle for power against

---

42. Mazrui, "The Multiple Marginality of the Sudan." Ali Mazrui does not see Sudan's marginality in terms of a crisis but rather as a more positive linkage among the various elements of identity involved. The crisis dimension in the sentence summarizing his paper is therefore this author's, not Mazrui's.

the NIF regime but the non-Arabs too will continue to fight either for their own self-determination or for a new Sudan in which Arabism and its association with Islam will not be bases for racial, ethnic, cultural, and religious marginalization or discrimination. In both cases, opposition groups could still expect support from an independent South for reasons of both national interest and racial solidarity.

Regional actors complicate the picture even more. Egypt, operating both individually and multilaterally via the Arab League, has campaigned vigorously against self-determination, fearing that it would lead to the secession of the South and the creation of a non-Arab state in the upper Nile region, where it has strategic water interests. This concern is in addition to Egypt's traditional cultural ties with and "colonial" claims over Sudan, a country that Egypt still classifies as part of its own backyard.

Other important regional actors are in principle supportive of self-determination for the South. However, this support for the South runs against the general African bias against secession and their own national interest in confronting the regional threats of Islamic fundamentalism emanating from Sudan. Regional security, in their consideration, is better served by removing the NIF government and replacing it with a more ideologically amicable regime. Self-determination that might lead to the secession of the South risks enhancing the security of the NIF regime, enabling it to continue its Islamic agenda at the regional and international levels. Although the right of the South to self-determination is acknowledged, the internal politics of the civil war and regional and international dynamics tend to militate against the exercise of that right, largely because it is expected to lead to secession.

It has been argued that without the South there would be no North.[43] This is even more true of the South: without the confrontation with the North—the still vivid memory of rapacious invasions by northern slave raiders, which contemporary experience has rekindled—and the attempts by postindependence governments to subdue, dominate, and assimilate the southern people, there would be no South as a viable political entity. It is feared that once the North-South confrontation is removed, divisions within the North and the South would proliferate and aggravate internal conflicts. There would be no end to the demand for self-determination.

These internal divisions within the regions, especially in the South,

_____

43. John Obert Voll, "Northern Muslim Perspective," in John V. Montville, ed., *Conflict and Peacemaking in Multiethnic Societies,* (Lexington, Mass.: Lexington Books, 1990), p. 389.

are, however, accentuated if not initiated by external manipulation. Rather than foster unity within the region as a step toward broader national unity, leaders on both sides focus their attention on the short-term objective of dividing and weakening "the enemy." The fear that self-determination might lead to further disintegration in the South and perhaps in the North too is, at least in part, a self-fulfilling prophecy. Crawford Young, commenting on the lack of unanimous backing for southern movements among the southerners, noted that "Khartoum always had some room for maneuver by playing on local rivalries."[44]

There is also the argument that neither the South nor the North is economically viable alone. During the colonial period, the South was regarded as nonviable. But more recently, with the discovery of oil reserves in commercial quantities, the mammoth Jonglei project aimed at retrieving the vast waters of the Sudd region for irrigation in the North and Egypt, and the arable land with adequate rainwater, not to mention the yet unexplored mineral resources believed to exist, the South has emerged as a potential source of wealth. The concern for non-viability has therefore shifted to the North.

Negotiations to Resolve the Conflict

It is in the context of this national polarization that the countries of the Inter-Governmental Authority on Development (IGAD) undertook its daring initiative to go beyond just fostering talks and address the root causes of the conflict.[45] The IGAD Mediation Committee, consisting of Ethiopia, Eritrea, Kenya, and Uganda and chaired by President Daniel Arap Moi of Kenya, held to the premise that the conflict in Sudan was not merely national, since it had regional repercussions that affected the neighboring countries.

In May 1994 the mediators presented the Declaration of Principles (DOP) to the IGAD's Standing Committee of Ministers. The DOP tried to reconcile the competing perspectives in the conflict and ruled out no option. It strongly upheld the right of self-determination for the South

---

44. Crawford Young, "Self-Determination, Territorial Integrity, and the African State System," in Deng and Zartman, *Conflict Resolution in Africa,* p. 339.

45. The IGAD was originally known as the Inter-Governmental Authority on Drought and Development (IGADD). Because the IGADD initiative came in the aftermath of many failed peace efforts, the reaction to it was initially negative. See, for example, the following articles: Bona Malwal, "Avoiding the Abujanisation of the Nairobi Peace Talks," *Sudan Democratic Gazette: A Newsletter for Democratic Pluralism* 48 (May 1994); and "The Abujanisation of the Nairobi Talks: Can It Be Avoided?" in the same issue.

but recommended that unity be given a chance. The declaration suggested arrangements that could facilitate unity, including the separation of religion and state, regional decentralization, pluralistic democracy, and respect for fundamental rights and civil liberties. Finally, the conditions for unity would be created and tested during an interim period. Among these conditions would be separation of religion and the state (secularism), a system of government based on multiparty democracy, respect for fundamental rights, independence of the judiciary, and a large measure of decentralization through a loose federation or a confederacy. The interim period was to be long enough to allow time for creating those conditions and testing them but not so long as to create complacency and lethargy on the part of the controlling authorities. After the interim period, the people of the South and other areas that felt equally disadvantaged and have taken up arms with the SPLM/SPLA would be asked to decide by referendum whether to continue the unity arrangement or adopt alternative arrangements, including the right of secession.[46] These principles were eventually endorsed by the 1995 Asmara Declaration of the National Democratic Alliance, in which all opposition groups from the North and South are members.

At the July meeting, whereas the SPLM/SPLA factions accepted the DOP, the government initially resisted it but was eventually persuaded by the mediators to discuss the principles and register any objections to specific issues.[47] Although multiparty democracy and human rights are known to be contentious for the regime, the most divisive issues turned out to be the proposed separation between religion and the states as well as the right of self-determination.

At a contentious September meeting in Nairobi the SPLM/SPLA factions insisted on secularism and the right of self-determination; the government had three broad objections. First, secularism was out of the question; the commitment to *shari'a* was a religious and moral obligation to an Islamic mission that colonialism had interrupted not only in the South but, indeed, in Africa. Second, self-determination was a ploy for partitioning the country and was therefore unacceptable as a matter of principle. Third, the format of the negotiations was flawed. Finally, the government had initiated its own internal peace process and hoped

---

46. For a more detailed discussion of the principles, see Francis M. Deng, "Genesis of the Sudanese Conflict," *Sudan Democratic Gazette* 51 (August 1994); and Bona Malwal in the same issue, "The IGADD Mediators Oblige Khartoum to Discuss the Taboo Topics." For an advocacy of unity, see A. H. al-Sawi, "Some Preliminary Thoughts on Unity and Division in Sudan," in the same issue.

47. See Malwal, "The IGADD Mediators Oblige Khartoum to Discuss the Taboo Topics."

to surprise the world in the near future with news about the internal achievement of peace.[48]

Eventually, the negotiations came back on track. The internal settlement of April 1997 between the government and factions of the SPLM/SPLA that defected from the movement also concedes the right of self-determination to the South. And in the Nairobi talks of April 1998, the government also accepted self-determination for the first time in direct negotiations with the mainstream SPLM/SPLA.

There are several positive aspects to these recent developments: (1) the issues that divide and the positions of the parties on those issues have been clearly identified; (2) the will of the regional mediators to be engaged not as disinterested third parties but as neighbors with a stake has been manifested; (3) while assuming a major responsibility for the peace process with support from the international community, these mediators have declared their intention to collaborate with the international community in discharging this obligation; and (4) despite the ambiguities surrounding the agreement on self-determination, it represents a constructive development that can be improved upon.

All this means is that Sudan is now at a critical juncture between Islamic fundamentalism or revivalism in the North and a Western concept of a secular pluralistic state in the South. So polarizing has the conflict become that one can argue with a reasonable degree of accuracy that if the laws of the land were 99.9 percent Islamic but were labeled secular, they would be objected to by the Islamists; if they were 99.9 percent secular but were labeled Islamic, they would be opposed by the secularists. The issue is no longer the substantive content of the laws or the policies but deeply felt identities that have proved incompatible as they are represented and reflected by the political elites.

This assessment, carried to its logical conclusion, makes the quest for a uniting national identity sound increasingly utopian and unrealistic. This is indeed the conclusion that even some of the pro-NIF scholars, intellectuals, and politicians from the North have reached on the basis of the objective evidence. Kamal Osman Saleh of the Institute of Strategic Studies in Khartoum has observed, "The lack of progress in the Sudan during 1985–9 suggests that it is virtually impossible for a viable system of government and administration to be created, let alone survive, in a deeply divided and heterogeneous nation in which political

---

48. For a detailed discussion of the September meeting, see Bona Malwal's editorial in the September issue of the *Sudan Democratic Gazette*, "The Tightening Options for All at the IGADD September Round." See also Peter Nyot Kok, "NIF Accepts Self-determination by Definition," in the same issue of the *Gazette*.

parties are primarily organized on sectarian, ethnic, and religious lines.[49] Abdel Wahab El-Affendi articulated the same conclusion:

> It is thus unlikely in the given circumstances, that the conflicting demands of the two major camps could eventually be satisfied within one state. . . . A multi-state solution may be the only way to preserve what is left of that once much loved oasis, and could be the only substitute to an illusory "united country," like the costly fiction of Lebanon and Cyprus.[50]

Finally, in a book published before the rise of Muslim fundamentalists to power, Abel Alier, a southern statesman who, apart from President Nimeiri himself, made the 1972 Addis Ababa Agreement possible, has given a sobering assessment of the constitutional options open to the country in light of the dismal record of North-South relations: "Options which would be available within the unity frame of reference range from administrative decentralization which was tried in the northern Sudan in 1980, regional autonomy which was tried in the southern Sudan from 1972 to 1983 and federation which was partially tried in the form of regional autonomy, to confederation which has not been tried."[51]

The second option splits the nation-state into two or more sovereign entities. Separation, which was by agreement ruled out in the Addis Ababa Agreement of 1972 but which has been less remote since 1983, when the agreement was abrogated, is as yet outside our frame of reference. Splitting the state could be achieved either on the battlefield or by a violent and reactionary revolution in a northern Sudan determined to adopt a theocratic system of government and an all-out Arab nationalism that make no provision for African nationality. But if that stance were adopted in Khartoum, it could well spell the end of a Sudanese nation-state.[52]

Several alternative policy approaches recommend themselves. One assumes the overriding goal of national unity and then builds on those elements most likely to achieve it. A major factor in this approach is the argument that the composition of the country does not support any claims to Arab purity, since there is a significant African element in the North that still links the population to the non-Arab groups within the

---

49. "The Sudan, 1985–1989: The Fading Democracy," *Journal of Modern African Studies* 28, no. 2 (1990), pp. 199–224.

50. El-Affendi, *Turabi's Revolution*, pp. 388–389.

51. Alier, *The Southern Sudan: Too Many Agreements Dishonoured*, p. 277.

52. Ibid.

North and the South. If Arabism, both as a racial and a cultural concept, is not representative of the North, it certainly is not representative of the country as a whole. The message this argument contains is a bitter pill for those committed to the Arab identity: it essentially means telling the North that it has been laboring under a notion of Arab identity that is fictitious, not sufficiently supported by genetics or history, and has divided the nation in a way that can no longer be sustained. If northerners value the unity of their nation above their self-delusion that they are Arabs, then they must courageously scrutinize their self-perception, explore the bonds of common ancestry with their non-Arab compatriots, and endeavor to help build a nation that is grounded on the uniting factors and enriched by its diversities. A similar message would also be targeted to southerners to make them realize that what divides them from the North is not as profound as has always been assumed, that a significant part of the northern population comprises the progeny of their African ancestors who were captured and taken away from the South as slaves, and that the challenge of building a united and strong nation now makes it incumbent on them to close ranks and explore their common origins.

A second argument recognizes that the identities of North and South have evolved into sharply contrasting racial, cultural, and religious self-perceptions. North and South are further characterized by different standards of living and varying levels of economic, social, and cultural development. In the North the sense of pride and dignity the Sudanese Arabs gain from their self-perceived heritage would prevent them from shedding their Arab skin to resume their long-discarded African identity. The southern Sudanese, too, are proud of their tribally rooted ethnic and cultural identity—which has survived recurrent Arab invasions for slaves—and contemptuous of a race they consider bent on subjugating and humiliating the black race. They would rather take the northern Sudanese for what they claim to be—Arabs. The fact that these Arabs deny their visible black African genetic origins is all the more reason to condemn them as renegades. The only unity that can be sustained on the basis of this duality is one founded on a diversified confederal coexistence.

An extension of the logic in the second alternative would lead to a third choice of policy. If indeed the differences between the North and the South are so wide and deep, there is every reason to believe that problems based on race, ethnicity, religion, culture, and language, crowned with regionalism, will undermine any form of unity. The inevitable conclusion is that even a loose framework of unity may not be mutually accommodating enough to be sustainable. In that case, the only remaining option is to partition the country. Partition may indeed allow each side to consolidate its internal front on the basis of shared values and institutionalized practices. With the realization that friendly and cooperative relations are essential to regional security, economic growth, and prosperity, the two parts of the country may eventually begin to build new bridges and come back together on the basis of a genuine need for cooperation and regional integration without the domination of one by the other.

These three scenarios do not, of course, address the problem of internal divisions in both the North and the South and the danger they pose for the further disintegration of these entities. The danger for the South is admittedly greater than for the North, where Islam, the Arabic language, and a broad cultural assimilation may serve as unifying factors. But the case of the South has to be seen in the context of divisive maneuvers by the North. If an agreement were reached on a mutually acceptable arrangement, this complicating factor would be significantly reduced, if not removed. Both the North and the South would then deal with their internal diversities in much the same way other African and Arab countries manage their internal ethnic or tribal differences.

Indeed, the current problem of division and fragmentation in the South could be mitigated if several questions were addressed. First, does the South have a recognizable cause worth fighting for? The answer to that question is bound to be a resounding yes. Second, which factions are fighting for that cause? Again, it is obvious that whereas all the groups espouse objectives that are similar, if not identical, they pursue these objectives through a variety of ways, some more credible than others. All things considered, it should also be relatively easy to determine which of them is credible as representative of the southern cause. Giving support to that faction would significantly strengthen it, undermine its opponents, and provide an incentive for regional unity. Even the prospects for national unity would be significantly enhanced by reducing regional factionalism in both the North and the South.

Undoubtedly, unity is a laudable goal, but the best guarantee for unity is for the leadership, especially at the national level, to rise above factionalism and to offer the entire nation a vision that would inspire a cross-sectional majority of the Sudanese people, irrespective of race, ethnicity, region, or religion, to identify with the nation and to stand together in collective pursuit of their common destiny. Only through mutual recognition, respect, and harmonious interaction among African and Arab populations can Sudan achieve and ensure a just and lasting peace and live up to its postulated role as a true microcosm of Africa and a dynamic link between the continent and the Middle East.

Conclusion

The options for the country remain limited given the combination of the North-South dichotomy and the ambiguous, cross-cutting racial and cultural linkages across the dividing line. Either Sudan consolidates by rising above the divisive labels of race, ethnicity, religion, and culture; or it builds on its North-South differences within a framework of loose unity through a genuine federal or confederal arrangement; or it addresses the crisis more radically through partition.

If self-determination for the South is to leave some room for the interests of the North, it must not be seen as synonymous with southern secession. Rather, it should be viewed as offering the South the opportunity to choose between or among options with competing advantages. If unity is to be a competitive option, it should be made desirable enough to win voluntary support from the South rather than be imposed by the North. This should in turn motivate the North to strive harder to make conditions for unity more desirable to the South than they have been so far. Making the unity option more attractive would also improve the possibility of non-Arab northerners, such as the Nuba and the Ingassana, preferring to remain within a united Sudan even if the South were to opt for secession.

Since the parties have already agreed to an internationally supervised referendum for the South, they should also be induced to accept an international peacekeeping operation to monitor a cease-fire; contain the criminal elements engaged in rampant destruction, murder, looting, and slavery; and help create a climate conducive to the free exercise of self-determination. Details of the administrative arrangements during the interim period and the options to be voted on could then be negotiated between the warring parties in a relatively more cordial climate. The process could be used not only to end the war between the government and the SPLM/SPLA but also to forge consensus in the North. Since the problem of the South has been a major factor in the discord among northern parties, its solution should allow the North to develop a system of government that is based on its cultural and religious values, a goal all major political parties have shared in varying degrees since independence.

Whichever options are adopted, the Sudanese will still have to address the legitimate fears of minority groups within both halves of the country—that one domination may be replaced by another. Ultimately, national leaders must recognize that such manipulations of ethnicity for divisive purposes are not in the long-term interest of the country. Likewise, southern leaders must recognize that there can be no durable peace or unity in the South unless the legitimate claims of self-administration of every group are respected and genuinely accommodated.

The region and the international community remain concerned with the alleged destabilizing role of the Sudan government and its supposed connection to international terrorism, and there is little doubt that these are external manifestations of the internal crises. Whatever ideological linkages to radical Islam the Sudanese Islamists may have, it is their need for international alliances against what they see as the Christian Western and Zionist forces—which they believe support the cause of the non-Arab and non-Muslim South and their secular allies in the North—that instigates their solidarity with radical Arab or Islamic revolutionary elements or movements abroad. A Sudan that successfully resolves its identity crisis and is at peace with itself will by definition desist from policies and actions that are acutely polarizing to the nation. It will become the constructive crossroads and Afro-Arab bridge that it has always been postulated to be.

11

Can Democracies Accommodate Ethnic Nationalism? The Rise and Decline of Self-Determination Movements in India

Atul Kohli

Numerous ethnic movements have over the years confronted the central government presiding over India's multicultural democracy. India thus provides laboratory-like conditions for the study of these movements. In this chapter I analyze three such ethnic movements—those of Tamils in Tamil Nadu during the 1950s and 1960s, of the Sikhs in the Punjab during the 1980s, and of Muslims in Kashmir during the 1990s—with the aim of explaining both their rise and decline. The focus will be less on details of these movements and more on deriving some general conclusions.

I argue that periodic demands for more control and power by a variety of ethnic groups—that is, self-determination movements—ought to be expected in multicultural democracies, especially developing-country democracies. The fate of these movements—the degree of cohesiveness the groups forge; whether they are accommodated or their demands readily escalate into secessionist movements; and their relative longevity—largely reflects the nature of the political context,

I would like to thank the following for their helpful comments on earlier drafts: Amrita Basu, Ayesha Jalal, Pratap Mehta, Claus Offe, Pravesh Sharma, John Waterbury, and the anonymous reviewers. The suggestions made by Ashutosh Varshney need to be singled out for acknowledgment because they were very useful; I incorporated many of them. The chapter further benefited from comments of participants at the conference Political Violence in India at Amherst, Massachusetts, September 23–24, 1995, and at a seminar I gave at the Department of Political Science, University of Toronto, February 9, 1996. Earlier versions of this chapter were published in the *Journal of Asian Studies* and in a volume published by Oxford University Press.

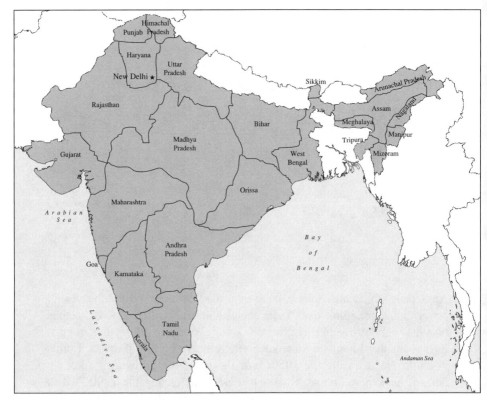

India

though group characteristics around which movements emerge and the resources these groups control are also consequential.

More specifically, two dimensions of the political context appear to be especially relevant, namely, how well central authority is institutionalized within the multicultural democracy and the willingness of the ruling groups to share some power and resources with mobilized groups. Given well-established central authority and firm but compromising leaders, self-determination movements typically follow the shape of an inverse U curve: A democratic polity in a developing country encourages group mobilization, which heightens group identities and facilitates a sense of increased group efficacy; mobilized groups then confront state authority, followed by a prolonged process of power negotiation; and such movements eventually decline as exhaustion sets in, some leaders are repressed, others are co-opted, and a modicum of genuine power sharing and mutual accommodation between the movement and the central state authorities is reached. Understood in this manner, self-determination movements constitute a political process whereby the central state and a variety of ethnic groups discover their relative power balances in developing-country democracies.

This bald argument requires some qualifications and caveats that are best stated at the outset. First, in addition to the domestic political context, the comparative analysis of these movements in India suggests that international factors can also alter the underlying power dynamics on which the predicted rise and decline of these movements rests. Second, the analysis is pitched at a fairly high level of generality. This not only obliterates complex details of individual movements but leads one to downplay important contrasts across movements: some identities (for example, those based on religion) may be better suited than others (for example, those based on language) for defining ethnic boundaries and thus may be more readily mobilizable and sustainable in the cause of self-determination movements. Finally, there is a need for a normative caveat. The focus on the state and the larger political context ought not to be read as endorsing the actions of state elites at the expense of the rights of ethnic movements. Established states often trample the rights of their minorities, sometimes ruthlessly. Whether a state or a demanding group has justice on its side is both important and controversial and is best decided on a case-by-case basis.

The chapter is organized as follows. I first discuss some general issues, explaining why a proliferation of group demands ought to be expected in a developing multicultural democracy such as India and why the institutionalization of central authority and the nature of the leadership are especially important aspects of the political context that shapes self-determination movements. Following this general discussion are case studies of three Indian self-determination movements—by Tamils, Sikhs, and Kashmiri Muslims—and comparisons of these movements. I then summarize the analysis and provide some general conclusions.

The Political Context: Some Generalizations

Politicization in Developing Democracies

The introduction of democracy to a developing country nearly always exacerbates political conflicts over the short to medium term. Some observers are surprised by such outcomes because, extrapolating from the Western experience, they expect democracy to be a solution to existing, rather than a source of new, power conflicts. In the West, however, democracy evolved over a long time, and both suffrage and political competition expanded slowly within the framework of centralized authority structures at the apex and growing popular pressures from below. Moreover, the question of who constituted a nation that was to be wedded to a specific state was often resolved prior to the introduction of mass suffrage. In this sense, democracy in the West indeed came to be a solution to growing power conflicts in society, especially among economic elites and across class lines. By contrast, democracy to most developing countries comes as imported ideas. As these ideas are translated into democratic institutions and these institutions provide new incentives for political actors to organize and mobilize, the results over the short to medium term are often disquieting. Several state-society traits of developing-country democracies help explain why this should be so.

First, prevailing cultural conditions in developing countries do not readily mesh with the imported model of political democracy. For example, mass suffrage is introduced in a context where identities and attachments often tend to be more local than national; authority in society tends to be dispersed but, within dispersed pockets, quite rigid and hierarchical; and community norms often prevail over narrow individualism. As democracy is introduced and competing elites undertake political mobilization, old identities are rekindled and reforged. Modern technology hastens the process (for instance, cassettes of the teachings of Ayatollah Khomeini and a television production of the *Ramayana*), and the collision of mobilized identities with each other or with the state ought not to be totally surprising. The spread of democratic norms also threatens traditional elites, who are more than willing to join hands with all those who perceive the spread of individualism as disruptive to traditional lifestyles. Again, a variety of reactionary movements ought to be expected.

Second, considerable state intervention is inherent to the overall design of "late development."[1] This structural trait in a low-income setting generates special problems when democracy is introduced. For example, ruling elites in developing-country democracies cannot readily claim that distributive problems are social (private) and not political (public); in other words, it is difficult in contemporary developing countries to establish the same separation between pubic and private realms that many Western democracies developed at early stages.

---

1. I have developed this argument in greater detail in the conclusion of Atul Kohli, *Democracy and Discontent: India's Growing Crisis of Governability* (New York: Cambridge University Press, 1991).

Accumulating distributive claims on these states thus partly reflect the politicization engendered by the state's attempts to penetrate and reorganize socioeconomic life. Relatedly, an interventionist state in a low-income setting controls large proportions of a society's economic resources, thus attracting the competitive energies of many of those who seek economic improvement. Intense competition over a state's resources, in turn, politicizes numerous cleavages, adding to problems of developing-country democracies.

Third, since democracy comes to most developing countries as an import, and since the transitions to democracy are over relatively short time periods, democratic institutions in most "follower" democracies tend to be weak. There is some variation on this dimension, and I will return later to the issue of relative institutionalization as a variable (India being more fortunate on this score). For the most part, however, norms of electoral politics, political parties, parliaments, constitutional separation of powers, and so on are not well established in developing-country democracies. Competitive mobilization that is unmediated by institutions, in turn, tends to spell trouble for most states. Of the problems generated by this well-known condition, the most significant is that power in these settings often comes to rest in individuals rather than in institutions. Barring exceptional individuals, leaders centralize personal power with detrimental long-term consequences. Because the centralization of power in individuals nearly always weakens fragile institutions—strong institutions do constrain the power of individuals— there is a built-in incentive in developing-country democracies for leaders to undertake periodic deinstitutionalization. Weak institutions and personal power thus tend to create a mutually reinforcing, vicious cycle. Typically, therefore, developing-country democracies tend to move toward situations in which centralizing, personalistic ruling elites confront a variety of oppositional elites who mobilize that which is most readily mobilizable, namely, community identities, and help transform them into rigid ethnic and group boundaries.

This observation brings the discussion to the fourth and last distinctive condition of developing-country democracies. The introduction of competitive elections, mass suffrage, and weak institutions will repeatedly generate expansionary political pressures in these democracies, that is, pressures toward a more equal distribution of power in society. A movement toward genuine devolution of political and economic power could accommodate such tendencies—by establishing a new equilibrium between demands and governance—and help strengthen new democracies. Any such trend, however, is likely to run up against two pervasive global constraints, both manifest as near intellectual hegemonies. These are first, a belief in strong, centralized states as a

necessity for the welfare of nations and, second, a widespread acceptance in recent years of orthodox economic models as appropriate models of economic development. Whereas the former privileges nationalists, the latter, in spite of the promised dismantling of the state and
related decentralization, pushes centralizing technocrats to the forefront.[2] In either case, power devolution in most developing-country
democracies is a fairly low priority. A typical outcome is the evolution
of these democracies toward two-track polities with a democratic track
in the sphere of electoral politics and a not-so-democratic track in the
state sphere, especially in the areas of economic policymaking. The
political society of many developing democracies is thus increasingly
characterized on the one hand by "too much democracy"—that is, by a
variety of conflicts, including ethnic conflicts—and, on the other hand,
by "not enough democracy" as the state increasingly insulates itself
from social demands and conflicts.

The cumulative impact of these distinctive state-societal traits is
that the introduction of democracy into developing countries rapidly
politicizes the body politic. Many different conflicts thus typically dot
the political landscape of these democracies. Broad contextual conditions, of course, do not fully explain either the variations across such
countries or the trajectories of specific conflicts; in the language of
social science, a focus on the context provides necessary but not sufficient conditions of specific conflicts. What can be said at the general
level, however, is that the four state-societal traits previously discussed
help explain why democracy in developing countries tends to be as
much a source of as a solution to power conflicts.

These conflicts may precipitate along cleavages of class, interest
groups, regions, or ethnic groups. Again, at a general level, it can be
noted that ethnic and regional groups are more likely than classes or
economic groups to demand self-determination because they can more
readily perceive themselves as total societies, as social groups with a
sufficiently complex division of labor to sustain ambitions of territorial
sovereignty. The possibility of a shared cultural heritage further encourages such imagining. The more such groups exist in a developing-
country democracy, the more likely it is that self-determination movements will emerge. If this much is relatively clear, the next interesting
question is why some such groups demanding greater power and control
are readily accommodated, whereas others move into a militancy-

---

2. This argument is developed in more detail elsewhere. See Atul Kohli,
"Democracy Amid Economic Orthodoxy: Trends in Developing Countries," *Third
World Quarterly* 14, no. 4 (1993), pp. 671–889.

repression cycle, escalating their demands into secessionist movements and threatening the territorial integrity of established states.

Institutionalization, Leadership, and Self-Determination Movements

Continuing the discussion at a fairly general level, I hypothesize that two proximate variables are especially important for understanding the varying trajectories of self-determination movements. The first of these is the level of institutionalization of the central state and the second concerns the degree to which the ruling strategy of leaders accommodates demands for self-determination. I use the concept of institutionalization in a fairly conventional sense (it has both a normative and an organizational component),[3] but my focus is narrowly on central state authority rather than on a host of other norms and political structures that may be more or less institutionalized. I also do not assume that state authorities are always agents of public order. The degree of institutionalization of the central state, then, influences the degree to which state authorities can impose their preferred vision of the political order on the societies they govern. The vision, of course, may be more or less accommodating of opposition demands; that is, when pressed, the leadership may be more willing in some instances to devolve power. The degree of institutionalization and leadership strategies are thus two important variables, two aspects of the broad political context discussed earlier that commonly vary within the developing world and influence the fate of self-determination movements. If one dichotomizes these two variables (which is clearly quite artificial), and if the mechanical quality of schematic depictions is excused, the resulting 2 x 2 matrix (Figure 11.1) helps clarify some of the issues succinctly.

The main hypothesis I propose is well depicted by the first quadrant: all other things being equal, the more the authority of the central state is institutionalized and the more accommodating the ruling strategy, the more likely it is that self-determination movements will traverse the shape of an inverse U curve. They will first rise because it is natural for them to do so in the political context of developing-country democracies. Second, after a more or less prolonged period of power negotiation with the central state, they will inevitably decline in intensity as exhaustion sets in and some genuine compromise is reached. The logic underlying this proposition is that, on the one hand, a well-institutional-

---

3. See, for example, Samuel Huntington, *Political Order in Changing Societies* (New Haven, Conn.: Yale University Press, 1968), passim but esp. chap. 1.

Figure 11.1   Developing Country Democracies: Political Context and the Trajectory of Self-Determination Movements

		Central Authority	
		Well Institutionalized	*Weakly Institutionalized*
	Accommodating	1. The inverse U curve of ethnic politics (e.g., Tamils in India in the 1950s and 1960s)	2. Peaceful breakup of the state (e.g., Czechoslovakia, 1990s)
Leadership Strategy			
	Unaccommodating	3. Demands and repression cycle (e.g., Sikhs in India's Punjab, 1980)	4. Turbulence and/or breakdown (e.g., Nigeria, first and second republics)

ized state sets firm boundaries within which political movements must operate, and, on the other hand, an accommodating leadership provides room (of course, within limits) for the movements to achieve some real gains.

The same logic can be readily extended to describe a few variations on the theme. A state's leadership may turn out to be not very accommodating to self-determination movements. This attitude may result from something as simple as a new and different type of leader coming to power or it may reflect something more complex, such as a leader's power resting on a new and different coalition. Whatever the underlying reasons, unaccommodating leaders in well-established states (quadrant 3) often channel self-determination movements into cycles of escalating demands and repression. The reason is that a well-institutionalized democratic state both provides room for self-determination movements to emerge and possesses a fair amount of legitimate coercion to repress these movements. Unaccommodating leaders, who define the state's good in terms of denying concessions to demanding groups, typically repress such movements only to push them further into more extreme directions of secession as a goal and militancy as a tactic. The situation depicted in quadrant 3 is then ripe for prolonged, militant self-determination movements. These situations are resolved either when overwhelming force is used and/or when a more accommodating leader comes to power.

Self-determination movements are deeply threatening to weakly institutionalized states (quadrants 2 and 4). If leaders of such states are relatively accommodating toward movements—such examples in the developing world are rare, suggesting that institutionalization of authority structures and leadership strategies may not be entirely independent of each other—the peaceful breakup or reorganization of the state is the most likely outcome. By contrast, unaccommodating leaders, especially those who control significant coercive resources, are likely to drive the situation toward considerable turbulence at minimum and, at maximum, toward a civil war and possibly even a violent breakup of the state.

In sum, how well the authority of the central state is institutionalized and the leadership strategy are two important aspects of the political context that influence the pattern of self-determination movements. The nature of the groups that are mobilized (the resources they control and whether they are organized around race, religion, or language) and how intensely such groups come to view their situation as unjust are issues that are by no means irrelevant to their fate. Some of these issues are by their very nature specific to given situations and will emerge in the empirical discussion of specific cases. At a general level, it is my central hypothesis that the nature of the broader political context is quite important for understanding self-determination movements.

Some Evidence from India

India is a noisy democracy. It has over the years experienced a variety of political conflicts. Conflicts around cleavages of class, caste, parties, language, religion, and regions thus dot India's political landscape. I have analyzed why this should be so in India in detail elsewhere;[4] some of the theoretical generalizations stemming from that analysis were also presented earlier in the chapter in a highly condensed form. Within that context, the focus here is mainly on ethnic movements demanding self-determination.[5] India has experienced quite a few of these, especially by groups who define their regional distinctiveness along criteria of language or religion. Three of the most significant of these movements, namely, those spearheaded by Tamils, Sikhs, and Kashmiri Muslims,

---

4. See Atul Kohli, *Democracy and Discontent: India's Growing Crisis of Governability.*

5. As suggested previously, I use the concept of self-determination movements fairly loosely. What I have in mind are mainly movements for greater power and control by groups that share some real or imagined characteristics and that are sufficiently large and complex to conceive of themselves as mini-nations. Within the Indian federation, then, demands of such minority groups have varied from minimum (for more power and resources within the federation and expressed through democratic channels) to maximum (for secession from the federation and expressed through militant means).

are analyzed further on.[6] Since I have proposed that institutionalization of state authority and leadership strategies influence the pattern of these movements, a few preliminary comments on how these contextual conditions have varied in India over time are in order.

India in the 1950s was a relatively well institutionalized polity, especially compared to other developing countries. This was manifest most strongly in a fairly well organized central state—especially in a highly professional national civil service and armed forces—but also in a well-functioning national political party, the Congress, that generally controlled the state. In addition, India possessed such effective institutions as a parliament, an independent judiciary, and a free national press. How and why India came to have such effective institutions is clearly a complex issue, well beyond the scope of this chapter. Suffice it to say that some state institutions were inherited from a colonial past and other more political ones were a product of a fairly prolonged and cohesive nationalist movement.[7] India's rigid and segmented social structure—especially the elaborate caste hierarchies, organized among numerous, relatively isolated villages—kept levels of political mobilization low and ironically may have further helped new institutions to take root in the early, postindependence phase.

Over time some of India's political institutions weakened. In terms of periodization, if the 1950s was a decade of relatively effective institutions, the 1960s is best thought of as a decade of transition during which the nationalist legacy declined, political competition and challenges to the hegemony of the Congress Party increased, and a new type of political system—a more populist one with noninstitutional methods of securing electoral majorities—was created by Indira Gandhi. During the two following decades, namely, the 1970s and 1980s, some of India's well-established institutions were battered, especially by leaders in power.

Since levels of institutionalization are relative, it is important to remember that even during the 1970s and 1980s, India's central state authority in comparison to most African and many Latin American countries was relatively well institutionalized. Nevertheless, in compar-

---

6. I estimate the significance of these movements by the following criteria: the number of people that were mobilized, the cohesiveness and longevity of the movement, and the degree to which it genuinely became a force that the central state could not ignore. It could be argued that this case selection is a little too convenient and that other cases, such as in eastern India, would not fit so well the argument of this chapter.

7. Among other writings on these themes, see Myron Weiner, *Party Building in a New Nation* (Chicago: University of Chicago Press, 1967); and Myron Weiner, *The Indian Paradox* (New Delhi: Sage, 1989).

ison to its own past, a fair amount of deinstitutionalization had occurred: The Congress Party as an organization was largely destroyed; the civil service, police, and even the armed forces became less professional and more politicized; parliament became less effective; and the autonomy of the judiciary was reduced. Once again, how and why these political changes occurred constitute a complex story, far beyond the scope of this chapter.[8]

As to the other variable of leadership strategy, India has had four main prime ministers who have ruled for more than two to three years: Nehru ruled India for nearly seventeen years (from 1947 until his death in 1964); his daughter, Indira Gandhi, dominated India for nearly as long as the father (1966–1977 and 1980–1984); then her son, Rajiv Gandhi, ruled from 1985 to 1989; Prime Minister Narasimha Rao was in power during 1991–1996.[9] Characterizing the leadership strategies of these leaders in a brief space is clearly to grossly oversimplify a fairly complex reality. I do so only reluctantly.

The main analytical concern here is how leaders typically respond to oppositional challenges, especially demands of mobilized groups for greater self-determination. On a dimension of leadership strategy that varies from accommodating to unaccommodating, Nehru was closer to the accommodating end of the spectrum. His approach was in part a function of his own personality and part a reflection of his relatively secure power position; a concession from Nehru here or there enhanced his magnanimity rather than threatened his hold on power. The political situation during his daughter's reign, however, was quite different, as were her political instincts. The Congress Party's hegemony had by then declined, and Indira consolidated her power against considerable odds. She was always suspicious of power challenges. She re-created a powerful political center in India mainly by portraying herself as a champion of the poor. As her personal popularity soared, opposition to her also became strident, culminating in the so-called Emergency in 1977, when democratic rights in India were suspended for some two years. When Indira Gandhi returned to power in 1980, she was less populist yet still needing to mobilize electoral pluralities; she started flirt-

---

8. A growing personalization of power was at the heart of the story; growing political fragmentation in society privileged personalism and, in turn, personalistic leaders damaged the institutions that constrained their discretionary powers. For details, see Kohli, *Democracy and Discontent.* Also see Paul Brass, *Politics of India Since Independence* (New York: Cambridge University Press, 1990); and Lloyd Rudolph and Susanne Rudolph, *In Pursuit of Lakshimi: The Political Economy of the Indian State* (Chicago: University of Chicago Press, 1987).

9. Other prime ministers, including the current one, Atal Bihari Vajapi, have not ruled for long enough periods to merit special attention.

ing with communal themes, occasionally courting India's Hindus (more than 80 percent of India's population) by railing against religious minorities, especially Sikhs. This strategy made her increasingly less accommodating toward minorities lest she be viewed as appeasing them. Overall, therefore, Indira Gandhi, in contrast to Nehru, was closer to the unaccommodating end of the leadership spectrum.

Both the subsequent leaders, Rajiv Gandhi and Narasimha Rao, were more flexible than Indira Gandhi.[10] Rajiv Gandhi was especially accommodating toward self-determination movements in the first two years of his rule. As his political situation became less secure, however, he too, like his mother, flirted with communalism, tilting occasionally in a pro-Muslim direction but mainly courting the Hindu vote, becoming more and more indecisive and unaccommodating in the second half of his rule. Narashimha Rao in the 1990s portrayed himself as a nonpersonalistic, flexible leader who, at a minimum, was not bent on a further centralization of power in his own hands. After the assassination of two prime ministers (both Indira and Rajiv were assassinated for political reasons), this ruling strategy appeared to have calmed an agitated polity, at least until 1998, when the right-wing, Hindu nationalist party, the Bharatiya Janata Party (BJP), came to power.

Thus, to oversimplify a rather complex reality, the Nehru period in India, say from 1950 to 1964, is best understood as a period when India's central state was relatively well institutionalized and leadership strategy, though firm, was also flexible and accommodating to demands for self-determination. Subsequently, especially since the mid-1960s, India's political institutions weakened, though they remain relatively effective by developing-country standards. The leadership strategy over these past three decades has varied. Whereas Indira Gandhi was quite unaccommodating toward demanding groups, both Rajiv and Rao appeared to be at least less threatening, if not actually more accommodating. With this context in mind, we are now in a position to turn our attention to a few specific self-determination movements within India.

Tamil Nationalism

Tamil Nadu is now one of India's important states, an integral part of the Indian federal system. No one now questions, not even those who live in Tamil Nadu, whether they are fully a part of the Indian union.

---

10. The contrast between these leaders and Indira Gandhi helps bolster the claim that leadership strategies are indeed somewhat independent of the degrees of institutionalization of state authority.

However, it was not always so. During the 1950s and the 1960s, Tamil leaders argued that Tamils were a distinctive people. They mobilized considerable support for a Tamil nation and demanded, at minimum, greater power and control over their own affairs vis-à-vis New Delhi or, at maximum, secession from India. A very brief recapitulation of the rise and decline of this movement, therefore, will serve our broader analytical interests.[11]

Tamil is a language and Tamils as a social group are, therefore, mainly a linguistically defined group. Tamil, along with a few other languages in South India but unlike most languages spoken in northern India, does not derive its roots from classical Sanskrit with its Indo-Germanic roots. Rather, Tamil is a Dravidian language. Tamil nationalists also used to insist that Tamils are a separate racial and cultural group with their roots in a Dravidian society that was indigenous to southern India prior to the historic arrival of and domination by "northern Aryans." Brahmans in Tamil society could thus be viewed not as natural hegemons of a caste society but rather as agents of northern domination. That some of the Tamil Brahmans were of lighter skin color than much of Tamil society only added to the plausibility of such an interpretation. Two other sets of "facts on the ground" are important for understanding the dynamics of Tamil nationalism. First, Brahmans in Tamil society constitute a relatively small caste group: less than 5 percent of the total (in comparison, say, to parts of northern India, where Brahmans often constitute nearly 10 percent of the total population). Second, for a variety of historical reasons, the area that is now Tamil Nadu was more urbanized by mid-century than many other parts of India.

The Congress Party in this part of India, as elsewhere, built its preindependence base on the Brahmans. That the Brahmans were few in number and that the non-Brahman castes were already active in city life provided the necessary conditions for the early rise of an anti-Brahman movement. Democratization and related power conflicts, in other words, came relatively early to this region of India. The first institutional manifestation of that movement was the Justice Party, which was led by the elite of the non-Brahman castes and sided with the British against both Brahmans and the Congress Party in the hope of securing concessions in government jobs and in education. The Justice Party eventually was delegitimized both because of its elitist nature and

---

11. The best book on this subject remains Marguerite Ross Barnett, *The Politics of Cultural Nationalism in South India* (Princeton: Princeton University Press, 1976).

because of the rising tide of nationalism. That had significant consequences, especially because the Congress Party became identified as a
Brahman party in a region where Brahmans had not been able to establish cultural and political hegemony. The early development of a cleavage between the Brahman and anti-Brahman forces opened up the political space for subsequent anti–Congress Party developments.

The link between the Congress Party and the Brahmans became the
target of Tamil nationalists in the postindependence period. The
Congress Party in Madras could not easily break out of that mold. The
continued Congress-Brahman alliance enabled the regional nationalists
to mobilize simultaneously against both caste domination and domination by northern Indians. Hammering on the theme of the distinctiveness of the Tamil tradition, and linking that with an opposition to northern Hindi rule and its allies, the southern Brahmans, the leaders of the
Dravidian movement found a ready audience among the numerous
backward castes that were already concentrated in the cities. To simpli-
fy a complex picture, Tamil nationalism and a petit bourgeois base
among the urban backward castes provided the core support for a
regional nationalist movement.

The early demands of this self-determination movement were for
greater power and control: over time, the broader movement came to
include a separatist movement demanding a Dravidistan, or a land for
the Dravidian people. A number of Indian states in the early 1950s
argued for reorganizing the Indian federation along linguistic lines.
Most such demands, of course, were not separatist. Nevertheless, in the
aftermath of India's separation with Pakistan, Nehru in the early 1950s
was reluctant to carry out a linguistic redesign lest it strengthen secessionist tendencies and lead to a further breakup of India. Tamil nationalists and their mobilized supporters were a point in case insofar as they
pressed their identity politics hard through demonstrations that occasionally turned violent and included public burning of the Indian flag
and constitution. When pressed by several states, Nehru recalculated
that the dangers of not devolving power to linguistic groups were
greater than those of doing so. Fully in control at the national center and
widely considered to be India's legitimate leader, Nehru set firm limits
on what powers the newly constituted states would have and what
would be controlled by New Delhi (which, by the way, was substantial).
Within these limits, then, India's federal system of states was reorganized along linguistic lines in 1956. This reorganization gave Tamil
nationalists a Tamil state, taking a fair amount of the separatist steam
out of the movement.

After Tamil nationalists gained a separate state (first called
Madras, subsequently relabeled Tamil Nadu, or home of the Tamils),

their struggle shifted to ousting the Congress Party from power within the state. For this effort, the Tamil nationalists utilized a political party, the DMK, and sought to broaden their power base. They adopted a radical rhetoric of land reform and eradication of the caste system, which further threatened the Brahmans. Many of the intermediate and lower caste dwellers in villages thus came to be attracted to the DMK. The DMK also successfully mobilized cultural themes. In this they were fortunate insofar as many Tamil nationalists were playwrights, literary figures, and theater and movie actors. Movies were the new emerging medium and they were used successfully by the Tamil Nationalist Party (Dravida Munnetra Kazhagam, or DMK) to popularize such themes as the injustices of the caste system, the glories of Tamil history, and the social need for Robin Hood–type heroes who would deliver the poor, weak, and dispossessed from the clutches of the rich and the wicked.

As Tamil nationalism became more populist, it simultaneously became less coherent yet more capable of winning elections. Following Nehru's death, for example, India's national leaders for a brief moment reattempted to impose Hindi as a national language on all states. Many states reacted negatively with Tamil Nadu reacting the most violently. Well mobilized to confront precisely such national policy shifts, it instigated language riots that broke out all over the state. Several students burned themselves to death, protesting the moves of the national government. For another brief moment the national government used a heavy coercive hand to deal with protests. As matters got worse, the national government backtracked. The principle was conceded that regional languages, such as Tamil, were "coequal" to the two national languages, namely Hindi and English. This proclamation was a major victory for the DMK. Enjoying considerable popularity, the DMK ousted the Congress Party from power within Tamil Nadu in the 1967 elections, and the party has since never returned to power in that state.

The rise and consolidation of power by the DMK had a profound impact on Tamil Nadu's politics. The highest leadership posts in the state slipped out of the hands of Brahmans and went to the well-educated elite of the non-Brahman castes. The intermediate and local leadership more accurately reflected the real power base of the DMK: the intermediate castes. Many of them gained access to more power and resources. As the DMK settled down to rule, the predictable happened. Over time, the DMK lost much of its self-determination, anticenter militancy, as well as its commitment to socioeconomic reforms. The reasons for that deradicalization in Tamil Nadu were the same as elsewhere. Once national leaders made important concessions (though within firm limits) and the DMK achieved its major goal of securing increased power, realpolitik concerns took over and mobilizing ideologies slowly lost their relevance for guiding governmental actions. Ethnic nationalism slowly declined, following the inverse U curve previously discussed.

Sikh Nationalism

Punjab is one of India's most prosperous states—the home of the green revolution—and Sikhs constitute about half of that state's population (the other half being Hindus). Sikh nationalism was a powerful political force in the state throughout the 1980s. Demands of Sikh groups varied from greater political and economic control within the Indian federation to secession from India and the creation of a sovereign state, Khalistan. The national government under Indira Gandhi, especially during the 1980s, was not only unaccommodating but actively sought to divide and rule the Sikhs. The strategy backfired as some Sikh groups turned sharply militant. The central state, in turn, met the militancy with considerable force. Punjab being a border state with Pakistan, its militant Sikhs were able to secure arms and support from across the border. Militant nationalists and a repressive state thus confronted each other in a vicious cycle of growing violence. Violence took its toll throughout the 1980s as nearly 1,000 people died every year, and it peaked in 1990, when some 4,000 people were killed in political violence. Since then, however, the situation has changed. Brutal state repression succeeded in eliminating many of the militants, and a more politically flexible Rao allowed state-level elections in Punjab in the early 1990s. As an elected government settled down to rule, an exhausted state went back to work, and both militancy and state repression fell into the background. In 1993 "only" 73 people died in political violence, and since then investment flows into Punjab have grown dramatically and violence has remained at a relatively low and sporadic level.

The underlying story behind the rise and decline of Sikh nationalism is complex and cannot be retold here in any detail.[12] What follows, therefore, is only a bare-bones account. Sikhs are a religious group, concentrated mainly in the Punjab. Sikh men are distinctive in that they wear religiously prescribed long hair and turbans. Sikhs and Hindus lived side by side, peacefully, for several centuries. Like the Hindus—from which Sikhism was initially derived in the late medieval period—

---

12. For a good account, see Paul Brass, "The Punjab Crisis and the Unity of India," in Atul Kohli, ed., *India's Democracy: An Analysis of Changing State-Society Relations* (Princeton: Princeton University Press, 1990), pp. 169–213.

Sikhs are internally differentiated along castelike lines. Most Sikhs are relatively prosperous agriculturalists. A sizable minority are urban traders and entrepreneurs; until recently intermarriage between these groups and their Hindu counterparts was common in the Punjab. Sikhs also have their own version of untouchables, the equivalent of the lowest Hindu castes that generally tend to be very poor and own no land.

Prior to the political turmoil that arose in the 1980s, caste and community divisions in Punjab had given rise to easily identifiable political divisions. In the past, the Hindus had generally supported the Congress Party, though a significant minority had also been loyal to a Hindu nationalist party. The Akali Dal (a predominantly Sikh party in the state), by contrast, had consistently counted on the Sikh vote but seldom succeeded in mobilizing all the Sikhs as an ethnic political bloc.

Given internal divisions among Sikhs, the Congress Party during the 1960s and 1970s was often in a position to form a government in Punjab with the help of Hindus and a significant Sikh minority. The Akalis, by contrast, could form only a coalition government, and that only with a seemingly unlikely partner: the pro-Hindu party. These basic political and community divisions provide the background essential for understanding the intensified political activities of the Sikhs during the 1980s. Akali militancy was aimed at mobilizing as many Sikhs as possible around a platform of Sikh nationalism. The analytical issue here is why those fairly normal political ambitions generated so much chaos and turmoil.

The Akali Dal as a political party has always exhibited a mixture of religious fervor and hard-nosed political realism aimed at capturing power. Being a primarily Sikh party, there is a close relationship between the party and Sikh religious organizations. The Sikh political elite thus periodically utilizes religious organizations to influence the political behavior of the laity. Over the years, the Akalis have been in and out of power. They first came to power in 1966 when they spearheaded a successful movement for a separate Punjabi Suba (or the land where Punjabi is spoken) and the current boundaries of the state of Punjab were drawn. Given the electoral arithmetic, however, the power position of the Akalis was never secure. Sikhs constituted a bare majority in the state, and Congress Party leaders consistently sought to draw away part of the Sikh vote through one machination or another. Unlike Tamil Nadu, therefore, where Tamil nationalists came to power around the same time, consolidated their hold, and settled on a slow but steady road toward deradicalization, Akalis in the Punjab have consistently needed to whip up religious and nationalist issues that would keep Sikhs united politically.

During the 1970s, as Indira Gandhi's popularity grew across India,

Congress Party leaders in the Punjab undertook aggressive efforts to divide Sikhs and to consolidate their own hold over state politics. A threatened Akali Dal had little choice but to raise the ante; it started demanding even greater control over the affairs of Sikhs, coming closer and closer in its formal statements to wanting a sovereign state for the Sikhs that it could control. Indira Gandhi countered with a combination of repression—labeling secessionists as seditious—and further attempts to divide the Sikhs. During the Emergency, many Sikh leaders were imprisoned. When Indira returned to power in 1980 and another round of elections were held in Punjab, the Congress Party won a clear majority and the Akalis secured only 27 percent of the popular vote. Congress Party leaders considered themselves the legitimate, elected rulers. The Akalis, by contrast, viewed Punjab as their state and thus one they ought to control. The Akalis were therefore cornered in their own state and decided they had to fight for their political life. Much of what followed—some anticipated but most of it unanticipated—makes sense mainly from this retrospective logic of competitive mobilization.

The battle lines were drawn. Indira Gandhi had the popular support and decided to use her position of advantage to launch a political offensive and consolidate her position vis-à-vis the Akalis. If she could use Sikh militants to split the ranks of the Akalis still further between the moderates and the extremists, victory would be hers. And this is what she attempted. The Akali Dal possessed another set of political resources, however, whose efficacy Indira Gandhi apparently underestimated. The Akalis still could organize around the issue of Sikh nationalism like no other party in Punjab. The chain of Sikh temples, moreover, provided a ready organizational network with money, personnel, and the proven ability to sway public opinion. A populist, centralizing, and unaccommodating national leader, Indira Gandhi, thus came to be pitted against a regional party, the Akali Dal, that had considerable potential to mobilize the forces of religious nationalism.

Both Indira Gandhi and the Akalis assembled militant forces for political ends. In retrospect, it is clear that over the next several years, the militancy led to civil disorder that took on a political life of its own, increasingly out of the control of both the Akalis and the national government. Whether that simply was not foreseen or was brazenly ignored under the short-term pressure to seize political advantage may never be known. What we do know is that once mobilized, Sikh militants very quickly gained political advantage over moderate Sikh leaders. If the political aim was indeed to create a separate Sikh state, namely, a Khalistan, then moderate Sikh leaders had little to contribute toward achieving such ends. A move toward secession was mainly a political ploy for most moderate Akalis. Having shifted the political discourse in that direction, however, they undermined their own legitimacy as moderates as well as any and all efforts to work with New Delhi; normal politics made the moderates look like opportunists unworthy of a leadership mantle. True believers, instead, became heroes of the day and gained public sympathy. Flushed with arms that often came from Afghanistan via Pakistan, Sikh militants unleashed a holy war aimed at establishing a sovereign Sikh state. Indira Gandhi countered by increasing government repression. As a militancy and repression cycle set in, Punjab, one of India's most prosperous states, became engulfed in a long decade of violence.

There were at least two important occasions during the 1980s when the Congress Party and Sikh moderates came close to a compromise. Among the demands of Akalis were a number of concrete bread-and-butter issues that fell well short of secession: control over river waters, the capital city of Punjab, and agricultural subsidies. Indira Gandhi during 1982–1984 refused these compromises lest she be viewed nationally as appeasing minorities. This policy weakened Sikh moderates and privileged those who wanted to use more militant tactics. A second and more important occasion arose when Rajiv Gandhi came to power in 1985. Flush with victory and committed to resolving the Punjab conflict, Rajiv offered broad compromises to Akalis. The results were dramatic. Elections were held in the state, Akalis came to power, and political violence dropped sharply during 1985. Unfortunately, all this progress was short lived. Very quickly Rajiv Gandhi found it impossible to implement the compromises he had offered to the Akali leaders. The details are complex, but the major obstacle to implementation was Rajiv's own growing political vulnerabilities: as his national popularity declined, starting sometime in 1986, he was increasingly pressed within his own party to not make any further concessions to minorities. Once it became clear, therefore, that concessions from Delhi were more apparent than real, the position of elected Akali leaders was again undermined and the militancy and repression cycle reappeared.

Had India been a weaker state during this period, it is conceivable that Sikh secessionists would have succeeded in establishing yet another state on the subcontinent. As it was, however, even though India's political institutions had weakened considerably over the previous decades, India remained a relatively well established state. The national legitimacy of elected leaders, an effective civil and police bureaucracy, and, most important, a loyal armed forces are critical components of the state. They were all utilized, especially brute force, to contain and repress the Sikh militants, who also became marginalized over time and lost popular support. Repression and political marginalization led to a dwindling number of Sikh militants undertaking violent acts to accomplish secessionist goals.

Rao finally called elections in the Punjab in the early 1990s. The Akalis boycotted the election, but a Sikh-led Congress Party government came to power. The Akalis eventually joined the government after municipal elections were held. For now, therefore, the militancy and repression of the 1980s has fallen into the background.

To sum up, Sikh nationalism in the Punjab also traversed the inverse U curve, but the top of the curve turned out to be prolonged. Among the important underlying contrasts with the earlier movement of Tamils was the contrasting approach of Nehru and Indira Gandhi; Nehru was accommodating and Indira was not. Of course, there were other factors at work: (1) Tamils dominate Tamil Nadu, whereas the Sikhs constitute only half of the Punjab's population; (2) Tamils are a linguistic group, whereas Sikhs are a religious group, and given the close marriage of politics and religion in Sikhism, the Sikh religion probably provides a more encompassing identity than does attachment to a language; (3) the threat posed by rapid socioeconomic change in the Punjab to Sikhism as a religious community was more serious than that posed to the linguistically defined community of Tamils; and (4) Tamils did not have as easy an access to arms and across-the-border sanctuaries as did Sikh militants. All of these factors played some role, but none on its own corresponds as neatly with the aforementioned pattern of the rise and decline of movements as do the degrees of institutionalization of state authority and the strategies of national leaders. Within a more turbulent polity, Indira Gandhi's commitment to dominate Punjab politics pushed Akalis into aggressive mobilization. Once mobilized, professional politicians lost control and militants took over. Finally, over time, militants were repressed out of existence and a tired population was relieved to accept some concessions from a more accommodating national leadership and to vote an elected provincial government back into power.

Muslim Nationalism in Kashmir

Since 1989 the state of Jammu and Kashmir, especially its northern valley of Kashmir, has been gripped by a militancy-repression cycle. The main protagonists of the conflict are Islamic groups that do not want Kashmir to be part of India, and a variety of Indian security forces. The dimensions of the conflict are quite severe: In a relatively sparsely populated state of some 8 million people (approximately 65 percent Muslim), at least 10,000 people (some estimates go as high as 40,000) died as a result of political violence during the second half of the 1990s; security forces deployed in the state by now consist of more than 300 paramilitary companies and several army divisions; and at least 100,000 Hindus have migrated away from the Muslim-dominated Kashmir valley, mainly to Jammu, the southern, Hindu-dominated part of the state. During the second half of the 1990s, India's central government pursued a two-pronged strategy: it came down very hard on recalcitrant Islamic militants, and the electoral process was resumed, strengthening the hands of those leaders who are willing to respect constitutional boundaries. Whether this strategy will generate a result similar to that in the case of the Sikhs in Punjab, namely, a return to normalcy, is not clear as yet, especially at present when a more hard-line BJP government may well rescind the special status that Kashmir enjoys within the Indian federation.

Once again, the full story behind this specific Indian case of ethnic politics need not be recalled here.[13] The following condensed account suggests that this case does not fit as neatly into the inverse U curve argument. I believe this partial anomaly exists partly because the conflict is more internationalized than the other two cases and partly because the conflict is still relatively young. The predicted decline of ethnic militancy and of the related fratricide may still set in over the next few years. Whatever the eventual outcome, some elements of how and why ethnic conflict flared up in Kashmir are still broadly consistent with the propositions previously developed.

Ever since India and Pakistan emerged as sovereign states in the late 1940s, Kashmir has been a focus of dispute. As a Muslim majority state that was contiguous to Pakistan, Kashmir arguably should have become a part of Pakistan. The Hindu head of the Kashmiri state instead chose to join India. Pakistan contested the legality of this decision, and as often happens in interstate relations, it was not legality but might that determined what was right; India and Pakistan fought two wars over the issue, and a large part of Kashmir was incorporated into India. What is important for our analytical purposes is that in spite of these international problems, for much of this period, say, 1950 to 1980, ethnic nationalism in Kashmir remained relatively mild. The memory and stories of ethnic injustices were probably kept alive. Nevertheless, Kashmir was accorded a special status within the Indian constitution giving it considerable autonomy within India's federal system; India's central government also provided a substantial financial subsidy to

---

13. A good account is to be found in Ashutosh Varshney, "India, Pakistan and Kashmir: Antinomies of Nationalism," *Asian Survey* 31, no. 11 (November 1991).

facilitate the economic development of Kashmir. This accommodation seemed to have succeeded. Although both New Delhi and Kashmiri leaders, especially Muslim leaders, viewed each other with suspicion, a working arrangement of sorts operated well into the early 1980s.

Several new factors came into play in the early 1980s. As discussed, the Indian polity as a whole was by now relatively more turbulent. Old nationalist institutions such as the Congress Party were in decline. A whole new postnationalist generation demanded a greater share of political and economic resources. Indira Gandhi was at the helm nationally. In her postpopulist phase, in the early 1980s she increasingly flirted with pro-Hindu themes to create a new national electoral coalition. This shift in strategy bode ill for states with considerable non-Hindu populations, such as the Sikhs in the Punjab and the Muslims in Kashmir. Given her centralizing and unaccommodating instincts, moreover, states like Kashmir came under increasing political pressure.

Within Kashmir, the state's founding father and much-revered leader, Sheikh Abdullah, died in 1982. His son Farooq Abdullah moved into the resulting political vacuum, both as the leader of the state's main non-Congress political party, the National Conference Party, and as the head of the state government. State-level elections in 1983 turned out to be quite important. Farooq successfully campaigned on an anti-Congress, anti-Delhi, and pro-Kashmiri autonomy platform. The campaign caught the imagination of a large majority, especially Kashmir's Muslim majority. Indira Gandhi herself campaigned in Kashmir on behalf of the state Congress Party, often appealing to the fears of Jammu Hindus. Communal polarization, although hardly new to Kashmir, increasingly came to be sponsored by competing elites and grew. Farooq's platform fell well short of secessionist demands. Nevertheless, his emphasis on regional autonomy for Kashmir turned out to be very popular, propelling the National Conference Party to a handsome electoral victory against the Congress Party.

Farooq in Kashmir had to tread a thin line between emphasizing Kashmiri autonomy on the one hand and not appearing as an antinational, Muslim Kashmiri secessionist on the other hand. In order to bolster this precarious position, he joined hands with other non–Congress Party heads of state governments. Hoping to be one of the many who were part of the loyal opposition, Farooq hosted a well-publicized conference in Kashmir of all major opposition leaders. Unfortunately, this was precisely the type of move that truly threatened Indira Gandhi. Hoping to clip Farooq's growing political wings, Indira appointed a close and tough personal aide, Jagmohan, to be Kashmir's governor. Jagmohan, in turn, initiated a series of machinations whereby a number of National Conference Party legislators defected to the Congress Party, further threatening Farooq's position. Jagmohan eventually dismissed Farooq as Kashmir's chief minister in 1984, claiming without proof that Farooq had lost the support of a majority in the legislature.

Farooq's dismissal—very much a part of an all India-pattern of a threatened Indira Gandhi bent on centralizing and weakening India's federal institutions—turned out to be a critical turning point. Public opinion data are not available, but it appears that the dismissal sent a strong message, especially to Kashmiri Muslims, that their democratic and legitimate efforts to create greater political spaces within India might well be thwarted.[14] This growing alienation of Muslims, especially of their urban youth, was not helped by political events that followed. As the 1987 state elections approached (Indira Gandhi was by now dead, replaced nationally by her son Rajiv), Farooq Abdullah, both pressed politically and sufficiently opportunistic, formed an electoral alliance with the Congress Party. This seemingly innocuous electoral opportunism had the profound impact of eliminating any major democratic outlet for Kashmiri Muslims who sought greater autonomy from Delhi. A number of Muslim groups hurriedly came together in an umbrella organization, the Muslim United Front. This organization, in turn, mobilized the urban youth, and its popularity grew. Elections and the aftermath turned out to be bitter. Mobilized and angry youth were confronted by security forces. Many were roughed up. Further alienated, some went across the border to Pakistan to be trained as militants and returned with Kalashnikovs. The National Front–Congress Party alliance won the election, but charges that it had rigged the elections were widespread. Whatever the reality, Kashmir was engulfed by a serious legitimacy crisis.

Meanwhile, the Soviet Union intervened in Afghanistan, the United States rearmed Pakistan, and Pakistani rulers regained a sense of confidence vis-à-vis India that they had lost during the 1971 war over Bangladesh. There is ample evidence to indicate that Pakistan trained alienated Muslim youths from Kashmir, providing them with arms and resources; and even when the Pakistani government was not directly involved, India's hostile neighbor became both a staging ground and a

---

14. See, for example, the essays by George Fernandez (a well-known Indian political leader who directly participated in Kashmiri affairs) and Riyaz Punjabi (a Kashmiri professor who lived through these events) in Raju Thomas, ed., *Perspectives on Kashmir: The Roots of Conflict in South Asia* (Boulder, Colo.: Westview Press, 1992).

sanctuary for Kashmiri militants. The number of Kashmiris trained in Pakistan by 1990 was estimated to be in the several thousands.[15]

Following the 1987 elections, Kashmiri Muslims, especially those in the valley (Muslims in Jammu tend to be ethnically distinct), confronted governments in Kashmir and in New Delhi simultaneously as hostile parties. Kashmiri militants and security forces increasingly met each other in growing cycles of militancy and repression. Human rights abuses occurred, and stories of such abuses must have further alienated the Muslim population. When elections were called again in 1989, militant groups boycotted them quite successfully. The more the democratic political process lost its meaning, the more a full-scale insurgency came to be unleashed.

Factionalism among Islamic militants has also increasingly come to the fore. The Jammu and Kashmir Liberation Front (JKLF)—a nominally secular group that is nevertheless controlled by Muslim leaders—argues for a sovereign state of Kashmir, including part of the Kashmir controlled by Pakistan, and remains the most popular group. The Hizbul Mujahideen are modeled after the Mujahids in Afghanistan and argue for accession of Kashmir to Pakistan. Although less popular than the JKLF, the Mujahideen receive more support from Pakistan, and its hardened militants are better trained and better armed. The popular JKLF faces the enormous obstacle that neither India nor Pakistan supports the possibility of a sovereign state of Kashmir. By contrast, the militant Mujahideen, although a potent armed force, are politically not so popular. The more the Hindus have migrated out of the Kashmir valley, the more the struggle has become one of Kashmiri Muslims versus India. Most Kashmiri Muslims, however, want a sovereign state; they do not want to join Pakistan. Aside from the fact that neither India nor Pakistan favors such an outcome, Kashmiri Muslims face another major hurdle: there are more than 100 million Muslims in India, of which Kashmiri Muslims constitute only about 5 million.

Fearing their own welfare in India if a Kashmiri Muslim state were established by force (such a move would be bound to encourage anti-

---

15. George Fernandez in 1990 estimated this figure to be in the range of 3,000–5,000. Since in his former capacity as India's minister for internal affairs (Janata government, 1989), he had access to all of Indian and other intelligence services data and since this estimate was provided in a public lecture at Harvard University, one is inclined to give some credence to it. See Thomas, *Perspectives on Kashmir*, p. 289. Subsequently, even the U.S. State Department has corroborated Pakistan's role in training terrorists. See, for example, Judith Miller, "South Asia Called Major Terror Hub in a Survey by US," *New York Times,* April 30, 2000, p. A1.

Muslim sentiments), Indian Muslims have generally refrained from openly supporting the cause of Kashmiri Muslims. The overall situation is thus a near stalemate: most Kashmiri Muslims are by now deeply alienated from India, and although divided among themselves, a majority would probably opt for a sovereign state of Kashmir. Not only will the powerful Indian state not let go of the Kashmiri Muslims, even Pakistan does not support such an outcome. Pakistani-trained militants, however, with arms left over from the Afghanistan civil war, remain a powerful militant force but one that Indian security forces have successfully fought to a standstill. The state-level elections of 1996 brought Farooq Abdullah back to power, and he continues to rule a fairly turbulent region.

Leaving the details of the tragic story aside, what are its analytical implications? It is clear that the roots of the militancy-repression cycle in Kashmir can be traced back to a power conflict in which a centralizing Indira Gandhi dislodged the elected government of Farooq Abdullah, precipitating a long-term legitimacy crisis. Had political institutions such as parties within Kashmir or the Indian federal system been stronger, the centralizing policies of one leader would have been not only difficult to pursue but easier to weather if pursued. The combination, however, of weakening institutions and an unaccommodating national leader helped push normal power struggles down the path of a militancy and repression cycle. The early trajectory of the Kashmir conflict thus broadly fits the analytical scheme developed earlier. That the conflict in Kashmir continues clearly defies the predicted journey (given certain conditions) of ethnic conflicts along an inverse U curve. Since India's democratic institutions, in spite of some weakening, remain relatively strong and since the leadership of Rao and of his successors—at least until the rise of the BJP—was more flexible than that of Indira Gandhi, how does one explain the persistence of a high-intensity ethnic conflict in Kashmir?

Three different answers (or three components of one answer) are possible to this question, each with different implications for the analytical argument proposed in this chapter. The first answer, and the one least compatible with the thesis of this chapter, focuses on the distinct values and discourse of Islam: it is possible that a political identity based on Islam is felt both more intensely and more comprehensively, and thus an Islam-based ethnic movement ought not to be expected to follow the same trajectory as followed by Tamil or Sikh nationalist movements. Such an argument, however, would have the burden of explaining why Muslim nationalism flared up mainly in Kashmir (and not in other parts of India) and why mainly in the 1990s.

The second answer focuses on the role of Pakistan in the Kashmir crisis. Unlike in Tamil Nadu and even more than in the Punjab, the

argument goes, Pakistan's continuing involvement in Kashmir has prolonged the conflict. Although I have not emphasized this explanation,
such an argument is compatible with the thesis of this chapter insofar as
the logic of the argument developed here is essentially political: ethnic
movements in developing-country democracies constitute a political
process whereby the central state and mobilized groups discover their
relative power balances. Intervention by an external actor, then, alters
the power-balancing process, at least prolonging, if not altering, the
overall trajectory.

Finally, the simple answer that is most readily compatible with this
chapter's thesis is that it is still too early to predict how the Kashmir
crisis will end. If Pakistan's role diminishes (a role that at the time of
writing seems to be actually increasing) and if the BJP government
maintains a firm but flexible set of policies, the ethnic conflict in
Kashmir may well decline over the next few years. However, if the BJP
government attempts to curtail the autonomy of Kashmir, moving further in the direction of centralization, the regional conflict may well be
exacerbated.

Conclusion

The argument of this chapter ought not to be taken too literally. It merely suggests that in an established multicultural democracy of the developing world, ethnic conflicts will come and go. Well, of course! The
real message of the chapter is thus not so much its literal interpretation
but rather some of the implications that flow from it. In conclusion,
therefore, I wish to spell out a few of these implications.

The first set of implications concerns analytical issues. Case studies
from within India suggest that ethnic conflicts are best thought of as
power conflicts. Ethnic conflicts are thus a subset of the larger set of
political conflicts that include conflicts along class, caste, or party lines
and that dot the political landscape of developing-country democracies.
Although one can readily emphasize the distinctiveness of ethnic as
opposed to other types of political conflicts, mobilized ethnic groups,
like other mobilized groups, seek greater power and control either as
ends in themselves or as the means to secure a society's other valued
resources. Such a perspective, in turn, also suggests what ethnic conflicts are not: They are not inevitable expressions of deep-rooted differences; they are not anomic responses to the disequilibrium generated by
modernization. Although ethnic identities can indeed be constructed
and manipulated, the process of identity formation and ethnic conflict is
also not so indeterminate as to defy a causal, generalizing analysis.

If ethnic conflicts are mainly power conflicts, how power is organized in state and society becomes important for understanding their patterns. I have suggested that in developing-country democracies, when state authority is well institutionalized and when national leaders act in a firm but accommodating manner, ethnic conflicts typically follow the shape of an inverse U curve. Both national leaders and leaders of ethnic movements may be quite calculating, and thus their strategies and counterstrategies may be amenable to a bargaining type of rationalist analysis. The shifts in values and discourses of the broader membership of an ethnic group that inevitably emerge during ethnic mobilization are, in turn, best understood from a close, anthropological type of research. As microapproaches, however, neither rational choice nor an anthropological approach readily aggregates into a macrogeneralization.[16] Generalizations about the conditions that help explain the rise and decline of ethnic movements, therefore, are best derived from a direct macrofocus on state and societal conditions. The emphasis on the degree of institutionalization of state authority in society and a focus on leadership hold up quite well against the Indian example. If persuasive, or at least suggestive, such an approach and hypothesis may be worth examining in cases other than India.

A second set of implications concerns normative and policy issues. To the extent that ethnic conflicts are power conflicts, it is often difficult to choose true heroes and villains. It is difficult on an a priori basis to determine whether established states are more right or wrong than are ethnic groups making demands. A lot depends on the situation. As a scholar, I believe it is important both to eschew the conservative bias that states necessarily act to preserve the public good and to resist the conclusion that all comers seeking self-determination have justice on their side. What is clearer is that leaders, especially national leaders but also leaders of ethnic movements, who persistently choose to be unaccommodating will channel normal power conflicts down a destructive path, a path where calculating leaders are replaced by true believers who utilize militant tactics as the cause becomes worth dying for. The true villains of ethnic conflicts are thus those leaders who refuse to see that the failure of timely compromise can only produce and exacerbate political problems, including their own downfall.

Finally, I turn to the question posed in the title of the chapter, name-

---

16. For a quick review of theoretical debates in the study of and for further references to the literature on politics of ethnicity, see Crawford Young, *The Rising Tide of Cultural Pluralism: The Nation-State at Bay?* (Madison: University of Wisconsin Press, 1993), pp. 21–25.

ly, Can democracies, especially developing-country democracies, accommodate ethnic nationalism? The Indian case suggests that the answer has to be a qualified yes.[17] It is ironic that the immediate effect of democracy and democratization in a developing-country setting is the encouragement of ethnic demands. A well-institutionalized state can put some limits on how far these demands may go. Of course, if the state itself is not well institutionalized, democracy and multiethnic competition spell great political problems—problems that constitute a set of cases not discussed here. Given an institutionalized state, however, if some of these demands are not accommodated, the sense of exclusion and injustice may well turn demanding groups toward militancy. That is why democratic leaders with inclusionary, accommodating ruling strategies fare better at dealing with ethnic conflicts. In sum, democracy in a developing country both encourages ethnic conflict and, under specific circumstances, provides a framework for dealing with them.

---

17. An important book that, after a great deal of valuable empirical work, reaches a conclusion that—though not identical—is broadly consistent with this conclusion is Donald L. Horowitz, *Ethnic Groups in Conflict* (Berkeley: University of California Press, 1985).

12

Self-Administration and Local Autonomy: Reconciling Conflicting Interests in China

MINXIN PEI

The twentieth century has been particularly unkind to multinational empires. World wars, nationalism, and democratic revolutions have toppled many. All but one of the multinational empires have gone the way of the fallen Humpty-Dumpty. The exception is China, which has survived the spectacular collapses of the Ottoman Empire, the Austro-Hungarian Empire and, recently, the former Soviet Union. To be sure, following the collapse of the Manchu dynasty in 1911, China disintegrated in all but name. It was ravaged internally by warlordism and communist insurgency. Externally, European and Japanese imperialism almost succeeded in partitioning China. After half a century of uninterrupted political turmoil and bloodshed, however, the fallen Humpty-Dumpty was miraculously restored by the victory of the communist revolution in 1949, despite the losses of huge tracts of territory during the twilight years of the Manchus.

Given the frailties of multinational empires, it is all the more remarkable that the People's Republic of China (PRC) has since managed to weather several horrendous domestic political crises and emerge relatively unscathed from both the Cold War and the collapse of communism. Today, for all its internal difficulties, China holds together fifty-six ethnic groups spread over a continent-sized country. The relative longevity of the Chinese multinational empire is no accident of history. Several unique demographic and geographic features set it apart from its less enduring historical counterparts and help to explain its durability.

First and foremost, there is the overwhelming majority of Han Chinese, who, as of the 1990 census, account for 92 percent of the

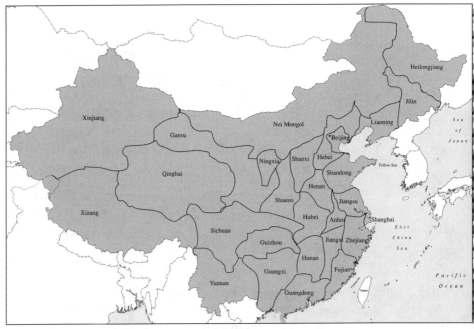

China

country's population.[1] This fact implies an unlimited capacity for Chinese migration, whether driven by government policy or economic forces, from the center to the periphery. In fact, since the founding of the PRC in 1949, several waves of Chinese migration have significantly altered the demographic structures of strategically important areas such as Inner Mongolia and Xinjiang. The demographic dominance of Han Chinese is the key to the maintenance of the empire: an implosion of the empire is almost inconceivable without a prior implosion of its Han Chinese core. And this is what has occurred in Chinese history: the fate of this multiethnic empire has been interwoven with the well-being of the central Chinese state. It is the decay within the center that has unleashed forces of disintegration on the periphery, and not the other way around.

Second, although numerically weak, China's fifty-five ethnic minorities populate many of the strategic areas vital to Chinese security as well as vast stretches of resource-rich land amounting to 64 percent

1. *Zhongguo minzu tongji 1992* (Beijing: Chinese Statistics, 1993), p. 53.
2. This official figure is based on the size of the territory covered by autonomous regions, prefects, and counties inhabited by ethnic minorities. *Zhongguo minzu tongji 1992*, p. 10.

of Chinese territory.[2] Government statistics show that mostly minority-inhabited areas contain rich mineral deposits; they also hold 56 percent of China's timber resources, 68 percent of the country's usable grassland, and 52 percent of its water resources suitable for hydropower generation.[3] Yet similar to other areas in the resource-rich third world, the minority regions of China remain at extremely low levels of economic development and lack the market institutions capable of mobilizing resources for rapid and sustained growth. Poor physical infrastructure in these areas makes communication within and among these groups extremely difficult and thus impedes coalition building against the dominant Han Chinese. Moreover, the complete absence of modern political institutions means that the traditional elites of these minority groups have little institutional capacity for effectively organizing mass support to counter the pressures from the core of the empire.

Finally, there is great diversity—in terms of size, economic development levels, production methods, social systems, and cultures—both among China's ethnic minorities and between these minorities and the Han Chinese. Of the fifty-five officially designated ethnic minorities, eighteen number over 1 million; fifteen have populations of between 1 million and 100,000; fifteen have populations of between 100,000 and 10,000; and seven number less than 10,000.[4] When the PRC was founded, about 30 million members of ethnic minorities lived under economic and social conditions (subsistence agrarian societies) similar to those of Han Chinese. Four million (including the Tibetans) were living under what Marxists termed the feudalist system of agrarian serfdom; 1 million lived in communities that maintained tribal serfdom.[5] This situation has essentially remained the same fifty years after the founding of the PRC. The overwhelming demographic dominance of the Han Chinese has hardly changed. It is this structural feature that has successfully counterbalanced centrifugal tendencies of diverse societies and maintained the territorial unity of the Chinese nation.

The enormous economic, cultural, and social differences between the Han Chinese majority and the other ethnic groups in China create two harsh political realities. First, direct and confrontational efforts by the ethnic minorities to achieve self-determination are likely to be costly and unsuccessful given the near certainty of repression and crackdown by the center. Second, the complexities of ethnic problems similarly compel the Chinese government to adopt a flexible system of rule

---

3. Ibid.
4. Liu Xianzhao, *Zhongguo minzu wenti yanjiu* (Beijing: Chinese Academy of Social Sciences, 1993), p. 220.
5. Ibid., pp. 222–223.

that can maintain the territorial integrity of the empire, exert the political authority of the center, and accommodate the economic and political demands of the minorities—especially those with large populations, high levels of concentration, distinct cultural values, and enduring social and political organizations. Beijing's draconian rule in non-Han Chinese areas is sure to be met with strong local resistance. The Chinese regime sees a system of limited autonomy as a realistic solution to the problems created by these two realities.

The institutional form of limited autonomy in China is the so-called regional autonomous government by minority nationalities, or *minzu zizhi*.[6] Although this system fails to grant minority nationalities full political autonomy or self-administration (let alone the rights to self-determination), it allows a slightly higher degree of decentralization of power to minority-inhabited areas than to Han Chinese–inhabited areas. In this chapter I first describe and analyze the extant institutional structure and the limitations of the regional self-administration system for China's ethnic minorities. I then analyze the evolution of this system since the founding of the PRC and the political and economic realism that has dominated China's policy toward the ethnic minorities. Finally, I propose a practical strategy for improving minority rights within the existing institutional framework of regional self-administration in China.

The Institutional Form of Self-Administration

As a concept, regional self-administration for China's ethnic minorities was introduced before the PRC's founding. In fact, when the Chinese Communist Party (CCP) was a fledgling underground organization in the 1920s, its radical charter even endorsed political federalism and advocated national self-determination for Tibet, Xinjiang, Mongolia, and Qinghai. This position remained virtually unchanged until the late 1940s, when the CCP became more confident about its impending military victory in China's civil war. As a functioning political institution, the system of limited self-administration by ethnic minorities was formally established in 1952 with the promulgation of "The People's Republic of China's Program of Implementation of Regional Self-administration by Minority Nationalities." The document stressed the principle of limited autonomy for ethnic minorities under the sovereign

---

6. For a discussion of the inadequacy of the system, see Thomas Herberer, *China and Its National Minorities: Autonomy or Assimilation?* (Armonk, N.Y.: M. E. Sharpe, 1989).

political authority of the PRC central government. It permitted the formation of local governments in minority areas that were given the de jure power of self-administration. Four provincial-level autonomous regions (Inner Mongolia, Guangxi, Ningxia, and Xinjiang) were formed under this law, and by the end of 1958, twenty-nine autonomous *zhou* (prefects) and fifty-four autonomous counties were established.

Aside from articulating a simple form of limited self-administration, the document accomplished very little. China's Leninist political system in reality allowed almost no genuine local autonomy. As Mao Zedong's regime began pursuing a radical version of socialism in the late 1950s, Beijing's policy toward the ethnic minorities grew less tolerant and local self-administration became nothing but an empty phrase. During the two decades of political radicalism in China (1957–1976), instead of emphasizing economic development and ethnic harmony in the economically backward areas inhabited by minorities, Mao's government advocated class struggle, imposed agrarian radicalism, and harshly repressed local ethnonationalism. A large number of ethnic minority leaders were persecuted, the cultural and religious heritages of the non-Han Chinese were devastated, and economic development was reversed.[7]

The end of the Cultural Revolution returned political moderation and pragmatism to Beijing. As a form of soft authoritarianism began to take shape at the center, China's minority policy became less intolerant. Gradual political relaxation also emboldened many minority groups to openly reclaim their identities. For example, in the 1982 census, only 67 million people identified themselves as members of ethnic minorities, whereas in the 1990 census, 91 million people did, most of them simply reclaiming their ethnic identities.[8] The most significant step taken by the government toward institutionalizing self-administration by minority groups was the revision of the 1952 document on self-administration and the issuance of the Law on Regional Autonomy for Minority Nationalities in May 1984 by the National People's Congress (NPC).[9] In a strict sense, genuine limited self-administration for ethnic

---

7. For a historical review of China's policy toward its ethnic minorities, see Colin Mackerras, *China's Minorities: Integration and Modernization in the Twentieth Century* (New York: Oxford University Press, 1994); June Teufel Dreyer, *China's Forty Millions: Minority Nationalities and National Integration in the People's Republic of China* (Cambridge: Harvard University Press, 1976), pp. 261–276; and Ya Hanzhang, "On Ethnic Relations in the Socialist Era," *Social Sciences in China,* no. 1 (1983), pp. 129–142.

8. Guo Dalie, *Lun dangdai zhongguo de minzu wenti* (On the nationality problem in contemporary China) (Beijing: Minzu, 1994), p. 91.

9. For a complete text of the law, see *Xinghua yuebao,* no. 5 (1984), pp. 33–37.

minorities was practiced in China only after the promulgation of the 1984 law.

Compared with the 1952 document, the 1984 law was more specific and liberal. Although reiterating the sovereign rule of the central government and the territorial integrity of China, the 1984 law formally grants a set of broad powers to the three levels of self-administrative governments (region, prefect, and county). The most important rights of self-administration specified in the law (Part 3) include the following:

1. Limited legislative power (Article 19): Although nominal legislative power is granted to autonomous regions, effective legislative power is held by the central government; laws passed by the legislatures of autonomous regions must also be approved by the Standing Committee of the NPC. Subregional legislatures, however, enjoy a greater degree of power under the 1984 law, as they are authorized to pass legislation subject to approval by the standing committees of the regional people's congress, not by the central government. This legal ambiguity is a potentially valuable vehicle to expand minority self-administration in subregional jurisdictions.

2. Limited power of appeal (Article 20): Self-administering governments at all levels may request a modification and suspension of central government policies that are unsuitable to local conditions.

3. Power of appointment (Articles 16 and 17): The chair or vice-chair of the standing committee of the people's congress of the self-administering jurisdiction must be a member of the local minority that administers the area. The same must be true for the governors of the autonomous regions and magistrates of the self-administering prefects and counties. Of course, since the CCP secretaries in these jurisdictions—usually Han Chinese appointed by the Central Committee of the CCP—control final decisions, these provisions amount to a very limited devolution of power from central Beijing.

4. Local fiscal power (Articles 33–35): Self-administering governments enjoy a greater degree of economic, rather than political, decisionmaking power. They have full control over most taxes and their use and may retain the surpluses according to a fixed formula negotiated between the local governments and the center.

Administratively, the Chinese system of limited ethnic autonomy consists of three levels of government:

1. Five autonomous regions (Inner Mongolia, Tibet, Guangxi, Xinjiang, and Ningxia) with their respective large minority groups (Mongolians, Tibetans, Zhuangs, Uighurs, and Huis).
2. Thirty autonomous prefects. Twenty prefects each feature one dominant local minority; the remaining ten each have two equally dominant minority groups.

3. One hundred twenty-four autonomous counties. These administrative units are designed to provide local autonomy to smaller ethnic minorities concentrated in localities surrounded by other larger minority groups.

This three-level structure of limited local autonomy represents an elaborate attempt to accommodate the demands of China's ethnic minorities within the country's constitutional framework. Its underlying logic is that the central government is willing to make provisions for limited decisionmaking power to ethnic minorities in exchange for minority groups' recognition of Beijing's sovereignty. The three-level model ensures that the largest non-Han Chinese minority groups (the Zhuangs, Huis, Mongolians, Uighurs, and Tibetans) receive a higher degree of autonomy than smaller minorities.

But to most foreign observers and minority ethnonationalist leaders in China, this system of limited self-administration is nothing but a facade—an institution designed to maintain Beijing's control in these outlying areas. However, in evaluating this framework of limited self-administration, two central facts about ethnic politics in China must not be ignored. First, as long as the core of the multiethnic Chinese empire remains under highly centralized political control from Beijing, there is little realistic chance for political decentralization or genuine self-administration to materialize in the minority-inhabited periphery. Second, as long as China's political system remains undemocratic, genuine self-administration by ethnic minorities that meets their nationalist aspirations is unlikely.

These two institutional impediments to genuine self-administration—centralized administration and authoritarian rule—are not immutable. Both are subject to gradualist changes caused by market forces as well as to incremental and endogenous institutional changes within the regime. Indeed, significant devolution of *economic* decisionmaking power following China's market-oriented reforms has already created a more decentralized *political* system with provinces enjoying greater real autonomy than prior to the introduction of the reforms. The consolidation of economic reforms and the rise of a new generation of pragmatic leaders at all levels of government in China similarly bode well for the slow and gradual evolution of a political system that will allow for greater popular participation and autonomy for minority groups. In the long run, this indirect route to self-administration—relying on market forces and the gradual evolution of Chinese political institutions—may be a less costly means to satisfy the nationalist yearnings of China's minorities.

An additional point to be made for the 1984 law on regional autonomy is that political institutions, once established and operational, usually take on a life of their own. They produce results that may not be anticipated by their original designers. The most dramatic effect of the 1984 law has been the steady increase in the number of minority officials recruited into the various levels of the PRC government bureaucracy, as well as in the number of delegates to China's representative bodies (such as the People's Congress). As Table 12.1 shows, ethnic minority representation in both the government and the Chinese Communist Party has increased dramatically.

The CCP has also striven to increase minority representation among the ordinary rank and file of the party; such representation did in fact increase by 460 percent between 1957 and 1989.[10] Although these increases in minority representation in Chinese government bodies and the CCP have not yet created a breakthrough in its policy toward the ethnic minorities, they are nevertheless important developments with long-term political consequences in advancing the political agenda of these minority groups.

Table 12.1   Increased Minority Representation

Year	Number of government officials of minority origins
Representation in the Chinese Government Bureaucracy	
1958	400,000
1977	789,000
1988	1,840,000 (an increase of over 100% over the past decade and representing 6% of the total government)[a]
1993	2,100,000 (45,000 of whom held government positions above the level of county government, including the governors of the five autonomous regions and magistrates of 30 autonomous prefects and 127 autonomous counties)[b]

Year	Number of Minority Full and Candidate Members of the Central Committee[c]
Representation in the Chinese Communist Party (CCP)	
1976	16 of 333 members (5% of the total)
1987	32 of 285 members (11% of the total)

Notes: a. Zi Yan, "A Historical Review of The Training and Employment of Cadres of Minority Ethnic Origins in China," *Shehui kexuejia,* no. 1 (1990), pp. 56–59.
    b. *Zijing Magazine* (Hong Kong), July 1993, p. 29.
    c. *Minzu zhishi shouche (*Handbook on ethnic minorities) (Beijing: People's Publishing, 1985), p. 826.

---

10. *Minzu gongzhuo tongji tiyao, 1949–1989* (Summary of work on ethnic minority issues) (Beijing: Minzu, 1990), p. 28.

The Political Economy
of Limited Self-Administration

The central objective of China's policy of limited self-administration for its ethnic minorities is the preservation of the country's territorial integrity and Beijing's sovereignty over the periphery. In fulfilling this strategic goal, the center has relied on three instruments: direct political control (chiefly through appointments of key regional and local officials, usually Han Chinese), recruitment of political elites from minority groups, and indirect economic control (through direct fiscal subsidies and economic integration).[11] The latter method of control over minority areas is facilitated by the historical economic backwardness of these areas. As the following statistics show, the level of economic development in minority areas is lower than that in the Han Chinese areas, and as a result the minority areas remain marginalized:

- Whereas 7.1 percent (80 million people) of the total population in China was living below the official poverty level in the early 1990s, 20 percent (18 million people) of China's minorities were living below the poverty level, and 10 million of them did not have access to safe housing and drinking water.[12]
- Minority areas have also lagged behind significantly in growth rates. Between 1950 and 1988, the value of China's gross industrial and agricultural output rose 3,910 percent; in minority areas the increase was only 1,950 percent, less than half the national rate.[13]
- The minority areas are predominantly agrarian. In 1991, the primary sector (agriculture) accounted for 40.7 percent of the GNP of minority areas (compared with 26.6 percent for China as a whole); industry contributed only 32.7 percent of the GNP (compared with 46.1 percent for China).[14]
- Personal income for minorities is also significantly behind. In 1989, net per capita peasant income in the five autonomous

---

11. For an overview of the economic development of China's minority areas, see Mackerras, *China's Minorities,* pp. 198–232.

12. Liu Xianzhao, *Zongguo minzu wenti yanji* (A study of the ethnic minority problem in China) (Beijing: Chinese Academy of Social Sciences, 1993), p. 298.

13. Ibid.

14. *Zhongguo minzu tongji 1992,* p. 14.

regions averaged only 484.6 yuan compared to the national average of 601.5 yuan—24 percent less.[15]

Such discrepancies persist despite large subsidies and investments provided to these areas by the central government. Between 1950 and 1988, the government invested 160 billion yuan in the state-owned enterprises in minority areas (82 billion yuan between 1979 and 1988).[16] In addition, the central government has provided large sums in direct budgetary subsidies to local governments in minority areas. Between 1978 and 1991, transfers from the central government to cover budget shortfalls in minority areas amounted to a staggering 123.7 billion yuan. In 1991 alone, the amount of direct fiscal subsidies was 14.28 billion yuan, about 4 percent of the central government's budget (but 25 percent of the central government's budget deficit).[17] Such massive transfers are necessitated by the dismal fiscal conditions in minority areas, where government revenues since the mid-1970s have covered only half of expenditures (although their fiscal picture brightened in the early 1990s, when revenues were about 85 percent of government expenditures).[18] Fiscal imbalances of this magnitude raise questions both about Beijing's long-term capacity to provide large budget subsidies to these areas and about these areas' fiscal well-being should the subsidies from the center be reduced or eliminated.

From a different perspective, one may treat Beijing's billions of yuan in fiscal subsidies to minority regions as a disguised form of payment for the abundant raw materials produced in these areas and transported to the industrialized core of the empire for processing at below-world-market prices. Although there are no official data on the total value of raw materials transferred from minority areas, the government statistics show that areas under minority self-administration are crucial sources of production of some commodities, especially livestock and timber (see Table 12.2).

An important question here is whether the center's massive investment in the state-owned enterprises in and fiscal transfers to minority areas have been used efficiently in developing a production base capable of generating wealth for the minorities. It is first important to recog-

---

15. Long Yunshu et al., "Minzu diqu nongchun chanye jiegou tiaozheng wenti xianxi" (A preliminary analysis of the adjustment of the economic structure in the rural areas in ethnic minority regions), *Xinan minzu xueyuan xuebao,* no. 5 (1991), p. 22.

16. Liu, *Zongguo minzu wenti yanji,* p. 226.

17. *Zhongguo minzu tongji 1992,* p. 205.

18. Ibid.

Table 12.2   Key Commodities Produced in Areas with High Concentrations of Ethnic Minorities (1991)

Commodities	Share of National Production (%)
Sheep	54.7
Timber	31.1
Cooking oil	14.0
Grain	12.7
Cotton	11.5
Coal	11.2

Source: Zhongguo minzu tongii 1992 (Beijing: Chinese Statistics, 1993), p. 13.

nize that the initial conditions for industrial development in these areas were so poor that the requirements for capital and other resource inputs were bound to be very large and the progress of development was most likely to be extremely slow. However, the main point to be made here is that China's investment and fiscal policies toward minority areas were driven primarily by political and strategic, not economic, concerns. Although the process of channeling resources from the center to the periphery was predictably successful at maintaining a system of limited autonomy that ensured central control, the policy was not economically efficient in the sense that the same resources could most probably have produced higher returns in other areas (such as the coast). In the case of industrialization, the central government's attempt to develop these areas through state-owned enterprises has been a total failure—in economic terms.

Official figures show that a very large proportion of state-owned enterprises in minority areas are unprofitable. In 1991, 2,993 of the 11,311 state-owned firms (26.4 percent) were loss-takers, going into the red for a total of 3.5 billion yuan that year.[19] Compared with counterparts in the Han Chinese–dominated areas, state-owned firms in minority areas are also much less productive. The average productivity for a full-time employee in state-owned firms in China was 32,304 yuan in 1991; the figure for a worker in a state-owned firm in minority areas was 25,761 yuan (about 20 percent less).[20] And owing to China's past misdirected investment policy that favored state-owned firms, the poorly performing state sector dominates the industrial sector in minority

19. Ibid., p. 132.
20. Sampling comes from state firms located in eight minority-dominated regions (Inner Mongolia, Guangxi, Tibet, Ningxia, Xinjiang, Guizhou, Yunnan, and Qinghai); Zhongguo minzu tongji 1992, p. 148.

areas. In 1991, state-owned enterprises contributed to 78.5 percent of the gross value of industrial output in minority areas (compared with 63.6 percent for the whole of China).[21] The persistent dominance by the inefficient state sector, coupled with the slow development of the private sector in minority areas, means that a structural transformation of the productive base will require a great length of time and a fundamental shift in the central government's investment strategy from favoring the state sector to supporting the private sector.

Finally, the economic structural transformation of China's minority areas is unlikely to benefit from the boom in foreign direct investment that has contributed significantly to the country's economic takeoff since the late 1970s. Of the tens of billions of dollars in foreign direct investment that China has received since the late 1970s, only a small amount has trickled into the minority areas. In 1991, total foreign direct investment actually disbursed in China came to $4.3 billion; the five autonomous regions received only $26.8 million, or 0.6 percent, of this.[22]

This analysis of the economic conditions in minority areas indicates that genuine self-administration in China faces not only serious political opposition from the central government, which is determined to maintain the country's territorial integrity and political sovereignty over these areas at all costs, but enormous economic structural obstacles as well. Shortages of managerial talent, the lack of a skilled labor force, a scarcity of capital, the state domination of the economy, low productivity, underdeveloped market institutions, and a poor infrastructure raise deep doubts about the economic prospects and viability of self-administered communities in those areas that are denied the benefits of trade and investment. Despite large central government fiscal support and capital investment, these areas remain the most backward in China, and there remains no convincing evidence that increasing the degree of self-administration will speed their economic development. In the near term, the economic well-being of these areas is most likely to be raised by the further expansion of market-oriented reforms emanating from the industrialized core of China. However, this market-oriented approach would, paradoxically, fuel resentment among ethnic minorities because they will interpret any reduction in direct support from the central government as evidence of neglect.

---

21. This figure applies only to firms at and above the township level. Ibid., p. 122.

22. Ibid., p. 199.

A Strategy for Expanded Self-Administration

China's three-pronged strategy for dealing with its ethnic minorities proved quite effective in maintaining the dominance of the Han Chinese majority, although the costs were extremely high (political repression of minorities, violations of human rights, destruction of minority cultures, and inefficient uses of economic resources). In the mid-1990s, this strategy became infeasible.

First, massive migration by Han Chinese to the outlying minority areas is no longer a viable option because of rising local resistance and overcrowding in places where arable land is already scarce. In some cases (such as Tibet), the policy continues to arouse international condemnation and pressure, which China, itself increasingly integrated into the world political and economic community, can no longer ignore as it did during the years of Maoist rule.[23] Furthermore, the Chinese government no longer has the same coercive power to force Han Chinese to emigrate to remote minority areas on a large scale.

Second, the economic interdependence between China's core and periphery, built on the planned-economy model, has also unraveled as a result of the market-oriented reforms that have continued since 1978. With the decentralization of public finance, the central government's capacity to sustain large transfers of financial aid to minority regions has declined significantly. This fiscal constraint will limit its available policy options in maintaining political dominance in these areas. Rising market-oriented economic interdependence between the core and the periphery will diminish the center's capacity to use administrative means to control the economic development of the regions.

Third, selective repression of open secessionist movements remains the only available option to the central government in the short term. But this approach is also becoming more costly: the minority groups demanding self-determination (Tibetans and Muslim groups in central Asia) not only have access to external moral and material support but may soon turn to more violent means in achieving their goals.

These factors require a new strategy to achieve a delicate balance

---

23. Economic development programs in minority areas have also become politically controversial. The most well publicized case was a World Bank–financed antipoverty program designed to move several thousand impoverished peasants (including Han Chinese) into parts of Qinghai Province, which Tibetans consider their traditional land. In 1999, well-organized campaigns in the West that supported the Tibetan cause greatly embarrassed the World Bank, although it did not cancel the loan program.

between maintaining China's territorial integrity and promoting genuine local autonomy. Although international forces may play a positive role in realizing this goal, political factors internal to China will remain paramount in promoting a peaceful evolution toward genuine self-determination for China's 75 million members of ethnic minority groups living in officially designated autonomous regions. Future progress in this direction should rely not on a change of individual leaders in Beijing but on the construction of more permanent institutional foundations that can ensure minority rights and political representation, as well as the development of economic federalism.

All these factors suggest that although expansion of self-administration by ethnic minorities in China at the county and prefect levels could be accomplished, drives for complete self-administration are infeasible. They would most likely lead to violent ethnic conflicts and bloody repression from the center. Truly democratic self-administration by minorities can become a political reality only with the emergence of a decentralized political system in the distant future.

It is well known that the Chinese government is extremely sensitive to demands for regional (that is, provincial) autonomy regardless of the region's ethnicity. In addition, since the Han Chinese demographically dominate all but two regions (Xinjiang and Tibet), a strategy toward achieving self-administration at the regional level is unlikely to work for most minority groups. A less ambitious but more practical alternative is to strive toward self-administration at the prefect and county levels, where minority groups are demographically predominant. As of 1990, minority groups made up an absolute majority in 20 of 30 autonomous prefects and in 78 of the 124 autonomous counties.[24] These 98 minority-dominated jurisdictions may have more favorable conditions for the expansion of self-administration, as the numerical advantage of the minorities would be felt in the relatively open local elections. Recent, albeit limited, progress in holding semi-free village elections in most parts of China has the potential of empowering members of ethnic minorities, at least at the grassroots level.

In addition to requiring political reforms, self-administration in China cannot be genuine or viable without a functioning form of economic federalism. Given the economic underdevelopment of most minority areas, it is vital that the institutions of economic federalism be

---

24. Calculated from data in Jiang Ping, ed., *Theories and Practice of China's Ethnic Problems* (Beijing: Chinese Communist Party Central Committee Institute, 1994), pp. 500–516.

constructed, especially those that maintain open markets and trade with the other regions of China (fully utilizing the local comparative advantage) and promote a system of local public finance. Of course, this is easier said than done, and in the short to medium term, minority areas will most likely continue to depend on economic transfers from the center, for which they may have to pay a high political price.

Self-administration by minority groups in China can thus be a workable compromise between complete independence and separate nationhood and the status quo. Political moderation, concessions, and cooperation are required from both Beijing and the various minorities yearning for political and economic autonomy. Barring a political implosion at the center similar to the collapse of the former Soviet Union, it is unrealistic to seek a quick breakthrough to independence at the regional level. Any such attempts are sure to cause massive violence and derail the evolutionary process toward self-administration at the subregional levels of government. The alternative path, despite its slow pace and uneven progress across regions, should not be dismissed as too conservative. Durable but slow evolutionary progress is here preferable to disruptive revolutionary changes.

The Positive Example of Hong Kong

For all the criticism China has received for mishandling ethnic issues and suppressing the legitimate demands for self-rule by its minority groups, the prospects of self-administration are ironically brighter in China than in many other states. The autonomy solution may in fact show the greatest promise in solving the PRC's three most difficult political problems: the resumption of Chinese sovereignty over Hong Kong, the ongoing Tibetan problem, and the dispute over the final status of Taiwan.

Under the formula of one country, two systems, Hong Kong is the only example of self-administration in China. Devised by the late Deng Xiaoping in the early 1980s to ensure Hong Kong's smooth transition from colonial to Chinese sovereignty, the formula pledges a high degree of autonomy for Hong Kong and a Hong Kong ruled by the people of Hong Kong. The formal transition occurred without incident on July 1, 1997, despite overwhelmingly negative coverage of the transition by Western media and dark predictions about the imminent death of Hong Kong as a vibrant international city. As of this writing, Beijing appears to have refrained from interfering directly in the affairs of Hong Kong (even though the government of this special administrative region has taken several controversial initiatives that were viewed as infringements on the rule of law, individual rights, and press freedom).[25] The Hong Kong media have not toned down their criticisms of China, and democratic activists continue to demonstrate against Chinese leaders and their policies. When the Hong Kong stock market crashed and the Hong Kong dollar was under speculative attack in late 1997, Beijing expressed full confidence in the local authorities' ability to deal with the crisis and avoided acts or gestures that would have further undermined investor confidence.

It is probable that Beijing's hands-off policy toward Hong Kong is only temporary, to be changed abruptly as a result of internal Chinese politics in the future. Such caution about the durability of autonomy and self-administration, however, should not prevent us from seriously examining the political and economic institutions of self-administration established in Hong Kong under the Basic Law, as they may offer useful clues to developing other self-administration frameworks.[26]

There are three pillars of the self-administration arrangement for Hong Kong: an autonomous economic system, a protected social system, and a semiautonomous political system. Hong Kong's economic autonomy is enshrined in three key institutions: (1) an independent monetary authority (Hong Kong's central bank) that makes monetary policy; (2) a separate fiscal system; and (3) a different regulatory and corporate governance system. Although the economies of China and Hong Kong have become closely integrated since the late 1970s, significant differences remain between the economic institutions in China and Hong Kong. Hong Kong's economic autonomy is institutionalized; the city has its own currency, tax system, and regulatory regimes. Even though Hong Kong is heavily dependent on China's markets and labor, its unique capitalist institutions have been preserved and remain distinct from China's semireformed state-socialist system. The viability of this system of self-administration depends on unpredictable political swings within China, but it is generally observed from the center that the setup poses little direct threat to one-party rule in the PRC and actually benefits both the Chinese economy and members of the ruling elite in Beijing.

A second key aspect of self-administration in Hong Kong is the physical insulation of the former British colony from the enormous population pressures in China. This is an important requirement for any

---

25. See Frank Ching, "Misreading Hong Kong," *Foreign Affairs* 76, no. 3 (May/June 1997), pp. 53–66.

26. For the complete text and several analyses of the Basic Law of Hong Kong, see Ming K. Chan and David J. Clark, eds., *The Hong Kong Basic Law* (Armonk, N.Y.: M. E. Sharpe, 1991).

viable self-administrative arrangement; for it to work, there must be a "country within a country." To ensure posttransition stability in Hong Kong, the Chinese government strengthened its border patrols and efforts to combat illegal immigration from the Chinese mainland. It even imposed a short-term ban on legitimate Chinese tour groups from visiting the city following the handover in July 1997.[27]

The third pillar of Hong Kong's autonomy, its political system, is the most vulnerable. The 1984 Joint Declaration between Great Britain and China was sufficiently vague on the issue of democratization that each side interpreted it differently. Ultimately, the two sides clashed over the pace of democratization in Hong Kong, a conflict that resulted in China's replacement of Hong Kong's directly elected Legislative Council with an appointed provisional legislature on July 1, 1997. Undoubtedly, this outcome represented a serious setback for both democracy and self-administration in Hong Kong; however, it is wrong to view it as evidence that political self-administration is infeasible there.

Three institutional arrangements in posttransition Hong Kong underpin its political self-administration. First, Hong Kong's legal system remains independent. The preservation of the rule of law will ensure local civil liberties and the enforcement of contracts. Second, although the restrictive electoral rules issued in late 1997 handicap the democratic opposition, they do contain provisions for competitive elections for the Legislative Council. The pro-democracy parties won 60 percent of the popular vote in the first posttransition elections in May 1998, giving them the full one-third of Legislative Council seats allowed by the electoral rules. On the Chinese mainland, there are no direct elections for public office (save for some of the village executive committees); thus Hong Kong is the most democratic region in China. Third, the chief executive of Hong Kong, who must be a native resident of the city, is subject to a degree of public scrutiny that is nonexistent in the rest of China. Although not directly elected by the public, he must gain enough support among the various local political groups to be nominated. His public and private behavior is closely watched and evaluated by the press.

Admittedly, it is premature to conclude that the current institutional arrangements of self-administration will endure in Hong Kong; they must be subject to a longer test period. The lack of democratic account-

---

27. As a result of this ban, the number of Chinese tourists fell dramatically, causing Hong Kong tourist industry representatives to complain to the Chinese government, which was persuaded to relax the ban.

ability of the Chinese government will be a constant hindrance to the durability, effectiveness, and stability of these arrangements. While remaining vigilant against Beijing's future encroachment on Hong Kong's autonomy, we should be prepared for the possibility that these arrangements will endure. They will gain political support—both in Hong Kong and in China—as the benefits of self-administration increase and become clear to all the interests involved.

The potential success of self-administration in Hong Kong will have far-reaching implications for the solution of the difficult problems posed by Tibet and Taiwan.[28] In the case of Tibet, complete independence seems impossible for the foreseeable future, as current Chinese policy will likely engender increasing Tibetan hostility and resistance. As for Taiwan, a formal declaration of independence by the island or a Chinese attempt at forceful reunification would be certain to spark a war across the Taiwan Strait that could even involve the United States. Self-administration seems the most desirable compromise in both cases.

As demonstrated by the ongoing experiment of self-administration in Hong Kong, the viability and success of this form of self-government depends on several important factors: (1) moderation of demands by both parties; (2) a recognition of the mutual benefits of self-administration; (3) consensus building within each party; and (4) external monitoring and support. For the moment, unfortunately, none of these conditions exist in either Tibet or Taiwan. The challenge for the leaders of China, Tibet, and Taiwan is thus to start thinking creatively about these issues and creating the necessary conducive conditions for self-administration.

---

28. See Melvyn Goldstein, *The Snow Lion and the Dragon* (Berkeley: University of California Press, 1997), pp. 100–131, for an excellent proposal for the principles of self-administration of Tibet.

Part 3

CONCLUSION

13

A Final Assessment

WOLFGANG DANSPECKGRUBER

Self-determination has had a diverse impact on the communities, states, and regions of the world—but at the beginning of the twenty-first century, the international system is changing, and so will the meaning and impact of self-determination. Its manyfold romantic as well as destructive and tumultuous capabilities and its power to create aspirations but also to cause upheaval, radicalize, and overcome rationality all demonstrate self-determination's ability to cause change. It alters borders, the shape and size of states; moves populations; and redistributes wealth—hence a state's power—and its relative position in the international system. But secession or self-determination—if sliding down the slippery slope to independence and sovereignty—can change entire regions and the situation on a continent. There is one fundamental issue: Bosnia, Somalia, Eritrea, Kosovo, Chechnya, and Kashmir have demonstrated that the single most important dimension is the effect on the individual human being—man, woman, and child, the family, the clan, the community. It is on them that the harsh reality of conflict, tension, expulsion, or death and destruction comes down. They are the ones who suffer from sanctions, blockades, or other grand strategic actions originally intended against a (many times remote) leadership. It is their fate that is frequently least considered by power-hungry, egocentric leadership. Human suffering, material destruction, seeding hatred for generations—they all go beyond the typical debate of strategies or the study of the notion of self-determination. The primary objective is to find mechanisms and policies to help avoid the danger of bloodshed and destruction for the future, to search for new avenues to satisfy both the aspirations of the communities and peoples concerned while maintaining stability and peace in the state and the region. An alteration of the often futile objective to secede or create a new independent state could help. The principal aim should be the amelioration of the situation of the individual citizen, promoting and supporting his or her rights, well-being, safety, and potential prosperity.

Conclusions

For the concept of self-determination to evolve in tandem with the changing international environment, political, strategic, economic, legal, ethnic, cultural, and other underpinnings are critical. Aspects inherent to globalization, such as immediate information and enhanced mobility, can contribute to the spread of secessionist ideas and hence to the widespread interest in self-determination. Generally there are three major dimensions to be considered in any problem of self-determination: the political strategic objectives of the leadership involved, the time needed to find and effect solutions, and human and material costs. These three dimensions have the potential to determine the extent and intensity of both the internal struggle and the external involvement (intervention). Typically all three favor determined nationalistic and autocratic governments who tend to settle self-determination claims from communities within their sovereign territory—hence high stakes for them—by employing time and disregarding costs.

Regarding the legal dimension of self-determination, Richard Falk argues that self-determination in its classical form undermines the legitimacy of political arrangements between distinct peoples that do not flow from genuine and continuing consent. He designates morality, politics, and law as the three paths along which the right of self-determination has matured and maintains that moral and political weight must be measured on a case-by-case basis and that legal interpretation is dependent on the antagonistic nature of the situation within the state.

Citing the collapse of the Soviet Union and Yugoslavia, Falk contends that the circumstances of secessionist movements of the former USSR and former Yugoslavia highlight opposite interpretations of the law. In discussing the theoretical debate surrounding the right of self-determination as it may pertain to indigenous peoples and the inhabitants of postcolonial territories, Falk argues that this right may be legally or politically upheld, consensually or nonconsensually, in symbolic or substantive terms.

Concerning the economic dimension of self-determination, the deliberate redistribution of wealth within one multiethnic state by the central government can contribute to the radicalization of feelings of injustice among communities—and thus to the intensified striving for greater independence by the targeted, wealthier community—and causes "economic nationalism," or nationalism fueled by economic considerations. This highlights several related problems: equal rights in a democracy, the moral dimension, the question of economic viability (size and capabilities), and the ultimate objective of the search for greater autonomy—classical independence and sovereignty or independent reintegration into a supranational regional organization.

In Chapter 1, Jeffrey Herbst emphasizes the great potential for the economic success of small states, citing as examples the Baltic republics, Slovenia, Eritrea, and the Asian Tigers. He concedes, however, the potential vulnerability of small states in terms of security. Indeed, sanctions can further contribute to the radicalization of the conflict and the suppression of independence movements by the central state while encouraging illegal operations and black marketeering. Herbst notes a general dearth of alternatives to independence in the form of the nation-state and sees a lack of alternative political theories of legitimacy that could replace nationalism with some other unifying ideal.

Movements for greater autonomy frequently demand secession, full independence, and sovereignty—a fact that obviously concerns the respective central authorities from the outset. Giving in to increased autonomy can lead to the slippery slope of decentralization and possibly eventual demands for full independence. Furthermore, granting greater independence to one community may eventually cause a domino effect, enticing other communities of the same state to look for similarly loosened relations with the central government and thus eventually endangering the territorial cohesion of the sovereign state. Obviously such movements also affect national and regional legal and administrative matters, political-ideological and moral dimensions, strategic considerations, economic perspectives, and, increasingly, even environmental concerns. They can produce direct effects such as the flows of refugees and the need for humanitarian and economic assistance. Indirect effects include radicalization of the region, economic and sociopolitical damage, and destabilizing influences from other states, corporations, organizations, or individual players.

Nevertheless, the understanding that economic specialization and interdependence may enable very small states to operate successfully and become highly prosperous encourages separation (see Jeffrey Herbst's Chapter 1).[1] That assumption does not always square with real-

---

1. For a very interesting study on the capabilities of and challenges for microstates see Jorri C. Duursma, *Fragmentation and the International Relations of Micro-States: Self-Determination and Statehood* (Cambridge: Cambridge University Press, 1996), esp. part 2.

ity, however, and works particularly in a nonthreatening regional environment. The key question relates to sovereign borders.[2] In practice, separatist tendencies still exist but are less violent in a highly integrated, nonthreatening environment such as the EU.

Concerning emerging dimensions of self-determination, frequent and intense international media coverage of struggles for independence—many even in real time and globally broadcasted—may lead to an immediate "demonstration effect"; that is, it can lead to encouragement to and support from other communities seeking greater autonomy as well as enticement for other communities elsewhere to intensify their respective struggles.[3] International media attention can also be used by communities in search of greater autonomy as a significant tool to broadcast their suffering and their situation. In light of the demonstration effect, sometimes even benign secessionist movements may search for ways to stir up international media interest. They may, for example, deliberately radicalize otherwise moderate aims, even causing bloodshed in order to attract media attention. The international community and media thus have to be aware of their responsibility regarding the potential radicalization of autonomy movements. International media attention can, however, also be of positive influence concerning the cause of the communities in question. Most governments care about their international reputation and will try—taking into account critical national interest—to avoid negative public relations abroad. This tendency can encourage them to contribute to an amenable and peaceful solution (see the successful case of the South Tyrol/Alto Adige "package deal," page 355).[4] These possible effects of global media coverage highlight the impact of the outside world on the relations between communities searching for greater self-governance and other communities as well as between them and their respective central authorities. The more positive or constructive strategic interest the outside world has in a particular state or region and its situation, the higher the chances of peaceful resolution. Inversely, absence of such interest, or especially negative, power-oriented interest, will unfortunately have detrimental

2. For an important caveat about the dangerous security implications of smallness, see John Thomson, "Commentary," in Wolfgang F. Danspeckgruber with Arthur Watts, eds., *Self-Determination and Self-Administration: A Sourcebook* (Boulder, Colo.: Lynne Rienner, 1997), p. 96.

3. I am grateful for this point to Stephen Kotkin, Princeton University. See Karl Rabl, *Das Selbstbestimmungsrecht der Völker* (Cologne: Böhlau, 1973). It became obvious as early as the nineteenth century that a community's striving for freedom against repression would entice not only those communities in the vicinity but also groups from afar to follow suit.

4. Discussion with Richard Falk, Woodrow Wilson School, Princeton University, September 16, 1998.

effects on the situation in and around a community searching for greater independence.

Another factor with potential for substantial influence in an evolving struggle for autonomy is the diaspora, that is, all those (former) citizens living abroad who originally emigrated from the state in question, or particularly from the community in question. Never before in history has their impact on the struggle of their community of origin been as immediate, extensive, and direct as today. Modern rapid global communications and transportion allow the diaspora immediate and direct influence in a struggle as well as the mobilization of international public opinion abroad. It may hold the key to critical support in financial and political matters, can communicate in real time (and thus with great effect), and can rapidly provide manpower, arms, and materials—either directly to the community or via neighboring states. The successful support of the Croat global diaspora during the conflict between Croatia and Serbia (1992–1995) documents these powers. The diaspora living in a powerful state abroad can stimulate and influence the media and national public opinion in that country. Through its impact on national elections in its host country, it may become rather influential in shaping foreign policy there through the democratic process (e.g., the influence of Indians in U.S. policies in the twenty-first century).

On the other side, the internationalization of organized crime with its significant power, equipment, motivation, and worldwide contacts may also affect certain self-determination conflicts. Secession movements frequently need money and all sorts of other support, particularly arms. Suppression by the central authorities leads to radicalization but fans the support for the secessionists from the like-minded abroad. This support may involve a range of both legal and illegal operations and goods: the illegal shipping of legally acquired or produced materials as well as legal transactions with illegal products or services (weapons and drugs, money laundering, human trafficking, etc.). A particularly dangerous situation could result from a secessionist group gaining access to weapons of mass destruction via illegal operations.[5]

Unfortunately, easy global access to scientific and military information has also contributed to the spreading of knowledge about and access to weapons of mass destruction. Even the threat of deployment could be used by radicals to pressure governments (local or abroad) into certain concessions. This potential to catapult any seemingly local and limited struggle for autonomy to global dimensions demands great attention, anticipation, and appropriate precautions from the interna-

---

5. Wolfgang Danspeckgruber, "EU and US Have an Important Role to Play in Beating Organised Crime in the Balkans," *Financial Times,* January, 6, 1999, p. 12; see <http://www.wws.princeton.edu:80/~lrpsd/ft99.html>.

tional community. The role of armed forces, paramilitary groups, and radical organizations in secessionist movements must be seen in a different framework today; the distinction between local, limited effects and continental or global effects is now blurred.[6]

Thus, the potentially wide-ranging effects of localized self-determination struggles and the consequent need for vigilance by the international community raise three sets of critical issues. The first concerns the balance between the rights of foreign powers to protect their own interests and the right to self-determination of communities. On the one hand, the international community must respond to a given self-determination crisis before that crisis escalates in terms of human and material costs. This response can be within the state itself or in the neighboring region. Anticipatory action will prevent too extensive a conflict and represents the most cost-effective position, as frequently, the longer a crisis broils, the more intense and costly it becomes. On the other hand, policymakers must consider the conditions under which they may legally and morally disregard another state's sovereignty and interfere.

Intervention has become a critical issue in the post–Cold War international system. In the words of Richard Falk, it so far depends on the "geopolitics of ambivalence," namely, on the national and strategic interests of the leading powers in a given struggle for autonomy and the respective geostrategic ramifications. Alas—highlighting the cruelty and injustice of this parameter—the deciding factors are geography, strategic interests, natural resources, energy, and so on and have little to do with justice or with the suffering of the individuals and communities involved.

One may assume a fundamental obligation of the international community to stop flagrant violations of human rights. Two kinds of intervention can be seen. The first, more benign "intervention from within," comprises international support and assistance for certain community or democratization movements, the creation of civil society, and encouragement to form working state structures. This type of support should further—without any active military or security involvement—peaceful processes and discourage violence and destruction. Once a conflict has already emerged and casualties, suffering, and destruction have taken

---

6. As the detonation of nuclear devices in 1999 by India and Pakistan demonstrated, it could be increasingly likely that struggles for independence or self-determination may one day include the use or threat of use of weapons of mass destruction. Wolfgang Danspeckgruber, "Self-Determination, Self-Governance and Security," *International Relations* 15 (April 2000), pp. 11–21.

place, the international response should be different. Then policymakers should consider the degree and scope of violations of human rights and the resulting humanitarian costs (casualties, displaced persons, and refugees), also beyond boundaries, as well as material and economic damages. When the scale of human suffering and destruction transcends acceptable standards, the outside community has a right, and indeed an obligation, to intervene in order to end the fighting and casualties. Timing is critical: early intervention can limit further suffering and devastation and thus reduce collateral damages and reconstruction and peace implementation costs for the international community. It may also help avoid a dangerous contagion across borders, especially in highly multiethnic areas such as the Caucasus and southeastern Europe. In addition, dealing with self-determination interests early, and thus anticipating negative outside influence, can help reduce military-strategic escalation. In a highly charged regional environment where the population is well armed, particularly along the former Soviet border (the Black Sea area, the Caucasus, and central Asia), such anticipatory attention may be critical for limiting the suffering caused by secessionist movements and the spread of violence.

In Chapter 3 of this book, Michael Doyle points to the freedom of interpretation regarding humanitarian concerns, troubled democracies, and the failure to extradite criminals in the context of increasing globalization and the shrinking sovereignty of states since the Cold War. He cites the original legitimacy of UN action in light of its multilateral nature and deplores the fact that multilateralism has not been fully employed: U.S.- and French-led UN initiatives have often been veiled examples of unilateral action, and the available political resources of regional groups have largely been ignored. He attributes this inefficacy, or at least the less-than-optimal outcomes of UN interventions in Bosnia and Somalia, to the overly restrictive nature of UN action—delimited as the UN is by its member states—as well as to the UN's tendency to commit beyond its capabilities or beyond the wishes of its member states. The UN has, furthermore, prevented states from upholding their own sovereignty through embargoes, disarmament, and revocation of the right to receive foreign assistance, and imperfect UN intervention strategy has facilitated, if not precipitated, renewed conflict. The inadvertent misdirection of UN punitive actions, which have failed to affect ruling elites but have worsened the condition of nonruling populations or heightened belligerency in the regions involved, are cases in point. Doyle suggests a new focus on those operations, including local-level, cooperation-based reform toward the reestablishment and maintenance of peace through the medium of UN peacemaking, peacekeeping, and peacebuilding activities. He also advises discontinuing UN peace-enforcement activities in view of the widespread lack of support for such efforts.

Moral concerns are raised on several levels by the democratic dilemma: Does a community that is neither repressed nor a colony have the right to break up an otherwise working state system against the will of the majority of other citizens in that state? What are the moral and legal obligations of those who would remain within the territory of the new state as minorities, and of those who would have to carry the burden of a split-up state and remain in the old states? The democratic dilemma, or the issue of minority versus majority, must be taken into consideration: Which groups within the state are opposed to separation, and which groups constitute minorities within the community that wants to secede? Self-determination is rarely just a zero-sum situation; it concerns not only the community in search of autonomy and its relations with the central government but frequently also with other communities and regions within the state. Occasionally, part of the community in question may reside just across the international boundary, introducing the relevance of external and internal/administrative borders; then, outside actors get involved. (See Figure 13.1, page 350.)

What justification can we advance for a minority in a democracy drumming up enough national and international support to obtain a "qualified majority" sufficient to convince its leaders to file for secession (see the problem in Canada regarding Quebec's desire to secede)?[7] Michael Walzer perceives (a sense of) oppression, estrangement, and cultural differences as the "crucial moral feature" in the search for self-determination.[8] But even when secession is morally justified, there will always be the rule of the majority or of the more powerful. The question, then, concerns the legitimacy of the claim for self-determination by a few. And who has the right to self-determination—a group, its individual members, a minority and subgroup, or the majority of the population of the state?

The more flexible an institution and government in dealing with its minorities and their demands, the greater the chances of negotiating a

---

7. Anthony DePalma, "Canadian Court Rules Québec Cannot Secede on Its Own," *New York Times,* August 21, 1998, p. A3; and "It's Québec, Again," *Economist,* August 29, 1998, p. 35. For the August 1998 decision of the Supreme Court of Canada on the legality of a unilateral declaration of independence, see <http://www.scc-csc.gc.ca/>.

8. See Michael Walzer, "Commentary," in Danspeckgruber with Watts, *Self-Determination and Self-Administration,* p. 127.

solution beneficial for all parties involved—not only for those who want to secede but also for the other communities and regions that intend to remain in the system, particularly the minorities. But the more the central authority tries to repress and ignore such initiatives, the greater the chance for radicalization and explosive outbursts calling for secession.[9]

An emerging issue has to do with the tension between intensified integration and globalization on the one hand and the search for communal autonomy and self-determination on the other. Continued demands for autonomy in the face of ever-increasing integration can be understood only by a voluntary differentiation, on the part of communities concerned, between sociocultural interests and economic-technologic goals. Most communities accept the need for and overall benefits of economic and technological interdependence and integration, but they may at the same time want to maintain their cultural and communal heritage.[10] They may envisage their struggle for complete independence as the first step toward unhindered participation in a global economy.

Herbst believes that the shattering of states—having defined the twentieth century—will continue due to powerful political, economic, and military forces and the inefficacy of international sanctions. He does not see the trend toward a substantial increase in the number of countries seeking autonomy as a serious challenge to the predominant political form of the nation-state. He points out that if the Europeans can tolerate the instability of the former Yugoslavia, the instability caused by other countries shattering will probably not move the great powers to react decisively.

---

9. See Atul Kohli, "The Bell Curve of Ethnic Politics: Rise and Decline of Self-Determination Movements in India," in Danspeckgruber with Watts, *Self-Determination and Self-Administration*, pp. 309–313.

10. Daniel Elazar finds that there is a general move from statism to federalism in our interdependent time. "[This] is not [because] states are disappearing, but the state system is acquiring a new dimension, one that began as a supplement and is now coming to overlay . . . a network of agreements and arrangements that are not only military and economically binding but are becoming constitutionally binding as well. This overlay increasingly restricts . . . sovereignty and forces states into various combinations of self-rule and shared rule." Elazar suggests that under these conditions autonomy "is needed as a means to satisfy demands for self-determination that cannot be satisfied by independent statehood. This fits well into the new federalist paradigm." He recommends that the "international community should recognize autonomy as an equally legitimate form of self-determination and provide a set of guidelines" to determine what can be considered true autonomy. Daniel Elazar, "Commentary," in Danspeckgruber with Watts, *Self-Determination and Self-Administration*, p. 94.

Emilio Cárdenas and María Cañás assert that subnational groups or minorities do not have—in principle—a legal entitlement to independence ("external self-determination") but do have a right to autonomy (an expression of "internal self-determination"). They agree with the general idea that an excessive push for self-determination can lead to "inner isolation," fragmentation, increased interethnic strife, and concrete threats to international peace and security. They praise decentralized forms of government and self-administration, including the concept of consociationalism.

Referring to the cases of the Åland Islands and the Azores and the islands of Faroe, Greenland, and Madeira, Cárdenas and Cañás suggest legal measures such as international guarantees of autonomy, demilitarization, neutralization, granting greater political autonomy within an existing state, and better internal political representation combined with guarantees of continued cultural autonomy, without necessarily offering full independence.[11] Today's self-determination, they argue, is too readily associated with independence, an idea—in their view—correlated with the decolonization process. They attribute "countless wars and conflicts" to the misuse of self-determination.

John Waterbury argues that the issue of self-determination needs to be treated with caution, that current guidelines to the definition of distinct groups are weak, that such identities are often artificially or ahistorically grounded, and that honoring self-determination claims is not always politically feasible or attentive to the rights of all involved. He maintains that effective, just political systems must be consent based and impartially just to members of all groups and to each group as a whole and that national power is best won by parties via cross-ethnic and cross-lingual coalitions.

Waterbury recognizes some merit in Amitai Etzioni's communitarian theory but argues that the definition of distinct communities almost inevitably leads to animosity between groups. He maintains that near total freedom should be granted to groups desiring to organize nonviolently, on any premise, in states capable of drafting and implementing law and of governing effectively. Waterbury suggests that the legal "naming of [group] names" should in most cases be avoided, that the law should remain permissive and neutral toward all groups residing within a state, and that cross-ethnic and cross-linguistic coalitions will provide stability, peace, and just governance.

---

11. See the Declaration on the Rights of Persons Belonging to National, or Ethnic, Religious and Linguistic Minorities, adopted by the UN General Assembly in December 1992, which grants minorities the right to enjoy their own culture.

Case Study Results

The case studies deal with specific problems in six different cases—Guatemala, Russia, Europe in general, the Middle East, Sudan, India, and China—and offer several conclusions.

John Waterbury's case studies address southern Sudan, Lebanon, and the Kurds. In the case of Sudan, he highlights the high toll of violence associated with strict northern and southern identities and microlevel cantonization. In the Lebanese case, he cites the successful effects of proportional representation and of Christian and Muslim vows not to seek the outside international intervention of related religious powers. As regards the Kurds, he cites their historic, ethnic, cultural, and linguistic rights to self-determination, discusses the means they use to achieve various levels of representation in the countries where they are most prominent—Iraq, Turkey, and Iran—and reveals the impracticality of Kurdish bids for political autonomy as a national state.

Kay Warren centers her study on language as a key determinant of cultural, political, and economic enfranchisement within Guatemalan society. She enumerates the dramatic problems of illiteracy and lack of education beyond the first years of primary school among indigenous populations, the total lack of rights to political participation for indigenous-language speakers, the nearly complete absence of economic opportunity, and the continued governmental suppression of the Mayan language and culture by the Ladino, Spanish-speaking state.

Warren sees three principal approaches to the handling of that situation: first, the status quo, that is, continued efforts to assimilate the adherents of Mayan culture into Ladino, Spanish-speaking culture coupled with continued economic, political, and cultural disenfranchisement; second, the culturalist argument in favor of establishing all-indigenous-language schools and the development of an indigenous society and politics in order to preserve Mayan culture. Third, having argued against the first two approaches, Warren proposes to reinvent Guatemalan cultural identity by providing mixed-language and cultural instruction in the indigenous language of the region as well as in Spanish, and the option of monolingual education for the stubborn few.

In my chapter I consider cases of the search for self-determination on the European continent; there, the search for self-determination is not necessarily always directed toward full independence and classical sovereignty. On the one hand, the EU's drive toward deeper economic-industrial and political-strategic integration and wider cooperation has intensified the appeal of self-determination and self-realization among communities. Regionalization and subsidiarity—developed within the framework of the EU's Maastricht agreement—provide a means of continued self-realization at the communal level in spite of profound economic and industrial integration. Moreover, new international entities within the EU would automatically belong to the supranational unit—the EU. This integration process has the potential to alter the role, position, and meaning of sovereign entities in Europe and beyond and to possibly change the very meaning of international borders. Sovereign entities will perhaps continue to retain their exclusionary powers over the transit of humans and (certain) goods but will be more permeable in terms of the exchange and movement of information, money, services, and people.

Three arguments result. First, interest in increased self-government (anti-deepening) in Western Europe focuses primarily on issues of culture, language, education, and related administrative, economic, and policy dimensions but does not necessarily involve issues of industrial, technological, economic, or security policy, where the need for integration is acknowledged. Second, self-determination need not necessarily result in classic sovereignty and full independence but can be successful with maximum autonomy, self-governance, and integration. Third, each case is unique, as each community has its own specific history, tradition, location, and aspirations; this holds for those states within the EU and those outside.

Ian Lustick discusses self-determination and state contraction in Britain and Ireland, France and Algeria, and Israel, the West Bank, and Gaza. He outlines the phenomenon of the contraction of states and suggests that state contraction can actually benefit the contracting state. He sees three primary issues: (1) whether cost-benefit calculations are politically relevant, (2) whether hegemonic beliefs prevent issues of costs from being posed as pertinent to public policy, and (3) whether qualitatively larger fears about the stability of the regime inhibit elites from acting on calculations of cost and benefit for them and their constituencies.

Regarding Russia and the former Soviet Union, William Wohlforth and Tyler Felgenhauer warn that mishandling the self-determination conflict in Chechnya could eventually lead to dire ramifications for all of Russia. They find that the legacy of Soviet-drawn administrative boundaries determines the extent and nature of today's self-determination claims in the region. What has helped avoid the state-shattering outcome of such claims so far is apparently the factor of demography, an institutional balance of power between the central government and regional governments, economics, ideas, and Moscow's policies and strategies, particularly under President Yeltsin. "Opportunistic adaptation" helps to forestall "more destabilizing pressures" from secessionist movements. In 2000, Russia's president, Vladimir Putin, launched an initiative on recentralization that would put an "end to the decade of negotiated bilateral deals where the center gave in to regions under implicit threat of secession."

In Chapter 10 Francis Deng outlines the origins and history of the Sudanese North-South conflict. Paying close attention to diverse perceptions and definitions of culture and identity, he elaborates on the question of mixed identity, exemplified in the North by Islamic Arab influences and attachments to the Middle East and in the South by Christian, Western influences and attachments to East Africa. He examines the issues from Middle Eastern, British, northern Sudanese, and southern Sudanese perspectives and discusses possible policy solutions to the problem as propounded by each of the interested groups and by disinterested policymakers.

Deng presents the political options of territorial division into two Sudanese states: territorial unification of the North with a member of the Arab Middle East and unification of the South with other African states, a unified Sudan, a confederated Sudan with North and South enjoying varying degrees of autonomy, and other possible confederations linking the North to the Arab Middle East and the South to the rest of black Africa. He further suggests cultural options, including continued division of the Arab-influenced northern and Western-influenced southern groups, the coexistence of the two linked with the groups' mutual tolerance, and the development of a new national Sudanese identity to be shared by all Sudanese irrespective of their current northern and southern identities. Deng believes that only "mutual recognition, respect, and harmonious interaction among African and Arab populations" throughout the country can ensure a just and lasting peace for the Sudan.

Atul Kohli analyses the movements for greater autonomy in India. He specifically looks at the Tamil Nadu Tamils, the Punjabi Sikhs, and the Kashmiri Moslems in the context of the Jawaharlal Nehru, Indira Gandhi, Rajiv Gandhi, and Narasimha Rao governments. He suggests that ethnic conflicts are in essence power conflicts developed along class, caste, or party lines and incited by groups seeking greater power and control to secure society's valued resources. As such, they are not emblematic of primordial ethnic conflict, anemic responses to the disequilibrium generated by modernization, or even causally linked to the formation of ethnic identity.

Because movements for greater autonomy are deeply threatening to weakly institutionalized states, threatened leaders often repress them, provoking them to be more extreme and temporarily worsening the situation, escalating the conflict to severe repression and violence. When states and leaders of democracies in developing countries are institutionally secure and accommodating, ethnic group mobilization occurs according to the pattern of a bell curve, first mobilizing, then entering a prolonged period of negotiations, then declining in intensity as exhaustion sets in, some leaders are co-opted, and a degree of power sharing and mutual accommodation between the movement and central government has been reached.

Minxin Pei relates that genuine self-administration in China faces not only serious political opposition from the center, which is determined to maintain the PRC's territorial integrity and political sovereignty at all costs, but also enormous structural economic problems (the intensely backward state of economic development of the minority-dominated jurisdictions). In China, the decentralization of public finance has diminished the central government's capacity to subsidize minority-inhabited areas and hence limits its political control. The growing market orientation enhances interdependence between center and periphery and will reduce the core's ability to control the administration of the periphery.

Pei recognizes that precipitous moves threatening the hegemony of the core would only prompt violent reprisals. Instead, he suggests evolutionary development toward greater autonomy for minorities as the most sustainable and peaceful means of achieving change. He relates that Han Chinese demographically dominate all Chinese regions except Xinjian and Tibet and that this domination makes self-administration at the regional level unlikely to work for most minority groups. Pei proposes "a less ambitious but more practical alternative," striving toward self-administration, to include semiopen local elections and economic federalism "at the prefect and county levels where minority groups are demographically predominant." He sees four critical issues as determining success of the Hong Kong–style experiment of self-administration: moderation of demands by both parties, recognition of the mutual benefits of self-administration, consensus building within each party, and external monitoring and support.

Options for Anticipating Tensions Offer
Solutions for Potential Self-Determination Crises

There exist two general possibilities for communities to find an acceptable and predictable way out of a potential self-determination dilemma: (1) clearly delineating self-determination modes and mechanisms in the constitution of a state, and (2) finding a feasible and acceptable alternative to classical self-determination, that is, secession and independence. This alternative should be in line with the emerging globalized international system and can help to avoid fractionation and separation, bloodshed and destruction, while providing for a peaceful and lasting solution. Communal self-governance plus regional integration seems to be the answer.

As has been demonstrated previously, however (see also Figure 13.1), potential secession frequently affects neighboring communities and states; their concerns also ought to be considered in order to create a viable and lasting solution for the future.

Figure 13.1 should assist in explaining the intricacies of self-governance of communities, states, and regions in an area with a supranational organization. On the vertical axis, multiple actors exist in a situation where authority travels from the higher level or institution to the lower, as implemented via supranational organizations and regional, subregional, state, and community institutions. Third-party, outside power interests in a community's demands for self-determination can have a decisive impact, as they can determine the intensity and extent of the problem.

On the horizontal level, communities begin to exercise treaty-making and financial powers as they achieve increased self-governance and concomitant rights and legal-administrative authority. Within a multiethnic state, the powers and rights of one community can frequently be increased only at the expense of the rights of other communities; consequently, efforts for self-governance are a zero-sum game not only between the community and the central government but among communities as well.

In certain circumstances, one homogenous community divided by an (imposed) external sovereign border may influence the relationship between several communities and their national government. Any demand for greater autonomy hence warrants bilateral intercommunal or even intergovernmental and subregional agreements on the effects of increasing the independence of the one community in relation to other communities and minorities. As antagonistic neighbor governments become involved, the relationship between the community and the government becomes more complex.

Finally, a complicating internal dimension often exists within communities that seek self-governance. The majority community has to consider the interests and aspirations of its own subcommunities or minorities, a psychologically demanding and difficult task as multiethnic rivalries in the Baltic and Balkan countries, Indonesia, and India demonstrated. Such consideration is a prerequisite to the democratic and successful implementation of self-governance.

Figure 13.1   Graphical Representation of Community in Space and Authority

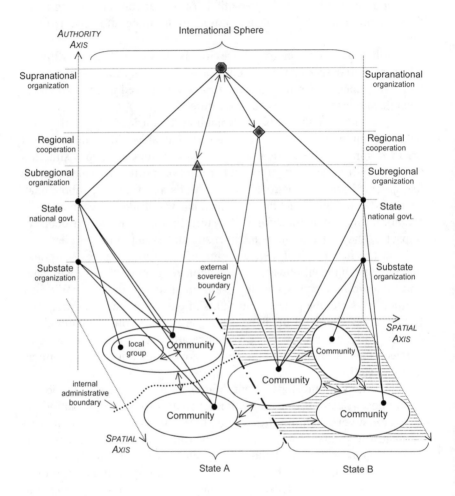

The Institutionalization of Self-Determination

In light of a more general trend to introduce meaningful democratic principles into daily life, several states have recently tried to offer provisions permitting classical self-determination, that is, secession, to their communities. It seems the intention is not to encourage disintegration of the sovereign state but to make a symbolic gesture demonstrating the ability of the state to conduct democracy to its fullest extent.

In essence these provisions represent an attempt to incorporate self-determination–related concepts into domestic legal structures, that is, constitutions, and hence to provide for a top-down effect on other national institutions and the legal framework. They should provide the means and mechanisms to offer predictability for communities that search for greater autonomy in a manner that is acceptable to the central authorities and electorate. No central government wants its territory to be changed or reduced. Equally, the majority of the international community will prefer the continued existence of sovereign boundaries and no change to the status quo. Nevertheless, it seems that offering communities as much say as possible in the political and legal-administrative decisionmaking process on the national, regional, and supranational level, even the maximization of their ideal of independence, will turn out to be more advantageous than restricting or denying it (see Atul Kohli's arguments). Inversely, it can be hoped that some kind of objective cost-benefit analysis on the part of the concerned community may come to the clear reasoning that the costs of achieving independence, as well as the costs of maintaining an independent state, typically outweigh the benefits.[12] Furthermore, options such as subsidiarity in EU Europe and self-governance cum regionalization may offer attractive alternatives that *à la longue* may benefit the community and region much more.

Two constitutions can be seen as examples for specifically enumerating the right of self-determination: the constitution of Ethiopia and the constitution of South Africa. Article 39(1) of the Ethiopian constitution reads, "Every Nation, Nationality and People in Ethiopia has an unconditional right to self-determination, including the right to secession." Chapter XIV, section 235, of the constitution of South African stipulates,

---

12. This holds true if considering the expenses for a full-fledged foreign service, defense, and currency policy—particularly if the to-be-created state is weak in power and population and lacks exceptional natural resources.

The right of the South African people as a whole to self-determination, as manifested in this Constitution, does not preclude, within the framework of this right, recognition of the notion of the right of self-determination of any community sharing a common cultural and language heritage, within a territorial entity in the Republic or in any other way, determined by national legislation.

The Principality of Liechtenstein is considering amending its constitution to include the right of self-determination. The Princely House suggests including the following passage on self-determination in order to offer communities the possibility to search for new legal arrangements:

Chapter 1: The Principality
Article 4
1. The change in the boundaries of the territory of the state can be accomplished only by law. Changes of boundaries between communities require a majority vote of the Liechtenstein citizens in the communities in question.
2. Each community has the right to secede. Secession is to be regulated by law or on a case-by-case basis by contract. Secession must be approved by a majority of Liechtenstein citizens resident in the community in question. In the case a majority approves secession the reigning prince shall have the right to order within thirty days a vote of reconsideration six months later.

Obviously this is a novel proposition—certainly for Europe. On an internal level, the Liechtenstein Draft Convention on Self-Determination (through self-administration) has been instigated and discussed over many years, and will be adopted by popular decision.

Communal Self-Governance Plus Regional Integration

Self-governance is defined as maximum autonomy along with the rights to self-administration in the areas of culture, education, language, religion, finance, judicial administration, and public safety, as well as in certain industrial, energy, and infrastructure projects. Self-governance should allow for the local administration of daily communal or regional affairs and offer more freedom for creativity to adapt the institutions, organs, laws, and regulations to the specific needs of the community. Their freedoms and competencies exceed self-administration on the local level, which is basically the right to execute and administer according to predetermined rules. In turn, the enhanced rights under a system of self-governance plus integration oblige the community to recognize and respect the rights of minorities within its territory. Self-governance increases and expands competencies and costs of self-administration, and consequently enhances the meaning of internal administrative, boundaries between the community and other areas within the state as it increases decentralization and avoids the creation of a new international entity.

Self-governance is a concept that is more positive, extensive, humane, and future oriented than classical self-determination; it also avoids secession and is less loaded with historical and legal-political baggage. The "self" addresses the community, just as the "self" in "self-determination." In contrast to self-determination, however, self-governance avoids the slippery slope to state-shattering secession, and new state formation. To the extent that self-governance would affect the character of borders at all, it does so gradually—through regional integration. Ideally this gradual softening of boundaries is accompanied by a process in accord with accepted international norms, OSCE standards, and, of course, the goals of the parties concerned.

Self-governance is distinct from self-administration, which, strictly speaking, is the right to execute and administer decisions from above according to predetermined rules and procedures. Self-governance is of a more flexible character, as it includes administrative duties but also tasks innate to the local governance of the region. It is also progressive, naturally leading to increased representation for women, nondiscriminatory politics, environmental awareness, and cultural flexibility.[13] In sum, self-governance should enable the classical concept of self-determination to advance from the traditional orientation of state-shattering toward a more benign, stable, and mutually satisfying notion of maximized autonomy within existing international boundaries while permitting rewarding participation in global economic integration.

Self-governance requires stability, predictability, and, most important, communal security. The experiences during the creation of the Conference on Security and Cooperation in Europe in the early 1970s may be of relevance. The major regional issues were divided into military-strategic, socioeconomic, and humanitarian "baskets." In order to establish a benevolent and encouraging framework in a region, such considerations are important. Otherwise, the existence of arms and armed forces or paramilitary groupings, as well as criminal elements organized locally or internationally, will hinder effective self-governance. Demilitarization and decriminalization of the region are

---

13. Richard Falk, *On Humane Governance* (University Park: Pennsylvania State University Press, 1997).

thus required for the successful introduction of self-governance. This process of stabilization may be taken one step further to neutralization, thus denying foreign actors the right to use the territory as a staging ground for military operations and also reducing the danger of armed clashes. A guarantee of the inviolability of the territory of the community in question may be offered by regional powers or an international organization. Self-governance should not include diplomatic representation abroad, the protection of sovereign borders, or customs and national defense; these responsibilities should be left to the central government. However, the community should have its own local security apparatus.

In many cases the community in question inhabits an area covering one or two (sometimes even more) states in a region; the community is thus separated from its other parts by external boundaries. Yet through the proposed parallel regional integration process, inhabitants of the entire area can interact through trade, economic development, and sociocultural exchanges irrespective of borders. These processes will gradually soften borders among the members of the region and eventually transform the boundaries from hard international to softer administrative ones. As borders are softened, their relevance is reduced and the primary objective (to become independent) is replaced by concerns regarding economic development and participation in the global market (ideally with the four European Economic Area [EEA] freedoms of movement of goods, services, capital, and citizens).[14]

The territory of the former Yugoslavia, for example, is surrounded by EU members and membership applicants—the former being Austria and Greece, the latter being Hungary, Slovenia, Romania, and Bulgaria. It would thus make sense if the EU were to push through various incentives for economic and technological cooperation in the region.

For instance, Swedish emissary Carl Bildt detailed the institutional forging of closer links between the EU and the Balkan states. He suggests, "The EU should provide clear blueprints for reforms that would pave the way [for closer cooperation and integration] . . . if not full-blown [EU] membership [including] the possibility of making them part of a broader euro-zone."[15]

The concept of self-governance transcends classical self-determination to advance from the traditional orientation of state-shattering

14. Stanley Hoffmann, "Yugoslavia: Implications for Europe and the European Institutions," in Richard H. Ullman, ed., *The World and Yugoslavia's Wars* (New York: Council on Foreign Relations, 1996), pp. 97–121.

15. Carl Bildt, "Embracing the Balkans," *Financial Times,* February 19, 1999, p. 14. Bildt, former Swedish prime minister, was at that time the special representative of the UN Secretary-General.

toward a more benign, stable, and hence mutually satisfying notion of increased autonomy within existing international boundaries while permitting rewarding participation in regional integration and the global marketplace.

Some fundamental conditions for successful negotiations in self-determination crises include a clarity of terms and mutual understanding; differentiation between self-determination as a process and an objective; mutual trust, coinciding desires, and clear goals; and, most important, the readiness to compromise. The following accompanying measures are critical to the successful implementation of any solution:

- democratization
- demilitarization
- demobilization and reintegration into a regular and orderly life
- depoliticization of municipal administrations
- decriminalization
- detraumatization and reeducation of the younger and youngest—create a common oral history as depolemicized and neutral as possible
- dependence—establish positive dependence with relevant neighbors and in the regions
- feasible, credible, and immediate projects concerning reconstruction, reconciliation, repatriation, reestablishment of order, relegitimization, regionalization (that is, encouragement of meaningful regional interaction and cooperation), and revitalization on a regional level

Examples such as Catalonia, Corsica, and South Tyrol/Alto Adige demonstrate that continuous negotiation and readiness to compromise and the absence of absolute objectives (independence) provide acceptable results and contribute to both economic and social success, as does an encouraging, or predictable and stable, international environment. These regions show also that the integrative process is transforming member states' external boundaries into softer administrative borders within EU territory. Regional integration also diminishes the striving for that independence of communities there, as long as they can obtain the benefits from participation in the European integration process and the global marketplace.

Recommendations

Any final-status solution for a given community ought to include the following five guidelines as well. First, the idea of legitimate multiple identities must be introduced and accepted throughout the region. This appreciation of diversity allows for increasing flexibility in defining the relationship between geographical living space and local, state, and regional hierarchies. Once multiple identities are accepted, the influence of militant nationalism will wane and tolerance for other identities will increase. As we have seen in successful cases of self-governance, a person can be proud to be a Catalan as well as a Spaniard while being also a Mediterranean and a European. This evolution is a question of understanding, education, time, and continuous international encouragement.

Second, the involved parties must develop a flexible political culture based, ideally, on democratic values and notions such as tolerance, flexibility, forgiveness, and compromise. Such a culture allows minorities—even within the community that search for greater independence from the center—to contribute and play a role. Democratization in any of its forms is also the only just and appropriate way to ascertain a community's will and to ensure international acceptance and continued support.

Third, organized crime in all its forms needs to be eliminated. This measure is essential for the development of a positive and benign political culture.

Fourth, it is indispensable to create economic programs with immediate effects. Enhanced possibilities for employment, for example, especially for the young, will support hopes and aspirations and reduce illegal activities and out-migration.

The fifth guideline concerns education and the dissemination of reliable information in order to minimize negative interference, exaggeration, and to create a realistic picture of the immediate environment and the other communities concerned. Education serves also to introduce the notion of multiple identities; that is, an individual community member may be a member of his or her clan or community, a citizen of the state, an occupant of a certain region, and a member of a higher entity.

Establishing a standing international commission that includes antagonistic parties and members of the international community will help to facilitate the process and verify and control certain policies. This commission should assist in creating and implementing fundamental legal and administrative standards, evaluate the status of agreements and address cases of noncompliance, and limit the interference of outside states.

Last and most important, political leadership abroad and in the community and state must have the will and farsightedness to concern itself with the interest and fate of individual citizens, the young and the old, the rich and the poor, rather than concentrating on individual leaders and personal interests and advantages. Too many times, issues of self-determination have been employed to serve leadership interests rather than the true interest at the very core of self-determination—the safety, economic and political possibilities, and rights of individual men, women, and children. It is for them that we ought to implement and support, and if necessary enforce, feasible and acceptable solutions that will hold in the long run and provide peace, justice, and prosperity.

APPENDIXES

Appendix A

Abbreviations and Acronyms

AER	Assembly of the European Regions
ARGE	Arbeitsgemeinschaft Alpenländer (Alpine States Working Group)
ASSR	Autonomous Soviet Socialist Republic
BJP	Bharatiya Janata Party (India)
BSEC	Black Sea Economic Cooperation Pact
CCP	Chinese Communist Party
CEC	Commission of the European Communities
CDLR	Steering Committee of Local and Regional Authorities (Council of Europe)
CECC	Central European Cooperation Committee
CEE	Central and Eastern Europe
CEFTA	Central European Free Trade Agreement
CEI	Central European Initiative (formerly Pentagonale)
CFSP	Common Foreign and Security Policy (EU)
CIS	Commonwealth of Independent States
CIS	Center of International Studies (Princeton)
CLRAE	Congress of Local and Regional Authorities of Europe (Council of Europe)
CMEA	Council for Mutual Economic Assistance
COE	Council of Europe
COMG	Consejo de Organizaciones Mayas de Guatemala
CONAVIGUA	Coordinadora Nacional de Viudas de Guatemala (National Coordinator of Guatemalan Widows)
COPAZ	Commission on the Peace in El Salvador
COR	Committee of the Regions
COTRAO	Communauté de Travail des Alpes Occidentales (Working Community of the Western Alps)
CSCE	Conference on Security and Cooperation in Europe
CUC	Comité de Unidad Campesina (Committee for Campesino Unity) (Guatemala)
DMK	Dravida Munnetra Kazhagam (Tamil Nationalist Party) (India)
DOD	Department of Defense
DOP	Declaration of Principles (Sudan)
EBRD	European Bank for Reconstruction and Development
EC	European Community

361

ECOS	European Cities Cooperation System
EEA	European Economic Area
EFTA	European Free Trade Association
EIB	European Investment Bank
EMU	European Monetary Union
ERDF	European Regional Development Fund
EU	European Union
FBIS-NES	Foreign Broadcast Information Service—Near East and South Asia
FBIS-WEU	Foreign Broadcast Information Service—Western Europe
FLMN	Frente Farabundo Martí para la Liberacion Nacional (El Salavador)
FLN	National Liberation Front (Algeria)
GA Res.	UN General Assembly Resolution
GAP	Southeast Anatolian Project (Turkey)
GDP	gross domestic product
HEC	High Executive Council (Sudan)
ICJ	International Court of Justice (The Hague)
ICORC	International Committee on the Reconstruction of Cambodia
IGAD	Inter-Governmental Authority on Development
IIN	Instituto Indigenista Nacional (Guatemala)
IPA	International Peace Academy (UN)
IRA	Irish Republican Army
IRRCT	Select Committee of Experts on Transfrontier Cooperation
ISI	industrialization through import substitution
JCS	Joint Chiefs of Staff (U.S.)
JKLF	Jammu and Kashmir Liberation Front
JNA	Yugoslav National Army
LASA	Latin American Studies Association
LISD	Liechtenstein Institute on Self-Determination, Princeton University (formerly the Liechtenstein Research Program on Self-Determination [LRPSD])
NAFTA	North American Free Trade Agreement
NATO	North Atlantic Treaty Organization
NDA	National Democratic Alliance (Sudan)
NGO	nongovernmental organization
NIF	National Islamic Front (Sudan)
NPC	National People's Congress (China)
OAU	Organization of African Unity
ONUSAL	UN Observer Mission in El Salvador
ÖVP	Tyrolian Peoples Party
OSCE	Organization for Security and Cooperation in Europe
P-5	5 Permanent Members of the UN Security Council: China, Russia, France, the United Kingdom, and the United States
PHARE	Pologne et Hongrie: Actions pour la Reconversion Economique
PKK	Kurdish Workers Party
PLO	Palestine Liberation Organization
PRC	People's Republic of China
PRONEBI	Programa Nacional de Educación Biligüe (renamed DIGEBI)

PUK	Patriotic Union of Kurdistan
RECITE	Regions and Cities for Europe
RIIA	Royal Institute of International Affairs (London)
RSFSR	Russian Socialist Federated Soviet Republic
SEA	Single European Act
SEM	Single European Market
SIL	Summer Institute of Languages (Guatemala)
SNC	Supreme National Council of Cambodia
SPLA	Sudan People's Liberation Army
SPLM	Southern Sudan People's Liberation Movement
SSLM	Southern Sudan Liberation Movement
SVP	Südtiroler Volkspartei (South Tyrolian Peoples Party)
SWAPO	South West African People's Organization (Namibia)
TEN	Trans-European Network
UNICEF	UN Children's Fund
UNITA	National Union for the Total Liberation of Angola
UNITAF	Unified Task Force in Somalia
UNOSOM I	UN Operation in Somalia I (prior to 1992)
UNOSOM II	UN Operation in Somalia II (after 1992)
UNPROFOR	UN Protection Force for the Former Yugoslavia
UNTAES	UN Transitional Administration for Eastern Slavonia
UNTAC	UN Transitional Authority in Cambodia
UNTAG	UN Transition Assistance Group (Namibia)
Z-4	Russia, the United States, the EU, and the UN (the four Zagreb-based mediators for the war in Croatia)

Appendix B

The Liechtenstein Draft Convention on Self-Determination Through Self-Administration: A Commentary

Sir Arthur Watts

Liechtenstein's proposals for ways in which the general principle of self-determination, and in particular the idea of self-administration, might be developed have been described—though necessarily in relatively general terms—in the United Nations General Assembly and its Third Committee. From the outset, however, it was envisaged that the Liechtenstein initiative might result in an international convention and that the proposals therefore needed to be given the structure and detail appropriate for a formal international legal instrument.

A draft of a convention embodying the Liechtenstein proposals has been in existence (although not publicly available) since the early stages of the Liechtenstein initiative. This helped in developing ideas in sufficient detail to produce a coherent and practicable set of proposals and focused attention on the political, practical, and technical requirements of a text that would have to be acceptable to governments after a process of diplomatic consideration and negotiation—considerations that are particularly weighty, given that the Liechtenstein proposals touch on matters that are politically sensitive for some states and at the same time seek to establish a regime that would have some degree of precise content as well as being practical and effective.

A draft convention has the disadvantage of its treaty form. The structure of a treaty, as a legal instrument, reflects drafting practices that, although they give it an internal logic of its own, disable its provisions from giving a straightforward narrative account of its contents. The Liechtenstein Draft Convention, to be properly understood, accordingly needs some further commentary, to explain its sometimes terse language and the thinking underlying it, to draw attention to the interrelationships between various provisions, and to identify the origins of some of the language used.

The Liechtenstein Draft Convention on Self-Determination Through Self-Administration (see pp. 382–392 for the full text) is the text as it stood in 1994 and the same that the authors of the various papers in this volume had before them when preparing their chapters.

The Draft Convention

Preamble

Treaties do not need a preamble, and many do not have any introductory words beyond a bold statement that the states concerned "have agreed as follows." Even where there is a preamble, it is often one of the last parts of the text to be settled. Nevertheless, there is value in setting down in a preamble the general context in which the Convention has been prepared and the motivation underlying it. While the provisions of a preamble do not themselves embody the legal rights and obligations arising for the parties by virtue of the treaty, and in that respect they are to be distinguished from the substantive provisions of the treaty contained in its numbered articles, the preamble nevertheless affects the meaning attributable to the treaty's terms. Insofar as the preamble explains the parties' motivation in concluding the treaty, it may indicate its object and purpose, which are also relevant to the interpretation of the treaty's terms.

The first four substantive paragraphs of the preamble—those lettered (b) to (e)—relate in a general way to the principle of self-determination. Successively, they recognize self-determination to be part of the broad field of human rights and fundamental freedoms, acknowledge the important role it has played in relation to territories not enjoying full self-government (i.e., the decolonization process), note that the principle is not limited to such territories, and note further that while self-determination has often led to independence, this is not the only outcome to which self-determination may lead. The last two of these points call for some comment.

There has been considerable debate whether self-determination applies only in relation to colonial territories, or whether, particularly now that the colonial content of the principle has become largely a matter of history, it is a concept of continuing and universal application. Although the matter is dealt with more fully in the context of Article 1, it must here be observed that this question is linked to that of the entity that may benefit from self-determination. That "peoples" have the right to self-determination is now clear, as is (probably) the inclusion within that term of the local inhabitants of colonial territories. From this, however, it does not necessarily follow either that it is only such colonial peoples who may be considered beneficiaries of that right, or that that *right,* whoever may be its beneficiaries, is the complete manifestation of the *principle* of self-determination. State practice in recent years has frequently used the language of self-determination in other than traditional colonial contexts.

The other point, that self-determination is not coterminous with independence, is also important, both because it is often overlooked and because it establishes the Liechtenstein proposal for self-administration as a permissible option within the broad framework of self-determination. It is clear that independence is not the only outcome of the exercise of self-determination: this follows not only from the term itself (which suggests only that the beneficiary has the right to choose its own destiny, but not that that choice has to be exercised in any particular way) but also from practice within the UN. The permissibility of self-determination leading to situations other than full independence is, in particular, expressly recognized in General Assembly Resolutions 1541(XV)(1960) and 2625(XXV)(1970) (the so-called "Friendly Relations" Declaration). The latter, in its fifth principle, stipulated (in paragraph 1) that "all peoples have the right freely to determine . . . their political status," and (in paragraph 4) that modes of implementing a people's right of self-determination were the establishment of a sovereign and independent state, the free association or integration with an independent state, "or the emergence into any other political status freely determined by [that] people." While in direct terms those passages relate to the *right* of *a people* to self-determination, it would seem to be an *a fortiori* proposition in relation to the broader, underlying principle of self-determination.

This leads naturally to the question of self-administration and to preambular paragraph (f). Self-administration is, first, stated to be consistent with the right of self-determination; "consistency," it may be noted, is not necessarily the same as "in implementation of" (although that would, of course, exemplify consistency). The second proposition in paragraph (f) is as important as consistency, namely, that in many (but not necessarily in all) circumstances self-administration by itself may be a sufficient exercise of the right of self-determination, without the need to move on to full independence. Independence, which can be a complicated and traumatic option, is for many communities not always the best solution. There is no advantage to be gained by insisting on independence and thus excluding other kinds of status if, in particular circumstances, they would grant a community all it wants in order to be able to acknowledge its distinctive characteristics without forcing it to assume the additional burdens of a wholly independent existence.

This leads to paragraph (g) (which itself looks ahead to Article 3). The principles of self-determination and of the territorial integrity of states are inevitably potentially in conflict, and reassurance to states that their territorial integrity is not threatened has become an almost invariable balancing provision whenever considerations of self-determination are advanced.[1] In the context of self-*administration,* however, this reassurance is inherently strong, since it is of the very essence of the Liechtenstein proposals that while independence can never be completely excluded, it is not their central aim. On the contrary, it is felt that by providing for self-administration, communities may feel their aspirations to self-determination are adequately met and they are no longer compelled to seek full independence.

Paragraphs (h) and (i) mark a return to the human rights considerations that permeate the Liechtenstein proposals. They emphasize that state structures are essentially a means toward the realization of the needs of human beings,[2] and that states have a duty to secure to all individuals the enjoyment of human rights and fundamental freedoms. The further consideration is added that their ability to enjoy those rights and freedoms is closely connected with (though not

---

1. See, for example, GA Res. 1514(XV)(1960), 2625(XXV)(1970), and paragraph 2 of Section 1 of the Vienna Declaration and Programme of Action (on Human Rights) of 25 June 1993. A notable exception, however, is Article 1 of the Covenant on Civil and Political Rights 1966.

2. Compare the second preambular paragraph of the Vienna Declaration and Programme of Action, adopted on 25 June 1993: "Recognizing and affirming that all human rights derive from the dignity and worth inherent in the human person, and that the human person is the central subject of human rights and fundamental freedoms, and consequently should be the principal beneficiary and should participate actively in the realization of these rights and freedoms."

necessarily wholly dependent upon) individuals' ability to express views through democratic procedures and the standing within states of the communities of which they form a part.

It is a strong feature of the thinking underlying the Liechtenstein proposals that more is needed than just fine-sounding words and declarations of principles; measures are also needed to produce results that are effective in practice. If states are to acknowledge a degree of self-administration for communities within their territories, and if such communities are to be able effectively to seek self-administration, they may need international support and assistance in their efforts. Paragraphs (j) and (k) acknowledge the desirability of this.

The absence of suitable international arrangements in this area is apparent. While, in principle states accept self-determination, they are often less ready to acknowledge it in practice, even in the more limited form of self-administration. Furthermore, although in certain areas procedures are available to assist with the realization of the principle (such as the UN General Assembly's "Committee of Twenty-Four"[3]) no generally applicable rules and procedures are available to secure its effective implementation. Where the right of self-determination is denied, or where even an adequate degree of self-administration has not been acknowledged, the absence of recognized rules and procedures to deal with the situation has often resulted in war or other forms of conflict leading to extensive human suffering. With an echo of GA Resolution 1514(XV)(1960),[4] paragraph (l) notes this tragic state of affairs; and the final paragraph (m) states the resolve to improve matters by seeking to go some way toward making the peaceful application of the principle of self-determination more truly effective, at least in the limited context of self-administration, by facilitating the exercise of self-administration and by providing procedures to resolve differences that may arise.

Preliminary Provisions: Articles 1–3

The operation of the convention turns on two particularly important concepts, "community" and "self-administration." The latter does not call for definition, and in the context of the Convention is given meaning by the provisions of Articles 4, 5, and 6. "Community" does, however, call for particular consideration.

"Community" is not a concretely established term with an accepted meaning. It is used in the Convention precisely for this reason and, in particular, to underline the fact that the underlying concept is different from certain others used in this general field, such as "people," "minority," and "indigenous people" (although there is clearly a degree of overlap with those concepts). The use

---

3. The committee has responsibilities for the granting of independence to colonial territories.

4. The fourth preambular paragraph reads: "Aware of the increasing conflicts resulting from the denial of or impediments in the way of the freedom of such peoples in the attainment of their independence." The reference to "such peoples" is a reference back to "all dependent peoples" in the preceding paragraph; and the resolution as a whole is, of course, concerned only with questions of colonialism.

of the term "community" creates a new perspective on what should be the proper sociopolitical unit to benefit from self-administration.

In the final analysis, a definition of "community" could be dispensed with. The UN charter itself does not define the "peoples" to whom the principle of self-determination applies, nor have subsequent UN resolutions been concerned with the implementation of that principle and its associated right. Even the more legally formal Covenant on Civil and Political Rights 1966[5] did not, in establishing a clear legal right to self-determination, define the "peoples" who are its beneficiaries. Similarly, the Declaration on Minorities adopted by the General Assembly in 1992[6] did not define a "minority." As those examples show, although it may be not at all easy to find generally acceptable definitions of central concepts, difficulties of definition are no necessary bar to progress on matters of substance.

Nevertheless, at the present exploratory stage-defining "community" may be helpful in order to clarify at the outset this important component in the Liechtenstein proposal. Article 1(a) establishes a definition with three essential elements: (1) a "distinct group" must exist; (2) it should "inhabit a limited area within a State"; and (3) the group should have "a sufficient degree of organization as such a group for the effective application of the relevant provisions of [the] Convention."

The requirement that a community should constitute *a distinct group* does not specify any particular basis for the group's distinctive characteristics. If the other two essential elements of the definition are present, the distinctiveness of the group will, in all probability, be sufficiently established on grounds that will be relevant in the particular context. Relevance of that practical kind, and flexibility, are probably more important than the need to satisfy fixed, predetermined criteria. It would, of course, be possible to identify specific bases for the group's distinctive characteristics by reference to considerations that are commonly invoked in this sort of context, such as cultural (including linguistic), religious, or ethnic qualities, or to a sense of solidarity directed toward preserving the group's cultural, religious, or ethnic traditions.[7] Such qualifications, however, might prove too limiting in particular contexts and could worsen religious and other divisions within a state rather than diminish them. What seems important to acknowledge is that many groups frequently see themselves as distinct and coherent social units more on the basis of their deep-seated tribal, cultural, or other origins, than because of the impact of boundaries subsequently superimposed—sometimes arbitrarily so far as they are concerned—on the areas they inhabit.

---

5. GA Res. 2200(XXI)(1966).

6. Res. 47/135.

7. Thus, the definition of a "minority" was tentatively formulated in 1977 by the special rapporteur of the Sub-Commission on the Prevention of Discrimination and the Protection of Minorities (Professor Capotorti) as meaning "a group numerically inferior to the rest of the population of a State, in a nondominant position, whose members—being nationals of the State—possess ethnic, religious or linguistic characteristics different from those of the rest of the population and show, if only implicitly, a sense of solidarity, directed towards preserving their culture, traditions, religion or language": UN Doc. E/CN 4/Sub/2/384.

The group must not only be distinctive but must *inhabit a limited area within a state,* thus—for purposes of the convention—a "community" is limited to one with essentially local territorial characteristics. Such a requirement for a community to have a degree of territoriality is in practice essential to the kind of self-administration envisaged in the Convention. The optional levels of self-administration described in Articles 5 and 6 are expressly territorial in that certain of the entitlements of communities under those articles are directly linked to the geographical area the group inhabits. Other entitlements are not inherently or expressly territorial, although most are more readily understood and applied in a territorial context: this is particularly so with the mandatory elements of self-administration set out in Article 4. Since the proposals envisage a progression from the basic, mandatory level of self-administration in Article 4 through the further, optional levels in the two following articles, the express territoriality of certain of the provisions necessarily informs that group of articles taken as a whole.

It may be hard to determine the precise area that a community may be said to inhabit, and it is for this reason that in relation to the optional levels of self-administration provided for in Articles 5 and 6, it is provided in Article 8.1(b) that the declarations by which a contracting party exercises those options must identify the area within its territory that the community in question inhabits. Although members of the group must inhabit a particular area, it does not follow that they must be its sole inhabitants. The extent to which others also inhabit the area is something to be taken into account in the particular self-administration arrangements that are made for the community. The locality has to be a "limited" area within the state; this signifies that the area should be determinate and, relative to the size of the state as a whole, should not be disproportionately large. But it does not have to be of any particular size in absolute terms and may in practice be quite small or quite large. There is, in fact, some advantage in acknowledging that even quite small groupings may qualify as a community, since it underlines the inappropriateness in such cases of any fully sovereign and independent status. Questions of territorial size are less relevant to the existence of a group as a "community" than to the degree of self-administration that would be appropriate for it.

The Convention does not apply to groups whose members are dispersed throughout a state and who therefore inhabit no particular limited area within it; nor does it apply to groups insofar as their members inhabit trans-frontier areas in two or more adjacent states (although the members in one state may qualify as a "community" within that state alone). Their exclusion from the scope of this particular Convention does not mean (and, indeed, could not mean) that they are also being excluded from the benefits of the right of self-determination generally; in that respect their position is protected by Article 2.3. Nor does it mean that these groups are to be excluded from proper treatment as minorities.

The third requirement of the definition is that there has to be *a sufficient degree of organization as a group for the effective application of the relevant provisions of the Convention.* Self-administration involves responsibilities for communities, as well as rights. If the various levels of self-administration envisaged in the Draft Convention are to be applied effectively, a community must be sufficiently coherently organized for the purpose. This notion is flexible, and the nature and degree of organization called for is essentially relative to the level of self-administration in question in any particular case.

Even with a definition (and even more so if a definition is dispensed with), differences may arise over whether a particular group constitutes a "community." Article 16 (particularly paragraph 3(b)) provides that an advisory opinion on this issue may be sought from the court established under the Convention.

Article 1 also contains a second definition, that of "self-determination" (Article 1(b)). As the title of the Convention, its preamble, and the opening words of Article 2.2 make clear, the essential idea underlying the Convention is that of self-determination, even though the detailed proposals concern only that aspect of self-determination that is contained in the notion of self-administration. At the present stage there is thus merit in recalling, in Article 1(b), what is meant by the right of self-determination and, in particular, that it not only envisages independence but may also involve other forms of freely chosen political status; eventually, however, such a definition may be dispensed with. The terms of Article 1(b) are drawn from Article 1.1 of the Covenant on Civil and Political Rights 1966, and paragraph 4 of the fifth principle of the "Friendly Relations" Declaration 1970.

Article 2. The opening paragraph, in asserting the general right of self-determination, repeats language taken from Article 1.1 of the Covenant on Civil and Political Rights 1966. Paragraph 2 places the goal of self-administration within the broad framework of self-determination. The substantive obligation that a state will undertake by virtue of this provision is to "respect the aspirations" of all communities within its territory to "an appropriate degree" of self-administration and to secure that degree of self-administration to them. This is a very flexible commitment, since the degree of self-administration "appropriate" in any particular case will, of course, depend on the circumstances.

Self-administration is not the whole content of self-determination but only one way of achieving it. Other ways in which the right of self-determination may properly be exercised are not in any way prejudiced by the Convention, and if a community is entitled to exercise a right of self-determination in some other way it remains free to do so. Paragraph 3 of Article 2 makes this clear. It also makes it clear that whatever rights of self-determination may be possessed by groups that do not come within the definition of a "community" are untouched by the present provisions.

The "exercise" of the right of self-determination is not just a matter of the goal that may be sought, but also concerns the means by which those goals may be attained. As paragraphs (k) and (m) of the preamble make clear, the Convention is concerned with enhancing the *peaceful* application of the principle of self-determination. This is its essential precondition. It is not, however, intended to assert the unlawfulness of resort to armed force by groups seeking to exercise the right of self-determination. There is much room for debate as to the circumstances in which such resort to force is lawful as a matter of general international law, but to the extent that it may be lawful, paragraph 3 leaves it also untouched.

Article 3. Self-determination is one of the most important principles of contemporary international law and international relations; without it, human rights and fundamental freedoms suffer. Equally important is respect for the territorial integrity and political unity of states; without it, a cornerstone of the international order is destroyed, and states fragment—a danger to which the

Secretary-General of the United Nations drew proper attention in his *Agenda for Peace*.[8] A balance has to be struck between them. The need for such a balance is recognized in many international instruments, which match declarations on the right of self-determination with reminders of the importance of territorial integrity.[9]

Against this background, and expanding upon paragraph (g) of the preamble, Article 3—which applies both to the contracting parties and to the institutions to be established under the Convention—establishes appropriate respect for the territorial integrity and political unity of states.[10]

The precise commitments for states and Convention institutions under this article are three. They must: (1) acknowledge the importance of the territorial integrity and political unity of states; (2) seek to the fullest extent possible and in conformity with the Convention to support peaceful efforts to preserve them; and, (3) seek to avoid any action that would impair them. While these legal obligations are far-reaching, they fall short of an absolute obligation to give priority in all circumstances to the territorial integrity and political unity of states over the requirements of the right of self-determination. There is, in fact, a classic case here of a conflict between two legal norms of equivalent weight, and there is no clear, theoretical solution for the resolution of that conflict. Both norms are charter-based, both have good claims to now being rules of *jus cogens,* and both serve equally important ends in securing a politically acceptable international legal order.

In large part this conflict may be thought to be extraneous to the principal aims of the Convention. Its emphasis, as already noted, is on self-administration rather than independence, and a community having a degree of self-administration remains part of the state to which the community belongs. Self-administration itself, by definition, does not violate the territorial integrity of the state or its unity as a political structure. To that extent, therefore, Article 3 might be considered unnecessary. Nevertheless, while self-administration is at the heart of the Convention, it is placed within the overall framework of self-determination, and that principle cannot exclude evolution toward independence; this is recognized in Article 7. To that extent Article 3 serves a necessary purpose in laying down a guiding principle for the application of the Convention. States may have reasonable concerns lest self-administration encourages their fragmentation, and firm reassurance that the Convention is not to be understood in that way will be of considerable political value in getting the Convention approved.

---

8. UN Doc A/47/277, of 17 June 1992: paragraph 17.

9. See above, n. 5.

10. It may be noted that the relevant language of the UN charter is "territorial integrity or political independence": Art. 2(4). While "political independence" is appropriate for a provision concerned with the prohibition of the threat or use of force, it is less so in the context of the possible breakup of states. Accordingly, in that context the usual and more appropriate term is now "political unity" or "national unity" (as, e.g., in the last two paragraphs of the fifth principle of the "Friendly Relations" Declaration of 1970 [GA Res. 2625(XXV)]).

Self-Administration: Articles 4–8

This group of articles sets out the content of the concept of self-administration as it is used in the Convention. Articles 4 to 6 cover the progressive levels of self-administration that may be appropriate for the stage of political and administrative development, Article 7 acknowledges the possibility of independence, and Article 8 covers certain procedural matters.

While the more advanced levels of self-administration are optional, the initial level dealt with in Article 4 is mandatory for all contracting parties (given, of course, that a "community," as defined in the Convention, exists in its territory). This article provides for the community and its members to enjoy certain very basic rights, as set out in subparagraphs (a) to (g). None of these rights is fundamentally novel or onerous for states to accord. To a considerable extent they reflect obligations that states have already assumed under various human rights instruments and will already be the practice adopted in many states.

Thus, the basic right in subparagraph (a)—to be able to enjoy the community's distinctive culture, religion, and language—is modeled on Article 27 of the Covenant on Civil and Political Rights 1966.[11] Subparagraph (b) provides for participation in the conduct of public affairs and voting and being elected at periodic elections; it is drawn from Article 25 of the covenant.[12] Subparagraphs (c) and (d) build, in ways appropriate for the Convention, on the provision in Article 25(a) of the Covenant that citizens have the right to take part in the conduct of public affairs directly or "through freely chosen representatives." This provision for representative participation in public affairs would seem implicitly to allow for the establishment of organizations to represent community interests (as subparagraph (c) provides), and for the members of the community freely to elect their representatives in such organizations (as subparagraph (d) provides). It is, of course, important to note that the "organization" referred to is one of "an appropriate form" (thus allowing flexibility to fit varied circumstances) and that it is an organization "*to represent* the community's interests" and is conceived more as a form of pressure group or political party rather than as, in any sense, a form of local government.

Subparagraph (e) requires states to establish organs of central, regional, and local government and administration to look after matters affecting the community's interests and to promote those interests "to the fullest extent possible." It is clear that what is required is the establishment not of a local government for the community but rather something more like a special department of the central government or a special administrative body operating within the state's governmental structure that is specifically concerned with the

---

11. That article relates to "States in which ethnic, religious or linguistic minorities exist." On the interpretation of that article, see General Comment No. 23(50), adopted on 6 April 1994 by the Human Rights Committee under Article 40.4 of the covenant: CCPR/C/21/Rev. 1/ Add.5, of 26 April 1994.

12. Article 25 applies to "every citizen," and thus will, in any case, already apply to members of communities if (as in most cases they will be) they are citizens of the state. Most states are already committed by that article to allowing periodic elections on the basis of "universal and equal suffrage" and "secret ballot, guaranteeing the free expression of the will of the electors."

community's affairs. There is also value in ensuring that the community's interests are taken into account when certain decisions that directly affect it are taken; this is covered in subparagraph (f). The commitment for states to "involve" elected community representatives in decision making does not necessarily mean granting them unrestricted veto power. Finally, subparagraph (g) adopts the principle prescribed in many human rights instruments, that discrimination against the community or its members is prohibited. Given that, as explained, Article 1(a) is not specific about the particular basis or bases for the community's distinctive characteristics, the prohibition of discrimination is related simply to whatever ground may in a particular case be directly associated with the community's distinctive characteristics.

There is considerable room for discussion about which rights are sufficiently basic that states should be *obliged* to confer on any community within their territories. Those prescribed in Article 4.1 of the Convention are probably an essential minimum.

Those obligatory rights, however, are not intended to be an exhaustive catalogue of the rights that a community may have, even before moving on to one of the more advanced, and optional, levels of self-administration. Other (i.e., additional) rights may always be agreed upon between the state and the community in question: that is a matter for them to decide for themselves and is a necessary part of the flexibility that needs to be built into the proposals to take account of the infinitely variable circumstances that may arise. These "other rights" may even include some specifically mentioned in the later articles that identify rights appropriate for subsequent, optional, levels of self-administration, even when the situation has not progressed formally to those levels by action under Article 5 or 6. Paragraph 2 of Article 4 makes this flexibility explicit, as do Articles 5.4 and 6.4. On the assumption that the very basic, mandatory level of self-administration has been accorded to communities within states, movement beyond that level is optional.

There remains a question whether a total of three levels of self-administration is enough, or whether additional stages might be better so as to allow for a more gradual progression to the most advanced level. While that could certainly be done, considerations of practicality seem to outweigh this unnecessary complication of the Convention. As long as the three levels are not rigidly separated and self-contained but allow for considerable flexibility in their application (as they do), it seems sufficient to provide for a basic (and mandatory) level of self-administration at one end of the scale (Article 4), a full (and optional) level amounting virtually to internal self-government at the other (Article 6), and just one intermediate (and also optional) level between the two (Article 5).

The optional character of the levels of self-administration set out in Articles 5 and 6 is established in each case by the first paragraph. Progress onward to these further levels takes place only if a state so choose;[13] in which case it must make an express declaration to that effect; the procedural aspects of such declarations are dealt with in Article 8. Here it may be noted that the declaration has to relate to a specified community in the state's territory; if

---

13. Subject, as already noted, to the possibility that a state may voluntarily choose to grant to a community certain of the more "advanced" rights and benefits even when the community is, formally, still only at the mandatory level of self-administration.

there are several communities within a state, it is open to it to deal with them differently if the circumstances so require.

Furthermore, it is important that the more advanced levels of self-administration should only be enjoyed by those communities that may reasonably be expected to be able to assume the responsibilities that come with the rights of self-administration. An appropriate basis for making this kind of assessment is the community's performance. Paragraph 1 of Article 5 (and, *mutatis mutandis,* of Article 6) accordingly requires that the community must have, over a "reasonable period," acquired satisfactory experience in fulfilling its role under the mandatory, basic level of self-administration provided for under Article 4. "Reasonable period" and "satisfactory experience" allow the necessary flexibility in applying this requirement to particular circumstances.

If the optional declaration envisaged by this article has been made, the community is to have the rights specified in paragraph 2. Since the rights set out in Article 4.1 are mandatory, those set out in paragraph 2 of Article 5 are in addition to those set out in Article 4. These additional rights concern the administration of state funds allocated for the community's benefit, community policing, the nomination of judges in certain lower courts, and the administration of community schools. In the exercise of these rights the community acts through its elected representatives—an implicit reference back to Article 4.1(c) and (d). Two of the rights—concerning judicial appointments and schooling—expressly relate to matters arising in "the community's area," as stipulated by Article 8.1(b).

The choice of these specified rights is in a sense arbitrary; they have no inherent or inescapable connection with a second stage of self-administration, and other rights could well be thought more appropriate. What is important, however, is the selection of rights that can reasonably be considered to be appropriate for a halfway stage between the basic, mandatory level of self-administration and the virtually full internal self-government provided for in Article 6.

While the rights listed in Article 5 undoubtedly touch on matters that are of considerable importance for communities in their search for ways of giving expression to their distinctive qualities, it is inevitable that states will be sensitive to granting any set of rights that marks a significant progress beyond the initial and very basic level of self-administration. Reassurance (over and above the inherently optional character of the whole provision) is provided by the requirement of paragraph 3(a) that these additional rights of self-administration operate within the basic constitutional structure of the state. That provision also draws attention to the fact that, from a practical point of view, the state and the community will in any case need to come to various agreements and arrangements in connection with the way in which the rights and responsibilities granted under this article are to be exercised. One important matter to elucidate is the financial relationship between the state and the community, as provided in paragraph 3(b).

Just as at the initial mandatory level the state and the community are free to agree on the rights that the community may possess, so, too at this optional level paragraph 4 allows them similarly to agree on additional rights to be enjoyed by the community. Now, however, only rights *additional* to ("other than") those specified in paragraph 2 may be agreed upon by the state and the community.

Article 6 follows the pattern established in Article 5, in that its paragraph 1 establishes that the Article is also optional, on the basis of a declaration to be made in accordance with Article 8, and similarly requires that before moving on to this yet more advanced level of self-administration, the community must have shown itself reasonably likely to be able to satisfactorily exercise the rights and responsibilities in question.

Once the option to move to this yet more advanced level of self-administration has been exercised, the rights and responsibilities of the community will be as set out in the second paragraph of the Article, which are in addition to those identified for the first optional level of self-administration (Article 5): The rights set out in paragraph 2 (affecting the creation of a representative legislature for the community, the right to enact laws and to raise taxes, and the administration of state functions other than matters of foreign affairs and defense) virtually amount to rights (and responsibilities) of internal self-government, with the reference to "the community's area" needing, again, to be read with Article 8.1(b). These rights affect only the community and its members. In practice, such a strict limitation is unlikely to be workable in all situations, as when governmental powers need to apply throughout the community's area over both members and non-members.

Paragraph 3 repeats the reassurances given in the equivalent provision of the preceding article, that this further level of self-administration still exists within the constitutional structure of the state and that additional agreements and arrangements between the state and the community will be needed in order to ensure the effective implementation of the rights and responsibilities in question, particularly in relation to financial matters.

The final paragraph repeats the equivalent provisions in paragraph 4 of each of the two preceding articles, giving the state and the community freedom to agree upon other (additional) rights. By the time a community has moved to this very advanced level of self-administration, other rights will probably become necessary under this provision. To that extent, the specific rights identified in paragraph 2 of the article must be regarded as representing only the key elements of this advanced level of self-administration and not as an exhaustive enumeration. Again, the nature and extent of any additional rights will likely vary considerably from case to case.

If the necessary flexibility is already built into the Draft Convention, is there any need for an elaborate specification of the rights appropriate to various levels of self-administration? Since—apart from the initial mandatory rights—all others are optional and may be flexibly agreed upon, adapted, and applied by states and communities on the basis of what is best for their infinitely variable circumstances, it might seem enough simply to allow for this to happen on a completely open-ended basis. There is some weight in that view. However, there are three counter-arguments: (1) dividing the process into three stages of self-administration clearly illustrates the step-by-step character of the overall concept; (2) the operation of the institutional elements set up by the Convention can more easily be understood within this three-stage structure, and (3) the structure gives the Secretary guidance for the exercise of his functions under later articles to assist in cases in which his good offices are invoked.

Although it is self-administration, and not independence, that is at the heart of the Convention, the eventual evolution of a community to full independence cannot be excluded. Instead, however, of establishing independence as a further option in accordance with the same basic pattern as that established in the three preceding articles, Article 7, which introduces the possibility of independence primarily for the sake of completeness, is much more limited.

Its opening paragraph, in effect, simply provides that when a community seeks independence, the matter shall first be discussed between the state concerned and the community. This is a description of what would be likely to happen in any event. The desired orderliness of the move to independence within the Convention's framework is underpinned by the stipulations that the community must have shown itself over a reasonable period to have satisfactorily fulfilled its role at the preceeding levels of self-administration, that its further progress is within the framework of self-determination, and that it is acting through its elected representatives. These stipulations do not purport to prohibit independence if they are not satisfied, but merely establish that in that event the move to independence is outside the ambit of the Convention.

The second paragraph notes that the parties in any such discussions "should bear in mind" four matters in which there "could be" value in including any independence arrangements: (1) the holding of a referendum among all inhabitants of the community's area on the question of moving to independence; (2) the democratic basis of the future state's government; (3) the future state's participation in human rights treaties; and, (4) the orderly determination of issues which usually arise in cases of state succession (including the allocation of state property, the state's financial resources and liabilities, and the future state's position under treaties other than human rights treaties). As usual, there is no obligation on the parties to includes those matters in their arrangements, nor even a categorical statement that the matters *are* of value in this context; the provision is thus primarily an *aide-mémoire* of certain potentially important topics.

Article 8 is an essentially procedural mechanism by which the community expresses its desire to advance to the next level of self-administration. A declaration to this effect is first communicated to the Secretary, who then informs the other contracting parties. In order to ensure a necessary element of stability, declarations once made may not, in principle, be withdrawn and are thus conceived as essentially permanent.

Exceptions, however, must be recognized where there has been a fundamental change in the circumstances that were essential to the making of the declaration in the first place.[14] If such a change has occurred, paragraph 3 allows a declaration to be withdrawn on giving six months' notice. The Convention does not attempt to spell out what the consequences of such a withdrawal might be, but they will clearly operate at two distinct levels—that of the Convention and that of the internal law of the state concerned. At the international level of the Convention, the withdrawal of a declaration will relieve the state making it from such obligations as might flow from it under the Convention; but in no case will the withdrawal affect the state's obligation to comply with the basic, mandatory level of self-administration, since it is independent of any state declaration. At the internal level, it will essentially be a matter for the state's own laws to determine the consequences.

---

14. Compare with the terms of Article 62 of the Vienna Convention on the Law of Treaties 1969, allowing fundamental change of circumstances as a ground for terminating or withdrawing from a treaty.

A further exception is needed to cover situations in which there is a public emergency that threatens the life of the nation. Paragraph 4 (drawing on Article 4 of the Covenant on Civil and Political Rights 1966)[15] accordingly permits a contracting party in such circumstances to derogate from its obligations under Article 5 or 6 on a temporary and nondiscriminatory basis. The secretary must be notified of such derogations when they are made and when they are subsequently lifted.

Institutional Provisions: Articles 9–14

For the Convention to be a truly effective system and not just a formal set of aspirations, some mechanisms are needed to ensure that the structure established by the Convention operates properly. Articles 9 to 14 accordingly provide for the setting up of basic institutions necessary for the Convention's effective implementation a Foundation (to be managed by a board), a Secretary, a Court, and (possibly) an Advisory Council. The detailed arrangements for these institutions are set out in the immediately following articles. The Foundation (Article 10) is to be an impersonal fund with its own legal personality.

Contributions to capital are to be made by contracting parties and private contributors. The involvement of private contributors in the financing of the Foundation, and by extension in the running of its affairs, introduces a hybrid public/private character to the institution, which may assist its creation. Contributions by private individuals would presumably by voluntary; contributions by contracting parties may need to be obligatory, although voluntary contributions from them need not be excluded. The basis on which any obligatory contributions are due needs further elaboration. The underlying assumption is that if the contracting parties wish the system established by the Convention to be a working reality, they will need to be prepared to provide the necessary finance. The financial requirements for the Convention system seem likely to be relatively modest.

The Foundation will need to have legal personality and the necessary legal capacities to enable it to perform its functions (essentially to have power over Foundation monies, to hold and acquire property, and to enter into contracts, all for the purpose of implementing the Convention). Paragraph 3(a) provides for this, and paragraph 3(b) provides for the Secretary to represent the Foundation in the exercise of its legal personality and capacities.

Left out, however, is how the Foundation's legal personality is to be established or under what system of law—either international law or that of a particular state. Creating the Foundation's legal personality will be an international obligation under the Convention, and will need to be reflected in the laws of the various contracting parties; it may even be desirable for the foundation to be established as a legal personality primarily under a particular state's law.

There is no need for the Foundation to enjoy a wide range of privileges and immunities. However, given the nature of its functions and purposes, it would seem necessary (particularly to the extent that private contributions are

---

15. See also Article 15 of the European Convention on Human Rights and Fundamental Freedoms 1950 and Article 27 of the American Convention on Human Rights 1969.

to be attracted, thus lessening the need for contributions from contracting parties) that contracting parties should not tax either the Foundation's assets or transfers of capital to the Foundation by private contributors. Paragraph 4 so provides.

The Foundation is to be managed by a Board, as provided in Article 11, with each contracting party being represented at its meetings. No limit to the number of members of the Board is prescribed; if the number of contracting parties becomes too great, there may be a need to make further provision to ensure that the management of the Foundation remains effective. Since private contributors are not members of the Board, it may be desirable to find some way of associating them with its activities.

An Advisory Council may be established for consultation by the Board and the Secretary. If this is done, the Board would determine its membership within certain specified limits. The Council would be restricted to a maximum of twenty members (plus the President of the Board), with no more than twelve representing the contracting state parties. The remaining eight members could be representatives of private contributors or of other relevant interests.

Article 12 provides for a Secretary who would oversee the day-to-day operations of the Foundation as well as operate the Convention's dispute resolution mechanism. In addition to these vitally important functions, the Secretary is also to submit to the Board an annual budget and an annual report on activities under the Convention, as well as serve the Board and the Advisory Council.

The Secretary is appointed by the Board for a four-year, renewable term. A limited staff will needed to assist the Secretary, and provision is made for the recruitment, due regard being paid to "the need for efficiency and economy." The Board authorizes the establishment of staff, and the Secretary appoints and directs them.

Paragraph 5 envisages, as perhaps a temporary function, that the Secretary would act as an International Research and Advisory Center on Self-Administration and Self-Determination. The Center would be open not only to contracting parties but also to other states, communities, international organizations, and other interested persons and bodies. Initially, the Center would form part of the Secretary's functions, assisted by such staff as may be needed. But circumstances may make it desirable to expand the Center's role, so that it ceases to be run by the Secretary and becomes instead a separate agency with its own Director and staff; paragraph 5(c) makes provision for this eventuality.

Later Articles, which deal with the settlement of differences, envisage the possibility of recourse to a Court if there are allegations of a breach of the Convention. Although such allegations will probably be rare, contingent provision for a Court needs to be made, as elaborated in Articles 13 and 14.

The Court would have seven members, elected by the Board. The President of the Court is initially elected by the Board, and subsequently by the Court. When it is operational the Court will need a Registrar, appointed by the Board. But it may well be some time before the Court needs to function, and in the meantime the Secretary would administer the Court as necessary. The rules governing the Court's operations, and the procedure to be adopted in cases before it, are matters for the Court to lay down.

Article 14 sets out the Court's jurisdiction and powers. It has jurisdiction over all cases concerning the interpretation or application of the Convention. Cases may be submitted to the Court by any contracting party, and, in certain circumstances envisaged in Article 16.6, by a community. The Secretary cannot submit a case to the Court for decision, but may request an advisory opinion. Paragraph 3 identifies the range of options the Court has in deciding cases submitted to it: it may reject the complaint, uphold the complaint, refer the complaint to the Secretary with a recommendation for further action, or decide on any combination of these outcomes. The Court's judgments are final, and the judges may deliver separate opinions if they are not unanimous.

Settlement of Differences: Articles 15 and 16

The evolution of communities at their various levels of self-administration will inevitably give rise to differences between them and the states concerned, or between two or more states with interests in the matter, and occasionally those differences may be serious. An essential part of the Convention is that it should provide procedures for the peaceful resolution of these disputes: assistance and involvement from the Secretary, and action by the Court and the Secretary in those cases where a breach of the Convention is alleged (Articles 15 and 16, respectively).

Under Article 15 the Secretary may become involved in a dispute, by providing its good offices or mediation services, in one of two ways. First, under paragraph 1, the Secretary may *volunteer* assistance if circumstances develop that threaten or have already given rise to a breach of the Convention. This assistance may be offered to contracting parties or to communities within their territories. It is for the Secretary to offer assistance; it is for the parties concerned to decide whether to accept the offer. Under paragraph 2, the Secretary's assistance may be *requested* by contracting parties or by communities within their territories. If such request are made, the Secretary is obliged to respond positively, except if: (1) as judged by the Secretary, involvement would be counterproductive to the maintenance of peace and security, or (2) if a request has come from a community and the state concerned does not agree to the Secretary's assistance being given. Finally, the Secretary is *obliged* under paragraph 3 to offer assistance if circumstances within the scope of the Convention give rise to the outbreak of armed conflict. If the offer of assistance is rejected, there is no continuing obligation to extend assistance, though it is assumed that the offer would not be withdrawn. In any of these three circumstances, the way in which the Secretary's assistance is given is to be agreed upon by the Secretary and the parties concerned.

Whereas Article 15 applies when the Convention continues to be observed, Article 16 applies to actions to be taken where a breach of the Convention has occurred or is alleged. The heart of the Convention is in those articles concerning the various levels of self-administration, Articles 4, 5, and 6. Disputes about these articles are likely to be as much about political relations as about strictly legal differences. It is with this in mind that Article 16 distinguishes between breaches of the "self-administration Articles" and breaches of the other Articles. In respect of breaches of these other Articles, any contracting party alleging a breach by any other contracting party may refer the matter to the Court. These would be normal inter-State proceedings, and the Court would render a decision.

Breaches of the "self-administration Articles" are a different matter. Disputes about such breaches will, in the first place, involve the Secretary rather than the Court. Notification of such alleged breaches is to be given by

either a contracting party or a community. There may be an important preliminary issue to determine, namely, whether a body submitting such a notification
is truly a "community" as defined in the Convention. Article 16 3(b) accordingly provides that if discussions fail to resolve the question, the Secretary may
seek an advisory opinion from the Court.

Allowing a community access to an international procedure of the kind
envisaged is to acknowledge that it has at least a degree of limited international
procedural capacity. This is likely to be a sensitive matter in some contexts, but
acknowledgment of that limited international capacity on the part of communities is both unavoidable if the principle of self-determination is to be effectively
implemented, and justifiable given the framework of the Convention. Even so,
it is a capacity of very limited scope: it is limited to those provisions of the
Convention which directly concern communities, it allows complaints only
against the state of which the community forms part, and it involves in the first
instance recourse only to the Secretary for investigation by him. Such capacity
is consistent with the general trend that accepts that beneficiaries of the right of
self-determination have a limited degree of international capacity.

Where the Secretary has been notified by a contracting party or by a community of an alleged breach of one of the "self-administration Articles," the
Secretary must investigate the allegation and is given considerable flexibility as
to how to do so. The Secretary can conclude that either a breach has or has not
occurred. If the former, the Secretary is obliged to make recommendations to
the parties concerned for remedying the breach and preventing any repetition.
If a contracting party or a community disagrees with the Secretary's conclusion
as to whether or not a breach of the Convention had occurred, it may refer the
matter to the Court, which will then decide on the matter.

Final Clauses: Articles 17 to 23

This group of articles contains the traditional "final clauses" that determine the
inadmissibility of reservations (Article 17); signature, ratification, and accession (Article 18); entry into force (Article 19); territorial application (Article
20); amendment (Article 21); depositary functions (Articles 22 and 23); and
authentic texts (Article 23). They follow provisions that are quite normal in
these contexts, although precise precedents vary from treaty to treaty. These
articles are included in the Convention at this stage primarily for completeness.

*   *   *

Draft Convention on Self-Determination
Through Self-Administration

Preamble

(a) The States Parties to the present Convention,

(b) Recognizing the right of self-determination as one of the human rights and fundamental freedoms;

(c) Noting with satisfaction the great achievements of the United Nations in securing the exercise of the right of self-determination by the inhabitants of territories not formerly enjoying full self-government;

(d) Recognizing that the principle of self-determination applies not only to such territories;

(e) Recognizing also that while the attainment of independence is one possible outcome of the exercise of the right of self-determination it is not the only possible outcome;

(f) Noting that the possession by communities within States of a degree of self-administration is consistent with the right of self-determination, and may in many circumstances be a sufficient exercise of that right;

(g) Noting also that the possession by communities within States of a degree of self-administration is consistent with the territorial integrity of States and thus avoids the risks of conflict often associated with the fragmentation of States;

(h) Recognizing that States are created by humans for humans;

(i) Recognizing also the duty resting on all States to secure the enjoyment of human rights and fundamental freedoms by all individuals, whose enjoyment of which is closely connected with their ability to express their views through democratic procedures and with the standing within the State of the communities of which they form part;

(j) Desiring to support States in their efforts to realize the principle of self-determination through the recognition of a suitable degree of self-administration on the part of communities within their territories;

(k) Desiring further to establish procedures which can assist communities in their quest for self-administration in pursuit of the peaceful exercise of the right of self-determination;

(l) Noting that violations of the right of self-determination, the absence of an adequate measure of self-administration, and the lack of relevant internationally recognized rules and procedures have led to countless wars and other conflicts;

(m) Being resolved to take steps to secure the effective and peaceful application of the principle of self-determination through the adoption of measures to facilitate the exercise of self-administration by certain communities, and to provide procedures for the resolution of differences which might arise in that context;

HAVE AGREED AS FOLLOWS:

SECTION I

Article 1

For the purposes of the present Convention:

(a) "community" means the members of a distinct group which inhabits a limited area within a State and possesses a sufficient degree of organization as such a group for the effective application of the relevant provisions of this Convention;

(b) "right of self-determination" involves the free determination by those possessing that right of their political status and their free pursuit of their economic, social and cultural development, and may be implemented by establishment as a sovereign and independent State, free association or integration with an independent State, or emergence into any other political status freely determined by the people concerned.

Article 2

1. All peoples have the right of self-determination.

2. Within the framework of that right, each State Party to the present Convention shall respect the aspirations of all communities within its territory to an appropriate degree of self-administration and shall secure that degree of self-administration to them.

3. The application of this Convention is without prejudice to the exercise of the right of self-determination to whatever further extent may be justified.

Article 3

In the implementation of this Convention the States Parties to the present Convention, and the institutions established under it, shall acknowledge the importance of the territorial integrity and political unity of sovereign and independent States. They shall accordingly seek, to the fullest extent possible and in conformity with the provisions of this Convention, to support peaceful efforts to preserve the territorial integrity and political unity of States and to avoid any action which would impair their territorial integrity and political unity.

SECTION II

Article 4

1. Each State Party to the present Convention shall, in relation to communities in its territory:

(a) allow members of the community the right, together with the other members of their group, to enjoy their own culture, to profess and practice their own religion, and to use their own language;

(b) allow members of the community to take part in the conduct of public affairs, and to vote and be elected at periodic elections by free and secret ballot to the central, regional and local elected institutions of the State;

(c) allow the community to establish an appropriate form of organization to represent the community's interests in public affairs;

(d) allow the members of the community to elect, by free and secret ballot, their representatives in such an organization;

(e) establish, to the fullest extent possible, organs of central, regional and local government and administration concerned primarily with matters affecting the community's interests, and in particular charged with the promotion of those interests;

(f) involve, to the fullest extent possible, the elected representatives of the community in decisions concerning the administration of State funds allocated for the benefit of the community and in any other decisions which directly affect the community;

(g) refrain from any discrimination against the community or its members on any ground directly associated with the distinctive characteristics of the community.

2. Nothing in the preceding paragraph of this Article shall prevent a State and a community agreeing that a community shall have rights other than those specified, even in the absence of any declaration allowing for the application of Articles 5 or 6 of this Convention.

Article 5

1. A State Party to the present Convention may at any time make a declaration in accordance with Article 8 of this Convention that it accepts the application of this article to a specified community in its territory, being a community which has over a reasonable period acquired satisfactory experience in fulfilling its role under the preceding article of this Convention.

2. When such a declaration has been made, the community so specified, acting through its elected representatives, shall have:
(a) the right to administer State funds allocated for the benefit of the community;
(b) the right to have its own police force;
(c) the right to nominate judges for the lower courts sitting in the community's area and dealing with matters directly affecting the community's interests;
(d) the right to administer schools in the community's area for use by children of members of the community.

3. (a) The community shall exercise these rights within the limits of the Constitution and laws of the State, and in accordance with agreements and arrangements to be made between the State and the community in connection with these rights.
(b) These arrangements shall include a financial compensation plan agreed between the State and the community, taking into account the income and administrative functions and responsibilities of the State and the community.

4. Nothing in the preceding paragraphs of this article shall prevent a State and a community agreeing that a community shall have rights other than those specified, or that, in the absence of a declaration under paragraph 1 of this article, a community shall have any or all of the rights specified in this article or any other rights.

Article 6

1. A State Party to the present Convention may at any time make a declaration in accordance with Article 8 of this Convention that it accepts the application of this article to a specified community in its territory, being a community which has over a reasonable period acquired satisfactory experience in fulfilling its role under the preceding article of this Convention.

2. When such a declaration has been made, the community so specified, acting through its elected representatives, shall have, in addition to the rights specified in Article 5 of this Agreement:
(a) the right to establish, through elections held by free and secret ballot, a representative legislature with powers over the community and its members;
(b) the right to enact laws having effect within the community's area and relating to the affairs of the community;
(c) the right to raise taxes payable by members of the community, to meet the expenses of the community;
(d) the right to assume responsibility for the administration of all State func-

tions within the community's area, with the exception of matters of foreign affairs or defense which shall remain the responsibility of the State.

3. (a) The community shall exercise these rights within the limits of the Constitution and laws of the State, and in accordance with agreements and arrangements to be made between the State and the community in connection with these rights.

(b) These arrangements shall include such adaptations to the financial compensation plan referred to in paragraph 3(b) of Article 5 as may be required to meet the new circumstances.

4. Nothing in the preceding paragraphs of this article shall prevent a State and a community agreeing that a community shall have rights other than those specified, or that, in the absence of a declaration under paragraph 1 of this article, a community shall have any or all of the rights specified in this Article or any other rights.

Article 7

1. Where a community which has over a reasonable period acquired satisfactory experience in fulfilling its role under the preceding article of this Convention seeks, within the framework of self-determination and acting through its elected representatives, to establish itself as a sovereign and independent State, the matter shall in the first place be discussed between the State Party concerned and the elected representatives of the community.

2. The parties participating in such discussion should bear in mind that there could be value in any arrangements for the peaceful attainment of independence including

(a) the holding of a referendum of all inhabitants in the community's area on the question whether that area should become an independent State;

(b) the community's system of government upon independence being such as to secure the proper observance of democracy in the community;

(c) the community undertaking to become a party to those treaties and other engagements for the protection of human rights and fundamental freedoms to which the State Party concerned is itself a party and which apply to the community's area, including those protecting the right of self-determination;

(d) arrangements being agreed between the State Party to the present Convention and the community for the orderly and peaceful allocation, as between them, of relevant rights, responsibilities, functions and powers, including:

(i) the allocation of State property, both in the State and abroad, including the allocation of the State's financial resources;

(ii) the allocation of the State's financial and other liabilities;

(iii) the future position under treaties (other than those referred to in subparagraph [c]) applying to the community's area.

Article 8

1. (a) A State Party to the present Convention wishing to make a declaration pursuant to Articles 5 or 6 of this Convention shall communicate its declaration to the secretary.

(b) The declaration shall state the article pursuant to which it is being made, shall specify the community to which it relates, and shall identify the limited area within the State's territory which the community inhabits.

2. The secretary shall inform the other States Parties to the present

Convention of all such declarations as soon as possible after they have been made.

3. A declaration made by a State Party to the present Convention may not be withdrawn unless there has been a fundamental change of circumstances essential to the making of the declaration, so as to make it no longer possible to continue to accord to the community in question the rights envisaged in the article pursuant to which the declaration was made. In such situations, the withdrawal of a declaration only takes effect after six months' notice in writing to the secretary.

4. (a) In time of public emergency which threatens the life of the nation and the existence of which is officially proclaimed a State Party to the present Convention which has made a declaration pursuant to Articles 5 or 6 may, on a non-discriminatory and temporary basis, take measures derogating from its obligations under the Article in question, to the extent strictly required by the exigencies of the situation.

(b) A State Party to the present Convention availing itself of the right of derogation shall immediately inform the secretary of the provisions from which it has derogated and of the reasons by which it was actuated, and shall make a further communication to the secretary on the date on which it terminates such derogation. The secretary shall immediately inform the other States Parties to the present Convention of all communications received under this provision.

SECTION III

Article 9
To provide for the effective implementation of this Convention there shall be established:
(a) the Foundation for Self-Administration and Self-Determination (referred to as "the Foundation") which shall be managed by the Board of the Foundation (referred to as "the Board");
(b) a secretary of the Convention (referred to as "the secretary");
(c) a Court of the Convention (referred to as "the Court"); and
(d) if so decided by the Board, an Advisory Council.

Article 10
1. The Foundation shall be established by contributions to capital made by
(a) the States Parties to the present Convention;
(b) private contributors.

2. The resources of the Foundation shall be devoted to meeting costs necessarily incurred in the implementation of this Convention, and to supporting research and other activities dedicated to the achievement of the purposes of this Convention.

3. (a) The Foundation shall have legal personality, and shall enjoy in the territory of each State Party to the present Convention the legal capacity to hold and acquire property and enter into contracts, and such other legal capacity as may be necessary to perform its functions.

(b) The Foundation, in the exercise of its legal personality and capacities, shall be represented by the secretary. Save with the consent of the Board, the secretary may not commit the Foundation to any contract which will be binding on the Foundation after the expiry of the secretary's current term of office.

4. The States Parties to the present Convention shall grant the Foundation immunity from taxation on its assets, and shall not impose taxes on transfers of capital to the Foundation by private contributors under paragraph 1 of this article.

Article 11
1. The Foundation shall be managed by a Board. Each State Party to the present Convention shall appoint a representative to attend meetings of the Board on its behalf. Representatives may be accompanied by experts and advisers.

2. The first meeting of the Board shall be convened by [State/organization] at [name of place] within three months after the entry into force of this Convention.

3. (a) At that meeting the Board will elect a President of the Board for a period of two years. The President cannot be re-elected.
(b) At the same meeting the Board will decide the timing and location of subsequent meetings.

4. (a) The Board shall, by a majority of the States Parties to the present Convention attending the meeting, adopt and later amend as necessary its rules of procedure, including provisions for the majorities required for the taking of decisions.
(b) Unless otherwise stipulated in this Convention or in the Board's rules of procedures, each decision of the Board shall require the favorable vote of a majority of the States Parties to the present Convention attending the meeting at which the decision is taken.

5. (a) The Board may set up an Advisory Council, composed of the President of the Board and not more than twenty other persons, not more than twelve of whom may be representatives of States Parties to the present Convention. The President of the Board will also take the chair at meetings of the Advisory Council.
(b) The Advisory Council shall give advice to the Board, and to the secretary, on any matters with which the Board or the secretary may be concerned, including the conduct and publication of research into matters relating to self-determination, and the raising of funds for the Foundation and the administration of those funds. The Advisory Council may act on the request of the Board or the secretary, or on its own initiative.

Article 12
1. The Board shall appoint the secretary on such terms and conditions as it may determine.

2. The secretary shall be appointed for a period of four years, and may be reappointed.

3. The secretary shall serve the Board and the Advisory Council, shall administer the Foundation, and shall perform such other functions as are entrusted to the secretary by this Convention or by the Board.

4. (a) The secretary shall submit an annual budget to the Board, for its approval, by a two thirds majority of the States Parties to the present Convention attending the meeting, before the beginning of the year to which it relates.
(b) The secretary shall submit to the Board an annual report on activities under this Convention during the preceding year, including a report on:

(i) the secretary's activities in relation to the resolution of any disputes or differences within the scope of this Convention;
(ii) the Foundation's income and expenditure;
(iii) the performance of the Foundation's investments; and
(iv) the Foundation's fund-raising activities.

5. (a) The secretary shall act as an International Research and Advisory Center on Self-Administration and Self-Determination (referred to as "the Center"), until such time as action is taken pursuant to subparagraph (c) of this paragraph.
(b) The Center shall be open to States, communities, international governmental and nongovernmental organizations, and other interested persons and bodies, for research and advice on matters related to self-administration and the exercise of the right of self-determination.
(c) If the activities of the Center make it desirable, the secretary may, with the approval of the Board, establish the Center as an agency with its own Director and staff, under the overall authority of the secretary. The detailed terms and conditions on which the Center, and its Director and staff, will operate as such an agency shall be determined by the secretary, with the approval of the Board.

6. The Board, with due regard to the need for efficiency and economy, shall authorize such staff establishment for a Secretariat to assist the secretary as it considers necessary for the performance of his functions, and the secretary shall appoint, direct and supervise such staff according to such rules and procedures and on such terms and conditions as the Board may determine.

Article 13
1. The Court shall consist of seven members, who shall be nationals of States Parties to the present Convention.
2. (a) Subject to subparagraph (b), the members of the Court shall be elected by the Board for a period of seven years. They may be re-elected.
(b) Of the members elected at the first election, the terms of six members shall expire after, respectively, one, two, three, four, five and six years. Immediately after the first election, those six members and the term for which each of them is elected, will be chosen by the President of the Board by lot.
(c) A member of the Court elected to replace a member whose term of office has not expired shall hold office for the remainder of his predecessor's term.
3. The President of the Court after the first election shall be elected by the Board for a period of [one] year. After that period, the President of the Court shall be elected by the members of the Court in accordance with such procedures as the Court may determine, for a period of [three] years. The President of the Court may be re-elected.
4. The Board shall appoint a Registrar when such an appointment becomes necessary, on such terms and conditions as it may determine. Until then, the secretary shall perform such administrative functions as may be necessary in support of the Court.
5. The Court shall draw up its own rules and shall determine its own procedure.

Article 14
1. (a) The jurisdiction of the Court shall extend to all cases concerning the interpretation or application of this Convention.

(b) In the event of a dispute as to whether the Court has jurisdiction, the matter shall be settled by decision of the Court.

2. (a) Cases may be submitted to the Court by any State Party to the present Convention, and, in the circumstances envisaged in paragraph 6 of Article 16, by any community.

(b) Requests for an advisory opinion on a matter of law arising out of the interpretation or application of this Convention may also be submitted to the Court by the secretary.

3. Unless the Court finds that it is without jurisdiction over a case submitted to it under paragraph 2(a) of this article, or that the case is otherwise inadmissible, it shall either:

(a) reject, as unfounded, the complaint on which the case was based; or

(b) decide that the complaint is to be upheld; or

(c) refer the complaint to the secretary with a recommendation for further action; or

(d) combine any or all of those courses of action, in respect of different parts of the case.

4. (a) The judgment of the Court on a case submitted to it under paragraph 2(a) of this article shall be final.

(b) If the judgment or opinion of the Court does not represent in whole or in part the unanimous opinion of the judges, any judge shall be entitled to deliver a separate opinion.

SECTION IV

Article 15

1. The secretary may at any time offer his assistance, by way of good offices or mediation, to States Parties to the present Convention or to communities within their territories if circumstances develop which in the secretary's opinion threaten to give rise to, or have already given rise to, a breach of this Convention.

2. (a) States Parties to the present Convention may at any time request the secretary to render assistance by way of good offices or mediation in respect of matters falling within the scope of this Convention.

(b) Communities within the territories of States Parties to the present Convention may similarly request the assistance of the secretary in respect of such matters.

(c) The secretary shall respond affirmatively to all such requests unless, in the secretary's opinion, it would be counter-productive to the maintenance of peace and security to do so or unless, in the case of a request from a community, the contracting party concerned does not agree to the secretary's assistance being given.

3. If circumstances within the scope of this Convention give rise to the outbreak of an armed conflict, the secretary shall offer assistance, by way of good offices or mediation, to the parties involved in the conflict, and shall maintain the offer for so long as the conflict continues.

4. If the secretary's offer of assistance under this Article is accepted, or he responds affirmatively to a request for assistance, the way in which the assistance is given shall be a matter for agreement between the secretary and the parties concerned.

Article 16

1. Any State Party to the present Convention which alleges that any other State Party to the present Convention is acting, or has acted, in breach of the provisions of this Convention other than Articles 4 to 6 inclusive may refer the matter to the Court for decision.

2. Any State Party to the present Convention which alleges that any other State Party to the present Convention is acting, or has acted, in breach of Articles 4 to 6 inclusive of this Convention, may refer the matter to the secretary by a notification in writing which shall set out the details of the allegation; it shall send a copy of the notification to the other Party. The secretary shall notify the members of the Board that a notification has been received.

3. (a) Any community may similarly refer to the secretary any allegation that the State Party to the present Convention part of whose territory the community inhabits is acting in breach of Articles 4 to 6 inclusive of this Convention; it shall send a copy of the notification to that State Party. The secretary shall notify the Board that a notification has been received.

(b) If there is any dispute whether the body referring the allegation to the secretary is a community as defined in Article 1 of this Convention, the secretary will seek to resolve the matter in discussion with the representatives of that body and the State Party in question; if such discussion fails to resolve the matter, the secretary may request an advisory opinion from the Court.

4. On receipt of notification from a State Party to the present Convention or a community alleging a breach of this Convention, the secretary shall investigate the allegation. For this purpose he may hold discussions with the parties concerned or any other persons or bodies who in the secretary's opinion may be able to assist, and may visit any relevant area within the territory of a State Party to the present Convention.

5. (a) If the secretary, in the light of the investigations, concludes that a breach of this Convention has occurred, the secretary shall so notify the parties concerned, shall make recommendations to them for remedying the breach and preventing any repetition, and shall notify the Board that the recommendations have been made.

(b) If the secretary, in the light of the investigations, concludes that no breach of this Convention has occurred, the secretary shall so notify the parties concerned and the Board.

6. Any State Party to the present Convention or community which disagrees with the conclusion of the secretary as to whether or not a breach of this Convention has occurred may refer the matter to the Court for decision.

SECTION V

Article 17

No reservations to this Convention shall be made.

Article 18

1. This Convention is open for signature at [place] until [date] by any State Member of the United Nations or member of any of its specialized agencies, by any State Party to the Statute of the International Court of Justice, and by any other State which has been invited by the Board to become a Party to this Convention.

2. This Convention is subject to ratification. Instruments of ratification shall be deposited with [the Secretary-General of the United Nations] [the Government of . . .] (referred to as the Depositary).

3. After the date referred to in paragraph 1 of this article, this Convention shall be open to accession by any State referred to in that paragraph.

4. Accession shall be effected by the deposit of an instrument accession with the Depositary.

5. The Depositary shall notify all States which have signed this Convention or acceded to it of the deposit of each instrument of ratification or accession.

Article 19

1. This Convention shall enter into force three months after the deposit with the Depositary of the [tenth] instrument of ratification or instrument of accession.

2. For each State ratifying the present Convention or acceding to it after the deposit of the [tenth] instrument of ratification or instrument of accession, this Convention shall enter into force three months after the date of the deposit of its own instrument of ratification or instrument of accession.

Article 20

The provisions of this Convention shall extend to all parts of federal States without any limitations or exceptions.

Article 21

1. Any State Party to the present Convention, the secretary, or the Advisory Council acting by a majority of the members present, may propose an amendment to this Convention and file it with the President of the Board. The President of the Board shall thereupon communicate any proposed amendments to the States Parties to the present Convention with a request that they notify him whether they favor a conference of States Parties to the present Convention for the purpose of considering and voting upon the proposals. If at least one third of the States Parties to the present Convention favours such a conference, the Depositary shall arrange for the convening of the conference. Any amendment adopted by a majority of the States Parties to the present Convention present and voting at the conference shall be regarded as adopted, and shall be submitted to all the States Parties to the present Convention for their further consideration and approval.

2. Amendments which are approved by a two thirds majority of the States Parties to the present Convention by notification in writing to the secretary shall come into force three months after the date of receipt by the secretary of the last notification necessary to constitute the required two thirds majority. The secretary shall inform all States Parties to the present Convention of the receipt by him of notifications of approval of amendments.

3. When amendments come into force, they shall be binding on those States Parties to the present Convention which have accepted them, other States Parties to the present Convention still being bound by the provisions of the present Convention and earlier amendments which are in force for them.

Article 22

In addition to the notifications made under paragraph 5 of Article 18 of this Convention, the Depositary shall inform all signatory and acceding States of the following particulars:

(a) signatures under Article 18;

(b) the date of the entry into force of this Convention under Article 19 and the date of the entry into force of any amendment under Article 21.

Article 23
1. This Convention, of which the Arabic, Chinese, English, French, Russian and Spanish texts are equally authentic, shall be deposited in the archives of . . .
2. The Depositary shall transmit certified copies of this Convention to all States Parties to the present Convention.
3. The Depositary shall register this Convention pursuant to Article 102 of the Charter of the United Nations.

Done at
this day of 200_

In witness whereof, the undersigned, duly authorized, have signed this Convention.

Appendix C Selected Self-Determination and Interstate Conflicts Since 1990

State(s) Claiming Sovereignty	Self-Determination Movement	Dispute Type	Violence	Significant Outside Political Involvement and/or Military Intervention	Period(s) of Dispute
		SUB-SAHARAN AFRICA			
Angola	Cabinda[a] (Cabindans)	substate	yes	—	1990–present
	Ovimbundu	substate	yes	—	mid-1960s–1997
Burundi	Hutu vs. Tutsi	intercommunal	yes	EU, UN, United States, OAU	1988–present
Cameroon	Westerners	substate	yes	—	1992–present
Cameroon, Nigeria	Bakassi Penninsula & borderlands	interstate border dispute	yes	International Court of Justice	1994–present
Chad	Southerners	substate	yes	—	1979–1986; 1992–1998
Comoros	Anjouan Island secession	substate	yes	OAU	1997–present
Djibouti	Afars	indigenous	yes	—	1991–1995
Ethiopia	Afars	indigenous	yes	—	1975–1998
	Eritreans	substate	yes	—	1961–1993 (independence)
	Oromos	substate	yes	—	1973–present
	Somalis	indigenous	yes	—	1963–present
Ethiopia vs. Eritrea	borderlands	interstate border dispute	yes	—	1997–?

(continues)

Appendix C   Continued

State(s) Claiming Sovereignty	Self-Determination Movement	Dispute Type	Violence	Significant Outside Political Involvement and/or Military Intervention	Period(s) of Dispute
		SUB-SAHARAN AFRICA			
Ghana	Konkmba vs. Dagombi	intercommunal	yes	—	1994–1995
Mali, Niger	Tuareg (Liberation Front of Air and Azawad, FLAA)	transstate, substate, indigenous	yes	—	1988–1993
Mauritania vs. Senegal	Reciprocal ethnic cleansing of black Africans (from Mauritania) & Arab Moors (from Senegal)	interstate	yes	—	1989–1990
Nigeria	Ogani[a]	substate	yes	—	1990–present
	Yoruba	substate	yes	—	1990–present
Rwanda	Batwa[a]	indigenous	yes	—	1994–present
	Hutu vs. Tutsi	intercommunal	yes	UN, France ("Operation Tourquoise," June 1994)	1994–present
Senegal	Casamancais	substate	yes	—	1991–present
Somalia	Somaliland (Isaaqs)	substate	yes	—	1986–1991
Sudan	Minority Christian South (SPLA)	control of govt., substate	yes	Egypt, Ethiopia, Eritrea	1956–1972; 1983–present
	Nuba	control of govt., substate	yes	—	1985–present
Tanzania	Zanzibar[a]	substate	yes	—	1964–present

(continues)

ASIA-PACIFIC

Country	Group	Type	Armed	External party	Dates
Afghanistan (Taliban-controlled)	Hazaras (and other non-Pashtun ethnicities)	substate	yes	Pakistan	1990s
	Tajiks	substate	yes	Pakistan	1979–1992; 1996–present
	Uzbeks	substate	yes	Pakistan	1996–present
Australia	Aboriginals[a]	indigenous	no	—	1951–present
Bangladesh	Bihari	substate	no	—	1971–present
	Chittagong Hill Peoples[a]	indigenous, substate	yes	—	1975–1997
Bhutan	Lhotsampa (Hindu-Nepali minority)	substate	yes	—	1990–1992
China	Xinjiang Province/East Turkestan[a] (Uighers and Turkoman)	substate, indigenous	yes	—	1990–present
	Hong Kong	substate	no	United Kingdom	1997 handover
	Inner Mongolia	substate, transstate, indigenous	yes	—	1995–present
	Taiwan[a]	substate	no	United States	1949–present
	Tibet[a] (Tibetans vs. Han Chinese)	substate, intercommunal	yes	—	1949–present
Fiji	Fijians vs. Indians	intercommunal, control of govt.	yes	—	1990s–present
(France)	Maohi (French Polynesia)[a]	anticolonial, indigenous	no	—	1994–present
	New Caledonia	anticolonial	no	—	1988–1998
India	Assamese vs. Bengalis	indigenous, intercommunal	yes	—	1990–present

(continues)

Appendix C   Continued

State(s) Claiming Sovereignty	Self-Determination Movement	Dispute Type	Violence	Significant Outside Political Involvement and/or Military Intervention	Period(s) of Dispute
			ASIA-PACIFIC		
	Bodos vs. Bengalis	indigenous, intercommunal	yes	—	1989–present
	Hindus vs. Muslims	intercommunal	yes	—	1948–present
	Jharkhand	substate	N/A	—	new state in India, 2000
	Manipur	substate	yes	—	1950s–present
	Nagaland[a] (Nagas)	substate, indigenous	yes	—	1952–1964; 1972–1996
	Punjab (Sikhs)	substate	yes	—	1978–1993
	Various Scheduled Tribes	indigenous	yes	—	1960–present
	Tripura (Tripuras vs. Bengalis)	indigenous, intercommunal	yes	—	1967–1972; 1979–present
India vs. Pakistan	Jammu and Kashmir (Kashmiri Moslems)	interstate border disupte, transstate	yes	UNMOGIP: UN Military Observer Group in India and Pakistan (Jan. 1949–present)	1949–present
Indonesia	Aceh/Sumatra[a] (Acehnese)	substate, indigenous	yes	—	1979–present
	West Kalimantan (Christian Dayaks vs. Muslim Madurese)	indigenous, intercommunal	yes	—	Dec. 1996–Feb. 1997
	East Timor[a] (East Timorese vs. pro-Indonesian militias)	substate, intercommunal	yes	UNTAET: UN Transitional Administration in East Timor (Oct. 1999–present); International Court of Justice	1974–present

(continues)

ASIA-PACIFIC

	Indonesians vs. Chinese	intercommunal	yes	—	Spring 1998
	Irian Jaya/West Papua[a] (Papuans)	substate, indigenous	yes	—	1965–present
	Republic of South Moluccas* (Christians vs. Muslims)	intercommunal	yes	—	1990s
Laos	Hmong	indigenous	yes	—	1945–1979; 1985–1996
Myanmar (Burma)	Kachins	indigenous	yes	—	1961–1994
	Karen[a]	indigenous	yes	—	1949–present
	Karenni	indigenous	yes	—	1945–present
	Mon[a]	indigenous	yes	—	1975–1997
	Arakan (Rohingyas)	indigenous	yes	—	1945–1985; 1991–1994
	Shan[a]	indigenous	yes	—	1962–1996
	Wa	indigenous	yes	—	1989–present
	Zomi (Chin)	indigenous	yes	—	1985–present
Papua New Guinea	Bougainville[a] (Bougainvilleans)	substate	yes	Australian-led multinational peace monitoring group	1989–1998
Phillippines	Cordillera[a] (Igorots)	indigenous	yes	—	1976–1993
	Mindanao (Moros)	substate	yes	—	1972–present
Sri Lanka	Tamils	substate	yes	India	1975–present
Thailand	Southern Muslims	substate	yes	—	1995–present

(continues)

Appendix C   Continued

State(s) Claiming Sovereignty	Self-Determination Movement	Dispute Type	Violence	Significant Outside Political Involvement and/or Military Intervention	Period(s) of Dispute
			EUROPE		
Albania	Greek minority[a]	substate	no	—	1990s
Belgium	Flemish-speaking Flanders	substate	no	—	1970s–1990s
	French-speaking Wallonia	substate	no	—	1970s–1990s
Bosnia-Herzegovina	Autonomous Province of Western Bosnia, Croatian Republic of B-H, and Serbian Republic of B-H	substate, intercommunal	yes	NATO-led implementation force (IFOR), and NATO-led stabilization force (SFOR), 1995–present; Russian Federation; and UNMIBH: UN Mission in Bosnia and Herzegovina (12/95–present)	1995–present
Croatia	Serbian Republic of Krajina (Serbs vs. Croats)	substate, intercommunal	yes	NATO; Russian Federation; UNCRO: UN Confidence Restoration Organization in Croatia (3/95–1/96); UNTAES: UN Transitional Administration for Eastern Slavonia; Baranja and Western Sirmium (1/96–1/98); UNPSG: UN Civilian Police Support Group (1/98–10/98); and UNMOP: UN Mission of Observers in Prevlaka (1/96–present)	1991–present

(continues)

EUROPE

Cyprus	Greece/Greek Cypriots vs. Turkey/Turkish Cypriots	substate, interstate, intercommunal	yes	Greece, Turkey, and UNFICYP: UN Peacekeeping Force in Cyprus (3/74–present)	1974–present
Czechoslovakia	Slovakia	substate	no	—	1991–1992
France	Brittany (Breton)	substate	no	—	N/A
	Corsica	substate	yes	—	N/A
(West) Germany	(East) Germany	substate	no	United States, United Kingdom, France, and the Russian Federation	1990–1991 reunification
Greece	Chameria[a] (Albanian Muslims)	substate	no	—	1990s–present
Italy	South Tyrol	substate	no	—	1918–1996
Macedonia	Albanian minority[a]	substate	no	—	1990s
Romania	Transylvania[a] (Hungarian minority)	substate	no	—	1989–1995
Serbia	Vojvodina (Hungarians)	substate	no	—	1990s
Serbia and Montenegro	Sanjak[a] (Muslims)	transstate	no	—	1990s
Spain	Catalonia	substate	no	—	N/A
Spain, France	Basques	transstate	yes	—	1959–present
Sweden	Scania[a]	substate, indigenous	no	—	1989–present

(continues)

Appendix C Continued

State(s) Claiming Sovereignty	Self-Determination Movement	Dispute Type	Violence	Significant Outside Political Involvement and/or Military Intervention	Period(s) of Dispute
		EUROPE			
Ukraine, Hungary, Poland	Rusyn People[a]	transstate	no	—	1939–present
United Kingdom	Northern Ireland (Catholic vs. Protestant)	substate, intercommunal	yes	United States, Ireland	1969–present
	Scotland	substate	no	—	1990s
	Wales	substate	no	—	1990s
Yugoslavia	Bosnia-Herzegovina	substate	yes	UNPROFOR: UN Protection Force (3/92–12/95)	1992–1995
	Croatia	substate	yes	UNPROFOR: UN Protection Force (3/92–12/95)	1991–1995
	Kosovo[a] (Kosovar Albanians vs. resident Serbs)	substate, intercommunal	yes	United States, NATO (International Security Force "KFOR"), Russian Federation, and UNMIK: UN Interim Administration Mission in Kosovo (1999–present) UNPREDEP: UN Preventive Deployment Force (3/95-2/99)	1997–present 1991–1995
	Macedonia (FYROM)	substate	no	—	
	Montenegro	substate	no	—	1990s
	Slovenia	substate	yes	—	June–July 1991

(continues)

FORMER SOVIET UNION

Azerbaijan vs. Armenia	Nagorno Karabakh (Armenians)	substate, transstate, interstate territorial conflict	yes	Russian Federation, OSCE Minsk Group (Armenia, Azerbaijan, Nagorno-Karabakh, Belarus, the Czech Republic, France, Germany, Italy, the Russian Federation, Sweden, Turkey, and the United States)	1988–present
Georgia	Abkhazia[a] (Abkhaz)	substate	yes	Russian Federation, UNOMIG UN Observer Mission in Georgia (8/93–present)	1992–1993; 1998
	Adjara	substate	yes	—	1991–1997
	South Ossetia	transstate	yes	Russian Federation	1991–1993
Moldova	Trans-Dniestria (Russians & Ukrainians)[a]	substate, transstate	yes	Russian Federation	1991–1997
	Gagauz (Turkish speaking)[a]	substate	yes	—	1991–1995
Russian Federation	Bashkortostan[a]	substate	no	—	1990–present
	Buryatia[a] (Buryat)	substate, indigenous	no	—	1990s
	Chechnya[a] (Chechens)	substate, indigenous	yes	OSCE	1991–present
	Chuvash[a]	substate	no	—	1990s
	Dagestan	substate	yes	—	1990s
	Ingushetia[a] (Ingush)	substate, indigenous	yes	—	1990s
	Inkeri[a]	substate, indigenous	no	—	1988–present
	Komi[a]	substate, indigenous	no	—	1990s
	Komyk[a]	substate	N/A	—	N/A
	Mari[a]	substate	no	—	1990s
	Sakha Republic (Yakutia)[a] (Yakut)	substate, indigenous	no	—	1990s

(continues)

Appendix C   Continued

FORMER SOVIET UNION

State(s) Claiming Sovereignty	Self-Determination Movement	Dispute Type	Violence	Significant Outside Political Involvement and/or Military Intervention	Period(s) of Dispute
	Tatarstan[a] (Tatars)	substate	no	—	1990s
	Tuva[a]	substate, indigenous	no	—	1990s
	Udmurt[a]	substate	no	—	1990s
Soviet Union	Armenia[b]	substate	no	—	1991
	Azerbaijan	substate	yes	—	1990–1991
	Belarus[b]	substate	no	—	1991
	Estonia[b]	substate	no	—	1991
	Georgia[b]	substate	no	—	1991
	Kazakhstan	substate	no	—	1991
	Kyrgyzstan	substate	no	—	1991
	Latvia[b]	substate	no	—	1991
	Lithuania	substate	yes	—	1991
	Moldova	substate	no	—	1991
	Russian Federation	substate	yes	—	1991
	Tajikistan	substate	yes	—	1991
	Turkmenistan	substate	no	—	1991
	Ukraine	substate	no	—	1991
	Uzbekistan	substate	no	—	1991
Ukraine	Crimea (Crimean Tatars)[a] and Russians	substate, transstate	no	Russian Federation	1988–1996

(continues)

MIDDLE EAST AND NORTH AFRICA

Chad vs. Libya	Aouzou Strip	interstate border dispute	yes	Algeria, UNASOG: UN Aouzou Strip Observer Group (5/94–6/94)	1994
Iran	Non-Shiites (Baha'is, Christians, & Azeris)	substate	N/A	—	N/A
Iran, Iraq, & Turkey	Kurdistan[a] (Kurds)	transstate	yes	United States during Gulf War, UN after Gulf War	1979–present
Iraq	Shi'a Muslims	substate	yes	—	spring 1991
Israel	West Bank and Gaza Strip (Palestinians)	substate	yes	United States, Egypt, Jordan	1968–present
Israel vs. Syria	The Golan Heights	interstate border dispute	yes	United States	1967–present
Israel vs. non-PLO groups (Hamas, Hizbollah, & Amal)	Buffer zone in southern Lebanon	interstate	yes	Syria, Lebanon	1982–2000
United States & Gulf War Coalition vs. Iraq	Kuwait	interstate	yes	United States, UN-sanctioned Gulf War Coalition. UNIKOM: UN Iraq-Kuwait Observation Mission (4/91–present)	1990–1991
United States & United Kingdom vs. Iraq	Iraqi government regime	interstate	yes	UNSCOM: UN Special Commission (on Iraq)	1991–present

(continues)

Appendix C   Continued

State(s) Claiming Sovereignty	Self-Determination Movement	Dispute Type	Violence	Significant Outside Political Involvement and/or Military Intervention	Period(s) of Dispute
MIDDLE EAST AND NORTH AFRICA					
Morocco	Western Sahara (Sahrawis)	substate	yes	Spain, United States, International Court of Justice, MINURSO: UN Mission for the Referendum in Western Sahara (4/91–present)	1973–present
Yemen	Southern Yemen	substate	yes	—	1990s, 1994
Yemen vs. Saudi Arabia	Border areas	interstate border dispute	yes	—	N/A
CENTRAL AND SOUTH AMERICA					
Brazil	Various Indian populations	indigenous	no	—	1990s
Chile, Argentina	Mapuche[a]	indigenous, transstate	no	—	1993–present
Ecuador	Indigenous highlanders	indigenous	no	—	N/A
Guatemala	Mayan tribes	indigenous	no	—	?–1996
Nicaragua	Miskitos	indigenous	no	—	N/A
Peru	Shining Path guerrillas	indigenous	yes	—	N/A
Peru vs. Ecuador	Border areas	interstate border dispute	yes	—	1994–1998

(continues)

NORTH AMERICA

Canada	Cree	indigenous	no	—	N/A
	Nunavut (Inuit)[a]	indigenous	no	—	N/A
	Nuxalk Nation[a]	indigenous	no	—	1982–present
	Quebec	substate	no	—	N/A
Mexico	Chiapas (Zapatistas)	indigenous	yes	—	N/A
	Maya	indigenous	no	—	N/A
	Popular Revolutionary Party (ERP)—state of Guerrero	indigenous	yes	—	N/A
United States	Guam	indigenous, anticolonial	no	—	N/A
	Kalahui Hawaii[a]	indigenous, anticolonial	no	—	1990s
	Lakota[a], Cherokee, and other Native America tribes	indigenous	no	—	1990s
	Puerto Rico	anticolonial	no	—	1990s

Sources: Compiled by Tyler Felgenhauer.
Center for Systemic Peace, "Current Status of the World's Major Episodes of Political Violence," (September 24, 1999): <http://members.aol.com/CSPmgm/cspframe.htm>; *CIA World Factbook:* <http://www.cia.gov/cia/publications/factbook/index.html>; *Conflict, Self-Determination, and Democracy 2000,* with a table prepared by Deepa Khosla, "Self-Determination and Ethnic Conflict," (New York: Carnegie Corporation, 2000): <http://www.bsos.umd.edu/cidcm/mar/autonomy/htm>; Ted Robert Gurr, *Peoples Versus States: Minorities at Risk in the New Century* (Washington, D.C.: U.S. Institute of Peace, 2000); Morton H. Halperin and David J. Scheffer with Patricia L. Small, *Self-Determination in the New World Order* (Washington, D.C.: Carnegie Endowment for International Peace, 1992); Human Rights Watch: <http://www.hrw.org/>; Charles W. Kegley Jr. and Eugene R. Wittkopf, eds., *World Politics: Trend and Transformation,* 8th ed. (Boston: Bedford/St. Martin's, 2001), pp. 212–213; *SIPRI Yearbook 1999: Armaments, Disarmament, and International Security,* Stockholm International Peace Research Institute (New York: Oxford University Press, 1999); United Nations, Department of Peacekeeping Operations: <http://www.un.org>; Unrepresented Nations and Peoples Organization (UNPO): <http://www.unpo.org>; and various articles from the *New York Times,* BBC, AP, and the *Washington Post.*

Notes: a. Current member of the Unrepresented Peoples and Nations Organization (UNPO).
b. Past member of the UNPO.

Appendix D

Principal Treaties and Agreements Relating to Self-Determination

1648   The Peace of Westphalia ends the Thirty Years War. The sovereignty of territorial rulers is legislated into international law, and religious toleration is established as part of the Holy Roman Empire, with each state adopting the religion of its ruler. Switzerland and the Netherlands are given their independence.

1783   The Treaty of Paris ends the American War of Independence. Great Britain recognizes the sovereignty of the United States, reaffirming this recognition in the Treaty of Ghent (1814). The North American colonies thereby set the pattern of New World inhabitants gaining self-rule through force with strategic support from European allies.

1816–1822   Treaties recognize the independence of Central and South American colonies: Argentina (1810), Chile (1810), Venezuela (1811), Columbia (1819), Peru (1821), Mexico (1821), and Brazil (1822). The Monroe Doctrine (1823) declares the opposition of the United States to the continued colonial presence of European states in the Americas, and Great Britain recognizes the new South American nations as a counterweight to Spanish conservatism in Europe (1825).

1830   A protocol crafted by Great Britain and France establishes the independence of Belgium from the Netherlands after a successful Belgian revolt. The Netherlands recognizes Belgium in the Treaty of London (1839).

1832   The Treaty of London grants Greece independence from the Ottoman Empire. This decision by the great powers is accepted by the Ottoman sultan and approved by the Greek National Assembly later that year.

1833   The Zollverein is established among seven German states. This agreement signals the first step toward unification of the German-speaking regions, held together by Prussian leadership.

1856   The Treaty of Paris ends the Crimean War. Plebiscites in Wallachia and Moldova set the precedent for their use in determining a region's allegiance.

1859   The Treaty of Zurich lays the groundwork for Italian unification and independence. The Kingdom of Italy is proclaimed in 1861, and unification is substantially completed by the acquisition of Venetia (1866) and of Rome (1870).

1866   The Treaty of Prague ends the Austro-Prussian War. German nationalism based on Prussia's "Small German" principle, rather than on the multinationalism of Austria, is victorious.

1871   The Peace of Versailles concludes the Franco-Prussian War. Alsace and Lorraine are ceded to the newly christened German empire. German national unification gains formal international recognition.

1878   The Treaty of Berlin grants international recognition to the newly independent states of Serbia and Romania; Bulgaria is set up as an autonomous region within the Ottoman Empire.

1919   The Treaty of Versailles establishes the League of Nations (see Article 1 et seq.) and recognizes the independence of Czechoslovakia (see Article 81 et seq.). Germany cedes its colonial possessions to the League of Nations to be held as mandates (see Article 22).

1919   The Treaty of St. Germain grants independence to the Czech regions of the Austro-Hungarian Empire, as well as to the Ruthene population of Austria (see Article 53 et seq.), and recognizes the independent Serb-Croat-Slovene state (see Article 46 et seq.). Italian-speaking areas of the monarchy are ceded to Italy. Austria's successor states are required to sign the Minorities Treaties, guaranteeing civil and political rights for ethnic minorities within their borders (see Articles 62–69).

1920   The Treaty of Trianon grants independence to the Slovak region in northern Hungary, and to the Slovenes and Croats in the south (see Article 41 et seq.). Hungary pledges to safeguard the rights of its ethnic minorities (see Articles 54–60).

1921   The Cairo Conference establishes constitutional monarchies in Iraq and Transjordan, thus taking a preparatory step toward Middle Eastern independence. British proclamations grant self-rule to Egypt (1922) and a constitution to Iraq (1924).

1922   The League of Nations grants Palestine to Great Britain as a mandate. This policy lays the foundation for the independence of Israel, recognized by the great powers after the termination of the mandate (1948).

1922   The Treaty of Lausanne grants independence from Ottoman rule to Arabia (see Article 16). The great powers formally recognize the independent Republic of Turkey, and Turkey agrees to respect the rights of its ethnic minorities (see Articles 37–45).

1922   The Anglo-Irish Treaty creates the Irish Free State, making possible the development of the independent Republic of Ireland (1949).

1927–1971   The Middle Eastern states achieve independence. Treaties of alliance establish the independent states of Iraq, Egypt, and Saudi Arabia (1927–1936). Morocco and Tunisia are granted independence by French declarations (1954–1956).

1945   The Charter of the United Nations is signed by fifty-one nations, along the lines agreed upon at the Dumbarton Oaks discussions in 1944. Self-determination is enshrined as one of the guiding principles of the UN (see Article 1, paragraph 2; Article 55, paragraphs [a]-[c]; Article 73, paragraph [b]; and Article 76, paragraph [b]). The Economic and Social Council is established as an organ of the UN to deal with the economic, political, and social development of the member states (see Articles 61–72).

1947   The Treaties of Paris reaffirm the sovereignties of the states absorbed by the Axis powers during World War II, including Czechoslovakia and Poland. Italy gives up its colonial possessions to the UN to be held as mandates (see Article 23), and Ethiopia is granted independence (see Article 33).

1947   The British Parliament's India Independence Act grants independence to the Republic of India.

1948   The Universal Declaration of Human Rights is adopted by the UN, setting forth a broad statement of political, civil, social, economic, and cultural rights of all people (see Article 22).

1948   The Charter of the Organization of American States declares the importance of national independence and self-government (see Articles 1, 2[b], and 3[e]).

1950   The European Convention on Human Rights binds signatories to respect the civil and political rights of their citizens and sets up institutions for the enforcement of the Convention's terms (see particularly Article 14).

1955   The Austrian State Treaty reestablishes the independence of Austria in international law (see Articles 1–5).

1957–1977   Independence of the African colonial states. A Belgian administrative agreement provides for independence in the Congo (1960), and an Italian proclamation grants independence to Somalia. A Franco-Algerian agreement endorses independence for Algeria (1962). European settlers in Rhodesia declare their independence from Great Britain (1965), but Rhodesia is not granted international recognition until a majority-rule government is established (1980).

1960   The Declaration on the Granting of Independence to Colonial Territories denounces colonialism and calls for self-determination in all non-self-governing territories (see particularly paragraphs 1–7).

1963   The Charter of the Organization of African Unity emphasizes national independence and self-government as a primary aspect of international relations (see Articles 2–3).

1966   The International Covenant on Economic, Social and Cultural Rights, and the International Covenant on Civil and Political Rights endorse personal freedoms for all persons in UN member states and establish self-determination as a legal right for all peoples (Article 1 of both covenants) and the cultural, religious, and linguistic rights of minorities (Article 27 of the Covenant on Civil and Political Rights).

1970   The Declaration on Principles of International Law Concerning Friendly Relations and Co-operation Among States stresses the importance of self-determination in the UN program (see preamble and statement of principles).

1972   The Simla Agreement ends the Third Indo-Pakistani War and lays the foundation for the independence of Bangladesh, recognized by Pakistan in 1974.

1973   The Paris Peace Accords remove colonial powers from Vietnam, leading to the unification of the independent state of Vietnam (1975).

1975   The Final Act of the Conference on Security and Cooperation in Europe (Helsinki Accords, later became the CSCE) endorses human rights principles and encourages the free movement of people and information (see Article 8).

1976   The International Covenant on Civil and Political Rights proclaims self-determination to be a fundamental human right and requires its signatories to uphold that principle within their own territories (see Article 1, Parts 1 and 3). The political rights of minorities are reiterated (see Article 27).

1981   The African Charter on Human and Peoples' Rights sets out self-determination and human rights as basic principles of government (see Articles 13, 19, 20, and 29).

1988   The Geneva Agreement lays the foundation for Namibian independence by endorsing the withdrawal of foreign troops, to be followed by elections.

1992   The Südtirol Packet is accepted by Austria and Italy, resolving the contentious issue of the northern Italian region Sudtirol/Alto Adige; it includes 137 detailed measures that guarantee ethnic, cultural, and economic rule to the German- and Ladin-speaking groups in that region.

1993   The Maastricht Treaty enters into effect, calling for the development of a European monetary union by the end of the 1990s and reinforcing the drive toward European unification embodied in the Single European Act (1986). The treaty acknowledges national identity to be a fundamental human freedom (see Article F).

1993   The Declaration on the Rights of Minorities proclaims the responsibility of signatory states to protect the identity and political rights of national, ethnic, religious, and linguistic minorities within their borders (see Articles 1–5).

1994   The Budapest Summit of the Conference on Security and Cooperation in Europe (CSCE) creates the Organization for Security and Cooperation in Europe (OSCE), dedicated to resolving security conflicts that threaten international stability and peace.

1994   Chechnya declares independence from Russia in 1991, as a result of which war erupts with Russia in December 1994, including the major battle of Grozny. In July 1995 a cease-fire is negotiated, which both sides have frequently violated. (Also see entry for 1996.)

1995   On September 28 in Washington, D.C., Israeli prime minister Yitzhak Rabin and PLO leader Yasser Arafat sign the Israeli-Palestinian Interim Agreement on the West Bank and the Gaza Strip, which transfers certain powers of autonomy to the Palestinian Authority in these areas.

1995   The Dayton Accords establish the independence of the Republic of Bosnia and Herzegovina from Yugoslavia.

1996   On August 31 the Russian Federation and Chechnya sign the Khasavyurt Agreement, which establishes quasi-independent status for Chechnya with a final decision on independence delayed for five years.

1997   Hong Kong returns to China peacefully, remaining a capitalist region within the officially communist nation.

1997   Ireland's Good Friday Accords are signed on April 19, and in May a referendum on the agreement wins with over 70 percent of the vote. The accords include a devolution of power from the central government to the Northern Ireland assembly.

1999   On August 30 the people of East Timor vote overwhelmingly for independence from Indonesia; after strong resistance, on October 20 Indonesia officially renounces all claims to East Timor.

BIBLIOGRAPHY

Abi-Saab, Georges. "Wars of National Liberation and the Laws of War." *Annales d'Etudes Internationales* 3 (1972).

Adams, Richard N. "Strategies of Ethnic Survival in Central America." In *Nation-States and Indians in Latin America,* Greg Urban and Joel Sherzer, eds. Austin: University of Texas Press, 1991.

Ahmed, Mohammed M.A. "Demographic Changes in Kurdistan-Iraq, 1957–1988." *Namah* 2, no. 1 (1994): 7–8.

Albino, Oliver. *The Sudan: A Southern Viewpoint.* London: Oxford University Press, 1970.

Alderman, G., ed., with J. Leslie and K. Pollmann. *Governments, Ethnic Groups, and Political Representation.* Strasbourg, France: European Science Foundation, 1992.

Alexander, Jeffrey. "Citizen and Enemy as Symbolic Classification: On the Polarizing Discourse of Civil Society." In *Cultivating Differences: Symbolic Boundaries and the Making of Inequality,* Michèle Lamont and Marcel Fournier, eds. Chicago: University of Chicago Press, 1992.

Alexander, Jeffrey, and Philip Smith. "The Discourse of American Civil Society: A New Proposal for Cultural Studies." *Theory and Society* 22, no. 2 (1993): 151–208.

Alexander, Yonah, and Robert A. Friedlaender, eds. *Self-Determination: National, Regional, and Global Dimensions.* Boulder, Colo.: Westview Press, 1980.

Alexseev, Mikhail A., ed. *Center-Periphery Conflict in Post-Soviet Russia: A Federation Imperiled.* New York: St. Martin's Press, 1999.

Alier, Abel. *The Southern Sudan: Too Many Agreements Dishonoured.* Exeter, N.Y.: Ithaca Press, 1990.

al-Mahdi, Sadiq. *Islam and the Problem of the South.* Khartoum: Author, 1984.

Almond, Gabriel A., and Sidney Verba. *The Civic Culture: Political Attitudes and Democracy in Five Nations.* Princeton: Princeton University Press, 1963.

Anaya, S. James. *Indigenous Peoples in International Law.* New York: Oxford University Press, 1996.

Anderson, Benedict. *Imagined Communities; Reflections on the Origin and Spread of Nationalism.* London: Verso, 1983.

Arnaud, Remy. *Panorama de l'économie française.* Paris: Bordas, 1986.

Assefa, Hizkias. *Mediation of Civil Wars: Approaches and Strategies—The Sudan Conflict.* Boulder, Colo.: Westview Press, 1987.

413

Aufderheide, Patricia. *Beyond P.C.: Toward a Politics of Understanding.* St. Paul, Minn.: Greywolf Press, 1991.

Avalishvili, Zourab, *The Independence of Georgia in International Politics, 1918–1921.* Westport, Conn.: Hyperion Press, 1981.

'Awda, 'Abd al-Malek. "Self-Determination in the Sudan," *al-Ahram al-Iqtisadi* 24 (January 1994): 90 (in Arabic).

Bachtler, John, ed. *Socio-Economic Situation and Development of the Regions in the Neighbouring Countries of the Community in Central and Eastern Europe: Final Report to the European Commission.* Brussels: Commission of the European Communities, Directorate-General for Regional Policies; Lanham, Md.: Unipub Distributor, 1992.

Baer, Douglas, Edward Grabb, and William Johnston. "National Character, Regional Culture, and the Values of Canadians and Americans." *Canadian Review of Sociology and Anthropology* 30, no. 1 (1993): 1336.

Balcells, Albert. *Catalan Nationalism: Past and Present.* New York: St. Martin's Press, 1996.

Baldwin, Peter. *The Politics of Social Solidarity: Class Bases of European Welfare State.* New York: Cambridge University Press, 1990.

Barnard, Frederick M. *Self-direction and Political Legitimacy: Rousseau and Herder.* Oxford: Clarendon Press; New York: Oxford University Press, 1988.

Barth, Frederick, ed. *Ethnic Groups and Boundaries: The Social Organization of Culture Differences.* Boston: Little, Brown, 1969.

Bashevkin, Sylvia B. *True Patriot Love: The Politics of Canadian Nationalism.* Toronto: Oxford University Press, 1991.

Bassand, Michel. *Self-Reliant Development in Europe: Theory, Problems, Actions.* Brookfield, Vt.: Gower, 1986.

Bassiouni, M. Cherif. *The Palestinians' Right of Self-Determination and National Independence.* Detroit: Association of Arab-American University Graduates, 1978.

Batliner, Gerard, ed. *Subsidiarität: ein interdisziplinares Symposium: Symposium Riklin. Liechtenstein-Institut in Bendern.* Vaduz: Verlag der Liechtensteinischen Akademischen Gesellschaft, 1994.

Baum, Gregory. "Ethical Reflections on the Language Debate." In *Boundaries of Identity: A Quebec Reader,* William Dodge, ed. Toronto: Lester, 1992.

Bayülken, Ümit Halûk. *Collective Security and Defence Organizations in the Changing World Conditions.* Ankara, 1976.

Beamish, Tufton Victor Hamilton. *The Kremlin's Dilemma: The Struggle for Human Rights in Eastern Europe.* London: Collins and Harvill, 1979.

Bechtold, Peter. "New Attempts at Arab Cooperation: The Federation of Arab Republics." *Middle East Journal* 27, no. 2 (1973): 152–172.

Behiels, Michael D. *Prelude to Quebec Quiet Revolution: Liberalism vs. Neo-Nationalism 1945–1960.* Kingston, Ontario: Queens University Press, 1985.

Bellah, Robert N. *The Broken Covenant: American Civil Religion in Time of War.* New York: Seabury Press, 1975.

Bellah, Robert N., Richard Madsen, William W. Sullivan, Ann Swidler, and Steven Tipton. *Habits of the Heart: Individualism and Commitment in American Life.* Berkeley: University of California Press, 1985.

Bennigsen, Marie. "Chechnia: Political Developments and Strategic

Implications for the North Caucasus." *Central Asian Survey* 18, no. 4 (December 1999): 535–574.

Bennigsen Broxup, Marie, ed. *The North Caucasus Barrier: The Russian Advance Towards the Muslim World.* New York: St. Martin's Press, 1992.

Berat, Lynn. *Decolonization and International Law.* New Haven: Yale University Press, 1990.

Berdal, Mats. *Whither UN Peacekeeping?* Adelphi Paper 281. London: International Institute for Strategic Studies (IISS), 1993.

Berg, Leo van den. *Governing Metropolitan Regions.* Aldershot: Avebury, 1993.

Berman, George A. "Taking Subsidiarity Seriously: Federalism in the European Community and the United States." *Columbia Law Review* 94, no. 2 (March 1994): 334.

Berman, Nathaniel. "Sovereignty in Abeyance: Self-Determination and International Law, 7." *Wisconsin International Law Journal* 51 (1988).

Berman, Paul, ed. *Debating P.C.: The Controversy over Political Correctness on College Campuses.* New York: Dell, 1992.

Bermeo, Nancy, ed., *Liberalization and Democratization—Change in the Soviet Union and Eastern Europe.* Baltimore, Md.: Johns Hopkins University Press, 1992.

Bernard, Phillippe. "La France ne parvient pas à endiguer les discriminations raciales." *Le Monde,* January 18, 1995: 10.

Beshir, Mohamed Omer. *The Southern Sudan: Background to Conflict.* London: C. Hurst, 1968; republished by Khartoum University Press, 1979.

Bettelheim, Peter, and Rudi Benedikter, eds. *Apartheid in Mitteleuropa? Sprache und Sprachenpolitik in Südtirol: La lingua e la politica delle lingue nel Sudtirolo.* Vienna: J & V, 1982.

Bhabha, Homi K. *Nation and Narration.* London: Routledge, 1990.

Bibo, Istvan. *The Paralysis of Internationale Institutions and the Remedies: A Study of Self-Determination, Concord Among the Major Powers, and Political Arbitration.* New York: Wiley, 1976.

Bissonnette, Lise. "Culture, Politics, and Society in Quebec." In *Boundaries of Identity: A Quebec Reader,* William Dodge, ed. Toronto: Lester, 1992.

Bitsch, Marie-Therese. *La Belgique entre la France et l'Allemagne, 1905–1914.* Preface by Rene Girault. Paris: Publications de la Sorbonne, 1994.

Black, Cyril Edwin, and Richard A. Falk. *The Future of the International Legal Order.* Princeton: Center of International Studies, Woodrow Wilson School of Public and International Affairs, Princeton University, 1982.

Blay, S.K.N. "Self-Determination Versus Territorial Integrity in Decolonization." *New York University Journal of International Law and Politics* 18, no. 441: 1985–1986.

Blum, John Morton. *Woodrow Wilson and the Politics of Morality.* Boston: Little, Brown, 1956.

Blum, Yehuda. "Reflections on the Changing Concept of Self-Determination." *Israel Law Review* 10, no. 511 (1975).

Blumenwitz, Dieter, and Boris Meissner, eds. *Das Selbstbestimmungsrecht der Völker und die Deutsche Frage.* Cologne: Verlag Wissenschaft und Politik, 1984.

Bobo, Lawrence, and Ryan A. Smith. "Antipoverty Policy, Affirmative Action, and Racial Attitudes." In *Confronting Poverty: Prescriptions for Change*, Sheldon H. Danziger, Gary D. Sandefur, and Daniel H. Weinberg, eds. New York: Russell Sage Foundation, 1994.

Boltanski, Luc, and Laurent Thevenot. *De la justification: Les économies de la grandeur.* Paris: Gallimard, 1991.

Bonnet, Jacques. *Lyon et son agglomeration: Les enjeux d'une métropole européenne.* Paris: La Documentation Française, 1987.

Bonneville, Marc, Marie André Buisson, Nicole Commeron, and Nicole Rouster. *Villes européennes et internationalisation.* Oullins, France: Bosc Frères, 1991.

Borkenhagen, Franz H.U. "Regions in Europe." *Aussenpolitik* (November 1994): 182–188.

Borys, Jurij. *The Sovietization of Ukraine, 1917–1923: The Communist Doctrine and Practice of National Self-Determination.* Edmonton: Canadian Institute of Ukrainian Studies, 1980.

Boutros-Ghali, Boutros. *An Agenda for Peace.* UN Doc A/47/277-S/2411. New York: UN, June 17, 1992.

Bowden, Mark. *Black Hawk Down.* New York: Atlantic Monthly Press, 1999.

Bowett, D. W. *The Law of International Institutions.* London: Stevens, 1963.

Brass, Paul. *Politics of India Since Independence.* New York: Cambridge University Press, 1990.

Bremmer, Ian, and Ray Taras, eds. *New States, New Politics: Building the Post-Soviet Nations.* Cambridge: Cambridge University Press, 1997.

Breton, Raymond. "The Production and Allocation of Symbolic Resources: An Analysis of the Linguistic and Ethnocultural Fields in Canada." *Canadian Review of Sociology and Anthropology* 21, no. 2 (1984): 123–144.

Breton, Raymond, Jeffrey G. Reitz, and Victor F. Valentine. *Cultural Boundaries and the Cohesion of Canada.* Montreal: Institute for Research on Public Policy, 1980.

Breuilly, John. *Nationalism and the State.* 2nd ed. Chicago: University of Chicago Press, 1994.

Brilmayer, Lea. "Secession and Self-Determination: A Territorial Interpretation." *Yale Journal of International Law* 16 (1991): 177–201.

Brinton, Jasper Yeates. *Federations in the Middle East.* Cairo: Brintonton, 1964.

Brittan, Leon. "Subsidiarity in the Constitution of the European Community." *Europe Documents,* English ed., no. 1786 (June 18, 1992): 1–6.

Brölmann, Catherine, Renè Lefébre, and Marjoleine Zieck. *Peoples and Minorities in International Law.* Boston: Martinus Nijhoff, 1993.

Brossard, Jacques. *L'accession a la souverainetè et le cas du Québec: Conditions et modalités politicojuridiques.* Montreal: Presses de l'Université de Montréal, 1976.

Brosted, Jens, ed. *Native Power: The Quest for Autonomy and Nationhood of Indigenous Peoples. Festschrift in Memory of Helge Kleivan (1924–1983).* Bergen: Universitetsförlaget, 1985.

Brown, Michael E. *The International Dimensions of Internal Conflict.* Cambridge: MIT Press, 1996.

Brubaker, William Rogers. "Immigration, Citizenship, and the Nation State in France and Germany: A Comparative Historical Analysis." *International Sociology* 54 (1990): 379–407.

Buchanan, Allen. *Secession: The Morality of Political Divorce from Fort Sumter to Lithuania and Quebec.* Boulder, Colo.: Westview Press, 1991.

―――. "Self-Determination and the Right to Secede." *Journal of International Affairs* 45, no. 2 (Winter 1992): 347–366.

Buchheit, Lee C. *Secession: The Legitimacy of Self-Determination.* New Haven: Yale University Press, 1978.

Burnett, Ron. "The Frontiers of Our Dreams Are No Longer the Same." In *Boundaries of Identity: A Quebec Reader,* William Dodge, ed. Toronto: Lester, 1992.

Calder, Kenneth J. *Britain and the Origins of the New Europe, 1914–1918.* New York: Cambridge University Press, 1976.

Camilleri, Joseph, and Jim Falk. *End of Sovereignty? The Politics of a Shrinking and Fragmenting World.* Brookfield, Vt.: Edward Elgar, 1992.

Cantori, Louis J., and Stephen L. Spiegel. *The International Politics of Regions: A Comparative Approach.* Englewood Cliffs, N.J.: Prentice Hall, 1970.

Cappellin, R., and P.W.J. Batey, eds. *Regional Networks, Border Regions, and European Integration.* London: Pion, 1993.

Card, Edgar Rouard de. *Etude de droit international public: Les annexions et les plebiscites dans l'histoire contemporaine.* Paris: Thorin, 1880.

Carey, Peter, and G. Carter Bentley, eds. *East Timor at the Crossroads: The Forging of a Nation.* London: Cassell, 1995.

Carothers, Thomas. "Democracy and Human Rights: Policy Allies or Rivals?" *Washington Quarterly* 17, no. 3 (Summer 1994): 109–120.

Carr, Edward H. *The Future of Nations: Independence, or Interdependence?* London: K. Paul, Trench, Trubner, 1941.

Cass, Deborah C. "The Word That Saves Maastricht? The Principle of Subsidiarity and the Division of Powers Within the European Community." *Common Market Law Review* 29 (December 1992): 1107–1136.

Cassese, Antonio. *International Law in a Divided World.* New York: Oxford University Press, 1986.

―――. *Self-Determination of Peoples: A Legal Reappraisal.* Cambridge: Cambridge University Press, 1995.

―――. "The International Court of Justice and the Right of Peoples to Self-Determination." In *Fifty Years of the International Court of Justice,* Lowe and Fitzmaurice, eds. Cambridge: Cambridge University Press, 1996.

―――, ed. *U.N. Law/Fundamental Rights: Two Topics in International Law.* Leiden: Sijthoff, 1979.

Cassese, Antonio, and Edmond Jouve, eds. *Pour un droit des peuples: Essais sur la déclaration d'Algérie.* Paris: Berger Levrault, 1978.

Centre for Economic Policy Research. *Making Sense of Subsidiarity: How Much Centralization for Europe?* London: CEPR, 1993.

Charpentier, Jean. "Autodetermination et decolonisation." In *Le droit des peuples à disposer d'eux-mêmes: Mélanges offerts à Charles Chaumont* 117, ^ Pedone, ed. Paris: 1984.

Chatterjee, Partha. *Nationalist Thought and the Colonial World.* London: Zed Books, 1988.

Chen, Lung-Chu. "Self-Determination and World Public Order." Notre Dame Law Review 66 (1991): 1287–1297.

Chou-Young, Hu. *Das Selbstbestimmungsrecht als eine Vorbedingung des völligen Genusses aller Menschenrechte: Eine Studie über Artikel der beiden Menschenrechtskonventionen vom 16. Dezember 1966.* Zurich: Schulthess Polygraphischer Verlag, 1972.

Clapham, Christopher S. *Africa and the International System: The Politics of State Survival.* New York: Cambridge University Press, 1996.

Clark, Donald, and Robert Williamson, eds. *Self-Determination: International Perspectives.* New York: St. Martin's Press, 1996.

Clark, Jeffrey. "Debacle in Somalia: The Failure of Collective Response." In *Enforcing Restraint,* Lori Damrosch, ed. New York: Council on Foreign Relations, 1993.

Clark, Roger S. "The Decolonization of East Timor and the United Nations Norms on Self-Determination and Aggression." *Yale Journal of World Public Order* 7, no. 2 (1980–1981).

Clark, Walter, and Jeffrey Herbst, eds. *Learning from Somalia: The Lessons of Armed Humanitarian Intervention.* Boulder, Colo.: Westview Press, 1997.

Clay, Jason W. "The Ethnic Future of Nations." *Third World Quarterly* (October 1989): 223.

———. "States, Nations and Resources: An Interdependent Relationship?" *Fletcher Forum of World Affairs* 19, no. 1 (1995): 11–20.

Cleveland, Harland. *Birth of a New World: An Open Moment for International Leadership.* San Francisco: Jossey-Bass, 1993.

Cloutier, Edouard, Jean Yves Gay, and Daniel Latouche. *Le Virage.* Montreal: HMH Hurtubise, 1992.

Cobban, Alfred, *National Self-Determination.* Chicago: University of Chicago Press, 1944.

———. *The Nation State and National Self-Determination.* New York: Thomas Y. Crowell, 1970.

COCADI. *Cultura maya y políticas de desarrollo.* Guatemala: Coordinadora Cakchiquel de Desarrollo Integral, Departamento de Investigaciones Culturales, 1989.

Codrington, Harold. "Country Size and Taxation in Developing Countries." *Journal of Development Studies* 25 (July 1989): 509.

Cohen, Hymen Ezra. *Recent Theories of Sovereignty.* Chicago: University of Chicago Press, 1937.

Cohen, Robin. "Diasporas and the Nation-State: From Victims to Challengers." *International Affairs* 72, no. 3 (July 1996): 507–520.

Cojtí Cuxil, Demetrio. "The Indian Movement in Contemporary Colonial Guatemala." Unpublished ms. Richard Adams, trans. N.d.

———. "Lingüística e idiomas mayas en Guatemala." In *Lecturas Sobre la Lingüística Maya,* Nora C. England and Stephen R. Elliott, eds. Guatemala: Centro de Investigaciones Regionales de Mesoamérica, 1990.

———. *Configuración del pensamiento político del Pueblo Maya.* Quetzaltenango, Guatemala: Asociación de Escritores Mayances de Guatemala, 1991a.

———. "Universidades guatemaltecas, universidades colonialistas." Paper presented at Latin American Studies Association (LASA), 1991b.

———. "Los contornos del pensamiento político del movimiento maya." Paper presented at LASA, 1992.

Cojtí Macario, Narciso. *Mapa de los idiomas de Guatemala y Belice.* Guatemala: Piedra Santa, 1988.

Colton, Timothy J., and Robert Legvold, eds. *After the Soviet Union: From Empire to Nations.* New York: W. W. Norton, 1992.

COMG (Consejo de Organizaciones Mayas de Guatemala). "Derechos específicos del Pueblo Maya/Rujunamil Ri Mayab' Amaq'." Guatemala: Mayab' Nimajay Cholsamaj, 1991.

Commission of the European Communities (CEC) Office in the United Kingdom. "The Subsidiarity Principle." Background Report no. 34 to the European Council and the European Parliament, London, November 1992.

Confer, Vincent. *France and Algeria: The Problem of Civil and Political Reform, 1870–1920.* Syracuse, N.Y.: Syracuse University Press, 1966.

Connor, Walker. "Ethnocentrism." In *Understanding Political Development,* Myron Weiner and Samuel Huntington, eds. Boston: Little, Brown, 1987.

Corba, Vittorio, and Fernando Ossa. "Small Open Economies: The Main Issues." In *Export-Oriented Development Strategies,* Vittorio Corba, Anne O. Krueger, and Fernando Ossa, eds. Boulder, Colo.: Westview Press, 1985.

Coughlin, Richard M. *Ideology, Public Opinion, and Welfare Policy.* Berkeley: Institute of International Studies, 1980.

Council of Europe. *International Conference. European Towns: Strategies and Programmes.* Strasbourg: Council of Europe, 1991.

———. *European Charter of Local Self-Government and Explanatory Report.* Council of Europe, 1996.

Crawford, James. *The Creation of States in International Law.* New York: Oxford University Press, 1979.

———. *The Rights of Peoples.* Oxford: Clarendon Press, 1988.

———. "The General Assembly, the International Court and Self-Determination." In *Fifty Years of the International Court of Justice: Essays in Honour of Sir Robert Jennings,* Vaughan Lowe and Malgosia Fitzmaurice, eds. Cambridge: Cambridge University Press, 1996.

Critescu, Aurelia. *El derecho a la libre determinación: Desarrollo histórico y actual sobre la base de los instrumentos de las Naciones Unidas* (E/CN.4/SUB 2/404/Rev. 1 (1981), as cited in Ian Brownlie, *Principles of Public International Law,* 4th ed. Oxford: Clarendon Press, 1990, p. 595.

Crocker, Chester A., and Fen Osler Hampson, eds. *Managing Global Chaos: Sources of and Responses to International Conflict.* Washington, D.C.: U.S. Institute of Peace Press, 1996.

Cruttwell, Charles. *A History of Peaceful Change in the Modern World.* London: Oxford University Press, 1937.

CSCE Geneva Report of the Meeting of Experts on National Minorities, as cited in Morton Halperin and David Scheffer with Patricia Small, *Self-Determination in the New World Order.* Washington, D.C.: Carnegie Endowment for International Peace, 1992.

Cukwurah, A. O. *The Settlement of Boundary Disputes in International Law.* Manchester: Manchester University Press, 1967.

Dahbour, Omar, and Micheline R. Ishay, eds. *The Nationalism Reader.* Atlantic Highlands, N.J.: Humanities Press, 1995.

Dahl, Robert A. *Dilemmas of Pluralist Democracy: Autonomy Is Control.* New Haven: Yale University Press, 1982.

Dahl, Robert, and Edward Tuftee. *Size and Democracy.* Stanford: Stanford University Press, 1973.

Dalie, Guo. *Lun dangdai zhongguo de minzu wenti* (On the nationality problem in contemporary China). Beijing: Minzu, 1994.

Dals, Erica-Irene A. "Some Considerations on the Rights of Indigenous Peoples to Self-Determination." *Transnational Law and Contemporary Problems* 3 (1993): 1–11.

Danspeckgruber, Wolfgang. "The European Economic Area, the Neutrals, and an Emerging Architecture." In *The Shape of the New Europe,* Gregory Treverton, ed. New York: Council on Foreign Relations, 1992.

———. *Classical Neutrality in Modern Europe—And Emerging Challenges: The Example of Technology,* Ph.D. dissertation, Graduate Institute of International Studies, Geneva, 1996.

———. "Regionalization, Sub-Regionalization, and Security in Central Eastern Europe." Princeton Pew Papers, Center of International Studies, Princeton University, 1996.

———. "Review Article: Borders, Self-Determination, and the Emerging Concept of 'Self-Governance.'" *Contemporary Austrian Studies* 7 (2000).

———. "Self-Determination, Self-Governance and Security." *International Relations* 15 (April 2000): 11–21.

———, ed. *Emerging Dimensions of European Security.* Boulder, Colo.: Westview Press, 1991.

Danspeckgruber, Wolfgang F., with Arthur Watts, eds. *Self-Determination and Self-Administration: A Sourcebook.* Boulder, Colo.: Lynne Rienner, 1997.

David Davies Memorial Institute of International Studies. *Small Is Dangerous: Micro States in a Macro World.* New York: St. Martin's Press, 1985.

Davison, W. Phillips, and Leon Gordenker. *Resolving Nationality Conflicts: The Role of Public Opinion Research.* New York: Praeger, 1980.

Deák, Francis, and Philip C. Jessup. *Neutrality: Its History, Economics, and Law.* New York: Columbia University Press, 1935.

———, eds. *A Collection of Neutrality Laws, Regulations and Treaties of Various Countries.* Westport, Conn.: Greenwood Press, 1974.

Deci, Edward L. *Intrinsic Motivation and Self-Determination in Human Behavior.* New York: Plenum, 1985.

Decker, Guenter. *Das Selbstbestimmungsrecht der Nationen.* N.p.: Schwartz, 1955.

Dehesa, Guillermo de la, and Paul Krugman. *EMU and the Regions.* Washington, D.C.: Group of Thirty, 1992.

Deibel, Terry L. "Internal Affairs and International Relations in the Post–Cold War World." *Washington Quarterly* 16, no. 3 (Summer 1993): 13–33.

Delcamp, Alain. *Definition and Limits of the Principle of Subsidiarity.* Report prepared for the Steering Committee on Local and Regional Authorities. Strasbourg: Council of Europe Press, 1994.

DeLupis, Ingrid Detter. *International Law and the Independent State,* 2nd ed. Brookfield, Vt.: Gower, 1974.

Democratic Republic of the Sudan. *The Southern Provinces Regional Self-Government Act.* Khartoum: Ministry of Culture and Information, 1972.

d'Encausse, Hélène Carrère. *The End of the Soviet Empire: The Triumph of the Nations.* New York: Basic Books, 1991.

Deng, Andrew. "Political Power and Decentralization in the Sudan." *Decentralization & Development Review* no. 1 (Spring 1981): 6–7.

Dennert, Jürgen. *Ursprung und Begriff der Souveränität.* Stuttgart: Fischer, 1964.

Denoeux, Guilain. *Urban Unrest in the Middle East: A Comparative Study of Informal Networks in Egypt, Iran, and Lebanon.* Albany: State University of New York Press, 1993.

Deschamps, Gilles. *Les communautés culturelles: Identification linguistique, rapport avec la societé francophone, et usages linguistiques.* Quebec: Ministère des communautes culturelles et de l'immigration, 1990.

d'Estaign, Valéry Giscard. *Report of the Committee on Institutional Affairs on the Principle of Subsidiarity.* EP doc A3–267/90/5p.

Devetak, Silvo, Sergej Flere, and Gerhard Seewann, eds. *Small Nations and Ethnic Minorities in an Emerging Europe.* Proceedings of the International Scientific Conference, Maribor, Slovenia, February 3–5, 1992. Munich: Slavica, 1993.

Devine, Pat, Yannis Katsoulacos, and Roger Sugden, eds. *Competitiveness, Subsidiarity and Industrial Policy.* New York: Routledge, 1996.

De Visscher, Charles. *Théories et réalités en droit international public,* 4th ed. Paris: Editions A. Pedone, 1970.

de Vries, Hent, and Samual Weber, eds. *Violence, Identity, and Self-Determination.* Proceedings of an international workshop held in Amsterdam, summer 1995. Stanford: Stanford University Press, 1997.

Díaz Polanco, Héctor. *Indigenous Peoples in Latin America: The Quest for Self-Determination,* trans. Lucia Rayas. Boulder, Colo.: Westview Press, 1997.

DiMaggio, Paul. "Classification in Art." *American Sociological Review* 52, no. 4 (1987): 440–455.

DiMaggio, Paul, and Bethany Bryson. "Americans' Attitudes Towards Cultural Diversity and Cultural Authority: Culture Wars, Social Closure, or Multiple Dimensions?" Department of Sociology, Princeton University, 1994.

Dock, Adolf. *Revolution und Restauration über die Soveränität.* Aalen: Scientia Verlag, 1972.

Dodge, William, ed. *Boundaries of Identity: A Quebec Reader.* Toronto: Lester, 1992.

Dodier, Nicolas. "Action as a Combination of 'Common Worlds.'" *Sociological Review* 41, no. 3 (1993): 556–571.

Döhring, Karl. *Das Selbstbestimmungsrecht der Völker als Grundsatz des Völkerrechts.* Karlsruhe: C. F. Müller, 1974.

Douglas, Mary. *Purity and Danger: An Analysis of the Concepts of Pollution and Taboo.* New York: Pantheon, 1966.

Downing, Brian M. *The Military Revolution and Political Change.* Princeton: Princeton University Press, 1992.

Doyle, Michael W. *Empires.* Ithaca, N.Y.: Cornell University Press, 1986.

———. "Forcing Peace." *Dissent* (Spring 1994): 167–171.

———. *UN Peacekeeping in Cambodia: UNTAC's Civil Mandate.* Boulder, Colo.: Lynne Rienner, 1995.

———. *Ways of War and Peace: Realism, Liberalism, and Socialism.* New York: W. W. Norton, 1997.

Drakulic, Slavenka. *The Balkan Express: Fragments from the Other Side of a War.* London: Hutchinson, 1994.

Drobizheva, Leokadiya. "Comparison of Élite Groups in Tatarstan, Sakha, Magadan, and Orenburg." *Post-Soviet Affairs* 15, no. 4 (October–December 1999): 387–406.

Dufour, Christian. *Le defi québecois*. Montréal: L'Hexagone, 1989.

Du Granrut, Claude. *Europe: Le temps des régions*. Paris: Librarie Générale du Droit et de la Jurisprudence, 1994.

Dunford, Mick, and Grigoris Kafkalas, eds. *Cities and Regions in the New Europe: The Global-Local Interplay and Spatial Development Strategies*. London: Belhaven Press; New York: Halsted Press, 1992.

Dunlop, John B. *The Rise of Russia and the Fall of the Soviet Union*. Princeton: Princeton University Press, 1993.

———. "Russia: In Search of an Identity?" In *New States, New Politics: Building the Post-Soviet Nations*, Ian Bremmer and Ray Taras, eds. Cambridge: Cambridge University Press, 1997.

Durch, William, ed. *The Evolution of UN Peacekeeping*. New York: St. Martin's Press, 1993.

Durkheim, Emile. *The Elementary Forms of Religious Life*. New York: Free Press, 1965.

Duursma, Jorri C., *Fragmentation and the International Relations of Micro-States: Self-Determination and Statehood*. Cambridge: Cambridge University Press, 1996.

———. *Self-Determination, Statehood, and International Relations of Micro-States: The Cases of Liechtenstein, San Marino, Monaco, Andorra, and the Vatican City*. Cambridge: Cambridge University Press, 1996.

Eagleton, Clyde. "Excesses of Self-Determination." *Foreign Affairs* 31, no. 4 (July 1953): 592–604.

———. "Self-Determination in the United Nations." *American Journal of International Law* 47, no. 1 (January 1953): 88–93.

Edsall T., and M. Edsall. *Chain Reaction: The Impact of Race, Rights and Taxes on American Politics*. New York: W. W. Norton, 1991.

El-Affendi, Abdel Wahab. *Turabi's Revolution: Islam and Power in Sudan*. London: Grey Seal, 1991.

Elkins, David J. *Beyond Sovereignty: Territory and Political Autonomy in the Twenty-First Century*. Toronto: University of Toronto Press, 1995.

El Shoush, Mohamed Ibrahim. "Some Background Notes on Modern Sudanese Policy." *Sudan Notes & Records* (Khartoum) 14 (1963): 21–42.

Elshtain, Jean Bethke. *Democracy on Trial*. New York: Basic Books, 1995.

Emerson, Rupert. *Self-Determination Revisited in the Era of Decolonization*. Cambridge: Harvard University, Center for International Affairs, 1964.

———. "Self Determination." *American Journal of International Law* 65 (1971): 459–475.

Emiliou, Nicholas. "Subsidiarity: An Effective Barrier Against the Enterprises of Ambition?" *European Law Review* 17, no. 5 (October 1992): 383–407.

England, Nora. *Autonomía de los idiomas mayas: Historia e identidad*. Guatemala: Cholsamaj, 1992.

England, Nora, and Stephen Elliot, eds. *Lecturas sobre la lingüística maya*. Guatemala: Centro de Investigaciones Regionales de Mesoamérica (CIRMA), 1990.

Entessar, Nader. *Kurdish Ethnonationalism*. Boulder, Colo.: Lynne Rienner, 1992.

Ermacora, Felix. *Die Selbstbestimmungsidee: Ihre Entwicklung von 1918–1974*. Vienna: Oestereichische Landsmannschaft, 1974.

———. "Die Entwicklung des Selbstbestimmungsrechts im Völkerrecht." In

Felix Ermacora et al., *Menschenrechte und Selbstbestimmung unter Berücksichtigung der Ostdeutschen.* Bonn, 1980.

———. *Südtirol: Die verhinderte Selbstbestimmung.* Vienna: Amalthea, 1991.

Espenshade, Thomas J., and Charles A. Calhoun. "An Analysis of Public Opinion Toward Undocumented Immigration." *Population Research and Policy Review* 12 (1994): 189–224.

Esping-Andersen, Gøsta. *The Three Worlds of Welfare Capitalism.* London: Polity Press, 1990.

Etzioni, Amitai. *Political Unification: A Comparative Study of Leaders and Forces.* New York: Holt, Rinehart and Winston, 1965.

———. "The Evils of Self-Determination." *Foreign Policy* 89 (Winter 1992–1993): 21–35.

———. "The Community of Communities." *Washington Quarterly* 19, no. 3 (Summer 1993): 127–138.

———. *The Spirit of Community.* New York: Crown, 1993.

———. *The New Golden Rule: Community and Morality in a Society.* New York: Basic Books, 1996.

Etzioni, Minerva M. *The Majority of One: Towards a Theory of Regional Compatibility.* New York: Sage, 1970.

Falk, Richard A. *Human Rights and State Sovereignty.* New York: Holmes & Meier, 1981.

———. *The Promise of World Order: Essays in Normative Relations.* Philadelphia: Temple University Press, 1987.

———. *Explorations at the Edge of Time: The Prospects Order.* Philadelphia: Temple University Press, 1992.

———. "Problems and Prospects for the Kurdish Struggle for Self-Determination After the End of the Gulf and Cold Wars." *Michigan Journal of International Law* 15, no. 2 (Winter 1994): 591–603.

———. *On Humane Governance: Toward a New Global Political World Order Models Project Report of the Global Initiative.* Cambridge, England: Polity Press, 1995.

———. *On Humane Governance.* University Park: Pennsylvania State University Press, 1997.

Falk, Richard A., Friedrich V. Kratochwil, and Saul Mendlovitz. *International Law: A Contemporary Perspective.* Boulder, Colo.: Westview Press, 1985.

Falk, Richard A., and Saul H. Mendlovitz. *Regional Politics and World Order.* San Francisco: W. H. Freeman, 1973.

Falk, Richard A., Samuel S. Kim, and Saul Mendlovitz, eds. *The United Nations and a Just World Order.* Boulder, Colo.: Westview Press, 1991.

Farah, Tawfic, ed. *Pan-Arabism and Arab Nationalism: The Continuing Debate.* Boulder, Colo.: Westview Press, 1987.

Farer, Tom. "Collectively Defending Democracy in a World of Sovereign States: The Western Hemisphere's Project." *Human Rights Quarterly* 15 (1993): 716–750.

Farij, Hanna Yusif. "The Kurdish National Question in Iraq and Foreign Intervention in the Region." *Political Readings* 2 (1993): 9–42.

Farley, Lawrence T. *Plebiscites and Sovereignty: The Crisis of Political Illegitimacy.* Boulder, Colo.: Westview Press, 1986.

Fawcett, Louise, and Andrew Hurrell. "Introduction." In *Regionalism in World*

Politics, Louise Fawcett and Andrew Hurrell, eds. Oxford: Oxford University Press, 1995.

Feron, François. "La droite, la gauche, et les tiers votant." *Liberation,* March 3, 1989: 15.

Fetherston, A. B. "Putting the Peace Back into Peacekeeping." *International Peacekeeping* 1, no. 2 (Spring 1994): 11.

Fitzmaurice, John. *The Politics of Belgium: A Unique Federalism.* Foreword, by Guy Spitaels. Boulder, Colo.: Westview Press, 1996.

Forman, James. *Self-Determination: An Examination of the Question and Its Application to the African-American People.* Washington, D.C.: Open Hand, 1984.

Fortin, André. *Passage de la modernité: Les intellectuels québecois et leurs revues.* Quebec: Les Presses de l'Université de Laval, 1993.

"Four Views." *New York Review of Books,* June 24, 1993.

Francisse, Anne Eudoxie. *The Problems of Minorities in the Nation-Building Process: The Kurds, the Copts, the Berbers.* New York: Vantage Press, 1971.

Franck, Thomas M. *The Power of Legitimacy Among Nations.* Oxford: Clarendon Press, 1990.

———. "The Emerging Right of Democratic Governance." *American Journal of International Law* 86, no. 1 (1992): 46–91.

Freiberg, Walter. *1911–1982: Südtirol und der italienische Nationalismus: Entstehung und Entwicklung einer europäischen Minderheitenfrage, quellenmässig dargestellt.* Innsbruck: Wagner, 1989.

Freschi, Louis. *Le Haut Adige-Tyrol du Sud: Autonomie et developpement.* Grenoble: Editions des Cahiers de l'Alpe de la Societé des Ecrivains Dauphinois, 1988.

Fuller, Graham. *Iraq in the Next Decade: Will Iraq Survive Until 2002?* N–3591-DAG. Santa Monica: Rand, 1993.

Gagnun, V. P., Jr. "Ethnic Nationalism and International Conflict: The Case of Serbia." *International Security* 19, no. 3 (Winter 1994–1995): 130–166.

Galbraith, Peter. "Washington, Erdut and Dayton." *Cornell International Law Journal* 30 (1997): 643–649.

Gall, Carlotta, and Thomas de Waal. *Chechnya: Calamity in the Caucasus.* New York: New York University Press, 1998.

Garbari, Maria, ed. *Convegno storico-giuridico sulle autonomie e sulle minoranze (1978: Trento, Italy).* Trento, Italy: Società di Studi Trentini di Scienze Storiche, 1981.

Gasòliba i Böhm, Carles Alfred. "The Application of Subsidiarity." In *Subsidiarity Within the European Community,* Andrew Duff, ed. London: Federal Trust for Education and Research, 1993, p. 71.

Gault, Michel. *Villes intermédiaires pour l'Europe?* Paris: Syros-Alternatives, 1989.

Geertz, Clifford. *The Interpretation of Cultures.* New York: Basic Books, 1973.

Geheimbericht der Südtiroler. *Delegation zur Pariser Konferenz 1946: Mit einer historischen und aktuellen Standortbestimmung.* Vienna: Amalthea, 1987.

Gellner, Ernest. *Nations and Nationalism.* London: Blackwell, 1983.

———. *Conditions of Liberty: Civil Society and Its Rivals.* New York: Penguin Press, 1994.

Gérard, Louis. "Des cessions déguisées de territoires en droit international public." Thesis, Université de Nancy, Faculté de Droit, 1903.

Germain, Annick, et al. "Cohabitation interethnique et vie de quartier." Unpublished document, Institut National de la Recherche Scientifique (INRS) Urbanisation, Université du Québec Montréal, 1994.

Getimis, Panayotis, and Grigoris Kafkalas, eds. *Urban and Regional Development in the New Europe: Policies and Institutions for the Development of Cities and Regions in the Single European Market.* Athens: Topos, 1993.

Geusau, F.A.M. Alting von. *Beyond the European Community.* Leiden: Sijthoff, 1969.

Ghaliyun, Burhan. *The Sectarian Order: From the State to the Tribe.* Beirut: Arab Cultural Center, 1990.

Ghisoni, Dominique, Wassissi Iopue, and Camille Rabin, eds. *Ces iles que l'on dit françaises: A partir des actes du colloque international de Lyon.* Preface by J. M. Tjibaou. Paris: Editions l'Harmattan, 1988.

Ghose, Aurobindo. *The Human Cycle: The Idea of Human Unity; War and Self-Determination.* Pondicherry: Ashram, 1971.

Ginther, Konrad. "Selbstbestimmung in Europa." Herbert-Miehsler Memorial Lecture at the University of Salzburg, June, 1992.

Ginther, Konrad, and Herbert Isak, eds. *Self-Determination in Europe.* Proceedings of an international workshop, Academy of Graz, Vienna, 1991.

Glenny, Misha. *The Fall of Yugoslavia: The Third Balkan War.* 3rd. rev. ed. New York: Penguin Books, 1996.

Goebel, Christopher M. "A Unified Concept of Population Transfer." *Denver Journal of International Law and Policy* 21, no. 1 (Fall 1992): 29.

Goldstein, Melvyn C., *The Snow Lion and the Dragon: China, Tibet, and the Dalai Lama.* Berkeley: University of California Press, 1997.

Gorenburg, Dmitry. "Regional Separatism in Russia: Ethnic Mobilisation or Power Grab?" *Europe-Asia Studies* 51, no. 2 (March 1999): 245–274.

Gottlieb, Gidon. *Nation Against State: A New Approach to Ethnic Conflicts and the Decline of Sovereignty.* New York: Council on Foreign Relations, 1993.

Gottlieb, Yosef. *Self-Determination in the Middle East.* New York: Praeger, 1982.

Goulding, Marrack. "The Evolution of United Nations Peacekeeping." *International Affairs* 69, no. 3 (July 1993): 451–464.

Gow, James. *Triumph of the Lack of Will: International Diplomacy and the Yugoslav War.* London: Hurst, 1997.

Gras, Pierre. *Du project au schéma: Lyon 2010: Une ville pour vivre et pour rêver.* Paris: Syros-Alternatives, 1990.

Gras, Solange. *La révolte des regions d'Europe occidentale: De 1916 a nos jours.* Preface by Roland Mousnier. Paris: Presses Universitaires de France, 1982.

Greenfeld, Liah. *Nationalism: Five Roads to Modernity,* Cambridge: Harvard University Press, 1992.

Gross, Feliks. *Ethnics in a Borderland: An Inquiry into the Nature of Ethnicity and Reduction of Ethnic Tensions in a One-Time Genocide Area.* Westport, Conn.: Greenwood Press, 1978.

Groupe de Reflection sur les Institutions et la Citoyenneté. "Pour un Québec concurrentiel et solidaire: Jalons d'un nouveau pacte social." *Le Devoir,* August 28, 1994: B2.

Grovogui, Siba N'Zatioula. *Sovereigns, Quasi Sovereigns, and Africans: Race and Self-Determination in International Law.* Minneapolis: University of Minnesota Press, 1996.

Gubek, Anthony B.Y. "Sudan: Rebel Disarray Delays Peace." *Civil Society* (June 15, 1994): 14–16.

———. "Ideology and Political System: Past and Present." *Civil Society* (August 1994).

Guber, Franz. *Das Selbstbestimmungsrecht in der Theorie Karl Renners: Eine soziologische Untersuchung; mit einem Geleitwort von Lothar Bossle.* Würzburg: Creator-Verlag, 1985.

Guehenno, Jean-Marie. *La fin de la democratie.* Paris: Flammarion, 1993.

Guilhaudis, Jean Françcois. *Le droit des peuples a disposer d'eux-mêmes.* Grenoble: Presses Universitaires de Grenoble, 1976.

Guillou, André. *Régionalisme et indépendance dans l'empire Byzantin au VIIe siècle.* Rome: Istito Storico Italiano per il Medio Evo, 1969.

Guiomar, Jean-Yves. *La nation entre l'histoire et la raison.* Paris: Editions la Découverte, 1990.

Gurr, Ted Robert. *Minorities at Risk: A Global View of Ethnopolitical Conflicts.* Washington, D.C.: U.S. Institute of Peace, 1993.

Gurr, Ted Robert, and Barbara Harff. *Ethnic Conflict in World Politics.* Boulder, Colo.: Westview Press, 1994.

Gurr, Ted Robert, and James R. Scaritti. "Minorities Rights at Risk: A Global Survey." *Human Rights Quarterly* 11 (August 1989): 375–405.

Gusfield, Hugh. "Poverty Politics." In *Confronting Poverty: Prescriptions for Change,* Sheldon H. Danziger, Gary D. Sandefur, and Daniel H. Weinberg, eds. New York: Russell Sage Foundation, 1994.

Haas, Ernst B. *The Obsolescence of Regional Integration Theory.* Berkeley: Institute of International Studies, University of California, 1975.

Hale, Henry E., ed. *Russian Election Watch,* no. 7 (February 4, 2000). Strengthening Democratic Institutions Project, Harvard University, p. 4.

Halperin, Morton H., and David J. Scheffer with Patricia L. Small. *Self-Determination in the New World Order.* Washington, D.C.: Carnegie Endowment for International Peace, 1992.

Hannum, Hurst. *Autonomy, Sovereignty, and Self-Determination: The Accommodation of Conflicting Rights.* Philadelphia: University of Pennsylvania Press, 1990.

———. "Rethinking Self-Determination." *Virginia Journal of International Law* 34, no. 1 (Fall 1993).

———. "Minority Rights: Introduction." *Fletcher Forum of World Affairs* 19, no. 1 (Winter/Spring 1995): 1–4.

———, ed. *Documents on Autonomy and Minority Rights.* Dordrecht, The Netherlands: Martinus Nijhoff, 1993.

Hanson, Stephen E. "Ideology, Interests, and Identity: Comparing the Soviet and Russian Secession Crises." In *Center-Periphery Conflict in Post-Soviet Russia: A Federation Imperiled,* Mikhail A. Alexseev, ed. New York: St. Martin's Press, 1999.

Harding, Alan, Jon Dawson, Richard Evans, and Michael Parkinson, eds.

European Cities Towards 2000: Profiles, Policies, and Prospects. New York: Manchester University Press, 1994.

Hassan bin Talal, Crown Prince of Jordan. *Palestinian Self-Determination: A Study of the West Bank and Gaza Strip.* New York: Quartet Books, 1981.

Haushofer, Karl. *Zum Freiheitskampf in Südostasien.* Berlin: Grunewald, Vorwinckel, 1923.

Hawtrey, Ralph George. *Economic Aspects of Sovereignty.* London: Longmans, Green, 1930.

Hayt, Franz, and Denise Galloy. *La Belgique: Dés tribus gauloises l'état fédéral.* Bruxelles: De Boeck Université, 1994.

Heater, Derek Benjamin. *National Self-Determination: Woodrow Wilson and His Legacy.* New York: St. Martin's Press, 1994.

Hecker, Hans, and Silke Spieler, eds. *Nationales Selbstverständnis und politische Ordnung: Abgrenzungen und Zusammenleben in Ost-Mitteleuropa bis zum Zweiten Weltkrieg.* Bonn: Kulturstiftung der Deutschen Vertriebenen, 1991.

Heidelmeyer, Wolfgang. *Das Selbstbestimmungsrecht der Völker; zur Geschichte und Bedeutung eines internationalen Prinzips in Praxis und Lehre von den Anfängen bis zu den Menschenrechtspakten der Vereinten Nationen.* Paderborn: Schöningh, 1973.

Heintze, Hans-Joachim, ed. *Selbstbestimmungsrecht der Völker— Herausforderung der Staatenwelt; Zerfällt die Internationale Staatenwelt in Hunderte von Staaten?* Bonn: Dietz Verlag, 1997.

Helman, Gerald, and Steven Ratner. "Saving Failed States." *Foreign Policy* (Winter 1992–1993): 3–21.

Henderson, Kenneth David Druit. *The Sudan Republic.* London: Ernest Benn, 1965.

Henze, Paul. "Caucasian Madness." *Turkish Times,* November 15, 1992.

Heraclides, Alexis. *The Self-Determination of Minorities in International Politics.* London: Cass, 1991.

———. "Secession and Third-Party Intervention." *Journal of International Affairs* 45, no. 2 (Winter 1992): 390–420.

———. "Secession, Self-Determination, and Nonintervention: In Quest of a Normative Symbiosis." *Journal of International Affairs* 45, no. 2 (1992): 399–420.

Herbst, Jeffrey. "War and the State in Africa." *International Security* 14, no. 4 (Spring 1990): 117–139.

———. *States and Power in Africa: Comparative Lessons in Authority and Control.* Princeton: Princeton University Press, 2000.

Herre, Paul. *Die südtirol Frage; Entstehung und Entwicklung eines europäischen Problems der Kriegs- und Nachkriegszeit.* München: Beck, 1927.

Herrera, Guillermina. *Estado del arte sobre educación en Guatemala.* Guatemala: Centro de Información y Documentación Educative de Guatemala and Universidad Rafael Landívar, 1987.

———. "Las lenguas guatemaltecas en la nueva constitución: Un desafio." In *Cultura maya y políticas de desarrollo,* Demetrio Rodríguez Guaján Raxché, ed. Guatemala: COCADI, 1989.

———. "Las lenguas indígenas de Guatemala: Situación actual y futuro." In *Lecturas sobre la lingüística maya,* Nora C. England and Stephen R.

Elliot, eds. La Antigua Guatemala, Guatemala: Centro de Investigaciones Regonales de Mesoamérica (CIRMA), 1990.

Hesse, Joachim Jens, ed. *Regionen in Europa = Regions in Europe = Régions en Europe*. Baden-Baden: Nomos, 1995.

Higgins, Rosalyn. "The New United Nations and the Former Yugoslavia." *International Affairs* 69, no. 3 (1993): 465–483.

———. *Problems and Progress: International Law and How We Use It*. New York: Oxford University Press, 1994.

Hitler, Adolf. *Mein Kampf*. Easton Press, 1994.

Hobsbawm, E. J. *Nations and Nationalism Since 1780: Programme, Myth, Reality*. Cambridge: Cambridge University Press, 1991.

Hoffmann, Stanley. "Yugoslavia: Implications for Europe and the European Institutions." In *The World and Yugoslavia's Wars*, Richard H. Ullman, ed. New York: Council on Foreign Relations, 1996.

Horowitz, Donald L. *Ethnic Groups in Conflict*. Berkeley: University of California Press, 1985.

———. "Self-Determination: Politics, Philosophy, and Law." In *National Self-Determination and Secession*, Margaret Moore, ed. New York: Oxford University Press, 1998.

Hu, Chou-Young. *Das Selbstbestimmungsrecht als eine Vorbedingung des völligen Genusses aller Menschenrechte: Eine Studie über Artikel der beiden Menschenrechtskonventionen vom 16. Dezember 1966*. Zurich: Schulthess Polygraphischer Verlag, 1972.

Hudson, Michael. *The Precarious Republic: Political Modernization in Lebanon*. New York: Random House, 1968.

Hula, Erich. *Nationalism and Internationalism: European and American Perspectives*. Preface by Kenneth W. Thompson. Lanham, Md.: University Press of America, 1984.

Huntington, Samuel P. "The Clash of Civilizations?" *Foreign Affairs* 72, no. 3 (Summer 1993): 22–49.

———. *The Third Wave: Democratization in the Late Twentieth Century*. Norman: University of Oklahoma Press, 1991.

Hutchinson, John, and Anthony D. Smith, eds. *Nationalism*. New York: Oxford University Press, 1994.

Huter, Franz, ed. *Südtirol: Frage des euopäischen Gewissens*. Vienna: Verlag für Geschichte und Politik, 1965.

Ibrahim, Sa'ad Elddin. *Considerations on the Question of Minorities*. Kuwait, Cairo: Dar Su'ad al-Sabah, 1992.

———. "The Wrong Side of History." *Civil Society* (May 14, 1994).

"Interinstitutional Declaration on Democracy, Transparency, and Subsidiarity," *Bulletin of the European Community*, no. 10 (1993): 118–120.

Isensee, Josef. *Subsidiaritätsprinzip und Verfassungsrecht*. Berlin: Duncker und Humblot, 1968.

Jacobson, John R., ed. *The Territorial Rights of Nations and Peoples: Essays from the Basic Issues Forum*. Lewiston, N.Y.: Mellen Press, 1989.

Jahrbuch der Oesterreichischen Aussenpolitik. Vienna: Ministry for Foreign Affairs, 1995.

Jardine, Matthew. *East Timor: Genocide in Paradise*. Introduction by Noam Chomsky. Tucson: Odonian Press, 1995.

Jeffery, Charlie, et al. "Federalism, Unification and European Integration, II," *German Politics* 1, no. 3 (December 1992): 58–118.

Jenson, Jane. "Mapping, Naming, and Remembering: Globalization at the End of the Twentieth Century." *Integration and Fragmentation: The Paradox of the Late Twentieth Century,* Guy Laforest and Douglas Brown, eds. Kingston, Ontario: Institute of Intergovernmental Relations, Queens University, 1994.

John, Harold S. *Self-Determination Within the Community of Nations.* Leiden: Sijthoff, 1967.

Johnson, Harold S. "Self Determination: Western European Perspective." In *Self-Determination: National, Regional, and Global Dimension,* Yonah Alexander and Robert A. Friedlander. Boulder, Colo.: Westview Press, 1980.

Johnston, R. J., David Knight, and Eleonore Kofman, eds. *Nationalism, Self-Determination & Political Geography.* London: Croom Helm, 1988.

Jones, Barry, and Michael Keating, eds. *The European Union and the Regions.* Oxford: Clarendon Press, 1995.

Jones, Lynne. "Nationalism and the Self." *Peace and Democracy News* 6, no. 2 (1992–1993): 20–27.

Kaiser, Robert John. *The Geography of Nationalism in Russia and the USSR.* Princeton: Princeton University Press, 1994.

Kalogeropoulas-Strates, Spyros. *Le droit des peuples à disposer d'eux-mêmes.* Bruxelles: E. Bruylant, 1973.

Kaltenbach, Frederick. *Self-Determination 1919: A Study in Frontier Making Between Germany and Poland.* London: Jarrolds, 1938.

Kampelman, Max M. "Secession and the Right of Self-Determination: An Urgent Need to Harmonize Principle with Pragmatism." *Washington Quarterly* 16, no. 3 (Summer 1993): 5–12.

Kann, Robert A. *Das Nationalitätenproblem der Habsburger Monarchie; Geschichte und Ideengehalt der nationalen Bestrebungen vom Vormärz bis zur Auflösung des Reiches im Jahre 1918.* 2 vols. Vienna: H. Böhlaus, 1964.

Kärntner Landesarchiv, ed. *Der 10. Oktober 1920: Kärntens Tag der Selbstbestimmung: Vorgeschichte, Ereignisse, Analysen. Mitarbeit von Alfred Ogris.* Klagenfurt: Verlag des Kärntner Landesarchivs, 1990.

Karny, Yo'av. *Highlanders: A Journey to the Caucasus in Quest of Memory.* New York: Farrar, Straus, and Giroux, 2000.

Kasfir, Nelson. "Explaining Ethnic Political Participation." *World Politics* 31, no. 3 (1979): 365–388.

Katz, Michael. *The Undeserving Poor: From the War on Poverty to the War on Welfare.* New York: Pantheon, 1989.

Keeton, George Williams. *National Sovereignty and International Order.* London: Peace Book Commission, 1939.

Kelsen, Hans. *Das Problem der Souveränität und die Theorie des Völkerrechts— Beitrag zu einer reinen Rechtslehre.* Tübingen: JCB Mohr, 1920.

Kennon, Patrick E. *The Twilight of Democracy.* New York: Doubleday, 1995.

Khalid, Mansur. *The Government They Deserve.* London: Kegan Paul International, 1990.

Khoury, Philip S., and Joseph Kostiner, eds. *Tribe and State Formation in the Middle East.* Berkeley: University of California Press, 1990.

Kicker, Renate, Joseph Marko, and Martin Steiner, eds. *Changing Borders, Legal and Economic Aspects of European Enlargement.* New York: Peter Lang Verlag, 2000.

Kincaid, John. "Peoples, Persons, and Places in Flux: International Integration Versus National Fragmentation." *Integration and Fragmentation: The Paradox of the Late Twentieth Century,* Guy Laforest and Douglas Brown, eds. Kingston, Ontario: Institute of Intergovernmental Relations, Queens University, 1994.

King, David Needen. *Financial and Economic Aspects of Regionalism and Separatism.* London: Her Majesty's Stationary Office, 1973.

King, Roger (with Chapter 8 by Graham Gibbs). *The State in Modern Society: New Directions in Political Sociology.* London: Macmillan, 1986.

Kingsbury, Benedict. "Claims by Non-State Groups in International Law." *Cornell International Law Journal* 25 (1992): 481.

Kirchner, Emil J., ed. *Decentralization and Transition in the Visegrad: Poland, Hungary, the Czech Republic, and Slovakia.* New York: St. Martin's Press, 1999.

Kiss, Alexandre Charles. "The Peoples' Right to Self-Determination." *Human Rights Journal* 7 (1986): 165–175.

Knight, David B. *Self-Determination: An Interdisciplinary Annotated Bibliography.* New York: Garland, 1987.

Kohli, Atul. *Democracy and Discontent: India's Growing Crisis of Governability.* New York: Cambridge University Press, 1991.

———. *The State and Poverty in India: The Politics of Reform.* Cambridge: Cambridge University Press, 1991.

Kolejka, Josef. *"'Narodnostni princip' a internacionalismus, 1789–1860: Vznik marxisticke teorie narodnostni otazky a 'zahranicni politiky.'"* Berne: Univerzita J. E. Purkyne v Brno, 1984.

Korowicz, Marek Stanislaw. *Organisations internationales et souverenité des états membres.* Paris: Pedone, 1961.

Kouchner, Bernard. *Les nouvelles solidarités: Actes dés assises internationales de 1989.* Paris: Presses Universitaires de France, 1989.

Kresl, Peter Karl. *The Urban Economy and Regional Trade Liberalization.* New York: Praeger, 1992.

Kreyenbroek, Philip G. "On the Kurdish Language." In *The Kurds: A Contemporary Overview,* Philip Kreyenbroek and Stefan Sperl, eds. London: Routledge, 1992.

Kristian, A. A. *The Right to Self-Determination and the Soviet Union.* London: Boreas, 1952.

Kristof, Erich. *Die Lehre der Selbstbestimmungsrechte in der Völkerrechtsdoktrin der DDR.* Frankfurt: Athenaeum-Verlag, 1973.

Kunz, Josef Laurenz. *Die völkerrechtliche Option.* Breslau: F. Hirt, 1928.

Kupchan, Clifford. "Devolution Drives Russian Reform." *Washington Quarterly* 23, no. 2 (Spring 2000): 67–77.

Laffan, Brigid. *Integration and Cooperation in Europe.* New York: Routledge, 1992.

Lafont, Robert. *La nation, l'état, les régions: Reflexions pour un fin de siècle et un commencement d'Europe.* Paris: Berg International, 1993.

Laitin, David D. "The National Uprisings in the Soviet Union." *World Politics* 44 (October 1991): 176.

Lâm, Maivân Clech. *At the Edge of the State: Indigenous Peoples and Self-Determination.* Ardsley, N.Y.: Transnational, 2000.

Lamont, Michèle. *Money, Morals, and Manners: The Culture of the French and American Upper Middle Class.* Chicago: University of Chicago Press, 1992.

Lamont, Michèle, and Marcel Fournier, eds. *Cultivating Differences: Symbolic Boundaries and the Making of Inequality.* Chicago: University of Chicago Press, 1992.

Landmann, Max. *Der Souveränitätsbegriff bei den französischen Theoretikern, von Jean Bodin bis auf Jean Jacques Rousseau.* Leipzig: Veit & Comp., 1896.

Landrieu, Josee. "Regions and French Society." *Futures* (February 1986).

Lansing, Robert. *Notes on Sovereignty from the Standpoint of the State and of the World.* Washington, D.C.: The Endowment, 1921.

Lapeyronnie, Didier. "France and Great Britain Faced with Their Immigrant Minorities." Paper presented at the Center for European Studies, Harvard University, 1994.

Lapidoth, Ruth. "Sovereignty in Transition." *Journal of International Affairs* (Winter 1992): 325–346.

———. "Autonomy: Potential and Limitations," *International Journal on Group Rights* 1 (1994): 269–290.

———. *Autonomy: Flexible Solutions to Ethnic Conflicts.* Washington, D.C.: U.S. Institute of Peace Press, 1996.

Lapidus, Gail, and Victor Zaslavsky, eds., with Philip Goldman. *From Union to Commonwealth: Nationalism and Separatism in the Soviet Republics.* Cambridge: Cambridge University Press, 1992.

Laski, Harold Joseph. *Studies in the Problem of Sovereignty.* New Haven: Yale University Press, 1917.

———. *A Grammar of Politics.* London:Allan and Unwin, 1934.

Lasok, D. "Subsidiarity and the Occupied Field." *New Law Journal* 142, no. 6567 (September 11, 1992): 1228–1230.

Lauterpacht, Hersh. *Régles générales du droit de la paix.* Hague: Academy of International Law, IV, 1938.

Lehmann, Susan G. "Islam and Ethnicity in the Republics of Russia," *Post-Soviet Affairs* 13 (January/March 1997): 78–103.

Lemberg, Eugen. *Die Geschichte des Nationalismus in Europa.* Linz: Brücken, c. 1950.

Lenin, Vladimir Il'ich. *The Right of Nations to Self-Determination: Selected Writings.* New York: International, 1951.

———. *Questions of National Policy and Proletarian Internationalism.* Moscow: Foreign Languages Publishing, 1970.

Leonardi, Robert, and Raffaella Y. Nanetti, eds. *The Regions and European Integration: The Case of Emilia-Romagna.* New York: Pinter, 1990.

Levin, Michael D., ed. *Ethnicity and Aboriginality: Case Studies in Ethnonationalism.* Toronto: University of Toronto Press, 1993.

Levy, Marion J., Jr. *Modernization and the Structure of Societies: A Setting for International Affairs.* Princeton: Princeton University Press, 1966.

Lieberson, Stanley. *A Piece of the Pie: Black and White Immigrants Since 1880.* Berkeley: University of California Press, 1980.

Liechtenstein, Prince Alois. "Der Liechtensteinische Entwurf für eine Konvention über das Selbstbestimmungsrecht im Vergleich zum Heutigen Völkerrecht." M.A. thesis, University of Salzburg, 1993, p. 12.

Liechtenstein, Prince Hans Adam II. "Die Grenzen des Staates." *Europäische Rundschau* (Summer 1997).

Liechtenstein Research Program on Self-Determination. *The Crisis in Chechnya: Causes, Prospects, Solutions.* Conference Proceedings, March 3–4, 2000. Princeton: Princeton University.

Lieven, Anatol. *Chechnya: Tombstone of Russian Power.* new ed. New Haven: Yale University Press, 1998.

Lijphart, Arend. "Consociational Democracy." *World Politics* 21, no. 2 (1969): 207–225.

———. "The Power-Sharing Approach." In *Conflict and Peacemaking in Multiethnic Societies,* Joseph Montville, ed. Lexington, Mass.: Lexington Books, 1987.

Link, Ewald. *Das Subsidiaritätsprinzip, sein Wesen und seine Bedeutung für die Sozialethik.* Freiburg: Herder, 1955.

Lipset, Seymour Martin. *The First New Nation: The United States in Historical and Comparative Perspective.* New York: W. W. Norton, 1979.

———. *Continental Divide: The Values and Institutions of the United States and Canada.* New York: Routledge, 1991.

Lisee, Jean François. "Interview with Pierre Lanctil." In *Boundaries of Identity: A Quebec Reader,* William Dodge, ed. Toronto: Lester, 1992.

Little, I.M.D., et al. *Boom, Crisis and Adjustment: The Macroeconomic Experience of Developing Countries.* New York: Oxford University Press, 1994.

Liu, Xianzhao. *Zongguo minzu wenti yanji* (A study of the ethnic minority problem in China). Beijing: Chinese Academy of Social Sciences, 1993.

Locher, Uli. *Les jeunes et la langue: Usages et attitudes linguistiques des jeunes qui étudient en français (de la 4e année du secondaire à la fin du collegial).* Quebec: Les Publications du Québec, 1993.

Lomax Cook, Fay. *Who Should Be Helped: Public Support for Social Services.* Beverly Hills: Sage, 1979.

López Raquec, Margarita. *Acerca de los alfabetos para escribir los idiomas mayas de Guatemala.* Guatemala: Ministerio de Cultura y Deportes, 1989.

Lowenstein, Karl. *Political Reconstruction.* New York: McMillan, 1946.

Luard, Evan. *The Globalization of Politics.* New York: New York University Press, 1990.

Lustick, Ian. *State-Building Failure in British Ireland and French Algeria.* Berkeley: Institute of International Studies, University of California, 1985.

———. "Becoming Problematic: Breakdown of Hegemonic Conception of Ireland in Nineteenth Century Britain." *Politics and Society* 18, no. 1 (1990): 39–73.

———. *Unsettled States, Disputed Lands: Britain and Ireland, France and Algeria, Israel and the West Bank/Gaza.* Ithaca, N.Y.: Cornell University Press, 1993.

———. "Ending Protracted Conflicts: The Oslo Peace Process Between Political Partnership and Legality." *Cornell International Law Journal* 30, no. 3 (1997): 741–757.

———. "Yerushalayim and Al-Quds: Political Catechism and Political Realities." *Journal of Palestine Studies* 30, no. 1 (2000): 5–21.

Macartney, W. J. Allan, ed. *Self-Determination in the Commonwealth.* Aberdeen: Aberdeen University Press, 1988.

Mackerras, Colin. *China's Minorities: Integration and Modernization in the Twentieth Century.* New York: Oxford University Press, 1994.

Magliana, Melissa. *The Autonomous Province of South Tyrol: A Model of Self-Governance?* Bolzano/Bozen: European Academy of Bolzano/Bozen, 1999.

Mandelbaum, Michael. ed. *Post-Communism: Four Perspectives.* New York: Council on Foreign Relations, 1996.

Manor, James. "Ethnicity and Politics in India." *International Affairs* 72, no. 3 (July 1996): 459–476.

Mansergh, Nicholas. *The Prelude to Partition: Concepts and Aims in Ireland and India.* New York: Cambridge University Press, 1978.

Marko, Joseph. *Autonomie und Integration—Rechtsinstitute des Nationalitätenrechts im funktionellen Vergleich: Studien zu Politik und Verwaltung, Band 51.* Vienna: Böhlau Verlag, 1995.

Masaryk, Tomas Garrigue. *The Makings of a State; Memories and Observations, 1914–18.* London: George Allen and Unwin, 1927.

Masse, Martin. *Identites collectives et civilisation: Pour une vision nonnationaliste d'un Québec independant.* Montreal: VLB Editeur, 1994.

Mayer, Nonna, and Pascal Perrineau. *Le Front National a decouvert.* Paris: Presses de la Fondation Nationale de Science Politique, 1989.

McAllister, Ian. *Regional Development and the European Community: A Canadian Perspective.* Quebec: Institute for Research on Public Policy, 1982.

McCorquodale, Robert. "Human Rights and Self-Determination." In *The New World Order: Sovereignty, Human Rights, and the Self-Determination of Peoples,* Mortimer Sellers, ed. Washington, D.C.: Berg, 1996.

McCorquodale, Robert, and Nicholas Orosz, eds. *Tibet: The Position in International Law.* Report of the Conference of International Lawyers on Issues Relating to Self-Determination and Independence for Tibet, London, January 6–10, 1993. London: Edition Hansjörg Mayer and Serindia, 1994.

McCrone, Gavin. "Subsidiarity: Its Implications for Economic Policy." *National Westminster Bank Quarterly Review* (November 1992): 46–56.

McDermott, F. E. *Self-Determination in Social Work: A Collection of Essays on Self-Determination and Related Concepts.* Boston: Routledge, 1975.

McKinlay, Peter. "Globalization, Subsidiarity, and Enabling the Governance of Communities."<http://www.mdl.co.nz/readingroom/governance/globalsub.html>, p. 4.

McRae, Kenneth Douglas. *Conflict and Compromise in Multilingual Societies.* Waterloo, Ontario: Wilfrid Laurier University Press, 1983.

Medrano, Juan Diez. *Divided Nations: Class, Politics and Nationalism in the Basque Country and Catalonia.* Ithaca, N.Y.: Cornell University Press, 1995.

Meissner, Boris, ed. *Das Selbstbestimmungsrecht der Völker in Osteuropa und China.* Cologne: Verlag für Wissenschaft und Politik, 1968.

Merelman, Richard M. *Making Something of Ourselves: On Culture and Politics in the United States.* Berkeley: University of California Press, 1984.

Merriam, Charles Edward. *History of the Theory of Sovereignty Since Rousseau.* New York: Columbia University Press, 1900.

Meunier, Sophie. "The French Exception." *Foreign Affairs* 79, no. 4 (July/August 2000): 104–107.

Millon-Delson, Chantal. *L'état subsidiaire: Ingerence et non-ingerence de l'état: Le principe de subsidiarité aux fondements de l'histoire européenne.* Paris: Presses Universitaires de France, 1992.

Minzu gongzhuo tongji tiyao 1949–1989 (Summary of work on ethnic minority issues). Beijing: Minzu, 1990.

Minzu zhishi shouche (Handbook on ethnic minorities). Beijing: People's Publishing, 1985.

Mitra, Subrata K., and R. Alison Lewis. *Subnational Movements in South Asia.* Boulder, Colo.: Westview Press, 1996.

Mommen, Andre. *The Belgian Economy in the Twentieth Century.* London: Routledge, 1994.

Monière, Denis L. *Le developpement des ideologies au Québec.* Montreal: Editions Québec/Amerique, 1977.

———. *L'indépendance: Essai.* Montreal: Québec/Amérique, 1992.

Monniér, Daniel. *Les choix linguistiques des travailleurs immigrants et allophones: Rapport d'une enquête réalisée en 1991.* Montreal: Publications du Québec, 1993.

Montcalm, Mary Beth. "Quebec Separatism in a Comparative Perspective." In *Quebec: State and Society,* Alain G. Gagnon, ed. New York: Methuen, 1984.

Moore, Barrington. *Social Origins of Dictatorship and Democracy: Lord and Peasant in the Making of the Modern World.* Boston: Beacon Press, 1966.

Moore, Margaret, ed. *National Self-Determination and Secession.* New York: Oxford University Press, 1998.

Moravcsik, Andrew. *The Choice for Europe: Social Purpose and State Power from Messina to Maastricht.* Ithaca, N.Y.: Cornell University Press, 1998.

Mordechai, Nisan. *Minorities in the Middle East: A History of Struggle and Self-Expression.* Jefferson, N.C.: McFarland, 1991.

Mouriaux, Rene. "Strategies syndicales face au chomage et a l'intervention industrielle de l'état dans la période 1962–87." In *Searching from the New France,* James F. Hollifield and George Ross, eds. New York: Routledge, 1991.

Moya, Ruth, and Otilia Lux de Cotí. "La mujer maya en Guatemala: El futuro de la memoria." Paper presented at the Conferencia Internacional Sobre Género, Etnicidad y Educación, Cochabamba, Bolivia, August 1999.

Moynihan, Daniel P. *On the Law of Nations.* Cambridge: Harvard University Press, 1990.

———. *Pandaemonium: Ethnicity in International Politics.* New York: Oxford University Press, 1993.

Mullerson, R. A. *International Law, Rights and Politics: Developments in Eastern Europe and the CIS.* London: Routledge, 1994.

Murlakov, Eli. *Das Recht der Völker auf Selbstbestimmung im israelisch-arabischen Konflikt.* Zurich: Schulthess, 1983.

Musgrave, Thomas D. *Self-Determination and National Minorities.* Oxford: Clarendon Press, 1997.

Naisbitt, John. *Global Paradox: The Bigger the World Economy, the More Powerful Its Smallest Players.* New York: W. Morrow, 1994.

Natali, Denise. "International Aid, Regional Politics, and the Kurdish Issue in Iraq After the Gulf War." Occasional Paper no. 31. Abu Dhabi: Emirates Center for Strategic Studies and Research, Spring 1999.

Necatigil, Zaim M. *The Cyprus Question and the Turkish Position in International Law.* 2nd ed. Oxford: Oxford University Press, 1993.

Neuberger, Ralph Benyamin. *National Self-Determination in Postcolonial Africa.* Boulder, Colo.: Lynne Rienner, 1986.

Neunreither, Karlz Heinz. "Subsidiarity as a Guiding Principle for European Community Activities." *Government and Opposition* 28, no. 2 (London, 1993): 206–220.

Newhouse, John, *Europe Adrift*. New York: Council on Foreign Relations, 1997.

Newman, Frank C. "A 'Nutshell' Approach to the U.N. Human Rights Law Protecting Minorities." *Fletcher Forum of World Affairs* 19, no. 1 (Winter/Spring 1995): 6–20.

Newman, Saul. "The Ethnic Dilemma: The Rise and Decline of Ethnoregional Political Parties in Scotland, Belgium and Quebec" Ph.D. dissertation, Princeton University, 1989.

Nincic, Djura. *The Problem of Sovereignty in the Charter and in the Practice of the United Nations*. The Hague: Nijhoff, 1970.

Noiriel, Gerard. *Le creuset français: Histoire de l'immigration, XlXe XXe siècle*. Paris: Seuil, 1988.

Nordiske, Rad. *Le coopération internordique*. Stockholm: Haesselby, 1965.

Norton, Richard A. "Lebanon After Ta'if: Is the Civil War Over?" *Middle East Journal* 45, no. 3 (1991): 457–473.

Núñez, Gabriela, Beatrice Bezmalinovic, Susan Clay, et al. *Primer encuentro nacional: Educando a la niña: Lograremos el desarrollo de Guatemala*. Guatemala: U.S. Agency for International Development (AID), 1991.

Nussbaum, Arthur. *A Concise History of the Law of Nations*. rev. ed. New York: Macmillan, 1954.

Nye, Joseph S. *Peace in Parts*. Boston: Little, Brown, 1971.

O'Corrain, Donnchadh. *Nationality and the Pursuit of National Independence*, T. W. Moody, ed. Belfast: Appletree Press for the Irish Committee of Historical Sciences, 1978.

Ofuatey-Kodjoe, W. *The Principle of Self-Determination in International Law*. New York: Nellen, 1977.

Oji, Umozurike. *Self-Determination in International Law*. Hamden, Conn.: Archon Books, 1972.

Operations des nations unies—Leçons de terrain: Cambodge, Somalie, Rwanda, ex-Yougoslavie. Paris: Fondation pour les Etudes de Défense, 1995.

"Orientations for a Union Approach Towards the Baltic Sea Region." Communication to the EU Council of Ministers, adopted by the European Commission, SEC (94) 1747 final, Brussels, 10/25/1994.

Ostrom, Elinor. *Governing the Commons: The Evolution of Institutions for Collective Action*. New York: Cambridge University Press, 1990.

Ott, David H. *Palestine in Perspective: Politics, Human Rights and the West Bank*. London: Quartet Books, 1981.

Otzoy, Irma. "Identity and Higher Education Among Mayan Women." Unpublished M.A. thesis, Department of Anthropology, University of Iowa, 1988.

Otzoy, Irma, and Enrique Sam. "Identidad etnica y modernización entre los Mayas de Guatemala." *Mesoamérica* 19 (June 1990): 97–100.

Oxlajuuj Keej Mayab' Ajtz'iib' [Ajpub', Ixkem, Lolmay, Nik'te', Pakal, Saqijix, and Waykan. *Mayab' Chii'; Idiomas mayas de Guatemala*. Guatemala: Cholsamaj, 1993.

Parkin, David, ed. *Continuity and Autonomy in Swahili Communities: Inland Influences and Strategies of Self-Determination*. London: School of Oriental and African Studies, University of London, 1994.

Parti Québecois. *Le programme économique*. Montréal: Editions du Parti Québecois, 1977.

Pasquali, Giancarlo. "Subsidiarity." *Journal of Regional Policy* 13, no. 1 (January-March 1993): 135–145.

Paugam, Serge. *La societé française et ses pauvres*. Paris: Presses Universitaires de France, 1993.

Pennings, Frans. "Is the Subsidiarity Principle Useful to Guide the European Integration Process?" *Tilburg Foreign Law Review* 2, no. 2 (1992): 153–163.

Perin, Constance. *Belonging in America*. Madison: University of Wisconsin Press, 1988.

Perrineau, Pascal. "Le Front National: Du désert a l'enracinement." In *Face au racisme*, vol. 2: *Analyses, hypotheses, perspectives*, Pierre-André Taguieff, ed. Paris: La Découverte, 1991.

Peterson, John. "Subsidiarity: A Definition to Suit Any Vision." *Parliamentary Affairs* 47 (January 1994): 116–132.

Peterson, Richard. "Understanding Audience Segmentation: From Elite and Mass to Omnivores and Univores." *Poetics* 21 (1992): 243–258.

Peterson, Scott A., and D. Millar. "Subsidiarity: A Europe of the Regions Versus the British Constitution?" *Journal of Common Market Studies* 32, no. 1 (March 1994): 46–47.

Pinto, Diana. "Toward a Mellowing of the French Identity?" *Yearbook of French Studies* 18 (1988): 1–19.

Poisson, Jacques. *Le romantisme et la souveraineté Enquête bibliographique*. Paris: J. Vrin, 1932.

Pomerance, Michla. *Self-Determination in Law and Practice: The New Doctrine in the United Nations*. The Hague: Nijhoff, 1982.

"Position of the European Commission of Defining and Implementing the Principle of Subsidiarity." *Europe Documents*, English ed., no. 1804–1805 (October 30, 1992): 1–16.

Prongue, Bernard, ed., with Cyrille Gigandet, Gilbert Ganguillet, and Daniel Kessler. *L'écart element: Espace jurassien et identité plurielle*. Introduction by Maurice Born. Saint-Imier, Canevas: Age d'Homme, 1991.

Protocol on the Application of the Principles of Subsidiarity and Proportionality of the Treaty of Amsterdam Amending the Treaty on European Union: The Treaties Establishing the European Communities, and Certain Related Acts (1997). European Union, Brussels.

Putin, Vladimir Vladimirovich, with Natalya Timakova Gevorkyan and Andrei Kolesnikov. *First Person: An Astonishingly Frank Self-Portrait by Russia's President*, trans. Catherine A. Fitzpatrick. New York: Public Affairs, 2000.

Putnam, Robert D., with Robert Leonardi and Raffaella Nanetti. *Making Democracy Work: Civic Traditions in Modern Italy*. Princeton: Princeton University Press, 1993.

Quaye, Christopher O. *Liberation Struggles in International Law*. Philadelphia: Temple University Press, 1991.

Quint, Wolfgang. *Souveränitätsbegriff und Souveränitätspolitik in Bayern, von der Mitte des 17. bis zur ersten Hälfte des 19. Jahrhunderts*. Berlin: Duncker und Humblot, 1971.

Rabl, Kurt O. *Das Selbstbestimmungsrecht der Völker: geschichtliche Grundlagen*. Cologne: Böhlau, 1973.

Ramcharang, B. G. "Individual, Collective and Group Rights: History, Theory, Practice and Contemporary Evolution." *International Journal on Group Rights* 1 (1993): 27–43.

Ranke, Leopold von. *Historisch-Politische Zeitschrift*. Vaduz: Topos, 1981.

Raschhofer, Hermann. *Das Selbstbestimmungsrecht. Sein Ursprung und sein Bedeutung*. Bonn, 1960.

Redslob, Robert. *Abhängige Länder: Eine Analyse des Begriffs von der ursprünglichen Herrschergewalt*. Leipzig: Veit & Comp., 1914.

Regional Research in an International Perspective. Munich: V. Florentz, 1984.

Regragui, Saad. *Le devoir d'assistance étrangère aux peuples en danger: La troisième dimension du droit des peuples*. Mohammedia, Morocco: Imprimerie de Fedala, 1991.

Reibstein, Ernst. *Volkssuveränität und Freiheitsrechte: Texte und Studien zur politischen Theorie des 14.–18 Jahrhunderts*. Freiburg: Karl Albert, 1972.

Reinarman, Craig. *American States of Mind: Political Beliefs and Behavior Among Private and Public Workers*. New Haven: Yale University Press, 1987.

Reitz, Jeffrey G., and Raymond Breton. *The Illusion of Difference: Realities of Ethnicity in Canada and the United States*. Toronto: C. D. Howe Institute, 1994.

Renaud, Marc. "Quebec's New Middle Class in Search of Social Hegemony: Causes and Political Consequences." *International Review of Community Development* 37, no. 40 (1989): 1–36.

Renner, Karl. *Das Selbstbestimmungsrecht der Nationen in besonderer Anwendung auf Oesterreich. Teil: Nation und Staat*. Leipzig: Franz Deuticke, 1918.

Report of the Secretary-General Pursuant to General Assembly Resolution 53/35, 1998.

Report on the Colloquim on Chechnya, Liechtenstein Research Program on Self-Determination, <http://www.princeton.edu/~lisd/chechnya.html.

Rescher, Nicholas. *Pluralism: Against the Demand for Consensus*. Oxford: Clarendon Press, 1993.

Resnick, Philip. *Letters to a Québecois Friend, with a Reply by Daniel Latouche*. Montreal: McGill Queen's University Press, 1990.

"Resolution of the Principle of Subsidiarity," Doc. A3–163/90.OJC231/1990/09/17/p. 163.

"Resolution on the Implementation of the Principle of Subsidiarity" (replacing B3–1514/92 and 1520/92). Session of November 1992, OJC337/1992/12/21/p. 116.

Rich, Norman, *The Age of Nationalism and Reform, 1850–1890*. New York: W. W. Norton, 1978.

Richards, Alan, and John Waterbury. *A Political Economy of the Middle East*. Boulder, Colo.: Westview Press, 1996.

Richards, Julia Becker, and Michael Richards. "Mayan Education: An Historical and Contemporary Analysis of Mayan Language Educational Policy." *Mayan Cultural Activism in Guatemala*, Edward Fischer and McKenna Brown, eds. Austin: University of Texas Press, 1966,

Richler, Mordicai. *Oh Canada, Oh Quebec: Requiem for a Divided Society*. Toronto: Viking, 1992.

Rigo, Sureda A. *The Evolution of the Right of Self-Determination: A Study of United Nations Practice.* Leiden: Sijthoff, 1973.

Roberts, Adam. "The United Nations and International Security." *Survival* 35, no. 2 (Summer 1993): 3–30.

Robertson, Patrick, ed. *Reshaping Europe in the Twenty-first Century.* London: Macmillan, 1992.

Roff, Sue Rabbitt. *Overreaching in Paradise: United States Policy in Palau Since 1945.* Juneau, Alaska: Denali Press, 1991.

Rohan, Henri duc de. *Intérêts et maximes des princes et des états souverains.* Cologne: Chez Iean du Pais, 1673.

———. *Maximes des princes et états souverains.* Colognes, 1673.

Rohan, Prinz Karl Anton. *Oesterreich, deutsch, europäisch: Neun metapolitische Aufsätze.* Bodman: Hohenstaufen Verlag, 1973.

Rondot, Pierre. "The Political Institutions of Lebanese Democracy." In *Politics in Lebanon,* Leonard Binder, ed. New York: John Wiley, 1966.

Ronen, Dov. *The Quest for Self-Determination.* New Haven: Yale University Press, 1979.

Rousseau, Jean-Jacques. *Essai sur le principe de la souveraineté.* London: Cox, Fils, et Baylis, 1804.

Rudd, Chris. *Coalition Formation in Belgium 1965–81.* Colchester, Essex: Deptartment of Government, University of Essex, 1985.

Sahlins, Peter. *Boundaries: The Making of France and Spain in the Pyrenees.* Berkeley: University of California Press, 1989.

Sahnoun, Mohammed. *Somalia: The Missed Opportunities.* Washington, D.C.: U.S. Institute of Peace, 1994.

Said, Abdul, and Luiz R. Simmons, eds. *Ethnicity in an International Context.* New Brunswick, N.J.: Transaction Books, 1976.

Salamé, Ghassan. "Small Is Pluralistic: Democracy as an Instrument of Civil Peace." In *Democracy Without Democrats? The Renewal of Politics in the Muslim World,* Ghassan Salamé, ed. London: I. B. Tauris, 1994.

Sam Colop, Luis Enrique. "Hacia una propuesta de ley de educación bilingüe." Unpublished thesis for the Licenciatura en Ciencias Jurídicas y Sociales, University Rafael Landívar, Guatemala, 1983.

Sathyamurthy, T. V. *Nationalism in the Contemporary World: Political and Sociological.* London: F. Pinter, 1983.

Sayn-Wittgenstein, Prinz Franz. *Südtirol und das Trentino.* Munich: Prestel, 1965.

Schaeffer, Robert K. *Warpaths: The Politics of Partition.* New York: Hill and Wang, 1990.

Schain, Martin. "The National Front in France and the Construction of Political Legitimacy." *West European Politics* 10, no. 2 (1987): 229–252.

Scherk, Nikolaus. *Dekolonisation und Soveränität: Die Unabhängigkeit und Abhängigkeit der Nachfolgestaaten Frankreichs in Schwarzafrika.* Vienna: Braumüller, 1969.

Schimm, Melvin G., ed. *European Regional Communities: A New Era on the Old Continent.* Dobbs Ferry, N.Y.: Oceana, 1962.

Schneider, Reinhard. *Grenzen und Grenzregionen herausgegeben von Wolfgang Haubrichts.* Saarbrücken: Saarbrückner Druckerei und Verlag, 1993.

Schoenberg, Harris O. "Limits of Self-Determination." In *Israel Yearbook on Human Rights.* Tel Aviv: Faculty of Law, Tel Aviv University, 1976.

Schoenborn, Walther. *Staatensukzession.* Berlin: Kohlhammer, 1913.

Schuman, Howard, Charlotte Steeh, and Lawrence Bobo. *Racial Attitudes in America: Trends and Interpretation.* Cambridge: Harvard University Press, 1985.

Seabury, Samuel. *The New Federalism: An Inquiry into the Means by Which Social Power May Be So Distributed Between State and People as to Insure Prosperity and Progress.* New York: Dutton, 1950.

Seers, Dudley, and Kjell Ostrom, eds. *The Crises of the European Regions.* New York: St. Martin's Press, 1983.

Selbstbestimmung fur Mittel-Schriftrenreihe, Sloboda und Osteuropa. Brugg: Adria, 1988.

Self-Determination and Indigenous Peoples: Sami Rights and Northern Perspectives. Compiled and edited from the seminar Self-Determination and Indigenous Peoples, organized by the Oslo and Copenhagen local groups of International Work Group for Indigenous Affairs (IWGIA). Copenhagen: IWGIA, 1987.

Sellers, Mortimer, ed. *The New World Order: Sovereignty, Human Rights, and the Self-Determination of Peoples.* Washington, D.C.: Berg, 1996.

Sever, Metin. *The Kurdish Question: What Our Intellectuals Think* (in Turkish). Istanbul: Cem Yayinevi, 1992.

Shafir, Gershon. *Immigrants and Nationalists: Ethnic Conflict and Accommodation in Catalonia, the Basque Country, Latvia, and Estonia.* Albany: State University of New York Press, 1995.

Shaheen, Samad. *The Communist (Bolshevik) Theory of National Self-Determination; Its Historical Evolution up to the October Revolution.* The Hague: W. van Hoeve, 1956.

Shain, Yossi. "Ethnic Diasporas and U.S. Foreign Policy." *Political Science Quarterly* 109, no. 5 (Winter 1994–1995): 811.

Shao-Chi, Liu. *Internationalism and Nationalism.* Peking: Foreign Languages Press, 1952.

Shapiro, Robert Y., and John T. Young. "Public Opinion and the Welfare State: The United States in Comparative Perspective." *Politique Science Quarterly* 104 (1989): 59–89.

Sharafutdinova, Gulnaz. "Chechnya Versus Tatarstan: Understanding Ethnopolitics in Post-Communist Russia." *Problems of Post-Communism* 47, no. 2 (March/April 2000): 13–22.

Shaw, Denis J.B. *Russia in the Modern World: A New Geography.* Oxford: Blackwell, 1999.

Shehadi, Kamal S. *Ethnic Self-Determination and the Break-up of States.* Adelphi Papers 283. London: IISS, 1994.

Shukri, Muhammad Aziz. *The Concept of Self-Determination in the United Nations.* Damascus: Al Jadidah Press, 1965.

Sidjanski, Pusan. *The Federal Future of Europe.* Ann Arbor: University of Michigan Press, 2000.

Silber, Laura, and Allan Little. *Yugoslavia: Death of a Nation.* New York: Penguin Books, 1996.

Silver, Hilary. "National Conceptions of the New Urban Poverty: Social Structural Change in Britain, France, and the United States." *International Journal of Urban and Regional Research* 17, no. 3 (1993): 336–354.

Silverman, Maxim. *Deconstructing the Nation: Immigration, Racism, and Citizenship in Modern France.* New York: Routledge, 1992.

Simonnot, Philippe. "A propos de l'équité." *Le Monde,* December 12, 1994, 1.

Simpson, Jerry J. "The Diffusion of Sovereignty: Self-Determination in the Post-Colonial Age." In *The New World Order: Sovereignty, Human Rights, and the Self-Determination of Peoples,* Mortimer Sellers, ed. Washington, D.C.: Berg, 1996.

Singh, Jaswant. "Against Nuclear Apartheid." *Foreign Affairs* 77, no. 5 (September/October 1998): 41–52.

Sleeper, Jim. *The Closest of Strangers: Liberalism and the Politics of Race in New York.* New York: W. W. Norton, 1991.

Slider, Darrell. "Regional and Local Politics." In *Developments in Russian Politics 4,* Stephen White, Alex Pravda, and Zvi Gitelman, eds. London: Macmillan, 1997.

Smith, Anthony D. *The Ethnic Origins of Nations.* Oxford: Basil Blackwell, 1986.

———. "The Myth of 'Modern Nations' and the Myths of Nations." *Ethnic and Racial Studies* 2 (1988): 1–26.

———. "The Ethnic Sources of Nationalism." *Survival* 35, no. 1 (Spring 1993).

Smith, Carol. *Guatemalan Indians and the State: 1540–1988.* Austin: University of Texas Press, 1990.

Smith, Stephen. "Subsidiarity and the Coordination of Indirect Taxes in the European Community." *Oxford Review of Economic Policy* 9, no. 1 (1993): 67–94.

Smyrniadis, Bion. *Les doctrines de Hobbes: Locke et Kant sur le droit d'insurrection.* Paris: La Vie Universitaire, 1921.

Snyder, Louis L. *Global Mini-Nationalisms: Autonomy or Independence.* Westport, Conn.: Greenwood Press, 1982.

Soroos, Marvin S. *Beyond Sovereignty: The Challenge of Global Policy.* Columbia: University of South Carolina Press, 1986.

Soysal, Yasemine Nuhoglu. "Changing Citizenship in Europe: Remarks on Postnational Membership and the National State." In *Citizenship, Nationality, and Migration in Europe.* London: Routledge, 1996.

Special Correspondent. "Khartoum's Greatest Challenge." *Merip Reports* (September 1985): 11–18.

Spencer, Metta, ed. *Separatism: Democracy and Disintegration.* Lanham, Md.: Rowman and Littlefield, 1998.

Spicker, Paul. "The Principle of Subsidiarity and the Social Policy of the European Community." *Journal of European Social Policy* 1, no. 1 (1991): 3–14.

Spruyt, Hendrik. *The Sovereign State and Its Competitor: An Analysis of Systems Change.* Princeton: Princeton University Press, 1994.

Stalin, Joseph. *Marxism and the National and Colonial Question: A Collection of Articles and Speeches.* (London, 1941), pp. 18–19. In *Self-Determination of Peoples: A Legal Reappraisal,* Antonio Cassese. Cambridge: Cambridge University Press, 1995, p. 14, n. 7.

Starushenko, G. *The Principle of National Self-Determination in Soviet Foreign Policy.* Moscow: Foreign Languages Publishing.

Stedman, Stephen. "The New Interventionism." *Foreign Affairs* 72, no. 1 (1993): 1–16.

Stevenson, Jonathan. "Hope Restored in Somalia." *Foreign Policy* 91 (Summer 1993): 138–154.

Stoner-Weiss, Kathryn. "Federalism and Regionalism." In *Developments in*

Russian Politics 4, Stephen White, Alex Pravda, and Zvi Gitelman, eds. London: Macmillan, 1997.

————. *Local Heroes: The Political Economy of Russian Regional Governance*. Princeton: Princeton University Press, 1997.

Strayer, Joseph R. *On the Medieval Origins of the Modern State*. Princeton: Princeton University Press, 1970.

Stremlan, John. "Antidote to Anarchy." *Washington Quarterly* 18, no. 1 (Winter 1995): 33.

Strobe, Talbott. "Self-Determination in an Interdependent World." *Foreign Policy,* no. 118 (Spring 2000): 152–163.

Strutzenberg, Beth E. "Urban Reawakening: International City Networks Within the European Union." Senior thesis, Princeton University, 1995.

"The Subsidiarity Principle." *Bulletin of the European Communities* 25, no. 10 (1992): 116–126.

Suleiman, Michael. *Political Parties in Lebanon*. Ithaca, N.Y.: Cornell University Press, 1967.

Suny, Ronald Grigor. "Provisional Stabilities: The Politics of Identities in Post-Soviet Eurasia." *International Security* 24, no. 3 (Winter 1999–2000): 139–178.

Supreme Court of Canada. Decision on the legality of a unilateral declaration of independence, August 1998, <http://www.scc-csc.gc.ca/>.

Szlechter, Emile. *Les options conventionelles de nationalité a la suite de cessions de territoires*. Paris: Recueit Sirey, 1948.

Taylor, Charles. *Multiculturalism and "The Politics of Recognition."* Princeton: Princeton University Press, 1992.

Taylor, Charles. *Rapprocher les solitudes: Ecrits sur le fédéralisme et le nationalisme au Canada*. Laval: Presses de l'Université Laval, 1992.

Taylor, Michael. *The Possibility of Cooperation*. Cambridge: Cambridge University Press, 1987.

Tempel, Stephan. "Staedtepartnerschaften in der deutsch-polnischen Zusammenarbeit." *Osteuropa* 47 (1997): 630–665.

Thornberry, Patrick. "Self-Determination, Minorities, Human Rights: A Review of International Instruments." *International and Comparative Law Quarterly* 38, pt. 4 (1989): 867–889.

Thorsell, William. "Canada: The Once and Future Nation." Lecture presented at Princeton University, October 4, 1994.

Thürer, Daniel. *Das Selbstbestimmungsrecht der Völker mit Excurs zur Jura-Frage*. Bern: Stámpfli, 1976.

————. "Das Selbstbestimmungsrecht der Völker: Ein Ueberblick." *Archiv des Völkerrechts,* H.-J. Schlochauer, ed., 22, no. 2 (1984): 113–137.

————. "National Minorities: A Global, European, and Swiss Perspective." *Fletcher Forum of World Affairs* 19, no. 1 (Winter/Spring 1995): 53–69.

Tocqueville, Alexis de. *Democracy in America*. New York: Vintage, 1945.

Tolz, Vera. "Conflicting 'Homeland Myths' and Nation-State Building in Postcommunist Russia." *Slavic Review* 57, no. 2 (Summer 1998): 267–294.

Tomuschat, Christian, ed. *Modern Law of Self-Determination*. Dordrecht, The Netherlands: Martinus Nijhoff, 1993.

Torunlu, Lamia. "100 Rich Kurds." *Nokta* (June 6–12, 1993): 12–18.

Toth, A. G. "The Principle of Subsidiarity in the Maastricht Treaty." *Common Market Law Review* 29, no. 6 (December 1992): 1079–1105.

Toynbee, Arnold J. "Self-Determination." *Quarterly Review,* no. 484 (1925).

Triesman, Daniel S. "Russia's 'Ethnic Revival': The Separatist Activism of Regional Leaders in a Post Communist Order." *World Politics* 49 (January 1997): 212–249.

———. "After Yeltsin Comes . . . Yeltsin." *Foreign Policy* (Spring 2000): 74–86.

Turp, Daniel. "Le droit de secession en droit international publique." *Canadian Yearbook of International Law* 20 (1982): 24–78.

Turpel, Mary Ellen. "Indigenous People's Rights of Political Participation and Self-Determination." *Cornell International Law Journal* 25 (1992).

Twining, William, ed. *Issues of Self-Determination.* Aberdeen: Aberdeen University Press, 1991.

Udechuku, E. C. *Liberation of Dependent Peoples in International Law.* London: African Publications Bureau, 1978.

Ullman, Richard H., ed. *The World and Yugoslavia's Wars.* New York: Council on Foreign Relations, 1996.

Umozurike, U. O. *Self-Determination in International Law.* Hamden, Conn.: Archon Books, 1972.

UNICEF. *Estado mundial de la infancia 1999.* New York: UNICEF, 1999.

Urbinati, Nadia. "Two Ideas of Nation." Unpublished paper, European Research Seminar, Princeton University, November 16, 1992.

Urquhart, Sir Brian. *Ralph Bunche: An American Life.* New York: W. W. Norton, 1993.

'Uthman, 'Ali. "The Kurdish Workers Party and the Future of the Kurdish Question in Turkey." *Political Readings* 2 (Tampa, Fla., 1993): 45–68 (in Arabic).

Varenne, Herve. *Americans Together: Structured Diversity in a Midwestern Town.* New York: Teachers College Press, 1977.

Veiter, Theodor. *Bibliographie zur Südtirolfrage (1945–1983).* Vienna: Braumüller, 1984.

Verter, Bradford. "Aiming the Canon: A Preliminary Investigation into Determinants of Public Opinion in the Curriculum Debate." Paper presented at the meetings of the American Sociological Association, Los Angeles, 1994.

Verzijl, J.H.W. *International Law in Historical Perspective.* Leiden: Sijthoff, 1968.

Viefhaus, Erwin. *Die Minderheitenfrage und die Entstehung der Minderheitenschutz-verträge auf der Pariser Friedenskonferenz 1919: Eine Studie zur Geschichte des Nationalitätenproblems im 19. und 20. Jahrhundert.* Würzburg: Holzner, 1960.

Vienna Declaration and Programme of Action. Adopted by the World Conference on Human Rights in 1993, para. I.8. Draft reference number A/CONF 157/23.

Waart, P.J.I.M. De. *Dynamics of Self-Determination in Palestine: Protection of Peoples as a Human Right.* Leiden: Brill, 1994.

Wagner, Peter. "Dispute, Uncertainty, and Institution in Recent French Debates." *Journal of Political Philosophy* 2, no. 3 (1994): 270–289.

Wagner, Wilfried. ed. *Rassendiskriminierung, Kolonialpolitik und ethnisch-nationale Identität: Referate des 2.* Münster: Lit, 1992.

Waldman, Moris David. *Beyond "National Self-Determination."* New York: American Jewish Committee, 1944.

Walker, R.B.J. *State Sovereignty, Global Civilization, and the Rearticulation of Political Space.* Princeton: Center of International Studies, Woodrow Wilson School of Public and International Affairs, Princeton University, 1988.

Wallace, William. "Regionalism in Europe: Model or Exception." In *Regionalism in World Politics,* Louise Fawcett and Andrew Hurrell, eds. New York: Oxford University Press, 1995.

Walt van Praag, M. C. *The Status of Tibet: History, Rights, and Prospects in International Law.* Foreword by Franz Michael; Introduction by Rikhi Jaipal. Boulder, Colo.: Westview Press, 1987.

Walzer, Michael. "Comment." In *Multiculturalism and the Politics of Recognition,* Charles Taylor, ed. Princeton: Princeton University Press, 1992.

————. *Thick and Thin: Moral Argument at Home and Abroad.* Notre Dame: University of Notre Dame Press, 1994.

Wambaugh, Sarah. *Plebiscites Since the World War, with a Collection of Official Documents.* Washington, D.C.: Carnegie Endowment for International Peace, 1933.

Wannow, Marianne. *Das Selbstbestimmungsrecht der Sowjetischen Völker.* Göttingen: N.p., 1965.

Ware, Robert Bruce. "Political Stability and Ethnic Parity: Why Is There Peace in Dagestan?" In *Center-Periphery Conflict in Post-Soviet Russia: A Federation Imperiled,* Mikhail A. Alexseev, ed. New York: St. Martin's Press, 1999.

Ware, Robert Bruce, and Envery Kisriev. "Political Stability in Dagestan: Ethnic Parity and Religious Polarization." *Problems of Post-Communism* 47, no. 2 (March/April 2000): 23–33.

Warren, Kay B. "Enduring Tensions and Changing Identities: Mayan Family Struggles in Guatemala." In *History in Person; The Mutual Construction of Endemic Struggles and Enduring Identities,* Dorothy Holand and Jean Lave, eds. Santa Fe: SAR Press, 1992.

————. "Transforming Memories and Histories: The Meanings of Ethnic Resurgence for Mayan Indians." In *Americas: New Interpretive Essays,* Alfred Stepan, ed. New York: Oxford University Press, 1992.

————. "Language and the Politics of Self-Expression: Mayan Revitalization in Guatemala." *Cultural Survival Quarterly* (Summer/Fall 1994): 81–86.

————. "Mayan Multiculturalism and the Violence of Memories." In *Violence, Political Agency, and the Construction of the Self,* Veena Das and Mamphela Ramphele, eds., 1996.

————. "Reading History as Resistance: Mayan Public Intellectuals in Guatemala." In *Mayan Cultural Activism in Guatemala,* Edward Fischer and McKenna Brown, eds. Austin: University of Texas Press, 1996.

————. *Indigenous Movements and Their Critics: Pan-Maya Activism in Guatemala.* Princeton: Princeton University Press, 1998.

————. "Indigenous Movements as a Challenge to a Unified Social Movement Paradigm for Guatemala." In *Cultures of Politics/Politics of Cultures: Re-*

visioning Latin American Social Movements, Sonia E. Alvarez, Evelina Dagnino, and Arturo Escobar, eds. Boulder, Colo.: Westview Press, 1998.

Waterbury, John. *The Egypt of Nasser and Sadat: The Political Economy of two Regimes*. Princeton: Princeton University Press, 1983.

———. *Exposed to Innumerable Delusions: Public Enterprise and State Power in Egypt, India, Mexico and Turkey*. New York: Cambridge University Press, 1993.

———. "Iraq's Future: Is Democracy the Only Way Out?" *Iranian Journal of International Affairs* (1993): 775–789.

Waterbury, John, and Mark Gersowitz, eds. *The Political Economy of Risk and Choice in Senegal*. London: Totowa, 1987.

Waterbury, John, and Farhad Kazemi, eds. *Peasants and Politics in the Modern Middle East*. Miami: Florida International University Press, 1991.

Waterbury, John, and Ezra N. Suleiman, eds. *Political Economy of Public Sector Reform and Privatization*. Boulder, Colo.: Westview Press, 1990.

Waters, Mary C. *Ethnic Options. Choosing Identities in America*. Berkeley: University of California Press, 1990.

Weber, Max. *The Protestant Ethic and the Spirit of Capitalism*. New York: Scribner, 1958.

———. *Economy and Society*. vol. 1. Berkeley: University of California Press, 1978.

Weiner, Myron, *The Indian Paradox*. New Delhi: Sage, 1989.

Weiner, Myron, and Samuel Huntington, eds. *Understanding Political Development*. Boston: Little, Brown, 1987.

Weiss, Klaus. *Das Südtirol-Problem in der Ersten Republik: dargestellt an Österreichs Innen-und Aussenpolitik im Jahre 1928*. Vienna: Verlag für Geschichte und Politik; Munich: R. Oldenbourg, 1989.

Werther, Guntram F.A. *Self-Determination in Western Democracies: Aboriginal Politics in a Comparative Perspective*. New York: Greenwood Press, 1992.

Weston, Burns H., Richard A. Falk, and Anthony D'Amato, eds. *Supplement of Basic Documents to International Law and World Order*. 3rd ed. St. Paul: West, 1997.

White, Robert H. *Tribal Assets: The Rebirth of Native America*. New York: H. Holt, 1990.

White, Robin C.A. "Self-Determination: Time for a Re-Assessment?" *Netherlands International Law Review* 28 (1981/1982): 147–170.

Wieviorka, Michel. *L'éspace du racisme*. Paris: Seuil, 1991.

———. *La France raciste*. Paris: Points, 1992.

Wilkinson, Herbert Arnold. *The American Doctrine of State Succession*. Baltimore, Md.: Johns Hopkins University Press, 1934.

Williams, Colin H., ed. *National Separatism*. Vancouver: University of British Columbia Press, 1982.

Willoughby, Westel Woodbury. *Types of Restricted Sovereignty and of Colonial Autonomy*. Washington, D.C.: GPO, 1919.

Wilson, Heather A. *International Law and the Use of Force by National Liberation Movements*. New York: Oxford University Press, 1988.

Wilson, Ian M. *The Influence of Hobbes and Locke in the Shaping of the Concept of Sovereignty in the Eighteenth Century*. Banbury, England: Voltaire Foundation, 1973.

Wolf, Werner. *Südtirol in Oesterreich: Die Südtirol Frage in der österreichischen Diskussion von 1945 bis 1969*. Würzburg: Holzner Verlag, 1972.

Wolfe, Alan. *Whose Keeper? Social Science and Moral Obligation.* Berkeley: University of California Press, 1989.

Woodward, Susan, L. *Balkan Tragedy: Chaos and Dissolution After the Cold War.* Washington, D.C.: Brookings Institution, 1995.

"The Wrong Side of History." *Civil Society* 3, no. 29 (1994).

Wylie, Lawrence. *Village in the Vaucluse.* New York: Harper and Row, 1961.

Young, Iris Marion. *Justice and the Politics of Difference.* Princeton: Princeton University Press, 1990.

Zaagman, Rob. "Commentary." In *Self-Determination and Self-Administration: A Sourcebook,* Wolfgang Danspeckgruber with Arthur Watts, eds. Boulder, Colo: Lynne Rienner, 1997.

Zavalloni, Roberto. *Self-Determination: The Psychology of Personal Freedom.* Chicago: Forum Books, 1962.

Zerubavel, Eviatar. *The Fine Line: Boundaries and Distinctions in Everyday Life.* New York: Free Press, 1991.

Ziehen, Ursula. *Vollendete Tatsachen bei Verletzungen der territorialen Unversehrtheit.* Würzburg: Holzner Verlag, 1962.

Zuck, Rüdiger. *Subsidiaritätsprinzip und Grundgesetz.* Munich: Beck, 1968.

Selected Websites Concerning Self-Determination and Related Topics

International Organizations

Association of South East Asian Nations (ASEAN)	www.aseansec.org
Central European Free Trade Agreement (CEFTA)	www.cefta.org
Central European Initiative (CEI), formerly Pentagonale	www.ceinet.org
Council of Baltic Sea States (CBSS)	www.baltinfo.org/CBSS.htm
Council of Europe	www.coe.int
Council of Europe, European Committee for the Prevention of Torture and Inhuman or Degrading Treatment or Punishment (CPT)	www.cpt.coe.int
European Bank for Reconstruction and Development (EBRD)	www.ebrd.org
European Union–European Commission Humanitarian Aid Office (ECHO)	europa.eu.int/comm/echo/
International Committee of the Red Cross	www.icrc.org
Organization of African Unity (OAU)	www.oau-oua.org
Organization of American States (OAS)	www.oas.org
Organization of the Black Sea Economic Cooperation (BSEC)	www.bsec.gov.tr
Organization for Security and Cooperation in Europe (OSCE)	www.osce.org
OSCE High Commissioner on National Minorities	www.osce.org/hcnm
United Nations (UN)	www.un.org

Rome Statute of the International Criminal   www.un.org/law/icc/
Court (ICC)
UN Department of Peacekeeping Operations   www.un.org/Depts/dpko
(UNDPKO)
UN High Commissioner for Human Rights   www.unhchr.ch
(UNHCHR)
UN High Commissioner for Refugees   www.unhcr.ch
(UNHCR)
Visegrád Group (V4), Visegrád Cooperation   www.visegrad.org

International NGOs

American Council for Voluntary International   www.interaction.org
Action (InterAction)
Amnesty International   www.amnesty.org
ARGE-Alp (Working Community of the Alps)   www.argealp.at
ARGE Alp–Adria   www.alpeadria.org
ARGE Danube Regions   www.argedonau.at
Care International   www.care-international.org
Carter Center   www.cartercenter.org
Coalition to Stop the Use of Child Soldiers   www.child-soldiers.org
Conference of Non-Governmental   www.conferenceofngos.org
Organizations in Consultative Relationship
with the United Nations (CONGO)
Federation of American Scientists;   fas.org/irp/threat/terror.htm
Terrorism—Intelligence Threat Assessments
Human Rights Watch (HRW)   www.hrw.org
International Interracial Association (IIA)   www.i3n.net/
Médecins du monde   www.medecinsdumonde.org
Médecins sans frontières (MSF)   www.msf.org
Millennium Forum   www.millenniumforum.org
Minority Electronic Resources (MINELRES)   www.riga.lv/minelres/
Minority Rights Group International (MRG)   www.minorityrights.org
Oxfam International   www.oxfam.org
Pugwash Conferences on Science and   www.pugwash.org
World Affairs
Save the Children   www.savethechildren.org
Terres des Hommes   www.tdh.ch
Unrepresented Nations and Peoples   www.unpo.org
Organization (UNPO)
Working Community of the Western Alps   www.unil.ch/cotrao
(COTRAO)

U.S. Government Agencies

Central Intelligence Agency (CIA), World   www.cia.gov/cia/
Factbook   publications/factbook/
U.S. Agency for International Development   www.usaid.gov/hum_response
(USAID), Office on Foreign Disaster   /ofda/
Assistance (OFDA)
U.S. Department of State, Country Background   www.state.gov/r/pa/bgn/
Notes

Institutes, Academia, and Think Tanks

Academic Council on the UN System (ACUNS) www.yale.edu/acuns/
Center for International Development and www.bsos.umd.edu/cidcm/
  Conflict Management (CIDCM), University
  of Maryland
  "Internal Wars and Failures of Governance, www.bsos.umd.edu/cidcm/
  1954-1996" database stfail/
  Minorities at Risk Project www.bsos.umd.edu/cidcm/
  mar/

Center for Multiethnic Research, Uppsala www.multietn.uu.se
  University
Center for Refugee Studies, York University www.yorku.ca/crs/
Center for Research in International Migration www.ceifo.su.se/
  and Ethnic Relations (CEIFO)
Center for Security Studies and Conflict www.fsk.ethz.ch
  Research (CSSCR)
Center for Systemic Peace members.aol.com/CSPmgm/
  cspframe.htm

European Center for Minority Issues www.ecmi.de
Foreign Policy in Focus, Self-Determination in www.fpif.org/
  Focus project selfdetermination/
  index.html

Initiative on Conflict Resolution and Ethnicity www.incore.ulst.ac.uk/
  (INCORE)
Institute for International Law of Peace and www.ruhr-uni-bochum.
  Armed Conflict (IFHV) de/ifhv/IndexE.htm
International Institute for Strategic Studies www.iiss.org
  (IISS)
International Peace Academy (IPA) www.ipacademy.org
International Relations and Security Network www.isn.ethz.ch
  (ISN)
Liechtenstein Institute on Self-Determination at www.princeton.edu/~lisd
  Princeton University
Norwegian Institute of International Affairs www.nupi.no
  (NUPI)
Overseas Development Council www.odc.org
Overseas Development Institute www.odi.org.uk/
Raoul Wallenberg Institute of Human Rights www.rwi.lu.se/
  and International Law, Lund University,
  Sweden
Stockholm International Peace Research www2.sipri.se/
  Institute (SIPRI)
United States Institute of Peace www.usip.org
University of Chicago Center for the Study of social-sciences.uchicago.
  Race, Politics, and Culture edu/ucrpc/

News Sources, Lists, and Journals

Columbia International Affairs Online	www.ciaonet.org
The Economist Intelligence Unit	www.eiu.com
Ethnic-L	www2.hawaii.edu/~fredr/ 6-eth5a.htm
Ethnic World Survey	www.partal.com/ciemen/ ethnic.html
Institute for War and Peace Reporting	www.iwpr.net
International Crisis Group	www.intl-crisis-group.org
Initiative on Conflict Resolution and Ethnicity (INCORE), *The Ethnic Conflict Research Digest*	www.incore.ulst.ac.uk/ecrd/
Janes Information Group	www.janes.com/security/
Nationalism and Ethnic Politics	www.frankcass.com/jnls/ nep.htm
Open Society Institute, Forced Migration Projects (archive)	www.soros.org/fmp2/index. html

THE CONTRIBUTORS

María Fernanda Cañás is counsellor in the Argentine Embassy to the United Kingdom.

Emilio J. Cárdenas is executive director of HSBC Argentina Holdings, S.A. He was formerly the Permanent Representative of Argentina to the United Nations and was President of the UN Security Council, January 1995.

Wolfgang Danspeckgruber is the founding director of the Liechtenstein Institute on Self-Determination at Princeton University. He is also chair of the Liechtenstein Colloquium on European and International Affaris, Vaduz, Liechtenstein.

Francis M. Deng is a senior fellow of foreign policy studies at the Brookings Institution.

Michael W. Doyle is former director of the Center of International Studies at the Woodrow Wilson School of Public and International Affairs, Princeton University. Currently he is assistant secretary-general of the United Nation Special Advisor to the UN Secretary-General.

Richard Falk is the Albert G. Milbank Professor of International Law and Practice and professor of politics and international affairs, Woodrow Wilson School of Public and International Affairs, Princeton University.

Tyler Felgenhauer is research associate and program manager for Eurasia at the Liechtenstein Institute on Self-Determination, Woodrow Wilson School of Public and International Affairs, Princeton University.

Prince Hans Adam II of Liechtenstein is the Ruling Prince of

Liechtenstein, Schloss Vaduz, Principality of Liechtenstein.

Jeffrey Herbst is chairman of the Department of Politics and professor of politics and international affairs, Woodrow Wilson School of Public and International Affairs, Princeton University.

Atul Kohli is professor of politics and international affairs, Woodrow Wilson School of Public and International Affairs, Princeton University.

Ian S. Lustick is a professor in the Department of Political Science, University of Pennsylvania.

Minxin Pei is a senior associate at the Democracy and Rule of Law Project, Carnegie Endowment for International Peace.

Kay B. Warren is a professor in the Department of Anthropology, Harvard University.

John Waterbury is president of the American University, Beirut, Lebanon, and William Stewart Tod Professor of Politics and International Affairs, Emeritus, Princeton University.

Sir Arthur Watts, QC, KCMG, is a former legal adviser at the Foreign Office, London.

William Wohlforth is associate professor, Dartmouth College, New Hampshire, and formerly an assistant professor at the Edmund A. Walsh School of Foreign Service, Georgetown University.

INDEX

ABOUT THE BOOK

With contentious issues of sovereignty and self-determination a focus of current world affairs, this comprehensive analysis is especially timely. The authors explore the conceptual, political, legal, cultural, economic, and strategic aspects of self-determination—encompassing both theory and practice—in the context of the evolving international system. Wide-ranging case studies enrich the collection.

The book serves as an excellent introduction to a central set of issues in international politics.

Wolfgang Danspeckgruber is the founding director of the Liechtenstein Institute on Self-Determination at Princeton University, and instructor in politics and international affairs at Princeton University.